Thomas Kingsmill Abbott

A Critical and Exegetical Commentary on the Epistles to the Ephesians

and to the Colossians

Thomas Kingsmill Abbott

A Critical and Exegetical Commentary on the Epistles to the Ephesians
and to the Colossians

ISBN/EAN: 9783337377977

Printed in Europe, USA, Canada, Australia, Japan

Cover: Foto ©ninafisch / pixelio.de

More available books at **www.hansebooks.com**

The International Critical Commentary

on the Holy Scriptures of the Old and New Testaments

UNDER THE EDITORSHIP OF

THE REV. CHARLES AUGUSTUS BRIGGS, D.D.
Edward Robinson Professor of Biblical Theology,
Union Theological Seminary, New York;

THE REV. SAMUEL ROLLES DRIVER, D.D.
Regius Professor of Hebrew, Oxford;

THE REV. ALFRED PLUMMER, M.A., D.D.
Master of University College, Durham.

The International Critical Commentary

on the Holy Scriptures of the Old and New Testaments.

EDITORS' PREFACE.

THERE are now before the public many Commentaries, written by British and American divines, of a popular or homiletical character. *The Cambridge Bible for Schools*, the *Handbooks for Bible Classes and Private Students*, *The Speaker's Commentary*, *The Popular Commentary* (Schaff), *The Expositor's Bible*, and other similar series, have their special place and importance. But they do not enter into the field of Critical Biblical scholarship occupied by such series of Commentaries as the *Kurzgefasstes exegetisches Handbuch zum A. T.;* De Wette's *Kurzgefasstes exegetisches Handbuch zum N. T.;* Meyer's *Kritisch-exegetischer Kommentar;* Keil and Delitzsch's *Biblischer Commentar über das A. T.;* Lange's *Theologisch-homiletisches Bibelwerk;* Nowack's *Handkommentar zum A. T.;* Holtzmann's *Handkommentar zum N. T.* Several of these have been translated, edited, and in some cases enlarged and adapted, for the English-speaking public; others are in process of translation. But no corresponding series by British or American divines has hitherto been produced. The way has been prepared by special Commentaries by Cheyne, Ellicott, Kalisch, Lightfoot, Perowne, Westcott, and others; and the time has come, in the judgment of the projectors of this enterprise, when it is practicable to combine British and American scholars in the production of a critical, comprehensive

Commentary that will be abreast of modern biblical scholarship, and in a measure lead its van.

Messrs. Charles Scribner's Sons of New York, and Messrs. T. & T. Clark of Edinburgh, propose to publish such a series of Commentaries on the Old and New Testaments, under the editorship of Prof. C. A. BRIGGS, D.D., in America, and of Prof. S. R. DRIVER, D.D., for the Old Testament, and the Rev. ALFRED PLUMMER, D.D., for the New Testament, in Great Britain.

The Commentaries will be international and inter-confessional, and will be free from polemical and ecclesiastical bias. They will be based upon a thorough critical study of the original texts of the Bible, and upon critical methods of interpretation. They are designed chiefly for students and clergymen, and will be written in a compact style. Each book will be preceded by an Introduction, stating the results of criticism upon it, and discussing impartially the questions still remaining open. The details of criticism will appear in their proper place in the body of the Commentary. Each section of the Text will be introduced with a paraphrase, or summary of contents. Technical details of textual and philological criticism will, as a rule, be kept distinct from matter of a more general character; and in the Old Testament the exegetical notes will be arranged, as far as possible, so as to be serviceable to students not acquainted with Hebrew. The History of Interpretation of the Books will be dealt with, when necessary, in the Introductions, with critical notices of the most important literature of the subject. Historical and Archæological questions, as well as questions of Biblical Theology, are included in the plan of the Commentaries, but not Practical or Homiletical Exegesis. The Volumes will constitute a uniform series.

THE INTERNATIONAL CRITICAL COMMENTARY.

THE following eminent Scholars are engaged upon the Volumes named below:—

THE OLD TESTAMENT.

Genesis. The Rev. T. K. CHEYNE, D.D., Oriel Professor of the Interpretation of Holy Scripture, Oxford.

Exodus. The Rev. A. R. S. KENNEDY, D.D., Professor of Hebrew, University of Edinburgh.

Leviticus. The Rev. H. A. WHITE, M.A., Fellow of New College, Oxford.

Numbers. G. BUCHANAN GRAY, B.A., Lecturer in Hebrew, Mansfield College, Oxford.

Deuteronomy. The Rev. S. R. DRIVER, D.D., Regius Professor of Hebrew, Oxford. [*Now Ready.*

Joshua. The Rev. GEORGE ADAM SMITH, D.D., Professor of Hebrew, Free Church College, Glasgow.

Judges. The Rev. GEORGE MOORE, D.D., Professor of Hebrew, Andover Theological Seminary, Andover, Mass. [*Now Ready.*

Samuel. The Rev. H. P. SMITH, D.D., late Professor of Hebrew, Lane Theological Seminary, Cincinnati, Ohio.

Kings. The Rev. FRANCIS BROWN, D.D., Professor of Hebrew and Cognate Languages, Union Theological Seminary, New York City.

Chronicles. The Rev. EDWARD L. CURTIS, D.D., Professor of Hebrew, Yale University, New Haven, Conn.

Ezra and Nehemiah. The Rev. L. W. BATTEN, Ph.D., Professor of Hebrew, P. E. Divinity School, Philadelphia.

Psalms. The Rev. CHARLES A. BRIGGS, D.D., Edward Robinson Professor of Biblical Theology, Union Theological Seminary, New York.

Proverbs. The Rev. C. H. TOY, D.D., Professor of Hebrew, Harvard University, Cambridge, Massachusetts.

Job. The Rev. S. R. DRIVER, D.D., Regius Professor of Hebrew, Oxford.

Isaiah. The Rev. A. B. DAVIDSON, D.D., LL.D., Professor of Hebrew, Free Church College, Edinburgh.

Jeremiah. The Rev. A. F. KIRKPATRICK, D.D., Regius Professor of Hebrew, Cambridge, England.

Minor Prophets. W. R. HARPER, Ph.D., President of the University of Chicago, Illinois.

Daniel. The Rev. JOHN P. PETERS, Ph.D., late Professor of Hebrew, P. E. Divinity School, Philadelphia, now Rector of St. Michael's Church, New York City.

THE INTERNATIONAL CRITICAL COMMENTARY. — Continued.

THE NEW TESTAMENT.

St. Mark.	The Rev. E. P. GOULD, D.D., Professor of New Testament Literature, P. E. Divinity School, Philadelphia. [*Now Ready.*]
St. Luke.	The Rev. ALFRED PLUMMER, D.D., Master of University College, Durham. [*Now Ready.*]
Harmony of the Gospels.	The Rev. WILLIAM SANDAY, D.D., Lady Margaret Professor of Divinity, Oxford, and the Rev. WILLOUGHBY C. ALLEN, M.A., Fellow of Exeter College, Oxford.
Acts.	The Rev. FREDERICK H. CHASE, D.D., Fellow of Christ's College, Cambridge.
Romans.	The Rev. WILLIAM SANDAY, D.D., Lady Margaret Professor of Divinity and Canon of Christ Church, Oxford, and the Rev. A. C. HEADLAM, M.A., Fellow of All Souls' College, Oxford. [*Now Ready.*]
Corinthians.	The Rev. ARCH. ROBERTSON, D.D., Principal of King's College, London.
Galatians.	The Rev. ERNEST D. BURTON, A.B., Professor of New Testament Literature, University of Chicago.
Ephesians and Colossians.	The Rev. T. K. ABBOTT, B.D., D. Lit., formerly Professor of Biblical Greek, Trinity College, Dublin. [*Now Ready.*]
Philippians and Philemon.	The Rev. MARVIN R. VINCENT, D.D., Professor of Biblical Literature, Union Theological Seminary, New York City. [*Now Ready.*]
Hebrews.	The Rev. T. C. EDWARDS, D.D., Principal of the Theological College, Bala; late Principal of University College of Wales, Aberystwyth.
St. James.	The Rev. JAMES H. ROPES, A.B., Instructor of New Testament Criticism in Harvard University.
The Pastoral Epistles.	The Rev. WALTER LOCK, M.A., Dean Ireland, Professor of Exegesis, Oxford.
Peter and Jude.	The Rev. CHARLES BIGG, D.D., Leamington, England.
Revelation.	The Rev. ROBERT H. CHARLES, M.A., Trinity College, Dublin, and Exeter College, Oxford.

Other engagements will be announced shortly.

THE EPISTLES TO THE EPHESIANS
AND TO THE COLOSSIANS

T. K. ABBOTT, B.D., D.LITT.

THE INTERNATIONAL CRITICAL COMMENTARY

A

CRITICAL AND EXEGETICAL COMMENTARY

ON THE

EPISTLES TO THE EPHESIANS AND TO THE COLOSSIANS

BY

REV. T. K. ABBOTT, B.D., D.LITT.

FORMERLY PROFESSOR OF BIBLICAL GREEK, NOW OF HEBREW,
TRINITY COLLEGE, DUBLIN

NEW YORK

CHARLES SCRIBNER'S SONS

1897

The Rights of Translation and of Reproduction are Reserved.

PREFACE

THE following Commentary is primarily philological. Its aim is to ascertain with as great precision as possible the actual meaning of the writer's language. The Commentaries which have been regularly consulted are those of Chrysostom and Theodore of Mopsuestia, amongst the ancients; and amongst the moderns, Alford, Barry, De Wette, Eadie, Ellicott, Meyer (W. Schmidt), Moule, von Soden, and the Speaker's; also for Ephesians, Harless, Stier, and Macpherson; and for Colossians, Lightfoot. The Commentary of von Soden, though concise, is very acute and independent. Mr. Moule's also, although bearing a modest title, is of great value. Other writers have been occasionally consulted. Much use has been made of Fritzsche's occasional notes in his various commentaries, especially in connexion with the illustration of the language of the Epistles from classical and late Greek authors. Wetstein, of course, has not been overlooked.

The text adopted is that of the Revisers, except where otherwise stated.

T. K. ABBOTT.

CONTENTS.

	PAGE
INTRODUCTION TO THE EPISTLE TO THE EPHESIANS	i–xlv
§ 1. To what Readers Written	i
On the reading ἐν Ἐφέσῳ	i
Not written to Ephesus	iii
Hypothesis of a circular letter	vi
§ 2. Genuineness of the Epistle	ix
External evidence	ix
Internal evidence	xiii
Objections from the language	xiv
Objections from the line of thought	xix
Paley on the internal evidence	xx
§ 3. Relation to the Epistle to the Colossians	xxiii
" " First Epistle of Peter	xxiv
" " Epistle to the Hebrews	xxvi
" " Apocalypse	xxviii
" " Gospel of St. John	xxviii
§ 6. Time and Place of Writing	xxix
§ 7. Vocabulary of the Epistle	xxxi
§ 8. Contents	xxxii
§ 9. Literature	xxxv
§ 10. On some Readings peculiar to one or two MSS.	xl
On the maxim "The more difficult reading is to be preferred"	xlv
Abbreviations	xlvi
INTRODUCTION TO THE EPISTLE TO THE COLOSSIANS	xlvii–lxv
§ 1. The Church at Colossæ	xlvii
The Colossian heresy	xlix
§ 2. Genuineness	l
Holtzmann's restoration of the supposed original	li
Alleged un-Pauline vocabulary	lii
Alleged Gnostic colouring	liv

		PAGE
§ 3. Place and Date of Writing		lix
§ 4. Relation to other N.T. Writings. . .		ib.
§ 5. Vocabulary of the Epistle		ib.
§ 6. Contents of the Epistle		lx
§ 7. Literature		lxii

COMMENTARY ON THE EPISTLE TO THE
    EPHESIANS 1–191
  Special Notes: On ἀπολύτρωσις 11
                On μυστήριον 15, 174
                On the angelic hierarchy 33
                On τέκνα φύσει ὀργῆς 45
                On ταπεινοφροσύνη 105
                On "It saith" 110
                On sacrifice 147

COMMENTARY ON THE EPISTLE TO THE
    COLOSSIANS 193–308
  Special Notes: On πρωτότοκος πάσης κτίσεως . . . 215
                On στοιχεῖα τοῦ κόσμου 247
                On ἀπεκδυσάμενος τὰς ἀρχάς, κ.τ.λ. . . 257
                On the Epistle "from Laodicea" . . 304
  Text of the spurious "Epistle to the Laodiceans" . . 308

INDEX TO THE NOTES
  1. Subjects and Names 309
  2. Greek Words 313
  3. Latin Words 315

INTRODUCTION.

§ 1. TO WHAT READERS WAS THE EPISTLE ADDRESSED?

THIS question cannot be treated apart from that of the genuineness of ἐν Ἐφέσῳ in i. 1.

MSS. All extant MS. authority, with three exceptions, is in favour of the words. The three exceptions are ℵ B 67².

In ℵ they are added by a later hand (ℵᶜ).

In B they are also added by a corrector (B³), although Hug was of opinion that the correction was by the first hand.

In 67 they were written by the original scribe, but are expunged by the corrector. Possibly this correction is not independent of B. Lightfoot observes that a reading in St. Paul's Epistles supported by ℵ B 67² almost always represents the original text.

In addition to these, however, we have the express testimony of Basil that the words were absent from the most ancient, or rather all the ancient, MSS. in his day. His words are: τοῖς Ἐφεσίοις ἐπιστέλλων, ὡς γνησίως ἡνωμένοις τῷ ὄντι δι' ἐπιγνώσεως, ὄντας αὐτοὺς ἰδιαζόντως ὠνόμασεν, εἰπών· τοῖς ἁγίοις τοῖς οὖσι καὶ πιστοῖς ἐν Χριστῷ Ἰησοῦ· οὕτω γὰρ καὶ οἱ πρὸ ἡμῶν παραδεδώκασι καὶ ἡμεῖς ἐν τοῖς παλαιοῖς τῶν ἀντιγράφων εὑρήκαμεν (*Adv. Eunom.* ii. 19). The hypothesis that he is referring, not to ἐν Ἐφέσῳ, but either to τοῖς or to οὖσιν, is quite untenable. How strange it would be that he should go on to quote the words καὶ πιστοῖς ἐν Χρ. Ἰ., which had no relation to the interpretation in question, and omit the intervening ἐν Ἐφέσῳ, the absence of which was no doubt what gave rise to it! The οὕτω γάρ must surely refer to the whole quotation as he gives it. Moreover, he distinguishes the MSS. from οἱ πρὸ ἡμῶν, by which he doubtless meant Origen, who omitted the words. Besides, his proof from this passage (against Eunomius), that Christ may be called ὁ ὤν, would have no foundation if he had read ἐν Ἐφέσῳ after οὖσιν.[1]

---

[1] It has been said that Basil's statement is not confirmed. The objection is doubly fallacious. His statement as to what he had himself seen does not need

Versions. All the Versions have the words, but it must be borne in mind that we have no MSS. of any of these as old as ℵ B.

Fathers, etc. Origen's commentary is quoted in Cramer's *Catena* as follows: Ὠριγένης δέ φησι, ἐπὶ μόνων Ἐφεσίων εὕρομεν κείμενον, τὸ "τοῖς ἁγίοις τοῖς οὖσι" καὶ ζητοῦμεν εἰ μὴ παρέλκει (*i.e.* is redundant) προσκείμενον τὸ "τοῖς ἁγίοις τοῖς οὖσι" τί δύναται σημαίνειν· ὅρα οὖν εἰ μὴ ὥσπερ ἐν τῇ Ἐξόδῳ ὄνομά φησιν ἑαυτοῦ ὁ χρηματίζων Μωσεῖ τὸ ὤν, οὕτως οἱ μετέχοντες τοῦ ὄντος, γίνονται ὄντες, καλούμενοι οἱονεὶ ἐκ τοῦ μὴ εἶναι εἰς τὸ εἶναι "ἐξελέξατο γὰρ ὁ Θεὸς τὰ μὴ ὄντα" φησὶν ὁ αὐτὸς Παῦλος "ἵνα τὰ ὄντα καταργήσῃ," κ.τ.λ. As τοῖς ἁγίοις τοῖς οὖσιν occurs with ἐν and the name of the place in other Epistles (2 Cor., Phil.; cf. Rom. i. 7), it is clear that what Origen refers to as used of the Ephesians only is τοῖς οὖσιν without ἐν Ἐφέσῳ.

Tertullian informs us that Marcion gave the Epistle the title "ad Laodicenos" (*Adv. Marc.* v. 17): "Ecclesiae quidem veritate epistolam istam ad Ephesios habemus emissam, non ad Laodicenos, sed Marcion ei titulum aliquando interpolare (*i.e.* falsify)[1] gestiit, quasi et in isto diligentissimus explorator; nihil autem de titulis interest, cum ad omnes apostolus scripserit, dum ad quosdam." Compare *ibid.* 11, "praetereo hic et de alia epistola, quam nos ad Ephesios praescriptum (*i.e.* superscribed) habemus, haeretici vero ad Laodicenos." It is clear from this that Marcion had not the words ἐν Ἐφέσῳ in his text. But it is also inferred with great probability that Tertullian himself had them not. For he does not charge Marcion with falsifying the text but the title, and he vindicates the title "ad Ephesios" by an appeal to the "veritas ecclesiae," not to the actual words in the text, which would have been conclusive. Moreover, how strange the remark, "nihil autem de titulis interest," etc., if he had ἐν Ἐφέσῳ in the text of the apostle! It is clear that "titulus" here means the superscription, not the address in the text.

Lightfoot points out that there are indications in the earlier Latin commentators that in the copies they used the word "Ephesi," if not absent, was in a different position, which would betray its later introduction. Thus in the middle of the fourth century, Victorinus Afer writes: "Sed haec cum dicit 'Sanctis qui sunt fidelibus Ephesi,' quid adjungitur? 'In Christo Jesu'" (*Mai. Script. Vett. Nova Coll.* iii. p. 87).

Ambrosiaster, in his Commentary, ignores "Ephesi": "Non solum fidelibus scribit, sed et sanctis: ut tunc vere fideles sint, si fuerint sancti in Christo Jesu."

confirmation, while as to the fact that the most ancient copies in his day did not contain the words, he is fully supported.

[1] "Interpolare" in Latin writers means usually to furbish up old articles so as to make them look new.

Sedulius Scotus (eighth or ninth century) writes: "Sanctis. Non omnibus Ephesiis, sed his qui credunt in Christo. Et fidelibus. Omnes sancti fideles sunt, non omnes fideles sancti, etc. Qui sunt in Christo Jesu. Plures fideles sunt, sed non in Christo," etc. The omission of "Ephesi" in the quotations from the text is of no importance; but the position of "qui sunt" is remarkable. It would seem as if some transcriber, finding "sanctis qui sunt et fidelibus in Christo Jesu," and stumbling at the order, transposed "qui sunt" into the position in which Sedulius, or some earlier writer whom he copies, appears to have found them.

Jerome is doubtless referring to Origen when he says (*in loc.*): "Quidam curiosius (*i.e.* with more refinement) quam necesse est, putant ex eo quod Moysi dictum sit 'Haec dices filiis Israel: qui est misit me,' etiam eos qui Ephesi sunt sancti et fideles, essentiae vocabulo nuncupatos. . . . Alii vero simpliciter non ad eos, qui sint, sed qui Ephesi sancti et fideles sint, scriptum arbitrantur." This is obscurely expressed, and it is not clear whether he means to refer to a difference of reading. But as we know that he had read Origen's commentary, he can hardly have been ignorant of the fact that the interpretation he quotes implied the omission of ἐν Ἐφέσῳ, and the reader will observe that the word is "scriptum," not "scriptam," as some commentators have quoted it. If this is taken strictly it must refer to the reading.

When we turn to the Epistle itself we find its whole tone and character out of keeping with the traditional designation. St. Paul had spent about three years at Ephesus "ceasing not to warn every one day and night with tears" (Acts xx. 31). On his last journey to Jerusalem he sent for the elders of Ephesus to meet him at Miletus. His address to them (Acts xx. 18 sqq.) is full of affectionate remembrance of his labours amongst them, and of earnest warnings. The parting is described in touching words: "They fell on his neck and kissed him, sorrowing most of all for the words which he spake, that they should see his face no more." There was no Church with which his relations were more close, nay, so close and affectionate, or in connexion with which he had such sacred and affecting memories. We might expect a letter written to Ephesus to be full of personal reminiscences, and allusions to his labours amongst them; instead of which we have a composition more like a treatise than a letter, and so absolutely destitute of local or personal colouring that it might have been written to a Church which St. Paul had never even visited. We need not attach much importance to the absence of personal greetings. There are no special salutations in the Epp. to the Corinthians and to the Philippians, for example, perhaps because, as Lightfoot says: "Where all alike are known to us, it becomes irksome, if not invidious, to select any for special salutation." But there is not even a general friendly greeting as in those Epistles; there is nothing but the impersonal εἰρήνη τοῖς ἀδελφοῖς, κ.τ.λ., vi. 23. But in addition to the general greeting in Phil., for example, ἀσπάσασθε πάντα ἅγιον ... ἀσπάζονται ὑμᾶς οἱ σὺν ἐμοὶ ἀδελφοί, κ.τ.λ., that Epistle abounds in personal reminiscences, to which there is no parallel here. Even the Epistle to the Colossians, whom St. Paul had never seen, betrays a more lively personal interest.

It is impossible to explain this on the supposition that the Epistle was addressed to the Ephesian Church, so loving to the apostle and so beloved.

But we may go farther than this, for there are expressions in the Epistle which seem impossible to reconcile with the supposition that it is addressed to that Church. Ch. i. 15, "Having heard of your faith," etc., may perhaps be explained, though not very naturally, as referring to the period since his departure from them. Not so the following: iii. 2, "For this cause, I Paul, the prisoner of Christ Jesus in behalf of you Gentiles,—if indeed ye have heard of (or 'were instructed in') the dispensation of the grace of God which was given me to you-ward"; iv. 21, 22, "But ye did not so learn Christ, if indeed ye heard of Him, and were taught in Him," etc.

Dr. Hort thinks the usual reply to the argument from the two latter passages true and sufficient, namely, that εἴγε "is not infrequently used with a rhetorical or appealing force where no real doubt is meant to be expressed," and St. Paul could not express any real doubt in either case about any Church of Proconsular Asia, any more than about the Ephesian Church.

Let it be granted that εἴγε does not imply the existence of a doubt, it certainly (as an intensified "if") implies that doubt is not inconceivable. It cannot mean more than "I am sure," "I do not doubt," "I know," "I am persuaded." But this is not the way in which a man expresses himself about a matter of his own experience, or in which he has himself been the agent. A preacher occupying a friend's pulpit may say "I know," or "if indeed ye have been taught," but not when addressing those whom he has himself taught.

Dr. Hort in confirmation of his remark about the appealing force of εἴγε refers to Ellicott's note, which is a notable instance of *petitio principii*. Having said that εἴγε "does not *in itself* imply the rectitude of the assumption made," as Hermann's *Canon* implies ("εἴγε usurpatur de re quae jure sumpta creditur"), but that this must be gathered from the context, he proceeds: "In the present case there could be no real doubt; 'neque enim ignorare quod hic dicitur (iii. 2) poterant Ephesii quibus Paulus ipse evangelium plusquam biennio praedicaverat,' Estius; comp. ch. iv. 21; 2 Cor. v. 3; Col. i. 23. No argument, then, can be fairly deduced from these words against the inscription of this Ep. to the Ephesians." That is to say, if εἴγε implied doubt, the Epistle could not be addressed to the Ephesians; but it was so addressed, therefore εἴγε does not imply doubt, and therefore is not inconsistent with such an address. The three passages referred to in illustration are singularly unsuitable for the purpose. Ch. iv. 21 belongs to the very Epistle in question. In 2 Cor. v. 3, εἴγε καὶ ἐνδυσάμενοι οὐ γυμνοὶ εὑρεθησόμεθα, and in Col. i. 23, εἴγε ἐπιμένετε τῇ πίστει, κ.τ.λ., it is the future that is spoken of, and the particle has its usual sense, "if, as I assume." Lightfoot, indeed (on Gal. iii. 4), expresses the opinion that in the N.T. εἴγε is even less affirmative than εἴπερ.

Eph. iii. 4 also (whether we adopt Hort's view that ἀναγινώσκοντες means "reading the O.T. Scriptures" or not) seems to imply that the author was not well known to his readers. The Ephesians had not now first to learn what St. Paul's knowledge of the mystery was.

In the early Church the Epistle was universally regarded as addressed to the Ephesians. It is so referred to in the Muratorian Canon; by Irenaeus (*Haer.* i. 3. 1, 4; i. 8. 4; v. 2. 36); by Tertullian (quoted above); by Clement of Alexandria (*Strom.* iv. 65); and by Origen, who, as we saw above, had not ἐν Ἐφέσῳ in his text (Comment. *in loc.*, and *Contra Celsum*, iii. 20).

There is one important exception to this general belief, namely, Marcion, who, as above mentioned, held the Epistle to be addressed to the Laodiceans. This fact has been generally put aside as of no importance, it being supposed that this was a mere critical conjecture of Marcion (as Tertullian assumes), and probably suggested by Col. iv. 16. But considering the antiquity of Marcion, who was of earlier date than any of the Catholic writers cited, we are hardly justified in treating his evidence so lightly, seeing that he could have no theological motive for changing the title. Even if his "ad Laodicenos" was only a critical conjecture, this would justify the inference that the destination of the Epistle was at that time to some extent an open question. But it is unlikely that he should have been led to adopt this title merely by the fact that mention is made elsewhere of an Epistle (not to, but) from Laodicea. There is nothing in the Epistle itself to suggest Laodicea. It is, then, not improbable that he had seen a copy with ἐν Λαοδικείᾳ in the text.

Passing by this, however, for the present, we have the following facts to account for: First, the early absence of ἐν Ἐφέσῳ. As Lightfoot puts it: "We have no direct evidence that a single Greek manuscript during this period (second and third centuries) contained the words in question. The recent manuscripts to which Basil refers in the latter half of the fourth century, are the earliest of which this can be distinctly affirmed" (*Biblical Essays*, p. 381). Secondly, the early and universal recognition in the Church of the Epistle as written to the Ephesians.

Writers who hold ἐν Ἐφέσῳ to have been an integral part of the original text suppose the words to have been omitted for critical reasons, namely, because they seemed not to agree with the character of the Epistle. This theory, to be plausible, would require the facts to be reversed, *i.e.* that the words should be omitted by the later not the earlier authorities, and that the opinion of the early Church should be vacillating. In fact, it explains the unanimity of early opinion by supposing that ἐν Ἐφέσῳ was read without question, and explains the early omission of the words by supposing that opinion was not unanimous.

Apart from this, the theory postulates a critical study of the relations between the apostle and the Churches which it would be a complete anachronism to ascribe to that early age. Much later, indeed, we find Theodore of Mopsuestia led by ἀκούσας in i. 15 to regard the Epistle as written by St. Paul before he had seen the Ephesians. "Numquam profecto dixisset se auditu de illis cognoscentem gratiarum pro illis facere actionem, si eos alicubi vel vidisset, vel ad notitiam ejus illa ratione venire potuissent." So also Severianus and Oecumenius. But it did not occur to Theodore or the others to question the correctness of the text.

An accidental omission of the words is out of the question. The only hypothesis that agrees with the facts is that the Epistle was in some sense an encyclical or circular letter. This seems to have been first suggested in a definite form by Ussher (*Ann. V. et N. Test.* A.D. 64): "Ubi notandum, in antiquis nonnullis codicibus (ut ex Basilii libro ii. adversus Eunomium, et Hieronymi in hunc Apostoli locum commentario, apparet) generatim inscriptam fuisse hanc epistolam, τοῖς ἁγίοις τοῖς οὖσι καὶ πιστοῖς ἐν Χριστῷ Ἰησοῦ, vel (ut in litterarum encyclicarum descriptione fieri solebat) *sanctis qui sunt . . . et fidelibus in Christo Jesu*, ac si Ephesum primo, ut praecipuam, Asiae metropolim missa ea fuisset; transmittenda inde ad reliquas (intersertis singularum nominibus) ejusdem provinciae ecclesias: ad quarum aliquot, quas Paulus ipse nunquam viderat, illa ipsius verba potissimum spectaverint."

There are two forms of this hypothesis. The first (agreeing with Ussher's view) supposes that a blank was originally left after τοῖς οὖσιν, which would be filled in with the names of the respective Churches for which the copies were intended, while in the Church at large some copies would be circulated with a vacant space, in which case, of course, in the copies made from these the blank would be disregarded. Or we might suppose, with Hort, that there was originally only one copy sent by the hand of Tychicus, the blank being filled orally when the Epistle was read in each place, and the name so supplied being naturally written in the copy or copies which would be made for preservation there.

The objection most strongly urged against this view is that there is no trace of copies with any other name in the place of Ἐφέσῳ in the text, and that it is highly improbable that none such should have been preserved. A little consideration will show that no weight is to be attached to this argument. The Epistle "from Laodicea" was either identical with the present Epistle or distinct from it. In the latter case, it has wholly perished, not a single copy having been preserved even to the time of Marcion. In the former case, only the copies bearing other names than that of Ephesus disappeared. Is not this quite natural? When copies were in demand, where would they be sought for but in the metropolitan city and commercial centre of Ephesus? No interest would attach to any particular address. Why, then, should it be thought much more probable that all copies should have been allowed to perish than that only those with names of minor importance should fail to be multiplied? Indeed, the fact itself is not certain, for it is not improbable that a transcript from the Laodicean copy was in Marcion's hands. In any case, we have a close parallel in the fact that the ancient copies which omitted ἐν Ἐφέσῳ had already before Basil's day been superseded by those which inserted the words, and although ℵ B remain (being on vellum), no succeeding copyists have a trace of the reading until we come to the late corrector of 67.

It must be admitted that this plan of leaving blanks savours more of modern than of ancient manner, and resembles the formality of a legal document more than the natural simplicity of St. Paul. Indeed, we have examples in 2 Cor. i. 1 and Gal. i. 2 of the form of address which he would be likely to adopt in an encyclical letter. Besides, any hypothesis which makes Ephesus the chief of the Churches addressed, is open, though in a less degree, to the objections alleged above against the traditional designation.

A second form of the hypothesis supposes the sentence to be complete without anything corresponding to ἐν Ἐφέσῳ. Origen's view of the meaning of the passage when these words are not read has been quoted above, viz. "to the saints who are."

This view has been recently espoused by Dr. Milligan (*Encycl. Brit.*, art. "Ephesians"), who translates: "To the saints existing and faithful in Christ Jesus." But the passages to which he refers in justification of this are by no means sufficient for the purpose. They are—Col. ii. 3, ἐν ᾧ εἰσι πάντες οἱ θησαυροί . . . ἀπόκρυφοι: *ib.* 10, καί ἐστε ἐν αὐτῷ πεπληρωμένοι: iii. 1, οὗ ὁ Χριστός ἐστιν ἐν δεξιᾷ τοῦ Θεοῦ καθήμενος.

In these the predicate is completed by ἐν ᾧ, ἐν αὐτῷ, οὗ, and so the passages supply no parallel to the supposed absolute use of τοῖς οὖσι here as "those existing." Besides, καὶ πιστοῖς comes in very awkwardly and weakly after such an epithet. Bengel, again, interprets: "*Sanctis et fidelibus qui sunt* in omnibus iis locis, quo Tychicus cum hac epistola venit," so that τοῖς οὖσιν = "qui praesto sunt," comparing Acts xiii. 1, κατὰ τὴν οὖσαν ἐκκλησίαν, and Rom. xiii. 1, αἱ δὲ οὖσαι ἐξουσίαι. But in the former case ἐν Ἀντιοχείᾳ had just preceded, so that only ἐκεῖ has to be supplied; in the latter the verb simply means "to be in existence." Not to dwell on the untenable suggestion that τοῖς οὖσιν should be taken with ἁγίοις ("the saints who are really such"), there remains the perfectly grammatical construction, "the saints who are also faithful" (see note *in loc.*). The difficulty of the construction is actually diminished by the absence of ἐν Ἐφέσῳ.

The Epistle, then, is best regarded as addressed, not to a Church, but to the Gentile converts in Laodicea, Hierapolis, and Colossae, and elsewhere in Phrygia and the neighbourhood of that province. This is the view adopted by Reiche, Ewald, and (independently) by Prof. Milligan (who, however, supposes the Epistle addressed only to the Gentile converts of Laodicea and Colossae). It meets most of the difficulties. It explains the absence of local references combined with the local limitation implied in vi. 22. It also escapes the difficulty of supposing a blank space in i. 1. Further, it explains the remarkable expression, Col. iv. 16, "the Epistle from Laodicea." That the Epistle referred to was not written to Laodicea appears highly probable from the fact that a salutation is sent through Colossae to the Laodiceans, which would be inexplicable if they were receiving by the same messenger a letter addressed to themselves; and the expression "from Laodicea" agrees with this, since Tychicus would reach Laodicea first, so that the Colossians would receive the letter from thence. Moreover, the hypothesis explains the remarkable fact that the Epistle contains no allusion to doctrinal errors such as had taken so great a hold in Colossae. Yet that such errors extended at least to Laodicea is not only probable, but is confirmed by the apostle's direction that the Epistle to Colossae should be read in Laodicea also.

There is no difficulty in understanding how the title "to the Ephesians" would come to be attached to the Epistle, since it was from Ephesus that copies would reach the Christian world generally. A parallel case is the title of the Epistle to the Hebrews, πρὸς Ἑβραίους, which, though of doubtful appropriateness, was never questioned. Once accepted as addressed to the Ephesians, the analogy of other Epistles in which τοῖς οὖσιν is followed by the name of a place would naturally suggest the insertion of ἐν Ἐφέσῳ.

The hypothesis that the Epistle is a "circular" letter has been adopted (with various modifications) by a very great number of scholars, including Bengel, Neander, Harless, Olshausen, Reuss, Arch. Robertson, Ellicott, Lightfoot, Hort, B. Weiss, Wold-Schmidt, Milligan.

§ 2. OF THE GENUINENESS OF THE EPISTLE.

External Evidence. — The earliest express reference to the Epistle as St. Paul's is that of Irenaeus; but inasmuch as, if not genuine, it must be much later than St. Paul, evidence of acquaintance with it on the part of early writers is important. When we add to this the fact that it professes to be St. Paul's, we are fairly justified in saying that evidence of its reception is evidence of its genuineness. We begin then with—

Clement of Rome, c. 64, ὁ ἐκλεξάμενος τὸν Κύριον Ἰησοῦν Χριστὸν καὶ ἡμᾶς δι' αὐτοῦ εἰς λαὸν περιούσιον. Compare Eph. i. 4, 5, καθὼς ἐξελέξατο ἡμᾶς ἐν αὐτῷ ... προορίσας ἡμᾶς ... διὰ Ἰησοῦ Χριστοῦ. Still closer is c. 46, ἢ οὐχὶ ἕνα Θεὸν ἔχομεν καὶ ἕνα Χριστόν; καὶ ἓν πνεῦμα τῆς χάριτος τὸ ἐκχυθὲν ἐφ' ἡμᾶς καὶ μία κλῆσις ἐν Χριστῷ; compare Eph. iv. 4–6. Again, c. 36, ἠνεῴχθησαν ἡμῶν οἱ ὀφθαλμοὶ τῆς καρδίας; cf. Eph. i. 18. And c. 38, ὑποτασσέσθω ἕκαστος τῷ πλησίον αὐτοῦ; cf. Eph. v. 21.

The part of the *Didaché* called the Two Ways contains the following (*Did.* iv. 10, 11, also worked up by Barnabas, xix. 7): οὐκ ἐπιτάξεις δούλῳ σου ἢ παιδίσκῃ τοῖς ἐπὶ τὸν αὐτὸν Θεὸν ἐλπίζουσιν, ἐν πικρίᾳ σου; and to servants: ὑμεῖς δὲ οἱ δοῦλοι ὑποταγήσεσθε τοῖς κυρίοις ὑμῶν ὡς τύπῳ Θεοῦ ἐν αἰσχύνῃ καὶ φόβῳ. Compare Eph. vi. 9, 5. The coincidence is in substance rather than in words, but it is best accounted for by supposing a knowledge of our Epistle.

Ignatius, *Ep. ad Eph.* c. 12, Παύλου συμμύσται (ἐστε), τοῦ ἡγιασμένου, ... ὃς ἐν πάσῃ ἐπιστολῇ μνημονεύει ὑμῶν ἐν Χριστῷ Ἰησοῦ. Many writers (including Hefele, *in loc.*, Alford, Harless, and, less decidedly, Westcott and Robertson) render this "in all his Epistle," viz. to you, or "in every part of his Epistle." But this is untenable. For, in the first place, it is ungrammatical; certainly no example has been produced which is quite parallel. Hefele adduces πᾶσα Ἱεροσόλυμα, Matt. ii. 3; and πᾶς Ἰσραήλ, Rom. xi. 26; but these are proper names. Other supposed parallels are examined by Lightfoot, *in loc.* Two have been relied on by later writers, viz. Acts xvii. 26, ἐπὶ παντὸς προσώπου τῆς γῆς, and Aristot. *Eth. Nic.* i. 13. 7, πᾶν σῶμα. But neither are these analogous. There is only one πρόσωπον τῆς γῆς, hence this term is used (not, indeed, with πᾶν) without the article in the

Sept. (Gen. iv. 14, vi. 7, xi. 8, πρ. πάσης τῆς γῆς = Luke xxi. 35). It is easy to understand, then, how it should come to be so used even with πᾶν preceding.

At first sight πᾶν σῶμα in Aristotle, *l.c.*, seems to present a closer parallel. The passage runs: δεῖ τὸν πολιτικὸν εἰδέναι πῶς τὰ περὶ ψυχῆς· ὥσπερ καὶ τὸν ὀφθαλμοὺς θεραπεύοντα, καὶ πᾶν σῶμα; *i.e.* he that heals the eyes must know the whole body. But σῶμα in the abstract sense, *i.e.* as meaning, not this or that individual body, but the body as opposed to the soul, is used by Aristotle without the article, just as ψυχή is also used (see, for example, *Eth. Nic.* i. 8. 2; 6. 12, etc.). In this particular instance the omission of the article was, in fact, necessary to precision; for πᾶν τὸ σῶμα might mean the body of him whose eyes were to be healed, whereas what is intended is the human body generally. Since, therefore, πᾶν σῶμα here does not mean the whole individual body, it furnishes no parallel to the alleged meaning of πάσῃ ἐπιστολῇ, and we are compelled to abide by the rendering "in every Epistle."

But, in the second place, the proposed rendering gives a wholly unsuitable sense. The fact of St. Paul devoting a letter to the Ephesians would deserve mention, but to what purpose to say, "in his whole letter to you he mentions you"? We do not speak of making mention of a man to himself, nor did the Greeks so use μνημονεύειν. But even if this were possible, it would be, as Lightfoot says, "singularly unmeaning, if not untrue," of the present Epistle. Alford, indeed, thinks the expression fully justified, and quotes Pearson, who says: "Tota enim Epistola ad Ephesios scripta, ipsos Ephesios, eorumque honorem et curam, maxime spectat, et summe honorificam eorum memoriam ad posteros transmittit. In aliis epistolis apostolus eos ad quos scribit saepe acriter objurgat aut parce laudat. Hic omnibus modis perpetuo se Ephesiis applicat," etc. All this if said of the Ephesians in a letter addressed to others might be called μνημονεύειν, although this would be a strangely weak word to use. Does not "acriter objurgare" involve μνημονεύειν as much as "laudare"? But the peculiarity of the Epistle is that nothing is mentioned or even alluded to which is personal to the Ephesians.

Kiene (*Stud. u. Krit.* 1869, p. 286) understands by πάσῃ ἐπιστολῇ "an entire letter," but without attempting to show the possibility of this rendering. But can we say that St. Paul mentions the Ephesians "in every letter"? Allowing for a natural hyperbole we may answer, Yes. Ephesus and the Christians there are referred to either alone or with others in Rom. xvi. 5; 1 Cor. xv. 32, xvi. 8, 19; 2 Cor. i. 8 sq.; and 1 and 2 Tim.

The longer recension of Ignatius has ὃς πάντοτε ἐν ταῖς δεήσεσιν αὐτοῦ μνημονεύει ὑμῶν. The Armenian Version reads μνημονεύω, which would be true to fact, for in five out of the six other

Epistles, Ignatius does mention the Ephesians. But the authority is insufficient.

Accepting, then, the usual reading and the grammatical rendering, we cannot infer from the words that Ignatius knew the Epistle as addressed to the Ephesians. Rather they would suggest the opposite conclusion. For, when Ignatius desired to remind his readers of St. Paul's regard for them, it would be strange that he should only refer to the mention of them in other Epistles, and not at all to that which had been specially addressed to them.

The word συμμύσται has been thought to have been suggested by Eph. i. 9, iii. 3, 4, 9, etc.; but this is very precarious, for St. Paul uses no expression there which would suggest Ignatius' word, and συμμύστης is used by Origen (*In Jes. Naue Hom.* 7, ii. p. 413), "ipse (Paulus) enim est symmystes Christi," and by Hippolytus (*in Dan.* p. 174, Lagarde).

The question as to Ignatius' knowledge and reception of the Epistle is quite a different one. In the address of his Epistle he has several expressions which may have been suggested by the early verses of our Epistle: τῇ εὐλογημένῃ, πληρώματι, προωρισμένη πρὸ αἰώνων εἶναι ... εἰς δόξαν, ἐκλελεγμένην, ἐν θελήματι τοῦ πατρός. More certain is cap. i., μιμηταὶ ὄντες τοῦ Θεοῦ, borrowed apparently from Eph. v. 1, and Polyc. 5, ἀγαπᾶν τὰς συμβίους ὡς ὁ Κύριος τὴν ἐκκλησίαν, a reminiscence of Eph. v. 29. In the following ch. vi. the reference to the Christian's πανοπλία was probably suggested by Eph. vi. 11, although the parts of the armour are differently assigned. Also Ign. *Eph.* c. 9, ὡς ὄντες λίθοι ναοῦ πατρός, ἡτοιμασμένοι εἰς οἰκοδομὴν Θεοῦ πατρός (Eph. ii. 20—22).

Contemporaneous with Ignatius is the *Epistle of Polycarp to the Philippians.* It contains two quotations from the present Epistle in cap. i., χάριτί ἐστε σεσωσμένοι, οὐκ ἐξ ἔργων, from Eph. ii. 5, 8, 9; and c. 12 (of which the Greek is lost), "ut his scripturis dictum est, *irascimini et nolite peccare et, sol non occidat super iracundiam vestram*, from Eph. iv. 26. Some commentators, indeed, suppose that Ignatius here is, independently of our Epistle, making the same combination of two O.T. texts, or that both adopt a combination made by some earlier writer. That is to say, they regard "let not the sun go down on your wrath" as a quotation from Deut. xxiv. 13, 15, verses which have nothing in common with this but the reference to the sun going down, for what they deal with is the hire of a poor man and the pledge taken from the poor. That two writers should independently connect the words in Deut. with those in Ps. iv., changing in the former "his hire" into "your anger," is beyond the bounds of probability. As to the difficulty which is found in Polycarp citing the N.T. as Scripture, perhaps the explanation may be that, recognising the first sentence as a quotation from the O.T., he hastily concluded that the second was so also. For in the context immediately preceding he confesses that his acquaintance with the Scriptures was not equal to that of the Philippians. This is at least more probable than an accidental coincidence.

Hermas, *Mand.* iii., has, ἀλήθειαν ἀγάπα καὶ πᾶσα ἀλήθεια ἐκ τοῦ στόματός σου ἐκπορευέσθω, doubtless from Eph. iv. 25, 29. A little after we have, μηδὲ λύπην ἐπάγειν τῷ πνεύματι τῷ σεμνῷ καὶ ἀληθεῖ; cf. *ib.* ver. 30. Again, *Sim.* ix. 13, ἔσονται εἰς ἓν πνεῦμα καὶ ἓν σῶμα, and 17, μία πίστις αὐτῶν ἐγένετο, seem to be reminiscences of Eph. iv. 4, 5.

The Valentinians also quoted the Epistle, iii. 4–18, as γράφη (Hipp. *Philos.* vi. 34).

By the close of the second century the Epistle was universally received as St. Paul's. Irenaeus, *adv. Haer.* v. 2. 3, has, καθὼς ὁ μακάριος Παῦλός φησιν, ἐν τῇ πρὸς Ἐφεσίους ἐπιστολῇ· ὅτι μέλη ἐσμὲν τοῦ σώματος, ἐκ τῆς σαρκὸς αὐτοῦ καὶ ἐκ τῶν ὀστέων αὐτοῦ (Eph. v. 30). Also i. 8. 5, he similarly quotes Eph. v. 13. Clem. Alex. *Strom.* iv. § 65, having quoted 1 Cor. xi. 3 and Gal. v. 16 sqq., with φησὶν ὁ ἀπόστολος, adds, διὸ καὶ ἐν τῇ πρὸς Ἐφεσίους γράφει· ὑποτασσόμενοι ἀλλήλοις ἐν φόβῳ Θεοῦ, κ.τ.λ., Eph. v. 21–25. Also *Paed.* i. § 18, ὁ ἀπόστολος ἐπιστέλλων πρὸς Κορινθίους φησὶν (2 Cor. xi. 2) . . . σαφέστατα δὲ Ἐφεσίοις γράφων . . . λέγων· μέχρι καταντήσωμεν οἱ πάντες, κ.τ.λ., Eph. iv. 13–15. Tertullian and Marcion have already been quoted.

From this evidence it is all but certain that the Epistle already existed about 95 A.D. (Clement), quite certain that it existed about 110 A.D. (Ignatius, Polycarp).

Not to be overlooked as an item of evidence of the genuineness of the Epistle is the mention, in Col. iv. 16, of an Epistle "from Laodicea." This has been already referred to for a different purpose. We learn from it that St. Paul wrote at or about the same time, besides the Epistles to Philemon and to the Colossians, an Epistle of a more or less encyclical character, not addressed to the Laodiceans, else it would be called the Epistle "to Laodicea," or "to the Laodiceans," and, for a similar reason, not addressed by name to any particular Church or Churches. It must also be considered highly probable that it was conveyed by the same messenger, Tychicus, for it was not every day that St. Paul would have the opportunity of a disciple travelling from Rome (or even from Caesarea) to Laodicea. It is hardly credible that a Church which carefully preserved and copied the unimportant private letter to Philemon, should allow this important encyclical to be lost. There was a further guarantee of its preservation in the fact that this did not depend on one single Church. Now, here we have an Epistle which satisfies these conditions; it is in some sort at least an encyclical letter; according to the best evidence, it was not addressed to a particular Church, and indirectly it purports to have been written about the same time and conveyed by the same messenger, as the Epp. to the Colossians and to Philemon. This would amount to nothing if there were reason to suspect a forgery suggested by Col. iv. 16. But this is entirely out of the question, for there is not the slightest indication in the Epistle which could lead an ordinary reader to that identification. So effectually, indeed, was it concealed, that with the exception of the heretic Marcion, it does not seem to have occurred to any ancient writer ; and on what ground Marcion judged that the Epistle was to the Laodiceans we do not know. We do know, however, that his adoption of that title did not lead others to think of Col. iv. 16, and even his own disciples seem not to have followed him.[1]

Whatever probability belongs to this identification (and the reasons alleged against it have little weight), goes directly to confirm the genuineness of the Epistle, and must in all fairness be taken into account. As the Canon of Marcion must have been drawn up before the middle of the second century, there is evidence of the general reception of the Epistle as St. Paul's at that period.

Many of the ablest opponents of the genuineness admit the early date of composition and reception of the Epistle. Ewald assigned it to about 75–80 A.D. Scholten also to 80. Holtzmann, Mangold, and others to about 100. The late date 140, assigned by some of the earlier critics, is irreconcilable with the evidence of its early recognition.

Internal Evidence.—Objections. The genuineness of the Epistle appears to have been first questioned by Schleiermacher (who suggested that Tychicus was commissioned to write it) and Usteri ; but the first to examine the internal evidence in detail was De Wette. His conclusion was that it is a verbose amplification ("wortreiche Erweiterung") of the Epistle to the Colossians, and in style shows a notable falling off from that of St. Paul. Against the subjective element of this estimate may be placed the judgment of Chrysostom, Erasmus, Grotius, and Coleridge. Chrysostom says : "The Epistle overflows with lofty thoughts and doctrines . . . Things which he scarcely anywhere else utters, he here expounds." ὑψηλῶν σφόδρα γέμει τῶν νοημάτων· ἃ γὰρ μηδαμοῦ ἐφθέγξατο, ταῦτα ἐνταῦθα δηλοῖ. Erasmus (although noting the difference in style, etc.): "Idem in hac epistola Pauli fervor, eadem profunditas, idem omnino spiritus ac pectus." He adds:

---

[1] This is Lightfoot's explanation of the perplexing passage in Epiphanius (*Haeres.* xlii.). Epiphanius speaks of Marcion as recognising the Ep. to the Eph., and also portions of the so-called Ep. to the Laodiceans. He blames Marcion for citing Eph. iv. 5, not from Eph., but from the Ep. to the Laodiceans. See Lightfoot, *Biblical Essays*, p. 383.

"Verum non alibi sermo hyperbatis, anapodotis, aliisque incommoditatibus molestior, sive id interpretis fuit, quo fuit usus in hac, sive sensuum sublimitatem sermonis facultas non est assequnta. Certe stilus tantum dissonat a caeteris Pauli epistolis ut alterius videri possit nisi pectus atque indoles Paulinae mentis hanc prossus illi vindicaret." Grotius: "Rerum sublimitatem adaequam verbis sublimioribus quam ulla unquam habuit lingua humana." Coleridge (*Table Talk*): "The Epistle to the Ephesians . . . is one of the divinest compositions of man. It embraces every doctrine of Christianity; - first, those doctrines peculiar to Christianity, and then those precepts common to it with natural religion." Others have also judged that, as compared with Colossians, it is in system "far deeper, and more recondite, and more exquisite" (Alford).

De Wette was answered by Lünemann, Meyer, and others. Some of the critics who followed De Wette went beyond him, rejecting the Ep. to the Colossians also, which he fully accepted, and assigning to both a much later date. Schwegler and Baur, finding in the Epistle traces of Gnostic and Montanist language and ideas, ascribed both Epistles to the middle of the second century. Similarly Hilgenfeld, who, however, attributed the Epistles to distinct authors. The fallacy of these latter speculations has been shown by Holtzmann, who has devoted an entire volume to the criticism of the two Epistles (*Kritik der Epheser und Kolosserbriefe auf Grund einer Analyse ihres Verwandtschaftsverhältnisses*, Leipz. 1872). His conclusion is that the writer of the present Epistle had before him a genuine, but much shorter, Epistle to the Colossians, on which he founded his encyclical, and that the same writer subsequently interpolated the Epistle to the Colossians. (This was first suggested by Hitzig, 1870.) Soden (in two articles in the *Jahrb. f. Prot. Theol.* 1885, 1887) maintained the genuineness of Col. with the exception of nine verses, and in his *Comm.* he withdraws this exception, regarding only i. 16b, 17 as a gloss.

Lastly, the most recent writer on the subject, Jülicher (*Einleitung in das Neue Testament*, 1894), will only go so far as to say that our Epistle cannot with certainty be reckoned as St. Paul's, while neither can its genuineness be unconditionally denied.

Objections from the Language of the Epistle.—Let us first notice the argument from the language of the Epistle. Holtzmann remarks, as favourable to the Pauline authorship, that it contains eighteen words not found elsewhere in the N.T. except in St. Paul. ἄρα οὖν occurs eight times in Romans, and besides only in Gal. i. and 2 Thess. and Eph. each once; διό, a favourite of St. Paul, occurs in Eph. five times (not in Col.). But the favourable impression created by this is outweighed by the peculiarities found in the Epistle. It is indeed admitted that the existence of ἅπαξ λεγόμενα would be no argument against the genuineness, if only they were not so numerous. There are, in fact, 42 words which are ἅ. λ. (in the N.T.), not including αἰχμαλωτεύειν, which is in a quotation. (Holtzmann reckoned only 37, but Thayer gives 42.[1]) This number, however, is not greater in proportion than that in admitted Epistles of St. Paul. Romans contains 100 (neglecting quotations); 1 Cor. 108; 2 Cor. 95; Gal. 33; Phil. 41 (Col. has 38). The percentage is, in fact, rather less in our Epistle (see Robertson, *Dict. of Bible*, i. 954*a*, note). It is, indeed, fair in such a comparison to take account of St. Paul's vocabulary rather than that of the N.T. generally. Accordingly, Holtzmann notes that there are here 39 words which, though occurring elsewhere in the N.T., are not found in St. Paul (the Pastoral Epp. and Col. are, of course, not counted). In Col. there are 15. Some of these, indeed, are such common words, that it is somewhat surprising that St. Paul has not used them elsewhere, such as ἄγνοια, ἀπατάω, δῶρον, φρόνησις, ὕψος, to which we may add, though not common, σωτήριον, εὔσπλαγχνος. But then, each of these occurs only once, and hence they cannot be regarded as indications of a different writer. Of the other words that have been noted as peculiar, some belong to the description of the Christian's armour, and for these there would be no obvious place except in connexion with a similar figure; while others, such as καταρτισμός, προσκαρτέρησις, ὁσιότης, cannot properly be reckoned as peculiar, since in other Epistles we find καταρτίζω, κατάρτισις, προσκαρτερεῖν, ὁσίως. So also, although ἄνοιξις does not occur elsewhere, ἄνοιξις τοῦ στόματος, vi. 19, is parallel to 2 Cor. vi. 11, τὸ στόμα ἡμῶν ἀνέῳγε. Even without making these allowances, there is little difference between this Epistle and that to the Galatians, for example, in this respect. The latter Epistle, which is rather shorter, contains, in addition to 32 ἅπαξ λεγόμενα, 42 words which, though occurring elsewhere in the N.T., are not found in the other Epistles of St. Paul. Such calculations are, indeed, futile, except in connexion with words so frequently used as to be characteristic of the writer.

More weight is to be given to the principle of the objection, that words are used here to express certain ideas which St. Paul is in the habit of expressing differently, and, again, that words used by him are here employed with a different meaning. But when we come to the instances we find them few, and for the most part unimportant. Of the first class, De Wette mentions τὰ ἐπουράνια for "heaven" (five times); τὰ πνευματικά for "spirits"; διάβολος twice (elsewhere only in 1 and 2 Tim.), κοσμοκράτωρ, σωτήριον. Soden adds, as favourite words of the writer, μεθοδεία (twice), and δέσμιος (twice). These, with τὰ ἐπουράνια and διάβολος, he says, it is strange not to find slipping from St. Paul's pen elsewhere. As to δέσμιος, however, it actually occurs in Philemon, and Holtz-

---

[1] See list at end of the Introduction.

mann had already pointed out that it was not to be expected except in Epistles written when St. Paul was a prisoner. As to διάβολος, of which much has been made because St. Paul elsewhere uses Σατανᾶς, if the writer of the Acts, or of the Fourth Gospel, and other N.T. writers, could use Σατανᾶς and διάβολος indifferently, why might not Paul use the former in his earlier Epistles, and the latter twice in this? The difference is only that between the Hebrew and the Greek forms, and is analogous to that between Πέτρος and Κηφᾶς, of which the former is used twice and the latter four times in the Epistle to the Galatians. Again, although τὰ ἐπουράνια (which is not = "the heavens") is not found elsewhere in St. Paul, the adjective occurs with the meaning "heavenly" in 1 Cor. xv. 40, 48, 49, and in Phil. ii. 10. Other un-Pauline expressions are found in τὰ θελήματα, αἱ διάνοιαι, πρὸ καταβολῆς κόσμου, φωτίζειν as a function of the apostle, ὁ ἄρχων τῆς ἐξουσίας τοῦ ἀέρος, ὁ Θεὸς τοῦ Κυρίου ἡμῶν Ἰησοῦ Χριστοῦ (i. 17. 3); πνεῦμα τοῦ νοός, ἡ ἁγία ἐκκλησία (ver. 27, not, however, in this form); οἱ ἅγιοι ἀπόστολοι καὶ προφῆται, ἴστε γινώσκοντες, διδοναί τινα τί (i. 22, iv. 11); ἀγαθὸς πρός τι (iv. 29); ἀγαπᾶν τὸν Κύριον (Paul has ἀγ. τὸν Θεόν), ἀγαπᾶν τὴν ἐκκλησίαν, of Christ; εἰς πάσας τὰς γενεὰς τοῦ αἰῶνος τῶν αἰώνων.

It is, for the most part, only by their number that these and similar instances can be supposed to carry weight as an objection to the Pauline authorship; two or three, however, are somewhat striking. On ὁ Θεὸς τοῦ Κυρίου ἡμῶν, see the note. It is certainly an unexpected expression, but it is one which no later imitator, holding such lofty views of Christ as are here expressed, would have ventured on without Pauline precedent. It has its parallel in John xx. 17. Again, although the expression ὁ Χριστὸς ἠγάπησε τὴν ἐκκλησίαν taken by itself sounds peculiar, it is not so when we find that it is suggested by the preceding words, οἱ ἄνδρες, ἀγαπᾶτε τὰς γυναῖκας καθὼς καί, κ.τ.λ.

The phrase which seems to create the greatest difficulty is τοῖς ἁγίοις ἀποστόλοις καὶ προφήταις. It is said that this, especially when compared with Col. i. 26, is strongly suggestive of a later generation which set the apostles and prophets (of the new dispensation) on a lofty pedestal as objects of veneration. Some of those critics who accept the Epistle as genuine have suggested that we have to do with a gloss (the whole or, at least, the latter half of ver. 5, Reuss; the word ἁγίοις, Jülicher), or a dislocation of the text (Robertson), ἁγίοις being the mediate or general (ἐφανερώθη, Col.), the ἀπ. κ. πρ. the immediate or special (ἀπεκαλύφθη) recipients of the revelation. Lachmann and Tregelles put a comma after ἁγίοις, so that ἀπ. κ. πρ. is in apposition with ἁγίοις. So far as the difficulty is in the writer's application of the term ἁγίοις, it appears to be due very much to the importation into ἁγίοις of the modern notion of holiness (see note). However this may be, the objection to the genuineness drawn from this word is deprived of all force by the words which follow presently in ver. 8, ἐμοὶ τῷ ἐλαχιστοτέρῳ πάντων ἁγίων. It is quite incredible that a writer otherwise so successful in assuming the character of St. Paul, should here in the same breath forget his part and (as it is thought) exaggerate it. The same consideration, in part at least, applies to the other difficulty found in the words, viz. that they represent the apostles as all recognising the principle of the calling of the Gentiles,—a principle which St. Paul elsewhere (and here also) claims as specially his gospel. The apostles are spoken of collectively also in 1 Cor. xv. 7; and as they had cordially assented to St. Paul's teaching as to the admission of the Gentiles (Gal. ii. 9), it is quite natural that he should speak of it here as revealed "to the apostles."

As examples of Pauline words used in a new sense, are quoted μυστήριον, οἰκονομία, περιποίησις. As to the first, there is really no difference between its meaning here and elsewhere in St. Paul; or if the sense in ver. 32 is thought to be different, that is a difference within this Epistle itself, in which the word occurs five times in its usual sense. οἰκονομία is found (besides Col. i. 25) in 1 Cor. ix. 17 of St. Paul's own stewardship, while in Eph. it is used of the ordering of the fulness of the times (i. 10), or of the grace of God (iii. 2), or of the mystery, etc. (iii. 9). Here, again, so little ground is there for assuming any serious difference in meaning, that in the last two passages the meaning "stewardship" (RV. marg.) is perfectly suitable. Again, περιποίησις in i. 14 is said to be concrete, whereas in 1 Thess. v. 9, 2 Thess. ii. 14, it is abstract. Admitting this (which is questioned), the difference is parallel to that, for example, in the meaning of ἀποκάλυψις in 1 Cor. xiv. 26 and i. 7.

In reference to these objections, and some others that have to be mentioned, it is important to remember that we are not dealing with an anonymous work. There are many points of difference which in such a case might be used with effect against the Pauline authorship, but which put on a different aspect when we consider that the Epistle makes a distinct claim to be the work of St. Paul,— so that, if not genuine, it is the work of a writer who designed that it should be mistaken for the work of that apostle,—and when we add to this the fact that it was received as such from the earliest times. For a writer of such ability as the author, and one so familiar with the writings of St. Paul, would take care to avoid, at least, obvious deviations from the style and language of the author whom he is imitating. From this point of view, not only ἅπαξ λεγόμενα, but still more the use of new expressions for Pauline ideas, instead of offering an argument against the Pauline author-

b

ship, become arguments against forgery. If, indeed, actual contradictions or inconsistencies could be shown, it would be different; but they cannot.

There are, it is true, at first sight, differences in the point of view taken in this Epistle and in others of St. Paul; but these have been exaggerated. For example, when in v. 1 the expression τέκνα ἀγαπητά occurs, Holtzmann remarks that this is elsewhere used by St. Paul, not to urge his readers as beloved children to imitate their Father, God, but because they owed their conversion to himself, so that he was himself their father (1 Cor. iv. 14, 17, cf. 2 Tim. i. 2). Yet the expression is quite naturally led up to here. "Forgive, for God has forgiven; therefore imitate God, whose children ye are." Addressing those to whom he was a stranger, he could not call on them to imitate himself (1 Cor. iv. 16, xi. 1), which, moreover, here, where the question is of forgiveness, would be an impossible bathos; nor could he call them his own children. As to the expression "children of God," we have a parallel in Rom. viii. 16, ὅτι ἐσμὲν τέκνα Θεοῦ.

Again, ἡ λεγομένη ἀκροβυστία, ἡ λεγομένη περιτομή (ii. 11), taken by themselves, may seem to deny any real significance to circumcision (contrary to Rom. iii. 1; Phil. iii. 5; Col. ii. 11, 13); yet a closer consideration will show that it is not so. "Ye who are contemptuously called uncircumcision by those who call themselves the circumcision, a circumcision in the flesh only (note the addition ἐν σαρκί), as if the mere fleshly circumcision had any spiritual value." Not only does the sense of the whole passage agree with Rom. ii. 26–29 (as Holtzmann allows), but the form of expression is natural as coming from the writer who in Phil. iii. 2 uses the strong and scornful word κατατομή, adding ἡμεῖς γάρ ἐσμεν ἡ περιτομή, οἱ πνεύματι Θεοῦ λατρεύοντες, κ.τ.λ.: to which we may add, for those who accept Colossians, Col. ii. 11. Holtzmann, indeed, thinks that Paul would not say, ἡ λεγομένη ἀκροβυστία, he being himself one of the Jews who so designated them (Rom. ii. 26, 27; iii. 30, iv. 9; Gal. ii. 7). But this corresponds to Col. iii. 11, οὐκ ἔνι . . . περιτομὴ καὶ ἀκροβυστία. (Compare the less forcible οὔτε περιτομή τι ἰσχύει, κ.τ.λ., Gal. v. 6, vi. 15.)

Holtzmann considers this way of speaking of circumcision as belonging to the general view of the Law taken in this Epistle, as merely typical. It is not spoken of, says v. Soden, as having a religious or moral significance, as παιδαγωγὸς εἰς Χριστόν, or as working κατάρα, but only in its formal character as the sum of ἐντολαὶ ἐν δόγμασιν, its content being left out of view. Compare, on the contrary, Rom. ix. 4; Gal. v. 23 (where, however, we have νόμος, not ὁ νόμος). Its significance consists in its causing a separation and even hostility between Jews and Gentiles. But this is not a greater difference than that between the ideas of a παιδαγωγός and a source of κατάρα, which we find within one epistle, that to the Galatians.

Objections from the line of thought in the Epistle.—It is said, further, that the whole view of the Church as regards the union of Jews and Gentiles is peculiar; St. Paul never represents it as the object or even an object of Christ's work to bring into one Jews and Gentiles (ii. 13-18, 19-22, iii. 5 sqq., iv. 7-16). This leads us further; we notice that the writer never speaks of local Churches, but only of the (one) Church. This has been supposed to indicate that he wrote at a time when the several local Churches were drawing together in resistance to a common danger, and binding themselves together by a single organisation. But the Church here is not represented as made up of individual Churches, but of individual men; nor is there any mention of external unity or common organisation. Nor is the conception of one "Church," which we find here, quite new. Not to mention passages where St. Paul speaks of himself as formerly persecuting "the Church of God" (1 Cor. xv. 9; Gal. i. 13; Phil. iii. 6), we have in 1 Cor. xii. 28, ἔθετο ὁ Θεὸς ἐν τῇ ἐκκλησίᾳ πρῶτον ἀποστόλους, κ.τ.λ. We may compare also Acts xx. 28, τὴν ἐκκλησίαν τοῦ Θεοῦ ἣν περιεποιήσατο, κ.τ.λ. In Col. we have ἡ ἐκκλησία in the same sense, as the universal Church (i. 18, 24), although it is also used of local Churches (iv. 15, 16). The encyclical character of the present Epistle sufficiently accounts for the predominance of the former view here. There is, however, no inconsistency in this advance upon the earlier conception. It is, indeed, remarkable that in Eph. the thought of the unity of the Church is so dominant that Christ's work is represented as having immediate reference to it rather than to individuals (compare v. 25-27, 29, 32, with Gal. ii. 20); of this He is the Saviour (ver. 23); it is this that He has sanctified by His offering of Himself (ver. 26). But it is essential to observe that all this occurs, not in an exposition of the nature of Christ's work, but in illustration of the duties of husbands to their wives. Any reference to His work in relation to individual men would have been entirely irrelevant. That reference comes in naturally in i. 7, v. 2, ii. 16 ff. But the first two passages, it is said, appear to be only verbal reminiscences of St. Paul. It is, however, much easier to conceive St. Paul writing as in *vv.* 25-32, than to suppose it the work of another who wishes to be mistaken for him. It is no doubt very remarkable that the whole circle of thought which in St. Paul has its centre in the death of Christ, here falls into the background. In i. 15-ii. 10, where the resurrection is twice mentioned, and the whole work of redemption dwelt on, the death is not mentioned. So also i. 11-14, iii. 1-21. In fact, with the exception of i. 7 (from Col. i. 14), it is only incidentally referred to as a pattern, and then with remarkable differences from St. Paul, that being attributed to Christ which is elsewhere attributed to God. (Yet, on the other hand, in iv. 32 it is God in Christ who is said to forgive, while in Col. iii. 13 it is Christ who forgives.) The only place in which the death of Christ is dealt with in greater detail is ii. 14-16; and there the interest is not in the reconciliation of individuals and the forgiveness of their sins, but in this, that the Law, and with it the enmity between Jew and Gentile, are removed. These and other differences that have been pointed out are no doubt striking, but they involve no inconsistencies; they are only developments of ideas of which the germ is found in St. Paul's other writings.

The representation of Christ as the Head of the Body, which is the Church, is common to Eph. and Col., and therefore cannot be alleged against the genuineness of the former by any who admit the latter. Elsewhere, when St. Paul uses the figure of the body, the whole body is said to be in Christ (Rom. xii. 4, 5), or to be Christ (1 Cor. xii. 12), and the head appears only as one member among many (*ib.* 21). But in those cases the point to be illustrated was the mutual relation of the members of the Church, and there is nothing inconsistent in the modification of the figure which we find in these Epp.

Again, as to the Person and Office of Christ, we have in both Epp. a notable advance beyond the earlier Epistles, as in Col. i. 16 ff., "in Him were all things created, in the heaven, and upon the earth . . . all things have been created through Him, and unto Him; and He is before all things, and in Him all things consist." But we have at least the germ of this in 1 Cor. viii. 6, εἷς Κύριος Ἰησοῦς Χριστός, δι' οὗ τὰ πάντα, καὶ ἡμεῖς δι' αὐτοῦ. In Eph., however, we have added to this the further thought that things in heaven as well as on earth have part in the reconciliation effected by Him (Eph. i. 10); and all this is referred to a purpose of the Divine will directed towards Christ Himself from the beginning.

Once more, the second coming of Christ has fallen into the background, and does not appear to have a part in bringing about the fulfilment of the promised blessings. Rather does the writer seem to anticipate a series of αἰῶνες ἐπερχόμενοι. But, as Hort observes, "nothing was more natural than that a change like this should come over St. Paul's mind, when year after year passed away, and still there was no sign of the Lord's coming, and when the spread of the faith through the Roman Empire, and the results which it was producing, would give force to all such ways of thinking as are represented by the image of the leaven leavening the lump" (*Prolegomena*, p. 142).

Paley on the Internal Evidence.—Paley in his *Horae Paulinae* has replied by anticipation to some, at least, of the objections to the genuineness of the Epistle, and has added some positive arguments which deserve attention. He remarks that "Whoever writes two letters or two discourses nearly upon the same subject and at no great distance of time, but without any express recollection of what he had written before, will find himself repeating some sentences in the very order of the words in which he had already used them; but he will more frequently find himself employing some principal terms, with the order inadvertently changed, or with the order disturbed by the intermixture of other words and phrases expressive of ideas rising up at the time; or in many instances repeating, not single words, nor yet whole sentences, but parts and fragments of sentences. Of all these varieties the examination of our two Epistles will furnish plain examples; and I should rely upon this class of instances more than upon the last; because, although an impostor might transcribe into a forgery entire sentences and phrases, yet the dislocation of words, the partial recollection of phrases and sentences, the intermixture of new terms and new ideas with terms and ideas before used, which will appear in the examples that follow, and which are the natural properties of writings produced under the circumstances in which these Epistles are represented to have been composed, would not, I think, have occurred to the invention of a forger; nor, if they had occurred, would they have been so easily executed. This studied variation was a refinement in forgery, which, I believe, did not exist; or if we can suppose it to have been practised in the instances adduced below, why, it may be asked, was not the same art exercised upon those which we have collected in the preceding class? [viz. Eph. i. 7 = Col. i. 14; Eph. i. 10 = Col. i. 20; Eph. iii. 2 = Col. i. 25; Eph. v. 19 = Col. iii. 16; and Eph. vi. 22 = Col. iv. 8]." Of the second class he specifies Eph. i. 19, ii. 5, which, if we take away the parentheses, leaves a sentence almost the same in terms as Col. ii. 12, 13; but it is in Eph. twice interrupted by incidental thoughts which St. Paul, as his manner was, enlarges upon by the way, and then returns to the thread of his discourse.

Amongst internal marks of genuineness, Paley specifies the frequent yet seemingly unaffected use of πλοῖτος used metaphorically as an augmentative of the idea to which it happens to be subjoined,—a figurative use familiar to St. Paul, but occurring in no other writer in the N.T. except once in Jas. ii. 5, "Hath not God chosen the poor of this world, rich in faith?", where it is manifestly suggested by the antithesis. (It occurs in 1 Tim. vi. 18.)

"There is another singularity in St. Paul's style which, wherever it is found, may be deemed a badge of authenticity; because, if it were noticed, it would not, I think, be imitated, inasmuch as it almost always produces embarrassment and interruption in the reasoning. This singularity is a species of digression which may properly, I think (says Paley), be denominated *going off at a word.* It is turning aside from the subject upon the occurrence of some particular word, forsaking the train of thought then in hand, and entering upon a parenthetic sentence in which that word is the prevailing term." An instance is 2 Cor. ii. 14, at the word ὀσμή (note *vv.* 15, 16). Another, 2 Cor. iii. 1, at ἐπιστολῶν, which gives birth to the following sentence, *vv.* 2, 3. A third is 2 Cor. iii. 13, at the word κάλυμμα. The whole allegory, *vv.* 14–18, arises out of the occurrence of this word in v. 13, and in iv. 1 he resumes the proper subject of his discourse almost in the words with which he had left it.

In Eph. we have two similar instances, viz. iv. 8-11, at the word ἀνέβη, and again, v. 13-15, at φῶς.

Again, in Eph. iv. 2-4 and Col. iii. 12-15, we have the words ταπεινοφροσύνη, πραότης, μακροθυμία, ἀνεχόμενοι ἀλλήλων in the same order; ἀγάπη is also in both, but in a different connexion; σύνδεσμος τῆς εἰρήνης answers to σ. τῆς τελειότητος; ἐκλήθητε ἐν ἑνὶ σώματι to ἓν σῶμα καθὼς καὶ ἐκλήθητε ἐν μιᾷ ἐλπίδι; yet is this similitude found in the midst of sentences otherwise very different.

Eph. v. 6-8, Col. iii. 6-8, afford, says Paley, a specimen of that *partial* resemblance which is only to be met with where no imitation is designed, but where the mind, exercised upon the same subject, is left to the spontaneous return of such terms and phrases as, having been used before, may happen to present themselves again. The sentiment of both passages is throughout alike: half of that sentiment, the denunciation of God's wrath, is expressed in identical words; the other half, viz. the admonition to quit their former conversation, in words entirely different.

Eph. vi. 19, 20, furnishes, according to Paley's very just remark, a coincidence (with the Acts) of that minute and less obvious kind which is of all others the most to be relied upon. It is the coincidence of πρεσβεύω ἐν ἁλύσει with Acts xxviii. 16. From the latter passage we learn that at Rome Paul was allowed to dwell by himself with one soldier that kept him. In such cases it was customary for the prisoner to be bound to the soldier by a single chain.

Accordingly, in ver. 20 St. Paul says, τὴν ἅλυσιν ταύτην περίκειμαι. It is to be observed that in the parallel passage in Col. the word used is δέομαι. A real prisoner might use either the general words δέομαι or ἐν δεσμοῖς, or the specific term. Paley, however, omits to notice the irony of πρεσβεύω ἐν ἁλύσει, to which the choice of the word is undoubtedly due. "Am an ambassador in chains" does not exactly express the force of the original, which is rather "act as an ambassador in chains." As Hort well remarks (p. 156), "the writer has in mind, not the mere general thought of being in bonds, but the visual image of an ambassador standing up to plead his sovereign's cause, and wearing, strangest of contradictions, a fetter by way of official adornment." ἐν δεσμοῖς would have meant "in prison."

3. RELATION TO THE EPISTLE TO THE COLOSSIANS.

It is impossible even to glance over these two Epistles without being struck by the many similarities, and even verbal coincidences, between them. On the other hand, the Epistle to the Ephesians differs markedly from its twin Epistle in the absence of controversial matter such as forms so important an element in the other. De Wette, admitting the genuineness of Col., thought it possible to account for the likeness by supposing that the writer of Eph. borrowed from the other Epistle. He gave a list of parallel passages (*Einl.* § 146a) as follows:—

Eph.		Col.		Eph.		Col.
,, i. 7	. .	,, i. 14.		,, iv. 22 f. .	.	,, iii. 8 ff.
,, i. 10	. .	,, i. 20.		,, iv. 25 f. .	.	,, iii. 8 f.
,, i. 15–17 .	.	,, i. 3, 4.		,, iv. 29 .	.	,, iii. 8, iv. 6.
,, i. 18	. .	,, i. 27.		,, iv. 31 .	.	,, iii. 8.
,, i. 21	. .	,, i. 16.		,, iv. 32 .	.	,, iii. 12 f.
,, i. 22 f.	. .	,, i. 18 f.		,, v. 3 .	.	,, iii. 5.
,, ii. 1, 12 .	.	,, i. 21.		,, v. 4 .	.	,, iii. 8.
,, ii. 5	. .	,, ii. 13.		,, v. 5 .	.	,, iii. 5.
,, ii. 15	. .	,, ii. 14.		,, v. 6 .	.	,, iii. 6.
,, ii. 16	. .	,, ii. 20.		,, v. 15 .	.	,, iv. 5.
,, iii. 1	. .	,, i. 24.		,, v. 19 f. .	.	,, iii. 16 f.
,, iii. 2	. .	,, i. 25.		,, v. 21 .	.	,, iii. 18.
,, iii. 3	. .	,, i. 26.		,, v. 25 .	.	,, iii. 19.
,, iii. 7	. .	,, i. 23, 25.		,, vi. 1 .	.	,, iii. 20.
,, iii. 8 f.	. .	,, i. 27.		,, vi. 4 .	.	,, iii. 21.
,, iv. 1	. .	,, i. 10.		,, vi. 5 ff. .	.	,, iii. 22 f.
,, iv. 2	. .	,, iii. 12 f		,, vi. 9 .	.	,, iv. 1.
,, iv. 3 f.	. .	,, iii. 14 f.		,, vi. 18 ff. .	.	,, iv. 2 f.
,, iv. 15 f. .	.	,, ii. 19.		,, vi. 21 f. .	.	,, iv. 7 f.
,, iv. 19	. .	,, iii. 1. 5.				

Holtzmann in his *Kritik der Epheser- und Kolosser-Briefe* examined the problem with great labour and minuteness. He argued strongly that in some of the parallels, the priority was on the side of Eph. The passages which he selected for detailed examination in support of this contention were, 1st, Eph. i. 4 (= Col. i. 22); 2nd, Eph. i. 6, 7 (= Col. i. 13, 14); 3rd, Eph. iii. 3, 5, 9 (= Col. i. 26, ii. 2); 4th, Eph. iii. 17, 18, iv. 16, ii. 20 (= Col. i. 23, ii. 2, 7); 5th, Eph. iv. 16 (= Col. ii. 19); 6th, Eph. iv. 22–24 (= Col. iii. 9, 10); and 7th, Eph. v. 19 (= Col. iii. 16). (With respect to the last three he seems to have changed his mind before publishing his *Einleitung*.) His conclusion was that there existed an Epistle to the Colossians by St. Paul, which was taken by the writer of Eph. as the basis of his work, and that the same writer subsequently interpolated the Epistle to the Colossians. He conjectures that this writer was the same who added the final doxology to the Epistle to the Romans.

In the introduction to the Epistle to the Colossians will be found a specimen of the result of his analysis of Colossians. The principal, indeed the only value of this part of his work is that it establishes the inadequacy of the more commonly accepted solution of the problem, namely, that Ephesians is simply a forgery based on Colossians. Some critics, however, such as Hausrath, Mangold, Pfleiderer, think that Holtzmann has at least indicated in what direction the solution is to be looked for. But all such attempts are attended with much greater difficulty than the traditional view.

There is another difficulty in this theory, and one which, from a literary point of view, is really fatal. It is that the words and phrases supposed to be borrowed from Col. are introduced into different contexts, and yet so as to fit in quite naturally with their new surroundings. (See, above, the passages mentioned by Paley.)

It may be asked, moreover, how is it that a writer so well acquainted with Pauline thought should have confined his borrowings almost exclusively to the Epistle to the Colossians, and that although the most characteristic element of that Epistle, its special polemic against the heretical teachers, seems to have had no interest for him. Indeed, it is strange how he succeeds in steering clear of all allusions to that subject. In the author of Col. this would be done unconsciously; it is not so easy to account for an imitator doing it.

§ 4. RELATION TO THE FIRST EPISTLE OF PETER.

The parallelisms between these two Epistles are so numerous that the Epistles may almost be compared throughout. The following comparison is chiefly from Holtzmann. After the address they begin thus—

1 Pet. i.	Eph. i.
3. εὐλογητὸς ὁ Θεὸς καὶ πατὴρ τοῦ Κυρίου ἡμῶν Ἰησοῦ Χριστοῦ, ὁ ἀναγεννήσας ἡμᾶς.	3. εὐλογητὸς ὁ Θεὸς καὶ πατὴρ τοῦ Κυρίου ἡμῶν Ἰησοῦ Χριστοῦ, ὁ εὐλογήσας ἡμᾶς.

This commencement, however, is found also in 2 Cor. i. 3. Then follows in each a long passage (1 Pet. i. 5–13; Eph. i. 5–15) in which the alternation of participles and relative pronouns is the same in both until the transition to the succeeding period is made in the one case by διό, in the other by διὰ τοῦτο. The substance of the passage in 1 Pet. i. 3–5 corresponds with that of the following passage in Eph. (i. 18–20), the "hope" being emphasised in both, and its object being designated the κληρονομία, the connexion with the resurrection of Christ as its ground being the same, and in both the δύναμις Θεοῦ being put in relation to the πίστις.

1 Pet. ii. 4–6 has much resemblance to Eph. ii. 18–22—

1 Pet. ii.	Eph. ii
4. πρὸς ὃν προσερχόμενοι λίθον ζῶντα . . .	18. δι᾽ αὐτοῦ ἔχομεν τὴν προσαγωγήν.
5. καὶ αὐτοὶ ὡς λίθοι ζῶντες οἰκοδομεῖσθε, οἶκος πνευματικός.	19. . . . οἰκεῖοι τοῦ Θεοῦ.
6. . . . λίθον ἀκρογωνιαῖον.	20. . . . ἐποικοδομηθέντες ἐπὶ τῷ θεμελίῳ . . . ὄντος ἀκρογωνιαίου αὐτοῦ Χριστοῦ Ἰησοῦ, κ.τ.λ.
	22. . . . συνοικοδομεῖσθε εἰς κατοικητήριον τοῦ Θεοῦ.

1 Pet., however, is here citing Ps. cxviii. 22 and Isa. xxviii. 16, and the former passage may have been in St. Paul's mind also. It had been applied by our Lord to Himself (Matt. xxi. 42), and is cited in St. Peter's speech, Acts iv. 11. Holtzmann thinks the citation of Isa. xxviii. 16 was suggested to 1 Pet. by the ἀκρογωνιαῖον of Eph.

1 Pet. iii. 18, ἵνα ἡμᾶς προσαγάγῃ τῷ Θεῷ, reminds us of Eph. ii. 18, δι᾽ αὐτοῦ ἔχομεν τὴν προσαγωγὴν πρὸς τὸν πατέρα, while the verses immediately following exhibit the ancient explanation of Eph. iv. 8–10. Then follows in 1 Pet. a striking parallel to Eph. i. 20–22—

1 Pet. iii.	Eph. i.
22. ὅς ἐστιν ἐν δεξιᾷ τοῦ Θεοῦ πορευθεὶς εἰς οὐρανόν, ὑποταγέντων αὐτῷ ἀγγέλων καὶ ἐξουσιῶν καὶ δυνάμεων.	20. ἐκάθισεν ἐν δεξιᾷ αὐτοῦ ἐν τοῖς ἐπουρανίοις.
	21. ὑπεράνω πάσης ἀρχῆς καὶ ἐξουσίας καὶ δυνάμεως . . .
	22. καὶ πάντα ὑπέταξεν.

Again, 1 Pet. i. 10–12 and Eph. iii. 5, 10 are strikingly parallel. They both contain the thought found here only in the N.T., that the meaning of the prophecies was not clearly known to the prophets themselves, but has first become so to us—

1 Pet. i.	Eph. iii.
10. προφῆται . . .	5. ὃ ἑτέραις γενεαῖς οὐκ ἐγνωρίσθη . . . ὡς νῦν ἀπεκαλύφθη τοῖς . . . προφήταις ἐν πνεύματι.
11. ἐρευνῶντες εἰς τίνα . . . καιρὸν ἐδήλου τὸ ἐν αὐτοῖς πνεῦμα.	10. ἵνα γνωρισθῇ νῦν . . .
12. οἷς ἀπεκαλύφθη ὅτι οὐχ ἑαυτοῖς, ἡμῖν δὲ διηκόνουν αὐτά, ἃ νῦν ἀνηγγέλη.	

Here 1 Pet. goes beyond Eph. in saying that the prophets themselves were made acquainted by revelation with their own

ignorance. (But on προφήταις in Eph. iii. 5 = New Test. prophets, see note.)

1 Pet. i. 20 and Eph. iii. 9 correspond in the same reference to the mystery ordained πρὸ καταβολῆς κόσμου, and hitherto hidden, but now revealed. And as in Eph. iii. 10 the wise purpose of God is now made known to angelic powers, so in 1 Pet. i. 12 they desire to search into these things.

These are but a selection from the parallelisms that have been indicated by Holtzmann and others. Some critics have explained them by the supposition that the writer of Eph. borrowed from 1 Pet. (Hilgenfeld, Weiss). But, in fact, the latter Epistle has affinities to other Epistles of St. Paul, and especially to that to the Romans, with which it has many striking coincidences (see Salmon, *Introduction*, Lect. xxii., and Seufert in Hilgenfeld's *Zeitschrift*, 1874, p. 360).

On the supposition that Eph. is genuine, and that St. Paul here borrowed from 1 Pet., we seem obliged to hold (as Weiss does) that in the other parallels the former was also the borrower. "Imagine," says Holtzmann, "the most original of all the N.T. writers, when composing the 12th chap. of his Ep. to the Romans, laboriously gleaning from 1 Pet. the exhortations which his own daily experience might have suggested to him, taking xii. 1 from 1 Pet. ii. 5 stripped of its symbolic clothing, then xii. 2 borrowing συσχηματίζεσθε from 1 Pet. i. 14; next in xii. 3-8 expanding 1 Pet. iv. 10, 11; taking xii. 9 out of 1 Pet. i. 22; xii. 10 from 1 Pet. ii. 17," etc.

Seufert, adopting an incidental suggestion of Holtzmann, has argued at length that Eph. and 1 Pet. are by the same author, possibly the same who wrote the third Gospel and the Acts (Hilgenfeld's *Zeitschrift*, 1881, pp. 179, 332). It is not necessary to discuss this theory in detail, since it appears to have gained no adherents. It may suffice to quote Salmon's remark, that the resemblances between 1 Pet. and Eph. are much less numerous and less striking than those between Ephesians and Colossians; whereas, in order to establish Seufert's theory, they ought to be very much stronger: "For we clearly can more readily recognise resemblances as tokens of common authorship in the case of two documents which purport to come from the same author, and which, from the very earliest times, have been accepted as so coming, than when the case is the reverse."

There remains the supposition that 1 Pet. borrowed from Ephesians. If the former be not genuine, there is, of course, no difficulty in this supposition, whether Eph. be genuine or not. Nor is there any real difficulty (except to those who will insist on putting the two apostles in opposition) in supposing that the Apostle Peter when in Rome should become familiar with the

Epistle to the Romans, and adopt some of its thoughts and language. It is difficult, however, to suppose him acquainted with Eph. and other Epistles. Salmon suggests another alternative, namely, that while Paul was in Rome, Peter may have arrived there, in which case there would be a good deal of *vivâ voce* intercourse between them, and Paul's discourses to the Christians at Rome may have been heard by Peter. This suggestion appears to have been made also by Schott (*Der erste Brief Petri*, 1851).[1] Holtzmann's objection to it is singularly weak, viz. first, that according to Gal. i. 18, ii. 1 sq., 11 sqq., we must regard the personal intercourse between the two apostles as limited to three widely separated moments, and broken off in some bitterness; and, secondly, that St. Peter could not in this way have become familiar with Rom. xii. xiii. The latter remark has been replied to by anticipation; as to the former, what sort of idea of the two apostles must Holtzmann have, to think that the incident at Antioch must have led to a permanent estrangement between them! Finally, if 1 Pet. was composed by Silvanus under the direction of the apostle, which is possibly what is meant by v. 12, the use of St. Paul's thoughts and language is sufficiently accounted for.

§ 5. RELATION TO OTHER NEW TESTAMENT WRITINGS

Epistle to the Hebrews.—Points of contact with the Ep. to the Hebrews have been noted. Lexically, *e.g.* αἷμα καὶ σάρξ (elsewhere σάρξ καὶ αἷμα), ἀγρυπνεῖν, κραυγή, ὑπεράνω. ὑπεράνω πάντων τῶν οὐρανῶν, εἰς ἀπολύτρωσιν, αἰὼν μέλλων, προσφορὰ καὶ θυσία, βουλή of God, παρρησία in the sense of spiritual assurance. There are also peculiar conceptions common to both Epistles: Eph. i. 20, ἐκάθισεν ἐν δεξιᾷ αὐτοῦ, Heb. i. 3, viii. 1, x. 12: Eph. i. 7, ἀπολύτρωσις διὰ τοῦ αἵματος, Heb. ix. 12: Eph. v. 25, 26, ἑαυτὸν παρέδωκεν ὑπὲρ αὐτῆς ἵνα αὐτὴν ἁγιάσῃ, Heb. xiii. 12, x. 10. St. Paul, it is said, does not represent ἁγιασμός as the object of Christ's atoning death, but rather justification. Eph. iii. 12, ἐν ᾧ ἔχομεν τὴν παρρησίαν καὶ τὴν προσαγωγήν, Heb. iv. 16, προσερχώμεθα μετὰ παρρησίας. The Christology, also, of the two Epp. is the same. Of course, if Eph. is genuine, there is no difficulty in admitting that the writer to the Hebrews used it. V. Soden, however, argues that the latter Epistle is the earlier. His reason is that 1 Pet. is dependent on Hebrews, and probably earlier than Eph. The former proposition is more than doubtful; but we need not discuss it, since, as we have seen, it is probably 1 Pet. that has used Eph.

---

[1] "Peter possessed an eminently sympathetic nature. He was one who received impressions easily, and could not without an effort avoid reflecting the tone of the company in which he lived" (Salmon, *Introd.*, 7th ed., p. 438).

The Apocalypse.—There are also noted points of correspondence with the Apocalypse, *e.g.* Eph. ii. 20, "foundation of the apostles and prophets"; Rev. xxi. 14 : Eph. iii. 5, (τῷ μυστηρίῳ) ὃ ... νῦν ἀπεκαλύφθη τοῖς ἁγίοις ἀποστόλοις αὐτοῦ καὶ προφήταις, Rev. x. 7, τὸ μυστήριον τοῦ Θεοῦ, ὡς εὐηγγέλισε τοὺς ἑαυτοῦ δούλους τοὺς προφήτας : Eph. v. 11, μὴ συγκοινωνεῖτε τοῖς ἔργοις τοῖς ἀκάρποις τοῦ σκότους, Rev. xviii. 4, ἵνα μὴ συγκοινωνήσητε ταῖς ἁμαρτίαις αὐτῆς : Eph. v. 25 ff., the comparison of the union of Christ and the Church to that of husband and wife; cf. Rev. xix. 7, *al.*[1] Many other coincidences are pointed out by Holtzmann, who concludes that the author of Eph. made use of the Apocalypse. V. Soden, however, judges that they do not prove any dependence either literary or spiritual on either side, but that they show that the author of Eph. stood much nearer than Paul to the modes of expression of Christianity which are attested in the Apocalypse; and he passes a similar judgment on the relation between Eph. and the Gospel of John, except that in the latter case the affinity extends also to the ideas.

As to the Apocalypse, it is hard to believe that the writer of Eph. v. 23 ff. had before him the fact that the Church had already by another writer been expressly designated the Bride of Christ. He seems, on the contrary, to have been led up to it step by step from the comparison of the headship of the man (= 1 Cor. xi. 3) to the headship of Christ. Rather does the exposition in the Apocalypse appear to be a development of the figure first suggested in Eph. The figure of the Bridegroom appears, indeed, in the Gospel of St. John iii. 29, but it is used there merely to illustrate the superiority of Christ to the Baptist. In fact, the Parable of the Ten Virgins in the Synoptic Gospels is much closer to the figure here.

Gospel of St. John.—Comparison with the Gospel of St. John gives results such as the following :—The Logos-idea is in substance indicated in i. 10, where Christ is represented as the point of union in which the divided universe is brought together. As to the special application of this fundamental thought to the relation of Jews and Gentiles (ii. 13–22, iii. 6), there are significant parallels in John (x. 16, xi. 52, xvii. 20, 21). Further, it is especially the ideas of γνῶσις and ἀγάπη that in both Epistle and Gospel dominate everything, and in most of the (ten) places in Eph. in which ἀγάπη occurs the thought is Johannine, as in i. 4, ii. 4. Christ is ὁ ἠγαπημένος (i. 6), the absolute object of Divine love, as in John iii. 35, x. 17, xv. 9, and especially xvii. 23, 24, 26. The words ἠγάπησάς με πρὸ καταβολῆς κόσμου in xvii. 24 particularly

---

[1] Compare also Eph. i. 17, Rev. xix. 10; Eph. i. 8, Rev. xiii. 18; Eph. ii. 13, Rev. v. 9; Eph. iii. 9, Rev. iv. 11, x. 6; Eph. iii. 18, Rev. xi. 1, xxi. 15–17; Eph. v. 32, Rev. i. 20.

are in touch both with ἠγαπημένος in i. 6, and with πρὸ καταβολῆς κόσμον in i. 4. The work of redemption is in John viewed especially as one of ἁγιάζειν (xvii. 17, 19); so also Eph. v. 26. This ἁγιάζειν is accomplished by Christ καθαρίσας ... ἐν ῥήματι, to which corresponds καθαρὸς διὰ τὸν λόγον, John xv. 3. Moreover, the effect produced on those who are sanctified is described as a quickening of the dead (John v. 21, 25, 28; Eph. ii. 5, 6). The contrast between the light which Christ brings and the opposing power of darkness is expressed in both with striking similarity.

EPH. v.

8. ὡς τέκνα φωτὸς περιπατεῖτε.
11. μᾶλλον δὲ καὶ ἐλέγχετε (τὰ ἔργα τοῦ σκότους).

13. τὰ δὲ πάντα ἐλεγχόμενα ὑπὸ τοῦ φωτὸς φανεροῦται· πᾶν γὰρ τὸ φανερούμενον φῶς ἐστι.

JOHN.

xii. 35. περιπατεῖτε ὡς τὸ φῶς ἔχετε.
iii. 20. πᾶς γὰρ ὁ φαῦλα πράσσων μισεῖ τὸ φῶς καὶ οὐκ ἔρχεται πρὸς τὸ φῶς ἵνα μὴ ἐλεγχθῇ τὰ ἔργα αὐτοῦ·
iii. 21. ὁ δὲ ποιῶν τὴν ἀλήθειαν ἔρχεται πρὸς τὸ φῶς ἵνα φανερωθῇ αὐτοῦ τὰ ἔργα.

Here what comes close together in Eph. appears in the Gospel of John in two separate places. The same thing occurs with Eph. iv. 8–10 compared with John iii. 31, vii. 39. Indeed, the parallels begin with Eph. iv. 7, ἡ χάρις κατὰ τὸ μέτρον τῆς δωρεᾶς τοῦ Χριστοῦ. In the Gospel the one exception in which the Spirit is given οὐκ ἐκ μέτρου is expressed in iii. 34 in a form which becomes intelligible only by presupposing the general statement in Eph. "to each of us," etc. The expressions, too, in Eph. iv. 9, 10, and John iii. 13. suggest a literary dependence. Eph.: τὸ δὲ ἀνέβη τί ἐστιν εἰ μὴ ὅτι καὶ κατέβη ... ὁ καταβὰς αὐτός ἐστιν καὶ ὁ ἀναβὰς ὑπεράνω πάντων τῶν οὐρανῶν.

John: οὐδεὶς ἀναβέβηκεν εἰς τὸν οὐρανὸν εἰ μὴ ὁ ἐκ τοῦ οὐρανοῦ καταβάς. Here again, says Holtzmann, the passage in the Gospel becomes quite clear only on supposition of a reminiscence.

The correspondence between Eph. and the Johannine writings is sufficiently accounted for by the supposition that "St. John read and valued St. Paul's writings," as Salmon remarks. This appears strongly confirmed by certain correspondences between the Apocalypse and the Ep. to the Colossians (see Introd. to Col.).

Pastoral Epistles.—It is not necessary to dwell on the coincidences with the Pastoral Epistles, since, whether these are accepted as genuine or not, it cannot be imagined that the writer of Eph. borrowed from them. In fact, no one who questions Eph. accepts the Pastorals.

§ 6. TIME AND PLACE OF WRITING.

The Epistle was written while St. Paul was a prisoner, iii. 1, iv. 1, vi. 20. From the mention of Tychicus as the bearer of it,

vi. 21 compared with Col. iv. 7 and Philemon 13, we may conclude that these three Epistles were written at the same time. Most commentators have supposed that they were written from Rome, but some moderns have advocated the claims of Caesarea (Acts xxiii. 35, xxiv. 27). The following reasons are adduced in favour of this view by Meyer. First, that it is more likely that the fugitive slave Onesimus would make his way from Colossae to Caesarea than by a long sea voyage to Rome. Wieseler's reply is sufficient, namely, that he would be safer from the pursuit of the *fugitivarii* in the great city. St. Paul, too, seems to have been under stricter guard at Caesarea, where only "his own" were allowed to attend him (Acts xxiv. 23), than at Rome, where he lived in his own hired house and received all that came to him. As to the circumstances of Onesimus' flight we know nothing. Secondly, if the Epistles were sent from Rome, Tychicus and his companion Onesimus would have arrived at Ephesus first, and we might therefore expect that, with Tychicus, Onesimus would be mentioned, in order to ensure him a kindly reception. This argument falls to the ground if the Ep. was not written to Ephesus.

Thirdly, he argues from Eph. vi. 21, ἵνα δὲ εἰδῆτε καὶ ὑμεῖς, that before Tychicus would arrive at Ephesus he would have previously fulfilled to others the commission here mentioned. But this is really to suppose that the readers of the Epistle had previously heard of the message to the Colossians. The meaning of καὶ ὑμεῖς is quite different (see note). Fourthly, it is argued that in Philem. 22 Paul asks Philemon to prepare him a lodging, and that soon (ἅμα δὲ καὶ). This presupposes, says Meyer, that his place of imprisonment was nearer to Colossae than Rome, and, which is the main point, that Paul intended on his expected release to go direct to Phrygia; whereas from Phil. ii. 24 we see that he intended to proceed to Macedonia after his liberation (not to Spain, as he had at first thought of doing, Rom. xv. 24). And Weiss thinks this decisive. But he might well take Philippi on his way to Colossae, Philippi being on the great high road between Europe and Asia (Lightfoot, *Philippians*, p. 48 f.). On the other hand, as Mangold observes (Bleek, *Einl.* p. 507), the desire to visit Rome lay so near the apostle's heart during his imprisonment in Caesarea (Acts xxiii. 11), that he would not think of making a journey thence to Phrygia for which he would order a lodging, even if Phrygia is looked on only as a station on the way to Rome. But the expression in Philem. implies more than a mere passing through. The fact is, however, that the argument treats the request too much in the light of a business arrangement instead of a friendly suggestion. When St. Paul says, "I hope that through your prayers I may be granted to you," without even adding "soon," it is clear that his hope was not definitely for a speedy release. Had it been so, he would doubtless have alluded to it in the Ep. to the Colossians. Jerome suggests the true explanation, viz. that he spoke "dispensatorie ut dum eum expectat Philemon ad se esse venturum, magis faciat quod rogatus est." As Hort puts it: "It is but a playful way of saying to Philemon, 'Remember that I mean to come and see with my own eyes whether you have really treated your Christian slave as I have been exhorting you'; and then giving the thought a serious turn by assuring him that, 'coming is no mere jest, for he does indeed hope some day to be set free through their prayers, and then he will haste to visit them.'"

Another argument has been founded on the absence from Col. of any reference to the earthquakes which visited the cities of the Lycus about this time. Under the year 60 (which includes the last part of the Caesarean imprisonment) Tacitus mentions an earthquake which destroyed Laodicea (*Ann.* xiv. 27). Four years later Eusebius' *Chronicle* mentions the destruction of Laodicea, Hierapolis, and Colossae by an earthquake (*Ol.* 210). It is not certain that these notices refer to the same event, but, even granting that they do, there is good reason to believe that Eusebius is more likely to be right in the date than Tacitus. The latter appears to be in error about the date of another earthquake of this reign (Schiller, *Nero*, 160, 172, referred to by Hort), whereas Eusebius appears to have followed unusually good authorities about these earthquakes; for in the case of the great earthquake in the reign of Tiberius, he adds Ephesus to the list of ruined cities mentioned by Tacitus and Pliny; and a monument at Naples proves his correctness. If Eusebius is right as to the date of the earthquake, it would be later than the Epistle. Or, again, if the earthquakes in question are not the same, there is no evidence that the earlier extended as far as Colossae.

Lightfoot, in his essay on the "Order of the Epistles of the Captivity" (*Comm. on Philippians*), argues strongly from language and style that the Epistle to the Philippians preceded these three. If so, and if, as is generally believed, that Epistle was written from Rome, we have in this a further proof of the Roman origin of Ephesians and the other two.

§ 7. VOCABULARY OF THE EPISTLE.

List of ἅπαξ λεγόμενα in the Epistle to the Ephesians.

ἄθεος, αἰσχρότης, αἰχμαλωτεύειν (but Text. Rec. in 2 Tim. iii. 6), ἀνανεόω, ἄνοιξις, ἀπαλγεῖν, ἄσοφος, βέλος, ἐκτρέφω, ἐλαχιστότερος, ἑνότης, ἐξισχύειν, ἐπιδύειν, ἐπιφαύσκειν, ἑτοιμασία, εὔνοια (Text. Rec.

has it in 1 Cor. vii. 3), εὐτραπελία, ὁ ἠγαπημένος (of Christ), θυρεός, καταρτισμός, κατώτερος, κληροῦν, κλυδωνίζεσθαι, κοσμοκράτωρ, κρυφῇ, κυβεία, μακροχρόνιος, μέγεθος, μεθοδεία, μεσότοιχον, μωρολογία, πάλη, παροργισμός, πολυποίκιλος, προελπίζειν, προσκαρτέρησις, ῥυτίς, συμμέτοχος, συμπολίτης, συναρμολογεῖν, συνοικοδομεῖν, σύσσωμος.

Words found elsewhere, but not in St. Paul.

The following words are found elsewhere in the N.T., but not in St. Paul: -ἄγνοια (Acts, 1 Pet.), ἀγρυπνεῖν (Mark, Luke, Heb.), ἀκρογωνιαῖος (1 Pet.), ἀμφότεροι, ἄνεμος, ἀνιέναι (Acts, Heb.), ἅπας, ἀπειλή (Acts), εὔσπλαγχνος (1 Pet.), μακράν, ὀργίζεσθαι, ὁσιότης (Luke), ὀσφύς, πανοπλία (Luke), πάροικος (Acts, 1 Pet.), περιζωννύναι, πλάτος (Apoc.), ποιμήν (= pastor, only 1 Pet., which also has ἀρχιποιμήν), πολιτεία (Acts), σαπρός, σπῖλος, συγκαθίζειν (Luke, but intrans.), σωτήριον (Luke, Acts), ὕδωρ, ὑποδεῖσθαι, ὕψος, φραγμός, φρόνησις (Luke), χαριτοῦν (Luke), χειροποιητός.

Holtzmann adds the following, which occur in the Pastorals, assuming, namely, that they are not genuine:—αἰχμαλωτεύειν (2 Tim. *Rec.*), ἄλυσις (2 Tim.), ἀπατᾶν (1 Tim.), ἀσωτία (Tit., 1 Pet. only), διάβολος (1 and 2 Tim. and Tit.), εὐαγγελιστής (Acts, 2 Tim. only), παιδεία (2 Tim.), τιμᾶν (1 Tim.).

Words common to the Epistles to the Ephesians and the Colossians, but not found elsewhere in N.T.

ἀνθρωπάρεσκος, ἁφή, ἀποκαταλλάσσειν, ἀπαλλοτριοῦσθαι, αὔξειν, αὔξησις, ὀφθαλμοδουλεία, ῥιζοῦν, συζωοποιεῖν, συμβιβάζειν.

Add the expression ἐκ ψυχῆς.

Words which are common to Ephesians and the Pauline Epistles (excluding the Pastorals), but which are not found in other N.T. writers.

ἀγαθωσύνη, ἀληθεύειν, ἀνεξιχνίαστος, ἐπιχορηγία, εὔνοια (1 Cor. vii. 3 Text. Rec., but not in the best texts), εὐωδία, θάλπειν, κάμπτειν, περικεφαλαία, πλεονέκτης, ποίημα, πρεσβεύειν, προετοιμάζειν, προσαγωγή, προτίθεσθαι, υἱοθεσία, ὑπερβάλλειν, ὑπερεκπερισσοῦ.

§ 8. CONTENTS OF THE EPISTLE.

Ch. i. 1, 2. Salutation.

3–8. Praise to God for the blessings of salvation. We were chosen in Christ as the recipients of these blessings before the Creation, and the object of this was that we should be holy and blameless, being admitted to the adoption of sons through Christ, in whom we received redemption.

9–11. God hath made known to us His purpose to sum up all things, whether in heaven or on earth, in Christ.

12–14. We Jews had even in former times been promised the Christ, and had fixed our hopes on Him; but ye Gentiles have also received the same blessings, and have been sealed with the Holy Spirit as an earnest of the inheritance.

15–19. Therefore having heard of your faith I always thank God for you, and pray that ye may attain the knowledge of the hope to which ye are called, the glory of your inheritance, and the greatness of the power of God, who gives this inheritance.

20–23. A striking example of this power was shown in the raising of Christ from the dead, who has now been set above all authorities and powers, by whatever name they may be called, whether earthly or heavenly, whether belonging to this world or to the next. To the Church, however, He stands in a closer relation, being the Head to which the Church is related as His Body.

ii. 1–10. A further instance of His power is that when we were dead through our sins He gave us life and made us partakers of the resurrection of Christ, and of His exaltation. This was not for any merit of our own, but was the undeserved gift of God, who loved us even when we were dead through our sins. But although our salvation was thus not of works but of grace, our new creation had good works in view as its result.

11–22. Ye Gentiles had formerly no share in the covenants of promise, but were aliens from the citizenship of Israel. Now, however, Christ, by His death, has done away with the barrier between you and the true Israel, and has reconciled both to God. So that equally with the Jews, and on the same terms, ye have access to the Father. All alike form part of the one holy temple in which God dwells.

iii. 1–9. This truth that the Gentiles are equally with the Jews heirs of the inheritance, members of the body and partakers of the promise, was hidden from former generations, but has now been revealed to the apostles and prophets; and to me, though unworthy, has been given the special privilege of preaching Christ to the Gentiles, and of making known to all men this mystery.

10–13. Hereby God designs that even the angelic powers may learn through the Church to know the varied wisdom of God exemplified in His eternal purpose in Christ.

14–19. Prayer that they may be given inward spiritual strength; that Christ may dwell in them through faith; and that being themselves well grounded in love they may learn to know the love of Christ, although, properly speaking, it surpasses knowledge.

c

20, 21. Doxology suggested by the thought of the great things which have been prayed for.

iv. 1–3. Exhortation to live a life corresponding to their calling, in lowliness, patience, love, and unity.

4–11. Essential unity of the Church as a spiritual organism, inspired by one Spirit, acknowledging one Master, into whose name they are all baptized, and all being children of the same Divine Father. Within this unity a diversity of gifts and offices is to be recognised.

12–16. The object of all is to make the saints perfect in unity of faith and maturity of knowledge, so that they may be secured against the changing winds of false doctrine, and that the whole body, deriving its supply of nourishment from the Head, even Christ, may grow up and be perfected in love.

17–24. Admonition that remembering the blessings of which they have been made partakers, they should put off their former life, their old man, and put on the new man.

25–31. Exhortations against special sins, falsehood, anger, theft, idleness, foul speaking, malice, etc.

32–v. 2. Exhortation to take the love of God in Christ as a pattern for imitation, especially in their forgiveness of one another.

3–14. Special warning against sins of uncleanness.

15–21. More general exhortation to regulate their conduct with wisdom, to make good use of opportunities, and, instead of indulging in riotous pleasure, to express their joy and thankfulness in spiritual songs.

22–33. Special injunctions to husbands and wives, illustrated by the relation of Christ to the Church, which is compared to that of the husband to the wife, so that as the Church is subject to Christ, so should the wife be to her husband; and, on the other hand, as Christ loved the Church even to the point of giving Himself up for it, so should the husband love his wife. There is, indeed, one important point of difference, namely, that Christ is the Saviour of the Church of which He is the Head.

vi. 1–9. Special injunction to children and fathers, slaves and masters; slaves to remember that they are doing service to Christ, masters that they also have a Master before whom master and slave are alike.

10–12. Exhortation to arm themselves with the whole armour of God in preparation for the conflict with the spiritual powers which are opposed to them.

13–18. Detailed specification of the parts of the spiritual armour.

19, 20. Request for their prayers for himself, that he may have freedom of speech to preach the mystery of the gospel.

21–24. Personal commendation of his messenger Tychicus, and final benediction.

§ 9. LITERATURE OF THE EPISTLE TO THE EPHESIANS.

Commentaries on the entire New Testament are not noticed here. For the older works, the lists in the English translation of Meyer, and in M'Clintock and Strong's *Cyclopaedia*, have been consulted.

Sixteenth and Seventeenth Centuries.

ALTHOFER (Christ.), *Animadversiones, etc.* Alt. 1641.
Annotationes in V.T. et in Ep. ad Ephesios (auctore incerto). Cantab. 1653; Amst. 1703.
BATTUS (Bartholomaeus), *Commentarius in Epistolam ad Ephesios.* Gryphisw. 1619.
BAYNE or BAYNES (Paul), *Commentary on the Ep. to the Ephesians.* Lond. 1643.
BINEMANN, *Expositio.* Lond. 1581.
BODIUS or BOYD (Robert), *In Ep. ad Ephesios Praelectiones.* Lond. 1652.
BUCER (Martin), *Praelectiones in Ep. ad Ephesios* (posthumous; ed. by Im. Tremellius). Basil, 1562.
BUGENHAGEN (Joh.), *Adnotatt. in Epp. ad Gal. Eph. Phil. Col. etc.* Basil, 1527.
CALIXTUS (G.), *Expositio litt. in Epp. ad Eph. Col. etc.* Helmst. 1664–66.
COCCEIUS (Joh.), *S. Apost. Pauli Ep. ad Ephesios cum Comm.* Lugd. Bat. 1667.
CROCIUS (Joh.), *Comment. in Ep. ad Ephesios.* Cassellis, 1642.
CRELLIUS (Joh.), *Comment. et Paraphrasis in Ep. ad Ephesios.* Eleutherop. 1656.
DU BOSE (Pierre Th.), *Sermons sur l'Epître de St. Paul aux Ephésiens* (chs. i.–iii. only). 3 tom. Rotterd. 1699.
FERGUSON (Jas.), *A brief Exposition of the Epp. of Paul to the Gal. and Eph.* London, 1659.
GOODWIN (Thos.), *Exposition, etc.* Lond. 1681. Condensed, Lond. 1842. Works: Edinb. 1861.
HANNEKEN, *Explicatio, etc.* Marp. 1631; Lips. 1718, *al.*
HEMINGE or HEMMINGIUS, *Comment. in omnes Epp. Apostolorum, etc.* Argent, 1586.
LAGUS (Daniel), *Commentatio quadripertita super Ep. ad Ephesios.* Gryphisw. 1664.
LUTHER (Martin), *Die Ep. an die Epheser ausgelegt; aus seinem Schriften herausgegeben von Chr. G. Eberle.* Stuttg. 1878.
MAYER or MAJOR (Georg), *Enarratio Ep. Pauli scriptae ad Ephesios.* Vitemb. 1552.
MEELFÜHRER, *Commentarius.* Norimb. 1628.

MEGANDER, *Commentarius.* Basil, 1534.
NAILANT, *Enarrationes.* Ven. 1554; Lond. 1570.
OLEVIANUS (Gaspar), *Notae ex [ejus] Concionibus, etc.* Herbosnae, 1588.
RIDLEY (Launcelot), *Comm. on Ephesians.* Lond. 1540. Republ. in Legh Richmond's *Selections of the Reformers, etc.* Lond. 1817.
ROLLOCK (Robert), *In Ep. Pauli ad Ephesios Commentarius.* Edinb. 1590.
SCHMID (Sebastian), *Paraphrasis super Ep. ad Ephesios.* Strassb. 1684.
STEUART (Peter), *Comment. in Ep. ad Ephesios.* Ingolstad. 1593.
TARNOVIUS, *Commentarius.* Rost. 1636.
WANDALIN, *Paraphrasis.* Slesw. 1650.
WEINRICH, *Explicatio.* Lips. 1613.
VELLERUS or WELLER (Hieron.), *Comment. in Ep. ad Ephesios.* Noriberg. 1550.
WOODHEAD (Abraham), ALLESTRY (Rich), and WALKER (Obadiah), *Paraphrase and Annot. on all the Epistles of St. Paul.* Oxford, 1682, etc.; republ. Oxford, 1852.
ZANCHIUS (Hieron.), *Comm. in Ep. ad Ephesios.* Neostad. 1594.

Eighteenth Century.

BAUMGARTEN (Sigmund Jakob), *Auslegung der Briefe Pauli an die Galater, Epheser, Philip. Col. Philemon u. Thess.* Halle, 1767.
CHANDLER (Sam.), *Paraphrase and Notes on the Epp. of St. Paul to the Gal. and Eph. (with Comm. on Thess.).* London, 1777.
CRAMER (Joh. Andr.), *Neue Uebersetzung des Briefs an die Epheser, nebst einer Auslegung desselben.* Hamb. 1782.
DINANT (Petrus), *De Brief aan die van Efeze verklaart en toegepast.* Rotterd. 1711. (In Latin), *Commentarii, etc.* Rotterd. 1721, *al.*
ESMARCH (H. P. C.), *Brief an die Epheser übersetzt.* Altona, 1785.
FEND, *Erläuterungen.* (s.l.) 1727.
GERBADEN, *Geopent Door.* Traj. ad Rhen. 1707.
GUDE (Gottlob Friedr.), *Gründliche Erläuterung des ... Briefes an die Epheser.* Lauban, 1735.
HAZEVOET, *Verklaar.* Leyden, 1718.
KRAUSE (Friedr. Aug. Wilh.), *Der Brief an die Epheser übersetzt u. mit Anmerkungen begleitet.* Frankf. a M. 1789.
LOCKE (John), *Paraphrase and Notes on the Epp. of St. Paul to the Gal. Cor. Rom. Eph.* London, 1707, *al.*

MOLDENHAUER, *Uebersetzung.* Hamb. 1773.
MICHAELIS (Joh. Dav.), *Paraphrase u. Anmerkungen über die Briefe Pauli an die Galater, Eph. Phil. Col.* Bremen u. Götting. 1750, 1769.
MORUS (S. F. N.), *Acroases in Epp. Paulinas ad Galatas et Ephesios.* Leipz. 1795.
MÜLLER, *Erklärung.* Heidelb. 1793.
PICONIO (Bernardinus a, *i.e.* Bernardin de Picquigny), *Epistolorum B. Pauli Apost. Triplex Expositio.* Paris, 1703; Vesont. et Paris, 1853.
POPP (G. C.), *Uebersetzung u. Erklärung der drei ersten Kapitel des Briefs an die Epheser.* Rostock, 1799.
ROELL (Herm. Alex.), *Commentarius in principium Ep. ad Ephesios.* Traj. ad Rhen. 1715. *Comm. pars altera cum brevi Ep. ad Col. exegesis;* ed. D. A. Roell. Traj. ad Rhen. 1731.
ROYAARDS (Albertus), *Paulus' Brief aan de Ephesen schriftmatig verklaart.* 3 deelen. Amsterd. 1735-38.
SCHMID (Sebastian), *Paraphrasis super Ep. ad Ephesios.* Strassb. 1684, *al.*
SCHNAPPINGER (Bonif. Martin W.), *Brief an die Epheser erklärt.* Heidelb. 1793.
SCHÜTZE (Theodore Joh. Abr.), *Comm. in Ep. Pauli ad Ephesios.* Leipz. 1778.
SPENER (Philip Jak.), *Erklärung der Episteln an die Epheser u. Colosser.* Halae, 1706, *al.*
VAN TIL (Solomon), *Comm. in quatuor Pauli Epp. nempe priorem ad Cor. Eph. Phil. ac Coloss.* Amstel. 1726.
ZACHARIAE (Gotthilf Trangott), *Paraphrastische Erklärung der Briefe Pauli an die Gal. Eph. Phil. Col. u. Thess.* Götting. 1771, 1787.

Nineteenth Century.

BARRY (Alfred, Bishop), "Commentary on Ephesians and Colossians" (Ellicott's *New Test. Comm. for English Readers*).
BAUMGARTEN-CRUSIUS (L. F. O.), *Comment. über d. Briefe Pauli an die Eph. u. Kol.* Jena, 1847.
BEET (J. A.), *Commentary on the Epistles to the Ephesians, Philippians, Colossians, and Philemon.* London, 1890.
BECK (J. T.), *Erklärung des Br. Pauli an die Epheser.* Gütersloh, 1891.
BLAIKIE (W. G.), "Ephesians, Exposition and Homiletics" (*Pulpit Commentary*). London, 1886.
BLEEK (Friedr.), *Vorlesungen über die Briefe an d. Kol. d. Philemon und d. Epheser.* Berlin, 1865.
BRAUNE (Karl) in Lange's *Bibelwerk,* 1867 and 1875. Translated by M. B. Riddle. New York, 1870.

DALE (R. W.), *Epistle to the Ephesians; its Doctrine and Ethics.* 3rd ed. 1884.
DAVIES (J. Llewelyn), *The Epistle to the Ephesians, Colossians, and Philemon.* 2nd ed. London, 1884.
EADIE (John), *Commentary on the Greek Text of the Epistle of Paul to the Ephesians.* 3rd ed. Edinb. 1883.
ELLICOTT (C. J., Bishop of Gloucester and Bristol), *Critical and Grammatical Commentary on Ephesians, with a Revised Translation.* London, 1855, etc. (many editions).
EWALD (G. H. A.), *Die Sendschreiben des Ap. P. übers. und erklärt.* Göttingen, 1856.
Ditto, *Sieben Sendschreiben des N. B.* Göttingen, 1870.
FINDLAY (G. G.), "Ephesians," in the *Expositor's Bible.* 1892.
FLATT (J. F. v.), *Vorlesungen über d. Br. an die Gal. u. die Epheser.* Tübingen, 1828.
GRAHAM (Wm.), *Lectures, etc.* Lond. [1870].
HARLESS, *Commentar über den Brief Pauli an die Epheser.* 2 Aufl. Stuttgart, 1858.
HODGE (Chas.), *Comm. on Ep. to the Ephesians.* New York, 1856, al.
V. HOFMANN (J. Chr. K.), *Der Brief Pauli an die Epheser*, Nördlingen, 1870.
HOLZHAUSEN (F. A.), *Der Br. an die Epheser übersetzt u. erklärt.* Hannov. 1833.
KLÖPPER (A.), *Der Brief an die Epheser.* Göttingen, 1891.
KAHLER, *Predigten.* Kiel, 1855.
LATHROP (Joseph), *Discourses.* Philad. 1864.
LIGHTFOOT (J. B., Bishop of Durham). "Notes on Epistles of St. Paul, from unpublished Commentaries by [him]." London, 1895. (Contains notes on the first 14 verses only.)
MACEVILLY (John, R.C. Bp. of Galway), *Exposition of the Epistles of St. Paul and of the Catholic Epistles.* Lond. 1856; Dublin, 1860.
MACPHERSON (John), *Commentary on St. Paul's Epistle to the Ephesians.* Edinb. 1892.
M'GHEE (Rob. J.), *Expository Lectures on the Ep. to the Ephesians.* 4th ed. London, 1861.
MEIER (Fr. K.), *Commentar über d. Br. Pauli an d. Epheser.* Berlin, 1834.
MEYER (H. A. W.), *Kritisch exegetisches Handbuch über d. Pauli an die Epheser.* 6te Aufl. Versorgt durch Dr. Woldemar Schmidt. Göttingen, 1886.
MEYRICK, "Ephesians," in the *Speaker's Commentary.*
MOULE (H. C. G.), "The Epistle to the Ephesians," in the *Cambridge Bible for Schools and Colleges.* Cambridge, 1895.
NEWLAND (Henry Garrett), *New Catena on St. Paul's Epp., A Practical and Exegetical Commentary.* Lond. 1860.

OLTRAMARE (Hugues), *Comm. sur les Epîtres de S. Paul aux Coloss. aux Ephes. et à Philemon.* 3 tom. Paris, 1891.

PASSAVANT (Theophilus), *Versuch einer praktischen Auslegung des Briefes Pauli an die Epheser.* Basel, 1836.

PERCEVAL (A. P.), *Lectures, etc.* Lond. 1846.

PRIDHAM (Arthur), *Notes, etc.* Lond. 1854.

PULSFORD (John), *Christ and His Seed: Expository Discourses on Paul's Ep. to the Ephesians.* Lond. 1872.

RÜCKERT (Leopold J.), *Der Br. Pauli an die Epheser erläutert u. Vertheidigt.* Leipz. 1834.

SADLER (M. F.), *Galatians, Ephesians, Philippians.* London, 1889.

SCHENKEL (Dan.), "Die Briefe an die Epheser, Philipper, Colosser" (1te Aufl. in Lange's *Bibelwerk*, 1862; 2te Aufl. 1867, when Braune's *Comm.* replaced it in Lange).

SCHMIDT (Woldemar). See MEYER.

SCHNEDERMANN (G.), in Strack and Zöckler's *Kurzgef. Komm.* Nördlingen, 1888.

SIMCOE (Henry A.), *Ep. to Eph. with Texts gathered, etc.* Lond. 1832.

VON SODEN (H.), "Die Briefe an die Kolosser, Epheser, Philemon; die Pastoralbriefe" (in *Hand-Commentar zum N.T.*; bearbeitet von H. T. Holtzmann, R. A. Lipsius, u. a.) 2te Aufl. Freiburg i. B., und Leipzig, 1893.

STIER (Rudolph E.), *Die Gemeinde in Christo; Auslegung des Br. an die Epheser.* Berlin, 1848, 1849.

TURNER (Samuel Hulbeart), *The Ep. to the Ephesians in Greek and English, with an Analysis and Exegetical Commentary.* New York, 1856.

WEISS (Bernhard), *Die Paulinischen Briefe in berichtigten Text, mit Kurzer Erläuterung.* Leipz. 1896.

WOHLENBERG (G.), "Die Briefe an die Epheser, an die Colosser, an Philem. u. an die Philipper ausgelegt (in Strack and Zöckler's *Kurzgef. Comm.*). München, 1895.

Critical Discussions.

General works on Introduction are not noticed here.

ALEXANDER (W. L.), art. "Ephesians" in Kitto's *Cyclopaedia of Biblical Literature.* Lond. 1863.

BAUR (F. C.), *Paulus der Apostel Jesu Christi.* Tübing. 1845. English trans. *St. Paul, His Life and Work.* London, 1873-75.

BEMMELEN (Van), *Epp. ad Eph. et Col. collatae.* Lugd. Bat. 1803.

HAENLEIN, *De lectoribus Ep. ad Ephesios.* Erlang. 1797.

Hönig (W.), "Ueber das Verhältniss des Briefes an die Epheser zum Br. an die Kolosser," in Hilgenfeld's *Zeitschrift*. 1872.

Holtzmann (H. J.), *Kritik der Epheser- und Kolosser-briefe*. 1872.

Hilgenfeld (Adolf), Review of the preceding, in his *Zeitschrift*, 1873, p. 188.

Hort (F. J. A.), *Prolegomena to St. Paul's Epistle to the Romans and the Ephesians*. (Posthumous.) Lond. 1895.

Huth, "Ep. ad Laod. in encycl. ad Eph." Erlangen, 1751.

Kiene (Adolf), "Der Epheserbrief ein Sendschreiben ... an die Heidenchristen der Sieben (?) Kleinasiat. Gemeinden," etc. *Studien u. Kritiken*, 1869, p. 285.

Koster, *De echtheid van de brieven aan de Kol. en aan de Eph.* Utrecht, 1877.

Köstlin (J.), *Der Lehrbegriff des Evang. u. der verwandten N.T. Lehrbegriffe*. Berlin, 1843.

Lightfoot (J. B., Bishop of Durham), "Destination of the Epistle to the Ephesians" in *Biblical Essays*. (Posthumous.) London, 1893.

Lünemann, *De Ep. ad Ephesios authentia*. Götting. 1842.

Milligan (W.), art. "Ephesians, Epistle to," in *Encyclopaedia Britannica*. 9th ed.

Montet (L.), *Introd. in Ep. ad Coloss*. Mont. 1841.

Robertson (Arch.), art. "Ephesians, Epistle to," in Smith's *Dictionary of the Bible*. 2nd ed. Lond. 1893.

Räbiger (J. Ferd.), *De Christologia Paulina contra Baurium Commentatio*. 1852.

Schenkel (Dan.), art. "Epheserbrief," in his *Bibellexicon*. 1869.

Schneckenburger (Matth.), *Ueber d. Alter d. judischen Proselyten Taufe, etc.* With Appendix, "Ueber d. Irrlehren zu Kolossae." 1828.

Soden (H. v.), "Epheserbrief" in *Jahrb. f. Prot. Theol*. 1887.

§ 10. ON SOME READINGS PECULIAR TO ONE OR TWO MSS.

Both Epistles are here taken together.

The more important readings are discussed in their respective places. Here are brought together a few isolated or nearly isolated readings of particular MSS., several of which are probably errors of the respective copyists.

ℵ stands alone—

Eph. i. 18, τῆς κληρονομίας τῆς δόξης for τῆς δ. τῆς κλ.

ii. 1, ἑαυτῶν for ὑμῶν.

ii. 4, ℵ* om. ἐν.

§ 10] READINGS PECULIAR TO ONE OR TWO MSS. xli

ii. 7, ℵ* omits the whole verse (passing from ἐν Χριστῷ Ἰησοῦ in ver. 6 to the same words in ver. 7), supplied by ℵᵃ.
ii. 10, ℵ*, Θεοῦ for αὐτοῦ.
v. 17, ℵ*, φρόνημα for θέλημα.
v. 20 om. ἡμῶν.
Col. ii. 10, ℵ*, τῆς ἀρχῆς ἐκκλησίας for ἀρχῆς καὶ ἐξουσίας.
ii. 18, ℵ*, before ἀγγέλων add. μελλόντων.
iii. 1, ὁ Θεός for ὁ Χριστός. But the first scribe seems to have himself corrected it (Tisch.).

In the following ℵ is not quite alone:—
Eph. i. 7, ℵ*, ἔσχομεν (ἔχομεν, ℵᶜ) = D*, Boh. Eth.
iii. 9, ℵ* om. ἐν. Expressly attributed to Marcion by Tertullian (*Marc.* v. 18), "rapuit haereticus in praepositionem, et ita legi fecit: occulti ab aeris deo," etc. So *Dial.* 870.
iv. 24, ℵ*, ἐν ὁσιότητι καὶ δικαιοσύνῃ for ἐν δικ. κ. ὁσ. = Ambrosiaster.
Col. i. 23, κῆρυξ καὶ ἀπόστολος (for διάκονος) = P.
A combines this and the genuine text; Eth. has κῆρυξ καὶ διάκονος; while Euthal. (cod.) has διάκονος καὶ ἀπόστολος.
i. 24, τοῖς παθήμασιν ὑμῶν for τοῖς π. ὑπὲρ ὑμῶν (= L 37*).

A alone has—
Eph. i. 10, κατὰ τὴν οἰκονομίαν for εἰς οἰκ.
iv. 14, ἤπιοι for νήπιοι (ν precedes).
iv. 19, ε[ἰς ἀκα]θαρσίαν πάσης for εἰς ἐργασίαν ἀκαθαρσίας πάσης.
vi. 23, ἔλεος for ἀγάπη.
Col. i. 23, κῆρυξ καὶ ἀπόστολος καὶ διάκονος for διάκονος. See under ℵ.
In Eph. i. 3 A* reads ὑμεῖς for ἡμεῖς, with D*.
In i. 11 A agrees with D G in reading ἐκλήθημεν for ἐκληρώθημεν.
i. 20, ὑμῖν for ἡμῖν = 39, 63.
v. 15, after οὖν A adds ἀδελφοί, with ℵᶜ Vulg. Boh.

B alone—
Eph. i. 13, ἐσφραγίσθη for ἐσφραγίσθητε (τῷ follows; the copyist's eye passed from τ to τ).
i. 21, ἐξουσίας καὶ ἀρχῆς for ἀρ. καὶ ἐξ.
ii. 1, ἐπιθυμίαις for ἁμαρτίαις.
ii. 5, after παραπτώμασιν B adds καὶ ταῖς ἐπιθυμίαις, thus repeating the expression of ver. 1 with the erroneous reading. These can hardly be regarded otherwise than as serious errors.
v. 17 after Κυρίου add ἡμῶν.

Col. i. 3 omits Χριστοῦ.
i. 4 omits ἣν ἔχετε.
i. 11, 12 after χαρᾶς adds ἅμα.
i. 12, καλέσαντι καὶ ἱκανώσαντι for ἱκανώσαντι, a complete reading.
ii. 15, after ἐξουσίας add καί.
In the following B is not without support:—
Eph. i. 3 om. καὶ πατήρ = Hil. (semel), Victorinus. But Hil. has also (bis) πατήρ without ὁ Θεὸς καί.
i. 18 om. ὑμῶν = 17 Arm.
i. 20, οὐρανοῖς for ἐπουρανίοις = 71, 213, Hil. Victorin.
ii. 5 before τοῖς παραπτ. adds ἐν = Arm (?).
iii. 3 om. ὅτι, with d, Victorin. Ambrosiaster. But G, Goth. have κατὰ ἀποκ. γάρ, which gives some probability to the omission of ὅτι.
iii. 5 om. ἀποστόλοις, with Ambrosiaster.
iii. 19, πληρωθῇ for πληρώθητε εἰς, with 17, 73, 116.
iv. 7, ὑμῶν for ἡμῶν = 38, 109, Theodoret.
vi. 10, δυναμοῦσθε for ἐνδυναμοῦσθε = 17.
Col. i. 14, ἔσχομεν, with Boh. Arab. (A non liquet).
ii. 23 om. καί before ἀφειδίᾳ, with m, Orig. (intp.) Ambrosiaster.
iii. 15 om. ἑνί = 67² Sah.
iv. 3, δι' ὅν for δι' ὅ = G (71 has δι' ου).

In D the following may be noted:—
D alone (E not being reckoned).
Eph. i. 6 adds τῆς before δόξης.
i. 16, παύσομαι for παύομαι (but so Victorinus).
ii. 15, D*, καταρτίσας for καταργήσας. (The Latin d has "destituens.")
iii. 12, D*, ἐν τῷ ἐλευθερωθῆναι for ἐν πεποιθήσει.
Col. i. 14, D* om. τὴν ἄφεσιν.
i. 26, φανερωθέν for ἐφανερώθη.
ii. 10, ἐκκλησίας for ἀρχῆς καὶ ἐξουσίας (compare ℵ*).
iv. 6, D*, ἡμῶν for ὑμῶν.
In the following it is supported by one or more:—
Eph. i. 6, D* adds υἱῷ αὐτοῦ, with G and one cursive, but many versions. See note.
i. 9 om. αὐτοῦ = G, Goth. Boh.
i. 12 om. αὐτοῦ = G.
ii. 5, D*, ταῖς ἁμαρτίαις for τοῖς παραπτώμασιν. So appy. Vulg. Hier. etc. (G has τῇ ἁμαρτίᾳ).
ib. after Χριστῷ add οὗ τῇ. G has οὗ. Some MSS. of the Vulg. have "cujus," with Ambrosiaster.
iii. 1 after ἐθνῶν adds πρεσβεύω = 10.

§ 10]   READINGS PECULIAR TO ONE OR TWO MSS.   xliii

iii. 21, ἐν Χριστῷ Ἰησοῦ καὶ τῇ ἐκκλησίᾳ = G, Victorin. Ambrosiaster.
iv. 29, πίστεως for χρείας = G, 46, some Verss. and FF.
v. 14, D*, ἐπιψαύσεις τοῦ Χριστοῦ, a reading mentioned by Chrys. Hier. al. = Ambrosiaster, al. A "Western" reading, WH.
vi. 11, εἰς for πρός = G.
Col. i. 21, τῆς διανοίας ὑμῶν for τῇ διανοίᾳ = G.
i. 22, ἀποκαταλλαγέντες = G. Goth. Ambrosiaster.
ii. 19, after κεφαλήν add Χριστόν = Syr-Harcl. Arm.
iii. 11, after ἔνι add ἄρσεν καὶ θῆλυ = G.
iii. 14, ἑνότητος for τελειότητος = G, Ambrosiaster.
iv. 10, D*, δέξασθαι for δέξασθε = G, Theoph. Ambrosiaster.
iv. 12, D*, Χριστοῦ for Θεοῦ (with one cursive).
iv. 13, D*, κόπον for πόνον = G.
It is to be remembered that D G are independent witnesses of a "Western" text.

From G we take the following:—
G alone (F not being reckoned).
Eph. i. 18, ἵνα οἴδατε for εἰς τὸ εἰδέναι ὑμᾶς (looks like a translation of the Latin "ut sciatis").
ii. 2, τούτου for τοῦ before πνεύματος (but Vulg. has "aeris hujus").
ii. 3 om. καὶ ἡμεῖς.
ii. 10, Κυρίῳ for Χριστῷ.
ii. 11, διὰ τοῦτο μνημονεύοντες for διὸ μνημονεύετε ὅτι (= Victorin.).
ii. 15, κοινόν for καινόν.
iii. 8, after αὕτη add τοῦ Θεοῦ.
iii. 11, om. τῷ Χρ. Ἰησοῦ.
iii. 12, τὴν προσαγωγὴν εἰς τὴν παρρησίαν.
v. 3, ὀνομαζέτω for ὀνομαζέσθω.
v. 5, εἰς τὴν βασιλείαν for ἐν τῇ βασιλείᾳ.
v. 20, ὑμῶν for πάντων (Theodoret combines both ὑπὲρ πάντων ὑμῶν).
Col. i. 6 om. ἧς.
i. 22 om. αὐτοῦ.
i. 26, after ἁγίοις add ἀποστόλοις.
i. 29, ἐν ᾧ for εἰς ὅ. Of course, no MS. but F agrees; but the Latin has "in quo."
iii. 8, κατά for τά, and add after ὑμῶν, μὴ ἐκπορευέσθω. Some Vss. agree, but in them the preceding word may be the nominative, e.g. "Stultiloquium."
iii. 13, ὀργήν for μομφήν.
iii. 24, τῷ Κυρίῳ ἡμῶν Ἰησοῦ Χριστοῦ ᾧ δουλεύετε.

iv. 9, after τὰ ὧδε add πραττόμενα. This looks like a translation from the Latin "quae hic aguntur," which cannot be cited as supporting G, for it is a fitting rendering of τὰ ὧδε.

In the following, G is not without support. (For the coincidences with D see above.)

Eph. ii. 6, om. ἐν Χριστῷ Ἰησοῦ = Victorin. Hil.

ii. 12, after ἐπαγγελίας add αὐτῶν = Tert. Victorin. Ambrosiaster, Eth.

ib. after κόσμῳ add τούτῳ = Victorin. Ambr. Vulg. (some mss.).

iii. 8, ἐλαχίστῳ for ἐλαχιστοτέρῳ = 49.

iii. 9, after αἰώνων add καὶ ἀπὸ τῶν γενεῶν = Syr-Harcl.

iii. 10 om. νῦν = Vulg. Syr-Pesh.

iii. 21 om. τοῦ αἰῶνος, with cod. tol. (of Vulg.) Ambrosiaster.

iv. 15, ἀλήθιαν δὲ ποιοῦντες for ἀληθεύοντες δέ = "veritatem autem facientes," Vulg. Victorin. Ambrosiaster, Hier. But the Latin is probably only an interpretation of ἀληθεύοντες, in which case the reading of G would have to be regarded as a translation of the Latin. Jerome in *Quaest.* 10 (*Algas.*) has "veritatem autem loquentes."

iv. 16 om. κατ' ἐνέργειαν, with Arm. (Usc.) Iren. (interp.) *al.*

iv. 23, om. δέ = Eth.

Col. i. 24, ἀναπληρῶ for ἀνταναπληρῶ = 43, 46, *al.*

ii. 15, τὴν σάρκα for τὰς ἀρχὰς καὶ = Hil. (*bis*) Novat. (Syr-Pesh. and Goth. seem to combine both). CAPKA may have originated from CAPXA, but this would not fully explain the change. It is more probable that the reading originated in an interpretation of ἀπεκδυσάμενος, the Syr. and Goth. having had our Greek text, but understanding ἀπεκδ. to mean "putting off his flesh." Hil. elsewhere has "spolians se carne et principatus et potestates ostentui fecit" (204). This interpretation being mistaken by a Greek scribe for a various reading, he conformed his text thereto.

ii. 23, after ταπεινοφροσύνῃ add τοῦ νόος = Syr-Harcl. Hil. Ambrosiaster. (Goth. Boh. add cordis.) This again looks like a rendering of a Latin expression.

It has to be noted that C is defective from Eph. i. 1, Παῦλος to προσαγωγήν, ii. 18, and from iv. 17, τοῦτο οὖν to καὶ τί αἰ in Phil. i. 22.

As E is only a copy of D (after correction), it has not been thought necessary or useful to cite it amongst the witnesses to various readings. Similarly, as F, if not copied from G (as Hort thinks), is, at best, an inferior copy of the same exemplar, it has not been cited. To cite D E, or F G, or D E F G, is to give the reader the trouble of calling to mind on each occasion the known relationship of the respective pairs.

It may not be out of place here to say a word on that much misapplied maxim: "The more difficult reading is to be preferred"; a maxim which, pressed to its logical conclusion, would oblige us to accept the unintelligible because of its unintelligibility; and which, indeed, is sometimes urged in support of a reading which cannot be interpreted without violence. Bengel with his usual terseness and precision expressed in four words the true maxim of which this is a perversion: "Proclivi scriptioni praestat ardua." "Proclivis scriptio" is not a reading easy to understand, but one into which the scribe would easily fall; and "scriptio ardua" is that which would come less naturally to him. The question is not of the interpreter, but of the scribe. This includes the former erroneous maxim so far as it is true; but it may, and often does happen that the "proclivis scriptio" is a "difficilis lectio." Bengel's maxim includes a variety of cases which he discusses in detail.

ABBREVIATIONS.

Versions.

Eth.	Ethiopic.
Arm.	Armenian.
Boh.	Bohairic. Cited by Tisch. as "Coptic," by Tregelles as "Memphitic," by WH. as "me."
It. or Ital.	Old Latin.
Sah.	The Sahidic or Thebaic ("the." WH.).
Syr-Pesh.	The Peshitto Syriac.
Syr-Harcl. or Hcl.	The Harclean Syriac.

The following represent MSS. of the Vulgate: viz. am. = Cod. Amiatinus; fuld. = Cod. Fuldensis; tol. = Cod. Toletanus.

Editors.

Tisch.	Tischendorf.
Treg.	Tregelles.
WH.	Westcott and Hort.
Alf.	Alford.
De W.	De Wette.
Ell.	Ellicott.
W. Schmidt	Woldemar Schmidt, Editor of Meyer's *Comm. on Ephesians*.
Theod. Mops.	Theodore of Mopsuestia.

Other abbreviations will create no difficulty.

THE EPISTLE TO THE COLOSSIANS.

INTRODUCTION.

§ 1. THE CHURCH AT COLOSSAE.

COLOSSAE (or Colassae, see i. 2) was situated in Phrygia, on the river Lycus, a tributary to the Maeander. Herodotus speaks of it as πόλις μεγάλη (vii. 30); Xenophon, as πόλις οἰκουμένη καὶ εὐδαίμων καὶ μεγάλη (*Anab.* i. 2. 6). Strabo, however (xii. 8), only reckons it as a πόλισμα. Pliny's mention of it amongst the "oppida celeberrima" (*H. N.* v. 32, 41) is not inconsistent with this. It is after enumerating the considerable towns that he speaks of "oppida celeberrima, praeter jam dicta," thus introducing along with Colossae, other small and decayed places. Eusebius (*Chron. Olymp.* 210. 4) records its destruction (with that of Laodicea and Hierapolis) in the tenth year of Nero. Tacitus (*Ann.* xiv. 27) states that Laodicea, "ex illustribus Asiae urbibus," was destroyed by an earthquake in the seventh year of Nero. (See Introduction to *Ephesians*.)

The Church at Colossae was not founded by St. Paul, nor had it been visited by him (i. 4, 7-9, ii. 1). These indications in the Epistle agree with the narrative in the Acts of the Apostles, which represents his journeys as following a route which would not bring him to Colossae. He is, indeed, related to have passed through Phrygia on his second and third missionary journeys; but Phrygia was a very comprehensive term, and on neither occasion does the direction of his route or anything in the context point to this somewhat isolated corner of Phrygia.

In his second missionary journey, after visiting the Churches of Pisidia and Lycaonia, he passes through τὴν Φρυγίαν καὶ Γαλατικὴν χώραν (Acts xvi. 6), *i.e.* the Phrygian region of the province of Galatia, or the Phrygo-Galatic region. (The τήν before Γαλατικήν in the Text. Rec. is not genuine.) Thence he travelled through Mysia (neglecting it, παρελθόντες) to Troas. Thus on this journey he kept to the east of the valley of the Lycus. On his third journey, he founded no new Churches in Asia Minor, but confined himself to revisiting and confirming those already founded (Acts xviii. 23). From the Galatic and Phrygian region he proceeded to Ephesus by the higher lying and more direct route, not the regular trade route down the valleys of the Lycus and the Maeander. On this Lightfoot and Ramsay are agreed, the former, however, thinking that Paul may have gone as far north as Pessinus before leaving Galatia; the latter (consistently with his view of the meaning of "Galatian" in Acts) supposing him to have gone directly westward from Antioch to Ephesus. Renan supposes him to have traversed the valley of the Lycus, but without preaching there, which is hardly consistent with the form of expression in ii. 1. The founder of the Church at Colossae was apparently Epaphras; at least it had been taught by him (see i. 7, where the correct reading is καθὼς ἐμάθετε, not καθὼς καὶ ἐμάθετε).

The Church appears to have consisted of Gentile converts (i. 21, 27, ii. 13); certainly there is no hint that any of the readers were Jews, and the circumstance that the founder was a Gentile Christian would have been unfavourable to the reception of his preaching by Jews. But they were clearly exposed to Jewish influences, and, in fact, we know that there was an important Jewish settlement in the neighbourhood, Antiochus the Great having transplanted two thousand Jewish families from Babylonia and Mesopotamia into Lydia and Phrygia (Joseph. *Antt.* xii. 3. 4), thus forming a colony which rapidly increased in numbers. See Lightfoot, *The Churches of the Lycus*, in his Introduction. He gives reasons for estimating the number of Jewish adult freemen in the district of which Laodicea was the capital in B.C. 62 at not less than eleven thousand (p. 20). The Colossians were now in danger of being misled by certain false teachers, whose doctrines we gather from the counter-statements and warnings of the apostle. That there was a Judaic element appears from ii. 11, 14, 16. It does not appear, indeed, that circumcision was urged upon them as a necessity, or even as a means of perfection. There is nothing in the Epistle even remotely resembling the energetic protest against such teaching which we have in the Epistle to the Galatians. The ascetic precepts alluded to in the Epistle were not based on the Mosaic law, for St. Paul says they were derived from the tradition of men. The law, too, laid down no general precepts about drinks (ii. 16). These rules seem to have been connected with the worship of angels (ii. 16-21). The false teachers claimed an exclusive and profound insight into the world of intermediate spirits, whose favour it was desirable to obtain, and by means of whom new revelations and new spiritual powers might be attained. It was with a view to this that the body was to be treated with severity.

In the three points of exclusiveness, asceticism, and angelology, the Colossian heresy shows affinities with Essenism, which, as Lightfoot remarks, had an affinity with Gnosticism, so that it might be called Gnostic Judaism. Historically, indeed, we do not know of any Essenism outside Palestine. But there is no need to assume an identity of origin of the Colossian heresy and Essenism; the tendencies were not confined to Palestine. And Phrygia provided a congenial soil for the growth of such a type of religion. It was the home of the worship of Cybele, and Sabazius, and the Ephesian Artemis. In philosophy it had produced Thales and Heraclitus. The former declared τὸν κόσμον ἔμψυχον καὶ δαιμόνων πλήρη (Diog. Laert. i. 27).

The natural phenomena of the region about Hierapolis, Laodicea, and Colossae were well calculated to encourage a belief in demoniac or angelic powers controlling the elementary forces of nature. There was, for example, at Hierapolis (and still is) an opening, called the Plutonium, which emitted a vapour (sulphuretted hydrogen) fatal to animals which came within its range. Strabo relates that the eunuchs employed about the temple were able to approach and bend over the opening with impunity—holding in their breath (μέχρι ποσοῦ συνεχόντας ὡς ἐπὶ τὸ πολὺ τὸ πνεῦμα), yet, as he adds, showing in their faces signs of a suffocating feeling. See Svoboda, *The Seven Churches of Asia*, 1869, p. 29 sqq.; Cockerell apud Leake, *Journal of a Tour in Asia Minor*, 1824, p. 342. A comparison of Cockerell and Svoboda's experiments shows that, as Lavorde also implies, the vapour is not always equally fatal. The region was noted for earthquakes.

Notwithstanding its affinities with Gnosticism, the Colossian heresy must be regarded as belonging to an earlier stage than the developed Gnosticism usually understood by that name, even earlier, indeed, than Cerinthus. There is, for example, no allusion to the aeons of later Gnosticism, nor to the properly Gnostic conception of the relation of the demiurgic agency to the supreme God. "That relation (says Lightfoot) was represented, first, as imperfect appreciation; next, as entire ignorance; lastly, as direct antagonism. The second and third are the standing points of Cerinthus and of the later Gnostic teachers respectively. The first was probably the position of the Colossian false teachers. The imperfections of the natural world, they would urge, were due to the limited capacities of these angels to whom the demiurgic

d

work was committed, and to their imperfect sympathy with the supreme God; but, at the same time, they might fitly receive worship as mediators between God and man; and, indeed, humanity seemed in its weakness to need the intervention of some such beings less remote from itself than the highest heaven." Hence the references in the Epistle to the ταπεινοφροσύνη in connexion with this angel worship.

St. Paul assures his readers, with an authority which he clearly expects them to accept, that the gospel they had learned from Epaphras required no such addition as the false teachers pressed upon them. He points out to them that they are members of a body of which the Head, Christ, was supreme above all these angelic powers of whatever kind.

§ 2. GENUINENESS OF THE EPISTLE TO THE COLOSSIANS.

There is no certain trace of the Epistle in Clemens Romanus or in Hermas. Barnabas, however, has a distinct allusion to Col. i. 16 in xii. 7, τὴν δόξαν τοῦ Ἰησοῦ, ὅτι ἐν αὐτῷ πάντα, καὶ εἰς αὐτόν. Ignatius, *Eph.* x. 3, has ἑδραῖοι τῇ πίστει, and so Polycarp, x. 1, doubtless from Col. i. 23. Probably also the division into ὁρατοὶ καὶ ἀόρατοί, in combination with τὰ ἐπουράνια, in Ign. *Smyrn.* vi. 1, may be another allusion to i. 16. The connexion also of idolatry and covetousness in Polyc. xi. 2 may have been suggested by Col. i. 23, 20, iii. 5. Justin, *Dial.* p. 311 (lxxxv), calls Christ πρωτότοκος πάσης κτίσεως, after Col. i. 15 (cf. πρωτότοκον τῶν πάντων ποιημάτων, p. 310); also p. 326 (xcvi), πρωτότοκον τοῦ Θεοῦ καὶ πρὸ πάντων τῶν κτισμάτων. Considering the frequent use of the Epistle to the Ephesians, it is remarkable that the traces of this Epistle previous to Irenaeus are so few and uncertain. Its shortness seems an inadequate explanation. Probably the true account is that, the Epistle being so largely controversial, its use would be less familiar to those who had no concern with the heresies with which it deals. About its early and uncontroverted reception as the work of St. Paul, there is no doubt. Irenaeus, iii. 14. 1, says: "Iterum in ea epistola quae est ad Colossenses ait: 'Salutat vos Lucas medicus dilectus.'" In the following section he quotes Col. i. 21, 22, and, indeed, he cites passages from every chapter.

Clement of Alexandria, *Strom.* i. 1, says: κἂν τῇ πρὸς Κολοσσαεῖς ἐπιστολῇ· νουθετοῦντες, γράφει, πάντα ἄνθρωπον, κ.τ.λ. = Col. i. 28, and again in several other places he cites the Epistle.

Tertullian also cites passages from each chapter. Origen, *contra Cels.* v. 8, quotes ii. 18, 19, as from St. Paul to the Colossians.

Marcion received the Ep. as St. Paul's, and the school of Valentinus also recognised it.

In the Muratorian Canon it has the same place as in our MSS. The external evidence for the genuineness is in no wise defective, nor was any question raised on the point until Mayerhoff (*Der Brief an die Kolosser, u.s.w.* 1838) contested it on the grounds of vocabulary, style, and differences from St. Paul in thought and expression; and, in addition to these, its relation to the Epistle to the Ephesians, which he considered to be genuine, and its supposed reference to Cerinthus. Many critics followed his lead, including Baur, Hilgenfeld, Pfleiderer, etc., rejecting, however, the Epistle to the Ephesians also. Ewald, partly followed by Renan, explained what seemed un-Pauline in the Epistle by the supposition that Timothy wrote it under the apostle's direction,—an hypothesis excluded by i. 23, ii. 1, 5. De Wette replied to Mayerhoff's arguments, rejecting, however, the Epistle to the Ephesians.

Holtzmann, as we have seen in the Introduction to the latter Epistle, regarded the present Epistle as an expansion by an interpolator of a short, genuine Epistle, being led to this conclusion by a careful critical examination of certain parallel passages in the two Epistles, the result of which was to show conclusively that it was impossible to maintain either, with Mayerhoff, the priority in every case of Eph., or, with De Wette, that of Col.[1]

As a specimen of his restoration of the original nucleus of the latter Epistle, the following may suffice. Ch. i. 9–29 reads as follows:—

Διὰ τοῦτο καὶ ἡμεῖς οὐ παυόμεθα ὑπὲρ ὑμῶν προσευχόμενοι περιπατῆσαι ὑμᾶς ἀξίως τοῦ Θεοῦ, ὃς ἐρρύσατο ἡμᾶς ἐκ τῆς ἐξουσίας τοῦ σκότους καὶ μετέστησεν εἰς τὴν βασιλείαν τοῦ υἱοῦ αὐτοῦ ὅτι ἐν αὐτῷ εὐδόκησεν καταλλάξαι, καὶ ὑμᾶς ποτὲ ὄντας ἐχθροὺς ἐν τοῖς ἔργοις τοῖς πονηροῖς, νυνὶ δὲ κατηλλάγητε ἐν τῷ σώματι τῆς σαρκὸς αὐτοῦ διὰ τοῦ θανάτου, εἴγε ἐπιμένετε τῇ πίστει ἑδραῖοι καὶ μὴ μετακινούμενοι ἀπὸ τοῦ εὐαγγελίου οὗ ἐγενόμην ἐγὼ Παῦλος διάκονος κατὰ τὴν οἰκονομίαν τοῦ Θεοῦ τὴν δοθεῖσάν μοι εἰς ὑμᾶς πληρῶσαι τὸν λόγον τοῦ Θεοῦ, εἰς ὃ καὶ κοπιῶ ἀγωνιζόμενος κατὰ τὴν ἐνέργειαν αὐτοῦ τὴν ἐνεργομένην ἐν ἐμοί.

Of ch. iii. Holtzmann regards as original only *vv.* 3, 12, 13, 17.

This is a very ingenious abridgment, and supposes extreme ingenuity on the part of the interpolator, who so cleverly dovetailed his own work into St. Paul's that, had Eph. not existed, no one would have suspected Col. of being interpolated. It would be strange, too, that the interpolated letter should so completely displace the Pauline original. It would seem, in fact, as if we were compelled to suppose it known only to this interpolator "who

---

[1] For a list of the principal passages compared, see Introduction to the *Ep. to the Ephesians*.

rescued it from oblivion" (*Kritik*, p. 305) only to consign it thither again. Holtzmann's theory is, as Jülicher says, too complicated to be accepted. In such a case, for example, as Col. i. 27 compared with Eph. i. 9, 10, and iii. 8, 9, 16, 17; or, again, Col. iii. 12–15 with Eph. iv. 2–4, 32, it is involved in inextricable difficulties. And as this seems to be generally felt, it is not necessary to examine his instances in detail.

Von Soden, in his article in the *Jahrb. f. Protest. Theol.* 1875, limited the interpolations to i. 15–20, ii. 10, 15, 18 (partly). In his Commentary he still further reduces the interpolation to i. 16*b*, 17, *i.e.* τὰ πάντα to συνέστηκε, which he regards as a gloss (*Einl.* p. 12).

Against the genuineness is alleged, first, the absence of St. Paul's favourite terms and turns of expression, together with the occurrence of others which are foreign to the acknowledged Epistles. For example, δίκαιος with its derivatives, ἀποκάλυψις, δοκιμάζειν, ὑπακοή, σωτηρία, κοινωνία, νόμος, πιστεύειν, are absent, as well as ἄρα, διό, διότι, while it is noted that γάρ occurs only five times (or six if it is read in iii. 24), as against thirty-six times in Gal. and some three hundred times in the three other great Epistles. But these phenomena are not without parallel in other Epistles or parts of Epistles of similar length. δικαιοσύνη occurs in 1 Cor. only once (i. 30), δίκαιος not at all. Both adjective and substantive are absent from 1 Thess., as well as the verb. σωτηρία is not used in 1 Cor. or Gal., while in 2 Cor. σώζω occurs but once; ἀποκάλυψις is not used in Phil. or 1 Thess., and in 2 Cor. only in xii. 1, 7, so that the first eleven chs. are without it. πιστεύειν is found in 2 Cor. only in a quotation, iv. 13; ὑπακοή not in 1 Cor. Gal. Phil. 1 Thess.; νόμος not in 2 Cor. or Thess. Again, as to the conjunctions, ἄρα does not occur in Phil., while ἄρα οὖν, frequent in Rom., is not used in 1 or 2 Cor., and only once in Gal. διό occurs only once in Gal. (iv. 31, where Rec. has ἄρα), and διότι once in 1 Cor., not at all in 2 Cor. γάρ is hardly more frequent (relatively) in Eph., which Mayerhoff accepted, than in Col. Its comparative infrequency in both as compared with Rom. and Cor. is clearly due to the more argumentative character of the latter Epistles.

As to the ἅπαξ λεγόμενα, they are not more numerous than was to be expected in an Epistle dealing with novel questions. In addition to ten words found only here and in Eph., there are forty-eight which do not occur elsewhere in St. Paul. But as Soden remarks, Paul had for a considerable time been under the new linguistic influence of Rome. Salmon quotes a very pertinent remark of Dr. Mahaffy, who compares St. Paul to Xenophon in this matter of varying vocabulary. He says: "His (Xenophon's) later tracts are full of un-Attic words, picked up from his changing surroundings; and, what is more curious, in each of them there are many words only used by him once; so that on the ground of variation in diction each single book might be, and, indeed, has been, rejected as non-Xenophontic. This variation not only applies to words which might not be required again, but to such terms as εὐανδρία (*Comm.* iii. 3. 12), varied to εὐψυχία (*Ven.* 10. 21), εὐτολμία (quoted by Stobaeus), ἀνδρειότης (*Anab.* vi. 5. 14), all used only once. Every page in Sauppe's *Lexilogus Xen.* bristles with words only once used in this way. Now, of classical writers, Xenophon is perhaps (except Herodotus) the only man whose life corresponded to St. Paul's in its roving habits, which would bring him into contact with the spoken Greek of varying societies."

The long sentences, such as i. 9-20, ii. 8-12, are not without analogy in other Epistles, *e.g.* Rom. i. 1-7, ii. 5-10, 14-16, iii. 23-26; Gal. ii. 3-5, 6-9; Phil. iii. 8-11. The series of relatives in i. 13-22 and ii. 10-12 is remarkable, but not without parallel; and in both cases the connexion shows that what is added in the relative clauses, though evident, had been overlooked by the heretical teachers. It was therefore properly connected by a relative. Anacolutha are particularly frequent in St. Paul. There are also many turns of expression which are strikingly Pauline, as : ii. 4, 8, 17, 18, 23, iii. 14, iv. 6, 17. In comparing the general tone of the Epistle with that of the other Epistles, it must be observed that St. Paul had not here to contend with any opposition directed against him or his teaching, nor had he to defend himself against objections, but was simply called on to express his judgment on the novel additions to the gospel teaching which were being pressed on the Colossians. This new teaching had not yet gained acceptance or led to factious divisions amongst them. Nor has he any longer occasion to argue that Gentiles are admitted to the Christian Church on equal terms with Jews; this question is no longer agitated here; St. Paul's own solution of the problem is assumed. Nor was he concerned here with the conditions of salvation, whether by faith or by the works of the law. If he does not adduce proof from the O.T., neither does he do this in Phil., where there might seem to be more occasion for doing so.

The greater stress laid here on knowledge and wisdom is explained by the fact that the false teachers were endeavouring to dazzle their hearers by a show of profound wisdom to which the apostle opposes the true wisdom. Hence, also, his frequent use of such words as μυστήριον, ἀποκρύπτειν, ἀπόκρυφος, γνωρίζειν, φανεροῦν.

Mayerhoff notes the hunting after synonyms as an un-Pauline characteristic of this Epistle. Of his many examples it may suffice to give a few specimens : i. 6, καρποφορούμενον καὶ αὐξανόμενον ; *ib.* ἀκούειν καὶ ἐπιγινώσκειν ; 7, σύνδουλος [ἡμῶν], διάκονος [τοῦ Χριστοῦ] ; 11, ὑπομονὴ καὶ μακροθυμία ; 23, τεθεμελιωμένοι καὶ ἑδραῖοι καὶ μὴ μετακινούμενοι (see Eadie, p. xxvii). Many of the so-called synonyms are clearly not so; and even where they are justly so called, the other Epistles supply parallels. See, for example, Phil. i. 3, 7, 9, 10, 11, 15, 20, 24, 25.

An objection to the genuineness of the Epistle, which would be serious if well founded, is that the Epistle combats certain errors of a Gnostic character which cannot have existed at so early a date. It is not enough, however, to show that errors of an analogous kind, but more developed, existed in the middle of the second century; it is necessary to show that they could not have existed in the time of St. Paul. But we have absolutely no materials for forming an opinion on this point, except in the New Testament itself. The earliest Gnostic writer of whom we have definite information is Cerinthus.

Indeed, Mayerhoff supposed the writer's polemic to be directed against him. But although there is an affinity between the errors of Cerinthus and those of the Colossian teachers, a closer examination shows that the latter belong to an earlier stage of development. There is no trace in the Epistle of the notion of creation by a demiurge ignorant of the supreme God, still less of that by one opposed to Him (as in the later Gnostics). Nor did the teaching of Cerinthus include asceticism. As to the view of Christ held by the Colossian false teachers, it was clearly derogatory, as we may infer from the emphatic assertions in i. 19, ii. 9; but the generality of the language there used shows that their opinions had not been stated with such precision as was the case when St. John wrote his Gospel, or, not to assume his authorship, when the Gospel bearing his name was written.

Baur, on the other hand, regards the Epistle to the Colossians (as well as that to the Ephesians) as written from an early Gnostic point of view, at a time, namely, when Gnostic ideas first coming into vogue still appeared to be unobjectionable Christian speculation. The errors combated were, he thought, those of the Ebionites, who maintained circumcision, abstained from animal food, observed the Jewish Sabbath, and attached high importance to the doctrine of angels and religious worship of them, and, lastly, considered Christ to be only one of these: ἐκτίσθαι ὡς ἕνα τῶν ἀρχαγγέλων μείζονα δὲ αὐτῶν ὄντα, αὐτὸν δὲ κυριεύειν τῶν ἀγγέλων καὶ πάντων τῶν ἀπὸ τοῦ παντοκράτορος πεποιημένων (Epiph. *Haer.* xxx. 16).

In which of St. Paul's Epistles, says Baur, do we find τὰ ἐπουράνια classified as they are in Eph. and Col.?

The reply is obvious; the classification of the celestial hierarchy which we find in these Epistles is not Paul's at all (as will be shown in the exposition), but that of the false teachers.

In reference, again, to the assertion in Col. and Eph., that

Christ is the creative principle of everything existing, and therefore that to Him is attributed absolute pre-existence, Baur remarks that "it is true that we find certain hints of similar views in the homologoumena of the apostle, but they are no more than hints, the meaning of which is open to question; while here, on the contrary, the absolute premundane existence is the dominating, the pervading element within which the whole thought of these Epistles moves." For the idea that Christ's activity comprehends heavenly and earthly things at once and in the same degree, there is, he says, no analogy in Paul's writings, but we are here transported to a circle of ideas which belongs to a different era, namely, the period of Gnosticism (*St. Paul*, Eng. tr. p. 7). The Gnostic systems, says Baur, rest on the root idea that all spiritual life which has proceeded from the supreme God has to return to its original unity, and to be taken back again into the absolute principle, so that every discord which has arisen shall be resolved into harmony. And so in these Epistles Christ's work is mainly that of restoring, bringing back, and making unity. His work is contemplated as a mediation and atonement whose effects extend to the whole universe.

Accepting Holtzmann's caution (p. 296), that when critics like Baur and himself speak of Gnostic colouring in the Epistle, they do not mean Gnosticism proper, we may reply, first, that according to the above statement of Baur, the root idea of Gnostic systems includes the emanation of inferior spiritual existences from the Supreme; and this can hardly be separated from the idea of the creation of matter by the inferior spirits, since it was just to explain the evil of matter that the theory of emanations, etc., was devised. Of these ideas there is no trace in the Epistle except by way of opposition. The notion of successive evolutions from the Divine nature, forming the links of a chain which binds the finite to the Infinite, is utterly opposed to the teaching of the Epistle; nor is it conceivable as a later development of anything that the writer himself says. It is, however, quite consistent with the teaching that he condemns. Secondly, the idea of reconciliation is wholly different from that of return to the unity of the Divine nature of that which has emanated or been evolved from it.

Baur, indeed, admits the possibility that the conception of the work of Christ which is exhibited in these Epistles may be harmonised with the Pauline Christology and doctrine of atonement; yet it is certain, he adds, that with Paul these ideas never assume the prominence which they have here. It is a transcendental region into which Paul looked now and then, but of which he had no definite views, and which he never introduced into his Epistles from a taste for metaphysical speculation.

"As even the Christology of these Epistles bears unmistakably the impress of Gnosticism," says Baur, "we meet also with other Gnostic conceptions"; and he draws attention especially to πλήρωμα. The Gnostic πλήρωμα is not the Absolute itself, but it is that in which the Absolute realises the conception of itself. According to the doctrine of the Valentinians, it is the sum of the aeons by which the original Divine source is filled.

Now this, says Baur, is just the conception of the Pleroma which we find in both our Epistles; the only difference being that there is no express mention here of a plurality of aeons as the complement of the Pleroma, and that not the supreme God Himself, but Christ, is the Pleroma, since only in Christ does the self-existent God unfold Himself in the fulness of concrete life. He finds a further remarkable agreement with the Valentinians in the comparison of the relation of husband to wife with that of Christ to the Church, since, according to the Valentinians, the aeons were divided into male and female, united in pairs called syzygies. Hence he explains how as Christ is the πλήρωμα, so also is the Church—that is to say, she is the πλήρωμα of Christ; since He is the πλήρωμα in the highest sense, she is τὸ πλήρωμα τοῦ τὰ πάντα ἐν πᾶσι πληρουμένου.

The latter suggestion scarcely merits a serious refutation. To compare the position of Christ as viewed by the writer with that of one of the aeons of the Valentinians, is to contradict the fundamental thesis of the Epistles, namely, that Christ is exalted far above all existences, earthly and heavenly, by whatever name they may be called. Equally remote from the writer's thought, and irreconcilable with it, is the conception of ἐκκλησία as an aeon co-ordinate with Christ. Indeed, the whole system of syzygies or duads was devised as a theory of successive generation. Nothing in the remotest degree resembling this appears in the Epistles. Throughout both, the relation of Christ to the Church is that of the head to the body; the figure of marriage is introduced only incidentally, not with the view of illustrating or explaining the union of Christ and the Church by that of man and wife, but in order to set forth the love of Christ as the Head, for His Body, the Church, as a pattern for the Christian husband; and it is the headship of Christ that is used to illustrate the headship of the man—"For we are members of His body." The idea of the thing illustrated reacts in the writer's mind on the conception of that with which it was compared, and so there grows up a new representation of the relation of Christ to the Church.

As to the word πλήρωμα, so far is the conception in our Epistles from being just the same as that of the Valentinians, that the difference which Baur himself mentions is a vital one. What the writer so emphatically asserts is that the whole πλήρωμα resides in Christ, not a mere fraction of it, not a single Divine power only, as the Gnostic use of the word would suggest. That some such view as this, of a part only of the πλήρωμα residing in Christ, was held by the Colossian false teachers, may be fairly inferred from the writer's insistence on πᾶν τὸ πλήρωμα, κ.τ.λ. It is simple and natural, then, to suppose that he purposely employs a term common to himself and them in such a way as to combat directly their erroneous views. How can such a fact be supposed to indicate a Gnostic tendency on the part of the writer?

In fact, once it is admitted that the thoughts expressed in this Epistle (or that to the Ephesians) are capable of being reconciled to those of St. Paul, it is no longer possible to use the (supposed) Gnostic colouring as an argument against the genuineness of a writing which bears the name of Paul, and which in addition has such strong external support. It is true these thoughts have more prominence and are more developed here than in the acknowledged Epistles, but this is fully accounted for by the nature of the errors with which the apostle had to contend. The circumstances of Rome, Corinth, and Galatia were not such as to call for such an exposition as we find here; indeed, in the Epistles to the last two Churches, at least, it would have been singularly out of place. It is not to a taste for indulging in metaphysical speculation that we are to trace its presence here, but to the exigencies of the case. But, then, it is said that although St. Paul did now and then look into this transcendental region, he had no definite views of it. What then? If the Epistles are genuine, several years had elapsed since the writing of the four great Epistles. Was the apostle's mind so rigid that we cannot conceive his views becoming more developed and more distinct in the interval of five or six years? Nothing was more likely to further their development than the presence of erroneous teaching. Just as the articles of the Church's creed took form only gradually as errors sprang up, so in an individual mind, even in that of the apostle, a particular truth would be more distinctly recognised and more precisely formulated when the opposing error presented itself.

It may be remarked that Baur found traces of Gnostic thought in the Epistle to the Philippians also, the genuineness of which has, however, been acknowledged by almost all subsequent critics, including Hausrath (who supposes it made up of two Epistles), Hilgenfeld, Holtzmann, Pfleiderer, Reuss, Renan, Schenkel. Indeed, it may be regarded as practically beyond question. This is not without importance for the Epistle to the Colossians, for it supplies an answer to the objections to the latter Ep. founded on the loftiness of the attributes assigned to Christ. For it contains nothing that goes beyond Phil. ii. 6-11. On the other hand, the Epistle to the Colossians, as Renan observes, cannot be separated from the Epistle to Philemon. The coincidence in some of the names mentioned might be explained by the hypothesis that the forger of the longer Epistle made use of the shorter. But the differences exclude this supposition (see Salmon, *Introduction*, ch. xx.). Col. mentions Jesus, surnamed Justus, an otherwise unknown person, in addition to those mentioned in Philem., while Philemon is not mentioned at all. Again, while Aristarchus and Epaphras are mentioned in both Epp., it is the former that is called fellow-prisoner in Col., the latter in Philemon. But there is nothing in the Ep. to Philemon to suggest Colossae as the city of his residence. We learn his connexion with it only by finding his runaway slave Onesimus mentioned in Col. as "one of you." Having learned this we observe further that Archippus, who in the private Epistle appears as an intimate, perhaps son, of Philemon, is mentioned in Col. in such a way as to suggest that he held office either there or in Laodicea. Certainly the way in which his name is introduced there is as unlike as possible to the contrivance of a forger. That Onesimus alone should be mentioned as Paul's messenger in the letter to Philemon, but Tychicus with him in the public Epistle, is perfectly natural.

Now the genuineness of the Epistle to Philemon is beyond question; in fact, in the whole range of literature there is no piece which bears more unmistakably the stamp of originality and genuineness. To quote Renan: "Paul seul, autant qu'il semble, a pu écrire ce petit chef d'oeuvre." Baur, indeed, felt himself compelled to reject it in consequence of its intimate connexion with Col. and Eph., and then set himself to confirm his rejection by an examination of the diction of the Epistle and of the circumstances supposed. His argument is valuable as a *reductio ad absurdum* of his whole method.

V. Soden remarks that there is a striking correspondence both in language and thought between the Ep. to the Colossians and to the only other document which we possess from the apostle's hand during his Roman imprisonment, viz. the Ep. to the Philippians (as he does not accept Eph.). Thus as to language he compares πληροῦν in Col. three times, in Phil. four times: σπλάγχνα οἰκτιρμοῦ, Col. iii. 12, Phil. ii. 1: λόγος τοῦ Θεοῦ, Col. i. 25, Phil. i. 14: περιτομή (figurative), Col. ii. 11, Phil. iii. 3: ἀγών, Col. ii. 1, Phil. i. 30: ἀπεῖναι, Col. ii. 5, Phil. i. 27: δεσμοί, Col. iv. 18, Phil. i. 7, 13 f., 17: τὰ κατ' ἐμέ, Col. iv. 7, Phil. i. 12: ταπεινοφροσύνη, Col. ii. 23, iii. 12, Phil. ii. 3: καρποφοροῦντες, Col. i. 10, πεπληρωμένοι καρπόν, Phil. i. 11: ἄμωμος, Col. i. 22, Phil. ii. 15: τέλειος, Col. i. 28, Phil. iii. 15: κατὰ τὴν ἐνέργειαν, κ.τ.λ., Col. i. 29, Phil. iii. 21: ἄνω, Col. iii. 1, Phil. iii. 14: τὰ ἐπὶ τῆς γῆς, Col. iii. 2, ἐπίγεια, Phil. iii. 19: βραβεῖον, Phil. iii. 14, καταβραβεύειν, Col. ii. 18. As to style, he compares the brevity of

Col. iv. 17 and Phil. iv. 2; the introduction of a judgment by a relative, Col. ii. 23, Phil. i. 28, iii. 19: the sentences, Col. i. 9, Phil. i. 11: the prayer for ἐπίγνωσις, Col. i. 9 f.; Phil. i. 9: the wish καὶ ἡ εἰρήνη, κ.τ.λ., Col. iii. 15, Phil. iv. 7: the similar ideas, Col. i. 24 and Phil. iii. 10; Col. ii. 18 and Phil. iii. 3; Col. i. 24 and Phil. ii. 30: the references to what the readers had heard, Col. i. 7, Phil. iv. 9: and, lastly, the close correspondence of some peculiar dogmatic expressions; see i. 19 ff.

§ 3. PLACE AND DATE OF WRITING.

For these see Introduction to the *Epistle to the Ephesians*, where it is shown to be probable that the Epistle was written from Rome about A.D. 63. The occasion seems to have been the information furnished by Epaphras of the dangers to which the Church at Colossae was exposed from heretical teachers.

§ 4. RELATION TO OTHER NEW TESTAMENT WRITINGS.

For the relation to the Epistle to the Ephesians, see the Introduction to that Epistle.

The relation to the Apocalypse deserves particular notice. It is especially in the Epistle to Laodicea, Rev. iii. 14–21, that we find resemblances. In that Epistle, St. John, speaking in the person of the Lord, declares almost in the language of St. Paul that He is the Amen, the faithful and true Witness, ἡ ἀρχὴ τῆς κτίσεως τοῦ Θεοῦ,—an expression which does not occur (nor anything like it) in any of the other six Epistles. Compare Col. i. 15, πρωτότοκος πάσης κτίσεως. Doubtless there still remained some trace of the heresy which St. Paul combated. Again, Rev. iii. 21, δώσω αὐτῷ καθίσαι μετ' ἐμοῦ ἐν τῷ θρόνῳ μου, κ.τ.λ., is very parallel to Col. iii. 1 and Eph. ii. 6, and here again there is nothing similar in the other Epistles. "This double coincidence (says Lightfoot), affecting the two ideas which may be said to cover the whole ground in the Epistle to the Colossians, can hardly, I think, be fortuitous, and suggests an acquaintance with and recognition of the earlier apostle's teaching on the part of St. John" (p. 42).

§ 5. VOCABULARY OF THE EPISTLE.

List of ἅπαξ λεγόμενα *in the Epistle to the Colossians.*

ἀθυμεῖν, αἰσχρολογία, ἀνεψιός, ἀνταναπληροῦν, ἀνταπόδοσις, ἀπεκδύεσθαι, ἀπέκδυσις, ἀπόχρησις, ἀρέσκεια, ἀφειδία, βραβεύειν, δογματίζεσθαι, δυναμοῦν (see Eph. vi. 10), ἐθελοθρησκεία, εἰρηνοποιεῖν, ἐμβατεύειν, εὐχάριστος, θεότης, καταβραβεύειν, μετακινεῖν, μομφή, νουμηνία, ὁρατός, παρηγορία, πιθανολογία, πλησμονή, προακούειν, προσηλοῦν, πρωτεύειν, στερέωμα, συλαγωγεῖν, σωματικῶς, φιλοσοφία, χειρόγραφον. More than half of these (18) are in ch. ii. only.

Words which occur in other Writers of the N.T., but not in St. Paul.

ἅλας, ἀποκρίνεσθαι, ἀπόκρυφος, ἀρτύειν, γεύεσθαι, δειγματίζειν, ἐξαλείφειν, παραλογίζεσθαι, πικραίνειν, πόνος, σκιά, σύνδουλος. The following are found in the Pastorals: ἀποκεῖσθαι, κρύπτειν, πλουσίως.

Pauline Words.

The following are found only in St. Paul: ἀπεῖναι, ἑδραῖος, εἰκῆ, ἐρεθίζειν, θριαμβεύειν, ἱκανοῦν, ἰσότης, πάθος, συναιχμάλωτος, συνθάπτειν, φυσιοῦν.

§ 6. CONTENTS OF THE EPISTLE.

i. 1, 2. Salutation, briefly specifying Paul's designation as an apostle, not by men, but by the will of God.

Although the apostle's purpose in writing to the Colossians was to warn them against the errors that threatened to creep in amongst them, yet with admirable delicacy, as writing to those to whom he was not personally known, he does not introduce his admonition until he has prepared the way for its favourable reception by a comparatively long introduction, which begins and ends with commendation.

3-8. Thanksgiving for their faith and love, resting on the heavenly hope laid up for them. Mention of the hope leads naturally to the assurance that the gospel which they had been taught by Epaphras was the true gospel, universal and unchangeable, and proving its genuineness by the fruit which it was bearing, both amongst them and in all the world.

9-12. Prayer that they may advance further in spiritual knowledge, and that not speculative but practical, so that their life may be worthy of their profession.

13 ff. The prayer passes insensibly into the positive instruction which will help to its fulfilment, and furnish a safeguard against the attempts that are made to mislead them. They have already been transferred into the kingdom of God's beloved Son. It is in Him that they have their redemption.

15-17. The pre-eminence of Christ, in His nature and in His office. In His nature He is superior to all created things, being the visible image of the invisible God, and all things having been created through Him, and holding together by Him.

18–20. In the spiritual order also He is first, the firstborn from the dead, and the Head of the Church, all the fulness of God dwelling in Him. The work of reconciliation wrought through Him extends even to things in the heavens.

21–23. The Colossians have their share in this reconciliation, the object of which is that they may be without blemish and without reproof in the sight of God. But this depends on their continuing steadfast in the faith which they have been taught.

24–29. The apostle's own qualifications as a minister of this gospel, privileged to know and make known the mystery hidden from preceding ages, namely, Christ dwelling in them. It is his business to proclaim this, and so to admonish and teach, that he may present every man perfect; and this he strenuously labours to do through the power of Christ.

ii. 1–7. This effort and anxiety of his extend even to those to whom he had not personally preached, that they may be confirmed in the faith and united in love, and, further, may learn to know the mystery of God. What they have to aim at is to be established in the faith which they have already been taught, firmly rooted in Christ, and living accordingly.

8–15. The apostle has learned (no doubt from Epaphras) that there are amongst them teachers who are endeavouring to propagate mischievous heresies which would undermine their faith. He does not, indeed, adopt this rude manner of expression, but cautions them against being led astray. The philosophy of which these false teachers make a display is mere deceit, and of human origin; it is not a more advanced teaching, but, on the contrary, belongs to an elementary stage. Ye have already been made full in Christ, who is above all these angelic beings of whom they speak, since the whole fulness of the Godhead dwells in Him. Ye need no circumcision of the flesh, for ye have received in Him the true circumcision of the Spirit; it is by Him that ye have been raised from death to life, and nothing remains to be added to His work, for He has completely removed the bond that was against you.

16–23. Application of these principles to the practices inculcated by the false teachers. With their precepts about meat and drink and days they would have you rest in the shadow, as if you had not already the reality. The angel worship which they inculcate is not the outcome of true humility, but of carnal pride in the fancied possession of superior knowledge; and it leads to a setting aside of the Head, through union with which alone can the body derive its nourishment and growth.

iii. 1–4. Your aims and thoughts must be more lofty. Ye

have been raised with Christ, and your life is now hid with Him. Seek therefore the things where He is, at God's right hand.

5-11. Sins to be avoided : not only the grosser ones of appetite, but the more subtle sins of temper, etc.

12-17. Virtues to be cultivated : kindness, love, forgiveness, of which we have such a lofty example in God's forgiveness of us, mutual teaching, and in everything thankfulness to God. Everything to be done in the name of the Lord Jesus Christ.

18-iv. 1. Special precepts for the several relations of life : wives and husbands, children and parents, slaves and masters, the motive always being "in the Lord."

2-6. Exhortation to constant prayer and thanksgiving, with request for prayer for the apostle himself in his work, to which he adds further practical hints as to wisdom in action and speech.

7-18. Personal commendations and salutations.

§ 7. LITERATURE OF THE EPISTLE TO THE COLOSSIANS.

Commentaries on the entire New Testament are not included.

Sixteenth and Seventeenth Centuries.

ALTING (J.), *Analysis exegetica in Ep. ad Coloss.* Opp. Amstel. 1687.
ARETIUS (Bened.), *Comm.* Morgis. 1580.
BAYNE (Paul), *Comm. on Ep. to Colossians.* Lond. 1634.
BUGENHAGEN. See *Ephesians.*
BYFIELD (Nicholas), *An Exposition on the Ep. to the Col.* Lond. 1617, *al.*
CALIXTUS. See *Ephesians.*
CARTWRIGHT (Thos.), *Comm.* Lond. 1603.
CRELLIUS, *Comm. et Paraphrasis in Col.*
DAVENANT (John, Bp. of Salisbury), *Expositio Ep. Pauli ad Coloss.* Cantab. 1627; transl. Lond. 1831.
DAILLÉ or DALLAEUS (Joannes), *Sermons sur l'Epistre aux Col.* 3 tom. Gen. 1662; transl. Lond. 1672, again Lond. 1841.
D'OUTREIN (Joh.), *Sendbrief, etc.* Amst. 1695. (In German) Frankf. 1696.
ELTON (Edw.), *Exposition of the Ep. to the Colossians . . . in Sundry Sermons.* Lond. 1615, *al.*
FERGUSON (Jas.), *A brief Exposition of the Epp. to the Phil. and Col.* Edinb. 1656, *al.*
GRYNAEUS (Jo. Jac.), *Explicatio . . .* Basil, 1585.

§ 7] LITERATURE OF EPISTLE TO THE COLOSSIANS lxiii

MELANCHTHON (Phil.), *Enarratio Epistolae Pauli ad Coloss.* Witenb. 1559.
MUSCULUS (Wolfg.), *Comm. in Epp. ad Philip. Coloss. etc.* Basil, 1565.
OLEVIANUS (Gaspar), *Notae, etc.* Gen. 1580.
QUIROS (Aug. de), *Comment.* Lugd. 1623.
ROLLOCK (Rob.), *In Ep. Pauli ad Col. Comm.* Edin. 1600.
SLICHTINGIUS, *Comm. in plerosque N.T. libros.* Eleutherop. 1656.
SCHMID (Seb.), *Paraphrasis super Ep. ad Col.* Strassb. 1696, *al.*
SUICER (J. H.), *In Ep. S. Pauli ad Col. Comment. crit. exeget. theolog.* Tiguri, 1669.
WOODHEAD. See *Ephesians.*
ZANCHIUS (Hier.), *Comm.* Opp. Gen. 1619.
ZUINGLIUS (Ulr.), *Comm.* Opp. Tiguri [1545].

Eighteenth Century.

BAUMGARTEN. See *Ephesians.*
BOYSEN, *Erklärung, u.s.w.* Quedlinb. 1766–81.
GLEICH, *Predigten.* Dresd. 1717.
HAZEVOET, *Verklaering.* Leyden, 1720.
KONING, *Openlegging.* Leyden, 1739.
LUTKEN, *Predigten.* Gardel. 1718, *al.*
MICHAELIS. See *Ephesians.*
PEIRCE (Jas.), *A Paraphrase and Notes on the Epp. to the Col. Phil. and Heb. after the manner of Mr. Locke.* Lond. 1727, *al.*
ROELL, *Ep. Pauli ad Col. exegesis.* Traj. 1731.
STORR (Gottlob Chr.), *Dissertatio exegetica in Epistolae ad Col. partem priorem [et poster].* Tübing. 1783–87; transl. Edinb. 1842.
STRESO, *Meditationes.* Amst. 1708.
TIL (Salomon v.). See *Ephesians.*
ZACHARIAE (G. T.). See *Ephesians.*

Nineteenth Century.

ALEXANDER (Wm., Archbishop of Armagh), *Commentary*; in the "*Speaker's Commentary.*" London
BÄHR (Felix), *Comment. über d. Brief Pauli au die Kol. mit stäter Berücksichtigung d. ältern u. neuern Ausleger.* Basel, 1833.
BARRY. See *Ephesians.*
BAUMGARTEN-CRUSIUS. See *Ephesians.*
BEET. See *Ephesians.*
BISPING, *Erklärung.* Münster, 1855.

BLEEK. See *Ephesians*.
BÖHMER (W.), *Theol. Auslegung des Pauli Sendschreiben an die Col.* Breslau, 1835.
BRAUNE. See *Ephesians*.
DALMER (Ed. Fr.), *Auslegung, u.s.w.* Gotha, 1855.
DECKER, *Bearbeitung.* Hamb. 1848.
EADIE (John), *Commentary on the Greek Text of the Ep. of Paul to the Colossians.* Edinb. 1855, 1884.
ELLICOTT (C. J., Bishop of Gloucester and Bristol), *A Critical and Grammatical Comm. on St. Paul's Epp. to the Philippians, Colossians, and to Philemon, with a Revised Translation.* Lond. 1857, *al.*
EWALD. See *Ephesians*.
FINDLAY (G. G.), "Colossians" in *Pulpit Commentary.*
FLATT (J. F. v.), *Vorlesung. über d. Br. Pauli an die Phil. Kol. etc.* Tübing. 1829.
GISBORNE (Thos.), *Exposition and Application . . . in Eight Sermons.* Lond. 1816.
HEINRICHS (J. H.), *In Koppe's Nov. Test. Graec. etc.* Götting. 1803, *al.*
HOFMANN (J. Chr. v.), *Die Briefe Pauli an die Col. u. an Philemon.* Nördlingen, 1870.
HUTHER (Joh. Ed.), *Comm. u.s.w.* Hamb. 1841.
JUNKER (Friedr.), *Histor. Krit. u. philolog. Comm.* München, 1828.
KÄHLER (C. R.), *Auslegung.* Eislehen, 1853.
KLÖPPER (A.), *Der Brief an die Kolosser.* Berlin, 1882.
LIGHTFOOT (J. B., Bishop of Durham), *St. Paul's Epistles to the Colossians and to Philemon, A Revised Text with Introductions, Notes, and Dissertations.* Lond. 1875, *al.*
MACLAREN (Alex.), "Colossians" in *The Expositor's Bible.*
MESSNER, *Erklärung.* Brixen, 1863.
MOULE (H. C. G.), "The Epp. to Colossians and to Philemon" in the *Cambridge Bible for Schools and Colleges.* Camb. 1893.
SCHNEDERMANN. See *Ephesians*.
STEIGER (W.), *Der Brief Pauli an die Epheser; Uebersetzung, Erklärung, einleitende u. epikritische Abhandlungen.* Erlangen, 1835.
THOMASIUS (G.), *Praktische Auslegung, u.s.w.* Erlang. 1869.
WATSON (Thos.), *Discourses.* 3rd ed. Lond. 1838.
WILSON (Dan., Bishop of Calcutta), *Lectures, etc.* Lond. 1845, *al.*
WIESINGER (J. C. Aug.), In *Olshausen's Comm.* Königsb. 1850; transl. Edinb. 1851.
WOHLENBERG. See *Ephesians*.
WEISS. See *Ephesians*.

Critical Discussions.

See *Ephesians*, and add the following :—

NEANDER, *Pflanzung u. Leitung d. christlichen Kirche*, bk. iii. ch. 9, Eng. trans. (*Biblical Cabinet*), vol. i. p. 374.

SANDAY (W.), art. "Colossians, Ep. to," in Smith's *Dictionary of the Bible*, 2nd ed. Lond. 1893.

SCHMIEDEL (P. W.), art. "Kolossae" in *Ersch. u. Gruber's Allgem. Encyclopädie.* 1885.

SMITH (W. Saumarez, Bp. of Sydney, N.S.W.), art. "Colossians" in *Encyclopaedia Britannica*, 9th ed. 1877.

WIGGERS (J.), "Das Verhältniss des Ap. Paulus zu der christlichen Gemeinde in Kolossae," *Theol. Studien u. Kritiken*, 1838, p. 165.

THE
EPISTLE TO THE EPHESIANS.

I. 1, 2. SALUTATION.

1, 2. *Paul, a divinely appointed apostle, gives Christian greeting to the Church at Ephesus. May the heavenly Father, and the Lord Jesus Messiah grant you free grace and the peace which none else can bestow.*

1. Παῦλος. It is observable that he does not associate with himself Timothy as in Col. and Philemon; perhaps because it was a circular letter without any personal allusions.

ἀπόστολος Χριστοῦ Ἰησοῦ. Χρ. Ἰη. in this order with B D P 17, Syr-Harcl. Boh. Ἰησοῦ Χρ. ℵ A G K L, Syr-Pesh. Arm. The genitive is not simply a genitive of possession (as with δοῦλος, Rom. i. 1), although from a purely grammatical point of view it may be so called. But the term ἀπόστολος gives it a further import. This word had not lost its proper signification, as we see in 2 Cor. viii. 23. Phil. ii. 25, "A commissioned messenger of—" clearly implies, not merely "belonging to," but "sent by," as "Ambassador of the King of France" obviously means one sent from him. The addition of κατ' ἐπιταγὴν Θεοῦ in 1 Tim. i. 1 is no objection to this. See on Rom. i. 1.

διὰ θελήματος Θεοῦ. These words are also found in 1 Cor. i. 1; 2 Cor. i. 1; Col. i. 1; 2 Tim. i. 1. Their occurrence in 2 Tim. sufficiently proves (to those who accept the Pauline authorship of that Ep.) that they are not added in order to enhance the writer's apostolic authority, or to justify his undertaking to instruct a Church to which he was a stranger (von Soden on Col.), nor yet because he has in his mind "the great subject of what he is about to treat, and himself as the authorised expositor of it" (Alford). It simply expresses what was always present to his mind, that his mission was due to the special and undeserved providence of God, not to any merit of his own. Compare 2 Cor. viii. 5. The same idea is expressed in 1 Tim. i. 1 by κατ' ἐπιταγὴν Θεοῦ.

τοῖς ἁγίοις (= Phil., Col.). In the earlier Epistles the address is τῇ ἐκκλησίᾳ (Cor., Gal., Thess.). The substitution is not to be attributed to any incompleteness of organisation, for ἐκκλησία is used in Philem. 2, and ἐκκλ. does not seem to include the idea of organisation. The use of ἅγιοι certainly gives a more personal colouring to the Epistle as if addressed to the members of the Church as individuals rather than as a body.

οἱ ἅγιοι, frequent in the N.T., is always a substantive (except perhaps Heb. iii. 1). It was a term transferred from the Israel of the Old Testament to the Christians as the true people of God, its primary sense, like that of the corresponding Hebrew word, being "consecrated to God." The notion of inward personal holiness becomes attached to it from the thought of the obligation laid on those who are so set apart to a "holy" God; and God Himself is so called as the object of supremest reverence.

τοῖς οὖσιν [ἐν Ἐφέσῳ], κ.τ.λ. The evidence for and against the bracketed words may be here summarily stated (for a fuller discussion see Introduction). They are omitted in ℵ B (but supplied in both by later hands). In cod. 67 they are expunged by the later corrector (who records many very ancient readings). To these we must add the MSS. mentioned by S. Basil (fourth cent.) and the text used by Origen. They are present in all other MSS., and Fathers and all versions.

Their omission, if they are genuine, would be hard to account for. That they should be omitted in consequence of critical doubts as to the destination of the Epistle founded on its contents is beyond the bounds of probability. On the other hand, if the Epistle was addressed to a circle of Churches of which Ephesus was chief, the insertion of the words would be natural.

If we have to interpret τοῖς οὖσιν καὶ πιστοῖς, κ.τ.λ. the rendering will be: "the saints who are also faithful." This would by no means imply that there might be ἅγιοι who were not πιστοί, but would rather give prominence to the thought that the apostle did not recognise any as ἅγιοι, in the technical sense, unless they were also πιστοί. The only difficulty is that τοῖς οὖσιν or τῇ οὔσῃ (with ἐκκλησίᾳ) is elsewhere followed by the name of the place (Rom., Cor., Phil.). Of course, if we suppose a blank space to have been left in the original letter the difficulty does not arise. But it is observable that in Col. i. 1 the same thought is expressed, τοῖς ἁγίοις καὶ πιστοῖς ἀδελφοῖς ἐν Χριστῷ, where τοῖς ἁγίοις is to be taken as a substantive (see note there).

Others connect οὖσιν with ἁγίοις, "who are truly saints" (Schneckenb.), or with both ἁγ. and πιστ. in the same sense, or understand τοῖς οὖσιν as = who are in every place where Tychicus comes with the Epistle (Bengel, comparing Acts xiii. 1). Origen's interpretation, "those who are," need only be alluded to here.

πιστοῖς may mean either "believing" or "faithful, steadfast." The former sense is adopted by Ellicott, Eadie, Meyer, *al.*, on the ground that here in the address τοῖς ἁγίοις alone would not adequately define the readers as Christians, and that if we adopt the other sense we must either suppose the apostle to distinguish the faithful from those who were not so, or to assume that all the professed ἅγιοι were faithful. It is alleged also that "faithful to Christ" would have required the single dative as in Heb. iii. 2. The phrase in 1 Cor. iv. 17, ἀγαπητὸν καὶ πιστὸν ἐν Κυρίῳ, being not parallel, since ἐν Κυρίῳ belongs to both adjectives, Grotius, Stier, Lightfoot, *al.*, adopt the other signification, which the word certainly has in Eph. vi. 21; Col. iv. 9; 1 Tim. i. 12; 2 Tim. ii. 2; 1 Pet. v. 12. If it meant here "believing," says Lightfoot, it would add nothing to what is contained in ἁγίοις. The use of the word with ἀδελφοῖς in Col. i. 2 is in favour of the latter view, which agrees with the classical use; but when used in such a connexion as here and in Col. i. 2, this presupposes "believing." Since all the ἅγιοι ought to be "faithful," it would be quite in St. Paul's manner to designate them as such, unless he had positive reason to the contrary. Whether we take the word as meaning "believing" or not, we are not to connect it directly with ἐν Χριστῷ as if = "believing in Christ Jesus" (πιστεύοντες εἰς), for the adjective is never so construed. Ἐν Χριστῷ Ἰησοῦ is best taken with the whole conception ἅγιοι καὶ πιστοί. Such they are, but only "in Christ." Compare vi. 21; 1 Cor. iv. 17; Col. i. 2.

2. Καὶ Κυρίου Ἰησοῦ Χριστοῦ. "And (from) the Lord Jesus Christ." The rendering of Erasmus, "Father of us and of the Lord," is sufficiently disproved by Tit. ii. 4, ἀπὸ Θεοῦ πατρὸς καὶ Χριστοῦ Ἰησοῦ τοῦ σωτῆρος ἡμῶν. See on Rom. i. 7.

3–8. *Praise to God for the blessings of salvation. The granting of these was no new thing in God's purposes, but had been determined before the creation of the world. The object to be attained was that we should be holy and blameless, and with a view to this He has admitted us to the adoption of sons through Christ, in whom we have received our redemption.*

3. Εὐλογητός, according to the analogy of verbals in -τος, means properly, not "on whom blessing is pronounced" (εὐλογημένος), but "worthy of blessing," ἐπαινεῖσθαι καὶ θαυμάζεσθαι ἄξιος Theod. Mops. Cf. μεμπτός, "blameworthy"; ὁρατός, "visible"; πιστός, "trustworthy." In the N.T. it is used exclusively of God, and so almost always in the Sept. In Mark xiv. 61, ὁ εὐλογητός stands alone for "the Blessed One," *i.e.* God, this being a frequent Jewish mode of avoiding the needless utterance of the sacred name. Here, then, we supply, not ἔστω, but ἔστι. See on Lk. i. 68.

ὁ Θεὸς καὶ πατὴρ τοῦ Κ. The natural rendering is "the God and Father of our Lord Jesus Christ," Θεός and πατήρ being in apposition (so Jerome, Theophylact, Alford, Eadie, Olshausen, W. Schmidt, Stier). But Syr., Theodoret, Theod. Mops., followed by Harless, Meyer, Ellicott, take the genitive to depend on πατήρ only. It is said, indeed, that the former rendering would require τε before καί; but cf. iv. 6, εἷς Θεὸς καὶ πατὴρ πάντων; 1 Pet. ii. 25, τὸν ποιμένα καὶ ἐπίσκοπον. The expression, "God of our Lord Jesus Christ," is used in ver. 17, and the fact that it does not occur oftener can be no objection. See also John xx. 17, "My God and your God." Θεὸς μὲν ὡς σαρκωθέντος, πατὴρ δὲ ὡς Θεοῦ λόγου, Theophylact. Chrysostom also prefers this view. We have the same combination, ὁ Θεὸς καὶ πατὴρ τοῦ Κ., Rom. xv. 6; 2 Cor. i. 3, xi. 31; Col. i. 3 (*v.l.*); 1 Pet. i. 3.

ὁ εὐλογήσας ἡμᾶς. "Who blessed us," viz. at the time of our becoming members of the Christian Church, or simply on sending His Son. Theodoret well remarks that men in blessing God can only offer Him words that cannot benefit Him, whereas God in blessing confirms His words by deed, and bestows manifold benefits upon us. Koppe strangely understands ἡμᾶς of Paul himself. Besides the unsuitableness of this in the initial thanksgiving, κἀγώ, in ver. 15, is decisive against it. ἐν πάσῃ εὐλογίᾳ πνευματικῇ. Blessings belonging to the spiritual sphere to which the πνεῦμα of man properly belongs. This is not quite the same as "referring to the mind or soul of man." Compare Rom. viii. 4, 9, 10, where πνεῦμα is contrasted with σάρξ, and 1 Cor. ii. 15, where it is opposed to ψυχή. That these blessings proceed from the Holy Spirit is true, but that is not the signification of the word, which characterises the nature of the blessings, not their source. Nor is the meaning "blessings of the Spirit" made out by the passages usually alleged in support of it, such as Rom. i. 11, "that I may impart some χάρισμα πνευματικόν"; 1 Cor. xii. 1, "About spiritual [gifts]"; xiv. 1, "desire spiritual [gifts]." Compare Rom. xv. 27, "The Gentiles have been made partakers of these spiritual things"; 1 Cor. ix. 11, "We have sown τὰ πν."; x. 3, 4; Eph. vi. 19, "spiritual songs," and 1 Cor. xv. 44, σῶμα πνευματικόν. Surely, if "from the Spirit" had been intended, it would have been more naturally expressed by τοῦ πνεύματος.

Chrysostom interprets the "spiritual blessings" as meant to be contrasted with the material and temporal blessings of the Old Covenant, in which he is followed by Grotius and others. But there is no hint of such antithesis in the context.

These blessings are not to be limited to the extraordinary gifts of the Spirit, as πάσῃ sufficiently shows. As Theodoret remarks, they include "the hope of the resurrection, the promises of immortality, the promise of the kingdom of heaven, the dignity of adoption," or more generally what St. Paul enumerates as the fruit of the Spirit in Gal. v. 22, love, joy, peace, and all Christian virtues.

ἐν τοῖς ἐπουρανίοις. The adjective is found several times in the N.T. in the sense "belonging to or seated in heaven." Sometimes opposed to τὰ ἐπίγεια, as in John iii. 12; 1 Cor. xv. 40, 48, 49; Phil. ii. 10; with κλῆσις, Heb. iii. 1; δωρεά, ib. vi. 4; πατρίς, ib. xi. 16; βασιλεία, 2 Tim. iv. 18. It will be seen that a local sense cannot be insisted on in all these places. The contrasted word ἐπίγειος also has a transferred sense in Phil. iii. 19, τὰ ἐπίγεια φρονοῦντες, and Jas. iii. 15, (σοφία) ἐπίγειος, ψυχική.

In the present passage τὰ ἐπουρ. appears to be interpreted by Theodoret as = heavenly things, ἐπουράνια γὰρ τὰ δῶρα ταῦτα, and so Bengel, "declaratur τὸ spirituali." But this would be to explain the clear and familiar term by one which is less clear. It might, however, be taken, not as an explanation, but as a further definition of the nature of the blessings. The article is not against this view, since it may properly be used to mark a class. It is, however, an objection that the phrase ἐν τοῖς ἐπ., not found elsewhere, occurs five times in this Epistle, and in three of these places has certainly a local signification, viz. i. 20, ii. 6, iii. 10. The fifth (vi. 12) cannot be quoted as certainly local, so that it is not correct to say, with some expositors, that everywhere else in this Epistle the signification is local. Those who adopt this interpretation, "in the heavenly regions," are not agreed as to the connexion. Beza and others refer the words to God (ὁ ἐν τοῖς οὐρανοῖς εὐλόγησας), but this is against the order of the words. Meyer takes them as a local definition added to εὐλ. πν., "with every spiritual blessing in heaven." The blessings of the Spirit are regarded as in heaven, and from thence brought down to us. Compare the description of the Spirit itself as ἡ δωρεὰ ἡ ἐπουράνιος. It seems more natural to connect the words with εὐλόγησας (Lightfoot), or rather with the whole clause εὐλ. ἐν. π. εὐλ. πν. Not, however, taking the words as expressing literal locality, but as designating the heavenly region in which our citizenship is (Phil. iii. 20), where the believer has already been seated with Christ (ii. 6), "the heaven which lies within and about the true Christian" (Lightfoot). "Those spiritual blessings conferred on us create heaven within us, and the scenes of Divine benefaction are 'heavenly places'; for wherever the light and love of God's presence are to be enjoyed, there is heaven." So substantially Harless, but connecting the words (as does Eadie) with εὐλογίᾳ.

ἐν Χριστῷ.[1] By virtue of our union with Him, and as members of His body. But it must not be left out of sight that

---

[1] On ἐν Χριστῷ in St. Paul, see Weiss, *Theol. Studien u. Kritiken*, 1896, p. 7 ff.

it is also in Christ that God confers the blessing (iv. 32). Not as if = διὰ Χριστοῦ (Chrys.), as if Christ were merely the instrument.

It answers the question, How? as the preceding clauses answered the questions, With what? and Where? the participle answering When? ἐν is omitted in a few cursive MSS., and in the edd. of Erasmus, Steph. 3, and Beza; but the omission is too slightly supported to deserve notice, except as accounting for the explanations of some commentators.

4. καθώς, frequent in later Greek (from Aristotle) for the more classical καθάπερ, "according as," expressing that the blessing was in harmony with what follows, so that it has a certain argumentative force, but does not mean (as the word sometimes does) "because." The blessing realised the election.

ἐξελέξατο. Generally understood as implying, (1) the choosing out from the mass of mankind, (2) for Himself. As to (1), although the idea of choice from amongst others who are not chosen is involved in the form of the word, this is not always prominent. For example, in Luke ix. 35, ὁ υἱός μου ὁ ἐκλελεγμένος (the true reading), we can hardly say, with Meyer, that it is as chosen out of all that is man that Christ is so called (cf. Luke xxiii. 35, ὁ τοῦ Θεοῦ ἐκλεκτός). Here what is chiefly in view is not the fact of "selection" (Alford), but the end for which the choice was made, εἶναι ἡμᾶς, κ.τ.λ. Oltramare argues from the aorist being used, that the election is an act repeated whenever the call is heard. God, before the creation of the world, formed the plan of saving man (all sinners) in Christ. The condition of faith is implicitly contained. The plan is historically realised under the forms of κλῆσις and ἐκλογή. Every man who by faith accepts the call is ἐκλεκτός. The second element, for Himself, as implied in the middle voice, must not be pressed too far; cf. Acts vi. 5, "They chose Stephen" (ἐξελέξαντο); xv. 22, 25, "to choose out men and send them." See Dale, *On Eph.*, Lect. ii. p. 31.

ἐν αὐτῷ, not ἐν αὑτῷ, as Morus, Holzh. (and G, which has ἑαυτῷ without ἐν), which would be quite superfluous, but ἐν Χριστῷ, as the context also shows. In Christ as our Head, not merely διὰ τῆς εἰς αὐτὸν πίστεως, as Chrysostom. Christ is the spiritual Head as Adam was the natural. Compare 1 Cor. xv. 22, "As in Adam all die, so also in Christ shall all be made alive"; and Gal. iii. 16, "thy seed ὅς ἐστι Χριστός." Believers were viewed in God's purpose as being in Christ adopted as sons through Him, it being God's purpose to sum up all things in Him (ver. 10). Comp. 1 Cor. xi. 3.

πρὸ καταβολῆς κόσμου. The same expression occurs John xvii. 24; 1 Pet. i. 20. ἀπὸ κατ. κ. is found several times (twice in Heb.), but neither expression occurs elsewhere in St. Paul. It is = ἀπὸ τῶν αἰώνων, iii. 9, "from all eternity."

εἶναι ἡμᾶς. The infinitive completes the notion of the verb, expressing the purpose of the ἐκλογή = ἐπὶ τούτῳ ἵνα ἅγιοι ὦμεν καὶ ἄμωμοι, Chrys. Cf. Col. i. 22, ἀποκατήλλαξεν παραστῆσαι ὑμᾶς, κ.τ.λ. The usage is quite classical.

ἅγιοι and ἄμωμοι give the positive and negative sides of the idea. ἄμωμος properly means "without blame." In the Sept. it is used of sacrificial victims, in the sense "without blemish"; the word μῶμος having been adopted by the translators as the rendering of the Hebrew for "blemish," "spot," on account of its resemblance in sound to the Hebrew *mûm*. In this sense μῶμος occurs in 2 Pet. ii. 13, σπίλοι καὶ μῶμοι. The adj. ἄμωμος is used in the signification "without blemish" in Heb. ix. 14; 1 Pet. i. 19. St. Paul uses the word here and v. 27, also Phil. ii. 15 (true text) and Col. i. 22. In the last-mentioned place ἀνεγκλήτους is added to ἁγίους καὶ ἀμώμους, and this favours the interpretation "blameless." In Phil. ii. 15, also, ἄμωμα seems parallel to ἄμεμπτοι, and is the opposite of μωμητά in the passage Deut. xxxii. 5, which is there alluded to. On the other hand, in Eph. v. 27 the reference to σπῖλον ἢ ῥυτίδα in the context favours the other sense. However, as there is no reference to a victim in any of these three places, there seems to be no sufficient reason for departing from the proper Greek sense. In Jude 24 either sense would be suitable, but in Rev. xiv. 5 "blameless" is better, for the connexion is "in their mouth." The word is so understood here by Chrysostom and Theophylact, ἅγιος ὁ τῆς πίστεως μετέχων· ἄμωμος δὲ ὁ κατὰ τὸν βίον ἀνεπίληπτος, Theoph.; ἄμωμος ὁ ἀνεπίληπτον βίον μετιών (ἔχων, *Catena*), Chrys.

Is this ἅγ. καὶ ἄμ. εἶναι to be understood of the actual spiritual and moral state (sanctification), or of righteousness imputed (justification)? Harless and Meyer strongly maintain the latter view, which is also adopted by Moule on the ground of the context, while Harless even thinks that this alone agrees with apostolic teaching. The fact appears to be the very opposite. The ultimate end of God's choice, as of Christ's work, is sanctification. Compare Phil. ii. 14, "Do all things without murmurings and disputings, that ye may be blameless and harmless children of God ἄμωμα (true text), . . . among whom ye are seen as lights in the world." In v. 27 words similar to the present are used of a future ideal not yet attained. So Col. i. 22 compared with 21, 23, 28, 29; 1 Thess. iv. 7, "God hath called us, not ἐπὶ ἀκαθαρσίᾳ, but ἐν ἁγιασμῷ." Compare the same Ep. v. 23; 2 Thess. ii. 13, "God chose you from the beginning εἰς σωτηρίαν ἐν ἁγιασμῷ πνεύματος." And very distinctly Tit. ii. 14, "Gave Himself for us, that He might redeem us from all iniquity, and purify unto Himself a people. . . . zealous of good works." Indeed, as Eadie observes, "the phrase 'holy and without blame' is never once applied to our complete justification before God. ... Men are not regarded by God as innocent or sinless, for the fact of their sin remains unaltered; but they are treated as righteous." It is no objection to this that this perfection is not attained here, nor need we modify the meaning by understanding "as far as can be." What is here specified as the purpose of the ἐκλέγεσθαι must be the ultimate purpose to be achieved, and that is perfect holiness. This is the view adopted by Chrysostom, Theophylact, Calvin, and, amongst recent expositors, Alford, Ellicott, Eadie, Macpherson, Oltramare, Stier. It is confirmed by the following words; nor is it really against the subsequent context; see on υἱοθεσία. κατενώπιον αὐτοῦ, *i.e.* not merely before men, says Chrysostom ; ἁγιωσύνην ζητεῖ ἣν ὁ τοῦ Θεοῦ ὀφθαλμὸς ὁρᾷ.

ἐν ἀγάπῃ has been variously joined with ἐξελέξατο, with ἁγ. καὶ ἀμ., and with προορίσας. It is, however, too far removed from ἐξελέξατο (although Macpherson regards this as no objection); but it is less easy to decide between the other possible connexions. In support of the connexion with the preceding words it is alleged that the words ἐν ἀγάπῃ stand after the clause to which they belong in iv. 2, 15, 16, v. 2 ; Col. ii. 2 ; 1 Thess. v. 13 (Lightfoot). But in all these cases the words preceding are verbs, or express a verbal notion (iv. 16), and are such that they could not be placed after ἐν ἀγάπῃ. Alford strenuously maintains that, "in the whole construction of this long sentence, the verbs and participles ... precede their qualifying clauses," *e.g. vv.* 3, 4, 6, 8, 9, 10. But this is no reason why the qualifying clause should not be placed before its verb here, if the writer's purpose so required. Alford adds that this qualification of the preceding words is in the highest degree appropriate, love being the element in which all Christian graces subsist, and in which all perfection before God must be found. Nevertheless, the connexion with the adjectives "holy and blameless (or without blemish) in love," appears less natural than with the verb, "having in love foreordained us." It is fitting, too, at the beginning of the Epistle that God's love should be the first to be mentioned, and very fitting that emphasis should be given to the love which moved Him so to preordain, by placing ἐν ἀγάπῃ first. So Chrysostom and the other Greek comm., Jerome, and, among moderns, Bengel, Harless, Meyer, Stier, Eadie, Ellicott, Soden, *al.*

5. προορίσας gives the reason of ἐξελέξατο, it is logically prior; but in the counsels of God there is no priority or order in time. Compare Rom. viii. 30, οὓς προώρισεν τούτους καὶ ἐκάλεσεν. The verb appears not to be found in any writer before St. Paul. The prefix προ has reference only to the future realisation, and does not of itself indicate that the act was πρὸ καταβολῆς κόσμου.

εἰς υἱοθεσίαν διὰ Ἰ. Χ. εἰς αὐτόν. These words belong closely together, "unto adoption through Jesus Christ unto Him as His sons." Christ is υἱὸς γνήσιος, Son by His nature; we are sons only by adoption through Him. Cf. Gal. iv. 5, "God sent forth His Son ... that we might receive the adoption of sons"; also Gal. iii. 26, "Ye are sons of God, through faith, in Christ Jesus"; and Heb. ii. 10 f. But this υἱοθεσία is not yet complete; we are still looking forward to its completion, υἱοθεσίαν ἀπεκδεχόμενοι τὴν ἀπολύτρωσιν τοῦ σώματος ἡμῶν, Rom. viii. 23. The figure of adoption is borrowed from Roman law; the practice was unknown to the Jews. εἰς αὐτόν most simply and naturally joined with υἱοθεσία, "adoption unto Him," viz. as His sons. It is putting too much into the preposition to find in it the idea of inward union, or to compare with 2 Pet. i. 4, "partakers of the Divine nature." αὐτόν is obviously the Father, not Christ, through whom the adoption is. V. Soden, however, argues strongly that thus εἰς αὐτόν would be superfluous, as υἱοθ. is a fixed terminus for the relation to God. The prominence of ἐν αὐτῷ in vv. 3-14 makes the reference to Christ more natural. The ἀνακεφαλαιώσασθαι ἐν Χρ., ver. 10, is the realisation of the προορίζειν εἰς αὐτόν. Col. i. 16 is a close parallel.

κατὰ τὴν εὐδοκίαν. According to Jerome the word εὐδοκία was coined by the Sept. "rebus novis nova verba fingentes." It means either "good pleasure, purpose," εὖ δοκεῖν, "as it seems good to"; or "good will," according as the satisfaction is conceived as in the action, or as felt towards a person. The latter is the common signification in the Sept., but it also occurs there in the sense of "purpose," Eccles. xi. 17, ἡ εὐδοκία αὐτοῦ εὐοδωθήσεται. Where the context does not point to a person towards whom the satisfaction is felt, the former meaning must be adopted; cf. Matt. xi. 26, οὕτως ἐγένετο εὐδοκία ἔμπροσθέν σου. Here, then, it corresponds to ἡ βουλὴ τοῦ θελήματος αὐτοῦ, ver. 11.

In the Sept. εὐδοκία is used frequently in the Psalms to render the Hebrew *râtsón*, and, with the exception of a passage in Canticles (where it corresponds to *Tirzah*), it is not found in the other canonical books at all. Their usual rendering of the Hebrew word is δεκτός.[1] It cannot, then, be fairly said that "the translators" exhibit "purpose" or "discrimination" in their employment of the word. One translator often uses it, and sometimes uses θέλημα when εὐδοκία would have been more correct; the others never. In Ecclus., however, εὐδοκία occurs fourteen times.

Fritzsche (on Rom. x. 1) has discussed the meaning of the word at length. The verb εὐδοκεῖν (which is an exception to Scaliger's rule about the composition of verbs) is found only in later Greek writers, Polybius, Diodorus, Dionys. Hal., in the signification "to choose or think fit (to do a thing)," sometimes with the idea of being glad to do it, as 1 Thess. ii. 8. Greek writers also said εὐδοκῶ τινι or ἐπί τινι, "to be content with something, or pleased with some person." The construction εὐδοκεῖν ἔν τινι originated with the Alexandrian writers (1 Macc. x. 47; cf. Matt. iii. 17; 1 Cor. x. 5, etc.).

---

[1] The word is rendered θέλημα several times in the Psalms, including xxx. 5, 7. In the latter place Symmachus substitutes εὐδοκία.

They also said εὐδοκεῖν τι, a usage not followed in the N.T., and εἴς τινα (2 Pet. i. 17); but in the meaning of the verb the Biblical writers do not differ from the later Greek. The significations of the substantive follow those of the text. It means first *voluntas*, as in Matt. xi. 26, then "contentment," Ecclus. xxix. 23, "delight," and as in Sept. most frequently "good will." See on Lk. ii. 14 and on Rom. x. 1.

6. εἰς ἔπαινον τῆς δόξης τῆς χάριτος αὐτοῦ. With a view to the praise of the glory (glorious manifestation) of His grace. The interpretations which make δόξης a mere adjectival attribute, either of ἔπαινος (Grotius) or of χάρις (Beza), are weak and inadmissible. Chrysostom gives the truer view, ἵνα ἡ τῆς χάριτος αὐτοῦ δόξα δειχθῇ.

"His grace." We are so accustomed to use the word "grace" in a technical religious sense, that we are prone to forget the simple meaning which it so often has, "undeserved bounty," "free gift," δωρεὰν τῇ αὐτοῦ χάριτι, Rom. iii. 24; κατ' ἐκλογὴν χάριτος, Rom. xi. 5; χάριτί ἐστε σεσωσμένοι, Eph. ii. 5. "Herein lies the magnificence, the glory, of God's work of redemption, that it has not the character of a contract, but of a largess" (Lightfoot). This glorious manifestation (cf. Col. i. 27) fills the mind of the apostle. He repeats in ver. 7 "wealth of His grace," and in ver. 12 "praise of His glory," and again in ii. 7, more emphatically still, "the exceeding wealth of His grace." Hence the verb χαρίζομαι has its signification "to grant of free favour."

ἧς ἐχαρίτωσεν ἡμᾶς. ἧς is the reading of ℵ A B Aeth. Syr., and is adopted by Lachm. Tisch.[8] Treg. Westcott and Hort. ἐν ᾗ is the reading of D G K L and most cursives with the Vulg. It was probably a resolution of the somewhat difficult attraction. The substitution of ἧς for ἐν ᾗ, especially when ἐν is so frequent in the context, is very unlikely.

The attraction is accounted for by the construction χάριν χαριτοῦν, like ἀγάπην ἀγαπᾶν, ii. 4. Compare χάριτας χαρίζεσθαι, Dem. 306. 28.

Χαριτόω, by the analogy of verbs in όω, means "gratia afficere." Cf. χρυσόω, πυργόω, θανατόω, μορφόω. Admitting this, two meanings are possible, according as the χάρις bestowed is taken subjectively or objectively, that is to say, as expressing the state of the individual or the grace of God. Chrysostom takes the former view, οὐ μόνον ἁμαρτημάτων ἀπήλλαξεν, ἀλλὰ καὶ ἐπεραστοὺς ἐποίησεν, "rendered us loveable," followed by Theodoret, Corn. à Lapide, "gratiosos nos reddidit," and most Roman Catholic interpreters, some of whom even use this as an argument for "justitia inhærens." Chrysostom says, it is as if one were to take a leper and change him into a lovely youth. Thus God has adorned our soul and made it an object of beauty and love. The partic. κεχαριτωμένος has this sense in Ecclus. xviii. 17. Clem. Alex., loosely quoting Ecclus. ix. 8, substitutes it for εὐμόρφου of the original (*Paed.* iii. 11).

But both the prevailing meaning of χάρις in St. Paul, and more particularly the context, seem decisive for the other sense, for ver. 7 states in what respect God ἐν τῷ ἠγαπ., ἐχαρίτωσεν being joined to this by ἐν ᾧ. And the leading idea of the passage is the undeserved goodness of God. With the reading ἧς there can hardly be any question that this latter meaning is alone possible. It resumes the εὐλόγησας ἡμᾶς ἐν τῷ Χρ. of ver. 3.

ἐν τῷ ἠγαπημένῳ. The MSS. D* G with the Vulgate add υἱῷ αὐτοῦ, a manifest gloss. The expression is not found elsewhere in the N.T. of Christ, but in the Apostolic Fathers it is used of our Lord, e.g. Ep. Barn. 3, ὃν ἡτοίμασεν ἐν τῷ ἠγαπημένῳ αὐτοῦ.

7. ἐν ᾧ (= Col. i. 14), not = διά or *per quem*; it has a certain argumentative force, and can hardly be given a different meaning from the ἐν before τῷ ἠγ. "In him, in whom." Rom. iii. 24, διὰ τῆς ἀπολυτ. τῆς ἐν Χριστῷ Ἰησοῦ, though parallel in substance is not parallel in construction, since here ἐν is closely connected with ἔχομεν. It is not apart from Him, but in Him alone, that we have our redemption.

ἔχομεν. D, Boh. read ἔσχομεν, which B, Boh. have in Col. i. 14.

τὴν ἀπολύτρωσιν. The article appears to indicate that which you know of, τὴν προσαγωγήν, ii. 18 (but see Heb. xi. 35).

On ἀπολύτρωσις Meyer remarks, "the redemption, namely, from God's wrath and penalties." . . . "The purchase price was His (Christ's) blood." Other commentators also say that the word "does not mean simply deliverance, but deliverance effected by the special means of purchase. Even where the term is used in the New Testament, without any accompanying statement of the price paid, the idea of a ransom price is still present" (Macpherson). The usage of the word and of its cognates by no means bears out this statement.

First, as to the simple verb λυτροῦν. In the active it means primarily "to release on receipt of a ransom." The idea "redeem by payment of a price," is expressed by the middle. Quite similarly, when Homer speaks of the ransom of Hector's body, it is Achilles who is always said λύειν, while Priam is said λύεσθαι. In the Sept. the middle λυτροῦσθαι is of very frequent occurrence, but not always with the idea of a price paid. On the contrary, it often means simply "to deliver." Thus it is used of the deliverance from Egypt, for which no price was paid. Isaiah (xliii. 3) says, "I give Egypt for thee." Compare 2 Sam. iv. 9, "As the LORD liveth, who hath redeemed my soul out of all adversity"; Ps. cvii. (cvi.) 2, "Whom He hath redeemed from the hand of the enemy."

So the English word "redeem" sometimes means "deliver," as in *Romeo and Juliet*, "Before the time that Romeo come to redeem me."

In the N.T. λυτροῦσθαι occurs thrice: Luke xxiv. 21 ("to deliver Israel"); Tit. ii. 14, " . . . from all iniquity"; 1 Pet. i. 18, " . . . from our vain conversation."

The substantive λύτρωσις occurs in Plut. *Arat*. xi. in the sense of "redemption" (of captives). In the Sept. it is used Lev. xxv. 48 of the 'right of redemption,' and Num. xviii. 16. In the Psalms it occurs thrice in the sense of "deliverance," viz. cxi. (cx.) 9, and cxxx. (cxxix.) 7. In the N.T. it occurs three times: Luke i. 68, ἐποίησεν λύτρωσιν τῷ λαῷ αὐτοῦ; ii. 38, τοῖς προσδεχομένοις λύτρωσιν Ἰσραήλ; Heb. ix. 12, αἰωνίαν λύτρωσιν εὑράμενος.

λυτρωτής is used Acts vii. 35 of Moses simply in the sense of "deliverer."

The verb ἀπολυτροῦν signifies properly, not "to redeem" (λυτροῦσθαι), but to release on receiving a ransom. *Epist. [Phil.] ap. Demosth.* p. 159, Ἀμφίλοχον . . . συλλαβὼν καὶ τὰς ἐσχάτας ἀνάγκας ἐπιθεὶς ἀπελύτρωσε ταλάντων ἐννέα. Plutarch, *Pomp.* xxiv. 4, p. 631 D, ἥλω δὲ καὶ θυγάτηρ Ἀντωνίου . . . καὶ πολλῶν χρημάτων ἀπελυτρώθη. Plato, *Legg.* xi. 919 A, ὅποταν ὡς ἐχθροὺς αἰχμαλώτους κεχειρωμένους ἀπολυτρώσῃ. Polyb. xxii. 21. 8, καὶ χρυσίου συχνοῦ διομολογηθέντος ὑπὲρ τῆς γυναικός, ἦγεν αὐτὴν ἀπολυτρώσων (*vid.* also ii. 6. 6). Lucian, of Achilles, χρημάτων ὀλίγων τὸν Ἕκτορος νεκρὸν ἀπολύτρωσας. The verb occurs twice in the Sept. viz. Ex. xxi. 8, of a master parting with a female slave (E.V. "he shall let her be redeemed"), and Zeph. iii. 1 (where the Hebrew word means "licentious," but was mistaken for one similarly written, which means "ransomed").

The substantive ἀπολύτρωσις is rare. Rost and Pahn give only one reference in Greek writers, viz. Plutarch, *Pomp.* xxiv. 2, p. 631 B (speaking of the pirates), σωμάτων ἡγεμονικῶν ἁρπαγαὶ καὶ πόλεων αἰχμαλώτων ἀπολυτρώσεις ("holding to ransom") ὄνειδος ἦσαν τῆς Ῥωμαίων ἡγεμονίας. Thayer adds other references, Joseph. *Antt.* xii. 2. 3, πλειόνων δὲ ἢ τετρακοσίων ταλάντων τῆς ἀπολυτρώσεως γενήσεσθαι φαμένων, ταῦτα τε συνεχώρει (of Aristæus paying the soldiers for their prisoners). Philo, *Quod omnis probus liber*, § 17, p. 882, ἀπογνοὺς ἀπολύτρωσιν ἀσμενος ἑαυτὸν διεχρήσατο. Diod. *Fragm.* lib. 37. 5. 3 (Didot's ed. ii. p. 564, of a slave who had agreed with his masters for the purchase of his freedom); Scaevola, φθάσας τὴν ἀπολύτρωσιν . . . ἀνεσταύρωσεν. In the Sept. it occurs only in Dan. iv. 30, ὁ χρόνος μου τῆς ἀπολυτρώσεως ἦλθε, *i.e.* of Nebuchadnezzar's recovery.

As far as usage goes, then, it would seem that if we are to attach to ἀπολύτρωσις the idea of ransom, the word will mean "holding to ransom" or "release on receipt of ransom," not "payment of ransom." In the New Testament the word occurs ten times, and in some of these instances it is only by a forced explanation that the idea of payment of a price can be brought in. In Heb. xi. 35, "were beaten, not accepting τὴν ἀπολύτρωσιν," the meaning connects itself easily with the classical use. It is "not accepting release." If the idea of price is brought in, it can only be apostasy; but those who offer the ἀπολ. are the captors. Again in Heb. ix. 15, ἀπολύτρωσις τῶν παραβάσεων is nearly equivalent to καθαρισμὸς τῶν ἁμαρτιῶν in i. 3. The transgressions were put away; there was deliverance from them. In Luke xxi. 28, "lift up your heads, for your ἀπολ. draweth nigh," there is no suggestion of a price. The opinion that the price is the destruction of Jerusalem is very forced.

In Rom. viii. 23, υἱοθεσίαν ἀπεκδεχόμενοι τὴν ἀπολύτρωσιν τοῦ σώματος, whatever interpretation is given of the latter words, they do not suggest the idea of a price paid. Nor does ἡμέρα ἀπολυτρώσεως, Eph. iv. 30, lend itself readily to this view. There are no doubt other passages in which it is easy to introduce the idea of payment of a price, but as the only ground for insisting on introducing this in every case is an erroneous view of the primary meaning of the word, further proof is required in each instance.[1] Certainly, however, the word implies deliverance from a state of slavery. The slavery from which we are delivered is a slavery to sin, Rom. vii. 23. "Captive to the law of sin"; it is not death as a punishment, but spiritual death as a state. Christ gave Himself for us, to redeem us from all iniquity, Tit. ii. 14. We were redeemed by the blood of Christ "from our vain conversation,"

---

[1] On ἀπολύτρωσις compare Westcott, *Heb.* pp. 295, 296; Ritschl, *Rechtf. u. Versöhn.* ii. 222 ff.; and Oltramare, *in loc.*

1 Pet. i. 18. Release from punishment is so far from being the chief idea, that it sinks into insignificance in comparison with that of deliverance from sin, without which it could not be. Here there is an insuperable difficulty in applying the idea of ransom by payment of a price. To whom is the ransom paid? We were not in slavery to God, nor is release from punishment to be obtained by any sort of payment of ransom. Hence the notion of early writers, that the ransom was paid to Satan. So Origen: ἀπολύτρωσις is ransom of those who are captives and in the power of the enemies; we were subject to the enemies, the ruler of this world and the evil powers under him; the Saviour therefore gave the ransom for us. This was at least logical.

Grotesque as this conception may seem to us, it kept in view the truth that it is release from the power of evil that is the main thing; and this was rather put out of sight by the later view, which gave most prominence to the release from punishment. But this, apart from deliverance from sin, is what is truly impossible; whereas given deliverance from sin, though suffering may remain, one ground for it has ceased, and it will be felt more as chastisement than as punishment.

For the notion of purchase, cf. 1 Cor. vi. 20, vii. 23, Christ, whose slaves we are there called because He bought us with a price, surely did not purchase us from God. So in the O.T. God is said to have purchased His people (Ex. xv. 16, etc.). See Dale, Lect. v.

διὰ τοῦ αἵματος αὐτοῦ. This suggests a different figure, that of sacrifice. On the idea of Christ's blood in the N.T., see Westcott, *Epistles of St. John*, p. 34 sq. He argues that "in accordance with the typical teaching of the Levitical ordinances, the Blood of Christ represents Christ's Life (1) as rendered in free self-sacrifice to God for man, and (2) as brought into perfect fellowship with God, having been set free by death. The Blood of Christ is, as shed, the Life of Christ given for man; and, as offered, the Life of Christ now given to man, the Life which is the spring of their life." The thought of Christ's Blood (as shed) includes all that is involved in His Death, and more, for it "always includes the thought of the life preserved and active beyond death." See especially John vi. 53–56.

It is observable that in the parallel passage Col. i. 14, the words διὰ τοῦ αἵματος αὐτοῦ are not added (in the genuine text).

τὴν ἄφεσιν τῶν ἁμαρτημάτων (ἁμαρτιῶν, Col.). Why was this further definition of the ἀπολύτρωσις so carefully added both here and in Col.? Lightfoot (on Col. i. 14) suggests that this points to some false conception of the ἀπολ. put forward by heretical teachers, as we know was the case with the later Gnostics, who applied the term to their own formularies of initiation. Thus Irenaeus (i. 13. 6) relates of the Marcosians, διὰ τὴν ἀπολύτρωσιν ἀκρατήτους καὶ ἀοράτους γίνεσθαι τῷ κριτῇ, and (i. 21. 4) εἶναι δὲ τελείαν ἀπολύτρωσιν αὐτὴν τὴν ἐπίγνωσιν τοῦ ἀρρήτου μεγέθους. Not that any direct historical connexion between the Colossian heretics and the later Gnostics is likely, but the passages (and others cited by Lightfoot) "show how a false idea of ἀπολύτρωσις would naturally be associated with an esoteric doctrine of angelic powers."

κατὰ τὸ πλοῦτος, κ.τ.λ. A term of which St. Paul is particularly fond. Paley calls it one of his "cant" words; "wealth of grace," "wealth of glory," "wealth of wisdom." Not to be resolved into "His rich grace"; but "the great fulness of His bounty." The wealth of His grace, *i.e.* bounty, is shown by the great price paid for our ransom; cf. ii. 7, and Rom. ii. 4, τοῦ πλούτου τῆς χρηστότητος αὐτοῦ.

8. ἧς ἐπερίσσευσεν. The verb is transitive, for the attraction of the dative, very rare in classical writers, is not found in the N.T. (not Rom. iv. 17). For the transitive use of περισσεύω, cf. 2 Cor. ix. 8, δυνατεῖ ὁ Θεὸς πᾶσαν χάριν περισσεῦσαι (2 Cor. iv. 15 is uncertain); 1 Thess. iii. 12. The meaning then is, "which He made to abound" (overflow); ἀφθόνως ἐξέχεε, Theoph. The AV. with Calvin, *al.*, takes the verb intransitively, and therefore ἧς as attraction for ᾗ, "in which He hath abounded." A third construction is possible, viz. that ἧς depends directly on περισσεύειν, since π. τινός may mean "to abound in." Cf. Luke xv. 17 (περισσεύουσιν ἄρτων, some texts; but WH περισσεύονται); ἵνα ... παντὸς χαρίσματος περισσεύῃς, Ignat. *Pol.* 2; so Beza, "qua redundavit"; or, as has been suggested (Ellicott, p. 164), περισσεύειν might mean "to make an abundance of." The first-mentioned rendering best agrees with the context.

ἐν πάσῃ σοφίᾳ καὶ φρονήσει. The distinction between these two words is clearly and pretty unanimously stated by several Greek writers. Aristotle (*Eth. Nic.* vi. 7) says that σοφία is τῶν τιμιωτάτων, while φρόνησις is περὶ τὰ ἀνθρώπινα καὶ περὶ ὧν ἔστι βουλεύσασθαι; and in *Magna Moralia*, i. 35, φρον. is περὶ τὰ συμφέροντα. Philo (*De Prom. et Poen.* 14) says σοφία is πρὸς θεραπείαν Θεοῦ, φρόνησις, πρὸς ἀνθρωπίνου βίου διοίκησιν. So Plutarch (*Mor.* p. 443 F) says that φρόν. is deliberative and practical in matters which concern us; and Cicero (*Off.* i. 43) states that it is "rerum expetendarum fugiendarumque scientia," while σοφία is "rerum divinarum atque humanarum scientia," which last is the common definition of σοφία, *i.e.* in Sextus Empir. and [Plato] *Def.* 411. φρόνησις in the same place is defined (*inter alia*) διάθεσις καθ' ἣν κρίνομεν τί πρακτέον καὶ τί οὐ πρακτέον. It is clear from this that φρόνησις cannot be predicated of God; nor is this refuted by the fact that in Prov. iii. 19 and Jer. x. 12 it is so used. It is very fallacious to call each individual translator of an O.T. book "the Seventy," and to regard such an occasional use as any evidence as to what was possible to an original author like St. Paul. With more reason might it be alleged that "discretion" might be properly predicated of God, because it is so used in the English Version in Jer. x. 12. In both instances a word was wanted to balance σοφία in the parallel clause (in the parallel passage in Jer. li. the word used is σύνεσις). 1 Kings iii. 28 is irrelevant. Solomon is there said to have possessed φρόνησις Θεοῦ. This is a literal rendering of the Hebrew idiom, expressive of the highest degree of prudence.

Nor is πᾶσα σοφία applicable to God, for πᾶσα is not "Summa" (Wahl, *al.*); it expresses, as Harless remarks, never intension, but extension; πᾶσα δύναμις = "every power there is," Col. i. 11. πᾶσα ὑπομονή, "all possible patience" (*ib.*). This is not invalidated by πᾶσα ἐξουσία, Matt. xxviii. 18; πᾶσα ἀσφάλεια, Acts v. 23; or πᾶσα ἀποδοχή, 1 Tim. i. 15; or the classical π. ἀνάγκη π. κίνδυνος, etc. In all these πᾶς is extensive not intensive. To say of God that He has done something πάσῃ σοφίᾳ, would imply that, conceivably, the wisdom might have been only partial. ἡ πολυποίκιλος σοφία, iii. 10, is wholly different, being the very varied manifestation or exercise of His wisdom.

Hence, whether we connect the words with ἐπερ. or with γνωρίσας they are to be understood of believers. This is confirmed by the parallel, Col. i. 9, ἵνα πληρωθῆτε τὴν ἐπίγνωσιν τοῦ θελήματος αὐτοῦ ἐν πάσῃ σοφίᾳ καὶ συνέσει. Moreover, the main idea in the context is the knowledge of the Christian. The connexion with ἐπερ. seems decidedly to be preferred to that with γνωρίσας, against which is the consideration that the making known of the "mystery" is not the proof of the abundance of grace, but of its abounding in the particular matter of σοφία καὶ φρ. Meyer notes the climax from the simple ἧς ἐχαρίτωσεν ἡμᾶς to ἧς ἐπερίσσευσεν εἰς ἡμᾶς.

9-11. *God hath made known to us His purpose to sum up all things in Christ, whether they be things in heaven or on earth.*

9. γνωρίσας, *i.e.* "In that He made known," cf. Col. ii. 3.

τὸ μυστήριον. We must be on our guard against importing into this word (as is done by some expositors) the meaning of the English "mystery," as in Shakespeare's "Mysteries which heaven will not have earth to know." It signifies simply "a truth once hidden but now revealed." The truth may be "mysterious," in the modern sense, but that is not implied in the word (so Lightfoot also, who, however, refers to 1 Cor. xv. 51 and Eph. v. 32 as instances of this accidental idea; but see *post*). Lightfoot thinks the term was borrowed from the ancient mysteries, with an intentional paradox, as the Christian "mysteries" are freely communicated to all, and so the idea of *secrecy* or *reserve* disappears. (Note on Col. i. 26.) In fact, it is almost always placed in connexion with words expressing revelation or publication. But there is no need to suppose that St. Paul had the heathen mysteries in his mind when he used the word. It appears to have been much more frequent colloquially than we should have supposed from the extant works of classical writers. In these the singular is found once only, and that in a fragment of Menander, "Do not tell thy secret (μυστήριον) to thy friend." In Plato, *Theaet.* 156 A, the plural is used of secrets, "will tell you the secrets of these," but with allusion to the μυστήρια in the context. There are, however, other sources from which we may infer that it was not an uncommon word in the sense "secret," viz. the Apocrypha, the Hexaplar translators, and Cicero. In the Apocrypha we find it in Tob. xii. 7, 11, "It is good to conceal the μ. of a king"; Judith ii. 2, "He (Nebuchadnezzar) communicated to them the secret (μυστήριον) of his counsel"; 2 Macc. xiii. 21, "disclosed the 'secrets' to the enemies"; frequently in Ecclus., and, as in Menander, in connexion with warnings against revealing a friend's secret, *e.g.* xxii. 22, xxvii. 16, 17, 21. In Wisd. xiv. 15, 23 the word is used of heathen "mysteries," E.V. "ceremonies," but in vi. 22, "I will tell you, and will not hide 'mysteries' from you."

In two places in Proverbs the Hexaplar translators have μυστήριον, "A talebearer revealeth secrets," μυστήρια; xi. 13 Sym., xx. 19 Theod. So in Ps. xxv. 14, μ. κυρίου; Theod. "secret of the Lord." It occurs several times in Daniel, where the AV. has "secret," as ii. 18, 19, 27, 29. Cicero is fond of using Greek words in his letters, and no doubt the words he uses were familiar. Writing to Atticus he says, "Our letters contain so much 'mysteriorum' that we usually do not trust them even to secretaries" (iv. 18). And in another place he writes a short passage entirely in Greek, because it is about some private domestic matter, saying, "illud ad te μυστικώτερον scribam," *i.e.* more privately (vi. 4). Ausonius again has "Accipe congestas, mysteria frivola, nugas" (Ep. iv. 67).[1] From all this we may conclude that μυστήριον was an ordinary, or rather the ordinary, word for "a secret." In the N.T. the same meaning holds, only that there it is always (except in the Apocalypse) "a secret revealed," and hence is applied to doctrines of revelation. Indeed, Rom. xvi. 25 might almost be taken as a definition μ. χρόνοις αἰωνίοις σεσιγημένου φανερωθέντος δὲ νῦν (= Col. i. 26). Such doctrines are the "mysteries of the kingdom of heaven," Matt. xiii. 11 (cf. ver. 35), which were communicated by the Lord in parables, Luke viii. 10. There is not one passage in which this meaning is not suitable. Lightfoot mentions two in which, although the signification of the word is the same, there comes in from the special circumstances of the case the accidental idea of mysteriousness. They are 1 Cor. xv. 51 and Eph. v. 32. In neither place is this contained in the word. There is, indeed, one place in which other writers suppose this idea to be contained in the word itself, viz. 1 Cor. xiv. 2. But the true interpretation of that passage is, "He is indeed telling secrets, but to no purpose,

[1] In the Liturgies, when the priest is directed to pray "secretly," μυστικῶς is the word used.

for no one understands." It is not because no one understands that they are μυστήρια. This is, on the contrary, a polite concession, as in ver. 17. In the Apocalypse the meaning "secret" still holds good, "the secret of the seven stars," "the secret of the woman.'

The one doctrine which St. Paul frequently calls the mystery of the gospel was the admission of the Gentiles. It was for this that he was in bonds.

τοῦ θελήματος αὐτοῦ. Gen. of the object, the secret concerning His will.

κατὰ τὴν εὐδοκίαν αὐτοῦ. Not to be joined to μυστ., which would be tautologous with τοῦ θελ. αὐτ., but with γνωρίσας. It qualifies γνωρίσας here as προορίσας in ver. 5. εὐδ. = purpose (ver. 5). Compare Book of Enoch xlix. 4, "according to His good pleasure."

10. προέθετο. The prefix in προτίθεσθαι is local, not temporal. "Set before oneself = to purpose" (Rom. i. 13), or "before others" (Rom. iii. 25). These three are the only places where the verb occurs in the N.T., but the substantive πρόθεσις is frequent = purpose, either Divine or human (Acts xi. 23, xxvii. 13; 2 Tim. iii. 10. Cf. προχειρίζεσθαι, Acts iii. 20; προαιρεῖσθαι, 2 Cor. ix. 7).

εἰς οἰκονομίαν, κ.τ.λ. "With a view to a dispensation belonging to the fulness of the seasons." οἰκονομία means either actual administration of a household, etc., or the office of an administrator. In the latter sense the English "stewardship" correctly represents it; in the former, which is the meaning here, though "dispensation" in its original sense well corresponds, it does not suggest to the reader the idea of "house management," which is contained in οἰκονομία. This is founded on the conception of the Church as God's household, 1 Tim. iii. 5; Heb. x. 21; 1 Pet. iv. 17; hence in this Epistle believers are called οἰκεῖοι τοῦ Θεοῦ, ii. 19. In the Gospels in five parables God is figured as οἰκοδεσπότης, e.g. Matt. xx. 1, 11. In classical writers the word οἰκονομία extended its meaning from the management of a household to that of a state. Thus Aristotle says that as household management is a sort of kingdom of a house, so a kingdom is οἰκονομία. It was also applied to systematic arrangement or management generally, as of the topics of a speech, of the parts of a building, etc. The kingdom of God had its own οἰκονομία, it involved a place or system of administration, the officers or οἰκονόμοι of which were the apostles and the ministers, 1 Cor. iv. 1; Tit. i. 7. For the later use of the term as specifically = the Incarnation, see Lightfoot's note, Eph. i. 10; Col. i. 25.

<small>V. Soden maintains that οἰκ. here has the same meaning as elsewhere, viz. stewardship. The thought is that the object of the Divine purpose should come to its achievement through an οἰκονόμος. Until the οἰκονομία</small>

began the plan rested in God. Who the οἰκονόμος is, is not said in the text; probably, in the first place, God Himself (iii. 1). Moule more suitably regards the Son as the οἰκονόμος, the "purpose" being that He should be the manifested Dispenser of the period of grace.

τ. πληρώματος τῶν καιρῶν. In substance equivalent to πλ. τοῦ χρόνου, as in Gal. iv. 4, but includes the conception of a series of καιροί, or seasons, the last of which is marked by the mission and work of the Messiah, so that now the series is closed. Cf. Mark i. 15, πεπλήρωται ὁ καιρός. Καιρός includes the notion of fitness or propriety. The καιροί are conceived as spaces filled with events. Since a κ. is not properly the object of an οἰκονομία the genitive πληρώματος is not gen. of object but of nearer definition; cf. κρίσις μεγάλης ἡμέρας, Jude 6.

ἀνακεφαλαιώσασθαι, "to gather up into one," seems to be an explanatory infinitive supplying at once the content of the μυστήριον, the object of the εὐδοκία, and the object reserved for the οἰκ. But as a matter of construction most easily connected with the nearest, viz. οἰκονομία. Some commentators prefer connecting it with προέθετο, others with μυστήριον. In classical writers κεφάλαιον means "chief point," cf. Heb. viii. 1; and both κεφαλαιόω and ἀνακεφαλαιόω mean to sum up, summarise. So Rom. xiii. 9, τὸ γὰρ οὐ μοιχεύσεις... ἐν τούτῳ τῷ λόγῳ ἀνακεφαλαιοῦται. So in a fragment of Aristotle, ἀνακεφαλαιώσασθαι πρὸς ἀνάμνησιν. And so Quintilian defines the substantive ἀνακεφαλαίωσις, "Rerum repetitio et congregatio quae Graece dicitur ἀν.... et totam simul causam ponit ante oculos" (*Inst.* vi. 1. 1). Compare the late Latin *recapitulo*, formed in imitation of the Greek. Thus there is no ground for assigning to the prefix the signification "again," as if there was in the word a reference to a bringing back to a former state, "in Christo omnia revocantur ad initium" (Tert. *Monog.* 5) (Meyer, *al.*). The Vulgate, indeed, expresses this idea to the exclusion of κεφάλαιον, "instaurare." But as it has the same rendering in Rom. xiii. 9, we cannot consider it as meant for anything but a verbal equivalent. ἀνα- here has the same force as in ἀναγινώσκειν, ἀναλογίζεσθαι, ἀναμετρεῖν, viz. the idea "one by one." So Lightfoot, who remarks that in the interpretation alluded to Tertullian found a serviceable weapon against Marcion, who maintained a direct opposition between the work of the Demiurge and the work of Christ. Chrysostom asks, τί ἐστιν ἀνακεφαλαιώσασθαι; and replies, συνάψαι. When he afterwards says, πάντας ὑπὸ μίαν ἤγαγε κεφαλήν, we may suppose that he only meant a rhetorical play on words, since the verb is not derived from κεφαλή, but from κεφάλαιον.

The middle voice is appropriate as implying the interest which God Himself has herein; cf. εἰς αὐτόν in 1 Cor. viii. 6; Rom. xi. 36.

τὰ ἐπὶ τοῖς οὐρανοῖς καὶ τὰ ἐπὶ τῆς γῆς. This is the reading of ℵ* B D L, Theodoret,[1] Oec. and some cursives, and is adopted by Lachm. Tisch. Treg. WH. But A G K, most cursives, have ἐν τοῖς οὐρ., with Chrys. Theodoret,[1] Theophyl. The variation in case after the same preposition has frequent parallels in classical writers.

On the other hand, the usual contrast is ἐν τοῖς οὐρανοῖς and ἐπὶ τῆς γῆς (iii. 15; Col. i. 20, in which latter place there is a poorly attested reading ἐπί, perhaps from this passage). It must be admitted also (with Harless) that there is something strange in the use of ἐπί, "upon," with τοῖς οὐρανοῖς, for the nature of the case as well as the antithesis forbid us to understand it as "above the heavens."

τὰ πάντα shows that it is not the uniting of things in heaven with things on earth that is expressed. These are named in order to express the greatest universality. Hence also here, as with πᾶσα ἡ κτίσις, Rom. viii. 19 sqq., there is no occasion to introduce any limitation except such as the context demands. To the spiritual as to the poetic eye all nature seems to share in what strictly and literally belongs only to intelligent beings; nor is it hard to see that there is a profound truth in such a view. The introduction here of this view (new in St. Paul) of the extension of Christ's work to things in heaven, is accounted for by his having in his mind the teaching derogatory to Christ, which is more distinctly referred to in the Ep. to the Colossians.

The things in the heavens were understood by Locke to mean the Jews (those on earth being the Gentiles), in support of which interpretation he refers to Matt. xxiv. 29. He is followed by Schoettgen, Ernesti, and others. Chrysostom understands the angels, while others interpret the words of the spirits of the just of the O.T. (Beza and many others).

11. **ἐκληρώθημεν**, ℵ B cursives generally, Vulg., Chrys. etc.

ἐκλήθημεν, A D G, probably not a gloss but a result of "parablepsy," assisted by the greater familiarity of the latter word. The converse substitution would be wholly unaccountable.

ἐν ᾧ καὶ ἐκληρώθημεν. καὶ obviously is joined with the verb "for whom also," not "we also," as if it were καὶ ἡμεῖς. The purpose was "also" carried out. κλῆρος, properly a lot, then, like the English "lot," "a portion allotted," or "portion" generally. It is common in both senses in the Sept. as well as in classical Greek. It is not = "inheritance." The verb κληρόω = "to choose by lot" or "assign by lot," hence in the passive, to be assigned, as "ἐκληρώθην δουλή." In this sense Chrysostom, Estius, etc., understand it here, κλῆρον γενομένου ἡμᾶς ἐξελέξατο, the word being chosen, according to Estius, to indicate that the election was not by our merit, and then προορισθέντες being added to exclude the idea of chance (Chrys.).

The Vulgate agrees, "sorte vocati sumus," and many modern interpreters. But this would be entirely without parallel in the language of St. Paul, with whom it is God's gracious will that is the determining source of the ἐκλογή, not any θεῖα τύχη.

Many interpreters adopt the rendering, "we were chosen as His lot or heritage," deriving the meaning of the verb from the second sense of κλῆρος. So Bengel, Alford, Ellicott. The sense is good, but this meaning of κληρόω, in which the idea of chance is lost, is not sufficiently supported, and the idea of "heritage" is without justification. On the other hand, the interpretation, "we have obtained κλῆρος" (κλῆρος τῶν ἁγίων, Col. i. 12), is unobjectionable in point of language; for κληροῦν τινι is classical, *e.g.* ἐν ἑκάστῳ ἐκλήρωσαν, Thuc. vi. 42, and it would be quite in accordance with analogy that κληροῦσθαι should be used in the sense "to be assigned a portion," cf. φθονοῦμαι, διακονοῦμαι, Matt. xx. 28; πιστεύομαι, Gal. ii. 7. It is probably in this way that we are to explain the usage in later Greek writers, exemplified in Aelian, *Nat. Hist.* v. 31, and Hippocrates, 1287. 15. In the former passage the serpent is said to have his heart near his throat. τὴν καρδίαν κεκλήρωται, κ.τ.λ. In the latter, Hippocrates says, πλείονα μεμψιμοιρίην ἢ τιμὴν κεκληρῶσθαι τὴν τέχνην. In both cases the verb seems to mean, not simply "to have," but "to have as one's portion or κλῆρος." The sense suits well, as it corresponds to the notions κληρονομία and περιποίησις in ver. 14, as well as to the ἐν τοῖς ἐπουρανίοις, ver. 3, and coincides with that of Col. i. 12 above referred to; we may compare also Acts xxvi. 18, τοῦ λαβεῖν . . . κλῆρον ἐν τοῖς ἡγιασμένοις, and xvii. 4, προσεκληρώθησαν τῷ Παύλῳ. The selection of the word is explained by the O.T. use of κλῆρος, which made it appropriate for the possession allotted to the Jewish Christians (so Meyer, Soden, Eadie). That these are intended here, although ἡμεῖς is not expressed before ver. 12, seems probable from the close logical connexion with ver. 12. Besides, if ὑμεῖς be included here, vv. 13*b*, 14 would be a weak repetition.

κατὰ τὴν βουλὴν τοῦ θελήματος αὐτοῦ. This specification seems meant to exclude all idea of any merit of the Jews in their κληροῦσθαι. As to the distinction between βουλή and θέλημα, and between the respective verbs, scholars are at issue. The best supported opinion is that βουλή involves the idea of purpose and deliberation, θέλειν and θέλημα denoting simply will. So Ammonius states that β. is used only of rational beings, θ. also of irrational. Thus, as Grimm says, θέλω would express the will that proceeds from inclination, βούλομαι that from deliberation. Cf. Matt. i. 19, "not willing (θέλων) to make her a public example, was minded, ἐβουλήθη," etc.; 1 Cor. vii. 36, ὃ θέλει ποιείτω; *ib.* 39, xiv. 35, εἰ δέ τι μαθεῖν θέλουσιν. θέλω as the less definite may be used there, but βούλομαι would be quite suitable. Some scholars, however, reverse this distinction. Here the combination "counsel of His will" seems intended to express emphatically the absolute self-determination of God. Compare 1 Pet. iii. 17, εἰ θέλοι τὸ θέλημα τοῦ Θεοῦ.

12–14. *We Jews had even in former times the promise of the Christ, which has now been fulfilled; but the same blessings are now extended to you the Gentiles, and as the earnest of your inheritance, ye have been sealed with the Holy Spirit.*

12. εἰς τὸ εἶναι, κ.τ.λ. It seems best to take τοὺς προηλπικότας as the predicate, according to the analogy of εἰς ἐπ. in ver. 6 and ver. 14, and εἰς ἔπαινον δόξης αὐτοῦ parenthetically. The article is necessary, since what has to be expressed is not that the ἡμεῖς were to have had the attribute of having previously hoped, but that it was their special privilege to be those amongst the Christians who had had a previous hope. And if προηλπ. is the subject, what reason can be given why προορισθ. εἰς ἔπ. δ. should be confined to them, seeing it applies equally to the ὑμεῖς ἀκούσαντες? Besides, this would be only a repetition of vv. 4, 5. The chief objection made to this interpretation is that the distinction between Jewish and Gentile Christians does not come in before ver. 13; but this is only an assumption, as the exposition of ver. 11, just given, shows. We translate, therefore (with Harless, Olsh. Soden), "That we, to the praise of His glory, should be those who have before had hopes in Christ."

Meyer's interpretation of τοὺς προηλ. as "quippe qui" is inconsistent with the article.

To what does the προ. refer? προελπίζω might, of course, mean simply hope before the event, as προορίζω implies an ὁρισμός before the object of it appeared; and so Ellicott, Meyer, understand the word here, explaining the perfect as indicating that the action still continues; but this seems fallacious; ἐλπίζειν continues, but not προελπίζειν.

It seems better then, with Beza, Bengel, v. Soden, to understand the προ. as referring to the time prior to the conversion of the heathen. Whether it be understood thus or as "before the coming of Christ," it is appropriate to the Jewish Christians as distinguished from the Gentile. But some expositors deny that there is any such distinction here (De Wette), and understand προ. as "before the Parousia." But the καὶ ὑμεῖς of ver. 13, together with the ἀκούσαντες which is antithetical to προηλπ., seems decisive. Compare Rom. xv. 8, 9, λέγω δέ, Χριστὸν διάκονον γεγενῆσθαι περιτομῆς ὑπὲρ ἀληθείας Θεοῦ, εἰς τὸ βεβαιῶσαι τὰς ἐπαγγελίας τῶν πατέρων· τὰ δὲ ἔθνη ὑπέρ, ἐλέους (*i.e.* not ὑπὲρ ἀληθείας) δοξάσαι τὸν Θεόν (not might glorify, as AV. and RV.).

13. ἐν ᾧ καὶ ὑμεῖς. "In whom ye also." There is much difference of opinion as to the connexion. Beza, Calvin, *al.*, supply ἠλπίκατε. But if προηλπ. is to suggest the supplement, it would be προηλπίκατε, which is inadmissible. Meyer and Alford supply the substantive in accordance with the current expression ἐν Χριστῷ εἶναι, "in whom ye also are." Not only is this extremely tame, but, considering the pregnant meaning of εἶναι in this phrase, it is hardly possible that it should be omitted, not having occurred in the previous clause. Erasmus, à Lapide, Harless, *al.*, supply ἐκληρώθητε. The objection of Meyer and Ellicott, that ἐκληρ. would thus be limited to Gentile Christians, though it formerly referred to both Jews and Gentiles, loses its force if the interpretation of ver. 11 above given be adopted. But it is awkward to go back so far, and a much simpler solution is that ἐν ᾧ is connected with ἐσφραγίσθητε, the second ἐν ᾧ being a resumption of the first, as in RV. with Theodore Mops., Bengel, Eadie, Ellicott, Soden. Thus the thought ἐν Χριστῷ, which governs the whole section 3 to 14, is with the second ἐν ᾧ once more emphatically brought forward, while πιστεύσαντες, as the necessary antecedent of ἐσφραγ., is given its proper prominence as distinguished from the prior condition ἀκούσαντες. The repetition of ὑμεῖς before πιστεύσαντες is so far from being necessary that it would obscure the importance of that word.

τὸν λόγον τῆς ἀληθείας. Cf. Col. i. 5. The word whose content is truth, *i.e.* the gospel, κατ' ἐξοχὴν sermo veritatis quasi extra ipsum nulla esset proprie veritas (Calvin), in apposition with τὸ εὐαγγέλιον τῆς σωτηρίας ὑμῶν, the gospel, or good tidings, whose subject-matter was salvation.

"In whom I say, when ye also believed, ye were sealed." ἐν ᾧ, not to be taken with πιστ., for which there is no parallel in St. Paul, but with ἐσφρ. Meyer, however, with Calvin, Beza, *al.*, refers ἐν ᾧ to τὸ εὐαγγ., comparing Mark i. 15, πιστεύετε ἐν τῷ εὐαγγελίῳ, and Gal. iii. 26, πίστις ἐν Χρ. Ἰ. But it is much more natural to understand it as = ἐν Χριστῷ; and, of course, if the account just given of the first ἐν ᾧ be adopted, this alone is possible. Compare Acts xix. 2, εἰ πνεῦμα ἅγιον ἐλάβετε πιστεύσαντες = "when ye believed."

ἐσφραγίσθητε. Compare 2 Cor. i. 22, ὁ καὶ σφραγισάμενος ἡμᾶς καὶ δοὺς τὸν ἀρραβῶνα τοῦ πνεύματος. The figure is such an obvious one that it is needless to seek for its origin in any allusion to circumcision, called a seal in Rom. iv. 11, or in the στίγματα of certain worshippers of heathen deities. In later writers σφραγίς is used simply for "baptism"; but there is no reason to suppose such a reference here, which would be too obscure.

τῷ πν. τῆς ἐπ. "The spirit of promise," *i.e.* which had been promised, ὅτι κατὰ ἐπαγγ. αὐτὸ ἐλάβομεν, Chrys., who, however, also gives a different view, as does Theoph. ἢ ὅτι ἐξ ἐπαγγελίας ἐδόθη ἢ ὅτι τὴν τῶν μελλόντων ἀγαθῶν ἐπαγγελίαν τὸ πν. βεβαιοῖ. The latter interpretation must be rejected, because the word πνεῦμα does not contain the idea of βεβαίωσις. "The Spirit which brings a promise" would be a possible interpretation; but it is not the Spirit that is the immediate bringer of the promise, and, moreover, the other view agrees better with the connexion. τῷ ἁγίῳ added with emphasis, "even the Holy Spirit."

14. ἀρραβών, a Semitic word (Heb. עֲרָבוֹן), which probably (we may say certainly) passed from the Phoenicians to the Greeks, and from them to the Romans in the sense of our word "earnest," a portion of the purchase money given to ratify the contract, and so as a pledge of full payment. In the N.T. it is found only here and 2 Cor. i. 22, ver. 5 (in both places ἀρρ. τοῦ πνεύματος). It is to be noted, first, that the earnest is of the same kind as the full payment. Compare Clem. Alex., *Ecl. Proph.* xii. p. 982, οὔτε γὰρ πᾶν κεκομίσμεθα οὔτε παντὸς ὑστεροῦμεν, ἀλλ' οἷον ἀρραβῶνα. . . . προσειλήφαμεν. So Irenaeus, "hoc est, pars ejus honoris qui a Deo nobis promissus est," v. 8. 1. To this corresponds ἡ ἀπαρχὴ τοῦ πν. Rom. viii. 23. "The actual spiritual life of the Christian is the same in kind as his future glorified life; the kingdom of heaven is a present kingdom; the believer is already seated at the right hand of God," Lightfoot, who adds that the metaphor suggests and doubtless was intended to convey another idea, namely, that the recipient of the earnest money pledges himself to accomplish his side of the contract. ὅς is attracted into the gender of ἀρρ. according to a usual idiom; cf. Mark xv. 16, τῆς αὐλῆς ὅ ἐστι πραιτώριον, and Gal. iii. 16, τῷ σπέρματί σου ὅς ἐστι Χριστός; also, perhaps, 1 Tim. iii. 16; Col. i. 27. ὅ is, however, found in A B G L, Athan. Cyril, Chrys., and is adopted by Lachm., WH.

εἰς ἀπολύτρωσιν τῆς περιποιήσεως. περιποιεῖν means properly "to cause to remain over, to preserve alive, save." It is so used both in classical writers and in the Sept. In the middle voice it means to acquire for oneself. So in N.T. Acts xx. 28, ἣν περιεποιήσατο διὰ τοῦ αἵματος τοῦ ἰδίου. The substantive περιποίησις occurs once in the Sept. in the sense of survival, 2 Chron. xiv. 13, καὶ ἔπεσον Αἰθίοπες ὥστε μὴ εἶναι ἐν αὐτοῖς περιποίησιν. This appears to be the sense intended here by the Sept. "for the redemption of those who live."

Most commentators compare the expression λαὸς εἰς περιποίησιν, 1 Pet. ii. 9, which is taken from Mal. iii. 17, ἔσονταί μοι . . . εἰς π., where εἰς π. represents the Hebrew that is elsewhere rendered περιούσιος; so RV. "*God's* own possession." It is a serious objection to this that π. by itself has not the meaning "people for a possession," or "God's possession." In 1 Pet. it is λαός, and in Malachi μοι, that determines the meaning: indeed, as St. Peter is quoting from Malachi, his words do not supply a second instance of even this limited use of the word, nor any at all of N.T. usage.

Meyer attempts to evade this objection by making αὐτοῦ refer to περιπ. as well as δόξης, which is very forced. Another very strong objection is from the context. It is our inheritance that is in question; it is of it that the earnest is received, and we should naturally expect that what follows εἰς would have reference to the complete reception of it. Instead of this, the interpretation quoted supposes the figure entirely changed, so that, instead of receiving an inheritance, it is we that are the possession; a figure proper in its place, but here involving a confusion of thought which we can hardly attribute to St. Paul. Augustine seems to have understood the word as = "haereditas acquisita," perhaps only following the Latin version, "acquisitionis." So Calovius, "plena fruitio redemtionis haereditatis nobis acquisitae," a meaning of π. which is unsupported.

Beza remarks that we have to distinguish two deliverances or ἀπολυτρώσεις; the one which is past and finished, the other, the complete deliverance to which we have to look forward in the hereafter. The former, he says, might be called "docendi causa," ἀπολύτρωσις ἐλευθερώσεως, and, correspondingly, the latter ἀπ. περιποιήσεως, "liberatio vindicationis or assertionis." His explanation of the construction, not the meaning of π., seems to be essentially the same as that of Theodore Mops., Theodoret, and Severianus. They, however, understand π. as ἡ πρὸς τὸν Θεόν οἰκείωσις. Thus Sever. says we are redeemed ἵνα περιποιηθῶμεν καὶ οἰκειωθῶμεν τῷ Θεῷ, so that the meaning is, "With a view to our full recovery of our privileges as sons of God." But this is open to the objection just now brought against the RV., that τῷ Θεῷ required to be expressed. We are compelled, therefore, by the necessity of the context, to understand περιποίησις of our acquisition; only it is not a thing possessed, the object of ἀπολ., but possession or acquisition, the result of the complete ἀπολ. (so Soden, and, in substance, Macpherson), "With a view to a complete redemption which will give possession." In the three other passages in which π. occurs in the N.T. it means acquisition or saving, in accordance with the classical usage, viz. 1 Thess. v. 9, σωτηρίας; 2 Thess. ii. 14, δόξης; Heb. x. 39, ψυχῆς (cf. Luke xxi. 19, κτήσεσθε τὰς ψυχὰς ὑμῶν).

15-19. *Therefore having heard of your faith, I thank God, and I pray that ye may attain a deeper knowledge of the glory of the inheritance, and of the mighty power of God who confers it upon you.*

15. Διὰ τοῦτο. Connected by some with *vv.* 13, 14, only, *i.e.*, "Because ye also are in Christ, and have been sealed," etc., since it is only in ver. 13 that the writer turns to the Ephesians. But better connected with the whole paragraph, *vv.* 3–14, "because this blessing which we share is so mighty." So Oecum., διὰ τὰ ἀποκείμενα ἀγαθὰ τοῖς ὀρθῶς πιστεύουσι καὶ βιοῦσι καὶ διὰ τὰ ἐν τοῖς σωθησομένοις τετάχθαι ὑμᾶς. This is to be preferred, if only because διὰ τοῦτο is too emphatic for so limited a reference as the former. It is used in transition to a new paragraph in Rom. v. 12; 2 Cor. iv. 1; Col. i. 9. The last passage is closely parallel to the present.

κἀγώ. "I also," does not express co-operation with the readers in their prayers, or with others, of whom there is no hint; nor is it "I who first preached to you"; but it simply notes the transition from ὑμεῖς. It is exactly parallel to καὶ ἡμεῖς in Col. i. 9, where the plural is used because Timothy is associated with Paul in the address.

ἀκούσας is certainly in favour of the view that the Epistle was written, not to the Ephesians, but to readers to whom Paul had not personally preached; and this appears to be confirmed by the similar expression in Col. i. 4. On the other hand, it must be observed that the same expression occurs in the Epistle to Philemon (ver. 5), Paul's beloved fellow-worker, except that the participle is present tense. But this makes all the difference. Theodoret explains ἀκούσας here as referring to the progress the Ephesians had made more recently; and so many moderns. But against this is the fact that in vv. 17 ff. this is prayed for. A frequentative force of the participle cannot be admitted. The frequentative force of the aor. ind. is only the result of its indefiniteness (Luke i. 55 ff.). The time of the participle is defined by the principal verb.

τὴν καθ' ὑμᾶς πίστιν. "Apud vos" = "among you," but in sense equivalent to τ. π. ὑμῶν, Col. i. 4. Compare Acts xvii. 28, τῶν καθ' ὑμᾶς ποιητῶν; xviii. 15, νόμου τοῦ καθ' ὑμᾶς = "the law that obtains among you"; xxvi. 3, τῶν κατὰ Ἰουδαίους ἐθῶν. This periphrasis for the genitive seems to have been frequent in later Greek; cf. Aelian, *V. H.* ii. 12, ἡ κατ' αὐτὸν ἀρετή, Diod. S. i. 65. ἡ κατὰ τὴν ἀρχὴν ἀπόθεσις (laying down the government). There seems, therefore, no good reason to say, with Harless and Ellicott, that the phrase here denotes the faith of the community viewed objectively (the thing in itself), in contradistinction to ἡ π. ὑμῶν, which expresses the subjective faith of individuals; or with Alford, that it implies the possibility of some not having this faith (whereas all are addressed as πιστοί). At most, perhaps, we may say that the form of expression was suggested by a view of the different classes of believers. That ἡ π. ὑμῶν could have been used is shown by Col. i. 4.

πίστιν ἐν τῷ Κυρίῳ Ἰησοῦ. ἐν indicates that in which the faith rests, as εἰς expresses that to which it is directed, "fidem in Christo repositam." The absence of the article before ἐν marks the binding of πίστις ἐν τ. Κυρίῳ into one conception.

καὶ τὴν ἀγάπην τὴν εἰς πάντας τοὺς ἁγίους. τὴν ἀγάπην is omitted by ℵ* A B P, Orig. Hier., inserted by ℵ° D G K L, Syr. Boh., Chrys. The insertion is supported by the parallel, Col. i. 4. Internal evidence is strongly in its favour, as πίστιν εἰς τοὺς ἁγίους would be an unexampled expression (Philem. 6 is not an instance). The omission, too, is very easily accounted for by the passing of a copyist's eye from the first to the second τήν. Lachm. and Westcott and Hort and RV. omit the words, but Tisch. Treg (not mg.) retain them.

16. οὐ παύομαι εὐχαριστῶν, κ.τ.λ. εὐχαριστεῖν, in the sense "giving thanks, being thankful," belongs to the later Greek (from Polybius onward). Its earlier meaning was "to do a good turn to," and hence to "return a favour," to be grateful.

οὐ παύομαι is usually joined directly with εὐχ., while μνείαν π. is made subordinate, as specifying the further direction of the εὐχαριστία. But the following ἵνα seems to require us to take μν. π. as the principal notion, "I cease not while giving thanks for you to make mention," etc. It is not clear whether μνείαν ποιεῖσθαι, which also occurs ver. 16, Rom. i. 9, Philem. 4, means "to remember" or "to mention." It is used in the latter sense by Plato (*Protag.* 317 E; *Phaed.* 254 A) and other writers. Cf. Ps. cxi. 4; Sept. μν. ἐπ. τῶν θαυμασίων αὐτοῦ.

For ἐπὶ τῶν προσευχῶν cf. Rom. i. 10; 1 Thess. i. 2.

ὑμῶν (after μνείαν) of the Text. Rec. is om. by א A B D*, added by De K L P; Vulg. Syr. (both) Boh., Orig. Chrys. G have ὑμῶν after ποιούμενος. Compare the readings in 1 Thess. i. 2, where ὑμῶν is om. by א* A B.

17. ἵνα. If this passage were to be considered without reference to the parallel in Col. i. 9, the rendering "in order that" would be tenable (though it would be strange to say, "I mention you in order that"). But in Col. the preceding verb is αἰτούμενοι. A verb of asking must be followed by words expressing the content of the request. And there is an abundance of examples to show that in this and similar cases ἵνα has almost or rather entirely lost its final sense. Thus we have δεῖσθαι ἵνα in Dion. Hal. εἰπὲ ἵνα, κελεύειν, ἐπιτρέπειν ἵνα.

Also with θέλειν, e.g. Matt. vii. 12, ὅσα ἂν θέλητε ἵνα ποιῶσιν: Mark vi. 25, Θέλω ἵνα μοι δῷς τὴν κεφαλήν Ἰωάννου: ix. 30, οὐκ ἤθελεν ἵνα τις γνῷ: x. 37, δὸς ἡμῖν ἵνα: Matt. x. 25, ἀρκετὸν τῷ μαθητῇ ἵνα γένηται: xviii. 6, συμφέρει αὐτῷ ἵνα κρεμασθῇ: cf. ἔδει ἵνα ἐπὶ ξύλου πάθῃ, Barn. *Ep.* v. 13: ἐλάχιστόν μοι ἐστιν ἵνα, 1 Cor. iv. 3: ἔστιν συνηθεία ἵνα . . . ἀπολύσω, John xviii. 39: μίσθος ἵνα, 1 Cor. ix. 18.

In modern Greek νὰ is used as a sign of the infinitive = "to." Winer quotes from the *Confessio Orthod.* πρέπει νᾶ, λέγεται νά. The usage above illustrated indicates the transition to this complete weakening of the original force of the word.

ὁ Θεὸς τοῦ Κυρίου, κ.τ.λ. Many of the early commentators in order to avoid the obvious sense of these words, of which the

Arians made use against the Divinity of Christ, interpreted δόξα as signifying the Divine nature, κύριος the human. Thus Theodoret, Θεὸν μὲν ὡς ἀνθρώπου, πατέρα δὲ ὡς Θεοῦ, δόξαν γὰρ τὴν θείαν φύσιν ὠνόμασεν. Similarly Athanasius, δόξαν τὸν μονογενῆ καλεῖ. But this would surely require αὐτοῦ to be added, and the distinction would be out of place in this context. The apostle refers to the relation of God to the Lord Jesus Christ as an encouragement to hope for the fulfilment of his prayer. More inadmissible, and only worthy of note as a singularity of interpretation, is the view of Menochius, who takes τοῦ κ. ἡ. 'I. X. as a parenthesis, or that of Estius, "Deus, qui est Domini nostri Jesu Christi pater gloriosus." These devices are unnecessary, since the Lord Himself calls God "My God," John xx. 17; Matt. xxvii. 46. The expression is neither more nor less expressive of subordination than this, "the Father is greater than I," which, as Pearson shows, was understood by the Fathers as spoken of the Divine nature of Christ. They did not hesitate to call the Father the Source, Fountain, Author, etc., of the Son or the whole Divinity.

ὁ πατὴρ τῆς δόξης. "The Father to whom belongs glory," cf. Acts vii. 2; "the God of glory," 1 Cor. ii. 8; "the Lord of glory," cf. Jas. ii. 1; and πατὴρ τῶν οἰκτιρμῶν, 2 Cor. i. 3; also χερουβὶμ δόξης, Heb. ix. 5.

The interpretation "author or source of glory," if it were tenable, would give a good sense. So Chrys. ὁ μεγάλα ἡμῖν δεδωκὼς ἀγαθά. But the possibility of the interpretation is not proved. Poetical expressions, such as Pindar's ἀοιδᾶν πατήρ (of Orpheus, which, moreover, is not = "creator," but "inventor"), are not to the point, nor "hath the rain a father"? in Job xxxviii. 28; cf. xvii. 14. "Father of spirits," Heb. xii. 9, proves nothing, for the term there is introduced only as an antithesis to "fathers of our flesh," and besides with the word "spirits," "father" preserves the double notion of "creator" and "ruler," as indeed the context there implies. The nearest parallel is Jas. i. 17, πατὴρ τῶν φώτων, where "the lights" are personified, and the notion of control is not absent. But there is no parallel to this in St. Paul, whose usage is shown by the passages above referred to. Alford's view is that as God and Father of our Lord Jesus Christ, God is the Father of the glory of the Godhead which shone forth in the manhood of the Son.

δῴη by Lachm. pointed δῴη as an Ionic conjunctive. The sense points to a conjunctive, but the form appears to be known only as epic. WH. give it in the margin, but in the text adopt δῴη, a later form for the opt. δοίη. B has δῷ, to which WH. give the second place in the margin. If the ἵνα were truly final, the optative would create a difficulty, being properly used after the present, when the attainment of the object is doubtful (Kost and Palm).

πνεῦμα σοφίας, κ.τ.λ. According to Eadie, Ellicott, Meyer, definitely the Holy Spirit, characterised here suitably to the subject. On the absence of the article cf. Gal. v. 5, 16. But these instances, where πν. is used as a proper name without a genitive following, are not parallel.

It is better to understand with RV. after Chrys. Theodoret, al., "a spirit of wisdom," etc.; cf. 2 Tim. i. 7, "God did not give you πν. δειλίας, ἀλλὰ δυνάμεως καὶ ἀγάπης καὶ σωφρονισμοῦ"; Rom. viii. 15, πν. δουλείας; Gal. vi. 1, πν. πραότητος; Rom. xi. 8, πν. κατανύξεως (Sept.). That the spirit of wisdom here is the effect of the Holy Spirit, is naturally understood but not expressed.

σοφία appears to be the more general term, ἀποκάλυψις having reference specially to the "mysteries" revealed to believers, not to the gift of prophecy, to which there is no reference in what follows, and to which the apostle did not attach so much importance (see 1 Cor. xiii., xiv.). Harless, followed in substance by Eadie, regards ἀποκ. as the medium by which σοφία is communicated. This relation would be more naturally expressed by ἀποκαλύψεως καὶ σοφίας.

ἐν ἐπιγνώσει αὐτοῦ, *i.e.* of God, as appears from αὐτοῦ in vv. 18, 19, Christ being first referred to in ver. 20. ἐπίγνωσις, "full knowledge," "major exactiorque cognitio," Grot.; see 1 Cor. xiii. 12, ἄρτι γινώσκω ἐκ μέρους, τότε δὲ ἐπιγνώσομαι καθὼς καὶ ἐπεγνώσθην. This is generally joined with the preceding, some taking ἐν for εἰς (à Lapide, Bengel, al.), or as = "by," which reverses the relation of the knowledge of God with the gift of σοφία. Meyer and Ellicott understand it as marking the sphere or element in which they were to receive wisdom and revelation; Stier and Eadie, connecting the words especially with ἀποκ., suppose them, while formally denoting the sphere, to indicate virtually the material of the revelation. If this punctuation be adopted, the latter view seems preferable. But all difficulty disappears if, with Lachm. WH. (after Chrysostom and Theoph.), we connect the words with what follows. The abruptness of πεφωτισμένους is much softened by the previous mention of the means. Indeed, the bold figure of enlightenment of the eyes of the heart seems to require some such definition as ἐν ἐπιγνώσει, which then naturally precedes, because of its connexion in sense with ἀποκάλυψις.

18. πεφωτισμένους τοὺς ὀφθαλμοὺς, κ.τ.λ. A difficult construction. The most probable explanation appears to be that the words are in apposition with πνεῦμα as the immediate effect, and so dependent on δῴη, in which case, however, according to the sound observation of Bengel, "articulus praesupponit oculos jam praesentes," we must render "the eyes of your heart enlightened," πεφ. being a tertiary predicate (so Harless, Olsh. Wold. Schmidt,

Soden). It is also possible to regard πεφ. as by anacoluthon referring to ὑμῖν, τοὺς ὀφθ. being the accusative of nearer definition. Somewhat similar examples of the accusative being used where the dative has preceded, and might be expected to be repeated, are found in classical writers, *e.g.* ὕπεστί μοι θράσος ἀδυπνόων κλύουσιν ἀρτίως ὀνειράτων, Soph. *El.* 479. The sense would be 'enlightened as to the eyes of your heart," *i.e.* "so that ye may be enlightened." Such an irregularity of construction is intelligible where it makes the sentence run more simply, not where it makes it obscure.

A third construction is adopted by Bengel, Eadie, *al.*, according to whom the πεφ. agrees with ὀφθ., the three words together being an accus. absolute, "the eyes, etc., being enlightened." That is, the words are taken as equivalent to πεφωτισμένων τῶν ὀφθαλμῶν. The possibility of this is questionable. Bernhardy (p. 133) maintains that absolute accusatives of participles should be banished from Greek grammars (cf. Jelf, § 581. 1). Acts xxvi. 3, cited by Pengel, is not in point, being a case of anacoluthon (Winer).

καρδίας. This reading rests on decisive authority. It is that of א A B D G K L P, Vulg. Syr., Orig. Chrys. etc. The T.R. διανοίας is supported only by a few cursives, Theodoret and Oecum.

ὀφθαλμοὺς τῆς καρδίας, "eyes of the heart"; cf. Plato, *Rep.* p. 533 Α, τὸ τῆς ψυχῆς ὄμμα. Aristotle in *Eth. Nic.* calls δεινότης, τὸ ὄμμα τῆς ψυχῆς (vi. 12. 10). Clement's ἠνεῴχθησαν ἡμῶν οἱ ὀφθ. τῆς καρδίας may be an allusion to this passage. It is to be observed that καρδία, with the ancients, was not only the seat of emotion, but of thought and moral perception. Here clearly it is as the seat of knowledge that it is referred to, hence "eyes of the heart." See the contrary state, the darkening of the heart, Rom. i. 21.

τίς ἐστιν ἡ ἐλπίς. Not "of what nature," nor "quanta," but simply "quae," which includes "qualis, quanta et quam certa." ἐλπὶς τῆς κλ., the hope which belongs to or is implied in our calling, *i.e.* not merely the subjective emotion produced by our calling (taking τῆς κλ. as gen. of efficient cause, Meyer, Ell.), the knowledge of which does not require a special grace, but certainly including the content of this hope, not the object in itself, but as a conception (compare the use of our word "ambition," "what is his ambition?" *i.e.* the object of it as a mental conception). From the nature of the case the certainty is assumed. Compare Col. i. 5, "the hope laid up for you in the heavens (= Tit. ii. 13), Heb. vi. 18, προσδεχόμενοι τὴν μακαρίαν ἐλπίδα. The κλῆσις gives the guarantee for this, and includes it; it is, in fact, to this hope that believers are called; ἐπὶ ποίαις ἐλπίσι κεκλήμεθα, Theodoret.

τίς ὁ πλοῦτος τῆς δόξης τῆς κληρονομίας αὐτοῦ. Not to be weakened into "rich glory" or "glorious inheritance." "What a full grandiose cumulation, picturing, as it were, the weightiness of the matter!" Meyer. Glory is the essential attribute of the inheritance to be received, and the apostle wishes the readers to know how great the rich fulness of this glory is; cf. Col. i. 27, "riches of the glory of this mystery."

ἐν τοῖς ἁγίοις. "Among the saints." This is by most commentators connected with κληρονομία, a connexion which is naturally suggested by Acts xx. 32, δοῦναι κληρονομίαν ἐν τοῖς ἡγιασμένοις πᾶσιν: cf. *ib.* xxvi. 18, κλῆρον ἐν τοῖς ἡγιασμένοις. It is a serious if not fatal objection to this that it would require the article τήν to be repeated before ἐν τ. ἁγ., not simply because αὐτοῦ comes between, but because ἡ κληρονομία Θεοῦ is completely defined by this αὐτοῦ. In fact, with this connexion the words would mean, "the inheritance which God has in the saints," which is actually the meaning adopted by Stier, conjoining ἐκληρώθημεν, ver. 11, which he interprets, "were made an inheritance." This, however, would be out of harmony with the use of the word in the N.T. (cf. ver. 14; ch. v. 5; Acts xx. 32, above), as well as with the context. Such phrases as τῶν συγγενῶν μου κατὰ σάρκα (where σ. is an adj., Rom. ix. 3); τὸν Ἰσραὴλ κατὰ σάρκα, 1 Cor. x. 18; τὰ ἔθνη ἐν σαρκί, Eph. ii. 11; τὸν ὑμῶν ζῆλον ὑπὲρ ἐμοῦ, 2 Cor. vii. 7, are not analogous.

The construction then is, "What the riches of the glory of His inheritance is among the saints." The community of believers is the sphere in which alone this πλοῦτος, κ.τ.λ., is found. This does not require the repetition of ὁ before ἐν τ. ἁγ., nor does it give too great emphasis to the latter words. The object of the κληρονομία is, of course, the future kingdom of God; but this future glory is treated by St. Paul as if present.

19. καὶ τί τὸ ὑπερβάλλον μέγεθος, κ.τ.λ. Supply, as in the previous clause, ἐστί, to which then we are to attach εἰς ἡμᾶς, not δυνάμεως, "And what the exceeding greatness of His power is to usward." Thus the two clauses are symmetrical, εἰς ἡμᾶς corresponding in position to ἐν τοῖς ἁγίοις.

The three objects of εἰδέναι are in reality one and the same under different points of view; the content of the "hope of the calling" is the inheritance of Heb. ix. 15, and this again in its realisation is an effect and proof of the δύναμις of God. Thus the object of the ἐπίγνωσις is the blessing to be obtained in the future kingdom of God.

κατὰ τὴν ἐνέργειαν, κ.τ.λ. Many commentators connect these words with τοῖς πιστ., understanding them as expressing the fact that faith itself is the result of God's ἐνέργεια. But this would make the whole solemn exposition in ver. 20 subservient to πιστ., which is only incidental in the sentence. The connexion would be interrupted by a reference to the origin of faith. Besides, this would require us to give to κατά some such meaning as "by virtue of," since our faith is not according to the measure of His power. The three objects of εἰδέναι are so closely connected in themselves that it matters little whether we refer the words κατὰ τ. ἐ. to the last only or to all three; naturally, however, the ἐνέργεια is immediately connected with the last. This ἐν. supplies the measure by which to estimate the power of God.

As to the three words ἰσχύς, κράτος, ἐνέργεια, the distinction appears to be that ἰσχύς is inherent power, κράτος power expressing itself in overcoming resistance, and ἐνέργεια the actual exercise of power. The Vulgate has "secundum operationem potentiae virtutis ejus." Each term has here its appropriate meaning, and there is no occasion to have recourse to a Hebraism, or to such a resolution as κράτος ἰσχυρόν.

20-23. *This power of God was shown in His raising Christ from the dead, and setting Him above all created powers by whatever name they may be called, whether on earth or in heaven. His relation to the Church, however, is more intimate. It is the Body of which He is the Head.*

20. ἣν ἐνήργησεν or ἐνήργηκεν. The latter is read by AB, Cyr., the former by א D G K L P. The versions naturally do not help. Lachm. Tisch. WH. adopt the perfect, WH. placing the aorist in the margin. Tregelles puts the perfect in the margin. The neighbouring aorist might readily lead to the substitution of the aorist for the perfect. The counter change would not be so easily accounted for. The perfect is properly employed, because the effect continues while the separate acts in which this ἐνεργεῖν realised itself follow in aorists.

ἐγείρας. The time is contemporaneous with that of the principal verb; not "having raised him"; but as AV. "when He raised him"; or "in that He raised Him."

21. καὶ καθίσας. This is the reading of א A B, Vulg. The Rec. καὶ ἐκάθισεν is found in D G K L P, Chrys. etc.; αὐτόν is added in א A, Boh. Syr. (both), but not in B D G K L P, Vulg. Tischendorf, who reads καὶ καθίσας αὐτόν with א A, thinks a difficulty was found in this reading for two reasons, first, that although the verb occurs frequently in the N.T. it is transitive only in 1 Cor. vi. 4 (compare συνεκάθισεν, Eph. ii. 6); and, secondly, because nowhere else is God said to have placed Christ at His right hand, but Christ is said to have sat down at God's right hand.

Those who adopt the reading ἐκάθισεν think that more emphasis is thereby given to ἐγείρας as the principal illustration of the Divine power. The words seem to be an indirect quotation of Ps. cx. 1. Compare Ps. xvi. 11, and the request of the sons of Zebedee, Mark x. 37; and for the ground of the figure, 1 Sam. xx. 25; 1 Kings ii. 19. Harless quotes from Pindar (of Minerva), δεξιὰν κατὰ χεῖρα πατρὸς ἵζεαι (*Fragm.* xi. 9). The words express participation in the highest honour and power. So Stephen beholds Jesus standing ἐκ δεξιῶν τοῦ Θεοῦ, Acts vii. 56.

ἐν τοῖς ἐπουρανίοις has, of course, primarily a local signification.

But so also have καθίσας and δεξιά. It is said that these "distinctly local expressions" "tend to invalidate the vague and idealistic 'status coelestis' urged by Harless" (Ellicott). But these expressions tell rather the other way. For surely no one will interpret the right hand of God locally, or the "sitting." These words are but figurative expressions of honour and dignity. Some writers, indeed, lay stress on Stephen's beholding of Jesus at the right hand of God. "As Stephen saw Him, so He veritably is," says Alford; and Stier holds fast the "*certum που* of heaven, yea of the throne of God in it." With so literal a view as this τὰ ἐπουράνια can be nothing but extra-terrestrial space, or more properly (considering the earth's motion), space in general. "The distressed mind instinctively looks *upward* (says Eadie) to the throne of God." And Stier calls a similar observation of Passavant decisive. (How about the Antipodes, or ourselves at a later hour?) We look upward in order to look away from visible things.

B reads ἐν τοῖς οὐρανοῖς, which is adopted by Lachmann.

21. ὑπεράνω, "over above," is not intensive, ἵνα τὸ ἀκρότατον ὕψος δηλώσῃ, "far above," AV. See Heb. ix. 5, ὑπεράνω αὐτῆς χερουβίμ; Ezek. xliii. 15, ὑπ. τῶν κεράτων πῆχυς; also *ib.* viii. 2, x. 19.

Compare also ὑποκάτω, Mark vi. 11, ὑ. τῶν ποδῶν ὑμῶν, and Heb. ii. 8. There was a tendency to such compounds in later Greek.

πάσης ἀρχῆς καὶ ἐξουσίας καὶ δυνάμεως καὶ κυριότητος. These words cannot be considered apart from the parallel enumeration in Col. i. 16, τὰ πάντα ἐν τοῖς οὐρανοῖς καὶ ἐπὶ τῆς γῆς τὰ ὁρατὰ καὶ τὰ ἀόρατα εἴτε θρόνοι εἴτε κυριότητες εἴτε ἀρχαὶ εἴτε ἐξουσίαι. In Col. the abstracts are obviously used for the concrete; it does not, however, follow that the same is the case here where the nouns are singular. There St. Paul is contending definitely against the doctrine of angelic mediators; here he is only alluding to it. Vitringa takes the words here as abstract, understanding them as titles which belonged to the Messiah. In either case there is probably a reference to the use of the words as names of classes of angelic powers. The view that limits the meaning of the words to earthly powers may be set aside, as this would have little point in connexion with such a lofty expression of Christ's exaltation. But the questions remain, Are the powers referred to only heavenly, or both earthly and heavenly? Are these heavenly powers good or bad, or both? and what conclusion, if any, can we draw as to the ranks and subordination of the angels? It will be convenient to answer the last question first, which we do without hesitation in the words of Lightfoot (on Col.), "In this catalogue St. Paul does not profess to describe objective realities, but contents himself with repeating subjective opinions." First, neither here nor elsewhere does he make any positive statement about the orders of angelic powers. To do so here would be, not to assist, but to interrupt his exposition of the doctrine of Christ's exaltation. Nor, indeed, is it likely that here and in Col., writing to those who were in danger of giving too much prominence to angelology, and priding themselves on their knowledge of the unseen (Col. ii. 18), St. Paul should enlighten them by "an incidental revelation" (Ellicott), which could have no effect but to assist them in their futile speculations. The very manner in which he expresses himself here, καὶ παντὸς ὀνόματος ὀνομαζομένου, κ.τ.λ., indicates the contrary. As Lightfoot well remarks, "He brushes away all these speculations without inquiring how much or how little truth there may be in them, because they are altogether beside the question." It is as if he said, "It matters not by what title they are called, or whether real or imaginary, Christ is elevated above them all." The εἴτε ... εἴτε in Col. gives a similar indication. He is impatient with this elaborate angelology.

No doubt St. Paul took these names from the speculations to which he refers in Col. ii. 18, with which the Asiatic readers of this Epistle also were familiar. This is not mere conjecture. In the *Testaments of the Twelve Patriarchs*, an early Jewish-Christian work (probably before A.D. 131), seven orders of spirits are named, the two highest, which are in the seventh heaven, being called θρόνοι and ἐξουσίαι. The others are described by their offices (Levi 3). Origen enumerates five classes, called in the Latin in an ascending series, "sancti angeli, principatus (=ἀρχαί), potentates (=ἐξουσίαι), sedes or throni (=θρόνοι), dominationes (=κυριότητες)," *Opp.* 1733, pp. 66, 70. But this cannot be regarded as independent of St. Paul. Ephrem Syrus, commenting on Deut. i. 15, gives three great divisions, subdivided thus: (1) θεοί, θρόνοι, κυριότητες; (2) ἀρχάγγελοι, ἀρχαί, ἐξουσίαι; (3) ἄγγελοι, δυνάμεις, χερουβίμ, σεραφίμ (*Opp. Syr.* i. p. 270). (Compare Milton's "thrones, dominations, princedoms, virtues, powers.")

The treatise of the pseudo-Dionysius "on the Celestial Hierarchy," written about A.D. 500, and very popular in the Middle Ages, gives three classes each with three subdivisions, viz.: (1) θρόνοι, χερουβίμ, σεραφίμ; (2) ἐξουσίαι, κυριότητες, δυνάμεις; (3) ἄγγελοι, ἀρχάγγελοι, ἀρχαί. Perhaps too much importance has been attached in this connexion to these quotations by some expositors, as if it might be assumed that they were derived from independent sources. Origen seems wholly dependent on St. Paul, saying that he does not know whence the apostle took the names.

It follows from what has been said that it is to no purpose to inquire whether the names are arranged in ascending or descending order, especially as the order in Colossians is not the same as in Ephesians, nor the reverse; whence Alford supposes that here the first two descend, the next two ascend. More wisely Chrysostom calls the names ἄσημα καὶ οὐ γνωριζόμενα, and Augustine, "dicant, qui possunt, si tamen possunt probare quod dicunt; ego ista ignorare fateor."

The universality of expression both here and in Colossians, where the enumeration is preceded by the words "in heaven and on earth, visible and invisible," leads us to infer that earthly powers as well as heavenly are included. The terms ἀρχαί, ἐξουσίαι are used of earthly powers in Tit. iii. 1, and in this Epistle in vi. 12 of evil powers. κυριότης occurs in 2 Pet. ii. 10; Jude 8. Compare the Book of Enoch lxi. 10, "angels of power and angels of principality" (ed. Charles, p. 46).

καὶ παντὸς ὀνόματος, κ.τ.λ. καί here = and in general, cf. Demosth. *De Contrib.* xxxi. 4, καὶ τιμῆς καὶ ἀρχῆς καὶ ἀγαθοῦ τινος μεταλαμβάνειν, and Aeschin. *adv. Tim.*, Σόλων ἐκεῖνος, ὁ παλαιὸς νομοθέτης καὶ ὁ Δράκων καὶ οἱ κατὰ τοὺς χρόνους ἐκείνους νομοθέται (Fritzsche, *Matth.* pp. 786, 870). ὄνομα ὀνομαζόμενον is understood by many (including Lightfoot) to mean "every dignity or title (whether real or imaginary) which is reverenced." But ὄνομα never of itself contains the idea of dignity; in such phrases as "the name of God," it is because of the word with which it is joined that it acquires this sense; so again in such phrases as ποιεῖν ὄν., ἔχειν ὄν., ἐν ὀνόματι εἶναι, the idea of dignity does not reside in the word ὄνομα any more than in our word "name," which is similarly used when we say "to make a name," etc. The participle ὀνομαζομένου also shows that the word is to be taken in its simple meaning. Nor is it "every such name," which is quite arbitrary.

οὐ μόνον, κ.τ.λ. Chrysostom and Theodoret suppose these words to refer to our possible knowledge in the future life; but it is not our knowledge that is in question, but the exaltation of Christ, which is thus declared to be, not temporary, but eternal. The form of expression is common in Jewish writers, who, however, by "the world to come" understand the time of the Messiah. Cf. Matt. xii. 32.

22. καὶ πάντα, κ.τ.λ., a reminiscence (not a citation as in 1 Cor. xv. 27) of Ps. viii. 7, where the words are spoken of man. Here the apostle adopts them as typically applicable to Christ, in whom they received a higher and more complete fulfilment. The context in the psalm itself, "all sheep and oxen," etc., shows that this is not to be regarded as an interpretation of the psalm, but an application of its language in a manner familiar with Jewish writers. In Christ, humility was raised to a dignity far surpassing that which was assigned to it at its first creation.

καὶ ἔδωκεν αὐτὸν κεφαλὴν ὑπὲρ πάντα τῇ ἐκκλησίᾳ. The verb ἔδωκεν is not for ἔθηκεν, but with its proper sense, "gave," is directly connected with τῇ ἐκκλ. The order of the words is not against this, for not only is the position of κεφαλὴν ὑ. π. most appropriate to the general sense of the passage, which concerns, not the giving, but the giving as Head, but it is also necessary to clearness, in order that ἥτις may follow ἐκκλ. directly. κεφαλὴν ὑπὲρ πάντα is not = summum caput, as if there were more heads than one, but simply "Head over all."

23. ἥτις = not the simple relative, but "which, in fact, is," "ut quae." In order, says Oecumenius, that hearing of the head you may not think merely of rule and authority, σωματικῶς ἡμῶν ἐστι κεφαλή. There is an organic connexion; the life of the Church springs from its union with Christ as its Head.

τὸ πλήρωμα τοῦ τὰ πάντα ἐν πᾶσιν πληρουμένου. A much vexed passage, which is ably discussed by Soden, to the following effect.

We find in iv. 10 that it is the function of Christ to fill all things, having ascended to heaven and thence descending with the gifts communicated to the Church. He is here, therefore, called ὁ πληρούμενος τὰ πάντα.

This He is able to do by virtue of His being the head over all. How this is to be understood is suggested by Rom. xiii. 9 sq., where that by which the law is fulfilled, namely, ἀγάπη, is also that in which the law with all its parts ἀνακεφαλαιοῦται. If we transfer this to the present passage, it gives the result that the fact that τὰ πάντα are filled by Christ coincides with this; but τὰ πάντα ἀνακεφαλαιοῦται in Christ, ch. i. 10. And this expression corresponds with the conception that the Church, whose function is to be the means of this πληροῦσθαι, is so because Christ is given to her as Head.

If Christ is to fill all things through the medium of the Church, He must first fill the Church. And with this the figure of σῶμα agrees, since in a man the head fills the body with its thoughts and purposes, so that each member is determined by it and filled by it, and that the more, the maturer the man is: comp. iv. 13, 16, where the πλήρωμα τοῦ Χρ. is attained in proportion as the σῶμα is, so to speak, full grown. In this view πλήρωμα τοῦ Χρ. is understood to mean that which is filled with Christ, and with some modifications this is the view adopted by most moderns.

The difficulty is in the genitive relation, πλ. τοῦ Χρ. The word πλήρωμα has been very fully discussed, from a lexical point of view, by Fritzsche (*Rom.* vii. p. 469), to whom later commentators are indebted for their references; also by Lightfoot in an excursus on Col., and by others. The verb πληρόω means either to fill or to fulfil, complete. The meanings of the substantive have been generally derived from the former signification, but it is important to keep the latter in mind. Like all verbals in -μα, the substantive has a passive signification. There are, indeed, one or two passages cited by Fritzsche and the lexicons as examples of an active sense, *e.g.* Eur. *Troad.* 824, Ζηνὸς ἔχεις κυλίκων πλήρωμα καλλίσταν λατρείαν, *i.e.* filling the cups of Zeus, and Philo, *de Abr.* (ii. p. 39), πίστις ἡ πρὸς τὸν Θεόν, παρηγόρημα βίου, πλήρωμα χρηστῶν ἐλπίδων = bonae spei ad eventum adductio (for faith is not the fulfilment of hope). These are not admitted by Lightfoot, but they are cited as examples of what would be properly called an "active" sense of πλήρωμα. That which is usually so called is really passive; for since the action of the verb has an indirect as well as a direct object, the substantive may mean either, "id quo res impletur s. impleta est," or "id quod completur." ναῦς πληροῦν is a familiar phrase for "to man ships," and hence τὸ πλήρωμα and τὰ πληρώματα of ships are the full complement of their crews or fighters, or both, cf. Xen.

Hell. i. 6. 16, ἐκ πολλῶν πληρωμάτων ἐκλελέχθαι τοὺς ἀρίστους ἐρέτας. It is also used of the cargo, as by Philo, *de vita Mosis* (ii. 144), who speaks of τὸ πλ. of the ark. Suidas, too, gives πληρώματα ὁ τῶν νηῶν φόρτος. The passive force in these cases will be more clear if we compare Xen. *Hell.* vi. 2. 14, where Iphicrates τὰς ναῦς ἐπλήρου. The action was that of Iphicrates, but neither he nor his action was πλήρωμα. The word is also used of the ship itself, as in Lucian, *Ver. Hist.* ii. 37, ἀπὸ δύο πληρωμάτων ἐμάχοντο; 38, πέντε γὰρ εἶχον πληρώματα,—a usage explained by Fritzsche from the sense "id quod completur," but more simply as a figure of the same kind as that by which in naval histories the admiral's ship is called "the admiral."

But we want to know the meaning of πλ. with a genitive. There appears to be no example of a ship being called πλ. ἐπιβατῶν or the like. πλήρωμα τῆς πόλεως occurs pretty often, of the full population of the city, or of a combination of artisans, etc. complete enough to form a city (Arist. *Pol.* iv. 4, p. 1291, ταῦτα πάντα, *i.e.* all these workmen, γίνεται πλήρωμα τῆς πρώτης πόλεως. In the Sept. we have πλ. τῆς γῆς, τῆς θαλάσσης, etc., and in Eccles. iv. 6, πλ. δρακός, a handful. In the N.T., still in the same sense, Mk. viii. 20, σπυρίδων πληρώματα. The sense "abundance," often found, does not concern us here. The only example quoted to justify the interpretation of πλ. with a genitive, as = πεπληρωμένον, is from Philo, *De Praem. et Poen.* (ii. p. 418), "The soul by these three excellent things, nature, learning, exercise, γενομένη πλήρωμα ἀρετῶν, leaving in itself no empty space for the entry of other things." But the plural ἀρετῶν here prevents our accepting the passage as a satisfactory parallel to πλ. Χριστοῦ (or Θεοῦ). The article also forms an objection to this interpretation. Since Christ, in the same sentence, is said to fill all things, how can the Church be defined as τὸ πλήρωμα, "that which is filled by Him"? Moreover, there is on this view no such parallelism between σῶμα and πλ. as the supposition would lead us to expect. The idea of the head filling the body is too remote from common notions to be left to the reader to supply.

Fritzsche suggests two alternatives, either "those who are filled by Christ, namely, with blessings," or taking πλ. = "multitudo," "plenum Christi agmen," the paronomasia in the latter case being verbal. Eadie and Ellicott as well as some others do not seem to distinguish the two notions "filled with" and "filled by," calling the Church "the filled-up receptacle of spiritual blessing from Him" (Eadie, adopted by Ell.). If this is their view it is irrelevant to quote πλ. ἀρετῶν or, as Fritzsche, πληροῦσθαι Θεοῦ (from Pollux). If they understand "filled with Christ's presence or life" (as we surely must if this signification of πλ. is adopted), the words just quoted are inadequate.

Lightfoot's view is that "all the divine graces which reside in Him are imparted to her; His fulness is communicated to her; and thus she may be said to be His pleroma." But this thought is not suggested by the connexion, and, besides, the interpretation makes σῶμα and πλήρωμα convey quite heterogeneous ideas.

There is, however, another meaning of πλήρωμα which would give an excellent sense, and which has been adopted by Chrysostom, Oecumenius, Thomas Aquinas, and many others, namely, "complement" in the second sense of that word, viz. that which makes complete. This appears to be the signification in which the word occurs in Matt. ix. 16, Mark ii. 21, where τὸ ἐπίβλημα, the patch put on the old garment, is called τὸ πλήρωμα (although Lightfoot interprets the word otherwise). This agrees with the use of the verb in connexion with χρείαν = to supply (Thucyd.). The expression is then seen to be easy and natural; the Church as the body of Christ is the πλήρωμα or complement of Him, its Head. "He says πλήρωμα," observes Chrysostom, "just as the head is completed by the body, for the body is composed of all the parts and has need of each one. See how he brings Him in as needing all. For unless we be many, and one a hand, another a foot, and another some other part, the whole body is not completed. By all then is His body completed. Then the head is completed, then the body becomes perfect when we are all joined and united together." To this it is objected that it supposes that Christ without the Church would be deficient, since πλήρωμα implies a previous ἥττημα. The objection leaves the figure out of account. When Christ is called Head, the figure implies that however complete He is in Himself, yet as Head He is not complete without His body. As Beza well remarks, "Such is Christ's love for the Church, that He, as it were, regards Himself as incomplete unless He has the Church united to Him as a body"; to which the apostle then adds, τοῦ τὰ πάντα, κ.τ.λ., to express that Christ does not of Himself need this complement, but that, on the contrary, all our completeness is from Him. There is here no inconsistency in thought, although a superficial inconsistency in words, in fact an oxymoron. Amongst recent expositors this view is adopted by Barry.

> Oltramare ably maintains the signification "perfection" for πλήρωμα. τὸ πλήρωμά τινος means "that by which a person or thing is filled," and hence, in speaking of persons, he says it signifies that by which a person is filled, perfected. John i. 16, ἐκ τοῦ πληρώματος αὐτοῦ ἐλάβομεν, i.e. of that with which he is filled,—an allusion to πλήρης χάριτος καὶ ἀληθείας, ver. 14. Usually it refers to qualities with which a person is filled, and which render him perfect, from πληροῦν, "to render perfect (things)," as in Phil. ii. 2, πληρώσατέ μου τὴν χαράν: Eph. iv. 10, ἵνα πληρώσῃ τὰ πάντα: 2 Thess. i. 11, ἵνα ... ὁ Θεὸς ἡμῶν ... πληρώσῃ πᾶσαν εὐδοκίαν ἀγαθωσύνης. So πληροῦσθαι, John iii. 29, ἡ χαρὰ ἡ ἐμὴ πεπλήρωται: xv. 11, ἵνα ... ἡ χαρὰ ὑμῶν πληρωθῇ: 2 Cor. x. 6, ὅταν πληρωθῇ ὑμῶν ἡ ὑπακοή: cf. Eph. iii. 19, v. 18; Col. i. 9. Hence πεπληρωμένος, "made complete, perfect," John xvi. 24,

xvii. 13; Phil. i. 11, πεπλ. καρπὸν δικαιοσύνης, "perfect as regards the fruit," etc., not as in Rec. καρπῶν, "filled with"; Col. ii. 10, ἐστε ἐν αὐτῷ πεπληρωμένοι: Apoc. iii. 2, οὐ γὰρ εὕρηκά σου τὰ ἔργα πεπληρωμένα, κ.τ.λ. Hence πλήρωμα, "perfection,"[1] Eph. iii. 19, ἵνα πληρωθῆτε εἰς πᾶν τὸ πλ. τοῦ Θεοῦ: Col. i. 19, πᾶν τὸ πλήρωμα: ii. 9, πᾶν τὸ πλ. τῆς θεότητος: Eph. iv. 13, τὸ πλ. τοῦ Χριστοῦ. Hence Oltramare renders here "the perfection (objectively, = the perfect work) of Him who makes all perfect." The difficulty in this interpretation is just in the equation "perfection = perfect work." This requires further justification.

We must decidedly reject the exposition which makes πλήρωμα to be in apposition with αὐτόν. This would make ἥτις ἐστιν τὸ σῶμα αὐτοῦ a useless insertion, and worse than useless, as serving only to separate πλ. from ἔδωκεν. Moreover, if the words were to mean "even Him who is," etc., they should come after αὐτόν; as they stand they could only depend on αὐτὸν ἔδωκεν, "gave Him to be πλ.," which does not yield a possible sense.

πληρουμένου, not passive, as Chrys. (see above) and Vulg. (adimpletur), which would make τὰ πάντα ἐν πᾶσι a solecism, but middle. We might interpret the middle here as = "for Himself," but the instance quoted above from Xen. *Hell.* vi. 2. 14, shows that the middle may be used simply in an active signification. The participle refers not to God, as Theodoret suggests, saying τοῦ μὲν Χριστοῦ σῶμα, τοῦ δὲ πατρὸς πλήρωμα, but to Christ, as the parallelism shows as well as iv. 12, where ἵνα πληρώσῃ τὰ πάντα is said of Christ. ἐν πᾶσι "in all" rather than "with all."

II. 1-10. *This exhibition of God's power has not stopped there. He has made us partakers of Christ's resurrection and exaltation, having given us life when we were dead through our sins. Not for any merit of our own, but of His own free grace, for it was when we were dead in our sins that He thus loved us. But though our salvation was not on account of any works of ours, it was God's purpose in His new creation of us that we should walk in the path of holiness which He designed.*

1. καὶ ὑμᾶς from its position means "and you, too." Resumed in ver. 5, where first the verb συνεζωοποίησε is expressed. Some commentators, indeed, have closely connected this with the preceding verse, so as to make ὑμᾶς depend on πληρουμένου. But the relation between νεκρούς and συνεζ. is decisive against this. Lachmann, while taking ὑμᾶς to be dependent on συνεζ., puts only a comma after i. 23, so as to co-ordinate καὶ (συνεζ.) ὑμᾶς with αὐτὸν ἔδωκε. But in this case we should certainly expect ἡμᾶς here, since the apostle would be passing from what God has done with respect to Christ, to what He has done to Christians; cf. i. 19, εἰς ἡμᾶς τοὺς πιστ. Moreover, i. 23 has the character of a solemn close, not of a parenthetical insertion; while the exposition which begins in ii. 1 is too important to be regarded as a

[1] Compare Plutarch, *De Plac. Phil.* i. 7. 9, ἤτοι ἐνέλειπεν εἰς εὐδαιμονίαν ἢ ἐπεπλήρωτο ἐν μακαριότητι, "either he lacked something for happiness, or he was complete in happiness."

mere appendage to the foregoing. Hence, also, it is not a mere exemplification of the general act of grace referred to in i. 23. Rather are we to understand that the apostle, having spoken of the exceeding power of God towards those that believe, which might be recognised by reflection on what He had done in raising and exalting Christ, now, applying this to his readers, reminds them that in them also God had shown that exceeding power (Meyer). The grammatical structure is interrupted before the subject or the verb is expressed. It is taken up again with δέ in ver. 4, where the subject is expressed, and in ver. 5 the object is repeated, which, however, is now changed to the first person in consequence of the καὶ ἡμεῖς introduced in ver. 3.

ὄντας νεκροὺς τοῖς παραπτώμασιν καὶ ταῖς ἁμαρτίαις ὑμῶν. ὑμῶν is added with ℵ B D G, Syr. (both) Vulg., Theodoret, etc. It is omitted by K L, most cursives, Chrys. Oec. A has ἑαυτῶν ὄντας ν., "dead as ye were through your trespasses and sins." Many attempts have been made to distinguish between ἁμαρτίαι and παραπτώματα. Tittmann, following Augustine's distinction (*ad Lev.* qu. 20), supposes the former to be deliberate sins, the latter sins of thoughtlessness. Augustine himself in the same place suggests a different view, viz. that π. meant "desertio boni," and ἁμ. "perpetratio mali." He seems then to have been guessing. Certainly these distinctions are both untenable. Jerome takes παρ. to refer to the beginnings of sin in thought, ἁμ. to the actual deeds, which is not admissible. Many understand ἁμ., which is the more general term, as meant to include the sinful disposition, παρ. being only concrete acts. However reasonable this may be with the singular ἁμαρτία, it can hardly be maintained of the plural. Etymology gives no help, for παραπίπτω means to fall or go aside from, to miss, *e.g.* τῆς ὁδοῦ, Polyb. iii. 54. 5; τῆς ἀληθείας, *ib.* xii. 7. 2, also without a genitive, to err. So that etymologically παρ. is the same as ἁμαρτία. St. Paul appears to use the words as synonymous, see Rom. v. 20, ἵνα πλεονάσῃ τὸ παράπτωμα; οὗ δὲ ἐπλεόνασεν ἡ ἁμαρτία, κ.τ.λ. Comp. also Rom. iv. 25 with 1 Cor. xv. 3.

νεκρούς is here taken by Meyer to mean liable to eternal death. That νεκροί may be used proleptically appears from Rom. viii. 10. In that case the dative is instrumental. But this is hard to reconcile with the tense of συνεζωοποίησε. And surely it is very improbable that the apostle in speaking of the working of God's power towards them, would mention only their future deliverance from death, and not their actual deliverance from spiritual death. Nor could the readers fail to think of spiritual death. This sense is sufficiently indicated by τοῖς παρ. κ.τ.λ., as well as by the following verse. So Chrysostom, εἰς ἔσχατον κακίας ἠλάσατε (τοῦτο γάρ ἐστι νεκρωθῆναι). This figure of spiritual (or moral) death is frequent amongst the ancients. Clement of Alexandria says that ἐν τῇ βαρβάρῳ φιλοσοφίᾳ νεκροὺς καλοῦσι τοὺς ἐκπεσόντας τῶν δογμάτων καὶ καθυποτάξαντας τὸν νοῦν τοῖς πάθεσι τοῖς ψυχικοῖς. The Jewish Rabbis have similar expressions. But Christianity has given a much deeper meaning to "death" in this connexion. We have the same phrase in Col. ii. 13, where ἐν is not part of the genuine text, and τῇ ἀκροβυστίᾳ τῆς σαρκὸς ὑμῶν is against the mere instrumental sense of the dative. It expresses that in which the death consisted.

2. ἐν αἷς refers to both substantives, though agreeing in gender with the nearer. περιπατεῖν in this sense is a Hebraism. The figure has disappeared, so that we are not to press the preposition as if marking "the walk which they trod"; see Rom. xiii. 13, περιπατήσωμεν, μὴ κώμοις καὶ μέθαις, κ.τ.λ., and the parallel use of πορεύεσθαι, Acts ix. 31, π. τῷ φόβῳ τοῦ κυρίου. It is of frequent occurrence in St. Paul and St. John, but is not found in St. James or St. Peter, who use ἀναστρέφεσθαι (a classical word, though not before Polybius); cf. 1 Pet. i. 17.

κατὰ τὸν αἰῶνα τοῦ κόσμου τούτου. "In accordance with the course of this world." This combination of αἰών and κόσμος creates some difficulty. Elsewhere we have ὁ αἰὼν οὗτος (1 Cor. i. 20, ii. 6, iii. 18, etc.), or ὁ κόσμος οὗτος, 1 Cor. iii. 19. ἡ σοφία τοῦ κ. τούτου in the latter passage being synonymous with ἡ σοφία τοῦ αἰ. τούτου in 1 Cor. ii. 6. But the two substantives are not synonymous; αἰών means a period of time; κόσμος, the world existing in that period. Thus Antoninus (ii. 12) says that all things quickly vanish, τῷ μὲν κόσμῳ αὐτὰ τὰ σώματα, τῷ δὲ αἰῶνι αἱ μνῆμαι αὐτῶν. The signification "life," frequent in classical Greek, especially in the tragic poets, is never found in the N.T. As a paraphrase, however, "spirit of the age" fairly represents the sense, except that "age" refers to the whole period of this κόσμος. Comp. Tacitus, "corrumpere et corrumpi saeculum vocatur" (*Germ.* i. 9). αἰών being a technical word with the Gnostics, it was to be expected that some expositors would adopt a similar meaning here. Accordingly, this has been done by Michaelis, who supposes the words αἰὼν τοῦ κ. τ. to mean "the devil," with a polemic reference to the Gnostic aeons; and by Baur, who regards the expression itself as Gnostic, and equivalent to κοσμοκράτωρ, vi. 12, meaning "the devil." Holtzmann regards it as representing a transition stage between Paulinism and Gnosticism. As the ordinary signification of αἰών yields a perfectly good and Pauline sense, there is no ground for such hypotheses. If the devil were intended to be designated here as ruler of this world, we might expect some such expression as ὁ θεὸς τοῦ αἰῶνος τούτου, as in 2 Cor. iv. 4.

κατὰ τὸν ἄρχοντα τῆς ἐξουσίας τοῦ ἀέρος. Most expositors take ἐξ. here collectively = αἱ ἐξουσίαι, understanding τοῦ ἀέρος as expressing the sphere of their existence. Such words as συμμαχία for σύμμαχοι, δουλεία for δοῦλοι, πρεσβεία for πρέσβεις, etc., exemplify this collective use of abstract for concrete terms. So occasionally in English, as "embassy," "flight" (of arrows). The present case, however, is not quite parallel, since the distribution for which ἐξ. is supposed to stand is the plural of this word itself, viz. αἱ ἐξουσίαι. This implies that the singular might be used of one of the ἐξουσίαι; cf. Rom. xiii. 2, 3, where, however, ἡ ἐξ. does not mean a ruling person. To use it collectively for αἱ ἐξ. is, therefore, very different from using ἡ συμμαχία for οἱ σύμμαχοι. Besides, we must not assume that the word can be treated apart from the following genitive. ὁ ἄρχων is defined, not by τῆς ἐξ., but by τῆς ἐξ. τοῦ ἀέρος. For this reason, too, we cannot take τ. ἐ. as a genitive of apposition = "princeps potentissimus." Now, the genitive following ἐξουσία is elsewhere either subjective, as ἡ ἐξ. τοῦ σατανᾶ, Acts xxvi. 18; τοῦ ἡγεμόνος, Lk. xx. 20; ὑμῶν, 1 Cor. viii. 9; or objective, πάσης σαρκός, John xvii. 2; πνευμάτων, Matt. x. 1; ὑμῶν, 1 Cor. ix. 12. It is possible, therefore, to understand the words as meaning "the ruler to whom belongs the power over the region of the air"; but this would create a difficulty in connexion with πνεύματος. It is therefore perhaps best to take ἡ ἐξ. τοῦ ἀ. as the power whose seat is in the air. Some commentators take ἀήρ here as = σκότος; and if this were possible we should have obvious parallels in vi. 12, κοσμοκράτορας τοῦ σκότους τούτου, and Col. i. 13, τῆς ἐξουσίας τοῦ σκότους. But although ἀήρ is used in Homer and elsewhere of "thick air" in contrast to αἰθήρ, as in Plutarch (of the first creation), ἔτι μὲν οὐρανὸν ἔκρυπτεν ἀήρ (*De esu carn. Or.* I. § 2), it does not appear that it can be used simply for σκότος, nor again that if so used figuratively, it could by another figure be used of spiritual darkness. What, then, does the expression mean? Oecumenius' view is that as the rule of Satan is under heaven, not above, it must be either in the earth or the air; but, being a spirit, it must be in the air, φύσις γὰρ τοῖς πνεύμασιν ἡ ἐναέριος διατριβή; and this is adopted by Harless and others. The air being understood to mean, not merely the region of the atmosphere, but "all that supra-terrestrial, but sub-celestial, region, which seems to be, if not the abode, yet the haunt of evil spirits," Ellicott, who compares Job i. 7 LXX, ἐμπεριπατήσαν τὴν ὑπ' οὐρανόν, which surely is not to be appealed to as giving any light. Eadie ingeniously suggests that "the ἀήρ and κόσμος must correspond in relation. As there is an atmosphere round the physical globe, so air, ἀήρ, envelops this spiritual κόσμος,"— an atmosphere "in which it breathes and moves." Compare our own phrases in which "atmosphere" is used figuratively, "an atmosphere of flattery," etc. But if such a figure were intended, some word must be added which would indicate the figure, such as the words "breathes and moves" in Eadie's explanation. Indeed, he admits that it is perhaps too ingenious to be true, and falls back on the alternative that either the apostle used current language, which did not convey error, as Satan is called Beelzebub, without reference to the meaning of the term "Lord of flies," or that he means to convey the idea of "near propinquity," or alludes to what he had more fully explained during his residence at Ephesus. That the notion of the air being the dwelling-place of spirits, and specially of evil spirits, was current, appears to be beyond doubt. Thus Pythagoras held εἶναι πάντα τὸν ἀέρα ψυχῶν ἔμπλεων (Diog. L. viii. 32). Philo says, οὓς ἄλλοι φιλόσοφοι δαίμονας, ἀγγέλους Μωσῆς εἴωθεν ὀνομάζειν· ψυχαὶ δ᾽ εἰσὶ κατὰ τὸν ἀέρα πετόμεναι. In the *Test. XII. Patr.* it is said of ὁ δεύτερος οὐρανός that it has fire, snow, ice ready for the day of the Lord's command, ἐν αὐτῷ εἰσὶ πάντα τὰ πνεύματα τῶν ἐπαγωγῶν εἰς ἐκδίκησιν τῶν ἀνόμων (Levi, *ap. Fabric. Cod. Apoc. V.T.* p. 547), and in *Test.* Benj. p. 729, Βελιάρ is called τὸ ἀέριον πνεῦμα. Drusius cites from the commentary on Aboth, "sciendum, a terra usque ad expansum omnia plena esse turmis et praefectis et infra plurimas esse creaturas credentes et accusantes, omnesque stare ac volitare in aere . . . quorum alii ad bonum, alii ad malum incitant." There is no difficulty in supposing that St. Paul is here alluding to such current notions. Nor are we to suppose that he is conveying any special revelation about the matter. Harless' objection, that according to the views referred to, the air was inhabited by good spirits as well as bad, is by no means fatal, since it is on the bad spirits that men's thoughts would chiefly dwell, and to them would be referred evil suggestions and desires.

τοῦ πνεύματος is understood by some (including Rückert and De Wette) as in apposition with τὸν ἄρχοντα. Winer, while rejecting this view, admits that in this case the apostle might most easily have wandered from the right construction, namely, on account of the preceding genitives. It is, however, unnecessary to suppose this, although it must be conceded that the only admissible alternative, viz. that πν. depends on ἄρχοντα, is more harsh as to sense, although the harshness is lessened by the distance from ἄρχοντα. Adopting this, the sense is, "the ruler of the spirit," etc. Here πνεῦμα is not to be understood collectively, which it cannot be: it is what in 1 Cor. ii. 12 is called τὸ πνεῦμα τοῦ κόσμου, the spiritual influence which works in the disobedient. It seems to be a sort of explanation of the preceding ἐξουσία.

νῦν. Not "even now," which would require καὶ νῦν, but in contrast to ποτέ, when this spirit operated in the readers also.

ἐν τοῖς υἱοῖς τῆς ἀπειθείας. A Hebrew form of expression. We have "son of misery," Prov. xxxi. 5; "sons of iniquity," 2 Sam. vii. 10; "sons of Belial (= worthlessness)." Compare ch. v. 6;

Col. iii. 6; 1 Thess. v. 5 ("sons of light"); 2 Thess. ii. 3 ("son of perdition"). Greek authors used the expression παῖδες ζωγράφων and the like, but not with abstracts. The opposite to υἱοὶ ἀπ. is τέκνα ὑπακοῆς, 1 Pet. i. 14. ἀπείθεια is not unbelief, but disobedience; compare Rom. xi. 30, καὶ ὑμεῖς ποτὲ ἠπειθήσατε τῷ Θεῷ. Chrysostom very curiously says, ὁρᾷς ὅτι οὐ βίᾳ οὐδὲ τυραννίδι ἀλλὰ πειθοῖ προσάγεται; ἀπείθειαν γὰρ εἶπεν, ὡς ἄν τις εἴποι, ἀπάτῃ καὶ πειθοῖ τοὺς πάντας ἐφέλκεται. But on Col. iii. 6 he says, δεικνὺς ὅτι παρὰ τὸ μὴ πεισθῆναι ἐν τούτοις εἰσιν. The former remark looks more like a rhetorical play on words than a serious comment.

3. **ἐν οἷς καὶ ἡμεῖς. καὶ ἡμεῖς,** "we also, we too." Having spoken specially of the Gentiles in the preceding verses, the apostle now passes to the Jews. The πάντες is certainly no objection to this. "Even amongst us (the chosen people) there was no exception." What more natural than to say "all of us also." If πάντες included both Jews and Gentiles, ἡμεῖς would be quite superfluous; and the emphatic καὶ ἡμεῖς would be unintelligible if it included ὑμεῖς of vv. 1 and 2. ἐν οἷς is connected by Stier with παραπτώμασιν (which he thinks appropriate to Jews, as ἁμαρτίαις to Gentiles). His reasons are, first, that as υἱοὶ τῆς ἀπ. are the heathen, not all the unbelieving, it would not be suitable to reckon the Jews amongst them; secondly, that the harshness of supposing that ἐν just now used with ἐνεργοῦντος is immediately used with the same object in a different signification; and thirdly, that the parallelism of 2 and 3 compels us to take ἐν αἷς and ἐν οἷς as parallel. With the reading ὑμῶν adopted above in ver. 1 it is impossible thus to separate παρ. from ἁμ. It might more plausibly be maintained that οἷς refers to both substantives, the feminine having been adopted only because ἁμ. was the nearest substantive, and the neuter being used where that reason does not exist. But we cannot well avoid referring the relative to the nearest antecedent when that gives a suitable sense, and the change of verb from περιπατεῖν to ἀναστρέφεσθαι, which is more suitable if οἷς be persons, is in favour of this; "amongst whom we also," belonging to the same class of the disobedient.

ἀνεστράφημεν. "Versabamur," "lived our life"; "speciosius quam ambulare," Bengel, but rather perhaps adopted because περιπατεῖν ἐν τοῖς υἱοῖς could not be said.

ἐν ταῖς ἐπιθυμίαις τῆς σαρκός. σάρξ, though primarily signifying the matter of the body, and hence the appetites arising from the body, is not to be limited to these, but includes the whole of the lower or psychical nature. In Rom. vii. it appears in the natural man as opposed to νοῦς or ἐγώ in the higher sense; in Rom. viii. in the regenerate it is opposed to πνεῦμα. Amongst the works of σάρξ are "strifes," etc., Gal. v. 19, 22. Compare Col. ii. 18, "puffed up by the νοῦς of his σάρξ." The ἐπιθυμίαι of the flesh are therefore not merely the bodily appetites, but in general what Butler calls "particular propensions." So here it includes σάρξ proper and διάνοιαι.

ποιοῦντες τὰ θελήματα, κ.τ.λ., expresses the result in act of the ἐπιθυμίαι; there is no tautology. Διάνοιαι is not found elsewhere with a bad signification. In classical authors διάνοια means the understanding, or a thought or purpose. In Aristotle virtue is προαίρεσις μετὰ λόγου καὶ διανοίας. The plural also is used by Plutarch in a good sense. In the N.T. it occurs frequently in a good sense, 1 Pet. i. 13, "girding up the loins of your δ."; 2 Pet. iii. 1, "I stir up your pure δ."; 1 John v. 20, "hath given us a δ."; cf. also ch. i. 18. Harless conjectures that the plural here is used in the sense common in Greek writers, viz. purpose, the plural suggesting vacillation; and he compares the use of σοφίαι in Aristoph. *Ran.*, and "sapientiae" in Cic. *Tusc.* iii. 18. But this is too refined. It deserves notice that in ch. iv. 18 and Col. i. 20, St. Paul speaks of his readers having been "darkened in their διάνοια," and "enemies in their δ." Here, while by no means admitting a hendiadys, "cogitationes carnales," we must at least allow that διανοιῶν acquires its bad signification from the preceding σαρκός, so that it nearly = "the σάρξ and its διάνοιαι."

καὶ ἤμεθα τέκνα φύσει ὀργῆς. This order, which is that of the Text. Rec., is established by ℵ B K etc., Chrys. Lachmann adopted φύσει τέκνα, with A D G L P, Vulg. Syr-Harcl.

The change from the participle to the finite verb need occasion no difficulty; it is, in fact, required by the sense. Had ὄντες been written it would be co-ordinate with ποιοῦντες and subordinate to ἀνεστράφημεν, and explanatory of it, "doing the desires . . . and being the children . . ." Whatever view is taken of the latter clause, these two are not co-ordinate. Not merely, therefore, for emphasis, but because the latter is a distinct predication, co-ordinate with ἐν οἷς ἀνεστρ., or, more exactly, expressing a consequence of that, the verb is in the indicative,—"and so we were."

τέκνα ὀργῆς is understood by many as = actual objects of God's wrath, τέκνα being used as suitable to Israel, and then by a sort of irony is added, not "of Abraham" or "of God," but "by nature of wrath." There could be no objection to such an interpretation if it corresponded with the context; but here, if the actual wrath of God were intended, we should expect it to be defined by Θεοῦ or the article, or otherwise. But how strange, if not impossible, would be the expression "children of God's wrath"; and especially so here, where in the same breath they are described as at the same time objects of God's love, without anything to soften the apparent opposition! Nor can it be said that this is at all implied in the word τέκνα. On the contrary, we have several instances in the Old Testament in which "son of" followed by a word denoting punishment cannot reasonably be given any other meaning than either "worthy of," or "in danger of." Thus Deut. xxv. 2, "If the wicked man be a son of stripes, the judge shall ... cause him to be beaten before his face," etc.: rightly rendered in the Sept. ἐὰν ἄξιος ᾖ πληγῶν. 1 Sam. xxvi. 16 (David to Abner), "Ye are sons of death, because ye have not kept watch over your lord." 2 Sam. xii. 5 (David to Nathan), "The man that hath done this is a son of death." In these two passages the RV. has correctly "worthy to die," and in the former no other interpretation is possible. In 1 Sam. xx. 31, RV. has in the text (with AV.) "shall surely die," but in the margin "is worthy to die." In Ps. lxxix. 11 and cii. 20, "sons of death" are "those who are in danger of death."

These instances, together with the indefiniteness of ὀργῆς, justify us in understanding the words to mean "objects, *i.e.* fit objects of wrath," "deserving of wrath." And so they are interpreted by Chrysostom, "We have provoked God to wrath, τουτέστιν, ὀργὴ ἦμεν καὶ οὐδὲν ἕτερον" (explaining that he who is ἀνθρώπου τέκνον is ἄνθρωπος). "πάντες ἐπράττομεν ἄξια ὀργῆς." Similarly Oecumenius, "As those who do things worthy of perdition or of hell are called τέκνα ἀπωλείας καὶ γεέννης [*e.g.* 2 Thess. ii. 3; Matt. xxiii. 15] οὕτω καὶ τέκνα ὀργῆς οἱ ἄξια ὀργῆς."

Why is φύσει inserted? This question does not seem hard to answer. It must first be remarked that φύσει is opposed sometimes to νόμος, sometimes to θέσις, ἀνάγκη, etc., but does not necessarily mean "by birth." Rom. ii. 14, the Gentiles do φύσει τὰ τοῦ νόμου; 1 Cor. xi. 14, ἡ φύσις teaches that if a man have long hair it is a shame. Josephus says of David that he was φύσει δίκαιος καὶ θεοσεβής (*Ant.* vii. 7. 1), and of the Pharisees φύσει ἐπιεικῶς ἔχουσιν (xiii. 10. 6). We have φύσει φιλογεωργότατος in Xen. *Occ.* xx. 25. Compare also Philo, *De Conf. Ling.* p. 327 E, ἀλλ᾽ οὐκ ἀντιλογικοὶ γεγόνασιν ὅσοι τῆς ἐπιστήμης καὶ ἀρετῆς ζῆλον ἔσχον. It is, in fact, used like our word "naturally." Here the opposition suggested might be to χάριτι; but as the Jews are in question, it is more probably to θέσει, their covenant position as the people of God, by which they were holy branches of a holy root, to whom belonged the υἱοθεσία (Rom. xi. 16, 21). "We Jews, too, just as the heathen, were, apart from the covenant, τέκνα ὀργῆς."

> From the time of Augustine these words have been supposed by many to contain a direct assertion of original sin. Thus Calvin, "Paulus nos cum peccato gigni testatur, quemadmodum serpentes suum venenum ex utero afferunt."
> But, first, this gives a very great emphasis to φύσει, which its position forbids. Secondly, it supposes καὶ ἤμεθα to refer to, or at least include, a time prior to ἐν οἷς ἄν., which seems not possible. Thirdly, it does not harmonise with the context. That treats of actual sin (including, of course, character), and the immediate context of the Jews only. It would be natural

and intelligible that this description should be followed by mention of the wrath thereby incurred; it would also be intelligible, though less natural, that it should be followed by a statement that in addition to this we inherited a sinful and guilty nature. The interpretation in question supposes that neither of these is mentioned; the wrath incurred by actual sin is omitted, while that incurred by birth sin is mentioned without mention of its cause, which is left to be inferred. And fourthly, even this is stated expressly only of the Jews; it is assumed as self-evident of the Gentiles, οἱ λοιποί. The reader has to fill up the sentence somewhat in this way, "We fulfilled the desires of the flesh [and thus became objects of God's wrath; and, in addition to this, we were even before committing any actual sin inheritors of a sinful nature, and so] already by nature objects of His wrath."

It is true, indeed, that men are born with a sinful and corrupt nature; but to say this is not to say that the infant who has committed no actual sin is an actual object of God's wrath; still less does it prove that the apostle's words here imply it. Chrysostom has no trace of such an interpretation; in fact he seems even to regard these words as guarding against a similar interpretation of θελήματα σαρκός. "That is [he says], οὐδὲν πνευματικὸν φρονοῦντες. But that he may not be suspected of saying this in disparagement of the flesh, and lest one should think the offence not great, see how he guards himself. Fulfilling the desires, etc.; he (the apostle) says, we provoked God"; adding what has been quoted above. Jerome gives as alternatives, "Vel propter corpus humilitatis corpusque mortis et quod ab adolescentia mens hominum apposita sit ad malum." "Vel quod ex eo tempore quo possumus habere notitiam Dei, et ad pubertatem venimus, omnes aut opere aut lingua aut cogitatione peccemus." He mentions some who took φύσει here to mean "prorsus"; cf. ἀληθῶς or γνησίως, Oecum.; but the word never has this meaning.

οἱ λοιποί, the heathen, cf. 1 Thess. iv. 13.

4. ὁ δὲ Θεός resumes from ver. 1 after the interruption, and now with the subject; οὖν is more usual in such a resumption; but δέ is more suitable here, on account of the contrast of what is now to be said with what precedes. Jerome's comment is characteristic, "Conjunctionem causalem in eo loco in quo ait: Deus autem etc. arbitramur aut ab indoctis scriptoribus additum et vitium inolevisse paulatim, aut ab ipso Paulo, qui erat imperitus sermone et non scientia, superflue usurpatum." Erasmus' remark is more correct, "Hyperbati longioris ambitum ipse correxit Apostolus."

πλούσιος ὢν ἐν ἐλέει, "being as He is" (the participle assigning the reason), not simply ἐλεήμων, but "rich in mercy" (Chrys.). Compare Rom. ix. 23, "make known the riches of His glory on σκεύη ἐλέους." In classical writers πλούσιος is construed with a genitive of the thing, but in the N.T. with ἐν, see Jas. ii. 5, ἐν πίστει; and similarly the verbs πλουτεῖν, πλουτίζεσθαι (1 Cor. i. 5). Compare the correspondence of ἔλεος and ἀπείθεια in Rom. xi. 31. ἀγάπη is not a particular form of ἔλεος, but is the cause from which, or by reason of which, ἔλεος was exercised.

διὰ τὴν πολλὴν ἀγάπην, "propter," Vulg. "for His great love"; cf. Philem. 8, "for love's sake." ἥν, cognate accusative, a very common usage, both in classical and N.T. Greek. Here the

II. 5] QUICKENED WITH CHRIST 47

addition ἦν ἠγ. ἡμᾶς, being not necessary to the sense, gives great emphasis to the expression of the Divine love. Nor is αὐτοῦ to be neglected, "His love" marking more distinctly that it is from Him alone and His attitude of love that this mercy proceeds.

ἡμᾶς now includes both the ὑμεῖς of ver. 1 and the ἡμᾶς of ver. 3, and includes therefore both Jews and Gentiles.

5. καὶ ὄντας ἡμᾶς νεκρούς. The καί does not signify "us also altogether," which is forbidden by the position of ἡμᾶς (not καὶ ἡμᾶς), and for the same reason it does not resume the καί of ver. 1. It is best taken as "Even," "Even when we were dead," etc. It is objected, indeed, that it is only the dead who can be "brought to life," and for this reason Meyer takes καί as the copula, "on account of His great love, and when we were dead"; but these two ideas are not co-ordinate. Soden, for the same reason, joins the words with the preceding, "loved us even when," etc. This, no doubt, gives a good sense, although the antithesis between "loved" and "when dead" is not very natural, whereas that between νεκρούς and ἐζωοποίησε is striking. Besides, the proposed construction would require ἡμᾶς to be expressed with συνεζ. not with ὄντας, since ἠγάπησεν already has its object expressed. But the objection is hypercritical. The answer to it is, not that νεκ. is qualified by τοῖς παραπτ. which has no emphasis, nor that συνεζ. is defined by ἐν Χριστῷ. The true answer is found in the position of the verb. "Gave life even to the dead" would not be a natural mode of expression, but "Even the dead He restored to life" is perfectly natural. The καὶ ὄντας, κ.τ.λ. attracts the reader's attention to some striking instance of God's love about to be mentioned. Comp. Col. ii. 13, where the connexion is unambiguous. Indeed, it is not quite true that ζωοποιεῖν can be only of the dead. See John vi. 63 compared with ver. 54; also 1 Cor. xv. 36; 2 Cor. iii. 6.

τοῖς παραπτώμασιν = our trespasses, the trespasses already mentioned in ver. 1.

συνεζωοποίησε τῷ Χριστῷ.

> B adds ἐν after the verb with 17 Arm. and some other authorities,—a reading admitted to the margin by Westcott and Hort, and in brackets by Lachmann. It might, with equal ease, be omitted or inserted accidentally. There could be no reason for intentional omission, but it might be added intentionally from the construction being mistaken. It is observable that B, Arm. also insert ἐν after νεκροῖς, if, indeed, a version can be safely cited in such a case. Internal evidence is against ἐν, as we get a better sense by taking Χριστῷ as dependent on συν.

Meyer, having understood νεκρούς to refer to future eternal death, of course understands συνεζ. as referring to the eternal life which begins with the resurrection. This view he regards as alone consistent with the context in which the translation into heaven is expressed, and again in ver. 7 the times after the Parousia are referred to. His view then is, that God has made believers alive with Christ; that is, that by virtue of the dynamic connexion of Christ with His believers as the Head with its body, their revivification is objectively included in His; "quum autem fides suscipitur ea omnia a Deo applicantur homini et ab homine rata habentur," Bengel. The apostle therefore views this as having already taken place, although the subjective individual participation remains future, and he might have used the future as in 1 Cor. xv. 22. The peculiar use of the aorist here he refers to the principle thus stated by Fritzsche (on Rom. viii. 30, ii. p. 206), "Ponitur Aoristus de re, quae, quamvis futura sit, tamen pro peractâ recte censeatur, quum vel aliâ re jam factâ contineatur, ut h. l., vel a conditione suspensa cogitetur, quam jam obtinuisse finxeris, v. Hom. *Il.* iv. 161; John xv. 6." This usage was first explained by Hermann, "De emend. ratione graecae gr." pp. 190 ff., but, as stated by him, does not apply here.

Of the two passages to which Fritzsche after Hermann refers, that from Homer is, says Hermann, the only instance known to me in which it may be reasonably questioned whether the aorist has not the signification of the future, viz. Hom. *Il.* iv. 160–162. It is as follows :—

> εἴπερ γάρ τε καὶ αὐτίκ' Ὀλύμπιος οὐκ ἐτέλεσσεν,
> ἔκ τε καὶ ὀψὲ τελεῖ, σύν τε μεγάλῳ ἀπέτισαν,
> σὺν σφῆσιν κεφαλῇσι γυναιξί τε καὶ τεκέεσσιν.

Here the poet throws himself forward into the time of the verb τελεῖ, and sees the instantaneous carrying out of this vindication of oaths; as if he said, "And, lo! at once they have paid the penalty." "Rem futuram non ut futuram sed ut praeteritam narrat: nimirum post quam Troianos punierit Iuppiter tum illi poenas dederunt" (Hermann). The other example is from John xv. 6, ἐὰν μή τις μείνῃ ἐν ἐμοί, ἐβλήθη ἔξω ὡς τὸ κλῆμα, καὶ ἐξηράνθη. Here also a condition is expressed from which the consequence necessarily follows. Similarly Epictetus, cap. 59, ἂν ὑπὲρ δύναμιν ἀναλάβῃς τι πρόσωπον. καὶ ἐν τούτῳ ἠσχημόνησας, καὶ ὃ ἠδύνασο ἐκπληρῶσαι, παρέλιπες (see Jelf, § 403). In the present passage, if συνεζ. is referred to the future, there is no resemblance to these instances. We have already seen, however, that νεκρούς includes present spiritual death, and that indeed as its primary notion, although it cannot be limited to that, since the consequence, natural and eternal death, is necessarily suggested with it. Accordingly, the vivification, though primarily spiritual, includes in it our share in the resurrection and exaltation of Christ. In i. 20, 21 the writer has pointed to the resurrection and exaltation of Christ as an exhibition of Divine power; here he declares that by virtue of our union with Him as of members with the head, we participate in the same. "Quamvis salus nostra in spe sit adhuc abscondita quantum ad nos spectat: in Christo nihilominus beatam immortalitatem possidemus," Calvin. Col. ii. 13 is closely parallel. The fact that baptism is there referred to as the means by which the individual entered subjectively into fellowship with Christ, and is not mentioned here, does not justify the adoption of a different meaning for συνεζ. here, such as that of Harless, whose view is that the risen life and glorification of Christ are here spoken of as ours, because they are the glory of "our" Redeemer.

Chrysostom's comment is: εἰ ἡ ἀπαρχὴ ζῇ, καὶ ἡμεῖς· ἐζωοποίησε κἀκεῖνον καὶ ἡμᾶς, to which Theophylact adds: ἐκεῖνον ἐνεργείᾳ, ἡμᾶς δυνάμει νῦν, μετ' ὀλίγον δὲ καὶ ἐνεργείᾳ. συν- clearly "with Christ," Col. ii. 13.

χάριτί ἐστε σεσωσμένοι. "It is by grace that ye have been saved,"—a lively parenthetical reminder suggested by the preceding words, and vindicating the expression "vivified when dead." Being dead, ye could do nothing of yourselves, so that it must needs be all by grace, *i.e.* simply by God's free gift. We are so accustomed to use "grace" in a technical theological sense, that we are prone to think of that sense where it does not really come in. This technical sense of "grace" as something conferred is not in question here, and any reference to the distinction between prevenient and co-operating grace, etc., is out of place. The word is used just as in royal letters the words "by our special grace and mere motion."

D G, Vulg. *al.* prefix οὗ (D οὗ τῇ) to χάριτι.

The perfect ἐστε σεσωσμένοι here is in striking contrast with the aorist ἐσώθημεν in Rom. viii. 24, τῇ γὰρ ἐλπίδι ἐσ. But the perfect is as suitable here as it would have been unsuitable there, where it would contradict ἐλπίδι. Then, what was to be said had reference to the definite moment of the readers' introduction into the Christian Church, and the point was that the σωτηρία obtained at that definite moment was in part a matter of hope. Here it is not a past moment that is in question, as if χάρις was over and done with, but the readers' present condition as the continuing result of their conversion. In one sense their σωτηρία was complete, viz. regarded with respect to that from which they were delivered; in another incomplete, viz. with respect to that which was reserved for them. So to persons rescued from a wreck, but not yet arrived in port, we might say either ἐσώθητε or σεσωσμένοι ἐστε.

6. συνήγειρε is nearly synonymous with συνεζωοποίησε, but suggests more distinctly physical resurrection. In Col. iii. 1, as here, the ἐγερθῆναι σὺν Χριστῷ is treated as past, and is made the motive

for seeking those things which are above, ". . . for ye died, and your life is hid with Christ in God." The present passage expresses this more vividly and strikingly, συνεκάθισεν ἐν τοῖς ἐπουρανίοις. "Non dicit in dextra; Christo sua manet excellentia," Bengel (and so Estius less tersely). ἐν τοῖς ἐπ. denotes the true or ideal locality of the Church as the "kingdom of heaven." Comp. Heb. xii. 22, προσεληλύθατε . . . πόλει Θεοῦ ζῶντος, Ἰερουσαλὴμ ἐπουρανίῳ.

ἐν Χριστῷ after συν- has caused some perplexity, and led some commentators to understand the συν- in ver. 6 (not in ver. 5) as joining ὑμεῖς and ἡμεῖς together. But it seems better to understand ἐν Χ. as completing and defining with more precision what was intended by σύν, for it is not simply together with Christ that this vivification and exaltation takes place, but also *in* Him, by virtue of union with Him as the Head.

7. ἵνα ἐνδείξηται. The middle does not mean "for His own glory," nor does the language of the verse suggest the idea of showing as a sample or specimen. The verb seldom occurs in the active voice except as a legal expression, never in N.T. The middle involves no more than is already contained in αὐτοῦ, as the instances show: Rom. ii. 15, "show the work of the law written in their hearts"; 2 Cor. viii. 24, "showing the ἔνδειξις of your love and of our boasting"; 2 Tim. iv. 14, "Alexander the coppersmith πολλά μοι κακὰ ἐνεδείξατο." See also Tit. ii. 10, iii. 2; Heb. vi. 10, 11. These instances also show that the word means, not "make known," but "exhibit in fact or act."

ἐν τοῖς αἰῶσι τοῖς ἐπερχομένοις. "In the coming ages." It seems more suitable to the context, as well as to the use of parallel expressions, to understand this of the future life, ὁ αἰὼν ὁ μέλλων, in which the state described in the preceding words will be actually realised and made manifest. The present participle is not against this, for in Mark x. 30 we have ὁ αἰὼν ὁ ἐρχόμενος in this sense. The plural may at first sight seem against it, but is not really so; it only indicates that the apostle viewed the future age as involving stages of development in which the exceeding riches of God's grace will be more and more clearly manifested, and that becomes actual, the knowledge of which is mentioned as the object of desire in i. 18. Compare the frequent expression εἰς τοὺς αἰῶνας τῶν αἰώνων, also Jude 25, εἰς πάντας τοὺς αἰῶνας; and the remarkable expression, 1 Tim. i. 17, τῷ βασιλεῖ τῶν αἰώνων. These αἰῶνες may be regarded as constituting a whole in contrast to the present life, and so be named in the singular ὁ αἰ. ὁ μέλλων.

τὸ ὑπερβάλλον πλοῦτος τῆς χάριτος αὐτοῦ. The neuter πλοῦτος is best supported here. In modern Greek the word is indifferently masculine or neuter.

ἐν χρηστότητι ἐφ' ἡμᾶς. These words are to be so connected,

not ὑπερβάλλον ἐφ' ἡμᾶς. To exhibit χάρις in χρηστότης would be tautological. Nor is the absence of the article any objection, for χρηστότης implies, not merely an inherent quality, but one which involves in its idea exercise towards another, so that it requires to be completely defined by the expression of this object.

ἐν Χριστῷ Ἰησοῦ. The ground of this kindness shown towards us is in Christ, not in us. As Calvin remarks, "Notanda repetitio nominis Christi quia nihil gratiae neque amoris a Deo sperari vult, nisi ipso intercedente."

8. τῇ γὰρ χάριτι, κ.τ.λ. How justly I say "the exceeding riches of His grace," for, etc. The apostle now speaks in more detail about the truth of which his mind was so full. χάριτι has the article, because it is the grace already mentioned.

διὰ πίστεως without the article, ℵ A B D* G P 17, Chrys. Rec. has the article, with Dᵉ K L and most cursives.

This is the subjective condition, the "causa apprehendens," the necessary medium on the side of man, "the living capacity for receiving the powers of the higher world," Olshausen. The whole emphasis is on τῇ χάριτι. The article before πίστεως would imply that its possession was presupposed: "your faith."

καὶ τοῦτο, "and that" (for which καὶ ταῦτα is more frequent in classical writers), is referred by the Fathers, Chrysostom, Theodoret, and Jerome, to "faith." Thus Chrysostom says: οὐδὲ ἡ πίστις ἐξ ἡμῶν, εἰ γὰρ οὐκ ἦλθεν, εἰ γὰρ μὴ ἐκάλεσε, πῶς ἠδυνάμεθα πιστεῦσαι; πῶς γὰρ, φησὶ, πιστεύσουσιν ἐὰν μὴ ἀκούσωσιν. He proceeds to interpret the words Θεοῦ τὸ δῶρον as applying, not to faith, but to the grant of salvation on condition of faith, ἐπεὶ πῶς σώζει ἡ πίστις, εἰπέ μοι, ἄνευ ἔργων; τοῦτο αὐτὸ Θεοῦ δῶρόν ἐστιν. This is not very different from what Theophylact says: οὐ τὴν πίστιν λέγει δῶρον Θεοῦ, ἀλλὰ τὸ διὰ πίστεως σωθῆναι, τοῦτο δῶρόν ἐστι θεοῦ. Modern commentators (Erasmus, Beza, Bengel, etc.) who have adopted the view that τοῦτο refers to πίστις, understand the meaning to be that the power or exercise of faith (faith subjectively considered) is the gift of God (as Phil. i. 29), in which case καὶ τοῦτο to δῶρον must be parenthetical, since to say that faith is not ἐξ ἔργων would be trivial in the extreme.

The gender of τοῦτο is not fatal to the reference to πίστις, but to separate ἐξ ὑμῶν in this way from ἐξ ἔργων does violence to the connexion. The latter is a nearer definition of the former. Recent commentators refer καὶ τοῦτο to σεσωσμένοι ἐστε, or, better, to the whole clause; for after χάριτι had been expressed with σεσ., the emphatic καὶ τοῦτο would be out of place. In fact, the apostle emphasises and defines τῇ χ. more closely by denying the opposites; first, of the objective source χάρις by οὐκ ἐξ ὑμῶν; and, secondly, of the subjective element by οὐκ ἐξ ἔργων (Meyer).

Θεοῦ τὸ δῶρον. God's is the gift = Θεοῦ δῶρον τὸ δῶρόν ἐστι,

Θεοῦ being placed first for the sake of the emphatic contrast with ὑμῶν.

9. οὐκ ἐξ ἔργων. He does not say ἔργων νόμου, because not writing to Jewish believers. De Wette (who does not accept the Pauline authorship) thinks the opposition in οὐκ ἐξ ἔργων has no meaning, since the writer is not thinking of Jews, and heathen believers did not need to be warned against taking pride in the righteousness of works, especially after what had preceded in *vv.* 1 and 5. But the οὐκ ἐξ ἔργων was such an essential principle of St. Paul's teaching that no doubt he must have often repeated it amongst both Jews and Gentiles; nor is there any force in the reference to the past condition of the readers. Might not Gentile converts be tempted to regard their salvation as secured by their new holiness of life? and not the less because their former sins were when they were in darkness.

ἵνα μή τις καυχήσηται. Some commentators insist on giving ἵνα its full final force, "in order that"; so that to prevent boasting was God's purpose, or one of His purposes, in appointing that men should not be justified by works. Are we then to say that, in order that men should not boast, He has refused to allow salvation or justification by works? Nay; but no man can be justified by his works, and "when they have been betrayed by these," God appointed that He should save them χάριτι διὰ πίστεως. So in substance Chrysostom and Theophylact, whose words are: τὸ γὰρ ἵνα οὐκ αἰτιολογικόν ἐστι, ἀλλ᾽ ἐκ τῆς ἀποβάσεως τοῦ πράγματος. Yet the clause is not to be reduced to a mere statement of result, since it is a result inseparable from God's purpose. Stier suggests that ἵνα, κ.τ.λ., may be viewed as the expression of the writer's purpose: "This I say in order that," etc. This cannot fairly be called unnatural, but it would require the verb to be present.

10. αὐτοῦ γάρ ἐσμεν ποίημα κτισθέντες ἐν Χριστῷ ἐπὶ ἔργοις ἀγαθοῖς. Proof of the foregoing clauses from οὐκ ἐξ ὑμῶν, not of ἵνα τις . . . only, which is only a secondary thought. If we are God's workmanship, our salvation is not our own work, but the gift of God; and if we are created in Christ for good works, there could be no works preceding this creation from which any merit could arise. The argument turns on αὐτοῦ, which is emphatic, "His workmanship we are," and on κτισθέντες; and the following words still more distinctly express the impossibility of any merit preceding this κτίσις.

ποίημα, found again only Rom. i. 20 of the works of creation. Here, too, it is referred by Tert. Greg. Naz. and Basil to physical creation. This is refuted by the nearer definition given in κτισθέντες, κ.τ.λ. Pelagius includes both the physical and the spiritual, "quod vivimus, quod spiramus, quod intelligimus, quod credere possumus, ipsius est, quia ipse conditor nostri est." The word can hardly of itself be used simply of the new or spiritual creation; it may perhaps be chosen to suggest strongly the analogy of this to the first creation, the nature of this ποίημα being left to be defined by the following words. Perhaps we may better say that the apostle's mind was so full of the idea of the "new man," that he writes as if this new creation might be regarded as the first "making" of us.

κτισθέντες. "Created"; for if anyone is in Christ, he is καινὴ κτίσις, 2 Cor. v. 17; compare also Gal. vi. 15. κτίζειν is appropriately used of the καινὸς ἄνθρωπος, the coming into being of which is called παλιγγενεσία, Tit. iii. 5. We are not, then, to weaken it into "efficere."

ἐν Χριστῷ Ἰ. Cf. ver. 15 and 2 Cor. v. 17, above. ἐν expresses the fellowship in which that new creation takes place.

ἐπὶ ἔργοις ἀγαθοῖς. ἐπί, with the dative, is used to express the condition upon which a thing happens or is done; for instance, the conditions of a treaty ἐπ' ἴσοις, ἐπὶ πᾶσι δικαίοις, ἐπὶ ῥητοῖς, ἐπ' ἀργυρίῳ, ἐπὶ τῇ τοῦ ἀνδρὸς ψυχῇ (Plato, *Rep.* ix. p. 590 A); δανείζειν ἐπὶ ὑποθήκῃ (Dem. p. 908, 21). Hence the expression ἐφ' ᾧτε. Many, if not most, of the instances adduced in support of the meaning, "with a view to such and such an end," are better explained by this usage, *e.g.* δώρῳ ἔπι μεγάλῳ in Hom. *Il.* x. 304, τίς κέν μοι τόδε ἔργον ὑποσχόμενος τελέσειεν δώρῳ ἔπι μ., certainly not "with a view to," but "on the terms of receiving"; *Il.* ix. 482, μοῦνον, τηλύγετον, πολλοῖσιν ἐπὶ κτεάτεσσιν; and v. 154, "he begat no other son," ἐπὶ κτεάτεσσι λιπέσθαι, the possessions being an accompanying condition of the sonship. So also in such phrases as ἐπὶ ξενίᾳ δέχεσθαι or καλεῖν; φάσκοντες ἐπ' ἐλευθερίᾳ προεστάναι τῶν Ἑλλήνων (Dem. p. 661, 16); ἐπ' ἐλευθερίᾳ (τινὸς κατατιθέναι χρήματα) (*ib.* p. 1355, 18). καὶ ἐφ' ᾧ ἐν Κορίνθῳ μὴ ἐργάζεσθαι. Where the condition is (as in the last instance, not in that preceding) that something be granted, the meaning amounts to the same as "with a view to"; but this does not seem to be contained in the preposition. Indeed, the following words, καὶ ἐφ' ᾧ, κ.τ.λ., appear to decide the signification of ἐπί here.

Similarly in Gal. v. 13, ἐπ' ἐλευθερίᾳ ἐκλήθητε means, not that freedom was the end or object, but the condition of their calling, the terms on which they were called, viz. so as to be free. Again, 1 Thess. iv. 7, οὐ γὰρ ἐκάλεσεν ἡμᾶς ὁ Θεὸς ἐπὶ ἀκαθαρσίᾳ. Not on such terms were we called, not so that we should be impure. In the following words, ἀλλὰ ἐν ἁγιασμῷ, ἐν appears to be preferred, because ἁγιασμός did not express any outward condition. 2 Tim. ii. 14, ἐπὶ καταστροφῇ τῶν ἀκουόντων "with a view to," would be clearly out of place: "to the subverting" gives the sense correctly. It is the inevitable concomitant. Here ἔργα ἀγαθά are not the object of the new creation, but are involved in it as an inseparable condition.

οἷς προητοίμασεν ὁ Θεὸς ἵνα ἐν αὐτοῖς περιπατήσωμεν. The construction here is much disputed. The most obvious explanation is that οἷς is in the dative by attraction, "which God before prepared." Then we ask in what sense can works be said to have been prepared, since they have no existence previous to their being done. An easy answer appears to be, that they are appointed, and so, though not realised in fact, are realised in the divine thought or purpose. This is the view taken after Augustine by Harless, who thinks this the only possible sense here, since the apostle expressly adds that the actual realisation is expected from the believers. Thus St. Paul uses προετοιμάζειν here of things, in the same sense as he had used προορίζειν in i. 11 of persons. De Wette and Braune, etc., agree. The difficulty in this view is that ἑτοιμάζειν is not = ὁρίζειν. "Aliud est enim, *parare ἑτοιμάζειν*, aliud *definire ὁρίζειν*" (Fritzsche, *Rom.* iii. 339). The instance which Harless cites from Matt. xxv. 34, "the kingdom prepared," is not parallel, nor Gen. xxiv. 14.

For this reason Ellicott, Eadie, Meyer, etc., reject this view, but fail to give a satisfactory interpretation. "God (says Ellicott) *made ready* for us, prearranged, prepared a sphere of moral action, or (to use the simile of Chrys.) a road, with the intent that we should walk in it and not leave it: this sphere, this road, was ἔργα ἀγαθά." Similarly Eadie, who suggests that προορίζειν marks the destination, προετοιμ. the means: "they have been prescribed, defined, adapted to us," "by prearranging the works in their sphere, character, and suitability, and also by preordaining the law which commands, the inducement or appliances which impel, and the creation in Christ which qualifies and empowers us," etc. But he does not explain how things non-existent can be arranged except by ordaining. These interpretations do not essentially differ from the first.

The similes of a sphere or a road (used by Chrysostom for homiletical purposes) are inappropriate. A road exists objectively before one walks in it. A truer simile would be a path through the seas. Perhaps we might say that the word προετ. is chosen, not as being logically accurate, but in order to express in the most striking manner the truth that the good works do not proceed from ourselves; they are, as it were, received from the Creator as out of a treasure, which is thus figuratively conceived as being prepared before. But this hardly meets the difficulty. Olshausen understands that the circumstances and conditions under which it becomes possible to do good works are ordered by God, προετ. differing from προορίζειν only as relating more to details (compare Eadie, above).

Stier suggests taking the verb intransitively, οἷς being the dative of reference. "For which God made previous preparation." The simple verb ἑτοιμάζειν is used intransitively in Luke ix. 52, ὥστε ἑτοιμάσαι αὐτῷ. This, however, is not entirely parallel. The object to be understood there is readily supplied, "parare paranda"; just as in English we may say "prepare," "make ready," viz. "things." But here we should have to ask, Prepare what? The answer would perhaps be "us." And as Fritzsche points out, this ἡμᾶς as the object did not require to be expressed, since it is sufficiently indicated by the following words, ἵνα ἐν αὐτοῖς περιπατήσωμεν. This seems, after all, the most unobjectionable interpretation, and is adopted by Reuss, v. Soden, Oltramare, etc. Eadie also expresses himself as inclined to adopt it, if it could be fully justified, but he does not refer to the suggestion of ἡμᾶς contained in the following words. This interpretation cannot fairly be charged with making ἵνα ἐν αὐτοῖς περιπατήσωμεν a mere tautology. These words strongly accentuate the moral purpose of the preparation. The supposition of a Hebraism, as if οἷς . . . ἐν αὐτοῖς were = ἐν οἷς, is inadmissible.

προ has its proper force, not, however, as if it meant before the κτίσις, as ἑτ. expresses an act, not a purpose; and, of course, not after, because of προ-, therefore at the time of the κτίσις, so that ἑτοιμάζειν repeats κτίζειν ἐπὶ ἐρ. ἀγ., only with the addition of προ to express that the new creation is the primary thing but has this end in view, the works being only a result. It must be observed that ἔργα ἀγαθά is general; not τοῖς ἀγ. ἔργοις, the definite good works, etc.

There is no ground for saying that the weight here assigned to good works goes beyond what is elsewhere expressed by St. Paul, as Baur insists, or that the importance of faith is lessened. Here, as elsewhere, works have their ground in faith. Bengel well says: "ut *ambularemus*, non *salvaremur*, aut *viveremus*."

11-22. *Ye Gentiles were formerly aliens from the commonwealth of Israel, and had no share in the covenants of promise; but Christ by His death has cast down the barrier which separated you from the City of God, and has reconciled you both to God. Now, therefore, all alike have access to Him, the Father, and all alike form part of the holy temple which He inhabits.*

11. Διὸ μνημονεύετε. These blessings should move them to think more of their former state, so that they should be the more thankful. "Talis recordatio gratum animum acuit, et fidem roborat." Διό is best taken as referring to the whole section, vv. 1 to 10.

ὅτι ποτὲ ὑμεῖς in this order ℵ* A B D* Vulg. Rec. has ὑμεῖς ποτέ, with ℵᶜ Dᶜ G (prefixes οἱ to ποτέ), Syr. Harcl. But Syr. Pesh. Boh. and some other versions have ποτε after ἔθνη. ὅτι is resumed by ὅτι, ver. 12, and ποτέ by τῷ καιρῷ ἐκ. Hence we need not supply either ὄντες or ἦτε, but τὰ ἔθνη is in simple apposition to ὑμεῖς.

τὰ ἔθνη, with the article as indicating a class. Since ἔθνη ἐν σαρκί expresses one single idea, the article does not require repetition before ἐν. ἐν σαρκί must have the same sense here as in the following clause, since the former is explained by οἱ λεγόμενοι ἀκροβυστία, and this has its antithesis in τῆς λεγ. περιτομῆς. It therefore refers to their uncircumcision, not to their former carnal state, nor to their descent. Chrysostom and other Fathers take ἐν σαρκί as opposed to ἐν πνεύματι. Thus Jerome: "Ephesios in carne vocans ostendit in spiritu esse non gentes." This contradicts ποτέ and ver. 12. The apostle is not exalting them, but calling attention to their previous inferiority to the Jews.

"Remember that formerly ye Gentiles in the flesh called (in contempt) Uncircumcision by the so-called Circumcision in the flesh, a circumcision merely physical, made with hands." He reminds them of the ignominy which in the mind of the Jews attached to the name of heathen and of the uncircumcised. This contempt is already predicated in the words οἱ λεγόμενοι ἀκρ.; and the lowness of their condition is further shown by the following description of those who so despised them, those, namely, who prided themselves on a mere fleshly distinction made with hands. Why, in fact, does he say λεγομένης περιτομῆς, and why χειροποιήτου? There was no need to give the readers information on the name or the fact. The latter word is clearly depreciatory, "a merely external and artificial thing." But he is far from depreciating circumcision, in its true significance, as the sign of membership of the commonwealth of the people of God. Hence the use of λεγομένης, which by its adjectival connexion with περιτομῆς gets the signification "so called." This is readily explained from the apostle's use of περιτομή elsewhere in a spiritual, as contrasted with a merely physical sense, as in Rom. ii. 28, 29, "Neither is that circumcision which is outward in the flesh . . . circumcision is that of the heart, in the spirit, not in the letter." Phil. ii. 2, he calls the physical circumcision κατατομή, a term more contemptuous than χειροποιήτου here: adding in ver. 3, "We are the circumcision, who worship by the Spirit of God and glory in Christ Jesus, and have no confidence in the flesh"; and in Col. ii. 11, which is strikingly illustrative of the present passage, "in whom ye were circumcised with a circumcision not made with hands." Soden thinks that χειροποιήτου here is superfluous, because there is no reference (as in Col.) to a spiritual circumcision, and ἐν σαρκί sufficiently emphasises the merely external character of the sign; and hence he thinks the word introduced out of imitation of Col. ii. 11. But it seems, on the contrary, to give emphasis and completeness to the thought, and would naturally occur to the writer who about the same time wrote ἀχειροποιήτου in Col.

Although "circumcision" is not used figuratively in the O.T., "uncircumcision" is. Even in Lev. xxvi. 41 we have "their uncircumcised heart." Jeremiah speaks of the uncircumcised ear of those who will not hearken (vi. 10), and calls the house of Israel "uncircumcised in heart" (ix. 26). Comp. Ezek. xliv. 7, "uncircumcised in heart and uncircumcised in flesh," and Acts vii. 51.

12. ὅτι ἦτε τῷ καιρῷ ἐκείνῳ χωρὶς Χριστοῦ. Rec. has ἐν before τῷ καιρῷ. It is omitted by ℵ A B D G.

ὅτι resumes the former ὅτι. "Remember, I say, that."

χωρὶς Χριστοῦ is taken by De Wette and Bleek as, not a predicate, but a circumstantial addition, "being at that time without Christ." It would thus correspond with ἐν Χριστῷ, ver. 13, and would give the reason of their alienation from the commonwealth of Israel. But, considering the position of the words, this is a harsh construction, and would deprive the words of the emphasis which belongs to them as the opposite of the frequent ἐν Χρ. in this Epistle. χωρὶς Χρ. is, as Meyer says, the first tragic predicate. χωρίς is distinguished from ἄνευ by Tittmann as follows: "χωρίς ad subjectum quod ab objecto sejunctum est refertur, ἄνευ ad objectum quod a subjecto abesse cogitandum est." According to this, χωρὶς Χρ. would mean "ye were far from Christ"; ἄνευ Χρ. would be "Christ was not with you." But this must be received with hesitation, seeing that χωρίς occurs in the N.T. forty times, and ἄνευ only thrice (Ellicott), viz. Matt. x. 29; 1 Pet. iii. 1, iv. 9. In the last quoted passage ἄνευ γογγυσμοῦ is equivalent to χωρὶς γογγυσμῶν, Phil. ii. 14.

Schwegler sees here a concession to Judaism which is unlike St. Paul; but without reason, since the concession only relates to pre-Christian times, and the advantage possessed by the Jews in this respect is, as it must be, fully admitted by St. Paul (Rom. iii. 1 ff.).

What is meant by χωρὶς Χριστοῦ is explained in the following words:—

ἀπηλλοτριωμένοι τῆς πολιτείας τοῦ Ἰσραήλ. The verb ἀπαλλοτριόω occurs also in iv. 18, ἀπ. τῆς ζωῆς τοῦ Θεοῦ, and Col. i. 21, without a genitive. In Ezek. xiv. 5, 7 we have ἀπ. ἀπ' ἐμοῦ; in 3 Macc. i. 4, τῶν πατρίων δογμάτων. The active verb occurs in Eccles. xi. 34, ἀπ. σε τῶν ἰδίων σου.

The verb always means to estrange; here therefore "estranged from" as opposed to "being at home in."

πολιτεία was interpreted by the ancients in the sense "manner of life," "conversatio, Vulg., a meaning which the word frequently has in Christian writers, and not in these alone; see Athen. i. p. 19 A. But to take it so here would be contrary to ver. 19, where the opposite of ἀπ. κ.τ.λ. is συμπολῖται. It may mean either citizenship, or state, commonwealth. Many commentators have taken it in the former sense. It is questionable whether it could be so used with a genitive of the nation or city. Nor does the verb ἀπηλλ. suggest such a meaning. Besides, the Greek and Roman conception of citizenship would not be appropriate here, and, further, we should have to explain the exclusion from citizenship as arising from exclusion from the commonwealth. Naturally it is the theocratic constitution from which they were excluded; and the name Israel implies this, since this was the name of the people in their theocratic relation. Yet Chrysostom refers the words to the exclusion of the Gentiles from the temporal glories of Israel, εἶπε περὶ τῶν οὐρανίων πραγμάτων, λέγει καὶ περὶ τῶν ἐπὶ τῆς γῆς, ἐπειδὴ μεγάλην δόξαν εἶχον περὶ αὐτῶν οἱ Ἰουδαῖοι, in which he was followed by some moderns (as by Grotius). As if any Roman citizen or subject could regard as a misfortune the exclusion from a State which was an object of contempt!

Many commentators suppose that ἀπηλλ. implies a previous unity. Thus Bengel: "Abalienati, non alieni; participia praesupponunt gentes ante defectionem suam a fide patrum imo potius ante lapsum Adami fuisse participes lucis et vitae." However attractive this view may be in itself, the conception is too new and important to be introduced here on so slight a ground. If it had been in the apostle's mind, he would doubtless have referred to it more explicitly in some part of his writings. It is not hinted at in ver. 14, where we might have expected "again made" or the like. For an instance of the verb being used without reference to a previous state, see Ps. lvii. (lviii.) 3, ἀπηλλοτριώθησαν οἱ ἁμαρτωλοὶ ἀπὸ μήτρας. Olshausen's view is that the exclusion referred to is that which resulted from God's restriction of His peculiar operations of grace to Israel. As far as alienation from God is referred to, however, it is true that men are regarded as originally, and from an ideal point of view, at one with God.

καὶ ξένοι τῶν διαθηκῶν τῆς ἐπαγγελίας. A further specification of what is meant by the preceding clause. ξένος is followed by a genitive, not of "the point of view" ("extraneos quod ad pactorum promissiones attinet," Beza), but simply of separation or privation. So Soph. *Oed. R.* 219, ξένος λόγου τοῦδ' ἐξερῶ, ξένος δὲ τοῦ πραχθέντος. Plato, *Apol.* i., ξένως (ἔχειν) τῆς ἐνθάδε λέξεως.

"The covenants of the promise." ἐπαγγ. is connected with διαθηκῶν, not with ἐλπίδα, as the position of the word shows. The covenants were characterised by the promise of the Messiah (cf. Acts xiii. 32). The plural is used with reference to the covenants with the patriarchs, but the Mosaic covenant is not excluded, although it was primarily νομοθεσία.

ἐλπίδα μὴ ἔχοντες. The absence of the article shows that it is not the definite hope of the Messiah that is meant, but hope in the widest sense, so that the expression is so much the stronger, "having no hope." μή is used, not because the thought is dependent on what precedes, but because it is their own consciousness that is referred to. οὐκ ἔχοντες would express only the writer's judgment of their state. Cf. οὐκ εἰδότες Θεόν, Gal. iv. 8.

καὶ ἄθεοι. "The deepest stage of heathen misery," Meyer. The word ἄθεος is not found in the Sept. or Apocrypha, and only here in the N.T. In Greek writers it occurs in three senses, "not believing in God, atheist" (Plato, *Apol.* p. 26 C). Secondly, "impious, godless" (Plato, *Legg.* p. 966 E), or "without God, without God's help," Soph. *Oed. R.*, ἐπεὶ ἄθεος ἄφιλος ὅ τι πύματον ὀλοίμαν. To understand it here as "forsaken by God" would be to introduce a conception not warranted by the expressions in the text. They were truly "without God," as not knowing Him. Notwithstanding their many gods, they had no conception of a Creator and Governor to be loved and trusted. So far as their consciousness was concerned, they had no God. But God had not left Himself without a witness amongst them. The description is general, of the class to which the readers belonged. This was not the occasion for referring to the noble exceptions to the moral degradation of heathenism. It was, indeed, in Asia Minor that this degradation was lowest, so that the Romans traced to it the corruption which spread to the whole empire.

ἐν τῷ κόσμῳ, to be joined both with ἐλπίδα μὴ ἔχ. and with ἄθεοι, "in the world," with all its troubles, trials, and uncertainties, ye were without Divine help; generally understood as contrasted with πολιτεία.

13. νυνὶ δὲ ἐν Χριστῷ Ἰησοῦ, ὑμεῖς οἱ ποτὲ ὄντες μακρὰν ἐγενήθητε ἐγγύς. νυνὶ opposed to τῷ καιρῷ ἐκείνῳ. ἐν Χρ. Ἰ. opposed to χωρὶς Χριστοῦ. We are not to supply either ἐστέ or ὄντες. Since the being in Christ was not prior to the being brought near, the interpretation, "postquam in Christo estis recepti" (Calvin, Harless), is not admissible. Nor can we understand "cum in Christo sitis recepti," which would not only make these words a superfluous addition, but would be hard to reconcile with the aorist.

Ἰησοῦ is suitably added to Χριστῷ here, and indeed was almost necessary to the distinct expression of the thought. In ver. 12 it could not have been added, since that included times preceding the incarnation, and χωρὶς Χρ. Ἰ. would imply the existence of the historical Jesus then; whereas here, not only the Messiah as such is referred to, but the personal Jesus as the Christ and the Saviour.

ποτὲ ὄντες μακράν corresponds to the expressions ἀπηλλοτριωμένοι, κ.τ.λ. μακράν and ἐγγύς, then, have reference both to the πολιτεία τοῦ Ἰσ. with its διαθῆκαι, and to the ἐλπίς with God Himself. Accordingly in the following verses we have two points of view combined, viz. the reconciliation of the Gentiles to God, and their admission to the πολιτεία of Israel, namely, the true Israel—the Christian Church.

The terms μακράν and ἐγγύς were suggested by Isa. lvii. 19, "Peace, peace to him that is far off, and to him that is nigh." There, indeed, as in Acts ii. 39, the words have a local meaning, and have no reference to the admission of Gentiles to the theocracy; but they easily lend themselves to this conception, and, in fact, were frequently used by Rabbinic writers with reference to proselytes, who were said to be "brought near." Many passages may be seen in Schoettgen and Wetstein. One may be quoted. "A woman came to R. Eliezer confessing certain gross sins, and asked to be made a proselyte, saying, 'Rabbi, propinquam me fac'; on hearing her sin he rejected her. She went to R. Joshua, who received her. His disciples said, 'R. Eliezer illam removit, tu vero eam propinquam facis?'"

ἐγγὺς γίνεσθαι, frequent in classical writers, but not found elsewhere in the N.T.

> The order ἐγενήθητε ἐγγύς is that of ℵ A B, 17. Rec. has ἐγγ. ἐγεν., with D G K L P. Ellicott thinks the Rec. genuine, the order here adopted being due to a mistaken correction of the emphatic juxtaposition of μακράν and ἐγγύς. Harless is of the same opinion. But why should copyists correct this emphatic juxtaposition? It is just what would strike an ordinary reader. Looking closer, we see that the opposition is not merely between these two, but between ὄντες μακράν and ἐγενήθητε ἐγγύς, and that the verb is properly placed in the most emphatic position.

ἐν τῷ αἵματι τοῦ Χριστοῦ more particularly defines the instrumentality. It is not possible to draw any satisfactory distinction between this and διὰ τοῦ αἵ. i. 7.

14. αὐτὸς γάρ ἐστιν ἡ εἰρήνη ἡμῶν, "He Himself is our peace"; He has not brought about peace by a mere external action or arrangement; it is in His own person that He gives it. "Non modo pacificator nam sui impensa pacem peperit et ipse vinculum est utrorumque," Bengel. The context shows that what is primarily intended is the union of Jews and Gentiles; but as it was not this union of itself that was of importance, but the essential basis of it, as the union of both in one body of Christ, it is manifest that the idea of peace with God could not be absent from the mind of the apostle in writing ἡ εἰρήνη ἡμῶν. Comp. ver. 17.

Schoettgen quotes a Rabbinic writer who calls the Messiah "Peace," in allusion to Isa. ix. 6.

ὁ ποιήσας. "Quippe qui."

τὰ ἀμφότερα ἕν. Both, *i.e.* both Jews and Gentiles. There is no ellipsis (as of γένη, ἔθνη, or the like). It is simply an instance of the neuter being used of persons in a general sense; cf. Heb. vii. 7, τὸ ἔλαττον ὑπὸ τοῦ κρείττονος εὐλογεῖται; 1 Cor. i. 27, 28, τὰ μωρὰ τοῦ κόσμου ... τὰ ἀσθενῆ (opposed to ver. 26, οἱ σοφοί). So in classical Greek, *e.g.* Xen. *Anab.* vii. 3. 11, τὰ φεύγοντα ἱκανοὶ ἐσόμεθα διώκειν.

ἕν. Comp. Gal. iii. 28, πάντες ὑμεῖς εἷς ἐστε ἐν Χριστῷ Ἰησοῦ. Not, says Chrysostom, that He has brought us to that nobility of theirs, but both us and them to a greater; as if one should melt down a statue of silver and one of lead, and the two should come out gold.

καί, exegetical = inasmuch as, He, τὸ μεσότοιχον τοῦ φραγμοῦ λύσας, "brake down the partition wall of the fence."

μεσότοιχον is a rare word, found, besides the Fathers, only in Eratosth. *ap. Athen.* vii. 281 D (masc.), and Hesychius. The genitive has been variously explained, as of quality = "the separating partition" (against which is the fact that this adjectival notion belongs to μεσότοιχον itself); or of possession, "the wall which belonged to the fence"; or better, of apposition, "the partition which consisted in the fence." φραγμός means a fence, hedge, or enclosure, not a separation.

It seems probable that the figure was suggested by the partition which separated the Court of the Gentiles from the temple proper, and on which there was an inscription threatening death to any alien who passed it. That the Ephesian readers can hardly be supposed to be familiar with the arrangements of the temple, is no proof that these may not have been in the apostle's mind. But it is worth noticing that it was an Ephesian, Trophimus, that St. Paul was charged with bringing into the temple. A more serious objection seems to be, that when the Epistle was written the wall referred to was still standing. But the apostle is not speaking of the literal wall, but using it as an illustration. Any reference to the vail which was rent at the time of the crucifixion would be out of harmony with the context. That vail did not separate Jews and Gentiles.

λύσας is suitable to the figure; cf. John ii. 19, λύσατε τὸν ναὸν τοῦτον. It is equally suitable to the following ἔχθραν, since λύειν ἔχθραν is of frequent occurrence in classical writers.

Here it is questioned whether ἔχθραν is to be connected with the words preceding or those following, and if with the preceding, whether ἐν τῇ σαρκὶ αὐτοῦ is to be taken with λύσας or with καταργήσας. Another alternative will be mentioned presently. We have to choose, then, between the following renderings:—

Having done away with the middle wall, namely, the enmity; having in His flesh annulled the law.

Having in His flesh done away with the middle wall, namely, the enmity, etc.

Having done away with the middle wall, having in His flesh annulled the enmity, namely, the law, etc.

The view which connects ἐν τῇ σαρκὶ αὐτοῦ with ἔχθραν as = the enmity in his flesh, whether "his flesh" be understood to mean humanity in general (Chrys.) or the Jews (cf. Rom. xi. 14), must be set aside as inconsistent with the absence of the article before ἐν τῇ σαρκί. The first-mentioned interpretation gives an awkward isolation to ἔχθραν, and adds the harshness of making the specification of manner, ἐν τῇ σ., precede the object and its verb.

The third construction is objectionable, first, because the law cannot itself be called ἔχθρα (the designation of it as δύναμις τῆς ἁμαρτίας, 1 Cor. xv. 56, is not analogous); and, secondly, because the position of ἐν τῇ σ. αὐτοῦ would be inexplicable, coming, as it does on that supposition, between the two nouns in apposition, although it has no relation to either. Indeed, it may be added that καταργήσας is not a verb appropriate to ἔχθραν; it does not properly mean to destroy, but "to make of none effect," "to deprive of power"; of the faith of God, Rom. iii. 3; of the law, Rom. iii. 31; the promise, iv. 14; persons from the law, vii. 2, 6. It is, indeed, used of things coming to an end, as knowledge and prophecy, but coming to an end by being superseded.

The second construction mentioned above seems to have the advantage of these two, although it must be admitted that it is not without difficulty. For the enmity was not the wall of partition. It was not the law only, although that was the ultimate cause, but the separation, religious, moral, and social, which forbade fellowship between Jew and Gentile. This partition was broken down by the annulling of the law.

V. Soden has proposed a view of the passage which, if admissible, would meet the difficulties. It is that τὴν ἔχθραν is the beginning of the participial clause, which, having been interrupted by the statement of the process by which the effect was produced, is taken up again in ver. 16, where ἔχθραν is repeated. If the text had run thus, τὴν ἔχθραν, τὸν νόμον τῶν ἐντ. ἐν δογ. καταργήσας, ἀπέκτεινε, there would have been nothing harsh in the order of the words. As it is, the parenthesis is enlarged, as in the manner of this Epistle, ii. 1 and 4, 11 and 12, iii. 1 and 12, and the interrupted thought is resumed in ver. 16. The two participles, καταργήσας, ἀποκτείνας, in their relation to one another, correspond exactly with the two in ver. 14. Soden connects ἐν τῇ σ. αὐτοῦ with the following clause. The parenthetic digressions, however, with which Soden compares this, are not quite parallel. In each of them, while the train of thought is interrupted, it is easy to account for the interruption by the influence of some particular word; they are, in fact, instances of what Paley well calls St. Paul's habit of "going off at a word." Thus in ii. 1 he goes off at ἁμαρτίαις, ἐν αἷς; in ii. 11 at ἔθνη ἐν σαρκί; in iii. 1 at ὑπὲρ ὑμῶν τῶν ἐθνῶν.

The verbal connexion is in each instance easy. But here there is no similar connexion between the words which precede the digression and τὸν νόμον, κ.τ.λ.

The ἔχθρα is obviously that of Jews and Gentiles. This naturally loomed much larger in the apostle's eyes than it does in ours, or than it did in those of Chrysostom and his successors. With us as with them, the more pressing thought is of the enmity of both Jew and Gentile to God. So Oecumenius: μεσότοιχον φραγμοῦ φησι τὴν ἔχθραν τὴν πρὸς Θεόν, ἡμῶν τε καὶ Ἰουδαίων, ἥτις ἐκ τῶν ἡμετέρων παραπτωμάτων. And so Chrysostom interprets τὴν ἔχθραν ἐν τῇ σαρκί as being the μεσότοιχοντ ᾧ κοινὸν εἶναι διάφραγμα ἀπὸ Θεοῦ διατειχίζον ἡμᾶς, rejecting the interpretation which makes the law the ἔχθρα. But even though ἡ ἔχθρα is not = ὁ νόμος, it is the annulling of the law that removes the ἔχθρα, and the law is characterised in terms which exclude the natural law. Moreover, the reconciling of both to God is stated as a further object of the removal of the enmity and the creating of both into one new man.

τὸν νόμον τῶν ἐντολῶν ἐν δόγμασιν καταργήσας. τὸν ν. τῶν ἐντ. ἐν δ. belong together; "the law of commandments expressed in decrees." The law consisted of ἐντολαί, and the definite form in which these were expressed was that of δόγματα, authoritative decrees ("legem imperiosam," Erasm.). This connexion does not require the article to be repeated after ἐντολῶν. For we might with propriety say ἐντολὴν διδόναι ἐν δόγματι, and therefore ἐντολὴ ἐν δ. may form a single conception. So Winer in his later editions. Compare τὸν ὑμῶν ζῆλον ὑπὲρ ἐμοῦ, 2 Cor. vii. 7. In fact, τῶν ἐντ. τῶν ἐν δ. would denote the ἐντολαί as a particular class, "commandments, even those expressed in decrees."

Δόγμα in classical Greek means, first, an opinion or resolution. In the plural it is used of the "placita philosophorum," whence the use of the word in Christian writers in the sense of "dogma." But it also means a decree (Xen. Demosth. Plato), and this is the meaning which alone it has in the N.T. We have ἐξῆλθε δόγμα παρὰ Καίσαρος, Luke ii. 1; δόγματα Καίσαρος, Acts xvii. 7; τὰ δ. κεκριμένα ὑπὸ τῶν ἀποστ., ib. xvi. 4. The word occurs also in Lachmann's text, Heb. xi. 23, δ. τοῦ βασιλέως. The remaining passages are the present and Col. ii. 14. Chrysostom does not seem to have contemplated this meaning. He suggests that what is meant is either faith, δόγμα αὐτὴν καλῶν, for by faith alone He saved us, or the precept τὴν παραγγελίαν, as Christ said, ἐγὼ δὲ λέγω ὑμῖν. He is followed by Theophylact, Theodoret (δόγματα τὴν εὐαγγελικὴν διδασκαλίαν ἐκάλεσεν), and Oecumenius. Theodore Mops. also connects the word with καταργήσας, but interprets differently, understanding δόγματα of the facts and hopes of the Gospel, "διὰ τῶν ἰδίων δογμάτων· ἵνα εἴπῃ, τῆς ἀναστάσεως, τῆς ἀφθαρσίας, τῆς ἀθανασίας· δ. γματα καλέσας ταῦτα ὡς ἐν πράγμασιν ὄντα, the Divine grace working in us so that we do not need commandments and precepts." This interpretation, as well as Chrysostom's, would clearly require τοῖς δόγμασιν αὐτοῦ or the like. Against Chrysostom's view, indeed, it is decisive that it was not by doctrines or precepts that Christ annulled the law. Theodore's view avoids this error, but gives δόγμα an impossible sense. Of course, when once these commentators connected ἐν δ. with the following, taking ἐν as instrumental, they were driven to some such interpretation.

Harless also connects ἐν δ. with καταργήσας, thinking that the absence of the article forbids the connexion with ἐντολῶν. But his interpretation is that Christ annulled the law only in respect of δόγματα, comparing Cic. *Phil*. i. 7, "In maximis vero rebus, id est legibus, acta Caesaris dissolvi ferendum non puto," and such phrases as ἐν τῇ πάντι ὠνείδισε (Arrian, *Exp*. iii. 30; Bernhardy, p. 212). St. Paul has already indicated by τῶν ἐντ. that he is not speaking of the law so far as it belonged to the covenants of promise, and now, to avoid all misconception, he adds ἐν δόγμασι. Olshausen follows Harless, who had, indeed, been preceded in this interpretation by Crellius. But this would require the article before δόγμασιν. Moreover, while it is true that the law as σκιὰ τῶν μελλόντων or as παιδαγωγὸς εἰς Χριστόν was not annulled, it was superseded. Such a limitation of the statement as to the abolition of the law would be out of place here, and would require more explicit statement, since it is not elsewhere referred to. The Mosaic law as such, not merely in certain aspects of it, has come to an end in Christ. He is the "end of the law," Rom. x. 4. Faith having come, we are no longer ὑπὸ παιδαγωγόν (Gal. iii. 25).

If ἐν δ. be connected with καταργήσας, then, considering the absence of the article, the only grammatical interpretation seems to be Hofmann's, viz. that Christ deprived the O.T. law of validity, by putting an end to all precepts, "Satzungen." He compares the construction in 1 Cor. ii. 7, λαλοῦμεν σοφίαν Θεοῦ ἐν μυστηρίῳ, *i.e.* λαλοῦντες σοφίαν λαλοῦμεν μυστήριον. But surely the N.T. contains many specific precepts which may be properly called δόγματα. Comp. also τὸν νόμον τοῦ Χριστοῦ, Gal. vi. 2; ἔννομος Χριστοῦ, 1 Cor. ix. 21; and the parallel to the present passage in Col. ii. 14. As Meyer observes, the δόγματα of Christianity are the true ἀεὶ παρόντα δόγματα, Plato, *Theaet*. p. 1·8 D. Had the intention been what Hofmann supposes, St. Paul would doubtless have added some qualification, such as ἐν δόγμασι δουλείας. νόμος here is not to be limited to the ceremonial law; there is nothing in the connexion to show such a limitation, which, on the contrary, would make the statement very weak. No reader would fail to see that, as Theodoret says, οὐκ ἀνεῖλε τὸ οὐ μοιχεύσεις, κ.τ.λ. The moral law retains its obligation, not, however, because the

Jewish law is only partially annulled, but because its obligation was independent of the law and universal (Rom. ii. 14). If a Mohammedan becomes a Christian, we do not say that the Koran retains its obligation for him in its moral part, although he still acknowledges the obligation of many moral precepts contained in it. The Christian now fulfils the moral law, not because of external precepts, but because conformity with it is the natural fruit of the Spirit. Hence the contrast between the expressions, "works of the law," "fruits of the Spirit."

ἵνα τοὺς δύο κτίσῃ ἐν αὐτῷ εἰς ἕνα καινὸν ἄνθρωπον. The neuter was used in ver. 14 to express the general characteristics of the two classes; but here, where the Jews and Gentiles are conceived as concrete persons, the masculine was necessary.

καινόν is necessary because the one is neither Jew nor Greek. Both have put off their former religious condition, and have received the same new nature. Chrysostom says: ὁρᾷς οὐχὶ τὸν Ἕλληνα γενόμενον Ἰουδαῖον, ἀλλὰ καὶ τοῦτον κἀκεῖνον εἰς ἑτέραν κατάστασιν ἥκοντας. οὐχ ἵνα τοῦτον ἕτερον ἐργάσηται τὸν νόμον κατήργησεν, ἀλλ' ἵνα τοὺς δύο κτίσῃ. κ.τ.λ. On κτίζειν, cf. ver. 10. It is specially appropriate here with καινὸς ἄνθ. οὐκ εἶπε, Μεταβάλῃ, ἵνα δείξῃ τὸ ἐνεργὲς τοῦ γενομένου, says Chrysostom.

ἐν αὐτῷ. Rec. has ἑαυτῷ, with אᶜ D G K L and most cursives, Chrys. Jerome. αυτω is the reading of א A B P, 17. Lachmann, Tischendorf, and Tregelles write αὑτῷ, but Westcott and Hort αὐτῷ. The sense here is certainly reflexive.

"In Himself." Not δι' ἑαυτοῦ, as Chrys., but, Christ is Himself the principle and ground of the unity; "ne alibi quam in Christo unitatem quaerant," Calv. Cf. Gal. iii. 28, πάντες ὑμεῖς εἷς ἐστε ἐν Χριστῷ Ἰησοῦ. Chrysostom, indeed, gives another interpretation, as if it were only a development of the former. "Fusing both this and that, he produced one, an admirable one, Himself having first become this; which is a greater thing than the former creation. For this is the meaning of ἐν ἑαυτῷ, Himself first affording the type and pattern." Oecumenius states the two interpretations as alternatives, explaining the first as οὐ δι' ἀγγέλων ἢ ἄλλων τινων δυναμέων.

ποιῶν εἰρήνην, present participle, "making peace," *i.e.* so that by this new creation He makes (not "made") peace. The words explain αὐτός ἐστιν ἡ εἰρήνη ἡμῶν of ver. 14. The peace is, from the context, that between Jews and Gentiles; but as the basis of that is peace with God, the latter thought underlies the former, and to it the apostle now turns.

16. καὶ ἀποκαταλλάξῃ. The καί is not the mere copula, but indicates a logical sequence, "and consequently reconcile both, now one body, to God by the Cross, having on it slain the enmity previously existing between them."

ἀποκαταλλάσσειν is found only here and Col. i. 20. It seems to be only an intensified form of the usual Greek word ἀλλάσσειν. ἀπό in composition frequently has this intensive meaning; cf. ἀπεκδέχεσθαι, ἀποκαραδοκεῖν, to await patiently; so ἀποθαρρεῖν, ἀποθαυμάζειν, ἀποθεᾶσθαι, etc. In a few instances, indeed, it seems to be equivalent to re- and to mean "again," as in ἀποδίδωμι, ἀπολαμβάνω, ἀποκαθίστημι, ἀποκατορθόω. In the first two of these the idea is rather to give or take what belongs of right to the receiver, as ἀποδ. χάριν, ὑπόσχεσιν. Here it is the idea of remotion from, that explains the meaning of the verb. In the other two examples also this local idea is involved

In any case, as this use of ἀπο- is much less common than the intensive use, we are not justified in assuming it in a compound that does not elsewhere occur.

ἐν ἑνὶ σώματι is interpreted by Chrysostom as referring to the human body of Christ. So Bengel: "in uno corpore cruci affixo." But in that case we should expect "His body." Nor is it easy to see why that should be designated ἓν σῶμα. The order of the words indicates the correct interpretation, "both now united in one body." The ἓν σῶμα is the εἷς καινὸς ἄνθρωπος. So most commentators. It is not the Church, for it is only as reconciled that Jews and Greeks belong to the Church. But when reconciled they become the body of Christ, and so, the Church.

διὰ τοῦ σταυροῦ is joined by Soden with the following, αὐτῷ being read for αὐτῴ (so G, Vulg. and some Latin codices with other authorities). The connexion with the two notions, ἀποκτείνας and ἔχθρα, gives it a subtle point. "By His death He was slain; by death on the Cross, in which the ἔχθρα showed itself, He has overcome the ἔχθρα." We have a parallel in Col. i. 20, only that there, instead of the negative ἀποκτείνειν τὴν ἔ., we have the positive εἰρηνοποιεῖν; also in connexion with διὰ τοῦ σταυροῦ. ἐν αὐτῷ, then, as in 15*b*, echoes with emphasis the fundamental thought: "He Himself is our peace." If we read ἐν αὐτῷ, it could not be referred to σῶμα, because this σ. was just mentioned as the medium of reconciliation to God, whereas here it is the enmity between Jews and Gentiles that is in question.

17. καὶ ἐλθὼν εὐηγγελίσατο εἰρήνην. "And He came and preached good tidings of peace." The preceding verses showed how Christ secured peace; this, how He proclaimed it. This, therefore, is posterior, and hence cannot refer to His life on earth, as Harless, following Chrysostom, understands it. Bengel interprets the "coming and preaching," as that of Christ personally after the resurrection, "veniens a morte, profectione ad inferos, resurrectione victor laetus ipse *ultro* nuntiavit." But it is much better to understand the words of Christ preaching by His Spirit in the apostles and other messengers of His. Not that εὐηγγ. means "caused to be preached"

(as Harless objects), for what is thus done by Christ's Spirit is properly said to be done by Him; nor is ἐλθών superfluous, but, on the contrary, important as expressing the spiritual coming referred to in John xiv. 18, ἔρχομαι πρὸς ὑμᾶς, and in Acts xxvi. 23, (Χριστὸς) πρῶτος ἐξ ἀναστάσεως νεκρῶν φῶς μέλλει καταγγέλλειν τῷ τε λαῷ καὶ τοῖς ἔθνεσι.

ὑμῖν τοῖς μακρὰν καὶ εἰρήνην τοῖς ἐγγύς. The second εἰρήνην has preponderant authority in its favour, ℵ A B D G P, 17, Vulg. and other versions except Syr. Contra, K L, most cursives, Syr. The repetition is highly emphatic.

The datives depend on εὐηγγελίσατο. τοῖς μακράν comes first, because it is these that are addressed, and are chiefly in view in the whole passage. This also agrees with the view that it is not Christ's personal preaching that is intended, since that would have required τοῖς ἐγγύς to come first. The repetition of εἰρήνην excludes the interpretation of τοῖς ἐγγύς as in apposition with ὑμῖν, and so = the Jewish Christians in Ephesus.

18. ὅτι δι' αὐτοῦ ἔχομεν τὴν προσαγωγὴν οἱ ἀμφότεροι ἐν ἑνὶ Πνεύματι πρὸς τὸν πατέρα. "For through Him we both have our access (or introduction) in one Spirit unto the Father."

Proof of what precedes. The emphasis, therefore, is not on δι' αὐτοῦ, but on οἱ ἀμφ. ἐν ἑνὶ Πν. Since both have their προσ. in one Spirit to the Father, it follows that the same good tidings of peace have been brought to both by Him. ὅτι is "for," not "that," as if the verse contained the substance of the passage which has been already expressed in εἰρήνη. And it is not the common access as such that is in question, but the peace therein assured (between Jews and Gentiles).

ἔχομεν. Compare Rom. v. 2, "δι' οὗ καὶ τὴν προσαγωγὴν ἐσχήκαμεν . . . εἰς τὴν χάριν ταύτην ἐν ᾗ ἑστήκαμεν. There, the πρ. is into the present condition, and accordingly the perfect is suitable; here, it is the πρ. to the Father, which is a present privilege.

Προσαγωγή in classical writers is usually transitive, but is also found fairly frequently in an intransitive sense.

The word is understood transitively here by Ellicott, Eadie, Meyer, after Chrysostom, οὐκ εἶπεν πρόσοδον ἀλλὰ προσαγωγήν, οὐ γὰρ ἀφ' ἑαυτῶν προσήλθομεν, ἀλλ' ὑπ' αὐτοῦ προσήχθημεν; cf. 1 Pet. iii. 18, ἵνα ἡμᾶς προσαγάγῃ τῷ Θεῷ, and it is supposed that there may be an allusion to the προσαγωγεύς at Oriental courts. Such an allusion would not be in harmony with the context. The ἐν πνεύματι is decidedly against the supposition that the apostle intended this ceremonial figure. Apart from this, the transitive sense is not suitable in iii. 12, where the word is used absolutely, and here also the intransitive agrees better with ἔχομεν, especially as the tense is present. προσαγωγή is something we possess.

τὴν προσ. "Our access."

ἐν ἑνὶ Πνεύματι is understood by Anselm (and some moderns) of the human spirit (ὁμοθυμαδόν), against the clear reference to Father, Son, and Spirit, δι' αὐτοῦ, ἐν ἑνὶ Π., πρὸς τὸν Πατέρα.

19. ἄρα οὖν οὐκέτι ἐστὲ ξένοι καὶ πάροικοι. "So then ye are no more strangers and sojourners." ἄρα οὖν, a favourite combination with St. Paul, is not found in classical writers except in the interrogative form, ἆρ' οὖν. ξένοι καὶ πάροικοι, equivalent to ἀπηλλοτριωμένοι, ver. 12. ξένος is "foreigner" in general; πάροικος, a foreigner dwelling in a state, and not having rights of citizenship. In classical Greek, indeed, it seems to be found only in the sense of neighbour. Rost and Palm name the Pandects (without reference) as having the word in the sense "inquilinus." In the Sept. it occurs eleven times as the rendering of גֵּר, which is usually rendered προσήλυτος. None of these instances are in Leviticus or Numbers. Ten times it occurs as the rendering of תּוֹשָׁב, "a foreign sojourner." Of this it is the usual rendering. The verb παροικέω occurs in Philo with the corresponding verbal meaning; see on Luke xxiv. 18. The noun seems to be equivalent to μέτοικος, which the Sept. have only once (Jer. xx. 3). In 1 Pet. ii. 11 it is used of Christians in the world, and so παροικία, *ib.* i. 17.

The meaning "proselyte" (Anselm, Whitby) is clearly excluded by the context, *vv.* 11 to 13; the other sense is pressed thus by Estius: "accolas fuisse dicit Gentiles quatenus multi ex illis morabantur inter Judaeos . . . non tamen iisdem legibus aut moribus aut religione utentes." But such a reference to local settlement would be too trivial, and quite out of place in writing to Ephesians. Nor had the Gentiles in a figurative sense been sojourners in the commonwealth of Israel. The word is simply used as contrasted with πολῖται. Bengel, followed by Harless, Eadie, *al.*, supposed πάροικοι here to be specially opposed to οἰκεῖοι, and ξένοι to συμπολῖται, the metaphors being respectively from the house and the State. συμπ., says Harless, is sufficient to show in what sense ξένος is used, so that πάροικος is not required as a nearer definition. Accordingly, he interprets the word here by Lev. xvii. 10, where the παρ. of the priest is mentioned, *i.e.* "the guest in the priest's house," and thinks there may be even an allusion to that passage where the πάροικος of the priest is not allowed to eat of the holy things, but the οἰκογενεῖς αὐτοῦ are permitted. But this passage is quite insufficient to establish such an otherwise unknown sense of the Hebrew, and still less of the Greek word. The πάροικος of the priest is simply the π. who dwells in his house. Nor would the figure be suitable, for the Gentiles could not be called guests in the house of God.

ἀλλά ἐστε συμπολῖται τῶν ἁγίων καὶ οἰκεῖοι τοῦ Θεοῦ. "But

ye are fellow-citizens of the saints, and of the household of God." The second ἐστε is added on preponderant authority. It gives greater independence to the clause, an independence befitting its importance. Cf. Rom. viii. 15.

<small>Συμπολίτης is condemned by Phrynichus, and said by grammarians to be a word of later Greek (Josephus, Aelian). It seems strange that they overlooked its occurrence in Euripides (*Heracl.* 826), now noted in the Lexicons. (In Aesch. *Sept. c. Theb.* 601, the true reading is ξὺν πολίταις.)</small>

τῶν ἁγίων. The clear reference to the πολιτεία of Israel shows decisively that the ἅγιοι are those who constitute the people of God. Such formerly had been the Jews, but now are all Christians. These are now the Israel of God, Gal. vi. 16, the true seed of Abraham, *ib.* iii. 7, 16; Rom. iv. 16.

The ἅγιοι, then, are not the Jews, nor specially the patriarchs or Old Testament saints, τῶν περὶ Ἀβραὰμ καὶ Μωϋσῆν καὶ Ἠλίαν, as Chrysostom says, nor the angels, as some other commentators. Nor, again, does the word mean "holy men of all times and places." The word does not refer to personal holiness, but to membership of the spiritual commonwealth to which Jewish and Gentile Christians alike belong. Hence in ch. i. 1 the apostle addresses his readers as ἅγιοι.

οἰκεῖοι τοῦ Θεοῦ, " belonging to the οἶκος or household of God," the theocracy regarded as a family; cf. 1 Tim. iii. 15, "to conduct thyself ἐν οἴκῳ Θεοῦ, ἥτις ἐστὶν ἐκκλησία Θεοῦ ζῶντος"; Heb. x. 20; 1 Pet. iv. 17. In Gal. vi. 10 we have the adjective as here, πρὸς τοὺς οἰκείους τῆς πίστεως, "those that are of the household of faith." But as οἰκεῖος was common with such words as φιλοσοφίας, γεωγραφίας, etc., the reference to an οἶκος cannot be pressed there.

Harless, while supposing the word to be specially contrasted with πάροικοι, remarks that the house is itself nothing but the community of the faithful, they being themselves the stones of which is built the house in which God dwells. They are οἰκεῖοι as ἐποικοδομηθέντες. But this would be to confound two figures founded on two different senses of οἶκος. It is, however, safe to say that the idea of οἶκος in one sense suggested to the apostle the kindred figure. This is quite in accordance with St. Paul's mobility of thought.

20. ἐποικοδομηθέντες. The aorist refers to the time when they became Christians. The further building of which they were the subjects is referred to in ver. 22. The compound verb does not stand merely for the simple, but expresses "superaedificati." Comp. Col. ii. 7 and 1 Cor. iii. 10. As regards the use of the dative case, ἐπὶ τῷ θεμ., it is easy to see why the accusative is not used, as that would suggest the idea of motion towards; cf. 1 Cor. iii. 12, Rom. xv. 20. It is less easy to give a reason for the preference of the dative to the genitive. It can hardly be

maintained that the genitive expresses separable superposition (Ellicott), for in Luke iv. 29 we have the genitive used of the building of a city on a hill, ἐφ' οὗ ἡ πόλις αὐτῶν ᾠκοδόμητο. What that passage suggests is that ἐπί with the genitive expresses locality; cf. Matt. x. 27, ἐπὶ τῶν δωμάτων; xxi. 19, ἐπὶ τ. ὁδοῦ; xxiv. 30, ἐρχόμενον ἐπὶ τ. νεφελῶν; hence it is used loosely of proximity, like our "on the river," ἐπὶ τ. θαλάσσης, either "on the sea" or "on the seashore." Yet the dative is similarly used, ἐπὶ Στρυμόνι (Herod. vii. 75). But, in general, the dative seems to imply more close and exact superposition.

τῶν ἀποστόλων καὶ προφητῶν. The genitive has been understood in four ways: first, as the genitive of possession, "the foundation on which the apostles and prophets have built"; secondly, as the genitive auctoris, "the foundation they laid"; thirdly, as genitive of apposition, "the foundation which consists of the apostles and prophets"; fourthly, "the foundation on which they themselves have been built."

The first view is adopted by Anselm and Beza. Beza's paraphrase is, "Supra Christum qui est apostolicae et propheticae structurae fundamentum." But this interpretation mixes up the θεμέλιος and the ἀκρογων. Christ here is spoken of as the cornerstone, not the foundation. The same objection applies to the fourth view (Bucer, Alford). The second view is very generally adopted, and is supported by reference to 1 Cor. iii. 10. In Bengel's words: "Testimonium apostolorum et prophetarum substructum est fidei credentium omnium." Eadie interprets the foundation as εἰρήνη,—not so much Christ in person as Christ "our peace"; others more generally of the doctrine preached by the apostles and prophets.

But nowhere is the gospel or any doctrine called the foundation of the Church. Moreover, it would be rather incongruous to assume as the foundation the system of teaching about Christ, and as the corner-stone, Christ's person. If, in order to preserve the congruity of the figure, we identify "Christ preached" with "the preaching about Christ," we identify the corner-stone with the foundation. Moreover, the building consists of persons. In 1 Cor. iii. 10 the figure is different; the building there is of doctrine, and naturally the foundation is doctrinal, "Christ," *i.e.* teaching about Christ. Still further, if this view be adopted, the point that is brought out is an incidental one, quite unessential to the connexion. The important point was that the Gentiles were now along with Jewish believers members of one and the same theocracy, or, adopting the apostle's figure, were stones in the same building as the ἅγιοι. This would by no means be expressed by saying that they were built on a foundation laid by the apostles and prophets.

Hence the interpretation of Chrysostom, Oecumenius, etc., is preferable, viz. that the apostles and prophets are themselves the foundation. It is true that elsewhere, with the exception of Rev. xxi. 14, Christ is the foundation, not the apostles; but here Christ is the corner-stone, and the passage in Rev., although not precisely parallel, quite justifies our interpretation here. The fact that the words there are taken from a vision is surely no objection to this. What seems a graver objection is that Christ seems thus to be named only as "primus inter pares." The answer to this is that by Orientals the corner-stone was reckoned of greater importance than the foundation, and as connecting and concentrating on itself the weight of the building. Hence the expression in Isa. xxviii. 16, alluded to here, and 2 Pet. ii. 6; cf. Ps. cxviii. 22; Acts iv. 11; Matt. xxi. 42.

Amongst recent commentators, Soden and Macpherson have adopted this view. The latter further defends the reference to the apostles as the foundation by 2 Tim. ii. 19, "The firm foundation of God standeth," "where undoubtedly the true elect of God are intended, who resist all temptations to unfaithfulness." He adds, "In the building up a special rank is given to those who have been by immediate Divine calling and inspiration His witnesses unto all besides. They, in fellowship with Christ, as forming the first layer, are called the foundation."

ὄντος ἀκρογωνιαίου αὐτοῦ Χριστοῦ Ἰησοῦ. Showing, as Chrysostom says, that it is Christ that holds the whole together; for the corner-stone holds together both the walls and the foundations. "Participium ὄντος initio commatis hujus, valde demonstrat in praesenti tempore," Bengel. ἀκρογ. (λίθου understood, which is added in D* G). The figure of the corner-stone as uniting the two walls is pressed by Theodoret as referring to the union of Jews and Gentiles; and many expositors have followed him. But this is not only to press the figure unduly, it is also unsuitable. For the point is that Jews and Gentiles now indifferently are built into the one building, not as if the Jews were one wall and the Gentiles another.

αὐτοῦ is referred to θεμέλιος by Bengel, Soden, Macpherson. Bengel urges the absence of the article before Χριστοῦ Ἰησοῦ. But, in fact, the article would imply the previous mention of Christ Jesus, and the sense would be "He Himself, even Christ Jesus"; see Fritzsche on Matt. iii. 4, where αὐτὸς δὲ ὁ Ἰωάννης and αὐτὸς Ἰωάννης (as in D) are equally possible. Similarly John iv. 44, where the best texts have αὐτὸς Ἰησοῦς; but the article (as inserted in R, 69, al.) is admissible. Also Luke xx. 42, αὐτὸς Δαυείδ. It is better to connect αὐτοῦ with Χρ. Ἰ., since it is more to the purpose that Christ should be called the corner-stone of the building than of the foundation; and in this connexion the emphatic pronoun is by no means superfluous, but fittingly distinguishes Christ from the apostles and prophets.

Who are these apostles and prophets? According to Chrysostom they are the Old Testament prophets. The absence of the article before προφητῶν is against this, though not decisive, since the O.T. prophets and the apostles might possibly be regarded as constituting one class, though this would hardly be natural. The order of the words is also against it, and is not satisfactorily accounted for by the superior dignity of the apostles as having seen and heard Christ (Estius). Again, we have the analogy of iii. 5 and iv. 11, in both of which passages apostles and prophets are named together, and the prophets are New Testament prophets. These passages also disprove the suggestion that the apostles themselves are here called prophets. The absence of the article before προφητῶν is natural, since the apostles and prophets formed one class as teachers of the Church. The objection, that the prophets themselves were built on the foundation of the apostles (in whichever sense we take the genitive), loses all force when we consider, first, the high value which St. Paul sets on the gift of prophesying (1 Cor. xiv. 1 ff.); and, secondly, that with him "apostles" does not mean the Twelve only (see hereafter on iv. 11). Nor does there appear any reason here why the apostles should be called by this additional title.

21. ἐν ᾧ, *i.e.* ἐν Χρ. Ἰησοῦ, not ἀκρογωνιαίῳ, as Theophylact, Beza, *al.*

πᾶσα οἰκοδομή. Rec. πᾶσα ἡ οἰκ.

The reading is difficult.

πᾶσα οἰκοδομή, ℵ* B D G K L and most others, Chrys. (*Comment.*), Theodoret.

πᾶσα ἡ οἰκοδομή, ℵ° A C P, Arm., Chrys. (text; but this is probably a copyist's error or correction). Thus the balance of documentary evidence is strongly against the insertion of the article. Before deciding in favour of this reading, we must consider the comparative likelihood of the article being either omitted or inserted in error. Reiche, for instance, thinks it probable that copyists either neglected the article from lack of exact knowledge of Greek, "quod in codicibus, qui articulo hic carent, saepe observatur," or misinterpreted the words of the apostle as referring to individual churches, or (as Chrysostom) to the various parts of each edifice (*Comment. Crit. in loc.*). He thinks ἡ might more easily be omitted because of the homoeoteleuton οἰκοδομή, and because in iv. 12, 16 the same word is without the article. But this is not a case of possible omission from homoeoteleuton; if the scribe's eye leaped from η to η, οικοδομη would be the word omitted. Itacism would be a more plausible explanation. In fact, the accidental omission of the article in cases where it is grammatically required is extremely rare, even in single MSS. Even where homoeoteleuton or other sources of parablepsy might have been expected to cause omission in one or two MSS., we find no variation, as in Matt. xxv. 7, πᾶσαι αἱ, or ὁ before words beginning with ο, as πᾶς ὁ ὄχλος, Matt. xiii. 2; Luke vi. 19. Intentional variation in the addition or omission of the article is pretty frequent, especially with such words as Θεός, Χριστός, πίστις. That the variation is intentional appears further from the grouping of the MSS. on each side, those to which the preference is given by recent critics being usually on the side of omission (not Rom. xv. 14 or Col. iii. 16). Nor does any reason appear for the intentional omission of the article in these cases. Where the article was omitted by the first scribe of ℵ and D (Epp.), it is generally supplied by a corrector. A remarkable instance of (probably) erroneous omission is in Eph. vi. 16, τά before πεπυρωμένα (om. B D* G). On the other hand, a striking example of the article (probably) added erroneously after πᾶς occurs Rom. xv. 14, πάσης τῆς γνώσεως (ℵ B P, but om. A C D and most). In Matt. iii. 5, πᾶσα ἡ Ἰουδαία, ἡ is om. by M Γ Δ and about twenty others, It is unnecessary before the proper name. In the present case, intentional addition is much more likely than intentional omission, since with the article the meaning is obvious, and without it there is a difficulty. Such a consideration as Reiche suggests does not seem sufficiently obtrusive to influence the scribes.

The word οἰκοδομή belongs to later Greek, and is condemned by Phrynichus. It is used both for οἰκοδόμημα and οἰκοδόμησις. For the former see 1 Chron. xxix. 1; for the latter, Ezek. xvi. 61, xvii. 17, where it represents the Hebrew infinitive. In the N.T. it seems to have a sort of intermediate sense, like the English "building." Thus in 1 Cor. iii. 9, "ye are God's husbandry (γεώργιον), ye are God's building (οἰκοδομή)," the word is not equivalent either to οἰκοδόμημα or to οἰκοδόμησις. As γεώργιον there is that which is cultivated by God, so οἰκ. is that which is builded up by God. In Matt. xxiv. 1 and Mark xiii. 1, 2, it is used of the buildings of the temple: ποταποὶ λίθοι καὶ ποταπαὶ οἰκοδομαί . . . βλέπεις ταύτας τὰς μεγάλας οἰκοδομάς. Here it does not appear to mean "edifices," for the temple could not properly be said to consist of several edifices. The separate λίθοι were not οἰκοδομαί, but every combination of them might be called an οἰκ. Just so we might say, "what carvings," "what outlines," or of a picture, "what harmonies." The Vulgate has in Matt. xxiv. 1 and Mk. xiii. 2, "aedificationes"; in Mk. xiii. 1, "structurae." In 2 Cor. v. 1, "we have a building from God," the word is nearly equivalent to "structure," yet it is plain that οἰκοδόμημα would not have been so suitable. It is "a house that God builds," not "has built." The English words "building, construction, structure" all have a similar ambiguity. The most common meaning of the word in the N.T. is the figurative one, "edification"; that sense it has in this Ep., iv. 12, 16. The meaning in iv. 29 is analogous.

Now let us turn to the text; and first, if the reading with the article is adopted, there is no obvious difficulty, "the whole building," that is, the whole organised body of believers. When we look closer, indeed, we find something strange in the expressions. συναρμολογουμένη is present. It seems strange that the whole building should be spoken of thus as in course of being framed together. Still more unexpected is αὔξει. The whole building is growing into a temple. The ambiguity of the English "building" disguises this strangeness, which is apparent when we substitute "edifice." "The whole edifice is growing into a temple." The words, "the whole building or edifice," express the conception of a thing completed. If the reading were well established, we might explain this as due to a want of precision in the metaphor; but, as we have seen, this reading is not so well supported as the other, to which we now turn.

Many expositors, including Eadie, Ellicott (more doubtfully), Barry, Moule, Meyrick, not Findlay, Macpherson, nor the Revisers, hold that πᾶσα οἰκοδομή may be rendered as if it were πᾶσα ἡ οἰκ., and they refer especially to Luke iv. 13, πάντα πειρασμόν: Acts ii. 36, πᾶς οἶκος Ἰσραήλ: vii. 22, πᾶσα σοφία Αἰγυπτίων: Homer, *Il.* xxiv. 407, πᾶσαν ἀληθείην. None of these passages bear out the assertion. πάντα πειρασμόν is not "all the temptation," but "every temptation," as RV., *i.e.* "every form of temptation." See on Luke iv. 13. So in Acts vii. 22, although the English version sufficiently expresses the sense, what is meant is not the totality of the wisdom of Egypt, but the wisdom in all its branches. In Hom. *Il.* xxiv. 407, ἄγε δή μοι πᾶσαν ἀληθείην κατάλεξον, the meaning clearly is: "Come, tell me the exact truth, nothing but the truth." The article here would not be appropriate. Similarly in Josephus, *Antiq.* iv. 5. 1, ποταμὸς διὰ πάσης ἐρήμου ῥέων is a river flowing through a country which is all desert.

οἶκος Ἰσραήλ in Acts ii. 36 is an expression borrowed from the O.T., where it occurs with πᾶς in Jer. ix. 26, Ezek. xxxvi. 10, xxxvii. 11, and is treated as a proper name, as it is without πᾶς in xxxix. 12, 22, 23, etc. So, too, οἶκος Κυρίου. So in classical writers γῆ, for example, is treated as a proper name. The general rule is that a word cannot be used with πᾶς without the article when the sense is "the whole," unless it is such that without πᾶς it can be employed definitely, or does not require the article to give it definiteness. A somewhat similar rule holds good in English, where we can say, not only "all England," but "all town," "all school," "all college," "all parliament"; but by no means "all house." It is, no doubt, immemorial use that has enabled such words to dispense with the article, when the thing meant, though only one of many, is marked out by its familiarity. We can also say "all night, "all day," as the Greeks did. Nor does it appear that π. οἰκ. would, to a reader of St. Paul's time, be any more likely to suggest "the whole building" than would "all building" to an English reader. We must therefore acquiesce in some such rendering as "every building," or "each several building," RV., modified, perhaps, as will be presently mentioned.

But what is meant by "every building"? Hardly "every church"; for to speak of the several local churches, or of the Jews and Gentiles as so many several buildings, would not be in accordance with the figure in ver. 20, or with St. Paul's language elsewhere. Moreover, he has just used a forcible figure to express the unity of the whole Church, and it would be strange if he now weakened it by speaking of several buildings. The individual believer, again, is spoken of in 1 Cor. iii. 16 as ναὸς Θεοῦ; but there the figure is explained by the context, as founded on the conception of the indwelling of the Spirit. This is very different from calling each believer an οἰκοδομή. The passages above referred to in Matthew and Mark suggest that what is intended is "everything that from time to time is builded in," "every constituent element of the building." The English words "all the building" would admit of being understood in this way, but are ambiguous. The image is that of an extensive pile of buildings in process of construction at different points on a common plan. The several parts are adjusted to each other so as to preserve the unity of design. So Findlay, who remarks that an author of the second century, writing in the interests of Catholic unity, would scarcely have omitted the article.

Hofmann compares πάσης κτίσεως, Col. i. 15, which he says does not mean "the whole creation," nor "every creature," but "all that is created," as πᾶσα σοφία καὶ φρόνησις in i. 8 is "all that is wisdom"; πᾶν θέλημα τοῦ Θεοῦ, Col. iv. 12, "all God's will," to which we may add πᾶσα γραφή, 2 Tim. iii. 16; π. ἀναστροφή, 1 Pet. i. 15. Soden's view is similar. Comp. iv. 16.

συναρμολογουμένη, "fitly joined together," present participle, because this harmonious framing together is a process still going on. The compound verb occurs only here and iv. 16. The simple verb ἁρμολογέω seems to be equally rare. The classical word is συναρμόζω. None of these is found in the Sept.

αὔξει, "groweth," the present, as in the former word, indicating the perpetual growth. The verb is neither rare nor poetical, as is sometimes stated; on the contrary, it is more frequent than αὐξάνω in the best Attic prose (Thuc. Xen. Plato), but the use of the active in an intransitive sense is later (Aristot. Polyb. Diod.). It occurs also in Col. ii. 19.

εἰς ναὸν ἅγιον ἐν Κυρίῳ. "Unto a holy temple (or sanctuary) in the Lord." Κύριος, according to the Pauline usage, must be Christ. ἐν Κ. seems best connected with ἅγιος, "holy in the Lord"; to join it with αὔξει alone would be a tautology.

22. ἐν ᾧ takes up the ἐν ᾧ of ver. 21; cf. ch. i. 11 and 12.

καὶ ὑμεῖς, "ye also"; cf. ver. 13.

συνοικοδομεῖσθε, not imperative, as Calvin: "Ephesios hortatur ut crescant in fide Christi magis et magis postquam in ea semel fuerunt fundati," but indicative, as is proved by vv. 19, 20, in which the apostle describes what the readers are, not what they ought to be. Note the present tense, because the building is still going on; cf. 1 Pet. ii. 5, "are being builded in together," *i.e.* together with the others; συν- as in συμπολῖται. The πᾶσα before οἰκ. looks forward to this καὶ ὑμεῖς συνοικ., and this is a fitting conclusion to the paragraph which commenced with "ye are no more strangers and foreigners." Meyer and Ellicott understand the συν- differently, viz. as referring to the putting together the single parts of the building; Meyer quoting Philo, *De Proem.* § 20, p. 928 E (ed. Mang. ii. p. 427), οἰκίαν εὖ συνῳκοδομημένην καὶ συνηρμοσμένην. But the whole context favours the interpretation "you together with others," and there is no reason to give any other sense to the συν- in συναρμολογουμένη.

εἰς κατοικητήριον τοῦ Θεοῦ. κατοικητήριον only in Rev. xviii. 2 in N.T., but freq. in the Sept. "Into a habitation of God," the same which was expressed by ναὸς ἅγιος, only further specifying the essential nature of this ναός. Harless, who reads πᾶσα ἡ οἰκ., supposes κατοικ. here to be used of each individual Christian in whom God dwells, the whole forming a ναὸς ἅγιος. Griesbach places ἐν ᾧ καὶ ὑμεῖς συνοικ. in a parenthesis, which is awkward and unnecessary.

ἐν πνεύματι, "in the Spirit." It is interpreted by Chrysostom as = spiritually, οἶκος πνευματικός, and so Theophyl. Oecum. Olshausen also thinks there is a glance at the ναὸς χειροποιητός. But there is no suggestion of this in the context; and as the whole is so distinctly figurative, it would be worse than superfluous to add this definition. Moreover, it does not appear that ἐν πνεύματι could be used with a substantive as = spiritual, except so far as the substantive involves a verbal notion, as περιτομὴ ἐν πν. = τὸ περιτέμνεσθαι ἐν πν., δέσμιος ἐν Χριστῷ = δεδεμένος ἐν Χρ.

But ἐν here is not merely instrumental, as if = διά. The Spirit is not the means or instrument only, but the medium by virtue of which God dwells in the Church. The ἐν refers to the act of κατοίκησις. He by or in His Spirit dwells in this temple. The article is not required, as πνεῦμα is frequently treated as a proper name where no ambiguity is caused thereby.

III. 1–7. *This truth, that the Gentiles are fellow-heirs with the Jews, was hidden from former generations, but has now been revealed to the apostles and prophets; and unworthy though I am, yet to me has been given the privilege of making it known, and of preaching Christ to the Gentiles.*

1. τούτου χάριν ἐγὼ Παῦλος ὁ δέσμιος τοῦ Χριστοῦ Ἰησοῦ ὑπὲρ ὑμῶν τῶν ἐθνῶν. (Tischendorf omits Ἰησοῦ, with ℵ* D* G.) "For this reason, I Paul, the prisoner of Christ Jesus in behalf of you Gentiles." "For this reason," "hujus rei gratiâ," Vulg., *i.e.*, as Theodoret says, "Knowing well both what ye were and how ye were called and on what conditions, I pray God to establish you in the faith."

Chrysostom supplies εἰμί. I am the prisoner of Christ Jesus, etc. So the Peshitto and many moderns, including Beza, Meyer,

Macpherson, "in order that ye may be built up to the habitation of God — in this behoof, that your Christian development may advance to that goal." But this is to give too great prominence to the assertion of his imprisonment, as if it were a main point in the discourse, instead of being incidental. Besides, we should expect in that case δέσμιος without the article. St. Paul was not likely thus to designate himself as "the prisoner of Christ Jesus," even with the addition "for you Gentiles." The notoriety of the fact does not explain this. Moreover, this view makes τούτου χάριν and ὑπὲρ ὑμῶν rather tautologous. The analogy of ch. iv. 1 is in favour of taking ὁ δ. in apposition with ἐγὼ Παῦλος.

Calvin's "legatione fungor" is a rendering of πρεσβεύω, the reading of D (from vi. 20). Three cursives add κεκαύχημαι.

Origen (*Catena*) supposes a solecism; that, in fact, what St. Paul ought to have written was τ. χαρ. ... ἐγνώρισα τὸ μυστ. Jerome also, following Origen, declares that after diligent search he could not find the continuation of the sense. But the true key was given by Theodore Mops., followed by Theodoret, viz. that vv. 2–13 is a parenthesis. ταῦτα πάντα ἐν μέσῳ τεθεικὼς ἀναλαμβάνει τὸν περὶ προσευχῆς λόγον, Theodoret. The apostle having described himself as a prisoner for the Gentiles, is quite characteristically drawn off into a digression on the grace granted to him in connexion with this ministry to the Gentiles. Oecumenius regards the sentence as resumed in ver. 8 with the change of the nominative to the dative, a change not without parallels, as he observes, in Thucydides and Demosthenes. On that view τούτου χάριν would mean "for this purpose," as in Tit. i. 5. But then ὁ δέσμιος would have no point, and, besides, ver. 8 is closely connected with 6 and 7. It is much more satisfactory to assume, with Theodore and Theodoret, that the sense is resumed with the same words, τούτου χάριν, in ver. 14. The supposition of a resumption in ch. iv. 1, adopted in the AV., rests apparently only on the repetition of ὁ δέσμιος, and unnecessarily lengthens the parenthesis.

"The prisoner of Christ Jesus," so he calls himself in 2 Tim. i. 8 and Philem. 9, and in this Ep. iv. 1, "prisoner in the Lord." He looks on his imprisonment, not merely as suffered in the service of the Lord, but as part of the lot assigned to him by Christ, so that he was Christ's prisoner. Somewhat similarly in ch. vi. 20, ὑπὲρ οὗ πρεσβεύω ἐν ἁλύσει.

"In behalf of you Gentiles." Since it was his preaching the free admission of the Gentiles that led to his persecution at the hands of the Jews and to his present imprisonment, Acts xxi. 21, 28, xxii. 22.

2. εἴγε ἠκούσατε τὴν οἰκονομίαν. "If, indeed, ye have heard of the dispensation." This seems decisive against the supposition that the Epistle was addressed to a Church which had been

personally instructed by the writer. The utmost force that can be claimed for εἴγε is that, in Hermann's words, it is used "de re quae jure sumpta creditur," "if, as I take for granted," being less hypothetical than εἴπερ. According to Lightfoot on Gal. iii. 4, this rule requires modification when applied to the N.T., where εἴγε is less directly affirmative than εἴπερ.

Eadie says it is "undeniable" that εἴγε is used in the N.T. of things that are certain, quoting iv. 21 and Col. i. 23. The former passage is in the same case with the present; in the latter, hope only is expressed, not certainty. The only other places where εἴγε occurs in the N.T. are Gal. iii. 4 and in the Received Text 2 Cor. v. 3 (εἴπερ, B D). It is found also in Rom. v. 6 in B. But allowing that the particle implies certainty as strongly as Hermann's rule asserts, it could not be used of a fact in the writer's own experience. A preacher addressing a strange congregation might say "I am sure," or even "I know that you have been taught so and so," but no preacher addressing those whom he himself had taught would ordinarily express himself in this way.[1]

It is said, indeed, that this argument proves too much, since "what was known of Paul in the Ephesian Church would practically be known of him throughout the missions of Asia" (Moule). But this is just the kind of case in which the particle may be properly used, viz. where the writer may be "practically" certain, but doubt is conceivable. Besides, the details which follow might be but imperfectly known to those who had not heard them from St. Paul's own lips. And again, would he, in writing to the Ephesians, refer them to what he has just now written, that they may appreciate his knowledge in the mystery of Christ? Had they not had much more full proof of this during his long ministry? Every other attempt to evade this conclusion is equally unsuccessful. Thus ἠκούσατε has been rendered "intellexistis" (Anselm, Grotius), a meaning which the verb can have only when "hearing" is included; or, again, "hearing" the Epistle read (alluding to earlier passages in this Epistle); but cf. ἀναγινώσκοντες, ver. 4. Calvin says: "Credibile est, quum ageret Ephesi, eum tacuisse de his rebus." Ellicott reasons in a circle, "There could be no real doubt; 'neque enim ignorare quod hic dicitur poterant Ephesii quibus Paulus ipse evangelium plusquam biennio praedicaverat,' Estius. . . . No argument, then, can be fairly deduced," etc. He supposes the apostle to convey the hope that his words had not been forgotten. Similarly Eadie, Alford, Macpherson, Meyer, (contra, W. Schmidt in last ed. of Meyer). But the words are not "if ye remember," or "if ye know"; but "if ye have heard"; and that, if written to the Ephesians, would be = "if I told you."

---

[1] On εἴγε and εἴπερ compare Sanday and Headlam, *Comm. on Romans*, iii. 30, with the quotation there from Monro's *Homeric Grammar*.

τὴν οἰκονομίαν τῆς χάριτος τοῦ Θεοῦ τῆς δοθείσης μοι εἰς ὑμᾶς. "The dispensation of the grace of God, the grace given me to you-ward."

As the explanation which follows is "that by revelation," etc., it is best to understand τ. χάριτος as the genitive of the object, viz. the dispensation or plan or arrangement (namely, God's arrangement) with respect to the grace," etc. Chrysostom, followed by Oecum., takes the genitive as that of the subject. οἰκ. χαρ. τὴν ἀποκάλυψιν φησίν, ὅτι οὐ παρὰ ἀνθρώπου ἔμαθεν, ἀλλ' οὕτως ᾠκονόμησεν ἡ χάρις ὥστε μοι ἐξ οὐρανοῦ ἀποκαλυφθῆναι, Oec. But this does not agree so well with the following words, which define the χάρις as ἡ δοθεῖσα εἰς ὑμᾶς. Alford, understanding the genitive as objective, takes οἰκ. as = "munus dispensandi." But it is not easy to see in what sense St. Paul could dispense the grace given to him. Many commentators suppose δοθείσης to be attracted into the genitive by χάριτος, either understanding that it is in and with the grace that the οἰκ. is entrusted to him (for which reason the participle has the case of χ., v. Soden), or taking τ. οἰκ. τ. χαρ. as = the gospel dispensation. But, while St. Paul might speak of the gospel dispensation as entrusted to him (οἰκονομίαν πεπίστευμαι, 1 Cor. ix. 17), he could hardly speak of it as "given to him." Nor does this interpretation agree with the circumstance that the following words take the form of an explanation. The explanation of οἰκ., as the apostolic office or stewardship, is also not consistent with the explanation, in which it is the act of God that is spoken of, not any conduct of the apostle. It is tempting to suppose, with some expositors, that the writer, in using the word οἰκονομία, has in his mind the building just referred to. But although οἶκος might suggest the idea of an οἰκονόμος, οἰκοδομή and οἰκητήριον do not; and the figurative use of οἰκονομία was so common, that if the apostle had intended such an allusion, he would have made it more distinct.

3. ὅτι κατὰ ἀποκάλυψιν ἐγνωρίσθη μοι τὸ μυστήριον. "That it was by way of revelation that the mystery was made known to me." Explanation of ver. 2; hence the emphasis is on κατὰ ἀπ., which is not really different from δι' ἀποκαλύψεως, Gal. i. 12. In the latter passage, κατά could not have been used on account of Ἰησοῦ Χριστοῦ following.

ἐγνωρίσθη is the reading of א A B C D* G P, Vulg. Boh. Arm., Chrys. The Rec. has ἐγνώρισε, with D^c K L, Theoph. Oec. For τὸ μυστήριον see on ch. i. 9. Here, not the "mystery" of redemption in general is meant, but the particular "mystery" of the inclusion of the heathen, for it is thus explained in ver. 6.

καθὼς προέγραψα ἐν ὀλίγῳ. "As I have just written in brief." προ- is local, not temporal (cf. Gal. iii. 1, προεγράφη), and the reference is to the present Epistle, not to an earlier one, as supposed by Chrysostom, Calvin, *al.*, contrary to the present participle ἀναγινώσκοντες. Theodoret and Theophylact have the right view. Comp. 1 Cor. v. 9, ἔγραψα ἐν τῇ ἐπιστολῇ; and 1 Pet. v. 12, ἔγραψα δι' ὀλίγων. The reference is doubtless to the whole preceding exposition about the Gentiles.

ἐν ὀλίγῳ, equivalent to ἐν βραχεῖ, used by Demosthenes. Theodoret, indeed, and some moderns connect this with the προ- in προέγραψα, as if it meant "paulo ante," which would be πρὸ ὀλίγου. ἐν ὀλ. in a temporal sense would mean, "in a short time" (Acts xxvi. 28). Wetstein correctly, " pauca tantum attigi cum multa dici possent." Oecumenius gives a peculiar turn, οὐκ ἔγραψεν ὅσα ἐχρῆν ἀλλ' ὅσα ἐχώρουν νοεῖν, as if the following πρὸς ὃ were = " prout," which would make ἀναγινώσκοντες unmeaning.

4. πρὸς ὃ is, "according to which, or looking to which," namely, to what I have said. Comp. "πρὸς ἃ ἔπραξεν," 2 Cor. v. 10; πρὸς τὴν ἀλήθειαν τοῦ εὐαγγ., Gal. ii. 14; πρὸς τὸ θέλημα αὐτοῦ, Luke xii. 47. But the usage is quite classical.

ἀναγινώσκοντες, present, because it is "while reading," or "as ye read."

νοῆσαι. Where it is indifferent whether the aorist or present infinitive is used, the aorist is more frequent (Winer, § 44. 7), especially after such verbs as δύναμαι, θέλω, etc. Hort thinks this ἀναγ. refers to reading the O.T. prophecies, comparing Matt. xxiv. 15. But there the passage "read" is distinctly specified, and although in Mark xiii. 14 Daniel is not named, he is quoted.

τὴν σύνεσίν μου ἐν τῷ μυστηρίῳ τοῦ Χριστοῦ. "My understanding in the mystery of Christ." The article is not required before ἐν τῷ μ., because συνιέναι ἐν is a frequent expression (Josh. i. 7; 2 Chron. xxxiv. 12).

μυστ. τοῦ Χρ. We have the same expression in Col. iv. 3, where it clearly means the doctrine of the free admission of the Gentiles (δι' ὃ καὶ δέδεμαι). It is the same here, as explained in ver. 6. Similarly, in Col. i. 27 we have τοῦ μ. τούτου ὅ ἐστιν Χριστὸς ἐν ὑμῖν. That passage has been used (by Alford, Ellicott, Meyer) to prove that the genitive here is one of apposition or identity; but it fails in this, since there it is not Χριστός, but Χριστὸς ἐν ὑμῖν, that constitutes the μ. It is better, therefore, to understand "the mystery (or doctrine) relating to the Christ"; the genitive being that of the object.

Critics who question the genuineness of the Epistle regard this verse as the expression of a boastfulness not in accordance with the dignity of an apostle, and only a clumsy imitation of 2 Cor. xi. 5, 6, where St. Paul is merely claiming for himself that in which his opponents claim to surpass him. But there is no self-laudation in this assertion of σύνεσις (see, on the contrary, ver. 8); nor even as high a claim to exceptional knowledge as is involved in κατὰ ἀποκάλυψιν, which it only serves to illustrate. Is it not quite natural that in writing to Churches where he was not personally known, and where there were teachers whose teaching was of a corrupt and paganising tendency (v. 11–14), and threatened to cause a schism between the Jewish and the Gentile members of the Church, the apostle, who was, in fact, combating these errors, and expounding the true nature of the privileges to which the Gentiles were admitted, should remind them in some such way that the subject was one on which he could speak with authority, and thus guard against objections which might possibly be urged by these unsound teachers? From this point of view it will be seen that this indirect and delicate way of meeting possible opposition is thoroughly Pauline. On the other hand, a writer who merely assumed the name of Paul, especially one of such power as the writer of this Epistle, would hardly put into his mouth an expression of such seeming self-complacency, without any hint of opposition. Still less would such a writer forthwith add so striking an expression of self-depreciation as is contained in ver. 8.

5. ὃ ἑτέραις γενεαῖς οὐκ ἐγνωρίσθη τοῖς υἱοῖς τῶν ἀνθρώπων. "Which in other ages was not made known to the sons of men." ἐν, which in the Received Text precedes ἑτέραις, rests on slight authority, but it expresses the right construction of ἑτ. γεν. Meyer, in his earlier editions, adopted the view that the meaning was "to other generations," τοῖς υἱοῖς, κ.τ.λ., being epexegetical. (So also v. Soden.) But the usual interpretation is simpler, and corresponds better with the antithetical νῦν. For γενεά in this sense, cf. Acts xiv. 16, ἐν ταῖς παρῳχημέναις γ.; and for the dative of time, ii. 12, ἑτέραις, *i.e.* other than the present.

"The sons of men," an expression frequent in the O.T. and simply = "men." Comp. Mark iii. 28 (the only N.T. parallel) with Matt. xii. 31. It is needless, therefore, to adopt Bengel's remark, "latissima appellatio, causam exprimens ignorantiae, ortum naturalem cui opponitur Spiritus." Bengel, indeed, thinks that the prophets are especially referred to, because Ezekiel, who writes largely of the temple, as St. Paul does here, calls himself the son of man; but this is peculiar to him. It seems equally erroneous to find in the words a marked contrast with "His holy apostles," namely, because these were Θεοῦ ἄνθρωποι (2 Pet. i. 21) (Ellicott). This is far-fetched. The apostles and prophets were not the less sons of men; and we might, with as much reason, follow Jerome, who would exclude the O.T. patriarchs and prophets because they were "sons of God."

ὡς νῦν ἀπεκαλύφθη τοῖς ἁγίοις ἀποστόλοις αὐτοῦ καὶ προφήταις ἐν Πνεύματι. "As it has now been revealed to His holy apostles and prophets in the Spirit."

ὡς is comparative, with such clearness as now. οὕτως ἀκριβῶς οὐκ ᾔδεισαν οἱ παλαιοὶ τὸ μυστήριον, Theoph.; "fuit illis hoc mysterium quasi procul et cum involucris ostensum," Beza.

ἀπεκαλύφθη, not now ἐγνωρίσθη, because the special manner in which the knowledge was given is to be brought out.

"His holy apostles." How can the writer, if himself an apostle, use such an expression? Some critics answer unhesitatingly that it is incredible that an apostle should do so, and that the expression betrays the view which belonged to a later age. Baur thinks the ἁγίοις an oversight. And the writer who was so unskilful as to be guilty of this palpable oversight, is so mindful of his assumed character that in the same breath he says, ἐμοὶ τῷ ἐλαχιστοτέρῳ πάντων ἁγίων. The difficulty seems to arise from the use of the word "holy," and the corresponding words in other modern languages, to express the personal character of "holiness." But ἅγιος is used of any thing that is set apart for a sacred purpose. So we have "holy prophets," Luke i. 70; Acts iii. 21. All Christians are by their calling ἅγιοι, and St. Paul frequently uses the word where he himself is included (*e.g.* 1 Cor. vi. 2 and Col. i. 26). When he calls all believers ἅγιοι, what delicacy should prevent him from calling the apostles by the same word? A clergyman is not expected to be prevented, by a feeling of delicacy, from speaking of his "reverend brethren," or a bishop of his "right reverend brethren."

Lachmann and Tregelles place a comma after ἁγίοις, the following words being in apposition: "to the saints, His apostles and prophets," or rather "apostles and prophets of His." But such a separation of the adjective from the following substantive is harsh, although it must be admitted that it is suggested by the parallel in Col. i. 26.

A more considerable difficulty seems to arise from the statement that the mystery of the free admission of the Gentiles had been revealed to "the apostles and prophets," viz. as a body. For this is precisely the special doctrine which St. Paul seems elsewhere, and here in ver. 3, to claim as his own, and which, at least at first, was not accepted by the other apostles (Gal. ii.). In ver. 8, also, this is recognised as the distinctive characteristic of St. Paul's apostleship. For this reason Reuss makes the suggestion that the second half of ver. 5 is a gloss. In favour of this suggestion, it may also be observed that αὐτοῦ has no expressed antecedent, unless, indeed, in opposition to most expositors, we take it to be Χριστοῦ. In the parallel in Col. i. 26, τοῖς ἁγίοις αὐτοῦ, the antecedent Θεοῦ occurs just before. But the authority of the MSS. is too strong for this suggestion to be accepted. B, indeed, omits ἀποστόλοις (with ps. Ambr.), while D G place the word after αὐτοῦ.

The difficulty, however, is met by the consideration that, notwithstanding the doubts which the other apostles at first entertained, they afterwards fully accepted the doctrine as taught by St. Paul, Acts xv., Gal. ii. 7 ff., and that long before the present Epistle was written. The "prophets" are manifestly Christian prophets. ἐν πνεύματι must be joined with the verb, not with προφήταις, to which it would be a superfluous addition, or ἁγίοις, or the following εἶναι.

6. εἶναι τὰ ἔθνη συγκληρονόμα καὶ σύσσωμα ... (namely) "that the Gentiles are fellow-heirs (or joint possessors) and fellow-members of the body." Epexegetical; stating, not the purpose, but the content of the μυστήριον. The "should be" of AV. is not grammatically tenable. συγκληρονόμα, fellow-heirs, not with Christ, as in Rom. viii. 17 (and Jerome here), for it is "in Christ," but with the believing Jews. The word συγκληρονόμος is found four times in the N.T. and once in Philo, but not elsewhere. σύσσωμα, incorporated with them into the body of which Christ is the Head. The word is not found elsewhere (except in the Fathers), and is supposed to have been perhaps formed by St. Paul. But as Aristotle has the compound συσσωματοποιεῖν (*De Mundo*, iv. 30), it is more probable that the adjective was in use.

καὶ συμμέτοχα τῆς ἐπαγγελίας ἐν Χριστῷ Ἰησοῦ.

The Received Text has αὐτοῦ after ἐπαγγ., with D^bc G K L, *al.*; but the word is absent from ℵ A B C D* P 17, *al.* Χριστῷ of the Text Rec. rests on nearly the same MS. authority, with the addition of D; while Χριστῷ Ἰησοῦ has the authority of ℵ A B C P 17.

"And joint-partakers of the promise in Christ Jesus." The accumulation of epithets is due to the importance of the matter; there is no climax, for συμμέτ. is not stronger than σύσσωμα. The former word is found outside this Epistle only in Josephus, but the verb συμμετέχω occurs in Xen. and Plato. Jerome renders the words "cohaeredes et concorporales et comparticipes promissionis," defending the inelegance of the Latin by the importance of correctly representing the Greek. The genitive ἐπαγγ. depends only on συμμετ. The promise is the promise of salvation, of a part in the kingdom of the Messiah; and to be partakers of the promise is to be joined with those to whom the promise is given. There is no need, then, to take ἡ ἐπαγ. as = the thing promised, still less to understand this specially of the Holy Spirit. In the passages to which Eadie and others refer in support of such a restriction, the Spirit is expressly named, *e.g.* Gal. iii. 14; ch. i. 13.

ἐν Χριστῷ Ἰησοῦ and διὰ τοῦ εὐαγγελίου refer to all three epithets. "In Christ Jesus through the gospel." In Christ, not διά, for He was not simply the means; it was in His person that this effect was produced. Cf. i. 7 ; and for an analogous distinction between ἐν and διά, even where both substantives are impersonal, 1 Pet. i. 5, ἐν δυνάμει Θεοῦ φρουρουμένους διὰ πίστεως, and Heb. x. 10, ἐν ᾧ θελήματι ἡγιασμένοι ἐστε διὰ τῆς προσφορᾶς, κ.τ.λ.

7. οὗ ἐγενήθην διάκονος. "Of which I became a minister" (ἐγενήθην, ℵ A B D* G; but ἐγενόμην, C D^c K L). The use of γενηθῆναι instead of the Attic γενέσθαι is condemned by Phrynichus, who calls it Doric; but it is frequent in later Greek writers (Polybius, Diodorus, Dion. Hal. etc.), as is shown by Lobeck (*ad Phryn.* p. 109). There is no ground, then, for assigning to the word here a passive shade of meaning, as is done by Oecum., οὐδὲν γὰρ ἐγὼ ἔργον ἐμὸν συνεισήνεγκα τῇ χάριτι ταύτῃ. Compare, on the contrary, Col. iv. 11, ἐγενήθησάν μοι παρηγορία; 1 Thess. ii. 14, μιμηταὶ ἐγενήθητε.

διάκονος. Harless maintains that δ. denotes the servant in his activity for that service, while ὑπηρέτης denotes him in his activity for the Master, apparently on the ground that διακονεῖν τι or τινί τι is said, and he compares 1 Cor. iv. 1 with Col. i. 7. But ὑπηρετεῖν τινί τι is also said (Xen. *Anab.* vii. 7. 46; Soph. *Phil.* 1012), and the distinction cannot be maintained; see 2 Cor. xi. 23, διάκονοι Χριστοῦ εἰσι; 1 Tim. iv. 6; and for ὑπηρέτης, Acts xxvi. 16; Luke i. 2.

κατὰ τὴν δωρεὰν τῆς χάριτος τοῦ Θεοῦ τῆς δοθείσης μοι κατὰ τὴν ἐνέργειαν τῆς δυνάμεως αὐτοῦ. According to the gift of that grace of God which was given to me "by virtue of the exercise of His power." τῆς δοθείσης is the reading of ℵ A B C D* G, Vulg. Boh. The accusative is read by D^c K L, Syr., Chrys. The genitive is one of apposition, the gift being the grace given, so that the two readings do not differ in sense; but logically the genitive has the advantage, as the grace required this further definition more than the gift.

κατὰ τὴν ἐν. αὐτοῦ. These words, which are to be connected with δοθείσης, are by no means superfluous, but express the ever-present consciousness of St. Paul that his mission as an apostle was not due to anything in himself, it was the grace of God given with Divine power that alone changed the persecutor into the apostle. Hence the accumulation δωρεά, χάρις, δοθείσης, ἐνέργεια, δύναμις, proceeding from the feeling of his own unworthiness, suggested by οὗ διάκ. ἐγενήθην. "Nolite respicere quid sim meritus, quia dominus ultro mihi sua liberalitate hoc contulit ut sim apostolus gentium; non mea dignitate sed ejus gratia. Nolite etiam respicere qualis fuerim; nam domini est homines nihili extollere. Haec est potentiae ejus efficacia, ex nihilo grande aliquid efficere." See Dale, Lect. xiii. p. 235.

8. ἐμοὶ τῷ ἐλαχιστοτέρῳ πάντων ἁγίων ἐδόθη ἡ χάρις αὕτη. τῶν is added before ἁγίων in the Received Text, against a great preponderance of authority. ἁγίων is used as a substantive. "To me who am less than the least of all saints" (*i.e.* all Christians) "was this grace given." Closely connected in thought with the preceding, as expressing his own unworthiness in contrast with God's grace. Ἐλαχιστότερος. Double forms of comparatives and superlatives are frequent in the poets. Wetstein quotes Eustathius, who has collected numerous instances. But they also occur in the later prose writers, *e.g.* μειζότερος (Malalas, 490. 9; also 3 John 4); ἐλαχιστότατος (Sextus Empir.; also Matt. iii. 54, ix. 406), apparently without any increase of meaning. The instances in earlier prose writers (Xen. Aristot.) seem to be invented by the respective writers. The present instance is remarkable as a combination of superlative and comparative. It has a curiously parallel form in Aristotle, *Metaph.* x. 4. 7 (Bekker), οὔτε γὰρ τοῦ ἐσχάτου ἐσχατώτερον εἴη ἄν τι; but there the form is introduced only as expressing an impossible conception, and is construed as a comparative; here, on the contrary, ἐλαχιστότερος appears to express a definite idea, not only least of all saints, but even less than this implies. It may therefore be considered a unique formation. The expression can hardly be interpreted, with some eminent expositors, as referring to his consciousness of enduring sinfulness, as to which he could not place himself lower than all saints. True it is, no doubt, that every Christian, when he looks into his own heart, and is conscious of the sin that still dwells there, and knows that he cannot see what is in the heart of others, may be ready to exclaim, ἐγὼ ἐλαχιστότερος πάντων ἁγίων; but this does not express a deliberate comparison, and whatever such a one may feel at such moments, he would act unwisely if, when instructing and exhorting others, he should thus proclaim his own inferiority to them. Such a confession would be likely to be misunderstood, and either called hypocritical or made the ground of the retort, Why, then, take upon you to instruct and reprove your betters? Certainly St. Paul gives us little reason to think that he would take such a view. He declares that he has "lived in all good conscience toward God"; that if any one might have confidence in the flesh, he might, being blameless as touching the righteousness which is in the law. And as one of the ἅγιοι, he does not reckon himself amongst the babes in Christ, but the mature, τέλειοι (Phil. iii. 15). He affirms that in nothing is he behind the ὑπερλίαν ἀπόστολοι; nay, he does not hesitate to call on his readers to be imitators of him, as he is of Christ. While never for a moment forgetting his own nothingness, and that it is only by the grace of God that he was what he was, he likewise never forgets his true position in Christ's service. And he was too much taken up with his work in that service to have time for indulging in that kind of self-examination which consists in analysing one's state of mind or one's feelings. In Rom. vii. 17, to which Harless refers, he is describing the state from which he has been delivered (*ib.* ver. 25, viii. 2).

His recollection, ever vivid, of his former career as a persecutor is quite sufficient explanation of the expression here used.

The same writers who hold that the ἅγιοι ἀπόστολοι, ver. 5, could proceed only from an imitator who forgot his part, are of opinion that the expression now before us is an exaggerated imitation of 1 Cor. xv. 9, "I am the least of the apostles, that am not meet to be called an apostle." But there was no occasion there for any comparison with believers in general; he is only speaking of himself as one of the apostles; here he speaks of a grace that distinguished him above other believers, and, "now undeservedly," is his natural feeling. Indeed, we may with more justice say that this striking and unique expression could not proceed from calculated imitation; it has the stamp of a spontaneous outflow of an intense feeling of unworthiness. Nor does it really go beyond the passage in 1 Cor.; for there he declares himself not only the least of the apostles, but not meet to be called an apostle; here he does not say that he is not meet to be reckoned amongst the ἅγιοι. For the reader will not fail to note that notwithstanding the depth of his self-depreciation he still counts himself (or is represented as counting himself), and that not with hesitation, amongst the ἅγιοι, the very term which when joined with ἀπόστολοι is thought to be unapostolic. Yet no one supposes that ἁγίων here is inconsistent with humility.

τοῖς ἔθνεσιν εὐαγγελίσασθαι τὸ ἀνεξιχνίαστον πλοῦτος τοῦ Χριστοῦ. The Rec. Text has ἐν before τοῖς ἔθ., with D G K L. It is absent from ℵ A B C P.

"To preach unto the Gentiles the unsearchable riches of Christ." This is what ἡ χάρις αὕτη consisted in. αὕτη refers to what follows. Harless regards the words as an exposition of δωρεά, ἐμοί to αὕτη being treated as a parenthesis in order to avoid what he thinks would be unnatural, the close of a period within the long parenthesis, whose unusual length is only explained by the uninterrupted flow of thought. In that case αὕτη would refer backward to ver. 7. But it is very awkward to separate εὐαγγελίσασθαι from the immediately preceding ἡ χάρις αὕτη. As to vv. 2–13, this is not grammatically a parenthesis, for the sentence in ver. 1 is completely broken off, and a new sentence begins in ver. 14.

ἀνεξιχνίαστον. Theodoret well remarks: καὶ πῶς κηρύττεις εἴπερ ὁ πλοῦτος ἀνεξιχνίαστος; τοῦτο γὰρ αὐτό, φησι, κηρύττω, ὅτι ἀνεξιχνίαστος. The neuter πλοῦτος, however, is the best supported reading in the text, being in ℵ* A B C D* G 17 67**, while ℵᶜ Dᶜ K L P have the masculine, "the riches of

Christ"; all the inexhaustible blessings contained in Him. Comp. Rom. xi. 33 (where the same word ἀνεξιχ. occurs), and 1 Cor. xiii. 9–12, "We know in part," etc., and Phil. iii. 10.

9. καὶ φωτίσαι [πάντας]. The reading is doubtful. φωτίσαι without πάντας is read by ℵ* A 67², Cyr. Hil. and apparently Jerome. πάντας is added by ℵᶜ B C D G K L P, Ital., Vulg. Syr., Chrys. *al.*; Tisch. Treg. Westcott and Hort leave out the word. The insertion seems easy to account for, as the verb seemed to require an accusative, which it usually has in the N.T. As to the sense, the advantage seems to be on the side of the omission. The general meaning is, indeed, pretty much the same with either reading, since the result of bringing the οἰκ. to light is that all men are enabled to see it. But πάντας would seem to represent this result as attained by opening the eyes of men, whereas, since it was by revelation that the apostle learned it, opening men's eyes would not be sufficient; the mystery itself had to be brought to light. Besides, the meaning given to φωτίσαι with the reading πάντας, viz. to enlighten by way of instruction, has no parallel in the N.T., although it is so used in a few passages in the Sept. (Judg. xiii. 8; 2 Kings xii. 2, xvii. 27, 28). Moreover, if πάντας is read, although it is not emphatic, it cannot be limited to the Gentiles, and it would hardly be in St. Paul's manner to claim as his the office of enlightening all men as to the mystery.

τίς ἡ οἰκονομία τοῦ μυστηρίου. The Rec. Text has κοινωνία, a remarkable variation, but found in few MSS. οἰκονομία is in all the uncials, most cursives, and the versions and Fathers.

"What is the arrangement, or administration, of the mystery?" The mystery is that indicated in ver. 6, and that which was ordered or arranged as to the carrying out of this is the οἰκ. τ. μυστ. This was entrusted to St. Paul; cf. ver. 2. This seems more natural than to interpret οἰκ. as the arrangement which consisted in hitherto concealing the mystery and now revealing it. Comp. Col. i. 25, τὴν οἰκ. τοῦ Θεοῦ τὴν δοθεῖσάν μοι εἰς ὑμᾶς πληρῶσαι τὸν λόγον τοῦ Θεοῦ τὸ μυστήριον τὸ ἀποκεκρυμμένον ἀπὸ τῶν αἰώνων.

τοῦ ἀποκεκρυμμένου, "which was hidden"=σεσιγημένου, Rom. xvi. 25. Comp. also 1 Cor. ii. 7, καλοῦμεν Θεοῦ σοφίαν ἐν μυστηρίῳ τὴν ἀποκεκρυμμένην.

ἀπὸ τῶν αἰώνων, equivalent to χρόνοις αἰωνίοις, Rom. xvi. 25, "from the beginning." The expression occurs only here and Col. i. 26 in the N.T. ἀπ' αἰῶνος (used also by Longinus) occurs in Luke i. 70; Acts iii. 21, xv. 18. ἐκ τοῦ αἰ., which is used by St John, ix. 32, is also found in Greek writers. Comp. πρὸ τῶν αἰώνων, 1 Cor. ii. 7.

ἐν τῷ Θεῷ τῷ τὰ πάντα κτίσαντι. "In God who created all things." The Rec. Text adds, διὰ Ἰησοῦ Χριστοῦ, with Dᶜ K L, Chrys. Theodoret, Oec. But the words are omitted by ℵ A B C D* G P, Vulg. Syr. Pesh. and Harcl. (text) and other versions, Tert. Jerome, Augustine, *al.*

It is not quite clear what is the point here of the words τῷ τὰ π. κτίσαντι. When the words διὰ Ἰ. Χρ. were read, a reference to the spiritual or new creation was naturally thought of; but these words being omitted, such a reference is excluded. But, in fact, it is remote from the context, and unsuitable to the emphatic and unrestricted πάντα, as well as to the simple κτίσαντι.

It is clear that κτίζειν cannot be applied to the μυστήριον, which is not a thing created. The simplest explanation seems to be that the Creator of all was free to make what arrangement He pleased as to the concealment and revelation of His purpose. As Bengel remarks: "Rerum omnium creatio fundamentum est omnis reliquae oeconomiae pro potestate Dei universali liberrime dispensatae." Harless connects the words with the following: "Created all things in order to reveal in the Church His varied wisdom." But so important an assertion as this would hardly be made in so incidental a manner in a subordinate clause, especially as it has no analogy elsewhere in the N.T. Moreover, νῦν in the following clause is against this view; see on ver. 10.

10–13. *It is God's purpose, that even the angelic powers should learn through the Church the varied wisdom of God as shown in His eternal purpose in Christ.*

10. ἵνα γνωρισθῇ νῦν ταῖς ἀρχαῖς καὶ ταῖς ἐξουσίαις ἐν τοῖς ἐπουρανίοις διὰ τῆς ἐκκλησίας ἡ πολυποίκιλος σοφία τοῦ Θεοῦ. "To the end that now might be made known to the principalities and the powers in the heavenly places the much varied wisdom of God." ἵνα is supposed by some to be connected with the whole of the preceding, or specially with ἐδόθη, κ.τ.λ. This would make St. Paul ascribe to his own preaching a result in which the other apostles had their share. But as γνωρισθῇ is directly opposed to ἀποκεκρ., and νῦν to ἀπὸ τῶν αἰώνων, the most natural interpretation is that the secret or mystery was concealed in former times in order that now the wisdom of God might be manifested in its fulfilment. Braune, however, connects ἵνα with τίς ἡ οἰκ. τοῦ μ. "The arrangement is directed to this end, that the wisdom of God," etc.

ταῖς ἀρχαῖς καὶ ταῖς ἐξουσίαις. Understood by some of the older expositors of earthly powers in general, or of Jewish rulers in particular (so Locke), or again of heathen priests, or of Church authorities; all from unwillingness to admit the sublime thought of the apostle, that God's wisdom in the scheme of redemption is an object of contemplation to heavenly intelligences. Comp., on the contrary, 1 Pet. i. 12, "which things angels desire to look into."

V. Soden, comparing Col. ii. 10–15, understands the words of the angelic powers which ministered the law on the one hand, and on the other hand the elemental spirits which claimed the veneration of the heathen. To both was it now made manifest that the enmity was at an end.

ἐν τοῖς ἐπουρανίοις, local, cf. i. 3, 20. It qualifies the preceding substantive notwithstanding the absence of the article, which is not necessary in the case of local definitions. Cf. Demosth. *c. Pantaen*, p. 967, τοῖς ἔργοις ἐν Μαρωνείᾳ: Aeschines, *Fals. Leg.* 42, τὴν τρίτην πρεσβείαν ἐπὶ τὸ κοινὸν τῶν 'Ἀμφικτυόνων (Bernhardy, p. 322 f.).

διὰ τῆς ἐκκλησίας, *i.e.* as Theodoret expresses it, διὰ τῆς περὶ τὴν ἐκκλησίαν οἰκονομίας. The Church is the phenomenon, which by its existence is a proof and exhibition of the Divine wisdom as manifested in a scheme of redemption which is world wide.

πολυποίκιλος does not mean "very wise," as has been hastily inferred from the use of ποίκιλος in Aesch. *Prom. Vinct.* 315, where, however, the word means "crafty." πολυποίκιλος is used by Eurip. *Iph. Taur.* 1149, of cloth; by Eubulus, *ap. Athen.* 15, p. 679*d*, of flowers. In a figurative sense, as here, it occurs in the *Orphica* (lxi. 4, of discourse), and in Theophilus. The Latin here has "multiformis." The word probably refers to the variety of God's dealings with Jews and Gentiles in former times, which are now seen to have worked to one end. Gregory of Nyssa (*Hom. viii. in Cant. Cant.* followed by Theoph. and Oecum.) gives a striking interpretation. "Before the incarnation of our Saviour the heavenly powers knew the wisdom of God only as simple and uniform, effecting wonders in a manner consonant with the nature of each thing. There was nothing ποίκιλον. But now by means of the οἰκονομία, with reference to the Church and the human race, the wisdom of God is known no longer as simple, but as πολυποίκιλος, producing contraries by contraries; by death, life; by dishonour, glory; by sin, righteousness; by a curse, blessing; by weakness, power. The invisible is manifested in flesh. He redeems captives, Himself the purchaser, and Himself the price." The thought is no doubt striking, but the adjective πολυπ. does not suggest παράδοξον. Perhaps, indeed, the word has been too much pressed by some expositors, and is only suggested by the thought of the great apparent difference and real harmony between the Christian dispensation and that which preceded it.

11. κατὰ πρόθεσιν τῶν αἰώνων. "According to the purpose of the ages." The genitive does not seem to be correctly taken as that of the object, the purpose concerning the ages, the foreordering of the ages (Whitby), since the writer is speaking of the one purpose carried out in Christ. Nor can πρόθεσις be taken as = foreknowledge (Chrys.). Modern commentators generally take it as = eternal. Ellicott compares πρόθεσιν . . . πρὸ χρόνων αἰωνίων, 2 Tim. i. 9; but then the latter words are connected with δοθεῖσαν, not with πρόθ. A better sense is obtained by taking the genitive as one of possession, "the purpose that runs through the ages." Cf. Tennyson, "through the ages one increasing purpose runs."

ἣν ἐποίησεν ἐν τῷ Χριστῷ Ἰησοῦ τῷ Κυρίῳ ἡμῶν. "Which He purposed in Christ Jesus our Lord." It is questioned whether ἐποίησεν means "formed" or "executed" the purpose. The immediate connexion favours the former view; but it is urged by Meyer, Ellicott, *al.*, that what follows belongs to the execution, not the formation of the purpose; and this has been thought also to account for Ἰησοῦ being added, since it was not the formation of the purpose, but its accomplishment that took place in the historical Jesus. For the use of ποιεῖν in this sense we are referred to ch. ii. 3; Matt. xxi. 31; John vi. 38, and in the Sept. 1 Kings v. 8; Isa. xliv. 28. But in all these passages the object of the verb is θέλημα, which primarily means that which is willed, so that the exact meaning of π. θέλημα is to perform that which God, *e.g.*, has willed. It could not mean to form a purpose. With πρόθεσις it is otherwise. This properly means the purpose as an act, although by a natural figure it may also be used of that which is purposed. The natural meaning of ποιεῖν πρ., therefore, is to form a purpose, and the passages cited do not prove that any other sense is possible. Meyer also compares ποιεῖν γνώμην, Rev. xvii. 17; but even if this were quite parallel, we cannot explain St. Paul's Greek by that of the Apocalypse. In any case, when it is a πρόθεσις τῶν αἰώνων that is in question, ποιεῖν would be a very weak verb to use. The addition of Ἰησοῦ is sufficiently accounted for by this, that the apostle desired to bring to the mind of his readers the thought that He whom they know as Jesus their Lord is none other than the Christ in whom God had from eternity formed His purpose. So likewise ch. i. 4.

12. ἐν ᾧ ἔχομεν τὴν παρρησίαν καὶ προσαγωγὴν ἐν πεποιθήσει διὰ τῆς πίστεως αὐτοῦ.

So ℵ A B 17 80, Greg.-Nyss. The Rec. Text has τήν before προσαγωγήν, with C D⁰ K L P, Ath. Chrys. *al.*

D*ᶜ have τὴν προσαγωγὴν καὶ τὴν παρρησίαν.

G: προσαγωγὴν εἰς τὴν παρρησίαν. The article seems more likely to have been inserted for grammatical reasons than omitted either accidentally or otherwise.

"In whom we have our boldness and access in confidence through our faith in Him." παρρησία is primarily freedom of speech, and is frequently found in that sense in the N.T., as well as in that of "plainness of speech," John xvi. 25, 26. It occurs in the sense of "confidence" in the Apocrypha and in Josephus, *e.g.* 1 Macc. iv. 18, λήψετε τὰ σκῦλα μετὰ π.; Wisd. v. 1, στήσεται ἐν π. πολλῇ ὁ δίκαιος; so Phil. i. 20; 1 Tim. iii. 13; Heb. x. 19; cf. 1 John ii. 28, iii. 21, iv. 17, v. 14. The transition of meaning seems not to be by way of generalisation from confidence in speaking to confidence generally; for the primary meaning is not "confidence," but "freedom, openness" of speech. But freedom of speech (in the active sense) implies the absence of fear or shame; see the passages just referred to in 1 John ii. 28, "have π., and not be ashamed"; iv. 17, "π. in the day of judgment." In John iii. 21 and iv. 12, π. is connected with prayer.

On προσαγωγή see ii. 18. The intransitive sense is obviously the more suitable here. If the article is not read we must either suppose παρρησία and προσαγωγή to form parts of one conception, or we must connect the following words with the latter only. What has just been said of παρρησία shows that the former alternative is quite possible, παρρησία καὶ προσαγωγή being nearly equivalent to προσαγωγὴ μετὰ παρρησίας, and the idea would be the same that is expressed in Heb. iv. 16, προσερχώμεθα μετὰ παρρησίας τῷ θρόνῳ τῆς χάριτος. The other alternative would leave παρρησία very indefinite.

How grandly is this confidence expressed in Rom. viii. 38, 39! (Meyer.)

πεποίθησις is a word of the later Greek. It occurs several times in Josephus, also in Sextus Empiricus and in Philo, but only once in the Sept. 2 Kings xviii. 19.

διὰ τῆς πίστεως αὐτοῦ. The genitive is that of the object, the πίστις is defined by its object. So in Mark xi. 22, ἔχετε π. Θεοῦ; Rom. iii. 22, 26; James ii. 1, μὴ ἐν προσωπολημψίαις ἔχετε τὴν πίστιν τοῦ Κυρίου ἡμῶν, and elsewhere. The words are to be connected with ἔχομεν, not with πεποιθήσει.

13. Διὸ αἰτοῦμαι μὴ ἐγκακεῖν ἐν ταῖς θλίψεσί μου ὑπὲρ ὑμῶν. Διό, viz. because I am the minister of so great a matter; connected, not with the preceding verse only, but with 8-12. The greater the office, the less becoming would it be to lose heart.

The following words, however, admit of two interpretations. Either, I pray that I may not lose heart, or, I entreat you, not to lose heart. The latter view is adopted by the Syr., Theodoret, Jerome, Bengel, Harless, Olshausen, Braune. In its favour it is alleged that it is much more natural to supply the subject of the infinitive from that of the substantive verb; and, secondly, that it is difficult to understand ἐν on the other view. But the chief objection to the first-mentioned interpretation, according to Harless, is from the structure of the whole passage. Either St. Paul resumes in these words the course of thought begun in ver. 1, or he does not. Now it is the thought of supplication for his readers that separates the subsequent context from the parenthesis. If, then, he does not here resume ver. 1, how can we suppose that he could express the same thought in the parenthesis itself without observing that the parenthesis was thereby removed? If he does here resume ver. 1, the τούτου χάριν after διό, instead of καί, is inexplicable, or rather intolerable. The argument assumes that αἰτοῦμαι means, I pray (God), and is set aside by taking that word as = I entreat you. The difficulties in Theodoret's interpretation are greater. First, if αἰτοῦμαι is, I pray God, Θεόν could hardly be omitted. The passages cited as parallel, viz. Col. i. 9 and Jas. i. 6, are not really so. In the former, αἰτούμενοι only expresses the content of the prayer mentioned in προσευχόμενοι, which, of course, means prayer to God. In the latter, αἰτείτω repeats the αἰτείτω of the previous verse, which is defined by παρὰ τοῦ διδόντος Θεοῦ πᾶσιν. Moreover, the words ἥτις ἐστι δόξα ὑμῶν supply much more naturally a motive for the readers than for the apostle. The μου after θλίψεσι, too, would be superfluous if the apostle were praying for himself. And we may add that the implied apprehension lest he should be disheartened by persecution is not in harmony with the apostle's character or with his other utterances. He gloried in tribulation, and took pleasure in persecution (Rom. v. 3; 2 Cor. xii. 10; Col. i. 24). Compare also the passage just referred to in Rom. viii. 38, 39. But he might have reason to fear that some of the Gentile converts might be tempted to lose heart when they saw the persecution to which the apostle was subjected just because of his proclaiming the doctrine, here insisted on, of the free and equal participation of the Gentiles in the blessings of the Messiah's kingdom.

ἐν ταῖς θλίψεσί μου ὑπὲρ ὑμῶν. "In my tribulations on your behalf." Namely, those which came upon him by reason of his being the Apostle of the Gentiles. Compare his touching words, Phil. ii. 17, "Even if I am offered on the sacrifice of your faith, I rejoice." ἐν denotes the circumstances in which, etc.; ὑπὲρ ὑμῶν is clearly to be joined to θλίψεσί μου, not to αἰτοῦμαι (as Harless). The article is not required, since θλίβεσθαι ὑπέρ τινος is possible (2 Cor. i. 6); cf. Gal. iv. 14.

ἥτις ἐστι δόξα ὑμῶν. ἥτις introduces a reason; it is not simply equivalent to ἥ, but implies that what is predicated belongs to the nature of the thing, "quippe qui," "inasmuch as this." It is referred to μὴ ἐγκακεῖν by Theodoret, followed by Harless, Olshausen, Braune, *al.* This, of course, supposes the preceding prayer to be for the apostle himself. On this view it would be his personal fortitude that is the glory of the Ephesians, which would be a strange expression. If it be asked how his afflictions could be their glory, Chrysostom replies, "Because God so loved them as to give His Son for them, and to afflict His servants; for in order that they should obtain so great blessings Paul was imprisoned."

14–19. *Prayer for the readers, that they may be given spiritual* *strength; that Christ may dwell in their hearts; and that they may learn to know His love, which surpasses knowledge.*

14. τούτου χάριν κάμπτω τὰ γόνατά μου. Resumes ver. 1, "On this account," referring to the train of thought in the latter part of ch. ii. Although the construction was broken off in ver. 2, the thought has continued to turn on the same ideas. "I bend my knees," this expresses the earnestness of the prayer, τὴν καταγεγυμμένην δέησιν ἐδήλωσεν, Chrys. "A signo rem denotat," Calvin. Some, as Calv., have with strange literality supposed that the apostle actually knelt while writing; (against πρός, see below). The usual posture in praying was standing: "when ye stand praying," Mark xi. 25; "stood and prayed," Luke xviii. 11; "the publican standing afar off," *ib.* 13. But kneeling is mentioned, 1 Kings viii. 54 (Solomon); Dan. vi. 10; and, in the N.T., Luke xxii. 41; Acts vii. 60, xx. 36, xxi. 5. Eusebius mentions it as the custom proper to the Christians: τὸ οἰκεῖον τοῖς χριστιανοῖς τῶν εὐχῶν ἔθος (*H.E.* v. 5). Justin Martyr and Basil represent kneeling as a symbol of our fall by sin. See on Luke xxii. 41.

πρὸς τὸν Πατέρα. κάμπτειν γόνυ in the literal sense takes the dative (Rom. xi. 4, xiv. 11; both places, however, being quotations). Here as the words were equivalent to προσεύχομαι, πρός is used as indicating the direction of the prayer.

<small>After Πατέρα the Rec. Text has τοῦ κυρίου ἡμῶν Ἰησοῦ Χριστοῦ, with ℵ^c D G K L, Syr. Vulg., Chrys. *al.*</small>

<small>The words are wanting in ℵ* A B C P 17 67**, Boh. Aeth., Jerome (expressly), and many others. The insertion of the words is easily accounted for; there would be no reason for their omission. Although Jerome expressly states, "quod sequitur . . . non ut in Latinis Codicibus additum est, *ad patrem domini nostri Jesu Christi*, sed simpliciter *ad patrem* legendum ut dei patris nomen non domino nostro Jesu Christo sed omnibus creaturis rationabilibus coaptetur" (vii. 599), yet a little before he had himself written, "ad patrem domini nostri Jesu Christi." Whether the reading there is due to him or to a copyist, it serves as an illustration of the fact that the evidence of readings furnished by quotations in the Fathers as distinguished from express statements must be used with caution.</small>

15. ἐξ οὗ πᾶσα πατριὰ ἐν οὐρανοῖς καὶ ἐπὶ γῆς ὀνομάζεται. "From whom every family in heaven and on earth is named." We meet here with a perplexity similar to that in ii. 21 (πᾶσα οἰκοδομή), except that here no MSS. appear to have the article. We should rather have expected the apostle to say "the whole family," which would require πᾶσα ἡ πατριά. Indeed, many commentators and translators have so taken the words as they stand. This was perhaps even more natural in the case of those who read the addition τοῦ Κυρίου ἡμῶν Ἰησοῦ Χριστοῦ, since it appeared easy to take these words as the antecedent to οὗ, the sense thus yielded being that "the whole family" was named from Christ. Whether that addition be accepted or not, if πᾶσα π. is rendered "every family," the antecedent must be τὸν Πατέρα. But if those words are omitted, the rendering "the whole family" loses much of its plausibility. Grammatically it cannot be maintained.

Πατριά is a quite classical word (although in classical writers πάτρα is more common). It occurs in Herodot. in the sense "race" or "tribe," as when he says there are three πατριαί of the Babylonians (i. 200). In the Sept. it occurs in a similar sense of those descended from a common ancestor, narrower, however, than φυλή, and wider than οἶκος; see Ex. xii. 3; Num. xxxii. 28; but also in a wider sense, as in Ps. xxi. (xxii.) 28, πᾶσαι αἱ πατριαὶ τῶν ἐθνῶν. So in Acts iii. 25, πᾶσαι αἱ πατριαὶ τῆς γῆς, for which we have in Gen. xii. 3 and xxviii. 14 φυλαί, and in xxii. 18 and xxvi. 4 ἔθνη. In Luke ii. 4 we have ἐξ οἴκου καὶ πατριᾶς Δαβίδ. See note *ad loc*.

Some of the ancients take π. in the present passage as = fatherhood, πατρότης. Thus Theodoret says: ὃς ἀληθῶς ὑπάρχει πατήρ, ὃς οὐ παρ' ἄλλου τοῦτο λαβὼν ἔχει, ἀλλ' αὐτὸς τοῖς ἄλλοις μεταδέδωκε τοῦτο. And Athanasius: "God as Father of the Son is the only true Father, and all created paternity is a shadow of the true" (*Orat. in Arian.* i. 24). But, not to insist on the consideration that this conception is of a kind foreign to St. Paul's mode of thought, the word itself does not admit such a meaning; and those who have adopted it are involved in a difficulty with respect to the πατριαί in heaven,—a difficulty which Theodoret solves by understanding spiritual fathers to be called heavenly fathers; Jerome, by supposing the archangels to be alluded to as fathers.

Setting aside this interpretation, we take the words as = "every family." This cannot be understood of "the family on earth" and "the family in heaven," in whatever way these respectively are interpreted, for πᾶσα implies a plurality. By the πατριαί on earth are doubtless meant the nations, with the fundamental division into Jews and Gentiles; by those in heaven, angels regarded as belonging to certain groups or "tribes."

ὀνομάζεται, *i.e.* gets the name πατριά, not, are called "sons of God," which is not in the words. Nor is it merely the fact of creation that is referred to; for the relation of intelligent beings to their author is something deeper than that of things to their creator. Of things merely material God is the creator; of personal intelligences He is the Father. Hence the words suggest a motive for the prayer, and a reason for expecting its fulfilment, for those addressed were also πατριά, of whom God was the Father. The rendering "every family" is therefore not only more grammatical, but more to the purpose than "the whole family," and the addition of the words τοῦ Κυρίου, κ.τ.λ., injures the sense.

ὀνομάζεται has been taken by some to mean "exists," or "is

called into existence"; but the verb never has this meaning, certainly not in i. 21 or v. 3. Even were it true that καλεῖν meant "to call into existence," this would prove nothing as to ὀνομάζειν, for καλεῖν means to call in the sense "bid one come," which in certain circumstances might signify to call into existence; whereas ὀν. is simply to give a name to a thing. Nor is it true that καλεῖν of itself has the alleged meaning: it is certainly not proved by Philo's words, "τὰ μὴ ὄντα ἐκάλεσεν εἰς τὸ εἶναι." For ὀνομάζεσθαι ἔκ τινος, cf. Soph. *Oed. Tyr.* 1036, ὥστ' ὠνομάσθης ἐκ τύχης ταύτης, ὃς εἶ.

ἵνα δῷ ὑμῖν κατὰ τὸ πλοῦτος τῆς δόξης αὐτοῦ. "That He would grant you according to the riches of His glory." δῷ is the reading of ℵ A B C G, whilst δώη is read by D K L and most MSS. The ἵνα depends on the idea of προσεύχομαι implied in the preceding, so that this and the following verses express the content of the prayer. For ἵνα cf. Col. i. 9. "Riches of His glory," Rom. ix. 23. Not to be limited to power or to grace, but in accordance with His whole glorious perfection. The term πλοῦτος is particularly suitable when the thought is of God as a giver.

δυνάμει κραταιωθῆναι διὰ τοῦ Πνεύματος αὐτοῦ εἰς τὸν ἔσω ἄνθρωπον. "To be strengthened with power through His Spirit in the inward man." δυνάμει is instrumental, "ut virtute seu fortitudine ab eo acceptâ corroboremini," Estius. Harless understands it as denoting the form in which the strengthening takes place, viz. a strengthening in power, not in knowledge or the like, comparing Acts iv. 33, "with great power gave the apostles witness"; but this does not seem parallel. In the present case this would be a tautology, "be strengthened with strength."

κραταιόω, from the poetic κραταιός (used also in later prose and in Sept.), is a later form for κρατύνω.

εἰς indicates the direction of the gift. The meaning of ὁ ἔσω ἄνθρωπος appears to be decided by Rom. vii. 22, "I delight in the law of God," κατὰ τὸν ἔσω ἄνθρωπον. It is not therefore the καινὸς ἄνθρ., but is the higher moral and rational nature, the Reason, which, by its constitution, is in harmony with the Divine Law, but in the unregenerate is enslaved to the power of sin in the flesh, that is, to the appetites and desires which constitute man's lower nature (compare Butler's *Sermons on Human Nature*). ὁ ἔσω ἄνθ. requires renewal, and undergoes renewal from day to day, ἀνακαινοῦται ἡμέρᾳ καὶ ἡμέρᾳ, 2 Cor. iv. 16.

It has been maintained, not without plausibility, that the expressions ὁ ἔσω ἄνθρ. and ὁ ἔξω ἄνθρ. are derived from the school of Plato, not directly, but through Plato's use having influenced common speech. We find in Plato, τοῦ ἀνθρώπου ὁ ἐντὸς ἄνθρωπος (*Rep.* ix. p. 589); in Plotinus, ὁ εἴσω ἄνθρ. (*Enn.* v. 1. 10) and ὁ ἔξω ἄνθρ. The threefold division, πνεῦμα, νοῦς, σῶμα, in 1 Thess. v. 23, points in the same direction. With St. Paul, however, the contrast between the inward man and the outward man is not that between the pure and the impure. The inward man includes not only the Reason, which accepts the law of God and approves of it, and the Conscience, which pronounces the obligation and condemns the violation of it, but also the Will from which action proceeds; see Rom. vii. 17, 18, where ἐγώ is used of both parts. St. Paul's view of the relation of the man to virtue and vice is much more like that of Aristotle. The man knows the right, but at the moment of action appetite blinds him.

It deserves notice also that St. Paul does not use πνεῦμα of the unregenerate. In them the higher principle is νοῦς, which ineffectively protests against the σάρξ, while in the regenerate πνεῦμα is superior (Rom. vii. 25, viii. 4, 9). That he does not mean πνεῦμα and ψυχή to be a complete division of the human faculties, would appear from 1 Cor. xiv. 14, 15.

17. κατοικῆσαι τὸν Χριστὸν διὰ τῆς πίστεως ἐν ταῖς καρδίαις ὑμῶν. "That Christ may dwell in your hearts by faith." κατοικῆσαι is, by many expositors, taken as the end or result of κραταιωθῆναι on account of, 1st, the asyndeton; 2nd, the emphatic position of the verb; and 3rd, the difference in the construction of the two clauses, which otherwise must be taken as co-ordinate. But although the use of the infinitive of end or result is often very lax, none of the instances cited in the grammars are parallel to this. Setting aside the cases in which the principal verb is one which means "to will, order," etc., or which otherwise involves the notion of purpose, in those which remain the subject of the infinitive is the same as that of the verb on which it depends. The emphatic position of κατοικῆσαι seems sufficiently accounted for by the importance of the idea it expresses, and the rhetorical advantage of giving it a position parallel to that of κραταιωθῆναι. The asyndeton need cause no difficulty, considering the structure of the whole sentence. κατοικ. is not something added to κραται., but is a further definition of it. κατοικεῖν is found in N.T. only here and Col. i. 19, ii. 9 (but ἐγκατοικεῖν, 2 Pet. ii. 8). It is very frequent in Sept. (as in classical authors also), and is opposed to παροικεῖν as the permanent to the transitory; cf. Gen. xxxvii. 1, κατῴκει Ἰακὼβ ἐν τῇ γῇ οὗ παρῴκησεν ὁ πατὴρ αὐτοῦ; and Philo, *de Sacrif. Ab. et Cain*, § 10, ὁ γὰρ τοῖς ἐγκυκλίοις μόνοις ἐπανέχων παροικεῖ σοφίᾳ, οὐ κατοικεῖ (Thayer). It is hardly probable that there is any allusion to the figure in ii. 21, 22, for the indwelling here spoken of is not in the Church, but in the individual hearts. "How does Christ dwell in the hearts?" says Chrysostom. Listen to Christ Himself saying, "I and the Father will come and make our abode with him." "In your hearts," "ut sciamus non satis esse si in linguâ versetur aut in cerebro volitet," Calvin.

18. ἐν ἀγάπῃ ἐρριζωμένοι καὶ τεθεμελιωμένοι. "Rooted and grounded in love." These words seem best taken as an irregular nominative, a construction of which there are frequent examples, especially with participles. Thus iv. 2, παρακαλῶ ὑμᾶς περιπατῆσαι ... ἀνεχόμενοι; Col. ii. 2, ἵνα παρακληθῶσιν αἱ καρδίαι αὐτῶν, συμβιβασθέντες; *ib.* iii. 16, ὁ λόγος τοῦ Χρ. ἐνοικείτω ἐν ὑμῖν. . . .

διδάσκοντες; 2 Cor. ix. 10, 11, and 12, 13. Examples in classical authors are frequent.

More prominence is thus given to the thought, and the transition to the following clause is made more easy. The result of Christ dwelling in their hearts is that they are firmly rooted in love, and the consequence is that they are enabled to comprehend, etc. This is the view adopted by Origen, Chrysostom, the ancient versions (except the Gothic); and amongst moderns, Harless, Olsh. De Wette, Ellicott, Eadie, Alford. The principal objection made to it is founded on the tense of the participles, which, being the perfect, would express, not the condition into which the readers are to come, but that in which they are already assumed to be. This, it is said, would be very illogical in connexion with the wish that they should be strengthened, and that Christ might dwell in their hearts. The perfect ἐρριζωμένοι in Col. ii. 7 is, it is alleged, not parallel, since there the reception of Christ is represented as preceding παρελάβετε τὸν Χριστόν. To this it may be replied, first, that in ch. ii. 20 the readers are said to be ἐποικοδομηθέντες, and yet in ver. 22 there is still a συνοικοδομεῖσθε necessary; secondly, that the participles here express their complete fixedness on the foundation, which does not imply that their building up is complete; and accordingly in Col. ii. 7 we have ἐρριζωμένοι καὶ ἐποικοδομούμενοι, the former perfect, the latter present. The fixedness, too, is clearly the result of κατοικῆσαι. The present participle would be here quite out of place, "ye being in process of being rooted and grounded." What follows depends, not on the progress, but on the completion of their grounding.

The alternative construction adopted by Photius (ap. Oecum.), also Meyer, Braune, Oltram., the English Versions (Authorised and Revised), is to take the participles with the following clause: "to the end that ye, being rooted," etc. This construction is hardly justified by the passages cited in support of it. In Rom. xi. 31 we have τῷ ὑμετέρῳ ἐλέει ἵνα . . . ; in 2 Cor. ii. 4, τὴν ἀγάπην ἵνα γνῶτε: 1 Cor. ix. 15, ἢ τὸ καύχημά μου ἵνα τις κενώσῃ (but here the best texts read οὐδεὶς κενώσει): Gal. ii. 10, μόνον τῶν πτωχῶν ἵνα μνημονεύωμεν: John xiii. 29, τοῖς πτωχοῖς ἵνα τι δῷ: Acts xix. 4, λέγων εἰς τὸν ἐρχόμενον μετ' αὐτὸν ἵνα πιστεύσωσι. In all these instances there is a particular emphasis on the words which precede ἵνα, here there is none; the emphasis is on the words that follow it.

That there is a mixture of metaphors here, as in Col. ii. 7 and 1 Cor. iii. 9, is not to be denied; nor is this disproved by showing that ῥιζόω was often used without reference to its primitive meaning as simply = "to establish firmly," *e.g.* a tyranny, Herodot. i. 64, or the city (Plutarch), or even a road (Soph. *Oed. Col.* 1591). All that this proves is that there is no reason to suppose that the apostle had two images present to his mind. The best ancient writers were less critical in this matter than the moderns. Cicero, for example, has sometimes a strange mixture of metaphors (see *In Cat.* i. 12). Lucian has ῥίζαι καὶ θεμέλιοι τῆς ὀρχήσεως (*De Saltat.* 34).

It may be inferred from the use of the two words that St. Paul (like Lucian in the place cited) did not intend the reader to think definitely of either image, but used the words in their applied sense. This seems the true answer to the difficulty that has been raised as to the designation of love as the foundation,—a position elsewhere ascribed to faith (Col. i. 23, ii. 7), from which love springs (1 Tim. i. 6). Beza asks: "Radicis et fundamenti nomen quomodo fructibus tribuas?" Harless meets the difficulty by supplying the missing object of the participles from the clause to which they belong, viz. ἐν Χριστῷ; for which there is no sufficient reason, especially as we have already a definition by ἐν, so that the readers could not think of applying another ἐν. Love is, as it were, the soil in which they are firmly fixed. This is not to be understood of Christ's love or God's love, either of which would require some defining genitive, but the grace of love in general as the "fundamental" principle of the Christian character. Faith retains its usual position (διὰ τῆς π.), but it is love that is the working principle.[1]

There is no difficulty about the absence of the article before ἀγάπῃ. Such omission before names of virtues, vices, etc., is frequent in classical writers and in N.T. For ἀγάπη, cf. 2 Cor. ii. 8; Gal. v. 6.

Westcott and Hort connect ἐν ἀγάπῃ with the foregoing (so also Holzhausen), but this overweights that clause. Besides, to say that Christ dwells in the heart in love is a strange expression. We might, at least, expect "by faith and love" rather than "by faith in love." Further, this construction leaves ἐρρ. καὶ τεθ. without any modal definition, which they seem to demand.

ἵνα ἐξισχύσητε. "That ye may be fully able." καταλαβέσθαι, "to comprehend." The active alone seems to occur in classical writers in this signification (Plato, *Phaedr.* 250 D), but the middle is interpreted by Hesychius as = κατανοεῖσθαι. It occurs in this sense in Acts iv. 13, "perceiving that they were unlearned"; x. 34, "of a truth I perceive"; and xxv. 25, "finding that he had committed nothing," etc. The first and last of these instances are sufficient to show that there is no need to call in the idea of "the earnestness or spiritual energy with which the action is performed"; the voice simply implies, "to grasp for oneself." Kypke (*Obs.* vol. ii. p. 294) takes the word to mean "occupare,"

---

[1] A somewhat analogous difficulty has been raised in connexion with Luke vii. 47: see note *ad loc.*

"ut possitis occupare ... latitudinem quandam," etc., comparing the sense to that in ver. 19, as if ("mutato accentu") τί τὸ πλάτος stood for τὸ πλάτος τι; as by a similar transposition we have in Acts viii. 36, ἐπί τι ὕδωρ. Apart from other objections, the article is fatal to this.

τί τὸ πλάτος καὶ μῆκος καὶ ὕψος καὶ βάθος. "What is the breadth, and length, and height, and depth." As to the order of the words, ὕψος precedes βάθος in B C D G 17, Vulg. Boh. *al.*; the contrary, ℵ A K L, Syr. *al.*

The four words seem intended to indicate, not so much the thoroughness of the comprehension as the vastness of the thing to be comprehended; hardly, however, "metaphysically considered by the ordinary dimensions of space," which has only three dimensions.

But what is it of which the readers are to learn the dimensions? Chrysostom replies, "the mystery," τοῦτ' ἐστι τὸ. μυστήριον τὸ ὑπὲρ ἡμῶν οἰκονομηθὲν μετὰ ἀκριβείας εἰδέναι. So Theodoret and Theophylact, Beza, Harless, Olshausen, Barry. In support of this, Harless remarks that the article shows that the substantives refer to something already mentioned. This is fallacious, the words being names of attributes, and the article is necessary to define them as the breadth, etc., of a definite thing, whether that is expressed or implied. Against the interpretation is the consideration that a new section of the discourse began in ver. 14, after which μυστήριον is not mentioned; and, besides, the μυστήριον of vv. 4–10 is the admission of the Gentiles, not the whole scheme of grace, as some of these expositors interpret.

Bengel understands the words as referring to the dimensions of the Christian temple. Eadie remarks, "The figure of a temple still loomed before the writer's fancy, and naturally supplied the distinctive imagery of the prayer." This has much plausibility; but the image has not been dwelt on since the first introduction of it, nor is it St. Paul's habit to work out a figure at such length. If the remoteness of the substantive was a good reason for not adding a pronoun in the genitive, it made it the more necessary to repeat the noun. The preceding τεθεμελιωμένοι is so far from keeping up the figure, or showing that it was still in the apostle's mind, that it rather tells the opposite way, unless, indeed, with Harless, we suppose ἐν Χριστῷ to be understood. Indeed, in any case it is not the foundation of the corporate body that is there alluded to, but that of individuals. It may, perhaps, be replied that in ver. 14 the writer has resumed the thought interrupted at ver. 2, and that the figure of the temple had immediately preceded. But a more serious objection is that the substantives simply express magnitude, and the mere magnitude of the temple was not likely to be dwelt on with such emphasis. Especially is the mention of the fourth dimension, "depth," adverse to this view, considering that the "depth" of the temple would be that of its foundation, and the foundation is either Christ or the apostles. This difficulty cannot be surmounted except by introducing ideas of which the text gives no hint, if, indeed, they are not inconsistent with the figure. Thus an old commentator (quoted by Wolf, ap. Eadie) says, "In its depth it descends to Christ." Bengel understands the depth as "*profunditas*, nulli creaturae percontanda"; the length, "*longitudo* per omnia secula."

V. Soden combines these two views, regarding the μυστήριον as the principal conception, the description of which, however, is finally summed up in the figure of the temple. De Wette finds the object in Col. ii. 3, which he supposes to have been before the writer's mind; thus taking it to be the wisdom of God; cf. Job xi. 8. Alford supposes the genitive to be left indefinite, "of all that God has revealed or done in and for us"; and this yields a very good sense. However, we need not travel beyond the immediate context to find a suitable object; it is given us in ἀγάπην τοῦ Χριστοῦ in the following verse. The thought comes to a climax; having spoken of apprehending the vastness of this, he checks himself before adding the genitive to advance a step further and declare that the ἀγάπη τοῦ Χριστοῦ is too vast to be comprehended. It has been objected to this, that the simple γνῶναι would be a weakening, not a strengthening, of ver. 18. But, first, γνῶναι is much stronger than καταλαβέσθαι, which only means to come to know a fact (see the passages cited above); and, secondly, it is not simply γνῶναι τὴν ἀγάπην, but γνῶναι τὴν ὑπερβάλλουσαν τῆς γνώσεως ἀγάπην. The particle τέ is not opposed to this view of the connexion. τέ expresses more an internal (logical) relation, καί an external (Winer, § 53. 2). Oltramare understands simply αὐτῆς, *i.e.* ἀγάπης.

Some of the ancients sought to find a special meaning in each of the four dimensions, and to such the Cross naturally suggested itself. We find this idea already in Origen, "All these the cross of Jesus has, by which He ascended on high and took captive a captivity, and descended to the lowest parts of the earth ... and has Himself run to all the earth, reaching to the breadth and length of it. And he that is crucified with Christ comprehends the breadth," etc. (*Catena*, p. 162). Gregory Nyssen also says that St. Paul describes the power which controls the whole by the figure of the Cross, τῷ σχήματι τοῦ σταυροῦ (Cont. Eunom. *Orat.* iv. p. 582). By the height he understands the portion above the crossbeam, by the depth that below; and so St. Augustine, who explains the mystery of the Cross, "sacramentum crucis," as signifying love in its breadth, hope in its height, patience in its length, and humility in its depth. But he was not writing as a commentator. According to Severianus, the height alludes to the Lord's divinity, the depth to His humanity, the length and breadth to the extent of the apostolic preaching. Jerome is still more fanciful, and finds in the height an allusion to the good angels, in the depth to the bad, in the length to men who are on the upward path, and in the breadth those on the broad way that leadeth to destruction. There are other varieties. Such fancies (not altogether extinct even in our own days) only deserve notice as a warning of the unprofitableness of such fanciful methods of interpretation. As Calvin well observes, "Haec subtilitate sua placent, sed quid ad mentem Pauli?" Nothing, indeed, could be more un-Pauline.

19. γνῶναί τε τὴν ὑπερβάλλουσαν τῆς γνώσεως ἀγάπην τοῦ Χριστοῦ. "And to know the love of Christ, which passeth knowledge."

A 74, Syr. Vulg. read or interpret τὴν ἀγάπην τῆς γνώσεως, "supereminentem scientiae charitatem," a reading interpreted by Grotius as meaning the love which flows from the knowledge of Christ. Both external and internal evidence are decisive against the reading, which may have originated from misunderstanding of the oxymoron. The genitive depends on the notion of comparison in ὑπερβ. Comp. Aesch. *Prom.* 923, βροντῆς ὑπερβάλλοντα κτύπον.

"Suavissima haec quasi correctio est," Bengel. As if the very word "know" at once suggested the thought that such knowledge was beyond human capacity. "But even though the love of Christ surpasses human knowledge, yet ye shall know it if ye have Christ dwelling in you," Theophylact. There is a relative knowledge which increases in proportion as the believer is filled with the spirit of Christ and thereby "rooted and grounded in love," for by love only is love known. γνῶναι, then, is used in a pregnant sense. τὸ γνῶναι, says Theodore Mops., ἀντὶ τοῦ ἀπολαῦσαι λέγει (referring to Ps. xv. 11). So also Theodoret, δυνατὸν ἡμᾶς διὰ τῆς πίστεως καὶ ἀγάπης τῆς πνευματικῆς χάριτος ἀπολαῦσαι καὶ διὰ ταύτης καταμαθεῖν. . . . For a similar oxymoron in St. Paul, see Rom. i. 20, τὰ ἀόρατα αὐτοῦ . . . καθορᾶται.

A quite different interpretation is adopted by Luther in his edition of 1545 (not the earlier), viz. "to love Christ is better than knowledge." Holzhausen defends a similar view, on the ground (amongst others) that to express the other meaning St. Paul would have said, as in Phil. ii. 4, ὑπερέχουσα πάντα νοῦν. But he desired to express the thought as an oxymoron, thus making it more striking. Dobree renders, "the exceeding love of God in bestowing on us the knowledge of Christ" (*Advers.* i. p. 573). He gives no reason, and it is hard to see how the rendering can be defended.

"The love of Christ," *i.e.* Christ's love to us. But knowledge of whatever kind is not the ultimate end, therefore he adds, not as a parallel clause, but as the end of the whole, ἵνα πληρωθῆτε εἰς πᾶν τὸ πλήρωμα τοῦ Θεοῦ, "that ye may be filled up to all the fulness of God."

This is not of easy interpretation. Chrysostom gives two alternatives, either the πλ. τοῦ Θεοῦ is the knowledge that God is worshipped in the Father, the Son, and the Holy Ghost, or he urges them to strive ὥστε πληροῦσθαι πάσης ἀρετῆς ἧς πλήρης ἐστιν ὁ Θεός. This is rendered by Newman, "of which God is the fountain-head," but has been usually taken to mean "be filled, even as God is full" (Alford, Olshausen, Ellicott, Eadie). It is indeed added, "each in your degree, but all to your utmost capacity"; or, again, "the difference between God and the saint will be, not in kind, but in degree and extent." But there is no such restriction in the text; it is not, "filled up to your capacity" (note πᾶν), and the expression is one of degree, not of kind. On the same principle of interpretation we might defend such an expression as "wise with all the wisdom of God"; yet the impropriety of this is obvious. Matt. v. 48, "ye shall be τέλειοι as (ὡς) your heavenly Father is τέλειος," is not in point, for what is there referred to is the single virtue of love, which is to be as all-embracing as that of God. "They who love those that love them are incomplete in love; they who love their enemies are τέλειοι," Euthymius, cf. 1 Pet. i. 15. To be filled as God is full, could at most be set forth as the ideal to be attained or rather approached in a future state. When it is urged (by Olsh. and Ellic.) that where Christ dwells there πᾶν τὸ πλήρ. τοῦ Θεοῦ is already (Col. ii. 9), this is really to confound two distinct interpretations. Oltramare, taking πλήρωμα to mean "perfection," and πληροῦσθαι "to be perfected," understands the words to mean, "that ye may be perfect even to the possession of all the perfection of God." "The highest moral ideal that can be presented to him in whose heart Christ dwells, who has comprehended the greatness of love, and has known the love of God."

Theodore Mops. appears to interpret the words of the Church, "ita ut et ipsi in portione communis corporis videamini in quod vel maxime inhabitat Deus"; and so some moderns, but does violence to the language.

Theodoret interprets: ἵνα τελείως αὐτὸν ἔνοικον δέξησθε; and this has much in its favour. εἰς, then, would be as in ii. 21, 22, so that ye become the πλήρ. (as the result of loading a ship is that it becomes a πλήρωμα). God, then, is that with which they are filled, as in i. 23 and iv. 13 it is Christ. So κατοικητήριον τοῦ Θεοῦ, ii. 22, is parallel to κατοικῆσαι τὸν Χρ. ἐν ταῖς καρδίαις, iii. 17 (v. Soden). But "to be filled with God" is an expression which, though capable of defence, would be open to misconception, and has no distinct parallel in the N.T. It appears more consonant with St. Paul's language generally to understand πλ. τοῦ Θεοῦ as the fulness of the riches of God, all that is "spiritually communicable to the saints, [who are] the 'partakers of Divine nature,' 2 Pet. i. 4" (Moule). This is substantially Meyer's view.

B has a peculiar reading: ἵνα πληρωθῇ πᾶν, which is also that of 17, 73, 116, of which, however, 17 reads εἰς ὑμᾶς instead of τοῦ Θεοῦ. Westcott and Hort admit the reading of B to their margin, "that all the fulness of God may be filled up." Comp., however, the loss of -τε of ἐσφραγίσθητε in B, cap. i. 13.

20, 21. *Doxology suggested by the thought of the glorious things prayed for.*

20. τῷ δὲ δυναμένῳ ὑπὲρ πάντα ποιῆσαι ὑπερεκπερισσοῦ ὧν αἰτούμεθα ἢ νοοῦμεν. "Now to Him who is able to do more than all abundantly beyond what we ask or think."

The object of the prayer was a lofty one; but, lofty as it is, God is able to give more than we ask, and even more than we understand. Neither the narrowness of our knowledge nor the feebleness of our prayer will limit the richness of His gifts. Surely a ground for this ascription of praise, which gives a solemn close to the first portion of the Epistle.

ὑπέρ is not adverbial; coming as it does close to πάντα, no reader could take it otherwise than as a preposition; besides, as an adverb it would be tautological. ὑπερεκπερισσοῦ, which occurs again 1 Thess. iii. 10, v. 13, is one of those compounds with ὑπέρ of which St. Paul was fond, cf. ὑπερλίαν, 2 Cor. xi. 5; ὑπερπερισσεύω, Rom. v. 20; 2 Cor. vii. 4. Indeed, St. Mark also has ὑπερπερισσῶς, vii. 37. Ellicott notes that of the twenty-eight words compounded with ὑπέρ, twenty-two are found in St. Paul's Epistles and Heb., and twenty of these are found there alone.

ὧν is not to be connected with πάντα, as there is no difficulty about joining it with ὑπερεκπερισσοῦ, which by the idea of comparison can govern the genitive (*i.e.* = τούτων ἅ).

κατὰ τὴν δύναμιν τὴν ἐνεργουμένην ἐν ἡμῖν. "According to (or by virtue of) the power that worketh in us." ἐνεργ. is clearly middle, not passive (as Estius). Onthovius, indeed, defends the latter view, maintaining that ἐνεργεῖται is always passive in the N.T., even Rom. vii. 5; 1 Thess. ii. 13; Jas. v. 16 (*Bibliotheca Bremensis, Classis 4ta*, p. 474). According to Winer, St. Paul uses the active of personal action, the middle of non-personal. Comp. Col. i. 29.

21. αὐτῷ ἡ δόξα ἐν τῇ ἐκκλησίᾳ καὶ ἐν Χριστῷ Ἰησοῦ. "To Him be glory in the Church and in Christ Jesus." So ℵ A B C 17, *al.*, Vulg. Boh., Jerome. But καί is omitted by D^b K L P, Syr. (both) Arm. Eth. Goth., Chrys. Theodoret, Theoph. Oecum. D* G transpose, and read: ἐν Χριστῷ Ἰησοῦ καὶ τῇ ἐκκλησίᾳ. This transposition is perhaps due to the thought that "Christ" should precede "the Church." It is not very easy to see why καί should have been omitted if genuine; on the other hand, it is easy to see a reason for its insertion. It is, however, hard to resist the documentary evidence for the insertion. If καί is omitted we understand "in the Church," in which thanks and praise are given, "in Christ Jesus," not simply "through"; but as St. Paul so often uses this expression, and "in the Lord"; He is not the medium merely, but by virtue of His union with the Church it is in Him that it gives glory to God. Olshausen and Braune, with some older commentators, connect ἐν Χριστῷ Ἰησοῦ with τῇ ἐκκλησίᾳ. The absence of the article is not inconsistent with this, but the addition would be superfluous, since the ἐκκλ. can only be that which is in Christ Jesus.

If καί, however, is read, we must apparently interpret ἐν similarly in both cases. The Church, then, is that by whose greatness and perfection the δόξα of God is exhibited, as it is also exhibited in Christ Jesus (v. Soden and Moule).

εἰς πάσας τὰς γενεὰς τοῦ αἰῶνος τῶν αἰώνων ἀμήν. "To all generations, for ever and ever. Amen." There seems to be a blending of the two formulae γενεαὶ γενεῶν and αἰῶνες, or αἰών, τῶν αἰώνων. εἰς τοὺς αἰῶνας τῶν αἰ. occurs Gal. i. 5; Phil. iv. 10; 1 Tim. i. 17; 2 Tim. iv. 18, besides the Apocalypse; εἰς τὸν αἰῶνα τῶν αἰώνων in 3 Esdr. iv. 38; and ἕως τοῦ αἰ. τῶν αἰ., Dan. vii. 18 (Theodot.). There seems to be no difference in the meaning. The phrase is understood by Meyer and others as designating the future αἰών, which begins with the Parousia, as the superlative age of all ages. It seems much more natural to explain it as the αἰών which includes many αἰῶνες, "in omnes generationes quas complectitur ὁ αἰών, qui terminatur in τοὺς αἰῶνας perpetuos," Bengel. But when we consider the difficulty of giving a logical analysis which shall be also grammatical of our own "world without end," we may be content to accept the meaning without seeking to analyse the expression.

IV. 1 ff. He now passes, as usually in his Epistles, after the doctrinal exposition to the practical exhortation, in the course of which, however, he is presently drawn back (ver. 4) to doctrinal teaching to support his exhortation to unity.

1–4. *Exhortation to live in a manner worthy of their calling, in lowliness, patience, love, and unity.*

1. παρακαλῶ οὖν ὑμᾶς ἐγὼ ὁ δέσμιος ἐν Κυρίῳ. "I therefore, the prisoner in the Lord, entreat you." οὖν may indicate inference from the immediately preceding verse, or more probably (since it is the transition between two sections of the Epistle) from the whole former part, ὁ δέσμιος ἐν Κ. This is not to excite their sympathy, or as desiring that they should cheer him in his troubles by their obedience; for, as Theodoret remarks, "he exults in his bonds for Christ's sake more than a king in his diadem"; but rather to add force to his exhortation. "In the Lord" for "in Domini vinculis constrictus est qui ἐν Κυρίῳ ὢν vinctus est," Fritzsche (*Rom.* ii. p. 84). It does not signify "for Christ's sake"; compare συνεργὸς ἐν Χριστῷ, Rom. xvi. 3, 9; ἀγαπητὸς ἐν Κυρίῳ, *ib.* 8. It assigns rather the special character which distinguished this captivity from others.

παρακαλῶ may be either "exhort" or "entreat, beseech";

and in both senses it is used either with an infinitive or with a conjunction (ἵνα or ὅπως). Either sense would suit here, but "exhort" seems too weak for the connexion; comp. Rom. xii. 1, where it is followed by "by the mercies of God," a strong form of appeal. More than exhortation is implied, especially as it is an absolute duty to which he calls them.

ἀξίως περιπατῆσαι τῆς κλήσεως ἧς ἐκλήθητε. "To walk worthily of the calling wherewith ye were called." ἧς attracted for ἥν the cognate accusative; cf. i. 6; 2 Cor. i. 4. True, the dative might be used with καλεῖν (see 2 Tim. i. 9); but the attraction of the dative would not be in accordance with N.T. practice.

2. μετὰ πάσης ταπεινοφροσύνης καὶ πρᾳότητος. "With all lowliness and meekness." μετά is used of accompanying actions or dispositions (see Acts xvii. 11; 2 Cor. vii. 15); πάσης belongs to both substantives. What is ταπεινοφροσύνη? Chrysostom says it is ὅταν τις μέγας ὢν ἑαυτὸν ταπεινοῖ; and elsewhere, ὅταν μεγάλα τις ἑαυτῷ συνειδώς, μηδὲν μέγα περὶ αὐτοῦ φαντάζηται. Trench says it is rather esteeming ourselves small, inasmuch as we are so, the thinking truly, and therefore lowlily of ourselves; adding that Chrysostom is bringing in pride again under the disguise of humility. In this he is followed by Alford and other English commentators. Yet surely this is not right. A man may be small, and know himself to be so, and yet not be humble. But every man cannot truly think himself smaller than his fellows; nor can this be the meaning of Phil. ii. 3. If a man is really greater than others in any quality or attainment, moral, intellectual, or spiritual, does the obligation of humility bind him to think falsely that he is less than they? It is no doubt true that the more a man advances in knowledge or in spiritual insight, the higher his ideal becomes, and so the more sensibly he feels how far he comes short of it. This is one aspect of humility, but it is not ταπεινοφροσύνη. And St. Paul is speaking of humility as a Christian social virtue. St. Paul declares himself to be not a whit inferior to οἱ ὑπερλίαν ἀπόστολοι, and in the same breath says that he humbled himself; he even exhorts his readers to imitate him, and yet he attributes this very virtue to himself, Acts xx. 19. And what of our Lord Himself, who was meek and lowly, πρᾷος καὶ ταπεινός, in heart? One who knows himself greater in relation to others, but who is contented to be treated as if he were less, such a one is certainly entitled to be called humble-minded; he exhibits ταπεινοφροσύνη. Chrysostom's definition, then, is far truer than Trench's; it only errs by limiting the possibility of the virtue to those who are great.

This is a peculiarly Christian virtue. The word occurs in Josephus and Epictetus, but only in a bad sense as = "meanness of spirit." πρᾳότης is understood by some expositors as meekness toward God and toward men; the spirit "which never rises in insubordination against God, nor in resentment against man" (Eadie); but its use in the N.T. does not justify the introduction of the former idea; compare 1 Cor. iv. 21, "Shall I come to you with a rod, or in the spirit of πρ."? 2 Tim. ii. 25, "correcting in πρ."; Tit. iii. 2, "showing all πρ. towards all men." Resignation toward God and meekness toward man are distinct though allied virtues. The same virtues are mentioned in Col. iii. 12.

μετὰ μακροθυμίας, "with long-suffering," connected by some expositors with the following; but ἀνεχόμενοι is already defined by ἐν ἀγάπῃ, which is best connected with that word. The repetition of μετά is rather in favour of than adverse to the parallelism with the preceding, ταπ. and πρᾳ. being taken more closely together as being nearly allied virtues.

μακροθυμία has two senses: steadfastness, especially in enduring suffering, as in Plutarch, "Never ask from God freedom from trouble, but μακροθυμία" (*Luc.* 32) cf. Jas. v. 10; Heb. vi. 12; but generally in N.T. slowness in avenging wrongs, forbearance, explained, in fact, in the following words. Fritzsche defines it, "*Clementia,* quâ irae temperans delictum non statim vindices, sed ei qui peccaverit poenitendi locum relinquas" (*Rom.* i. p. 98). Compare 1 Cor. xiii. 4, ἡ ἀγάπη μακροθυμεῖ, χρηστεύεται. In his comment on that passage, Chrysostom rather curiously says: μακρόθυμος διὰ τοῦτο λέγεται ἐπειδὴ μακράν τινα καὶ μεγάλην ἔχει ψυχήν.

ἀνεχόμενοι ἀλλήλων ἐν ἀγάπῃ. "Forbearing one another in love." This mutual forbearance is the expression in action of μακροθυμία. It involves bearing with one another's weaknesses, not ceasing to love our neighbour or friend because of those faults in him which perhaps offend or displease us.

The participles fall into the nominative by a common idiom, ὑμεῖς being the logical subject of ἀξίως περιπατ.; cf. ch. iii. 18 and Col. i. 10. There is no need, then, with some commentators, to supply ἐστέ or γίνεσθε.

3. σπουδάζοντες τηρεῖν τὴν ἑνότητα τοῦ πνεύματος ἐν τῷ συνδέσμῳ τῆς εἰρήνης, "giving diligence to keep the unity of the Spirit in the bond of peace." "Endeavouring," as in the AV., would imply the possibility, if not likelihood, of the endeavour failing. Trench (*On the Authorised Version*, p. 44) says that in the time of the translators "endeavouring" meant "giving all diligence." But in Acts xvi. 10 the word is used to render ἐζητήσαμεν, and except in this and two other passages it is not used for σπουδάζειν, which, in Tit. iii. 12 and 2 Pet. iii. 14, is rendered "be diligent"; in 2 Tim. iv. 9, 21, "do thy diligence"; 2 Tim. ii. 15, "study." The other passages where the rendering is "endeavour" are 1 Thess. ii. 17, where the endeavour did fail, and 2 Pet. i. 15, where failure might

have appeared possible. Theophylact well expresses the force of the word here: οὐκ ἀπόνως ἰσχύσομεν εἰρηνεύειν. The clause expresses the end to be attained by the exercise of the virtues mentioned in ver. 2.

τηρεῖν, "to preserve," for it is supposed already to exist. "Etiam ubi nulla fissura est, monitis opus est," Bengel. The existence of divisions, therefore, is not suggested. "The unity of the Spirit," *i.e.* the unity which the Spirit has given us. "The Spirit unites those who are separated by race and customs," Chrys., and so most recent commentators; and this seems to be proved by ἓν Πνεῦμα in the following verse. But Calvin, Estius, and others, following Anselm and ps-Ambrose, understand πν. here of the human spirit, "animorum concordia." De Wette, again, thinks that the analogy of ἑνότης τῆς πίστεως, in ver. 13, is against the received interpretation, and accordingly interprets "the unity of the spirit of the Christian community," taking πν. in ver. 4 similarly. Comp. Grotius, "unitatem ecclesiae quae est corpus spirituale." (Theodore Mops. agrees with Chrys. The quotation in Ellicott belongs to the next verse.)

ἐν τῷ συνδέσμῳ τῆς εἰρήνης. Genitive of apposition; peace is the bond in which the unity is kept; cf. σύνδεσμον ἀδικίας, Acts viii. 23, and σύνδεσμος εὐνοίας, Plut. *Num.* 6. The fact that love is called the bond of peace in Col. iii. 14 does not justify us in taking the words here as meaning "love," an interpretation adopted, probably, in consequence of ἐν being taken instrumentally; in which case, as peace could not be the instrument by which the unity of the Spirit is maintained, but is itself maintained thereby, the genitive could not be one of apposition. But the ἐν is parallel to the ἐν before ἀγάπῃ, and in any case it is not by the bond of peace that the unity of the Spirit is kept.

4–11. *Essential unity of the Church. It is one Body, animated by one Spirit, baptized into the name of the one Lord, and all being children of the same Father. But the members have their different gifts and offices.*

4. ἓν σῶμα καὶ ἓν Πνεῦμα καθὼς καὶ ἐκλήθητε ἐν μιᾷ ἐλπίδι τῆς κλήσεως ὑμῶν. "One Body, and one Spirit, even as ye were called in one hope of your calling." This and the two following verses express the objective unity belonging to the Christian dispensation in all its aspects. First, the oneness of the Church itself: one Body, one Spirit, one Hope. Next, the source and instruments of that unity, one Lord, one Faith, one Baptism; and lastly, the unity of the Divine Author, who is defined, in a threefold manner, as over all, through all, and in all.

Although there is no connecting particle, and γάρ is certainly not to be supplied, the declaration is introduced as supplying a motive for the exhortation, but the absence of any such particle makes it more vivid and impressive. We need not even supply ἐστί; it is rather to be viewed as an abrupt and emphatic reminder of what the readers well knew, as if the writer were addressing them in person. Still less are we to supply, with Theophylact and Oecumenius, "Be ye," or with others, "Ye are," neither of which would agree with vv. 5 and 6.

One Body; namely, the Church itself, so often thus described; one Spirit, the Holy Spirit, which dwells in and is the vivifying Spirit of that body; cf. 1 Cor. xii. 13. The parallelism εἷς Κύριος, εἷς Θεός seems to require this. Comp. 1 Cor. xii. 4–6, where τὸ αὐτὸ Πνεῦμα, ὁ αὐτὸς Κύριος, ὁ αὐτὸς Θεός. Chrysostom, however, interprets differently; indeed, he gives choice of several interpretations, none of them agreeing with this. "Showing (he says) that from one body there will be one spirit; or that there may be one body but not one spirit, as if one should be a friend of heretics; or that he shames them from that, that is, ye who have received one spirit and been made to drink from one fountain ought not to be differently minded; or by spirit here he means readiness, προθυμία."

καθώς is not used by Attic writers, who employ καθάπερ or καθό. It is called Alexandrian, but is not confined to Alexandrian or biblical writers.

ἐν μιᾷ ἐλπίδι. ἐν is not instrumental, as Meyer holds. Comp. καλεῖν ἐν χάριτι, Gal. i. 6; ἐν εἰρήνῃ, 1 Cor. vii. 15; ἐν ἁγιασμῷ, 1 Thess. iv. 7; nor is it = εἰς or ἐπί, as Chrysostom.

It is frequently said in this and similar cases that it indicates the "element" in which something takes place. But this is no explanation, it merely suggests an indefinite figure, which itself requires explanation. Indeed, the word "element" or "sphere" seems to imply something previously existing. What ἐν indicates is that the hope was an essential accompaniment of their calling, a "conditio" (not "condition" in the English sense). It differs from εἰς in this, that the latter preposition would suggest that the "hope," "peace," etc., followed the calling in time. In fact, the expression εἴς τι involves a figure taken from motion; he who is called is conceived as leaving the place in which the call reached him. But κλῆσις as applied to the Christian calling is pregnant, it includes the idea of the state into which the calling brings those who are called. "ἐν exprimit indolem rei," Bengel on 1 Thess. iv. 7; so also the verb. Hence such an expression as κλητοὶ ἅγιοι. They are so called as to be ἐν ἐλπίδι, ἐν εἰρήνῃ, by the very fact of their calling, not merely as a result of it. Hence, also, we are not to interpret "hope of your calling," or "the hope arising from your calling," which is hardly consistent, by the way, with the idea that hope is the "element." It is rather the hope belonging to your calling.

5. εἷς Κύριος, μία πίστις, ἓν βάπτισμα. "One Lord, one Faith,

one Baptism." One Lord, Christ; one faith, of which He is the object, one in its nature and essence; and one baptism, by which we are brought into the profession of this faith.

The question has been asked, Why is the other sacrament not mentioned? and various answers have been given, of which the one that is most to the point, perhaps, is that it is not a ground or antecedent condition of unity, but an expression of it. Yet it must be admitted that it would supply a strong motive for preserving unity, as in 1 Cor. x. 17. Probably, as it was not essential to mention it, the omission is due in part to the rhythmical arrangement of three triads.

6. εἶς Θεὸς καὶ πατὴρ πάντων. "One God and Father of all." Observe the climax: first, the Church, then Christ, then God; also the order of the three Persons—Spirit, Lord, Father. Ellicott quotes from Cocceius: "Etiamsi baptizamur in nomen Patris Filii et Spiritus Sancti, et filium unum Dominum nominamus, tamen non credimus nisi in unum Deum." It is arbitrary to limit πάντων to the faithful. It is true the context speaks only of Christians, but then πάντες has not been used. The writer advances from the Lord of the Church to the God and Father of all. For this notion of Fatherhood see Pearson, *On the Creed*, Art. 1.

ὁ ἐπὶ πάντων καὶ διὰ πάντων καὶ ἐν πᾶσιν. "Who is over all, and through all, and in all." The Received Text adds ὑμῖν, with a few cursives, and Chrys. (Comm. not text) Theoph. Oec. ἡμῖν is added in D G K L, Vulg. Syr. (both) Arm. Goth., Iren.

There is no pronoun in א A B C P 17 67², Ign. Orig. *al.* It was, no doubt, added as a gloss, πᾶσιν seeming to require a limitation.

As πᾶσιν is undoubtedly masculine, it is most natural to take πάντων in both places as masculine also. Ver. 7 individualises the πάντες by ἑνὶ ἑκάστῳ ἡμῶν. Erasmus and some later commentators, however, have taken the first and second πάντων as neuter, whilst the Vulg. so takes the second.

ὁ ἐπὶ πάντων; cf. Rom. ix. 5, ὁ ὢν ἐπὶ πάντων Θεὸς εὐλογητὸς εἰς τοὺς αἰῶνας. "Over all," as a sovereign ruler. It is less easy to say what are the distinct ideas meant to be expressed by διά and ἐν respectively. The latter is more individualising, the indwelling is an indwelling in each; whereas διὰ πάντων expresses a relation to the whole body, through the whole of which the influence and power of God are diffused. It is a sustaining and working presence. This does not involve the supplying of ἐνεργῶν.

We are not to suppose a direct reference to the Trinity in these three prepositional clauses, for here it is the Father that is specially mentioned in parallelism to the Spirit and the Son, previously spoken of.

7. ἑνὶ δὲ ἑκάστῳ ἡμῶν ἐδόθη ἡ χάρις κατὰ τὸ μέτρον τῆς δωρεᾶς τοῦ Χριστοῦ. "But to each one of us the grace was given according

to the measure of the gift of Christ." He passes from the relation to the whole to the relation to the individual. In the oneness of the body, etc., there is room for diversity, and no one is overlooked; each has his own position. Compare Rom. xii. 4–6; 1 Cor. xii. 4 ff., where the conception is carried out in detail. "The grace," *i.e.* the grace which he has. The article is omitted in B D* G L P*, but is present in ℵ A C D^c K P^{corr}, most others. The omission is easy to account for from the adjoining η in ἐδόθη. "According to the measure," etc., *i.e.* according to what Christ has given; cf. Rom. xii. 6, "gifts differing according to the grace that is given to us."

8. Διὸ λέγει. "Wherefore it saith" = "it is said." If any substantive is to be supplied it is ἡ γραφή; but the verb may well be taken impersonally, just as in colloquial English one may often hear: "it says," or the like. Many expositors, however, supply ὁ Θεός. Meyer even says, "Who says it is obvious of itself, namely, God, whose word the Scripture is." Similarly Alford and Ellicott. If it were St. Paul's habit to introduce quotations from the O.T., by whomsoever spoken in the original text, with the formula ὁ Θεὸς λέγει, then this supplement here might be defended. But it is not. In quoting he sometimes says λέγει, frequently ἡ γραφὴ λέγει, at other times Δαβὶδ λέγει, Ἡσαΐας λέγει. There is not a single instance in which ὁ Θεός is either expressed or implied as the subject, except where in the original context God is the speaker, as in Rom. ix. 15. Even when that is the case he does not hesitate to use a different subject, as in Rom. x. 19, 20, "Moses saith," "Isaiah is very bold, and saith"; Rom. ix. 17, "The Scripture saith to Pharaoh."

This being the case, we are certainly not justified in forcing upon the apostle here and in ch. v. 14 a form of expression consistent only with the extreme view of verbal inspiration. When Meyer (followed by Alford and Ellicott) says that ἡ γραφή must not be supplied unless it is given by the context, the reply is obvious, namely, that, as above stated, ἡ γραφὴ λέγει does, in fact, often occur, and therefore the apostle might have used it here, whereas ὁ Θεὸς λέγει does not occur (except in cases unlike this), and we have reason to believe could not be used by St. Paul here. It is some additional confirmation of this that both here and in ch. v. 14 (if that is a biblical quotation) he does not hesitate to make important alterations. This is the view taken by Braune, Macpherson, Moule; the latter, however, adding that for St. Paul "the word of the Scripture and the word of its Author are convertible terms."

It is objected that although φησί is used impersonally, λέγει is not. The present passage and ver. 14 are sufficient to prove the usage for St. Paul, and there are other passages in his Epistles where this sense is at least applicable; cf. Rom. xv. 10, where λέγει is parallel to γέγραπται in ver. 9; Gal. iii. 16, where it corresponds to ἐρρήθησαν. But, in fact, the impersonal use of φησί in Greek authors is quite different, namely = φασί, "they say" (so 1 Cor. x. 10). Classical authors had no opportunity of using λέγει as it is used here, as they did not possess any collection of writings which could be referred to as ἡ γραφή, or by any like word. They could say: ὁ νόμος λέγει, and τὸ λεγόμενον.

Ἀναβὰς εἰς ὕψος ᾐχμαλώτευσεν αἰχμαλωσίαν καὶ ἔδωκε δόματα τοῖς ἀνθρώποις. "When he ascended on high He led a captivity captive, and gave gifts unto men." The words appear to be taken from Ps. lxviii. 18 (where the verbs are in the second person); but there is an important divergence in the latter clause, which in the Hebrew is, "Thou has received gifts among men," the meaning being, received tributary gifts amongst the vanquished, or according to another interpretation, gifts consisting in the persons of the surrendered enemies (Ibn Ezra, Ewald). The Septuagint also has ἔλαβες δόματα ἐν ἀνθρώπῳ, or, according to another reading, ἀνθρώποις. Various attempts have been made to account for the divergence. Chrysostom simply says the one is the same as the other, τοῦτο ταὐτόν ἐστιν ἐκείνῳ; and so Theophylact, adding, "for God giving the gifts receives in return the service." Meyer, followed by Alford and Eadie, maintains that the Hebrew verb often has a proleptic signification, "to fetch," *i.e.* to take in order to give. The apostle, says Eadie, seizes on the latter portion of the sense, and renders—ἔδωκε. Most of the passages cited for this are irrelevant to the present purpose, the verb being followed by what we may call the dative of a pronoun, *e.g.* Gen. xv. 9, "Take for me"; xxvii. 13, "Fetch me them." In such cases it is plain that the notion of subsequent giving is in the "mihi," not in the verb, or rather the dative is simply analogous to the *dativus commodi*. This use is quite parallel to that of the English "get." In xviii. 5, "I will get a piece of bread and comfort ye your hearts," the pronoun is omitted as needless, the words that follow expressing the purpose for which the bread was to be fetched. In xlii. 16, "Send one of you and let him fetch your brother," there is no idea of giving. In no case is giving any part of the idea of the Hebrew verb any more than of the English "get" or "fetch." But whatever may be thought of this "proleptic use," this is not the sense of the verb in the psalm, so that it would not really help. The psalm speaks of receiving (material) gifts from men; the apostle, of giving (spiritual) gifts to men. Macpherson says, "The modification is quite justifiable, on the ground that Christ, to whom the words are applied, receives gifts among men only that He may bestow them upon men." But Christ did not receive amongst men the gifts which He is here said to bestow. The

Pulpit Commentary states: "Whereas in the psalm it is said *gave* gifts *to* men" [which is not in the psalm, but in the Epistle], as modified by the apostle it is said "*received* gifts *for* men," which is neither one nor the other, but a particular interpretation of the psalm adopted in the English version. Ellicott, admitting that the difference is not diminished by any of the proposed reconciliations, takes refuge in the apostolic authority of St. Paul. "The inspired apostle, by a slight (?) change of language and substitution of ἔδωκε for the more dubious לקח, succinctly, suggestively, and authoritatively unfolds." But he does not profess to be interpreting (as in Rom. x. 6, 7, 8), but quoting. Such a view, indeed, would open the door to the wildest freaks of interpretation; they might not, indeed, command assent as inspired, but they could never be rejected as unreasonable. The change here, far from being slight, is just in that point in which alone the quotation is connected either with what precedes or with what follows.

The supposition that St. Paul does not intend either to quote exactly or to interpret, but in the familiar Jewish fashion adapts the passage to his own use, knowing that those of his readers who were familiar with the psalm would recognise the alteration and see the purpose of it, namely, that instead of receiving gifts of homage Christ gives His gifts to men, is not open to any serious objection, since he does not found any argument on the passage. So Theodore Mops., who remarks that ὑπαλλάξας τὸ ἔλαβε δόματα οὕτως ἐν τῷ ψαλμῷ κείμενον, ἔδωκε δόματα εἶπε, τῇ ὑπαλλαγῇ περὶ τὴν οἰκείαν χρησάμενος ἀκολουθίαν· ἐκεῖ μὲν γὰρ πρὸς τὴν ὑπόθεσιν τὸ ἔλαβεν ἥρμοττεν, ἐνταῦθα δὲ τῷ προκειμένῳ τὸ ἔδωκεν ἀκόλουθον ἦν. As Oltramare observes: Paul wishes to speak of the spiritual gifts granted to the Christian in the measure of the gift of Christ, exalted to heaven. An expression of Scripture occurs to him, which strikes him as being "le mot de la situation." Depicting originally the triumph of God, it strikes him as expressing well (*mutatis mutandis*) the triumph of Christ, but he does not identify either the facts or the persons. It is, however, remarkable that the same interpretation of the words of the psalm is given in the Syriac Version and in the Targum. The former may have followed St. Paul, as the Arabic and Ethiopic, although made from the Septuagint, have done; and it has been suggested that the Targumist, finding a difficulty, followed the Syriac,—an improbable supposition. In his expansion he interprets the words of Moses, "Thou didst ascend to the firmament, Moses the prophet, thou didst take a captivity captive, thou didst teach the words of the law, thou gavest gifts to the sons of men." This Targum as we have it is of comparatively late date. But if we may assume, as no doubt we may, that it is giving us here an ancient interpretation, we have a solution of the difficulty so far as St. Paul is concerned; he simply made use of the Rabbinical interpretation as being suitable to his purpose. Compare 1 Cor. x. 4. No doubt the question remains, What led the Targumist to take this view of the passage? Hitzig suggests that as the receiving of gifts seemed not consonant with the majesty of God, the paraphrast mentally substituted for לקח the verb חלק, which has the same letters in a different order, and means "to divide, give a portion," etc. This verb is rendered δίδωσιν by the Sept. in Gen. xlix. 27 (EV. "divide"), while in 2 Chron. xxviii. 21, where it occurs in an otherwise unexampled sense "plunder" (EV. "took a portion out of"), the Sept. has ἔλαβεν (τὰ ἐν). The feeling that prompted the paraphrast here shows itself also in Rashi's comment, "took, that thou mightest give."

This renders needless a recourse to the supposition that the quotation is from a Christian hymn, which borrowed from the psalm. The objection raised to this and to the preceding view from the use of λέγει, has no force except on the assumption that Θεός is to be supplied; and, in fact, in ver. 14 many expositors suppose that it is a hymn that is quoted in the same manner. Nor can it be truly alleged that St. Paul here treats the words as belonging to canonical Scripture, for he draws no inference from them, as we shall see. Indeed, if he himself had altered them, instead of adopting an existing alteration, it would be equally impossible for him to argue from the altered text as if it were canonical.

ᾐχμαλώτευσεν αἰχμαλωσίαν. "Took captive a body of captives," the cognate accusative, abstract for concrete, as the same word is used in 1 Esdr. v. 45 and Judith ii. 9. We have the same expression in the song of Deborah: "Arise, Barak, and lead thy captivity captive, thou son of Abinoam," Judg. v. 12, which is perhaps the source of the expression in the psalm. The interpretation adopted in a popular hymn, "captivity is captive led," as if "captivity" meant the power that took captive, is quite untenable, and such a use of the abstract is foreign to Hebrew thought.

Who are these captives? Chrysostom replies: The enemies of Christ, viz. Satan, sin, and death. In substance this interpretation is no doubt correct, but it is unnecessary to define the enemies; the figure is general, that of a triumphant conqueror leading his conquered enemies in his train. Compare Col. ii. 15. To press the figure further would lead us into difficulties. These enemies are not yet finally destroyed, ἔσχατος ἐχθρὸς καταργεῖται ὁ θάνατος (1 Cor. xv. 25).

Theodoret interprets the "captives" as the redeemed (as Justin had already done), namely, as having been captives of the devil, οὐ γὰρ ἐλευθέρους ὄντας ἡμᾶς ᾐχμαλώτευσεν, ἀλλ' ὑπὸ τοῦ διαβόλου γεγενημένους ἀντηχμαλώτευσεν, καὶ τὴν ἐλευθερίαν ἡμῖν ἐδωρήσατο; and so many moderns. But this does not agree with the construction by which the αἰχμαλωσία must be the result of the action of the verb. Besides, the captives are distinguished from ἄνθρωποι. The same objections hold against the view that the captives are the souls of the righteous whom Christ delivered from Hades (Lyra, Estius).

"And gave gifts." καί is omitted in ℵ* A C² D* G 17, al.; but inserted in ℵᶜ B C* and ᶜ Dᶜ K L P, al. Syr. A tendency to assimilate to the passage in the psalm appears in the reading ᾐχμαλώτευσαις in A L and several MSS., which nevertheless read ἔδωκεν. For the gifts compare Acts ii. 33.

9. τὸ δὲ Ἀνέβη τί ἐστιν εἰ μὴ ὅτι καὶ κατέβη εἰς τὰ κατώτερα μέρη τῆς γῆς. "Now that He ascended, what is it but that He also descended into the lower parts of the earth?"

> There is here a very important variety of reading—
> κατέβη without πρῶτον is the reading of ℵ* A C* D G 17 67², Boh. Sahid. Eth. Amiat., Iren. Orig. Chrys. (Comm.) Aug. Jerome.
> κατέβη πρῶτον is read in ℵᶜ B Cᶜ K L P, most mss. Vulg. Goth. Syr. (both) Arm., Theodoret.
> The weight of authority is decidedly on the side of omission. Transcriptional evidence points the same way. The meaning which presented itself on the surface was that Christ who ascended had had His original seat in heaven, and that what the apostle intended, therefore, was that He descended before He ascended; hence πρῶτον would naturally suggest itself to the mind of a reader. On the other hand, it is not easy to see why it should be omitted. Reiche, indeed, takes the opposite view. The word, he says, might seem superfluous, since both in ver. 8 and ver. 10 we have ἀναβὰς εἰς ὕψος without πρῶτον; or, again, unsuitable, since Christ descended but once, supposing, namely, that the reference to ἀναβάς was missed. He thinks πρῶτον all but necessary to the argument of the apostle. This is just what some early copyists thought, and it is a consideration much more likely to have affected them than the opposite one, that the word was superfluous. It is rejected by most critics, but Westcott and Hort admit it to a place in the margin.
>
> μέρη after κατώτερα has the authority of ℵ A B C Dᶜ K L P, while it is omitted by D* G (not f). The versions and Fathers are divided. The word is read in Vulg. Boh. Arm. Syr-Pesh., Chrys. Theodoret, Aug., but omitted by Goth. Syr. (Sch.) Eth., Iren. Theodotus. The insertion or omission makes no difference in the sense. Most recent critical editors retain the word. Tischendorf rejected it in his seventh, but restored it in his eighth edition. Alford, Ellicott, and Meyer pronounce against it; the last-mentioned suggesting that it is a gloss due to the old explanation of the descent into hell, in order to mark the place as subterranean.

τὸ δὲ Ἀνέβη, *i.e.* not the word ἀνέβη, which had not occurred, but that which is implied in ἀναβάς. τί ἐστιν εἰ μή, κ.τ.λ., *i.e.* "what does this mean but," etc. τὰ κατώτερα τῆς γῆς. The genitive may be either partitive, the lower as distinguished from the higher parts of the earth, or of apposition, the lower regions, *i.e.* those of the earth. With the former interpretation we may understand either death simply, as Chrysostom and the other Greeks, τὰ κάτω μέρη τῆς γῆς τὸν θάνατόν φησιν, ἀπὸ τῆς τῶν ἀνθρώπων ὑπονοίας, quoting Gen. xliv. 29; Ps. cxlii. 7; or Hades, as the place where departed spirits live, which is the view of Tertullian, Irenaeus, Jerome, and many moderns, including Bengel, Olshausen, Meyer (later editions), Alford, Ellicott, Barry.

But there are serious objections to this. First, if the apostle had meant to say that Christ descended to a depth below which there was no deeper, as He ascended to a height above which was none higher, he would doubtless have used the superlative. τὰ κατώτερα μέρη τῆς γῆς, if the genitive is partitive, could mean "the low-lying regions of the earth," in opposition to τὰ ἀνωτερικὰ μέρη (Acts xix. 1). Meyer, indeed, takes the genitive as depending on the comparative; but this would be an awkward way of expressing what would more naturally have been expressed by an adverb. τὰ κατώτατα τῆς γῆς occurs in the Sept. Ps. lxiii. 9, cxxxix. 15 (κατωτάτω); but in the former place the words mean death and destruction; in the latter they figuratively denote what is hidden, the place of formation of the embryo. The corresponding Hebrew phrase is found in Ezek. xxxii. 18, 24, referring to death and destruction, but rendered βάθος τῆς γῆς. Cf. Matt. xi. 23, where ᾅδου is used similarly. Such passages would support Chrysostom's view rather than that under consideration. But, secondly, all these Old Testament expressions are poetic figures, and in a mere statement of fact like the present, St. Paul would hardly have given such a material local designation to the place of departed spirits, especially in connexion with the idea of Christ filling all things. Thirdly, the antithesis is between earth and heaven, between an ascent from earth to heaven, and a descent which is therefore probably from heaven to earth. Some, indeed, who adopt this view understand the descent as from heaven, some as from earth. For the argument from the connexion, see what follows.

For these reasons it seems preferable to take "the lower parts of the earth" as = "this lower earth." Those who adopt this view generally assume that the descent preceded the ascent, and therefore understand by the descent, the Incarnation. This view, however, is not free from difficulty. St. Paul is speaking of the unity of the whole on the one hand, and of the diversity of individual gifts on the other. The latter is the topic in ver. 7 and again in ver. 11. To what purpose would be an interpolation such as this? It is not brought in to prove the heavenly pre-existence of Christ; that is assumed as known; for ascent to heaven does not imply descent thence, except on that assumption. And why the emphatic assertion of the identity of Him who ascended with Him who had previously descended, which was self-evident?

But, in fact, this ascension is not what is in question, but the giving of gifts; what had to be shown was, that a descent was necessary, in order that He who ascended should give gifts. The descent, then, was contemporaneous with the giving, and, therefore, subsequent to the ascent. This seems to be indicated by the καί before κατέβη. It seems hardly possible to take καὶ κατέβη otherwise than as expressing something subsequent to ἀνέβη. The meaning then is, that the ascent would be without an object, unless it were followed by a descent. This is the descent of Christ to His Church alluded to in ii. 17, "came and preached"; in iii. 17, "that Christ may dwell in your hearts"; and which we also find in John xiv. 23, "we will come to Him"; also *ib.* 3 and xvi. 22. It is now clear why it was necessary to assert that ὁ καταβάς was the same as ὁ ἀναβάς. This interpretation is ably maintained by v. Soden.

10. ὁ καταβὰς αὐτός ἐστιν καὶ ὁ ἀναβὰς ὑπεράνω πάντων τῶν οὐρανῶν ἵνα πληρώσῃ τὰ πάντα. "He Himself that descended is also He that ascended high above all the heavens, that He might fill all things."

αὐτός is not "the same," which would be ὁ αὐτός, but emphatic. οὐ γὰρ ἄλλος κατελήλυθε καὶ ἄλλος ἀνελήλυθεν, Theodoret.

"All the heavens" is probably an allusion to the seven heavens of the Jews. Cf. 2 Cor. xii. 2, τρίτος οὐρανός, and Heb. iv. 14, διεληλυθότα τοὺς οὐρανούς, "that He might fill all things."

This has sometimes been understood to mean "that He might fill the universe," as when we read in Jer. xxiii. 24, μὴ οὐχὶ τὸν οὐρανὸν καὶ τὴν γῆν ἐγὼ πληρῶ; But how can the occupation of a special place in heaven have for its object presence throughout the universe? Moreover, this does not agree with the context, which refers to the gifts to men. In fact, in order to explain this connexion, the omnipresence is resolved by some commentators into the presence everywhere of His gifts (Harless), or else of His government (Chrys, *al.*). A similar result is reached by others, who take πληρώσῃ as meaning directly "fill with His gifts" (De Wette, Bleek, *al.*), τὰ πάντα being either the universe, or men, or members of the Church. But πληροῦν by itself can hardly mean "fill with gifts." Rückert explains, "accomplish all," viz. all that He had to accomplish. But the words must clearly be interpreted in accordance with i. 23, τὰ πάντα ἐν πᾶσιν πληρουμένου, which they obviously repeat. Oltramare interprets, "that He might render all perfect, and (in conformity with this purpose), He gave," etc.

11. καὶ αὐτὸς ἔδωκεν τοὺς μὲν ἀποστόλους, τοὺς δὲ προφήτας, τοὺς δὲ εὐαγγελιστάς, τοὺς δὲ ποιμένας καὶ διδασκάλους. "And He Himself gave some as apostles, some as prophets, some as evangelists, some as pastors and teachers."

ἔδωκεν is not a Hebraism for ἔθετο (1 Cor. xii. 28); it is obviously chosen because of ἔδωκεν δόματα in the quotation, as if the apostle had said, "the gifts He gave were," etc. It is not merely the fact of the institution of the offices that he wishes to bring into view, but the fact that they were gifts to the Church. Christ gave the persons; the Church appointed to the office (Acts xiii. 2, xiv. 23). The enumeration here must be compared with that in 1 Cor. xii. 28, "God hath set some in the Church, first, apostles; secondly, prophets; thirdly, teachers; then miraculous powers, then gifts of healing, helps, governments, divers kinds of tongues." There the order of the first three is expressly defined; the latter gifts are not mentioned here, perhaps, as not expressing offices, but special gifts which were only occasional; and, besides, they did not necessarily belong to distinct persons from the former.

"Apostles." This word is not to be limited to the Twelve, as Lightfoot has shown in detail in his excursus on Gal. i. 17. Besides St. Paul himself, Barnabas is certainly so called (Acts xiv. 4, 14); apparently also James the Lord's brother (1 Cor. xv. 7; Gal. i. 19), and Silvanus (1 Thess. ii. 6, "we might have been burdensome to you, being apostles of Christ"). In Irenaeus and Tertullian the Seventy are called apostles (Iren. ii. 21. 1; Tert. *adv. Marc.* iv. 24). According to the Greek Fathers, followed by Lightfoot, Andronicus and Junia are called apostles in Rom. xvi. 7. In 2 Cor. viii. 23 and Phil. ii. 25 the messengers of the Churches are called "apostles of the Churches." But to be an apostle of Christ it seems to have been a condition that he should have seen Christ, 1 Cor. ix. 1, 2, and have, moreover, been a witness of the resurrection (Acts i. 8, 21–23). Their office was not limited to any particular locality. Prophets are mentioned along with apostles in ii. 20, iii. 5. Chrysostom distinguishes them from "teachers" by this, that he who prophesies utters everything from the spirit, while he who teaches sometimes discourses from his own understanding. "Foretelling" is not implied in the word either etymologically or in classical or N.T. usage. In classical writers it is used of interpreters of the gods. For N.T. usage, compare Matt. xxvi. 68, "Prophesy, who is it that smote thee"; Tit. i. 12, "a prophet of their own," where it is used in the sense of the Latin "vates"; Matt. xv. 7, "well hath Isaiah prophesied of you"; and especially 1 Cor. xiv. 3, "He that prophesieth speaketh unto men to edification, and exhortation, and comfort." Also Acts xv. 32, "Judas and Silas, being themselves also prophets, exhorted the brethren . . . and confirmed them." The function of the prophet has its modern parallel in that of the Christian preacher, who discourses "to edification, exhortation, and comfort" to those who are already members of the Church. "Preaching," in the English Version of the N.T., means proclaiming the gospel to those who have not yet known it (κηρύττειν, εὐαγγελίζεσθαι).

By "evangelists" we are doubtless to understand those whose special function it was to preach the gospel to the heathen in subordination to the apostles. They did not possess the qualifications or the authority of the latter (περιϊόντες ἐκήρυττον, says Theodoret). One of the deacons is specially called an evangelist (Acts xxi. 8). Timothy is told by St. Paul to do the work of an evangelist, but his office included other functions.

τοὺς δὲ ποιμένας καὶ διδασκάλους. The first question is whether these words express distinct offices or two characters of the same office. Many commentators—both ancient and modern—adopt the former view, differing, however, greatly in their definitions. Theophylact understands by "pastors," bishops and presbyters, and by "teachers," deacons. But there is no ground for supposing that deacons would be called διδάσκαλοι. On the other hand, the circumstance that τοὺς δέ is not repeated before διδασκάλους is in favour of the view that the words express two aspects of the same office. So Jerome: "Non enim ait: alios autem pastores et alios magistros, sed alios pastores et magistros, ut qui pastor est, esse debeat et magister." This, indeed, is not quite decisive, since it might only mark that the gifts of pastors and of teachers are not so sharply distinguished from one another as from those that precede; and it must be admitted that in a concise enumeration such as the present, it is in some degree improbable that this particular class should have a double designation. This much is clear, that "pastors and teachers" differ from the preceding classes in being attached to particular Churches. The name "pastors" implies this, and this term no doubt includes ἐπίσκοποι and πρεσβύτεροι. Compare 1 Pet. v. 2 (addressing the πρεσβύτεροι), ποιμάνατε τὸ ἐν ὑμῖν ποίμνιον τοῦ Θεοῦ, ἐπισκοποῦντες (om. RV. mg.): 1 Pet. ii. 25, τὸν ποιμένα καὶ ἐπίσκοπον τῶν ψυχῶν ὑμῶν, where ἐπίσκοπον seems to explain ποιμήν: Acts xx. 28, τῷ ποιμνίῳ ἐν ᾧ ὑμᾶς τὸ Πνεῦμα τὸ ἅγιον ἔθετο ἐπισκόπους, ποιμαίνειν τὴν ἐκκλ. ποιμήν was used in the earliest classical writers of rulers of the people. Even in Homer we have Agamemnon, for instance, called ποιμὴν λαῶν. The ποιμήν of a Christian Church would, of course, be a teacher as well as a governor; it was his business to guide the sheep of the flock; cf. 1 Tim. iii. 2, δεῖ τὸν ἐπίσκοπον ... διδακτικὸν (εἶναι): also Tit. i. 9. But there would naturally be other teachers not invested with the same authority and not forming a distinct class, much less co-ordinate with the ἐπίσκοποι. Had τοὺς δέ been repeated, it might have seemed to separate sharply the function of teaching from the office of ποιμήν. It is easy to see that ἐπίσκοπος would have been a much less suitable word here, since it does not suggest the idea of a moral and spiritual relation.

12–16. *The object of all is the perfection of the saints, that they may be one in the faith, and mature in knowledge, so as not to be carried away by the winds of false doctrine; but that the whole body, as one organism deriving its nourishment from the Head, may be perfected in love.*

12. πρὸς τὸν καταρτισμὸν τῶν ἁγίων, εἰς ἔργον διακονίας, εἰς οἰκοδομὴν τοῦ σώματος τοῦ Χριστοῦ. "With a view to the perfecting of the saints unto the work of ministering, unto the building up of the body of Christ." The καταρτισμὸς τῶν ἁγ. is the ultimate purpose, with a view to which the teachers, etc., have been given εἰς ἔργον διακ. εἰς οἰκ. κ.τ.λ. The Authorised Version follows Chrysostom in treating the three clauses as co-ordinate, ἕκαστος οἰκοδομεῖ, ἕκαστος καταρτίζει, ἕκαστος διακονεῖ. The change in the prepositions is not decisive against this, for St. Paul is rather fond of such variety. But if the three members were parallel, ἔργον διακονίας should certainly come first as the more indefinite and the mediate object. In fact, Grotius and others suppose the thoughts transposed. A plausible view is that adopted by De Wette and many others, that the two latter members depend on the first. "With a view to the perfecting of the saints, so that they may be able to work in every way to the building up," etc. But in a connexion like this, where offices in the Church are in question, διακονία can only mean official service; and this does not belong to the saints in general.

Olshausen supposes the two latter members to be a subdivision of the first, thus: "for the perfecting of the saints, namely, on the one hand, of those who are endowed with gifts of teaching for the fulfilment of their office; and, on the other hand, as regards the hearers, for the building up of the Church." But it is impossible to read into the words this distinction, "on the one hand," "on the other hand"; and the οἰκοδομὴ τοῦ σώματος describes the function of teachers rather than of hearers. Besides, we cannot suppose the teachers themselves to be included among those who are the objects of the functions enumerated in ver. 11.

> The word καταρτισμός does not occur elsewhere in the N.T. Galen uses it of setting a dislocated joint. The verb καταρτίζω by its etymology means to restore or bring to the condition ἄρτιος, and is used Matt. v. 21 of "mending" nets; in Heb. xi. 3 of the "framing" of the world. It occurs Gal. vi. 1 in the figurative sense, "restore such one." In Luke vi. 40 the sense is as here, "to perfect," κατηρτισμένος πᾶς ἔσται ὡς ὁ διδάσκαλος αὐτοῦ. Also in 2 Cor. xiii. 11, καταρτίζεσθε. Comp. *ib.* 9, τὴν ὑμῶν κατάρτισιν. καταρτισμός is the completed result of κατάρτισις.

οἰκοδομὴν τοῦ σώματος. The confusion of metaphors is excused by the fact that οἰκοδομή had for the apostle ceased to suggest its primary meaning; cf. 1 Cor. viii. 10; 1 Thess. v. 11, and below, ver. 16. The fact that both οἰκοδομή and σῶμα τοῦ Χριστοῦ have a distinct metaphorical sense accounts for the confusion, but does not prove it non-existent. The ancients were less exacting in such matters than the moderns; even Cicero has some strange examples. See on iii. 18.

It is useful to bear this in mind when attempts are made elsewhere to press too far the figure involved in some word.

13. μέχρι καταντήσωμεν οἱ πάντες εἰς τὴν ἑνότητα τῆς πίστεως καὶ τῆς ἐπιγνώσεως τοῦ υἱοῦ τοῦ Θεοῦ εἰς ἄνδρα τέλειον, εἰς μέτρον ἡλικίας τοῦ πληρώματος τοῦ Χριστοῦ. "Till we all (we as a whole) attain to the oneness of the faith, and of the thorough knowledge of the Son of God, to a full-grown man, to the measure of the stature (or maturity) of the fulness of Christ." μέχρι is without ἄν because the result is not uncertain. οἱ πάντες, "we, the whole body of us," namely, all believers, not all men (as Jerome), which is against the preceding context (τῶν ἁγίων). The oneness of the faith is opposed to the κλυδωνιζόμενοι καὶ περιφερόμενοι, κ.τ.λ., ver. 14. "Contrarius unitati est omnis ventus," Bengel. ἐπίγνωσις is not merely explanatory of πίστις, which is indeed a condition of it, but a distinct notion. τοῦ υἱοῦ τοῦ Θεοῦ belongs to both substantives. The Son of God is the specific object of Christian faith as well as knowledge.

εἰς ἄνδρα τέλειον, a perfect, mature man, to which the following νήπιοι is opposed. Comp. Polyb. p. 523, ἐλπίσαντες ὡς παιδίῳ νηπίῳ χρήσασθαι τῷ Φιλίππῳ, διά τε τὴν ἡλικίαν καὶ τὴν ἀπειρίαν τὸν μὲν Φ. εὗρον τέλειον ἄνδρα. The singular is used because it refers to the Church as a whole; it corresponds to the εἰς καινὸς ἄνθρωπος. It is doubtful whether we are to take ἡλικία as "age" or "stature"; not only ἡλικία itself but μέτρον ἡλικίας occurs in both senses, the ripeness of full age, and the measure of stature. In the N.T. ἡλικία has the meaning "stature" in Luke xix. 3, ἡλικίᾳ μικρὸς ἦν, and "age" in John ix. 21, ἡλικίαν ἔχει. "Mature age" is the most common signification in Greek writers, whereas the adjective ἡλικός most frequently refers to magnitude. It would appear, therefore, that to a Greek reader it is only the connexion in which it stands that would decide. There is nothing here to decide for "stature"; μέτρον, indeed, might at first sight seem to favour this, but we have in Philostratus, *Vit. Soph.* p. 543, τὸ μέτρον τῆς ἡλικίας ταῖς μὲν ἄλλαις ἐπιστήμαις γήρως ἀρχή.

On the other hand, what the context refers to is the idea of "maturity"; if "stature" were unambiguously expressed, it could only be understood as a mark of maturity; any comparison with physical magnitude would be out of the question. See on Lk. ii. 52.

"Of the fulness of Christ," *i.e.* to which the fulness of Christ belongs.

Some expositors take πλήρωμα here as if used by a Hebraism

for πεπληρωμένος = perfect, complete, either agreeing with Χριστοῦ (πεπληρωμένου) or with ἡλικίας (πεπληρωμένης), thus interpreting either "the measure of the perfect (mature) Christ," or "of the perfect stature of Christ," which again may be explained as that which Christ produces. But this supposition is inadmissible. We cannot separate τὸ πλήρωμα τοῦ Χριστοῦ. Or, again, τὸ πλήρωμα τοῦ Χριστοῦ is understood to mean, "what is filled by Christ," *i.e.* the Church, which is so called in i. 23. But apart from the wrong sense thus given to πλήρωμα, there is a wide difference between predicating τὸ πλ. of the Church, and using the term as synonymous with ἐκκλησία. We may ask, too, How can we all arrive at the maturity of the Church? A better interpretation is that which makes τὸ πλ. τοῦ Χρ. = the fulness of Christ, *i.e.* the maturity is that to which belongs the full possession of the gifts of Christ. Oltramare objects that this interpretation rests on an erroneous view of the sense of πλήρωμα τοῦ Χρ., which does not mean the full possession of Christ, nor the full gracious presence of Christ. Moreover, it makes μέτρον superfluous, and makes the whole clause a mere repetition of εἰς ἄνδρα τέλειον. With his view of πλήρωμα = perfection (see i. 23), there is a distinct advance, "to the measure of the stature (*i.e.* to the height) of the perfection of Christ." This is also Rückert's view.

It is questioned whether St. Paul here conceives this ideal as one to be realised in the present life or only in the future. Amongst the ancients, Chrysostom, Theoph., Oecum., Jerome, took the former view, Theodoret the latter. It would probably be an error to suppose that the apostle meant definitely either one or the other. He speaks of an ideal which may be approximated to. But though it may not be perfectly attainable it must be aimed at, and this supposes that its attainment is not to be represented as impossible. See Dale, Lect. xv. p. 283.

14. ἵνα μηκέτι ὦμεν νήπιοι, κλυδωνιζόμενοι καὶ περιφερόμενοι παντὶ ἀνέμῳ τῆς διδασκαλίας. "That we may be no longer children tossed and borne to and fro by every wind of teaching." This does not depend on ver. 13, for one does not become a mature man in order to grow. Ver. 12 states the final goal of the work of the teachers; ver. 13, that which must take place in the meantime in order to the attainment of that end. κλυδωνιζόμενοι from κλύδων, a billow or surge, may mean either tossed by the waves or tossed like waves, as in Josephus, *Ant.* ix. 11. 3, ὁ δῆμος ταρασσόμενος καὶ κλυδωνιζόμενος. Here, as ἀνέμῳ is most naturally connected with it as well as with περιφ., the latter seems best; and this corresponds with Jas. i. 8, διακρινόμενος ἔοικε κλύδωνι θαλάσσης ἀνεμιζομένῳ. A similar figure occurs in Jude 12, νεφέλαι ἄνυδροι ὑπὸ ἀνέμων παραφερόμενοι: cf. Heb. xiii. 9, διδαχαῖς ποικίλαις μὴ παραφέρεσθε.

ἀνέμῳ does not refer to "emptiness" nor to "impulsive power," but rather is chosen as suitable to the idea of changeableness. So Theophylact : τῇ τροπῇ ἐμμένων καὶ ἀνέμους ἐκάλεσε τὰς διαφόρους διδασκαλίας. The article before διδ. does not "give definitive prominence to the teaching" (Eadie), but marks teaching in the abstract.

ἐν τῇ κυβείᾳ τῶν ἀνθρώπων. "Through the sleight of men." κυβεία, from κύβος, is properly "dice-playing," and hence "trickery, deceit." Soden prefers to take it as expressing conduct void of seriousness; these persons play with the conscience and the soul's health of the Christians. But this is not the ordinary sense of the word. ἐν is instrumental, the words expressing the means by which the περιφ. κ.τ.λ. is attained. There is no objection to this on the ground that it would thus be pleonastic after ἐν ἀνέμῳ (Ell.), since ἐν τῇ κ. is not connected with περιφερόμενοι, but with the whole clause. Ellicott himself says the preposition "appears rather to denote the *element*, the evil *atmosphere* as it were, *in* which the varying currents of doctrine exert their force." "Element" is itself figurative, and requires explanation; and if "evil atmosphere," etc., is intended as an explanation, it is clear that no such idea is implied in the Greek, nor would it be at all in St. Paul's way to carry out the figure in such detail, or to expect the reader to compare κυβεία to the atmosphere; see on v. 5.

ἐν πανουργίᾳ πρὸς τὴν μεθοδείαν τῆς πλάνης. "By craftiness, tending to the scheming of error." πανοῦργος and πανουργία are used in the Sept. generally, if not invariably, in a good or an indifferent sense, "prudent," Prov. xiii. 1; "prudence," Prov. i. 4, viii. 5; "shrewdness," Ecclus. xxi. 12; Josh. ix. 4 (though this latter may be thought an instance of a bad sense). Polybius also uses πανοῦργος in the sense of δεινός, "clever, shrewd." In classical writers the words have almost invariably a bad sense, the substantive meaning "knavery, unscrupulous conduct."

In the N.T. the substantive occurs five times, always in a bad sense (Luke xx. 23; 1 Cor. iii. 19; 2 Cor. iv. 2, xi. 3, and here); the adjective once, 2 Cor. xii. 16, in the sense "crafty."

μεθοδεία is found only here and ch. vi. 11. The verb μεθοδεύω is used, however, by Polybius, Diodorus, and the Sept., and means to deal craftily (cf. 2 Sam. xix. 27, where Mephibosheth says of Ziba, μεθώδευσεν ἐν τῷ δούλῳ σου); the substantive μέθοδος, from which it is derived, being used by later authors in the meaning "cunning device." πλάνη has its usual meaning "error," not "seduction" (a meaning which it never has, not even in 2 Thess. ii. 11), and the genitive is subjective, thus personifying error. In the Revised Version πρός is taken as = according to, "after the wiles of error," a comma being placed after πανουργίᾳ. This seems to leave the latter word too isolated. Moreover, this sense of πρός, though appropriate after verbs of action, being founded on the idea of "looking to," or the like, does not agree with the participles κλυδ. and περιφ. Codex A adds after πλάνης, τοῦ διαβόλου, an addition suggested probably by vi. 11.

15. ἀληθεύοντες δὲ ἐν ἀγάπῃ. "But cherishing truth in love." RV. has "speaking truth in love," only differing from AV. by the omission of the article before "truth," but with "dealing truly" in the margin. Meyer insists that ἀληθεύειν always means "to speak the truth." But the verb cannot be separated from ἀλήθεια. Verbs in -εύω express the doing of the action which is signified by the corresponding substantive in -εία. Of this we have two examples in ver. 14, κυβεία, which is the action of κυβεύειν, μεθοδεία of μεθοδεύειν. Comp. κολακεία, κολακεύω; βραβεύω, ἀριστεύω, ἀγγαρεύω with their substantives in -εία, and many others. Now ἀλήθεια is not limited to spoken truth, least of all in the N.T. In this Epistle observe iv. 24, δικαιοσύνη καὶ ὁσιότητι τῆς ἀληθείας, also iv. 21 and v. 9; and compare the expressions "walking in truth," "the way of truth," "not obeying the truth, but obeying unrighteousness, ἀδικία." Here, where the warning is not to the false teachers, but to those who were in danger of being misled like children by them, "speaking truth" appears out of place. As to the connexion of ἐν ἀγάπῃ, it seems most natural to join it with ἀληθεύοντες, not only because otherwise the latter word would be harshly isolated, but because the "growth" is so fully defined by the following words. If, indeed, love were not mentioned, as it is, at the end of ver. 16, there might be more reason to adopt the connexion with αὐξήσωμεν, on the ground that considering the frequent references to it, as in iv. 2, iii. 18, 19, it was not likely to have been omitted in speaking of growth. Connected with ἀληθεύειν, ἐν ἀγάπῃ is not a limitation, but a general characteristic of the Christian walk; "Not breaking up, but cementing brotherly love by walking in truth" (Alford). Probably, however, the apostle intended ἐν ἀγάπῃ to be connected both with the preceding and the following; his ideas progressing from ἀλήθεια to ἀγάπη, and thence to αὔξησις.

αὐξήσωμεν εἰς αὐτὸν τὰ πάντα ὅς ἐστιν ἡ κεφαλή, Χριστός. "May grow up unto Him in all things, who is the Head, even Christ."

αὐξήσωμεν is not transitive as in 1 Cor. iii. 6; 2 Cor. ix. 10, etc., and in the older classical writers and the Septuagint, but intransitive as in later Greek writers and Matt. vi. 28; Luke i. 80, ii. 40, and elsewhere; cf. here also ii. 21.

εἰς αὐτόν. Meyer understands this to mean "in relation to Him," with the explanation that Christ is the head of the body, the growth of whose members is therefore in constant relation to Him as determining and regulating it. The commentary on εἰς αὐτόν is, he says, given by ἐξ οὗ, κ.τ.λ., the one expressing the ascending, the other the descending direction of the relation of the growth to the head, He being thus the goal and the source of the development of the life of the Church. However correct this explanation may be in itself, it can hardly be extracted from the interpretation of εἰς as "in relation to," which is vague and feeble. Nor does it even appear that εἰς αὐτόν admits of such a rendering at all. Such expressions as ἐς ὅ = "in regard to which," εἰς ταῦτα = "quod attinet ad . . ." etc., are not parallel. Interpreted according to these analogies, the words would only mean "with respect to Him, that we should grow," and the order would be εἰς αὐτὸν αὐξ. Meyer has adopted this view from his reluctance to admit any interpretation which does not agree with the figure of the head. But that figure is not suggested until after this. We have first the Church as itself becoming ἀνὴρ τέλειος, then this figure is departed from, and the readers individually are represented as possible νήπιοι. The subjects of αὐξήσωμεν, then, are not yet conceived as members of a body, but as separate persons. But as soon as the pronoun introduces Christ, the idea that He is the head suggests itself, and leads to the further development in ver. 16.

We can hardly fail to see in αὐξ. εἰς αὐτόν a variation of καταντήσωμεν εἰς ἄνδρα τέλειον, εἰς μέτρον ἡλικίας τοῦ πλ. τοῦ Χρ. "Unto Him." This would seem to mean at once "unto Him as a standard," and "so as to become incorporated with Him"; not that εἰς αὐτόν by itself could combine both meanings, but that the thought of the apostle is passing on to the idea contained in the words that follow. He begins with the idea of children growing up to a certain standard of maturity, and with the word αὐτόν passes by a rapid transition to a deeper view of the relation of this growth to Christ the Head.

Harless, to escape the difficulty of αὐξ. εἰς αὐτόν, connects the latter words with ἐν ἀγάπῃ, "in love to Him." The order of the words is certainly not decisive against this view; instances of such a hyperbaton are sufficiently frequent, but there seems no reason for it here, and it would make the introduction of "Who is the Head" very abrupt.

τὰ πάντα, the ordinary accusative of definition, "in all the parts of our growth."

Χριστός. This use of the nominative in apposition with the relative, where we might have expected the accusative Χριστόν, is a usual Greek construction. Compare Plato, *Apol.* p. 41 A, εὑρήσει τοὺς ὡς ἀληθῶς δικαστάς, οἵπερ καὶ λέγονται ἐκεῖ δικάζειν Μίνως τε καὶ Ῥαδάμανθυς καὶ Αἴακος. The Received Text has ὁ Χριστός, with D G K L, Chrys. Theod. The article is wanting in ℵ A B C, Bas. Cyr.

16. ἐξ οὗ πᾶν τὸ σῶμα συναρμολογούμενον καὶ συμβιβαζόμενον. "From whom the whole body fitly framed and put together." ἐξ οὗ goes with αὔξησιν ποιεῖται. The present participles indicate that the process is still going on. On συναρμ. cf. ii. 21. The use of the word there forbids the supposition that the derivation from ἁρμός, a joint, was before the mind of the writer. συμβιβάζω is used by classical writers in the sense of bringing together, either persons figuratively (especially by way of reconciliation) or things. Compare Col. ii. 2, συμβ. ἐν ἀγάπῃ. As to the difference between the two verbs here, Bengel says: "συναρμ. pertinet ad τὸ regulare, ut partes omnes in situ suo et relatione mutua recte aptentur, συμβ. notat simul firmitudinem et consolidationem." So Alford and Eadie. Ellicott thinks the more exact view is that συμβ. refers to the *aggregation*, συναρμ. to the *interadaptation* of the component parts. This would seem to require that συμβ., as the condition of συναρμ., should precede. Perhaps it might be more correct to say that συναρμ. corresponds to the figure σῶμα, the apostle then, in the consciousness that he is speaking of persons, adding συμβιβ. (so Harless and, substantially, Meyer). In the parallel, Col. ii. 19, we have ἐπιχορηγούμενον καὶ συμβιβαζόμενον. In that Epistle the main theme is "the vital connexion with the Head; in the Ephesians, the unity in diversity among the members" (Lightfoot). Hence the substitution here of συναρμ. for ἐπιχορ. But the idea involved in the latter is here expressed in the corresponding substantive.

διὰ πάσης ἁφῆς τῆς ἐπιχορηγίας. "Through every contact with the supply." The parallel in Col. ii. 19 seems to decide that these words are to be connected with the participles.

ἁφή has some difficulty. It has been given the meaning "joint," "sensation," "contact." If by "joint" is understood those parts of two connected limbs which are close to the touching surfaces (which is no doubt the common use of the word), then ἁφή cannot be so understood; it means "touching" or "contact," and can no more mean "joint" in this sense than these English words can have that meaning. And what would be the meaning of "every joint of supply"? Eadie answers: "Every joint whose function it is to afford such aid." But this is not the function of a joint, and this notion of the supply being through joints would be a very strange one and strangely expressed. Besides, it would not be consistent with the fact that it is from Christ that the ἐπιχορηγία proceeds. Theodoret takes ἁφή to mean "sense" or "sensation." ἁφὴν τὴν αἴσθησιν προσηγόρευσεν, ἐπειδὴ καὶ αὐτὴ μία τῶν πέντε αἰσθήσεων, that is, "the apostle calls sensation 'touch,' because this is one of the five senses, and he names the whole from the part." Chrysostom is more obscure, and seems to make, not ἁφῆς alone, but ἁφῆς τῆς ἐπιχ. = αἰσθήσεως ; for when he proceeds to expound, he says: τὸ πνεῦμα ἐκεῖνο τὸ ἐπιχορηγούμενον τοῖς μέλεσιν ἀπὸ τῆς κεφαλῆς ἑκάστου μέλους ἁπτόμενον οὕτως ἐνεργεῖ. Theodoret's interpretation is adopted by Meyer, "every feeling in which the supply (namely, that which is given by Christ) is perceived." But although the singular ἀφή, which sometimes means the sense of touch, might naturally be used to signify "feeling" in general; yet we cannot separate this passage from that in Col. where we have the plural; and, as Lightfoot observes, until more cogent examples are forthcoming, "we are justified in saying that αἱ ἀφαί could no more be used for αἱ αἰσθήσεις, than in English 'the touches' could be taken as a synonym for 'the senses.'" Meyer, indeed, takes the word there as "the feelings, sensations"; but there is no evidence that ἀφαί could have this meaning either. Besides, "the conjunction of such incongruous things as τῶν ἀφῶν καὶ συνδέσμων, under the vinculum of the same article and preposition, would be unnatural." It remains that we take ἀφή in the sense of "contact," which suits both this passage and that in Col. Lightfoot, on Col. ii. 19, gives several passages from Galen and Aristotle in illustration of this signification. Here we need only notice the distinction which Aristotle makes between σύμφυσις and ἀφή, the latter signifying only "contact," the former "cohesion." ἡ ἀφὴ τῆς ἐπιχορηγίας, then, is the touching of, *i.e.* contact with, the supply. ἅπτεσθαι τῆς ἐπιχ. would mean "to take hold of, or get in touch with," the ἐπιχ.; hence διὰ πάσης ἀφῆς τῆς ἐπιχ may well mean "through each part being in touch with the ministration." So Oecumenius: ἡ ἀπὸ τοῦ Χριστοῦ κατιοῦσα πνευματικὴ δύναμις ἑνὸς ἑκάστου μέλους αὐτοῦ ἁπτομένη. Oltramare understands the gen. as gen. auctoris = ἐκ τῆς ἐπιχορ. = τῆς ἀφῆς ἧς ἐπεχορήγησε, "par toute sorte de jointures provenant de sa largesse." ἐπιχορηγία occurs again Phil. i. 19; it is found nowhere else except in ecclesiastical writers. But the verb ἐπιχορηγέω (which occurs five times in the N.T.) is also found, though rarely, in later Greek writers.

κατ' ἐνέργειαν ἐν μέτρῳ ἑνὸς ἑκάστου μέρους.

μέρους is the reading of ℵ B D G K L P, Arm., Theodoret, etc.; but A C, Vulg. Syr. Boh., Chrys. have μέλους. This is so naturally suggested by the figure of σῶμα that we can hardly doubt that it came in either by a natural mistake or as an intentional emendation. But μέρους is really much more suitable, as more general.

"According to the proportionate working of each several part." ἐνέργεια does not mean "power," but "acting power," "activity," "working," so that the interpretation of κατ' ἐνέργειαν as adverbial = "powerfully," is excluded. As to the connexion of the following words, ἐν μέτρῳ may be taken either with κατ' ἐνεργ. or as governing ἑνὸς ἑκ. μέρ. The latter is the view adopted by many commentators, with so little hesitation that they do not mention the other. Thus Eadie and Ellicott render "according to energy in the measure of each individual part." This is not very lucid, and Ellicott therefore explains "in the measure of (*sc.* commensurate with)." Alford's rendering is similar. If this is understood to mean "the energy which is distributed to every part," etc., as it apparently must be, we miss some word which should suggest the idea of distribution, which ἐν certainly does not. Moreover, ἐνέργεια, from its signification, requires to be followed by some defining word, and elsewhere in the N.T. always is so.

It is preferable, therefore, to join ἐν μέτρῳ closely with ἐνέργεια, which it qualifies, and which is then defined by the genitive following. It is as if the writer had been about to say κατ' ἐνεργ. ἑνὸς ἑκ., and then recalling the thought of ver. 7 inserted ἐν μέτρῳ. If this view (which is Bengel's) is correct, the reason assigned by Meyer for connecting these words with αὔξ. ποιεῖται instead of with the participles falls to the ground, viz. that μέτρῳ suits the idea of growth better than that of joining together. The RV. appears to agree with the view here taken.

τὴν αὔξησιν τοῦ σώματος ποιεῖται. "Carries on the growth of the body." In Col. ii. 19 we have αὔξει τὴν αὔξησιν; here the active participation of the body as a living organism in promoting its own growth is brought out, and this especially in order to introduce ἐν ἀγάπῃ. The middle ποιεῖται is not "intensive," but is appropriately used of the body promoting its own growth; ποιεῖ would imply that σῶμα and σώματος had a different reference. σώματος is used instead of ἑαυτοῦ, no doubt because of the remoteness of σῶμα, as well as because ἑαυτοῦ was required presently. Compare Luke iii. 19.

εἰς οἰκοδομὴν ἑαυτοῦ ἐν ἀγάπῃ. On the mixture of metaphors cf. ver. 12. οἰκοδομή is not suitable to the figure of a body, but is suggested by the idea of the thing signified to which the figure in οἰκ. is so familiarly applied. It would be awkward to separate ἐν ἀγάπῃ from οἰκ. and join it with αὔξησιν ποιεῖται, as Meyer does on account of the correspondence with ver. 15. Through the work of the several parts the building up of the whole is accomplished by means of love. Observe that it is the growth of the whole that is dwelt on, not that of the individual parts.

17-24. *Admonition, that knowing how great the blessings of which they have been made partakers, they should fashion their lives accordingly, putting off all that belongs to their old life, and putting on the new man.*

17. τοῦτο οὖν λέγω καὶ μαρτύρομαι ἐν Κυρίῳ. Resumes from *vv.* 1–3. As Theodoret observes: πάλιν ἀνέλαβε τῆς παραινέσεως τὸ προοίμιον. οὖν, as often, has simply this resumptive force, and does not indicate any inference from what precedes; for the exhortation begun *vv.* 1–3 was interrupted, and the ἀξίως περιπατεῖν of ver. 1 is repeated in the negative form in ver. 17. The τοῦτο looks forward.

μαρτύρομαι, "I protest, conjure" = διαμαρτύρομαι. Polyb. p. 1403, συνδραμόντων τῶν ἐγχωρίων καὶ μαρτυρομένων τοὺς ἄνδρας ἐπανάγειν ἐπὶ τὴν ἀρχήν. Thucydides, viii. 53, μαρτυρομένων καὶ ἐπιθειαζόντων μὴ κατάγειν. The notion of exhortation and precept is involved in this and λέγω by the nature of the following context, μηκέτι περιπ., as in the passage of Thucydides, so that there is no ellipsis of δεῖν.

ἐν Κυρίῳ. Not either "per Dominum" or "calling the Lord to witness." μάρτυρα τὸν Κύριον καλῶ, Chrys. Theodoret, etc. Some expositors have defended this on the ground that N.T. writers, following the Hebrew idiom, wrote ὀμόσαι ἔν τινι; but it by no means follows that ἔν τινι without ὀμόσαι could be used in this sense any more than κατὰ Διός could be used without ὀμόσαι instead of πρὸς Διός.

Ellicott says: "As usual, defining the element or sphere in which the declaration is made"; and so Eadie and Alford. This is not explanation. Meyer is a little clearer: "Paul does not speak in his own individuality, but Christ is the element in which his thought and will move." εἶναι ἔν τινι is a classical phrase expressing complete dependence on a person. Soph. *Oed. Col.* 247, ἐν ὑμῖν ὡς Θεῷ κείμεθα: *Oed. Tyr.* 314, ἐν σοὶ γάρ ἐσμεν: Eurip. *Alc.* 277, ἐν σοὶ δ' ἐσμὲν καὶ ζῆν καί μή. Compare Acts xvii. 28, ἐν αὐτῷ ζῶμεν καὶ κινούμεθα καὶ ἐσμέν. In the N.T., indeed, the expression acquires a new significance from the idea of fellowship and union with Christ and with God. Whatever the believer does, is done with a sense of dependence on Him and union with Him. For example, "speaking the truth" "marrying" (1 Cor. vii. 39).

Here, where an apostolic precept is concerned, it is implied that the apostle speaks with authority. But the expression would hardly have been suitable had he not been addressing those who, like himself, had fellowship with the Lord. This interpretation is so far from being "jejune," that it implies a personal and spiritual relation which is put out of sight by the impersonal figure of an "element."

μηκέτι ὑμᾶς περιπατεῖν καθὼς καὶ τὰ ἔθνη περιπατεῖ. For the infinitive present compare the passages above cited from Thucyd. and Polyb. Also Acts xxi. 2, λέγων μὴ περιτέμνειν: xxi. 4, ἔλεγον μὴ ἀναβαίνειν, where the imperative would be used in *oratio directa*. Demosth. xxvii. 7, λέγω πάντας ἐξιέναι. Aesch. *Agam.* 898, λέγω κατ' ἄνδρα, μὴ Θεόν, σέβειν ἐμέ.

Text. Rec. adds λοιπά before ἔθνη, with ℵ⁴ D^bb K L, Syr., Chrys. etc. The word is wanting in ℵ A B D* G, Vulg. Boh.

The λοιπά is more likely to have been added in error than omitted. Assuming that it is not genuine, this is an instance of St. Paul's habitual regard for the feelings of his readers. It suggests that they are no longer to be classed with the ἔθνη. They were ἔθνη only ἐν σαρκί, but were members of the true commonwealth of Israel.

ἐν ματαιότητι τοῦ νοὸς αὐτῶν. Although in the O.T. idols are frequently called μάταια (compare Acts xiv. 15), the substantive is not to be limited to idolatry, to which there is no special reference here. It is the falseness and emptiness of their thoughts that are in question (cf. Rom. i. 21, ἐματαιώθησαν ἐν τοῖς διαλογισμοῖς αὐτῶν). Nor, again, are we, with Grotius, to suppose any special reference to the philosophers, merely because in 1 Cor. iii. 20 it is said of the διαλογισμοὶ τῶν σοφῶν that they are μάταιοι. Rather, it refers to the whole moral and intellectual character of heathenism; their powers were wasted without fruit. As Photius (quoted by Harless) remarks: οὐ τὰ τῆς ἀληθείας φρονοῦντες καὶ πιστεύοντες καὶ ἀποδεχόμενοι ἀλλ᾽ ἅπερ ἂν ὁ νοῦς αὐτῶν μάτην ἀναπλάσῃ καὶ λογίσηται. νοῦς includes both the intellectual and the practical side of reason, except where there is some ground for giving prominence to one or the other in particular. Here we have both sides, ἐσκοτωμένοι referring to the intellectual, ἀπηλλοτριωμένοι to the practical.

18. ἐσκοτωμένοι τῇ διανοίᾳ ὄντες, ἀπηλλοτριωμένοι τῆς ζωῆς τοῦ Θεοῦ.

ἐσκοτωμένοι is the form in ℵ A B, while D G K L P have ἐσκοτισμένοι. The former appears to be the more classical.

ὄντες is better joined with the preceding than with the following. If ὄντες ἀπηλλ. be taken together, this would have to be regarded as assigning the ground of ἐσκοτ. But the darkness was not the effect of the alienation, which, on the contrary, was the result of the ἄγνοια. The position of ὄντες is not against this, since ἐσκοτ. τῇ δ. express a single notion. Meyer illustrates from Herod. i. 35, οὐ καθαρὸς χεῖρας ἐών, and Xen. *Ages.* xi. 10, πρᾳότατος φίλοις ὤν. The two participles thus stand in an emphatic position at the beginning, and this emphasis is lost by joining ὄντες with the following. The change of gender from ἔθνη to ἐσκοτωμένοι ὄντες corresponds to a change from the class to the person.

ἐσκοτωμένοι is opposed to πεφωτισμένοι (i. 18). We have the same expression Rom. i. 21, ἐσκοτίσθη ἡ ἀσύνετος αὐτῶν καρδία, and a remarkable parallel in Josephus, τὴν διάνοιαν ἐπεσκοτισμένους, *Ant.* ix. 4. 3. Διάνοια strictly means the understanding, but is not so limited in the N.T. Compare Col. i. 21, ἐχθροὺς τῇ διανοίᾳ: 2 Pet. iii. 1, διεγείρω ... τὴν εἰλικρινῆ διάνοιαν. Here, however, the connexion decides for the meaning "understanding." On ἀπηλλ. cf. ii. 12.

τῆς ζωῆς τοῦ Θεοῦ. Explained by Theodoret as = τῆς ἐν ἀρετῇ ζωῆς, *i.e.* as = the life approved by God, or "godly life." But ζωή in N.T. does not mean "course of life," βίος, but true life as opposed to θάνατος. In Gal. v. 25 we have it expressly distinguished from "course of conduct"; εἰ ζῶμεν πνεύματι, πνεύματι καὶ στοιχῶμεν. Moreover, ἀπηλλοτριωμένοι implies separation from something real. Erasmus' explanation of the genitive as one of apposition, "vera vita qui est Deus," is untenable. The analogy of ἡ εἰρήνη τοῦ Θεοῦ, Phil. iv. 7; αὔξησις τοῦ Θεοῦ, Col. ii. 19, suggests that the words mean "the life which proceeds from God"; "tota vita spiritualis quae in hoc seculo per fidem et justitiam inchoatur et in futura beatitudine perficitur, quae tota peculiariter vita Dei est, quatenus a Deo per gratiam datur," Estius. But something deeper than this is surely intended by the genitive, which naturally conveys the idea of a character or quality. It is the life "qua Deus vivit in suis," Beza (who, however, wrongly adds to this "quamque praecipit et approbat"). Somewhat similarly Bengel: "Vita spiritualis accenditur in credentibus ex ipsa Dei vita." Harless, indeed, argues that the life of regeneration is not here referred to, since what is in question is not the opposition of the heathen to Christianity, but to God; so that ζωὴ τ. Θεοῦ is to be compared to John i. 3, where the λόγος is said to be (from the beginning) the ζωή and φῶς of the world, and thus there was an original fellowship of man with God. So in part many expositors, regarding the perfect participles as indicating "gentes ante defectionem suam a fide patrum, imo potius ante lapsum Adami, fuisse participes lucis et *vitae*," Bengel. But St. Paul is here speaking of the contemporary heathen in contrast to those who had become Christians (ver. 17); and it is hard to think that if he meant to refer to this original divine life in man, he would not have expressed himself more fully and precisely. The idea is one which he nowhere states explicitly, and it is by no means involved of necessity in the tense of the participles, which is sufficiently explained as expressing a state. Indeed, the aorist ἀπηλλοτριωθέντες would more suitably suggest the idea of a time when they were not so; cf. 1 Pet. ii. 10, οἱ οὐκ ἠλεημένοι νῦν δὲ ἐλεηθέντες. And how can we think the Gentiles as at a prehistoric time τῇ διανοίᾳ not ἐσκοτωμένοι?

διὰ τὴν ἄγνοιαν τὴν οὖσαν ἐν αὐτοῖς διὰ τὴν πώρωσιν τῆς καρδίας αὐτῶν. The cause of their alienation from the Divine life is their ignorance, and this again results from their hardness of heart. Most expositors regard διά ... διά as co-ordinate, some connecting both clauses with ἀπηλλ. only (Origen, Alford, Eadie, Ellicott), others with both participles (Bengel, Harless, Olsh. De Wette). Bengel, followed by Olsh. and De Wette, refers διὰ τὴν ἄγν. to ἐσκ. and διὰ τὴν π. to ἀπηλλ. But this is rather too artificial for a letter. Nor does it yield a satisfactory sense; for ἄγνοια is not the cause of the darkness, but its effect. De Wette evades this by saying that ἄγνοια refers to speculative knowledge, ἐσκοτ. to practical. But there is no sufficient ground for this. The substantive ἄγνοια does not elsewhere occur in St. Paul's Epistles (it is in his speech, Acts xvii. 30, "the times of this ignorance"; and in 1 Pet. i. 14, besides Acts iii. 17); but the verb is of frequent occurrence, and always of ignorance only, not of the absence of a higher faculty of knowledge. Such ignorance was not inaccessible to light, as is shown by the instances of the converted Gentiles: but so far as it was due to the hardness of their hearts, it was culpable. It is only by the subordination of the latter clause to the former that the use of τὴν οὖσαν ἐν αὐτοῖς instead of the simple αὐτῶν finds a satisfactory explanation. Compare Rom. i. 18–33. Ellicott, following Harless, explains these words as pointing out the *indwelling deep-seated* nature of the ἄγνοια, and forming a sort of parallelism to τῆς καρδίας αὐτῶν, and so, as Harless adds, opposed to mere external occasions. But there is nothing of this in the context, nor in the words οὖσαν ἐν αὐτοῖς. The ignorance must be in them; and, unless we take the connexion as above (with Meyer), the words express nothing more than αὐτῶν.

πώρωσις is "hardness," not "blindness," as most of the ancient versions interpret. Indeed, it is so explained also by Suidas and Hesychius, as if derived from an adjective πωρός, "blind"; which seems, however, to be only an invention of the grammarians (perhaps from confusion with πηρός, with which it is often confounded by copyists). It is really derived (through πωρόω) from πῶρος, which originally meant "tufa," and then "callus," a callosity or hardening of the skin. (It is also used by medical writers of the "callus" formed at the end of fractured bones, and of "chalkstones" in the joints.) Hence, from the insensibility of the parts covered with hard skin, the verb means to make dull or insensible. It is thus correctly explained by Theodoret, πώρωσιν τὴν ἐσχάτην ἀναλγησίαν λέγει· καὶ γὰρ αἱ τῷ σώματι ἐγγινόμεναι πωρώσεις οὐδεμίαν αἴσθησιν ἔχουσι. Cicero frequently uses "callum" in a similar figurative sense, *e.g.* "ipse labor quasi callum quoddam obducit dolori," *Tusc. Disp.* ii. 15.

19. οἵτινες, "quippe qui," "being persons who." ἀπηλγηκότες, "being past feeling," a word appropriate to the figure in πώρωσις; it properly means to give over feeling pain, and is used by Thucydides with an accusative of the thing, ἀπαλγοῦντες τὰ ἴδια, ii. 61; hence it comes to mean "to be without feeling." The AV. "past feeling" expresses the sense very accurately. Polybius, however, has the expression ἀπαλγοῦντες ταῖς ἐλπίσι, and, indeed, elsewhere uses the verb in the sense "giving up," as Hesychius interprets, μηκέτι θέλοντες πονεῖν. This may be "giving up in despair," as in i. 58 of the Romans and Carthaginians, κάμνοντες ἤδη τοῖς πόνοις διὰ τὴν συνέχειαν τῶν κινδύνων, εἰς τέλος ἀπήλγουν. Hence some commentators have adopted "desperantes" here, which is the rendering of the Vulgate. Bengel cites from Cicero (*Epp. ad famil.* ii. 16) what looks like a paraphrase of the word: "diuturna desperatione serum obduruisse animum ad dolorem novum." "Dolor, says Bengel, "urget ad medicinam: dolore autem amisso, non modo spes sed etiam studium et cogitatio rerum bonarum amittitur, ut homo sit excors, effrons, exspes." Theophylact gives a similar interpretation: κατερρᾳθυμηκότες, καὶ μὴ θέλοντες καμεῖν πρὸς τὴν εὕρεσιν τοῦ καλοῦ, καὶ ἀναλγήτως διατεθέντες. The reading of D G is ἀπηλπικότες (ἀφ- G); but evidence for the textual reading is predominant, and, moreover, ἀπηλπικότες would give a very poor sense. Jerome appears to regard "desperantes" of the old Latin as an incorrect rendering of ἀπηλπικότες, for which he suggests "indolentes sive indolorios." But he did not alter the text of the translation. Probably the other versions which express the same meaning had not a different reading; and, on the other hand, the reading of D G may have arisen either from the influence of the versions or as a gloss.

ἑαυτούς. What is ascribed in Rom. i. 24 to God is ascribed here to themselves, in accordance with the hortatory purpose of the present passage, so as to fix attention on the part which they themselves had in the result.

ἀσελγής and ἀσέλγεια were used by earlier writers (Plato, Isaeus, Dem.) in the sense of "insolent, insolence, outrageous"; Later writers apply them in the sense "lasciviousness." The substantive has that meaning in 2 Cor. xii. 21; Gal. v. 19; 2 Pet. ii. 7, 18; Rom. xiii. 13. In Mark vii. 22; Jude 4; 1 Pet. iv. 3; 2 Pet. ii. 2, the meaning is less clearly defined. In the LXX it occurs only Wisd. xiv. 22 and 2 Macc. ii. 26. The derivation is probably from σέλγω, a form of θέλγω.

εἰς ἐργασίαν ἀκαθαρσίας πάσης. ἐργασία suggests the idea that they made a business of ἀκαθαρσία. So Chrysostom: οὐ παραπεσόντες, φησίν, ἥμαρτον, ἀλλ᾽ εἰργάζοντο αὐτὰ τὰ δεινά, καὶ μελέτῃ τῷ πράγματι ἐκέχρηντο. It is not, however, to be understood of literal trading in impurity, which could not be asserted with such generality of the Gentiles. Compare Luke xii. 58, ἐν τῇ ὁδῷ δὸς ἐργασίαν, "give diligence": see note *ad loc.*

ἐν πλεονεξίᾳ. πλεονεξία originally meant (like πλεονέκτης, πλεονεκτεῖν) only advantage over another, for example, superiority in battle, hence it passed to the idea of unfair advantage, and then to that of the desire to take unfair advantage, "covetousness." The verb occurs five times in 2 Cor. in the sense "take advantage of." The substantive πλεονέκτης is found (besides Eph. v. 5) in 1 Cor. v. 10, 11, vi. 16. πλεονεξία occurs in all ten times in N.T.

In Luke xii. 15 it is clearly "covetousness," and so in 2 Cor. ix. 5 ; 1 Thess. ii. 5. But all three words are so frequently associated with words relating to sins of the flesh, that many expositors, ancient and modern, have assigned to them some such special signification. Thus πλεονέκτης, 1 Cor. v. 10, 11 ; πλεονεξία, Col. iii. 5, πορνείαν, ἀκαθαρσίαν, πάθος, ἐπιθυμίαν κακήν, καὶ τὴν πλεονεξίαν, ἥτις ἐστὶν εἰδωλολατρεία: besides the present passage and Eph. v. 3, πᾶσα ἀκαθαρσία ἢ πλεονεξία, cf. also v. 5. In 2 Pet. ii. 14, καρδίαν γεγυμνασμένην πλεονεξίας ἔχοντες, "covetousness" does not suit the connexion as well as some more general term. But the most striking passage is 1 Thess. iv. 6, τὸ μὴ ὑπερβαίνειν καὶ πλεονεκτεῖν ἐν τῷ πράγματι τὸν ἀδελφὸν αὐτοῦ, where the verb is undoubtedly applied to adultery, viewed as an injustice to one's neighbour. And this suggests that possibly in Mark vii. 21, where the right order is κλοπαί, φόνοι, μοιχεῖαι, πλεονεξίαι, there is a similiar idea. In Rom. i. 29 also, something grosser than covetousness seems to be intended. In Polycarp, *Phil.* vi., which exists only in the Latin, "avaritia" undoubtedly represents the original πλεονεξία. Polycarp is lamenting the sin of Valens, and says: "moneo itaque vos ut abstineatis ab avaritia, et sitis casti et veraces," and a little after: "si quis non abstinuerit se ab avaritia, ab idololatria coinquinabitur ; et tanquam inter gentes judicabitur." In the present passage Theodoret says the word is used for ἀμετρία: "Πᾶσαν ἁμαρτίαν τολμῶσι, ὑπὲρ κόρον τῷ διεφθαρμένῳ καταχρώμενοι βίῳ πλεονεξίαν γὰρ τὴν ἀμετρίαν ἐκάλεσε." The association with idolatry in Eph. v. 5 and Col. iii. 5 favours the same view. Hammond on Rom. i. 29 has a learned note in support of this signification of πλεονεξία, which, however, he pushes too far. Of course it is not alleged that the word of itself had this special sense, but that it was with some degree of euphemism so applied, and in such a connexion as the present would be so understood.

It is alleged, on the other side, that covetousness and impurity are named together as the two leading sins of the Gentile world ; that they even proceed from the same source ; that covetousness especially is idolatry, as being the worship of Mammon.

Covetousness was not a peculiarly Gentile sin. The Pharisees were covetous (φιλάργυροι). Our Lord warns His own disciples against πλεονεξία, in the sense of covetousness, in Luke xii. 15 above referred to. And the form of the warning there shows that covetousness and impurity were not on the same level in respect of grossness. This may also be inferred from St. Paul's ὁ κλέπτων μηκέτι κλεπτέτω. Can we conceive him saying ὁ μοιχεύων μηκέτι μοιχευέτω?

That covetousness and impurity proceed from the same source, and that "the fierce longing of the creature which has turned from God to fill itself with the lower things of sense" (Trench, *Syn.*, after

Bengel), is psychologically false. Lust and impurity are excesses of a purely animal and bodily passion ; covetousness is a secondary desire, seeking as an end in itself that which was originally desired only as a means.

The explanation of ver. 5 by the observation that the covetous serve Mammon, not God, is due to Theodoret, who derives it from Matt. vi. 24. But that passage does not make it probable that the covetous man would be called an idolator without some explanation added. St. Paul himself speaks of persons who serve, not the Lord Christ, but their own belly (Rom. xvi. 18), and of others "whose god is their belly"; yet he probably would not call them, without qualification, "idolators." Indeed, other Greek commentators devised various explanations. Chrysostom, for instance, as one explanation, suggests that the covetous man treats his gold as sacred, because he does not touch it.

We may ask, further, why should covetousness be specified with impurity and filthy speaking as not to be even named? (Eph. v. 3). Impure words suggest impure thoughts, words about covetousness have no tendency to suggest covetous thoughts. It is said, indeed, that the ἤ there between ἀκαθαρσία πᾶσα and πλεονεξία implies that the two words cannot refer to sins of the same kind ; but this argument seems to be answered by the immediately following μωρολογία ἢ εὐτραπελία. In ver. 5, also, we have πόρνος ἢ ἀκάθαρτος ἢ πλεονέκτης. In the present passage we have, not καὶ πλ., but ἐν πλ. To take this as ἐν "covetousness," or the like, after the strong words that have preceded, would be an incredible weakening of the charge.

20. ὑμεῖς δὲ οὐχ οὕτως ἐμάθετε τὸν Χριστόν. "But ye, not so did ye learn Christ." Beza, followed by Braune, places a stop after οὕτως, "But not so ye. Ye have learned Christ." This, however, makes the second clause too abrupt. We should expect ὑμεῖς to be repeated, or ἀλλά inserted, as in Luke xxii. 26, ὑμεῖς δὲ οὐχ οὕτως· ἀλλ' ὁ μείζων ἐν ὑμῖν, κ.τ.λ. Besides, the connexion with ver. 21 is impaired, "ye learned Christ" is first stated absolutely, and then with a qualification.

οὐχ οὕτως, a litotes ; cf. Deut. xviii. 14. ἐμάθετε, "did learn," viz. when they became Christians. This use of μανθάνω with an accus. of a person seems to be without parallel. The instance cited by Raphelius from Xenophon, ἵνα ἀλλήλους μάθοιεν ὁπόσοι εἴησαν, is clearly not parallel, the object of the verb there being ὁπόσοι, κ.τ.λ. Hence the ancients and many moderns have taken Χριστόν as = "doctrinam Christi," which is feeble and unsupported. Others, as Rückert and Harless, understand ἐμάθετε as "learned to know," viz. "what He is and what He desires." But the key to the expression is supplied by the passages which speak of "preaching Christ," Gal. i. 16 ; 1 Cor. i. 23 ; 2 Cor. i. 19 ;

Phil. i. 15; indeed the following verse (21) speaks of "hearing Him." As Christ was the content of the preaching, He might properly be said to be learned. So Phil. iii. 10, τοῦ γνῶναι αὐτόν. Col. ii. 6, παρελάβετε τὸν Χρ., is similar.

21. εἴγε, "tum certe si," see on iii. 2. Here also the conjunction is unfavourable to the view that St. Paul is addressing those whom he had himself instructed. αὐτόν with emphasis placed first, "if Him, indeed, ye heard." ἐν αὐτῷ, not "by Him," as AV., a construction not admissible with a personal author, nor "illius nomine, quod ad illum attinet" (Bengel). But as those who believe are said to be ἐν Χριστῷ, so here they are said to have been taught in Him, *i.e.* as in fellowship with Him. There is a progress, as Meyer observes, from the first announcement of the gospel (ἠκούσατε) to the further instruction which then as converts they would have received (ἐν αὐτῷ ἐδιδ.), both being included in ἐμάθετε τὸν Χριστόν. John x. 27 is not parallel, since ἀκούειν in the sense "hearken to" would take the genitive.

Καθώς ἐστιν ἀλήθεια ἐν τῷ Ἰησοῦ. The AV. "as the truth is in Jesus" is incompatible with the absence of the article, but admits of being understood in the true sense of the Greek, which is not the case with the form in which the words are so often quoted, "the truth as it is in Jesus," which would be τὴν ἀλήθειαν καθώς ἐστιν, κ.τ.λ. Nor do the words mean, as Jerome interprets: "quomodo est veritas in Jesu, sic erit in vobis qui didicistis Christum,"—an interpretation which is followed by Estius and many others, and which makes Jesus be set forth as the pattern of truth, *i.e.* holiness. In addition to the difficulty of so understanding ἀλήθεια, this supposes ὑμᾶς to be emphatic, which its position forbids; the antithesis would also require that ἐν τῷ Ἰησοῦ should come after καθώς. Moreover, any interpretation which makes ἀποθέσθαι depend on ἐδιδάχθητε is open to the objection that in that case ὑμᾶς is superfluous. Ellicott, who adopts this construction, suggests that ὑμᾶς is introduced to mark their contrast, not only with other Gentiles, but with their own former state as implied in τὴν προτέραν ἀναστροφήν. But it is not clear how ὑμᾶς can mark such a contrast. Nor is ἐδιδ. suitable to ἀνανεοῦσθαι. It seems better to take ἀποθέσθαι ὑμᾶς as the subject of the clause, ἀλήθεια being understood in the sense "true teaching," opposed to ἀπάτη. Compare the use of ἀλήθεια in John iii. 21, "he that doeth the truth," and here, ver. 24. The sense will then be, "as is right teaching in Jesus: that ye put off." The change from Χριστόν to Ἰησοῦ is appropriate. Their introduction to Christianity or to the πολίτεια of Israel instructed them in the hope centred in the Messiah as a Redeemer. But when obedience to the practical teaching of a historical person is referred to, the historical name is used.

A very different view of the construction is taken by Credner, v. Soden, and Westcott and Hort mg., viz. that Χριστός is the subject of ἐστιν, in which case ἀλήθεια may be either nom. (Credner, Soden) or dative (WH. mg.). Soden remarks that considering the emphatic repetition of αὐτόν, ἐν αὐτῷ, which takes up τὸν Χρ. from the clause with οὕτως, the subject of this clause can only be Christ, viz. "as He is truth in Jesus," so that the thought is that they must not only believe in a Christ, but recognise Him in Jesus; and if they are to live in truth in Christ, they must live in Jesus. The thought is parallel to Heb. xiii. 18. The dative ἀληθείᾳ, as in WH. mg., seems preferable, "have been taught in Him, as He is in truth, in Jesus." On ἀληθείᾳ in this sense, comp. Phil. i. 18, εἴτε προφάσει εἴτε ἀληθείᾳ.

22. ἀποθέσθαι, a figure from putting off clothes = ἀπεκδυσάμενοι, Col. iii. 9, as ἐνδύσασθαι from putting them on. The frequency of the figure in Greek writers puts out of the question any reference to change of dress in baptism (Grotius).

It is rightly rendered in the Vulg. "deponere," not "deposuisse," which would require the perfect inf. The aorist expresses the singleness of the act, whereas ἀνανεοῦσθαι expresses a continuing process.[1] The infin. is not for the imperative (as in Phil. iii. 16), which is inconsistent with ὑμᾶς.

κατὰ τὴν προτέραν ἀναστροφήν. "As concerns your former manner of life," defining the particular respect in which the old man was to be put off. ἀναστροφή in this sense belongs to later Greek. The word originally meant a turning back, thence dwelling in a place; hence Aeschylus uses it of a "haunt." We find it in Polybius in the sense of "behaviour." κατά τε τὴν λοιπὴν ἀναστροφὴν καὶ τὰς πράξεις τεθαυμισμένος ὑπὲρ τὴν ἡλικίαν (iv. 82. 1); so also Epict. i. 9. 5. In the Sept. it occurs only in the Apocrypha, Tobit iv. 19; 2 Macc. v. 8; both times in this sense.

τὸν παλαιὸν ἄνθρωπον. The ἐγὼ σαρκικός of Rom. vii. 14; ἐγὼ σάρξ, ib. 18, opposed to ἄνθρωπος ὁ κατὰ Θεὸν κτισθείς. The adoption of the expression the old and the new ἄνθρωπος, indicates that the change affects, not some particulars only, but the whole personality or ἐγώ.

τὸν φθειρόμενον. "Which waxeth corrupt." This supplies a motive for the putting off. The present tense indicates a process that is going on. Compare Rom. viii. 21, "bondage of φθορά." Meyer thinks the reference is to eternal destruction, the present expressing either the future vividly conceived as perfect, or rather what already exists in tendency, "qui tendit ad exitium," Grot.

---

[1] "Except after verbs of saying, thinking, etc., the aorist in the infinitive has no preterite signification, and differs from the present only in this, that it expresses a single transient action; and even this bye-signification often falls away."—Madvig.

His reason is that the moral corruption of the old man is already existing, not "becoming." But though the corruption exists it is progressive. The tendency to perdition is expressed by St. Paul elsewhere by the term ἀπολλύμενον κατὰ τὰς ἐπιθυμίας τῆς ἀπάτης. Mark the contrast with ἀληθείας, ver. 24; τῆς ἀπάτης, not as in AV. a genitive of quality, but a subjective genitive, ἀπάτη being almost personified, not, indeed, by the article alone, but by the attributing to it of ἐπιθυμίαι. It is the deceitful power of sin. Cf. ἀπάτη τῆς ἁμαρτίας, Heb. iii. 13, and Rom. vii. 11, ἡ ἁμαρτία ἐξαπάτησέ με. Hence the ἐπιθυμίαι derive their power ἡ ἁμαρτία ... κατειργάσατο πᾶσαν ἐπιθυμίαν, *ib.* 8. It is quite against N.T. usage to understand ἀπάτη here as "error." Compare ἀπάτη τοῦ πλούτου, Matt. xiii. 22; ἀπ. ἀδικίας, 2 Thess. ii. 10.

κατά, "in accordance with," *i.e.* as their nature implies.

23. ἀνανεοῦσθαι. Passive, not middle, for the middle of this verb is always used transitively, in an active signification. Nor would it be Pauline to represent the renewal as springing from the man himself. Compare also ἀνακαινούμενον, Col. iii. 10.

It may be questioned whether ἀνα- here implies restoration to a former state, as is generally assumed. In classical writers ἀνανεοῦσθαι means "to restore"; but then the object expresses the original state, etc., which is thus brought into force or existence again, ἀν. ὅρκους, φιλίαν, etc. That is not the sense here, or in Col. iii. 10, of ἀνακαινοῦσθαι. Here the object is ὑμᾶς, and the meaning is, not that ye are to be brought out of a state of suspended existence, but that ye are to be changed so as to become νεοί. What ἀνα- implies, therefore, is simply change, and the meaning of the verb is to be illustrated by that of similar compounds of verbs derived from adjectives, where these adjectives would express the result of the action of the verbs. Such are: ἀνισόω, "to equalise"; ἀναπληρόω, "to fill"; ἀνακοινόω, "to communicate"; ἀνιερόω, "to consecrate," *i.e.* to make ἴσος, πλήρης, κοινός, ἱερός.

τῷ πνεύματι τοῦ νοὸς ὑμῶν. This is understood of the Holy Spirit by Oecumenius and Theophylact, followed by Fritzsche, Ellicott, and others (the genitive being thus possessive), the "(Divine) Spirit united with the human πνεῦμα, with which the νοῦς as subject is endued, and of which it is the *receptaculum*." But this would be entirely without parallel. The Holy Spirit is never called τὸ πνεῦμα ὑμῶν or τοῦ νοὸς ὑμῶν, nor, indeed, does it seem possible that it should be so designated. The spirit of the νοῦς of a man must be the man's spirit. πνεῦμα, in the sense of the Holy Spirit, is sometimes followed by a characterising genitive "of holiness," "of adoption," or, again, "of Christ," "of God"; never "of us," or "of you." This interpretation is particularly out of place if ἀνανεοῦσθαι is taken as depending on ἐδιδάχθητε. Bengel's interpretation is doubtless the correct one, "spiritus est intimum mentis," the higher principle of life. In Rom. vii. we see νοῦς pronouncing approval of the law, but unable to resist the motions of sin, for it has no motive power. In ch. viii. we see the πνεῦμα inspired by God, and we have a description of the man who is ἀνανεούμενος τῷ πνεύματι τοῦ νοὸς αὐτοῦ. For the distinction between νοῦς and πνεῦμα compare, further, 1 Cor. xiv. 14, τὸ πνεῦμά μου προσεύχεται, ὁ δὲ νοῦς μου ἄκαρπός ἐστι. The expression here used is thus quite in harmony with St. Paul's usage elsewhere. But in Rom. xii. 2 the νοῦς is said to be renewed, μεταμορφοῦσθε τῇ ἀνακαινώσει τοῦ νοός.

24. καὶ ἐνδύσασθαι τὸν καινὸν ἄνθρωπον. Note the correctness of the tenses: ἀποθέσθαι and ἐνδύσασθαι aorists, because a single act is meant; ἀνανεοῦσθαι present, because a continuing process. So in the parallel Col. iii. 9, 10, καινός differs from νέος in that the latter refers only to time, new, not long in existence, the former to quality also, as opposed to effeteness: cf. Heb. viii. 13. The καινὸς ἄνθρ., like the καινὴ διαθήκη, is always καινός, but not always νέος.

κατὰ Θεόν. Compare Col. iii. 10, τὸν νέον τὸν ἀνακαινούμενον εἰς ἐπίγνωσιν κατ᾽ εἰκόνα τοῦ κτίσαντος αὐτόν. From the parallel, Meyer and Ellicott conclude that κατὰ Θεόν = "ad exemplum Dei," there being an allusion to Gen. i. 27. Meyer compares Gal. iv. 28, κατὰ Ἰσαάκ. But in Col. it is just the word εἰκόνα that expresses the idea sought to be introduced here. That κατ᾽ εἰκόνα means "after the likeness of," is no proof that κατά = "after the likeness of." κατά in that phrase means "after the manner of," and if so taken here it would imply that the parallelism was in the action of the verb, i.e. that God was κτισθείς. For a similar reason 1 Pet. i. 15 is not parallel, κατὰ τὸν καλέσαντα ὑμᾶς ἅγιον, καὶ αὐτοὶ ἅγιοι.

κατὰ Θεόν occurs 2 Cor. vii. 9, 10, 11 = "in a godly manner," and this suggests the true interpretation, viz. "according to the will of God." It may be said that this is flat compared with the other view; but if so, that does not justify us in giving κατά an unexampled sense.

ἐν δικαιοσύνῃ καὶ ὁσιότητι τῆς ἀληθείας. The AV. "righteousness and true holiness" is doubly wrong; in connecting the genitive with the latter substantive only, and in resolving it adjectivally. The Bishops' Bible was correct, "in righteousness and holiness of truth." Yet Chrysostom understood the words as meaning true as opposed to false, δικ. and ὁσ. The usual distinction between these substantives is that ὁσιότης has reference to God, δικαιοσύνη to men; so Plato, Philo, and other Greek writers distinctively state; but Plato tells us in one place that δικαιοσύνη was a general term including ὁσιότης; in fact, it meant righteousness or propriety of conduct in itself. In the N.T. the adjectives are combined in Tit. i. 8, the adverbs in 1 Thess. ii. 10, and the substantives in Luke i. 75 and Clem. Rom. Cor. 48. In 1 Tim. ii. 8, ἐπαίροντας ὁσίους χεῖρας χωρὶς ὀργῆς καὶ διαλογισμῶν, the added words do not define the ὁσιότης. The hands are ὅσιοι when not unfitted to be lifted up in prayer. Nor is the use of ὅσιος with ἀρχιερεύς, Heb. vii. 26, at all peculiar. ὅσιος occurs thrice in the Acts in quotations from the O.T. which do not concern St. Paul's usage. Here, as in Luke i. 75 and Wisd. ix. 5, the words seem used in a way which had become familiar as a summary of human virtue. The suggestion that δικαιοσύνη is in contrast to πλεονεξία, and ὁσιότης to ἀκαθαρσία (Olsh. Alf. Ell.), has against it, not only the distance from ver. 19, and the ἐν there (not καί), but also the fact that these are not the proper opposites. The opposite of ἀκαθ. is not ὁσιότης but ἁγνότης; and δικαιοσύνη is very much more than the opposite of πλεονεξία in any sense of that word.

τῆς ἀληθείας. D¹ G, It., Cypr. Hil. read καὶ ἀληθείᾳ.

25-32. *Warning against special sins.*

25. Διὸ ἀποθέμενοι τὸ ψεῦδος. There is no need to render "having put away," which would seem to imply a separation in time between the two actions. The aorist suits the Greek idiom, as falsehood is to be put away once for all; but "putting away" agrees better with the English.

ψεῦδος, "falsehood," is, of course, suggested by ἀλήθεια; it is more general than "lying," which is mentioned immediately after as the most obvious example of it. So Col. iii. 8, μὴ ψεύδεσθε. But τὸ ψεῦδος is falsehood in all its forms; cf. Rom. i. 25; Rev. xxii. 15.

μετά is more forcible than πρός (Zech. viii. 16), implying "in your mutual intercourse."

ὅτι ἐσμὲν ἀλλήλων μέλη. Chrysostom carries out the figure in a striking manner, *e.g.* if the eye sees a serpent, does it deceive the foot? if the tongue tastes what is bitter, does it deceive the stomach? etc. This is passable in a homily, but in the text the argument is not at all founded on the figure, but on the fact that we are members of the body of Christ: "est enim monstrum si membra inter se non consentiant, imo se fraudulenter inter se agant," Calvin; cf. Rom. xii. 5, τὸ δὲ καθ' εἷς ἀλλήλων μέλη. As each member belongs to the rest, they may be called members one of the other. Comp. 1 Cor. xii. 15.

26. ὀργίζεσθε καὶ μὴ ἁμαρτάνετε. These words are a quotation from Ps. iv. 5 (EV. 4), LXX., "Stand in awe, and sin not." But expositors so diverse in their views as Hitzig and Delitzsch agree with the rendering of the LXX. The Hebrew verb primarily means "to tremble," and unless it were followed by "before me," or the like, could not mean definitely "stand in awe." It occurs in Prov. xxix. 9 and Isa. xxviii. 21 in the sense "to be angry." It is, however, superfluous, as far as the present passage is concerned, to inquire what the meaning of the original is. St. Paul is not arguing from the words, but adopting them as well known, and as expressing the precept he wishes to inculcate. The sense here is sufficiently intelligible, "ita irascamini ut ne peccetis." The key is Bengel's remark, "saepe vis modi cadit super partem duntaxat sermonis." Thus Matt. xi. 25, "I thank Thee that Thou hast hid these things," etc.; Rom. vi. 17, "Thanks be to God that ye were the servants of sin, but," etc. Had St. Paul not been quoting from the O.T., he would probably have expressed himself differently, *e.g.* ὀργιζόμενοι μὴ ἁμαρτάνετε, or the like. The phrase is frequently explained by reference to what is called the Hebrew idiom (which is by no means peculiarly Hebrew) of combining two imperatives, so that the former expresses the condition, the latter the result, as in Amos v. 4, "Seek Me and live." But this would make the words mean, "Be angry, and so ye shall not sin." Olshausen takes the first imperative hypothetically, "If ye are angry, as it is to be foreseen that it will happen, do not sin in anger." For, he says, "man's anger is never in itself just and permissible." God's alone is holy and just. This is fallacious, for anger is only in a figure attributed to God, and would not be so if all human anger were wrong. Besides, such a meaning would require ἀλλά, or the like, instead of καί. Indeed, no one acquainted with Butler's classical discourse on Resentment would accept Olshausen's statement. Apart from sudden (or instinctive) anger, which was intended to prevent sudden harm, deliberate anger is lawfully aroused by injustice. "It is in us connected with a sense of virtue and vice, and in the form of indignation on behalf of others is one of the common bonds by which society is held together" (cf. Rom. xiii. 4). Nor can the fact that the injury is done to ourselves make it unlawful. It becomes so when indulged where no injustice was intended, or when it is out of proportion, or when harm is inflicted merely to gratify it. Our Lord was angry, Mark iii. 5. Beza, Grotius, and others have taken ὀργίζεσθε interrogatively, which is inconsistent with its being a quotation.

ὁ ἥλιος μὴ ἐπιδυέτω ἐπὶ παροργισμῷ ὑμῶν.

τῷ is added before παροργισμῷ in Rec., with most MSS. and Fathers, but is absent from ℵ* A B. Alford thinks it may have been omitted to give indefiniteness. But it is much more likely to have been added for grammatical reasons.

<blockquote>
Παροργισμός is not found in profane authors; it occurs several times in the LXX., but usually of the sins by which Israel "provoked" the Lord, *e.g.* 1 Kings xv. 30. In Jer. xxi. 5, in Cod. Alex., it occurs in the sense "anger." The verb is found (in the passive) in Demosth. 805. 19; in the active, in this Epistle, vi. 4. παροργισμός appears to be distinguished from ὀργή as implying a less permanent state, "irritation."
</blockquote>

There is no reason to suppose a reference to the night as tending to nourish anger ("affectus noctu retentus alte insidet," Bengel after Chrys.). The precept simply means, as Estius observes, "let the day of your anger be the day of your reconciliation," for the new day began at sunset. The Pythagoreans, as Plutarch informs us, observed the same rule, εἴποτε προσαχθεῖεν εἰς λοιδορίας ὑπ' ὀργῆς, πρὶν ἢ τὸν ἥλιον δῦναι, τὰς δεξίας ἐμβάλλοντες ἀλλήλοις καὶ ἀσπασάμενοι διελύοντο (Plut. *De Am. Frat.* 488 B). Eadie quotes a quaint comment from Fuller, "Let us take the apostle's meaning rather than his words—with all possible speed to depose our passion, not understanding him so literally that we may take leave to be angry till sunset, then might our wrath lengthen with the days; and men in Greenland, where days last above a quarter of a year, have plentiful scope of revenge."

27. μηδὲ δίδοτε τόπον τῷ διαβόλῳ. The Rec. has μήτε, with most cursives; all the uncials apparently have μηδέ. μήτε would imply that St. Paul might have said μήτε . . . μήτε, but wrote μή in the first clause, because not then thinking of the second. Such a usage, μή . . . μήτε, is so rare in classical authors that some scholars have denied its existence, and it is not elsewhere found in St. Paul. The distinction between μήτε . . . μήτε and μηδέ . . . μηδέ, according to Hermann and others, is that the former divide a single negation into parts which are mutually exclusive; and neither negation gives a complete whole; thus corresponding to "neither . . . neither." Comp. Matt. vi. 26, οὐ σπείρουσιν οὐδὲ θερίζουσιν οὐδὲ συνάγουσιν, "they sow not, and they reap not, and gather not"; Matt. xii. 32, οὔτε ἐν τούτῳ τῷ αἰῶνι οὔτε ἐν τῷ μέλλοντι, "neither in this world nor in the future," these being the two divisions of οὐκ ἀρεθήσεται.

δίδοτε τόπον, *i.e.* room to act, since indulgence in angry feelings leads to hatred, malice, and all uncharitableness. Comp. Rom. xii. 19, δότε τόπον τῇ ὀργῇ.

τῷ διαβόλῳ. ὁ διάβολος is used by St. Paul only in this and the Pastorals. Erasmus, Luther, and others understand the word here as simply "calumniator," and so the Syriac. But elsewhere in N.T. ὁ διάβολος always means "the devil." In 1 Tim. iii. 11; 2 Tim. iii. 3; Tit. ii. 3, the word is used as an adjective.

28. ὁ κλέπτων μηκέτι κλεπτέτω. Not "qui furabatur," as Vulg., an attempt to soften the proper force of the word. Jerome mitigates the word in a different way, interpreting it of everything "quod alterius damno quaeritur," and favours the application to the "furtum spirituale" of the false prophets. The present participle seems intermediate between ὁ κλέψας and ὁ κλέπτης.

μᾶλλον δὲ κοπιάτω, rather, on the contrary, let him labour, ἐργαζόμενος ταῖς [ἰδίαις] χερσὶν τὸ ἀγαθόν.

There is a considerable variety of reading here—
ταῖς ἰδίαις χερσὶν τὸ ἀγαθόν, ℵ* A D G, Vulg. Clarom. Goth. Arm.
ταῖς χερσὶν τὸ ἀγαθόν, ℵ⁴ B, Amiat., Ambrosiaster.
τὸ ἀγαθὸν ταῖς ἰδίαις χερσίν, K 10 mss., Theodoret.

τὸ ἀγαθὸν ταῖς χερσίν, L most mss., Chrys. Theoph. Oecum.

The chief question is as to the genuineness of ἰδίαις. On the one hand, it is suggested that it may have been intentionally omitted because its force was not perceived, and so it was thought to be superfluous; on the other hand, that it may be an interpolation from 1 Cor. iv. 12. Against the former suggestion is the circumstance that in the passage in Cor., where the word might with even more reason be thought superfluous, no copyist has omitted it. The insertion, on the other hand, was very natural. The case of τὸ ἀγαθόν is very different. The variation in its position is, indeed, suspicious, and a nearer definition of ἐργαζόμενοι might have seemed necessary (since, as Chrys. observes, ὁ κλέπτων ἐργάζεται, ἀλλὰ κακόν), and Gal. vi. 10 would then suggest τὸ ἀγαθόν; but the only authority for its omission is Tertullian (*Res. Carn.* 45).

τὸ ἀγαθόν. "Antitheton ad furtum prius manu piccata male commissum," Bengel.

ἵνα ἔχῃ μεταδιδόναι τῷ χρείαν ἔχοντι. The motive here alleged is striking and characteristic, although surely we cannot say, with Olshausen and Ellicott, that this is the true specific object of all Christian labour; unless by "Christian labour" is meant labour over and above what is necessary for the labourer's own subsistence. That, by the law of nature, is the first object, unless we include with it the support of his own family.

Schoettgen infers from this clause that there were some who thought their thefts might be atoned for by almsgiving; and he quotes passages from Jewish writers which refer to such a delusion (Yalkut Rubeni, f. 110. 4; Vayyiqra Rabba, f. 147. 1). Not, indeed, that there was any such "Jewish opinion," as some writers assert. But the precept here is too general to be so understood, it simply (as Meyer remarks) opposes to unlawful taking, dutiful giving.

29. πᾶς λόγος σαπρὸς ἐκ τοῦ στόματος ὑμῶν μὴ ἐκπορευέσθω. The negative belongs to the verb; cf. Rom. iii. 20; Gal. ii. 16, οὐ δικαιωθήσεται πᾶσα σάρξ : 1 Cor. i. 29, ὅπως μὴ καυχήσηται πᾶσα σάρξ. The expression is quite logical; whereas in English, if we say "all flesh shall not be justified," the negative really belongs to "all," not to the verb.

σαπρός is primarily "rotten, diseased," hence in classical writers "disgusting." In the N.T. it is used of a "worthless" tree, Matt. vii. 17, xii. 33; fish, Matt. xiii. 48. It is clear, therefore, that the word does not of itself mean "filthy," and Chrys. interprets it as meaning ὃ μὴ τὴν ἰδίαν χρείαν πληροῖ (*Hom.* iv. on Tim.), and Theodoret makes it include αἰσχρολογία, λοιδορία, συκοφαντία, βλασφημία, ψευδολογία, καὶ τὰ τούτοις προσόμοια. With this we might compare πᾶν ῥῆμα ἀργόν, Matt. xii. 36. But although σαπρός, used of material things, may mean simply what is only fit to be thrown away, just as "rotten" is colloquially used by English schoolboys, it may be questioned whether in connexion with λόγος it must not have a more specific meaning, something, perhaps, like our word "foul" used of language, including, like it, not merely "filthy," but scurrilous language. So Arrian opposes σαπροὶ λόγοι to κομψοί (*Diss. Epict.* iii. 16, p. 298, ap. Kypke) ἀλλὰ εἴ τις ἀγαθὸς πρὸς οἰκοδομὴν τῆς χρείας. For χρείας there is a remarkable variant, πίστεως, in D*G, Vulg-Clem. (but Amiat. has χρείας) Goth. Jerome expressly says: "pro eo quod nos posuimus *ad aedificationem opportunitatis*, hoc est quod dicitur Graece τῆς χρείας, in Latinis codicibus propter euphoniam mutavit interpres et posuit *ad aedificationem fidei*."

> χρείας is the reading of ℵ A B K L P and nearly all mss. and versions.
> It is somewhat curious that in Rom. xii. 13, D*G substitute μνείαις for χρείαις.

εἰς οἰκοδομὴν τῆς χρείας, by no means for εἰς χρ. τῆς οἰκ., as AV. χρείας is the objective genitive; the actual "need" or "occasion" is that which is to be affected by the edifying influence of the discourse. In Acts vi. 3 the word seems to mean "occasion" or "matter in hand" ("whom we may set over this χρ."). Field aptly cites Plutarch, *Vit. Pericl.* viii., μηδὲ ῥῆμα μηδὲν ἐκπεσεῖν ἄκοντος αὐτοῦ πρὸς τὴν προκειμένην χρείαν ἀνάρμοστον. Thus the sense is "for the improvement of the occasion." So in substance Theophylact: ὅπερ οἰκοδομεῖ τὸν πλησίον ἀναγκαῖον ὂν τῇ προκειμένῃ χρείᾳ, and Jerome: "juxta opportunitatem loci temporis et personae aedificare audientes." Olshausen and Rückert take χρεία as abstract for concrete = those that have need, which would make τῆς χρείας superfluous.

ἵνα δῷ χάριν τοῖς ἀκούουσιν. "That it may give benefit to them that hear."

δῷ χάριν has been variously interpreted. Chrysostom somewhat strangely understands it to mean "make the hearer grateful," ἵνα χάριν σοι εἰδῇ ὁ ἀκούων, but adding as an alternative, ἵνα κεχαριτωμένους αὐτοὺς ἐργάσηται. Theodoret observes, χάριν τὴν θυμηδίαν ἐκάλεσε· τουτέστιν ἵνα φανῇ δεκτὸς τοῖς ἀκ. But edifying discourse cannot always be acceptable, nor should this be the object aimed at; nor, again, does διδόναι χάριν ever have this meaning. Said of persons, it means to grant a favour. But Plutarch has the phrase with reference to food given to invalids: οὐδεμίαν ἡδονὴν οὐδὲ χάριν ἀποδίδωσι, "it confers neither pleasure nor benefit." And in N.T. χάρις is similarly used, as in 2 Cor. i. 15, "that ye might have a second χ."; viii. 6, "that he would complete in you this χ. also." But as χάρις has a specially spiritual meaning in the N.T. generally, there is no reason to deny such a reference here.

30. καὶ μὴ λυπεῖτε τὸ Πνεῦμα τὸ Ἅγιον τοῦ Θεοῦ. The connexion with the foregoing is well expressed by Theophylact: ἐὰν εἴπῃς ῥῆμα σαπρὸν καὶ ἀνάξιον τοῦ χριστιανοῦ στόματος, οὐκ ἄνθρωπον ἐλύπησας, ἀλλὰ τὸ πνεῦμα τοῦ Θεοῦ. The warning assumes the

indwelling of the Spirit, and vividly expresses the offence done to that Spirit by such sins of the tongue. Aquinas weakens it by referring it to grieving the Spirit of God in others.

ἐν ᾧ ἐσφραγίσθητε. This supplies the ground of the motive. εἶτα καὶ ἡ προσθήκη τῆς εὐεργεσίας, ἵνα μείζων γένηται ἡ κατηγορία, Chrys. Some of the older as well as later commentators see in the words a suggestion that the Spirit may thus be led to depart, and the seal be lost. Had this been intended, μὴ παροξύνετε would have been more suitable. But there is no suggestion of a possible departure of the Spirit; even the tense of ἐσφραγίσθητε, referring as it does to a sealing once for all, is against this. But it would be equally erroneous to say that the doctrine of "final perseverance" is contained or implied. When a son is warned that if he acts in such and such a manner he will grieve his father, this does not suggest that his father may cast him off.

εἰς ἡμέραν ἀπολυτρώσεως, *i.e.* for, or with a view to, the day of complete redemption. On ἀπολ. cf. i. 14.

31. πᾶσα πικρία, "every kind of bitterness," the temper which cherishes resentful feelings. Aristotle defines the πικροί as "hard to be reconciled" (δυσδιάλυτοι), and retaining their anger for a long time.

καὶ θυμὸς καὶ ὀργή. These flow from the temper of πικρία, ῥίζα θυμοῦ καὶ ὀργῆς πικρία, Chrys. Of these two, θυμός expresses rather the temporary excitement of passion; ὀργή, the more settled anger. Thus Greg. Naz. *Carm.* 34, θυμὸς μέν ἐστιν ἀθρόος ζέσις φρενός, ὀργὴ δὲ θυμὸς ἐμμένων. Hence Ecclus. xlviii. 10, κοπάσαι ὀργὴν πρὸ θυμοῦ, before it bursts out. The Stoics defined θυμός as ὀργὴ ἀρχομένη (Diog. Laert. vii. 114).

καὶ κραυγὴ καὶ βλασφημία. Chrysostom well observes: ἵππος γάρ ἐστιν ἀναβάτην φέρων ἡ κραυγὴ τὴν ὀργήν· συμπόδισον τὸν ἵππον, καὶ κατέστρεψας τὸν ἀναβάτην. κραυγή leads to βλασφημία, which is clearly "reviling," not "blasphemy."

σὺν πάσῃ κακίᾳ. Associated also in Col. iii. 8 with ὀργή, θυμός, and βλασφημία, to which is there added αἰσχρολογία. It is not badness in general, but "malice," "animi pravitas, quae humanitati et aequitati est opposita." So Suidas: ἡ τοῦ κακῶσαι τὸν πέλας σπουδή. It is the very opposite of what follows.

32.-V. 2. *Exhortation to be tender-hearted and forgiving, following as a pattern God's forgiveness in Christ.*

32. γίνεσθε δέ, "become, show yourselves." Corresponding to ἀρθήτω ἀφ' ὑμῶν on the other side. χρηστοί, "kind." This is the only place in the Epistles where the adjective occurs; it is used of God in Luke vi. 35; so the substantive, ch. ii. 7; Tit. iii. 4, etc.

εὔσπλαγχνοι, "tender-hearted," in this sense only in biblical and ecclesiastical writers. Hippocrates has it in the physical sense, "having healthy bowels." Euripides uses the substantive εὐσπλαγχνία in the sense "firmness of heart." The adjective occurs in the same sense as here in the Prayer of Manasses, 7, and in *Test. XII Patr.*, of God. Comp. the parallel Col. iii. 12, σπλάγχνα οἰκτιρμοῦ.

χαριζόμενοι ἑαυτοῖς = Col. iii. 13. Origen presses ἑαυτοῖς as indicating that what was done to another was really done to themselves, διὰ τὸ συσσώμους ἡμᾶς εἶναι; Meyer and Alford think it implies that the forgiveness they are to show to others has as its pattern that which was shown to them as a body in Christ, ἑαυτοῖς being thus emphatic. In Col. iii. 12, also, we have ἀνεχόμενοι ἀλλήλων καὶ χαριζόμενοι ἑαυτοῖς, and again, 1 Pet. iv. 8–10, τὴν εἰς ἑαυτοὺς ἀγάπην ἐκτενῆ ἔχοντες . . . φιλόξενοι εἰς ἀλλήλους . . . εἰς ἑαυτοὺς [τὸ χάρισμα] διακονοῦντες. We are not justified in putting so much into the word as Meyer's explanation supposes; but so much is true, that ἑαυτοῖς suggests, more than ἀλλήλοις, that they are addressed as members of one corporate body. This use of the word is quite classical. Demosthenes has βούλεσθε . . . περιιόντες αὐτῶν πυνθάνεσθαι (p. 43, 10). Comp. also Xen. *Mem.* iii. 5. 16 (quoted by Lightfoot on Col.), ἀντὶ μὲν τοῦ συνεργεῖν ἑαυτοῖς τὰ συμφέροντα, ἐπηρεάζουσιν ἀλλήλοις, καὶ φθονοῦσιν ἑαυτοῖς μᾶλλον ἢ τοῖς ἄλλοις ἀνθρώποις . . . καὶ προαιροῦνται μᾶλλον οὕτω κερδαίνειν ἀπ' ἀλλήλων ἢ συνωφελοῦντες αὐτούς. Also Dem. *Mid.* 101, p. 547.

The Vulgate has erroneously "donantes," and Erasmus, "largientes," but the following context shows that the word must mean "forgiving."

καθὼς καί, the same motive that is appealed to in the Parable of the Unforgiving Servant.

ὁ Θεὸς ἐν Χριστῷ. "In Christ," not "for Christ's sake," as AV., for which there is no justification. The sense is the same as in 2 Cor. v. 19, "God was in Christ, reconciling the world unto Himself." Not "per Christum" (Calvin), nor even μετὰ τοῦ κινδύνου τοῦ υἱοῦ αὐτοῦ καὶ τῆς σφαγῆς αὐτοῦ (Theoph.), of which there is no hint in the ἐν; but, as in the passage in 2 Cor., God manifesting Himself in, acting in (not "through"), Christ. Hence in Col. iii. 13 it is ὁ Κύριος ἐχαρίσατο ὑμῖν.

ἐχαρίσατο ὑμῖν. The readings here and in ch. v. 2 vary between the second and the first person.

In iv. 32 ὑμῖν is read by ℵ A G P 37, Vulg. (Clem.) Goth. Sah. Boh. Eth.   ἡμῖν by D K L 17, 47, both Syr. Arm.

In v. 2 ὑμᾶς by ℵ A B P 37, Sah. Eth.   ἡμᾶς by ℵ^c D G K L 17 47, Vulg. Syr. (both) Boh. Goth. Arm.

Ib. ὑμῶν by B 37, Sah. Eth.   ἡμῶν by ℵ A D G K L P 17 47, Vulg. Syr. (both) Boh. Goth. Arm.

Or, to put it otherwise, we have—
ἡμ. in all three places, D K L 17 47, Syr. Arm.
ὑμ. in all three, Sah. Eth.
ὑμ. ὑμ. ἡμ., ℵ A P.

ὑμ. ἡμ. ἡμ., ℵ^c Vulg. Goth.
ἡμ. ὑμ. ὑμ., B.

Critics differ in their judgment. Lachmann (judging in the absence of ℵ) reads ἡμ. in all three places. Tischendorf (8th ed.) and Tregelles adopt ὑμ. ὑμ. ἡμ. (Treg., however, in iv. 32, giving ἡμῖν a place in the margin). So WH. (who place ἡμ. in the margin in the first and third places). So v. Soden and RV. (with ἡμ. in the mg. in the first place and ὑμ. in the third). Alford, Ellicott, and Eadie prefer ὑμ. ἡμ. ἡμ. The confusion of the two pronouns is very frequent. As far as documentary evidence is concerned, the reading adopted in RV. seems to have the advantage. The evidence for ὑμῶν in the third place is comparatively small, and it is very natural that St. Paul, while using the second person in close connexion with the precepts χαριζόμενοι, περιπατεῖτε ἐν ἀγάπῃ, should pass from that to the more general statement in the first person. Indeed, it is perhaps not going too far to say that while "God forgave you," "Christ loved you," are perfectly natural, it would not seem so natural to say, "Christ gave Himself for you," although the individual believer may say, "He gave Himself for me," Gal. ii. 20.

ἐχαρίσατο, "forgave," as referring to a past historical fact. Note that in Col. iii. 13 it is ὁ Κύριος, with ὁ Χριστός in some texts.

V. 1. γίνεσθε οὖν μιμηταὶ τοῦ Θεοῦ. "Become therefore imitators of God." γίνεσθε resumes the γίνεσθε of iv. 32. The words of that verse, "forgiving . . . as God forgave you," show that the imitation inculcated is in respect of this particular virtue, and the οὖν, therefore, connects this verse with that immediately preceding, not with the whole foregoing subject. Imitators of God! The idea is a grand and ennobling one; and our Lord Himself sets it before us, and in the same aspect, when He says, "Ye therefore shall be perfect, as your heavenly Father is perfect," namely, in that "He maketh His sun to rise on the evil and on the good, and sendeth rain on the just and the unjust" (Matt. v. 45, 48). So that we also should love our enemies.

The forgiveness inculcated is obviously free forgiveness, as in the passage just cited and in the Lord's Prayer. That this is here placed on the ground of imitation of God's forgiveness is a decisive proof that St. Paul did not view the Atonement in the light of payment of a debt or endurance of a penalty demanded by Divine justice. The most unforgiving of men, if not actually vindictive, might say, 'I am quite ready to forgive on the same terms on which you say that God forgives, viz. that the debt be fully paid, the offence fully atoned for. Chrysostom has a fine comment on this "forgiving one another." There is a great difference, he says, between God's forgiveness and ours, "for, if thou forgivest, the other will in turn forgive thee; but to God thou hast forgiven nought. And thou to thy fellow-servant, but God to His servant, and His enemy, and him that hateth Him. And He did not forgive simply without peril, but with the peril of His Son. For that He might forgive thee He sacrificed the Son,—τὸν Υἱὸν ἔθυσε,— but thou, although often seeing forgiveness to be without peril or expense, dost not exercise it."

ὡς τέκνα ἀγαπητά, *i.e.* as children beloved of God. He adds, says Chrys., another obligation of imitating God, not only because He has conferred benefits on us, but because we are His children, nay, His beloved children. "If God so loved us, we also ought to love one another."

2. καὶ περιπατεῖτε ἐν ἀγάπῃ, specifying, further, wherein the imitation of God is to be shown. Love is to be the rule of our life.

καθὼς καὶ ὁ Χριστὸς ἠγάπησεν ὑμᾶς, καὶ παρέδωκεν ἑαυτὸν ὑπὲρ ἡμῶν. Compare John xiii. 34, "as I have loved you, that ye also love one another." καὶ παρέδωκεν expresses wherein this love was shown. So ver. 25, "loved the Church, and gave Himself for it"; Gal. ii. 20, "loved me, and gave Himself for me." The verb requires no supplement, such as εἰς θάνατον or τῷ Θεῷ; see Rom. viii. 32; Gal. ii. 20, and ver. 25. ὑπέρ, "on behalf of."

προσφορὰν καὶ θυσίαν τῷ Θεῷ. τῷ Θεῷ is best connected with these words for the reason just mentioned; not with the following, since this would suppose the words placed emphatically before εἰς ὀσμήν, as if to exclude the idea of human pleasure, which is out of the question. προσφορά and θυσία are sometimes said to specify respectively an unbloody and a bloody offering; but such a distinction cannot be maintained either in classical or biblical Greek. The idea of "sacrifice" in θύω is not derived from that of slaying, but of "smoking," "burning incense." This was, according to Aristarchus, the meaning of the verb in Homer; cf. Latin "fumus," "subfio," which are from the same root. For biblical usage see Gen. iv. 3; Num. vii. 49, 73, etc. The alleged sense would be especially out of harmony with the figurative use of θυσία in St. Paul, θυσία ζῶσα, Rom. xii. 1; cf. Phil. ii. 17, iv. 18. Ellicott supposes that προσφορά is used as the more general term, relating, not to the death only, but to the life of obedience of our blessed Lord, His θυσία ζῶσα; while θυσία refers more particularly to His atoning death. The words appear, however, to be borrowed from Ps. xl. 6 (quoted Heb. x. 5), where they are used simply as together including all kinds of ceremonial offering.

εἰς ὀσμὴν εὐωδίας. "For a sweet-smelling savour." The figure was founded originally on the heathen idea that the smell of the burnt sacrifice did literally ascend to the gods, who thereby participated with the worshipper in the sacred feast. So in Homer often; see especially *Il.* xxiv. 69, 70, οὐ γάρ μοί ποτε βωμὸς ἐδεύετο δαιτὸς ἐΐσης, λοιβῆς τε κνίσης τε· τὸ γὰρ λάχομεν γέρας ἡμεῖς. It is appropriate only to a burnt-offering.

That St. Paul here speaks of Christ as a sacrifice cannot, of course, be denied. But does he do so by way of stating the nature or manner of the atonement? Surely not. There is not one word to hint at the relation of this sacrifice to God's forgiveness. On the contrary, God in Christ forgiving us, and Christ showing His love by His offering of Himself, are put forward as exactly parallel examples; indeed, in view of the parallel in Col., ὁ Κύριος ἐχαρίσατο, we might say as one and the same. It is this single aspect of Christ's sacrifice as a supreme exhibition of love on the part both of the Father and of the Son that is here presented. Indeed, in Rom. viii. 32 the very same word παρέδωκε is used of the Father that is here used of the Son. And if we cannot argue as if the apostle were here stating the essential nature of the atonement, still less are we justified in assuming that he had in his mind the "substitutionary" view of sacrifice. Whatever the original idea of sacrifice may have been (and certainly the substitutionary view is not the only one possible), neither psalmists nor apostles seem to have had this idea present to their minds whenever they spoke of sacrifice. The psalmist speaks of sacrificing thanksgiving and praise (Ps. l. 14); St. Paul, of his offering of the Gentiles (Rom. xv. 16). In Rom. xii. 1, already quoted, he calls on his readers to present their bodies as a sacrifice. In Phil. ii. 17 he represents himself as offering their faith as a sacrifice; and in the same Ep., iv. 18, he calls their present to him a sacrifice, an odour of a sweet savour. With the exception of 1 Cor. x. 18 ("they that eat of the sacrifices"), these are the only passages beside the present in which he uses the words. This gives little support to the notion that we are to interpret his words here as if we were dealing with a treatise on scientific theology.

Chrysostom certainly does not err in this way. He observes: ὁρᾷς, τὸ ὑπὲρ ἐχθρῶν παθεῖν, ὅτι ὀσμὴ εὐωδίας ἐστί, καὶ θυσία εὐπρόσδεκτος; κἂν ἀποθάνῃς, τότε ἔσῃ θυσία· τοῦτο μιμήσασθαί ἐστι τὸν Θεόν.

3–11. *Special warnings against sins of impurity.*

3. πορνεία δὲ καὶ ἀκαθαρσία πᾶσα ἢ πλεονεξία μηδὲ ὀνομαζέσθω ἐν ὑμῖν.

πορνεία is mentioned as being a sin of little account amongst the Gentiles. On πλεονεξία see iv. 19. This passage, says Moule, more perhaps than any other, suggests that the word (πλεονεξία) had acquired by usage, in St. Paul's time, a familiar though not fixed connexion with *sensual* greed, just such as our word "covetousness" has acquired with the greed of material property. It is urged here that ἢ indicates that the two words between which it stands belong to different classes. But in the following verse we have ἢ between μωρολογία and εὐτραπελία, which do not belong to different classes.

μηδὲ ὀνομαζέσθω. Herodotus says of the Persians: ἅσσα δέ σφι ποιέειν οὐκ ἔξεστι, ταῦτα οὐδὲ λέγειν ἔξεστι (i. 138). But St. Paul's precept refers to particular classes of sin only. Compare ver. 12. οἱ γὰρ λόγοι τῶν πραγμάτων εἰσὶν ὁδοί, Chrys. Bengel suggests for ὄνομ. "mentioned as committed," "ut facta"; cf. ἀκούεται ἐν ὑμῖν πορνεία, 1 Cor. v. 1. But, besides that ὄνομ. can hardly mean this, μηδέ, "not even," is decisive against it.

4. καὶ αἰσχρότης καὶ μωρολογία ἢ εὐτραπελία.
The MSS. and Vss. vary between καί and ἤ in the first and second places.
A D* G, It. Vulg. Sah. have ἤ . . . ἤ.
ℵ*ᵃ B D° K, Boh. Eth. have καί . . . καί.
ℵ* P, Syr-Harcl. Arm. have καί . . . ἤ.
Lachmann writes ἤ . . . ἤ, Tischendorf, RV. καί . . . ἤ, WH. καί . . . καί.

αἰσχρότης is not merely "foolish talking," which would be αἰσχρολογία, but "shameful conduct." Plato has (of Rhadamanthus inspecting the souls of the dead): ἀσυμμετρίας τε καὶ αἰσχρότητος γέμουσαν τὴν ψυχὴν εἶδεν (*Gorg.* 525 A); but there the word means the hideousness stamped on the soul by the vices of the living man.

μωρολογία, "stultiloquium," only here in bibl. Grk. It is a rare word also in classical writers, but occurs in Arist. (*Hist. An.* i. 11) and Plutarch (*Mor.* 504 B). Plautus uses "morologus," "Amoris vitio non meo nunc tibi morologus fio" (*Pers.* i. 1. 50).

εὐτραπελία. Aristotle defines εὐτρ. as πεπαιδευμένη ὕβρις. οἱ ἐμμελῶς παίζοντες εὐτράπελοι προσαγορεύονται. But he adds that, since most persons are pleased with excessive jesting, οἱ βωμολόχοι εὐτράπελοι προσαγορεύονται (*Eth. Nic.* iv. 14), *i.e.*, as in many other cases, the extreme usurps the name of the near. This would justify St. Paul's usage, were there nothing else. But for the adjective compare also Pindar, *Pyth.* i. 178, μὴ δολωθῇς εὐτραπέλοις κέρδεσσ', and iv. 104, where Jason boasts that he has never spoken ἔπος εὐτράπελον. According to Dissen, the word was used "cum levitatis et assentationis, simulationis notatione"; but this does not seem to be the meaning here, where the context clearly points to licentious speech; see ver. 5. Trench compares the history of the Latin "urbanitas" and the English "facetious." He notes that in the *Miles Gloriosus* of Plautus, the old man who describes himself as "cavillator facetus" says: "Ephesi sum natus; non enim in Apulis, non Animulae."

ἃ οὐκ ἀνῆκεν. So ℵ A B P. Rec. has τὰ οὐκ ἀνήκοντα, with D G K L and most.

ἀλλὰ μᾶλλον εὐχαριστία. Clement of Alex. understands εὐχ. here of "gracious speech"; and so Jerome (but with a "forsitan"): "juxta quam grati sive gratiosi et salsi apud homines appellamur," —an opinion followed by Calvin, Hammond, and many others, "gracious, pious, religious discourse in general," Hammond; who points to the ἵνα δῷ χάριν τοῖς ἀκ. in iv. 29, and "let your speech be always ἐν χάριτι," in Col. iv. 6. In Prov. xi. 16 we have γυνὴ εὐχάριστος, "a gracious, pious woman." The adjective is sometimes so used in classical authors: εὐχαριστότατοι λόγοι, Xen. *Cyr.* ii. 2. 1. This would suit the context very well; but as it is not only against St. Paul's use of the word elsewhere, but, moreover, there is no example of the substantive in this sense, it would be too bold to adopt it. We have to understand a suitable verb from ὀνομαζέσθω, both for this and the preceding substantives. The sense is not: "let not foolish speech be mentioned but thanksgiving," but: "let there not be," etc. Bengel understands ἀνῆκει to εὐχαριστία; and so Braune; which with the reading ἃ οὐκ ἀνῆκεν is not unnatural, but more harsh. In these cases of brachylogy there is really no need to look for a verb, the sense is obvious to the reader.

5. τοῦτο γὰρ ἴστε γινώσκοντες. ἴστε is the reading of ℵ A B D* G P, It. Vulg. Goth. Sah. Boh. Arm., Chrys.

ἐστε, that of D^c K L, Theodoret, Theoph. Internal as well as external evidence favours the former. ἐστε γιν. would be a feeble periphrasis for οἴδατε or γινώσκετε, since there is no hint here of an emphasis on the present tense.

The combination of the two verbs is not to be explained by reference to the Hebrew idiom, which combines a finite verb with the infinitive absolute (imitated in Greek by the participle with the finite verb), since the verbs here are different. Xenophon's ὁρῶν καὶ ἀκούων οἶδα (*Cyr.* iv. 1. 14) is nearer, but not exactly parallel, since there the participles define the kind of knowledge: "I know by observation and hearsay." The meaning is clear: "ye know full well, of your own knowledge." ἴστε is not imperative, as in the Vulgate and Bengel, etc., which does not at all agree with the addition γινώσκοντες. Hofmann puts a stop after ἴστε, so as to make τοῦτο refer to the preceding.

On πᾶς οὐκ cf. iv. 29.

ὅ ἐστιν εἰδωλολάτρης.

There are three readings—
ὅ ἐστιν εἰδωλολάτρης, ℵ B 67², Jerome.
ὅς ἐστιν εἰδωλολάτρης, A D K L P, Syr-Harcl. Boh. Arm., Chrys.
ὅ ἐστιν εἰδωλολατρεία, G, It. Vulg. Goth.; Syr-Pesh. (printed text) has "or," which points to ὅ.

The last is supposed by Meyer to have been an explanation of the second, which he thinks genuine, the first being produced from this by restoring εἰδωλολάτρης. But it is quite as easy to account for the third variety as arising from the first, because εἰδωλολάτρης was thought unsuitable to ὅ. If the second reading had been the original, it is not easy to see why it should have been changed; but ὅ would readily be changed to ὅς for grammatical reasons.

With the reading ὅς some commentators (Harless, Braune, etc.) refer the relative to all three antecedents; but this is not so natural as the reference to πλεονέκτης, which also corresponds with Col. iii. 5, πλεονεξίαν, ἥτις ἐστὶν εἰδωλολατρεία, although there also Harless regards ἥτις as by attraction for ἅτινα, as Eph. iii. 13. With the reading ὅ, the latter reference must, of course, be adopted. On the designation of πλ. as idolatry, see above on iv. 19. The passages from Rabbinical writers, quoted by Schöttgen and Wetstein, do not throw much light on the matter. They represent all kinds of wickedness and vice as idolatry; pride, anger, refusal to give alms. If πλεονεξία is simply "covetousness," the question is, why should this, any more than fornication and impurity, be singled out to be called idolatry? Meyer says that πορνεία and ἀκαθαρσία are also subtle idolatry (certainly not "more subtle forms," Ellicott), but that it was natural for St. Paul, whose own self-sacrificing spirit was so opposed to this self-seeking, to brand this especially as idolatry in order to make it κατ' ἐξοχήν abominable. There is nothing in his language elsewhere to support this idea. One of Chrysostom's explanations shows how difficult he found it to answer the question. Wouldst thou learn, says he, how πλ. is idolatry, and worse than idolatry? Idolaters worship God's creatures, but thou worshippest thy own creature, for God did not create πλεονεξία.

If we give πλεονεξία and πλεονέκτης the wider sense advocated on iv. 19, there is no difficulty.

οὐκ ἔχει κληρονομίαν. As κληρονομία does not necessarily imply actual possession, but the title to possession, it is not necessary to say that the present is used to express the certainty of future possession.

ἐν τῇ βασιλείᾳ τοῦ Χριστοῦ καὶ Θεοῦ. Many expositors (Bengel, Harless, etc.) argue from the absence of the article before Θεοῦ that the words mean "the kingdom of Him who is Christ and God." But Θεός is one of the words that do not require an article; comp. 1 Cor. vi. 9, 10, βασιλείαν Θεοῦ: also *ib*. xv. 50 and Gal. v. 21. See also Gal. i. 1, διὰ Ἰησοῦ Χριστοῦ καὶ Θεοῦ πατρός: Rom. xv. 8, ὑπὲρ ἀληθείας Θεοῦ: xiii. 4, Θεοῦ διάκονος, etc. There is in the context no dogmatic assertion about Christ, and to introduce such a prediction in this incidental way would be out of place. Nor does the apostle's language elsewhere lead us to suppose that he would thus absolutely designate Christ, God. Comp. iv. 6, "one Lord, one God." The absence of the article gives more unity to the conception; it is not "the kingdom of Christ, and also the kingdom of God," but being the kingdom of Christ it is the kingdom of God.

6. μηδεὶς ὑμᾶς ἀπατάτω κενοῖς λόγοις. λόγοι κενοί, "sermones a veritate alieni." Aeschines speaks of a decree written by Demosthenes as κενώτερον τῶν λόγων οὓς εἴωθε λέγειν καὶ τοῦ βίου ὃν βεβίωκε (*Cont. Ctes.* p. 288); and Plato says: τίς ἐν ξυνουσίᾳ τοιᾷδε μάτην κενοῖς λόγοις αὐτὸς αὐτὸν κοσμοῖ; (*Laches.* 169 B).

To what persons do these words refer? Grotius thinks, partly heathen philosophers, partly Jews, who thought that all Jews would have part in the world to come. Meyer sees in them the unbelieving heathen, which view he supports by reference to the following words; and so Eadie. But the Christians, as such, were separate from the unbelieving heathen, and the Epistle gives no reason to suppose that they would need to be warned against immoral teaching proceeding from them. Rather, we must understand persons amongst themselves who made light of sins of impurity, as too many in Christian communities still do. As Bullinger (ap. Harless) says: "Erant apud Ephesios homines corrupti, ut hodie apud nos plurimi sunt, qui haec salutaria Dei praecepta cachinno excipientes obstrepunt; humanum esse quod faciant amatores, utile quod foeneratores, facetum quod jaculatores, et idcirco Deum non usque adeo graviter animadvertere in istiusmodi lapsus." The context perfectly harmonises with this: "Be not ye Christians misled into such vices, for it is just these, etc., and by falling into them ye would be συμμέτοχοι with those who are in the darkness from which ye have been delivered."

διὰ ταῦτα γάρ, "for it is on account of these things"; not this teaching, but these sins.

ἔρχεται ἡ ὀργὴ τοῦ Θεοῦ. ὀργή is not to be limited to the ordinary judgments of this life, "quorum exempla sunt ante oculos" (Calv.); nor is there reason to limit it to the wrath of God in the day of judgment (Meyer). The wrath of God will be manifested then, but it exists now.

ἐπὶ τοὺς υἱοὺς τῆς ἀπειθείας, see ii. 2.

7. μὴ οὖν γίνεσθε συμμέτοχοι αὐτῶν. "Do not therefore become partakers with them." αὐτῶν refers to the persons, not the sins (as Braune). This sharing is by some understood of sharing in their punishment, but by most expositors of sharing in their sins; Stier combines both, and not unreasonably, since it has just been said that these sins bring punishment, and the sense naturally is: Have nothing in common with them, for ye surely do not desire to share the wrath with them.

8. ἦτε γάρ ποτε σκότος. μέν is quite properly absent. To quote Fritzsche: "Recte ibi non ponitur, ubi aut non sequitur membrum oppositum, aut scriptores oppositionem addere nondum constituerant, aut loquentes alterius membri oppositionem quacunque de causâ lectoribus non indixerunt" (Rom. x. 19, vol. ii. p. 423).

ἦτε. The emphasis is on the time past; cf. "Troja fuit, fuimus Troes." σκότος. Stronger than "were in darkness." They were not only in darkness; darkness was also in them. So νῦν δὲ φῶς ἐν Κυρίῳ. The whole nature of light was to belong to them as formerly the whole nature of darkness; they were not only in the light, but penetrated by it, so that they themselves became "the light of the world," Matt. v. 14.

ἐν Κυρίῳ, "in fellowship with the Lord."

ὡς τέκνα φωτὸς περιπατεῖτε. With τέκνα φωτός cf. υἱοὶ ἀπειθείας, ver. 6 and ii. 3. Alford argues from the absence of the article before φωτός (in contrast with τοῦ φωτός, ver. 9 and Luke xvi. 8), that "it is light *as light* that is spoken of." But the absence of the article is in accordance with the settled rule stated by Apollonius, that (subject to certain qualifications) nouns in regimen must have the article prefixed to both or to neither (see Middleton, *On the Greek Article*, iii. 1, 7; 3, 6).

9. ὁ γὰρ καρπὸς τοῦ φωτός. The walk to which I exhort you is that which becomes children of the light, for etc.

> The Rec. Text. has πνεύματος for φωτός, with D⁰ K L, Syr-Pesh., Chrys. and most cursives.
> φωτός is the reading of ℵ A B D* G P 67², It. Vulg. Goth. Boh. Arm., Origen, Jerome.
> It might be thought possible that φωτός had come in from recollection of the same word just preceding, but the figure of "light" governs the whole passage, and ἔργα ἄκαρπα σκότους, ver. 10, corresponds to καρπὸς φωτός here. Καρπὸς πνεύματος undoubtedly came in from the parallel, Gal. v. 22, where the contrast is with ἔργα σαρκός, ver. 19; cf. 17, 18. The variation is an important one for the estimate of the character of the authorities that support the two readings respectively.

ἐν πάσῃ ἀγαθωσύνῃ καὶ δικαιοσύνῃ καὶ ἀληθείᾳ. "In all (*i.e.* every kind of) goodness and righteousness and truth," the opposites of κακία, ἀδικία, ψεῦδος. ἀγαθωσύνη is not found in classical Greek, but is used by St. Paul in three other places, viz. Rom. xvi. 14; Gal. v. 22; 2 Thess. i. 11. The use of it in the Sept. gives us little help. In Eccles., where it occurs several times, it is used for "enjoyment." In Neh. ix. 25, 35, it is used of the goodness of God. In Ps. lii. 3 (li. Sept.) it is "good" in general as opposed to "evil"; and so in xxxviii. (xxxvii.) 20. In St. Paul it would seem to mean "goodness" in the special sense of benevolence; and thus the threefold enumeration here would correspond to that in the Gospels: "justice, mercy, and truth," and to Butler's "justice, truth, and regard to common good" (comp. Rom. v. 7).

As a metaphor the expression "fruit of the light" cannot be called "strictly correct," as if it referred to the necessity of light for the production of fruit, etc. The words "children of light" convey no intimation of such a figure.

10. δοκιμάζοντες τί ἐστιν εὐάρεστον τῷ Κυρίῳ. Compare Rom. xii. 2, εἰς τὸ δοκιμάζειν ὑμᾶς τί τὸ θέλημα τοῦ Θεοῦ, τὸ ἀγαθὸν καὶ εὐάρεστον καὶ τέλειον.

Putting to the proof, partly by thought and partly by experience. Stier and some others take the words imperatively, supplying ἐστε, as Rom. xii. 9-13 and *vv.* 19, 20; but here between two imperatives this is less natural.

11. καὶ μὴ συγκοινωνεῖτε τοῖς ἔργοις ἀκάρποις τοῦ σκότους. "Have no fellowship with." The thought joins on to ver. 7. The verb with the dative means (like the simple κοινωνεῖν) to have fellowship or partnership with. In the sense, "to have part in a thing," it takes the genitive. ἀκάρποις, for vice has no καρπός. Thus Jerome: "Vitia in semet ipsa finiuntur et pereunt, virtutes frugibus pullulant et redundant."

11, 12. μᾶλλον δὲ καὶ ἐλέγχετε, τὰ γὰρ κρυφῇ γινόμενα ὑπ' αὐτῶν αἰσχρόν ἐστι καὶ λέγειν. κρυφῇ γινόμενα cannot be merely synonymous with ἔργα σκότους, as Harless and Olshausen hold; σκότος and κρυφῇ are distinct notions, and ἔργα σκότους might be open offences. Besides, this would make κρυφῇ quite superfluous. καὶ λέγειν, "even to mention."

ἐλέγχετε is usually taken to mean "reprove." This seems to imply reproof by words; but then the reason assigned seems strange; they are to be reproved, because even to speak of them is shameful. If the conjunction had been "although" and not "for," it would be intelligible. Hence some expositors have actually supposed that γάρ here means "although," which is, of course, impossible. Another view that has been taken is "rebuke them openly, for to speak of them otherwise is shameful"; but this puts too much into λέγειν. Bengel's view is that the words assign, not the reason for ἐλ., but the reason of the apostle's speaking indefinitely of the vices, whilst he enumerates the virtues. This is forced, and against the emphatic position of κρυφῇ. Stier's view is that the reproof is to be by the life, not by words: "Ye would yourselves be sinning if ye were to name the secret vices"; hence the necessity for walking in the light, that so these deeds may be reproved. But St. Paul is not deterred by such scruples from speaking plainly of heathen vices when occasion required. Harless' view, that the words are connected with μὴ συγκ., "Do not commit these sins, for they are too bad even to mention," assumes that τὰ κρυφῇ γινόμενα simply = τὰ ἔργα τοῦ σκότους, which we have seen is untenable.

Meyer and Eadie assign as the connexion, "By all means reprove them; and there is the more need of this, for it is a shame even to speak of their secret sins." This seems to leave the difficulty unsolved. Barry says: "In such reproof it should be remembered that it would be disgraceful 'even to speak' in detail of the actual 'things done in secret.'" This again supposes that γάρ assigns a reason for what is not expressed, namely, for some qualification of ἐλέγχετε, not at all for ἐλέγχετε itself.

There is, however, another meaning of ἐλέγχω very common, especially when the object is a thing, not a person, and more particularly in connexion with derivatives of κρύπτω, viz. to expose or bring to light. Artemidorus, in his interpretations of dreams, when speaking of those dreams which forebode the revealing of secrets, always speaks of τὰ κρυπτὰ ἐλέγχεσθαι, *e.g.* ii. 36, ἥλιος ἀπὸ δύσεως ἐξανατέλλων τὰ κρυπτὰ ἐλέγχει τῶν λεληθέναι δοκούντων. Polybius says: ἐλέγχεσθαί φασιν τὰς φύσεις ὑπὸ τῶν περιστάσεων (p. 1382). He opposes to it διασκοτεῖσθαι (p. 1383). And Phavorinus defines ἐλέγχω. τὸ κεκρυμμένον ἀτόπημά τινος εἰς φῶς ἄγω. Cf. Aristoph. *Eccles.* 483.

So the substantive ὁ ἔλεγχος = proof. The connexion of this signification with that of "convict" is obvious. The *Etym. M.* has ἐλεγχύς ἐστιν ὁ τὰ πράγματα σαφηνίζων . . . ὁ γὰρ ἔλ. εἰς φῶς ἄγει τὰ πράγματα.

This appears to be the meaning of the verb in John iii. 20, οὐκ ἔρχεται πρὸς τὸ φῶς, ἵνα μὴ ἐλεγχθῇ τὰ ἔργα αὐτοῦ. Compare in the following verse, ἔρχεται πρὸς τὸ φῶς, ἵνα φανερωθῇ αὐτοῦ τὰ ἔργα. Compare also 1 Cor. xiv. 22, ἐλέγχεται ὑπὸ πάντων . . . τὰ κρυπτὰ τῆς καρδίας αὐτοῦ φανερὰ γίνεται. The occurrence of κρυφῇ here in the immediate context suggests that this meaning was present to the apostle's mind. Adopting it, we obtain as the interpretation: Have no participation with the works of darkness, nay, rather expose them, for the things they do secretly it is a shame even to mention; but all these things when exposed by the light are made manifest in their true character. Then follows the reason, not for 13*a*, but for the whole exhortation. This ἐλέγχειν is not useless, for it leads to φανεροῦσθαι, and so turns σκότος into φῶς. This is Soden's interpretation. A remarkable parallel is John iii. 20, just quoted. There also ἔργα are the object, ἔργα whose nature is σκότος (ver. 19); and it is the φῶς which effects ἐλέγχειν, ver. 20, and φανεροῦν, ver. 21.

13. τὰ δὲ πάντα ἐλεγχόμενα ὑπὸ τοῦ φωτὸς φανεροῦται· πᾶν γὰρ τὸ φανερούμενον φῶς ἐστι. The difficulty in tracing the connexion continues to be felt here. Meyer interprets: But everything (= those secret sins) when it is reproved is made manifest by the light; that is, by the light of Christian truth which operates in your reproof, it is brought to the light of day in its true moral character; I say, by the light, for—to prove that it can only be by the light— whatever is made manifest is light; it has ceased to have the nature of darkness. Assuming, namely, "quod est in effectu (φῶς ἐστι) id debet esse in causa (ὑπὸ τοῦ φωτός)." This is adopted by Ellicott. But it is open to serious objection: first, ὑπὸ τοῦ φωτός is not emphatic; on the contrary, its position is as unemphatic as possible; secondly, ἐλεγχόμενα is on this view not only superfluous but disturbing; thirdly, the assumption that what is in the effect must be in the cause, is much too recondite a principle to be silently assumed in such a discourse as this; and, lastly, this treats φανερούμενον as if it were πεφανερωμένον. Meyer, in fact, endeavours to obtain, by the help of a hidden metaphysical assumption, the

same sense which Eadie and others obtain by taking φανερούμενον as middle (= AV.).

Ellicott adds, "whatever is illumined is light." But φανερόω does not mean "to illumine," but to make φανερός. It occurs nearly fifty times in the N.T. and never = φωτίζειν. True, it is allied to φῶς, but not closely, for its nearest connexion is with the stem of φαίνω, viz. φάν, which is already far from φῶς. Again, when it is said by Alford (in reply to Eadie's objection that the transformation does not always take place) that, "objectively taken, it is universally true: *everything shone upon* IS LIGHT" (whether this tends to condemnation or not depending on whether the transformation takes place or not), this surely is just what is not true. A dark object shone upon does not become *lux* (the English word is ambiguous). He adds that the key text is John iii. 20, but in order to fit this in he interprets "brought into light" as "made light."

Bengel, followed by Stier, takes φανερούμενον as middle, "quod manifestari non refugit; confer mox, ἔγειραι καὶ ἀνάστα" [the correct reading is ἔγειρε]; and on πᾶν, "Abstractum pro concreto nam hic sermo jam est de homine ipso, coll. v. seq. *propterea*."

We seem almost driven (with Eadie, after Beza, Calvin, Grotius, etc.) to take φανερούμενον as middle, in this sense, "whatever makes manifest is light." The examples, indeed, of φανεροῦσθαι as middle, adduced by Eadie, are not quite to the point, viz. such as ἐφανερώθη in Mark xvi. 12, where the medial sense is much more marked than in the present passage. Bleek thinks it necessary to suppose an active sense here, but he proposes to read φανεροῦν τό. Oltramare interprets: "All the things done in secret, when reproved, are brought into open day by the light [which is salutary], for whatever is so brought out is light."

14. Διὸ λέγει. "Wherefore it is said." It is generally held that this formula introduces a quotation from canonical Scripture. Here the difficulty arises that this is not a quotation from canonical Scripture. Jerome admits this, saying, "omnes editiones veterum scripturarum ipsaque Hebraeorum volumina eventilans nunquam hoc scriptum reperi." He therefore suggests that it is from an apocryphal writing; not that the apostle accepted such a writing as authoritative, but that he quoted it as he has quoted Aratus, etc. He, at the same time, mentions others who supposed the words to be spoken by the apostle himself under inspiration. Many moderns, however, think that the original text is Isa. lx. 1, "Arise, shine, for thy light is come, and the glory of the LORD is risen upon thee," the words being, it is said, quoted, not verbally, but in essence. It would be more correct to say that the resemblance is verbal rather than in essence; for the differences are important. The very word ὁ Χριστός is fatal to the idea of a

quotation. Alford, indeed, says that it is a necessary inference from the form of the citation (viz. ὁ Χρ.) that St. Paul is citing the language of prophecy in the light of the fulfilment of prophecy, which obviously assumes the point in question. It is said, moreover, that no surprise can be felt at finding Christ substituted for the LORD (Jehovah) of the O.T., and the true Israel for Jerusalem. True: if the question were of the application of words from the O.T., as in 1 Pet. iii. 15, or of interpretation added to the quotation, as in Rom. xi. 6–8. Moreover, the words here are not addressed to the Church (ὁ καθεύδων), they seem rather addressed either to recent converts or to those who do not yet believe. And, further, there is nothing in Isaiah about awaking from sleep or arising from the dead (though Alford asserts the contrary); nor is the idea, "shall give thee light," at all the same as Isaiah's, "the glory of the Lord has risen upon thee."

Hence other commentators find it necessary to suppose a reference to other passages either separately or combined with this, viz. Isa. ix. 2, xxvi. 19, lii. 1. Such conjectures, in fact, refute themselves; for when the words of a prophet are so completely changed, we can no longer speak of a quotation, and λέγει would be quite out of place. Nor can we overlook the fact that the point of the connexion seems to lie in the word ἐπιφαύσει.

Others have adopted Jerome's suggestion as to an apocryphal source, some even going so far as to suggest the actual name of the book, Epiphanius naming the Prophecy of Elijah; George Syncellus, a book of Jeremiah; the margin of Codex G, the Book of Enoch. It is hardly sufficient to allege against this view that λέγει always introduces a quotation from canonical Scripture. But ὁ Χριστός is inconsistent with the idea of an O.T. apocryphon, and apart from that the whole expression has a Christian stamp.

Meyer endeavours to reconcile the assertion that λέγει introduces a citation from canonical Scripture with the fact that this is not such a citation, by the supposition that by a lapse of memory the apostle cites an apocryphon as if it were canonical. But was St. Paul's knowledge of the Scriptures so imperfect that he did not know, for example, that the promised deliverer is never in the O.T. distinctly called ὁ Χριστός?

Others conjecture that it may be a saying of Christ Himself that is quoted. The use of ὁ Χριστός in the third person is not inconsistent with this; nor, again, the fact that St. Paul does not elsewhere quote the sayings of Christ. Why might he not do it once? But it is impossible to supply ὁ Χριστός or Ἰησοῦς as a subject without something to suggest it. It is too forced to meet this by taking φῶς as the subject.

The difficulties disappear when we recognise that λέγει need not be taken to mean ὁ Θεὸς λέγει,—an assertion which has been shown in iv. 8 to be untenable. It means "it says," or "it is said," and the quotation may probably be from some liturgical formula or hymn,—a supposition with which its rhythmical character agrees very well. That the words were suggested originally by Isa. lx. 1 may be admitted. Theodoret mentions this opinion: τινὲς δὲ τῶν ἑρμηνευτῶν ἔφασαν πνευματικῆς χάριτος ἀξιωθέντας τινὰς ψαλμοὺς συγγράψαι, referring to 1 Cor. xiv. 26. He seems to have taken this from Severianus (*Cramer*, vi. 197), who concludes: δῆλον οὖν ὅτι ἐν ἑνὶ τούτων τῶν πνευματικῶν ψαλμῶν ἤτοι προσευχῶν ἔκειτο τοῦτο ὃ ἐμνημόνευσεν (compare also Origen in the *Catena*, *ib.*). Stier adopts a similar view, but endeavours to save the supposed limitation of the use of λέγει by saying that in the Church the Spirit speaks. As there are in the Church prophets and prophetic speakers and poets, so there are liturgical expressions and hymns which are holy words. Comparing *vv.* 18, 19, Col. iii. 16, it may be said that the apostle is here giving us an example of this self-admonition by new spiritual songs.

The view that the words are from a liturgical source is adopted by Barry, Ewald, Braune, v. Soden, the last-mentioned suggesting (after some older writers) that they may have been used in the reception after baptism. Compare 1 Tim. iii. 16, which is not improbably supposed to have a similar source.

ἔγειρε is the reading of a decisive preponderance of authorities, ℵ A B D G K L P, apparently all uncials, ἔγειραι being found only in cursives. In the other places where the word occurs (Matt. ix. 5; Mark ii. 9, 11, iii. 3, v. 41; Luke v. 23; John v. 8), ἔγειρε is likewise supported by preponderant authority, a third variation ἐγείρου occurring in some places. Fritzsche on Mark ii. 9 has ably defended the propriety of ἔγειρε, which is not to be understood either as active for middle or as if σεαυτόν were understood, but as a "formula excitandi," "Up!" like ἄγε, ἔπειγε (Eurip. *Orest.* 789). So in Eurip. *Iph. Aul.* 624, ἔγειρ' ἀδελφῆς ἐφ' ὑμέναιον εὐτυχῶς; and Aristoph. *Ran.* 340, ἔγειρε φλογέας λαμπάδας ἐν χερσὶ . . . τινάσσων. This use is limited to the single form ἔγειρε. ἔγειραι, says Fritzsche, would mean "excita mihi aliquem."

ἀνάστα for ἀνάστηθι = Acts xii. 7. This short form is also found in Theocritus and Menander. Compare κατάβα, Mark xv. 30 (in some MSS. including A C), and ἀνάβα, Apoc. iv. 1.

καὶ ἐπιφαύσει σοι ὁ Χριστός. ἐπιφαύσει from ἐπιφαύσκω, which is found several times in Job (Sept.); D* d e and MSS. mentioned by Chrysostom and by Jerome read ἐπιψαύσεις τοῦ Χριστοῦ. Jerome (quoted by Tisch.) relates that he heard some one disputing in the church, in order to please the people with something new, saying that this was said with reference to Adam, who was buried on Calvary, and that when the Lord on the Cross hung above his grave, the prophecy was fulfilled, "Rise Adam, who sleepest, and rise from the dead and Christ shall touch thee, ἐπιψαύσει," *i.e.* that by the touch of Christ's body and blood he should be brought to life. This story probably indicates how this reading arose.

15-21. *General exhortation to regulate their conduct with wisdom, to make their market of the opportunity, and, avoiding riotous indulgence, to express their joy and thankfulness in spiritual songs.*

15. βλέπετε οὖν ἀκριβῶς πῶς περιπατεῖτε.

This is the reading of ℵ* B 17 and some other mss., Origen, and probably Chrys. But πῶς ἀκριβῶς, ℵᶜ A D G K L P, with most mss., Vulg. Syr. (both) Arm., Theodoret, Jerome, etc. Chrysostom has ἀκριβῶς πῶς in text and comment, but in the latter πῶς ἀκριβῶς occurs presently after, also βλέπετε πῶς περιπατεῖτε. As πῶς ἀκρ. is the common later reading, it is probable that its occurrence in the second place in the comm. is due to a copyist of Chrys. The variation in the original text may have arisen from an accidental omission of πῶς after -βῶς (it is actually om. in Eth.), it being there inserted in the wrong place. In Eadie's comment. ed. 2, πῶς is similarly om.

οὖν is resumptive, "to return to our exhortation." Some, however, regard this as an inference from what immediately precedes, viz. "since ye are enlightened by Christ" (Ewald, Braune); but as the substance of the exhortation is clearly the same as in *vv.* 8-10, it is unnecessary to look on this as an inference from ver. 14. Harless follows Calvin, who says: "Si aliorum discutere tenebras fideles debent fulgore suo, quanto minus caecutire debent in proprio vitae instituto?" But this would seem to require an emphatic αὐτοί.

On ἀκριβῶς compare Acts xxvi. 5, κατὰ τὴν ἀκριβεστάτην αἵρεσιν. As περιπατεῖτε is a fact, the indicative is correctly used, and is exactly parallel to 1 Cor. iii. 11, ἕκαστος βλεπέτω πῶς ἐποικοδομεῖ. Most commentators expound the other reading. Fritzsche's view of this has been generally adopted (*Opuscula*, p. 209 n.), viz. that ἀκρ. περ. = "tanquam ad regulam et amussim vitam dirigere," the whole meaning πῶς τὸ ἀκριβῶς ἐργάζεσθε = "videte quomodo circumspecte vivatis h. e. quomodo illud efficiatis, ut provide vivatis." He exposes the fallacy of Winer's contention (subsequently abandoned), that the words were a concise expression for βλέπετε πῶς περιπατεῖτε, δεῖ δὲ ὑμᾶς ἀκριβῶς περιπατεῖν. He thinks the reading ἀκριβῶς πῶς was a correction on the part of those who, being familiar with ἀκ. βλέπειν, εἰδέναι, etc., were offended with ἀκρ. περιπατεῖν, which is, he says, most suitable to this place.

μὴ ὡς ἄσοφοι, explaining πῶς, and so dependent, like it, on βλέπετε, hence the subjective negation (Winer, § 55. 1). Then περιπατοῦντες need not be supplied.

16. ἐξαγοραζόμενοι τὸν καιρόν. "Seizing the opportunity," "making your market to the full from the opportunity of this life" (Ramsay, *St. Paul as Traveller*, etc., p. 149). The same expression is used in Col. iv. 5 with special reference to conduct towards those outside the Church, ἐν σοφίᾳ περιπατεῖτε πρὸς τοὺς ἔξω. τὸν κ. ἐξαγ. Lit. "buying up for yourselves," ἐξ being intensive, and corresponding to our "up." καιρὸν ὑμεῖς ἀγοράζετε occurs Dan. ii. 8, but in a different sense, viz. "wish to gain time." More parallel as to sense is κερδαντέον τὸ παρόν, Antonin. vi. 26. ἐξαγοράζω, in the sense "buy up," is found in Polyb. iii. 42. 2, ἐξηγόρασε παρ' αὐτῶν τά τε μονόξυλα πλοῖα πάντα, κ.τ.λ. In *Mart. Polyc.* 2 it has the wholly different sense: "buy off," διὰ μιᾶς ὥρας τὴν αἰώνιον κόλασιν ἐξαγοραζόμενοι. Chrysostom says the expression is obscure, and he illustrates it by the case of robbers entering a rich man's house to kill him, and when he gives much to purchase his life, we say that he ἐξηγόρασεν ἑαυτόν. So, he proceeds, "thou hast a great house, and true faith; they come on thee to take all; give whatever one asks, only save τὸ κεφάλαιον, that is τὴν πίστιν." This completely ignores τὸν καιρόν. Occum. is more to the point: ὁ κ. οὐκ ἔστιν ἡμῖν βέβαιος ... ἀγόρασον οὖν αὐτὸν καὶ ποίησον ἴδιον. So Theodore Mops., and so Severianus in *Catena*, adding that "the present opportunity δουλεύει τοῖς πονηροῖς, buy it up, therefore, so as to use it for piety." But it is futile to press the idea of "purchasing," or the force of ἐξ, so as to inquire from whom the opportunity is to be bought, as "from evil men" (Bengel, cf. Severianus, above), "the devil," Calvin; or what price is to be paid (τὰ πάντα, Chrys.). The price is the pains and effort required.

ὅτι αἱ ἡμέραι πονηραί εἰσιν. So that it is the more necessary τὸν καιρὸν ἐξαγ. The moments for sowing on receptive soil in such evil days being few, seize them when they offer themselves. πονηραί is "morally evil," not "distressful" (Beza, Hammond, etc.),—an idea foreign to the context, which contrasts the walk of the Christians with that of the heathen.

17. διὰ τοῦτο. Viz. because it is necessary to walk ἀκριβῶς. εἰ γὰρ ἔσεσθε ἄφρονες ἀκριβῶς οὐ περιπατήσετε, Schol. ap. Cat. Not "because the days are evil," which was only mentioned in support of ἐξαγ. τὸν καιρόν.

μὴ γίνεσθε ἄφρονες. "Do not show yourselves senseless." ἄφρων differs from ἄσοφος as referring rather to imprudence or folly in action.

ἀλλὰ συνίετε. So ℵ A B P 17, 67², etc. Rec. has συνιέντες, with Dᶜ E K L and most mss., It. Vulg. Syr-Pesh.; while D* G have συνίοντες, which Meyer, with little reason, prefers as the less usual form.

Somewhat stronger than γινώσκετε, "understand." τί τὸ θέλημα, cf. ver. 10.

18. καὶ μὴ μεθύσκεσθε οἴνῳ. καί marks a transition from the general to the particular, as in εἴπατε τοῖς μαθηταῖς αὐτοῦ καὶ τῷ Πέτρῳ, Mark xvi. 7; πᾶσα ἡ Ἰουδαία χώρα, καὶ οἱ Ἰεροσολυμῖται,

Mark i. 5. Fritzsche, in the latter place, remarks that καί in these instances is not = "imprimis," but "scriptores rem singularem jam comprehensam communiori propterea insuper adjiciunt copulae adjumento, quod illam tanquam gravem impensius inculcatam volunt lectori."

It is out of the question to suppose any reference here to such abuses as are mentioned in 1 Cor. xi., which would have called for a more explicit censure.

ἐν ᾧ ἐστιν ἀσωτία. ἐν ᾧ, not οἴνῳ, but μεθύσκεσθαι οἴνῳ. ἀσωτία, "a word in which heathen ethics said much more than they intended or knew," Trench. It is the character of the ἄσωτος "perditus," thus defined by Aristotle: τοὺς ἀκρατεῖς καὶ εἰς ἀκολασίαν δαπανηροὺς ἀσώτους καλοῦμεν (*Eth. Nic.* iv. 1). In classical authors the adjective varies in sense between "lost" and "prodigal," the latter, "qui servare nequit," being the more common. The substantive occurs also Tit. i. 6; 1 Pet. iv. 4; and the adverb Luke xv. 13, where see note. The Vulg. renders by "luxuria, luxuriose," words which in later Latin acquired the sense of profligate living. In mediæval Latin "luxuria" = "lasciviousness." But the meaning in the N.T. is clearly "dissoluteness." The remark of Clem. Alex., τὸ ἄσωστον τῆς μέθης διὰ τῆς ἀσωτίας αἰνιξάμενος, was natural to a Christian writer accustomed to the technical use of σώζειν, but no such idea seems implied in the use of the word in N.T. ἄσωτος is not derived from σώζω, but from σόω (Hom. *Il.* ix. 393, 424, 681).

ἀλλὰ πληροῦσθε ἐν πνεύματι. The antithesis is not directly between οἶνος and πνεῦμα, as the order of the words shows, but between the two states. Meyer remarks that the imperative passive is explained by the possibility of resistance; but what other form could be employed? The signification is middle, for they must co-operate. The present tense cannot very well be expressed in the English rendering; "be filled" is after all better than "become filled," which would suggest that the filling had yet to begin. ἐν πνεύματι is usually understood of the Holy Spirit, ἐν being instrumental (Meyer), or both instrumental and expressing the content of the filling (Ellicott, Macpherson, *al.*). But the use of ἐν with πληρόω to express the content with which a thing is filled would be quite unexampled. Phil. iv. 19 is not parallel (Ellicott admits it to be doubtful); still less Col. ii. 10, iv. 12 (where, moreover, the true reading is πεπληροφορημένοι). Plutarch's ἐπεπλήρωτο ἐν μακαριότητι (*Plac. Phil.* i. 7. 9) is not parallel; the words there (which are used of the Deity) mean "is complete in blessedness," the alternative being "something is wanting to Him." Meyer, indeed, says that as St. Paul uses genitive, dative, and accusative (Col. i. 9) with πληρόω, we cannot be surprised at his using ἐν,—a singular argument. The genitive and dative are both classical; the accusative in Col. i. 9 is not accusative of material. But such variety in no way justifies the use of ἐν, the meaning of which is wholly unsuitable to the idea "filled with." The nearest approach to this would be the instrumental sense (adopted by Meyer, *al.*, in i. 23). Where the material is only regarded as the means of making full, it may conceivably be spoken of as an instrument; but this would require the agent to be expressed, and, besides, would be quite inappropriate to the Holy Spirit. For these reasons the rendering mentioned in the margin RV. (Braune's also) is not to be hastily rejected. "Be filled in spirit," not in your carnal part, but in your spiritual. Alford attempts to combine both ideas, "let this be the region in, and the ingredient with which you are filled," πνεῦμα being the Christian's "own spirit dwelt in and informed by the Holy Spirit of God." This seems an impossible combination, or rather confusion of two distinct ideas. Macpherson, in order to secure a contrast between the "stimulation of much wine and the stimulation of a large measure of the Spirit," represents the apostle as saying, "conduct yourselves like those that are possessed, but see to it that the influence constraining you is that of the Holy Spirit." It is hardly too much to say that this is a *reductio ad absurdum* of the supposed antithesis. There is nothing about excitement, nor does St. Paul anywhere sanction such conduct.

19. λαλοῦντες ἑαυτοῖς. On ἑαυτοῖς = ἀλλήλοις, see iv. 32. Not "to yourselves," AV.; "meditantes vobiscum," Michaelis. Compare Pliny's description, "carmen Christo quasi Deo dicere secum invicem" (ἑαυτοῖς) (*Epp.* x. 97). But the reference cannot be specially to religious services, as the context shows; cf. Col. iii. 16.

ψαλμοῖς καὶ ὕμνοις καὶ ᾠδαῖς πνευματικαῖς = Col. iii. 16, except that the copulas are there wanting. The distinction between these words is not quite agreed upon. ψαλμός from ψάλλειν, primarily the plucking of the strings, is used by classical authors to mean the sound of the harp, and hence any strain of music. The Schol. on Aristoph. *Aves,* 218, says: ψαλμὸς κυρίως, ὁ τῆς κιθάρας ἦχος. Cyrilli *Lex.* and Basil on Ps. xxix. define it: λόγος μουσικός, ὅταν εὐρύθμως κατὰ τοὺς ἁρμονικοὺς λόγους πρὸς τὸ ὄργανον κρούεται. And to the same effect Greg. Nyss. It occurs frequently in the Sept., not always of sacred music, *e.g.* 1 Sam. xvi. 18 of young David, εἰδότα τὸν ψαλμόν, *i.e.* playing on the harp.

ὕμνος is properly a song of praise of some god or hero. Arrian says: ὕμνοι μὲν ἐς τοὺς θεοὺς ποιοῦνται, ἔπαινοι δὲ ἐς ἀνθρώπους (*Exped. Alex.* iv. 11. 3). Augustine's definition is well known: "Oportet ut, si sit hymnus, habeat haec tria, et laudem, et Dei, et canticum." Hence ὑμνεῖν, to praise by a hymn.

ᾠδή, from ἀείδω, ᾄδω, seems to have originally meant any kind of song, but was specially used of lyric poetry. It is frequently used in Sept. (Ex. xv. 1; Deut. xxxi. 19–22; Judg. v. 1, 12, etc.).

πνευματικαῖς is omitted by B d e, and bracketed by Lachmann. Not only is it attested by superabundant authority, but it seems essential as a further definition of the preceding word or words. Probably it is to be taken (as by Hofmann and Soden) with all three. ἐν is prefixed to ψαλμοῖς in B P 17 67², Vulg., Jerome, and admitted to the margin by WH. After πνευμ. A adds ἐν χάριτι, clearly from Col. iii. 16.

ᾄδοντες καὶ ψάλλοντες τῇ καρδίᾳ ὑμῶν τῷ Κυρίῳ.

Rec. has ἐν before τῇ κ., with K L most mss., Syr-Harcl. Arm., while Lachm. reads ἐν ταῖς καρδίαις, with №° A D G P, It. Vulg. Boh. Syr-Pesh. Harcl. *mg.* But ℵ* B have the singular without ἐν, and so Origen. In Col. iii. 16 all MSS. have ἐν, and most MSS. and Vss. the plural, D° K L reading the singular.

Chrysostom interprets ἐν τῇ καρδίᾳ as meaning "heartily or sincerely"; μετὰ συνέσεως προσέχοντες, *i.e.* from the heart, not merely with the mouth. But this would be ἐκ τῆς καρδίας without ὑμῶν.

20. εὐχαριστοῦντες πάντοτε ὑπὲρ πάντων. "Even," says Chrysostom, "if it be disease or poverty. It is nothing great or wonderful if when prosperous you give thanks. What is sought is that when in affliction you do so. Nay, why speak of afflictions here? we must thank God for hell," explaining that we who attend are much benefited by the fear of hell, which is placed as a bridle upon us: a profoundly selfish view, to which he was no doubt led only by the wish to give the fullest meaning to πάντων. Jerome is more sober: "Christianorum virtus est, etiam in his quae adversa putantur, referre gratias creatori." But St. Paul is not specially referring to adversity; on the contrary, the context shows that what he had particularly in his mind was occasion of rejoicing. Theodoret, however, takes πάντων as masc., that we must thank God for others who have received Divine blessing. But there is nothing in the context to favour this.

ἐν ὀνόματι τοῦ Κυρίου ἡμῶν Ἰησοῦ Χριστοῦ. When I speak of doing something in the name of another, this may mean either that I do it as representing him, that is, by his authority, or if the action is entirely my own, that I place its significance only in its reference to him. When an apostle commands in the name of Christ, this is in the former sense; when I pray or give thanks in the same name, it is as His disciple and dependent on Him.

τῷ Θεῷ καὶ Πατρί, see i. 3. There is no need to refer πατρί here to Christ; the article rather leads to the sense, "God, who is also the Father," namely, of us.

21. ὑποτασσόμενοι ἀλλήλοις ἐν φόβῳ Χριστοῦ.

Χριστοῦ with ℵ A B L P, Vulg. Syr. (both) Boh. etc. Θεοῦ of Rec. is in most cursives, and D has Χριστοῦ Ἰησοῦ; G,' Ἰησοῦ Χριστοῦ. As φόβος Χριστοῦ is not found elsewhere, copyists naturally wrote φόβος Θεοῦ, which was familiar.

"In the fear of Christ," *i.e.* with reference for Him as the guiding motive.

"Submitting yourselves." The connexion of this with the preceding seems rather loose. Ellicott says: "the first three [clauses] name three duties, more or less specially in regard to *God*, the last a comprehensive moral duty in regard to *man*," suggested by the thought of the humble and loving spirit which is the principle of εὐχαριστία. This does not meet the difficulty of the connexion. Alford refers back to μὴ μεθύσκ., "not blustering, but being subject," and Eadie is inclined to the same view; but this is forced, and requires us to interpolate something which is not indicated by anything in the text. Much the same may be said of Findlay's view. He illustrates by reference to the confusion in the Church meetings in the Corinthian Church (1 Cor. xiv. 26-34), "when he urges the Asian Christians to seek the full inspiration of the Spirit, and to give free utterance in song to the impulses of their new life, he adds this word of caution." This supplies too much, and besides, ὑποτασσόμενοι would be an unsuitable word to express such readiness to give way in the matter of prophesying as St. Paul directs in 1 Cor. Bloomfield, taking a similar view, supposes that what is insisted on is subordination to a leading authority. This preserves the sense of ὑποτ., but not of ἀλλήλοις. Blaikie refers back to ver. 15.

In considering the connexion it must be borne in mind that ὑποτάσσεσθε in the next verse is in all probability not genuine, so that the verb has to be supplied from ὑποτασσόμενοι. There is therefore no break between *vv.* 21 and 22. Further, the whole following section, which is not a mere digression, depends on the thought expressed in this clause of which it is a development. To suppose a direct connexion with πληροῦσθε ἐν πν. does not yield a suitable sense. The connexion with the preceding context is, in fact, only in form, that with what follows is in substance. From iv. 32 we have a series of precepts expressed in imperatives and participles depending on γίνεσθε, περιπατεῖτε; δοκιμάζοντες, ἐξαγοραζόμενοι, λαλοῦντες. Ver. 18 interrupts the series by a direct imperative, as in *vv.* 3 ff., 12 ff. St. Paul elsewhere (Rom. xii. 9) carries on in participles a series of precepts begun in a different construction, ἀποστυγοῦντες τὸ πονηρόν, κ.τ.λ. It is therefore quite natural that here, where the participles λαλοῦντες, εὐχαρ., though not put for imperatives, yet from their connexion involve a command, he should make the transition to the new section easy by continuing to use the participle. Comp. 1 Pet. ii. 18, iii. 1. Meyer admits that it is no objection to this that in what follows we have only the ὑπόταξις of the wives, while the ὑπακοή of the children and servants in ch. vi. cannot be connected with ὑποτασσ.; for in classical writers also, after the prefixing of such absolute nominatives which refer collectively to the whole, often the discourse passes over to one part only. But he thinks that in that case αἱ γυναῖκες would necessarily have a special verb correlative with ὑποτ. It is not easy to see the force of this.

22-33. *Special injunctions to husbands and wives. Wives to be subject to their husbands, husbands to love their wives. This relationship is illustrated by that of Christ and the Church. As Christ is the Head of the Church, which is subject to Christ, so the husband is the head of the wife, who is to be subject to the husband; and Christ's love for the Church is to be the pattern of the man's love for his wife. The analogy, indeed, is not perfect, for Christ is not only the Head of the Church which is His body, but is also the Saviour of it; but this does not affect the purpose of the comparison here.*

22. αἱ γυναῖκες τοῖς ἰδίοις ἀνδράσιν ὡς τῷ Κυρίῳ. So without a verb B, Clement (when citing *vv.* 21-25), Jerome's Greek MSS. His note is, "Hoc quod in Latinis exemplaribus additum est: *subditae sint*, in Graecis Codd. non habetur." ὑποτασσέσθωσαν is added after ἀνδράσιν in ℵ A P 17 *al.* Vulg. Goth. Arm. Boh. etc., and Clement (when citing ver. 22 only). ὑποτάσσεσθε in K L most mss., Syr. (both), Chrys. D G also have ὑποτάσσεσθε, but after γυναῖκες. Lachmann adopted ὑποτασσέσθωσαν, but later critical editors read without the verb. The testimony of Jerome, who knew of no Greek MSS. with the verb, is very important. No reason can be imagined for its omission if it had been in the text originally, whereas the reason for its insertion is obvious, and was stated even by Erasmus: "adjectum, ut apparet, quo et sensus sit lucidior, et capitulum hoc separatim legi queat, si res ita postulet." The latter reason is particularly to be noted. The diversity in the MSS. which have the verb is also of weight. The shorter reading agrees well with the succinct style of St. Paul in his practical admonitions.

ἰδίοις is more than a mere possessive, yet does not imply an antithesis to "other men"; it seems rather to emphasise the relationship, as in the passage quoted from Stobaeus by Harless (*Floril.* p. 22): Θεανὼ ἡ Πυθαγορικὴ φιλόσοφος ἐρωτηθεῖσα τί πρῶτον εἴη γυναικὶ τὸ τῷ ἰδίῳ, ἔφη, ἀρέσκειν ἀνδρί. Compare also *Acta Thomae*, p. 24 (ed. Thilo): οὕτως εἰ ὡς πολὺν χρόνον συμβιώσασα τῷ ἰδίῳ ἀνδρί. That the word was not required to prevent misconception of ἀνδράσι is shown by its absence in the parallel, Col. iii. 18.

ὡς τῷ Κυρίῳ, not "as to their lord," which would have been expressed in the plural, but "as to the Lord Christ," "as" not meaning in the same manner as, but expressing the view they are to take of their submission; compare vi. 6, 7. "*Subjectio* quae ab uxore praestatur viro simul praestatur ipsi Domino, Christo," Bengel. So Chrysostom: ὅταν ὑπείκῃς τῷ ἀνδρί, ὡς τῷ Κυρίῳ δουλεύουσα ἡγοῦ πείθεσθαι.

23. ὅτι ἀνήρ ἐστι κεφαλὴ τῆς γυναικός. Assigns the reason of ὡς τῷ Κυρίῳ. The article before ἀνήρ in Rec. has no uncial authority in its favour. "A husband is head of his wife."

ὡς καί, "as also." Compare 1 Cor. xi. 3, παντὸς ἀνδρὸς ἡ κεφαλὴ ὁ Χριστός ἐστι, κεφαλὴ δὲ γυναικὸς ὁ ἀνήρ, κεφαλὴ δὲ τοῦ Χριστοῦ ὁ Θεός.

ὁ Χριστὸς κεφαλὴ τῆς ἐκκλησίας αὐτὸς σωτὴρ τοῦ σώματος.

<small>Rec. has καὶ αὐτός ἐστι σ., with א^c D^{bc} K L P most mss., Syr. (both) Arm. But the shorter reading is that of א* A B D* G, Vulg. The added words are an obvious gloss. Boh. has ἐστι without καί, and Aeth. καί without ἐστι.</small>

The apostle having compared the headship of the husband to that of Christ, could not fail to think how imperfect the analogy was; he therefore emphatically calls attention to the point of difference; as if he would say: " A man is the head of his wife, even as Christ also is head of the Church, although there is a vast difference, since He is Himself the Saviour of the body, of which He is the head; but notwithstanding this difference," etc. Calvin already proposed this view: " Habet quidem id peculiare Christus, quod est servator ecclesiae; nihilominus sciant mulieres, sibi maritos praeesse, Christi exemplo, utcunque pari gratia non polleant." So Bengel concisely: "Vir autem non est servator uxoris; in eo Christus excellit; hinc *sed* sequitur." Chrys. Theoph. and Oecum., however, interpret this clause as equally applicable to the husband. καὶ γὰρ ἡ κεφαλὴ τοῦ σώματος σωτηρία ἐστίν, Chrys. And more fully Theoph.: ὥσπερ καὶ ὁ Χριστὸς τῆς ἐκκλησίας ὢν κεφαλή, προνοεῖται αὐτῆς καὶ σώζει· οὕτω τοίνυν καὶ ὁ ἀνήρ, σωτὴρ τοῦ σώματος αὐτοῦ, τουτέστι τῆς γυναικός. πῶς οὖν οὐκ ὀφείλει ὑποτάσσεσθαι τῇ κεφαλῇ τὸ σῶμα, τῇ προνοουμένῃ καὶ σωζούσῃ. So Hammond and many others. But αὐτός cannot refer to any subject but that which immediately precedes, viz. ὁ Χριστός. Moreover, to use σῶμα without some qualification for the wife would be unintelligible; nor is σωτήρ ever used in the N.T. except of Christ or God.

24. ἀλλὰ ὡς ἡ ἐκκλησία ὑποτάσσεται τῷ Χριστῷ, οὕτως καὶ αἱ γυναῖκες τοῖς ἀνδράσιν. There is much difference of opinion as to the force to be assigned to ἀλλά. Olshausen takes it as introducing the proof drawn from what precedes; and similarly De Wette, " But (aber) if the man is your head," a sense which ἀλλά (which is not = δέ) never has. Eadie gives the word "an antithetic reference," such as ἀλλά sometimes has after an implied negative. He interprets: "do not disallow the marital headship, for it is a divine institution,—ἀλλά,—but," etc. He refers for this use of ἀλλά to Luke vii. 7; John vii. 49; Rom. iii. 31, viii. 37; 1 Cor. vi. 8, ix. 12. The fact that in most of these cases we might not incorrectly render "Nay," or "Nay, on the contrary," shows how unlike the present passage they are. Nor are 2 Cor. viii. 7, xiii. 4; 1 Tim. i. 15, 16, or the other passages which he cites, at all parallel; and the negative to which he supposes ἀλλά to refer ("do not disallow," etc.) is not even hinted at in the text. His objection to the interpretation here adopted is that it sounds like a truism. Harless and others take ἀλλά to be simply resumptive; but the main thought has not been interrupted, and there is no reason for rejecting its adversative force. Hofmann, like Eadie, reads into the text an objection which ἀλλά repels, "but even where the husband is not this (namely, a σωτὴρ τοῦ σ., making happy his wife, as Christ the Church), yet," etc. The view here preferred is adopted by Meyer, Alford, Ellicott, Braune, Moule, etc.

ἐν παντί. It is presupposed that the authority of the husband is in accordance with their relation as corresponding to that of Christ to the Church. "ὡς εὐσεβέσι νομοθετῶν προστέθεικε τὸ ἐν πάντι," Theodoret.

ὥσπερ of the Rec. is the reading of D⁽ᶜ⁾ K L and most mss.; but ὡς, ℵ A D* G P 17 67² etc. (B omits.)

ἰδίοις is prefixed to ἀνδράσιν by A D⁽ᶜ⁾ K L P, Vss., but om. by ℵ B D* G 17 67². It has clearly been introduced from ver. 22.

25. οἱ ἄνδρες, ἀγαπᾶτε τὰς γυναῖκας.

Rec. adds ἑαυτῶν, with D K L, Syr. etc.; but ℵ A B 17, Clem. (when giving the whole passage) omit. G adds ὑμῶν.

καθὼς καὶ ὁ Χριστός, κ.τ.λ. "Si omnia rhetorum argumenta in unum conjicias, non tam persuaseris conjugibus dilectionem mutuam quam hic Paulus" (Bugenhagen). Meyer also well observes: "It is impossible to conceive a more lofty, more ideal regulation of married life, and yet flowing immediately from the living depth of the Christian consciousness, and, therefore, capable of practicable application to all concrete relations." Chrysostom's comment is very fine: "Hast thou seen the measure of obedience? hear also the measure of love. Wouldst thou that thy wife should obey thee as the Church doth Christ? have care thyself for her, as Christ for the Church; and if it should be needful that thou shouldest give thy life for her, or be cut to pieces a thousand times, or endure anything whatever, refuse it not; yea, if thou hast suffered this thou hast not done what Christ did, for thou doest this for one to whom thou wert already united, but He for her who rejected Him and hated Him . . . He brought her to His feet by His great care, not by threats nor fear nor any such thing; so do thou conduct thyself towards thy wife."

26. ἵνα αὐτὴν ἁγιάσῃ καθαρίσας τῷ λουτρῷ τοῦ ὕδατος ἐν ῥήματι.

The immediate purpose of ἑαυτὸν παρέδωκεν, ver. 25. ἁγιάσῃ is clearly not to be limited to "consecration"; it includes the actual sanctification or infusion of holiness. It is the positive side, καθαρίσας expressing the negative, the purification from her former sins. But as the remoter object is ἵνα παραστήσῃ, the ceremonial idea of ἁγιάζειν appears to be the prominent one here. Logically, καθαρίζειν precedes ἁγιάζειν, chronologically they are coincident; cf. 1 Cor. vi. 11, ἀλλὰ ἀπελούσασθε, ἀλλὰ ἡγιάσθητε. The tense of καθαρίσας by no means requires the translation "after He had purified" (cf. i. 9), which would probably have been expressed by a passive participle agreeing with αὐτήν, indeed καθαρίζων would have been quite inappropriate.

τῷ λουτρῷ τ. ὔ. "By the bath of water," distinctly referring to baptism, and probably with an allusion in λουτρῷ to the usual bath of the bride before the marriage; the figure in the immediate context being that of marriage.

ἐν ῥήματι. The first question is as to the connexion. By Augustine the phrase is supposed to qualify τῷ λουτρῷ τοῦ ὔδ., "accedit verbum ad elementum et fit sacramentum."

But as the combination is strange, and neither τὸ λουτρόν nor τὸ ὕδωρ can form with ἐν ῥήματι a single notion (like ἡ πίστις ἐν Χρ.), this would require the article to be repeated. The interpretation, "the bath resting on a command" (Storr, Peile, Klöpper), would require ἐν ῥ. Χριστοῦ. Meyer, following Jerome, connects the words with ἁγιάσῃ, "having purified with the bath of water, may sanctify her by the word." The order of the words is strongly against this, and, besides, we should expect some addition to καθαρ., which should suggest the spiritual signification of "purifying with water."

It is therefore best connected with καθαρίσας. But as to the meaning? Alford, Eadie, Ellicott, Meyer take ῥῆμα to mean the gospel or preached word taught preliminary to baptism. ῥῆμα is, no doubt, used in this sense (not in Acts x. 37 but) Rom. x. 17, ῥῆμα Χριστοῦ; but there it is defined by Χριστοῦ, as in ver. 8 by τῆς πίστεως; indeed, ῥῆμα is there used, not because of any special appropriateness, but for the sake of the quotation. Elsewhere we have ῥῆμα Θεοῦ, Eph. vi. 17. It is far, indeed, from being correct to say that "the gospel" is "the usual meaning of the Greek term," as Eadie states, referring, in addition to the passages mentioned above, to Heb. vi. 5 (where the words are Θεοῦ ῥῆμα): Acts x. 44, τὰ ῥήματα ταῦτα: xi. 14, λαλήσει ῥήματα πρός σε. In these last two places it is obvious that ῥήματα means simply "words" or "sayings," as in Acts xxvi. 25, where St. Paul says of his speech before Festus, ἀληθείας καὶ σωφροσύνης ῥήματα ἀποφθέγγομαι. See also Acts ii. 14, ἐνωτίσασθε τὰ ῥήματά μου. Needless to say that ῥῆμα is used of single sayings very frequently. There may be even πονηρὸν ῥῆμα or ἀργὸν ῥῆμα (not to mention cases where ῥῆμα is used for "a thing mentioned": see on Luke i. 65). That the word is most frequently used, not to signify a Divine or sacred saying, but where the connexion implies such a saying, is simply a result of the fact that there was little occasion (in the Epp. none) to refer to other ῥήματα. There is no example of ῥῆμα by itself meaning "the gospel" or anything like this. Had it the article here, indeed, there would be good reason for maintaining this interpretation.

The Greek commentators understand ῥῆμα of the formula of baptism. ποίῳ; says Chrysostom, ἐν ὀνόματι τοῦ Πατρὸς καὶ τοῦ Υἱοῦ καὶ τοῦ ἁγίου Πνεύματος. It is true, as Estius remarks, that if this were the sense we should expect καὶ ῥήματος; and Harless adds that these definite words could hardly be referred to except with the article, τῷ ῥήματι. But although "of water and ῥῆμα" might, perhaps, have been expected, ἐν is quite admissible; compare ἐν ἐπαγγελίᾳ, vi. 2. The objections from the absence of the article, and from the fact that ῥῆμα has not elsewhere this meaning, fall to the ground when we consider that it is not alleged or supposed that ῥῆμα of itself means the formula of baptism; it retains its indefinite meaning, and it is only the connexion with the reference to baptism in the preceding words that defines what ῥῆμα is intended. So Soden. Moule renders, "attended by, or conditioned by, an utterance," which would agree well with this interpretation. He explains it as "the revelation of salvation embodied in the name of the Father, the Son, and Holy Ghost." Macpherson denies the reference to baptism, and thinks it more natural to speak of the cleansing as effected by the bathing ("washing," AV.) rather than in the bath, especially as "of water" is added. "The reference is most probably to the bath of the bride before marriage." Yes, such a reference there is; but what is it which the reader is expected to compare with the bridal bath? As there is no particle of comparison, the words imply that there is a λουτρὸν ὕδατος, which is compared to the bath. And surely baptism could not fail to be suggested by these words to the original readers. As to λουτρόν, besides the meaning "water for bathing," it has the two senses of the English "bath," viz. the place for bathing and the action; but it does not mean "washing."

27. ἵνα παραστήσῃ αὐτὸς ἑαυτῷ, κ.τ.λ. The remoter object of παρέδωκεν depending on ἁγιάσῃ, etc. The verb is used, as in 2 Cor. xi. 2, of the presentation of the bride to the bridegroom, παρθένον ἁγνὴν παραστῆσαι τῷ Χριστῷ. The interpretation, "present as an offering" (Harless), is opposed to the context as well as inconsistent with ἑαυτῷ. αὐτός is the correct reading, and emphasises the fact that it is Christ who, as He gave Himself to sanctify the Church, also presents her to Himself. This presenta-

tion is not complete in this life, yet Bengel correctly says: "id valet suo modo jam de hac vita."

αὐτός is the reading of ℵ A B D* G L, Vulg. Syr-Harcl. etc. The Rec. has αὐτήν, with D^c K most mss., Syr-Pesh., Chrys. The latter is the reading which would most readily occur to the copyist; no copyist would be likely to depart from it if he had it before him, but αὐτός has a peculiar emphasis.

ἔνδοξον τὴν ἐκκλησίαν. The tertiary predicate ἔνδοξον is placed with emphasis before its substantive. Not "a glorious Church," but "the Church, glorious," "that He might present the Church to Himself, glorious."

μὴ ἔχουσαν σπίλον. σπίλος, which also occurs 2 Pet. ii. 13, is a word of later Greek (Plutarch, etc.) for κηλίς; ἄσπιλος occurs four times in N.T.

ἀλλ' ἵνα ᾖ. Changed structure, as if ἵνα μὴ ἔχῃ had preceded; compare ver. 33.

28. οὕτως is connected by Estius and Alford with ὡς following: "So ... as." This is not forbidden by grammatical considerations; for in spite of Hermann's rule, that the force of οὕτως is "ut eo confirmentur *praecedentia*," it is used with reference to what follows, introduced by ὡς or ὥσπερ, both in classical writers and in N.T. Compare τοὺς οὕτως ἐπισταμένους εἰπεῖν ὡς οὐδεὶς ἂν ἄλλος δύναιτο (Isocr. ap. Rost and Palm. ἔστιν γὰρ οὕτως ὥσπερ οὗτος ἐννέπει, Soph. *Trach*. 475, is not a good instance, for οὕτως may very well be referred to what precedes). And in N.T. 1 Cor. iii. 15, οὕτω δὲ ὡς διὰ πυρός: cf. iv. 1. But in such cases οὕτως has some emphasis on it, and apart from that it yields a better sense here to take οὕτως as referring to the preceding statement of Christ's love for the Church. "Even so ought husbands ..." If καί is read before οἱ ἄνδρες, as Treg. WH. and RV., the latter view is alone possible.

The position of ὀφείλουσιν varies in the MSS. ℵ^b K L 17 and most have it before οἱ ἄνδρες, A D G P after. The latter group add καί before οἱ ἄνδρες, and of the former group B 17. As the position of the verb would hardly be a reason for inserting καί, it may be presumed to be genuine.

ὡς τὰ ἑαυτῶν σώματα. The sense just ascertained for οὕτως determines this to mean "as being their own bodies"; and this agrees perfectly with what follows: "he that loveth his own wife loveth himself." Moreover, although we speak of a man's love for himself, we do not speak of him as loving his body or having an "affection" for it (Alford); and to compare a man's love for his wife to his love (?) for his "body," would be to suggest a degrading view of the wife, as, indeed, Grotius does, saying: "sicut corpus instrumentum animi, ita uxor instrumentum viri ad res domesticos, ad quaerendos liberos." Plutarch comes nearer to the apostle's view: κρατεῖν δεῖ τὸν ἄνδρα τῆς γυναικός, οὐχ ὡς δεσπότην κτήματος, ἀλλ' ὡς ψυχὴν σώματος, συμπαθοῦντα καὶ συμπεφυκότα τῇ εὐνοίᾳ. ὥσπερ οὖν σώματός ἐστι κήδεσθαι μὴ δουλεύοντα ταῖς ἡδοναῖς αὐτοῦ καὶ ταῖς ἐπιθυμίαις· οὕτω γυναικὸς ἄρχειν εὐφραίνοντα καὶ χαριζόμενον (*Conj. Praec.* p. 422, quoted by Harless). The meaning is, Even as Christ loved the Church as that which is His body, so also should husbands regard their wives as their own bodies, and love them as Christ did the Church.

ὁ ἀγαπῶν τὴν ἑαυτοῦ γυναῖκα ἑαυτὸν ἀγαπᾷ. This is neither identical with the preceding nor an inference from it, but rather an explanation of ὡς τὰ ἑαυτῶν σώματα. If the latter words meant, "as they do their own bodies," they would fall immeasurably short of this. It is, however, going beyond the bounds of psychological truth to say that a man's love for his wife is but "complying with the universal law of nature by which we all love ourselves," or that it "is in fact self-love," whether "a hallowed phasis" of it or not. If it were so, there would be no need to enforce it by precept. Although the husband's love for his wife may be compared to what is called his love for himself, inasmuch as it leads him to regard her welfare as his own, and to feel all that concerns her as if it concerned himself, the two mental facts are entirely different in their essence. There is no emotion in self-love; it is the product of reason, not of feeling; and it is a "law" of man's nature, not in the sense of obligation (although there is a certain obligation belonging to it), but in the sense that it necessarily belongs to a rational nature. The basis of conjugal love is wholly different, and is to be found, not in the rational part of man's nature, but in the affections. The love is reinforced by reflection, and made firm by the sense of duty; but it can never become a merely rational regard for another's happiness, as "self-love" is for one's own.

To refer to the stirring remarks of Chrysostom above cited, when a man gives his life for his wife, is that an exercise of "self-love"? Surely no more than when a mother gives her life for her child. There is none of this false philosophy in the language of St. Paul.

29. τὴν ἑαυτοῦ σάρκα. The word is, no doubt, chosen with reference to the σὰρξ μία, quoted ver. 31. It is not perhaps correct, however, to say that it is so chosen instead of σῶμα, for it is hardly probable that the apostle would have used σῶμα in this connexion in any case. Rather, the whole sentence is suggested by the thought of σὰρξ μία.

30. ὅτι μέλη ἐσμὲν τοῦ σώματος αὐτοῦ. Rec. adds ἐκ τῆς σαρκὸς αὐτοῦ καὶ ἐκ τῶν ὀστέων αὐτοῦ.

For the insertion are ℵ° D G L P (K has τοῦ σώματος for τῶν ὀστέων) nearly all cursive mss., It. Vulg. Syr. (both) Arm., Iren. Jerome, etc.

For the omission ℵ* A B 17 67², Boh. Eth., Method. Euthal. Ambrst. and apparently Origen.

It will be seen that the MSS. which omit decidedly outweigh those that insert. Ellicott speaks of the testimony of ℵ as "divided," which seems a singular way of neutralising the evidence of the earlier scribe by that of a seventh-century corrector.

It is an obvious suggestion that the words might have been omitted by homoeoteleuton. Reiche, who accepted the words (writing before the discovery of ℵ), rightly observes that this can hardly be admitted in the case of so many witnesses. He prefers to suppose that they were omitted in consequence of offence being taken at the apparently material conception presented; and some other critics have adopted the same view. The objection must have been very strong which would lead to such a deliberate omission. But there is no reason to suppose that the words would have given offence, especially considering such words as "a spirit hath not flesh and bones as ye see Me have," not to mention "eating My flesh and drinking My blood." Nor do the ancient commentators indicate that any such difficulty was felt. Irenaeus, after quoting the words, adds: "non de spirituali aliquo et invisibili homine dicens haec; spiritus enim neque ossa neque carnes habet," etc. Indeed, an ancient reader would be much more likely to regard the words as a natural expansion of μέλη τοῦ σώματος αὐτοῦ. On the other hand, nothing was more likely than that the words should be added from recollection of the passage in Genesis, quoted in ver. 31. It is objected to this, that the words are not quoted with exactness, "bone" preceding "flesh" in Gen. This is to assume an exactness of memory which is at least questionable. Once added, the ordinary copyist would, of course, prefer the longer text.

As to the internal evidence, on careful consideration it will be found strongly in favour of the shorter text. When Christ is called the Head or Foundation, and the Church the Body or House, the language is that of analogy, i.e. it suggests, not resemblance of the objects, but of relations; Christ in Himself does not resemble a Head or a Foundation-stone, but His relation to the Church resembles the relation of the head to the body and of the foundation-stone to the building. But what relation is suggested by the bones of Christ? Or if σώματος be understood of the figurative or mystical body, what conceivable meaning can be attached to the bones thereof? This fundamental difficulty is not faced by any commentator. While trying to attach some meaning to the clause, they do not attempt to show any appropriateness in the language. The utmost that could be said is that the words express an intimate connexion; but unless this was a proverbial form of expression, of which there is no evidence, this, besides losing the force of ἐκ, would leave the difficulty unsolved. Moreover, the clause is so far from carrying out the μέλη τοῦ σ., that it introduces an entirely different figure. This is disguised in the AV.

Had the words been "of His flesh and of His blood," we might have understood them as alluding to the Eucharist; and it is worth noting that several expositors have supposed that there is such an allusion; but the mention of "flesh and bones" instead of "flesh and blood" is fatal to this.

The reader may desire to know how the omitted clause has been interpreted. Chrysostom, in the first instance, explains it of the incarnation, by which, however, Christ might rather be said to be "from our flesh." It is no answer to this to say, with Estius, "in hac natura ipse caput est," which is to change the figure.

Besides, it is true of all men, not only of Christians, that in this sense they are of the same flesh as Christ; but this again is not the meaning of ἐκ. Alford says: "As the woman owed her natural being to the man, her source and head, so we owe our spiritual being to Christ, our Source and Head"; and similarly Ellicott, Meyer, etc. Surely a strange way of saying that our spiritual being is derived from Christ, to say that we are from His bones! Others, as above mentioned, interpret of communion in the Eucharist (so in part Theodoret and Theophylact, also Harless and Olshausen).

Not without reason did Rückert come to the conclusion that it was doubtful whether St. Paul had any definite meaning in the words at all.

31. ἀντὶ τούτου = ἕνεκεν τούτου. Compare the use of ἀντί in ἀνθ' ὧν. Then the sense will be: because a man is to love his wife as Christ the Church. V. Soden, however, takes ἀντὶ τούτου to mean "instead of this," viz. instead of hating (ver. 29), observing that the conclusion of this verse returns to the main idea there, i.e. ἡ ἑαυτοῦ σάρξ. See on Lk. xii. 3.

καταλείψει ἄνθρωπος, κ.τ.λ. A quotation from Gen. ii. 24, which might have been introduced by "as it is written"; but with words so familiar this was needless.

Most commentators interpret this verse of Christ, either primarily or secondarily. So Jerome: "primus vates Adam hoc de Christo et ecclesia prophetavit; quod reliquerit Dominus noster atque Salvator patrem suum Deum et matrem suam coelestem Jerusalem." So many moderns, including Alford, Ellicott, Meyer, the last mentioned, however, referring the words to the Second Coming, the tense being future. Ellicott thinks this is pressing the tense unnecessarily, whereas it may have the ethical force of the future, for which he refers to Winer, § 40. 6, whose examples are wholly irrelevant to Ellicott's purpose. If the passage is interpreted of Christ it refers to a definite fact, and the future must have its future sense. Understood of Christ, the expressions ἄνθρωπος for Christ, and "leave his father and mother," for "leave His seat in heaven," are so strange and so unlike anything else in St. Paul, that without an express intimation by the writer it is highly unreasonable so to interpret them. Can we imagine St. Paul writing, "Christ will leave His father and His mother and will cleave to His wife, the Church"? We might not be surprised at such an expression in a mystical writer of the Middle Ages, but we should certainly not recognise it as Pauline. It is, if possible, less likely that he should say the same thing, using ἄνθρωπος instead of Χριστός, and expect his readers to understand him. If the future is given its proper meaning, the expression "leaving His seat at the right hand of God" is inappropriate.

On the other hand, the whole passage treats of the duty of husbands, the reference to Christ and the Church being introduced only incidentally for the purpose of enforcing the practical lesson. It was, indeed, almost inevitable that where St. Paul was so full on the duty of the husband, he should refer to these words in Genesis in their proper original meaning. This meaning being so exactly adapted to enforce the practical precept, to take them otherwise, and to suppose that they are introduced allegorically, is to break the connexion, not to improve it.

There are some differences of reading. The articles before πατέρα and μητέρα are absent in B D* G, and are omitted by Lachm. and Treg., and bracketed by WH. Tischendorf omitted them in his 7th ed., but restored them in the 8th in consequence of the added evidence of ℵ. αὐτοῦ is added after πατέρα in ℵᶜ A Dᶜ K L P, Syr-Pesh. Boh. from LXX; not in ℵ* B D* G 17, Vulg. Arm. αὐτοῦ is added after μητέρα in P 47, Vss.

For πρὸς τὴν γυναῖκα, which is in ℵᶜ B Dᶜ K L, Orig., τῇ γυναικί is read by ℵ* A D* G. The readings in the Sept. also vary.

32. τὸ μυστήριον τοῦτο μέγα ἐστίν, ἐγὼ δὲ λέγω εἰς Χριστόν καὶ εἰς τὴν ἐκκλησίαν.

The second εἰς is om. by B K and some other authorities.

We must first determine the meaning of μυστήριον and of μέγα. On the former word see on i. 9. It does not mean "a mysterious thing or saying," "a saying of which the meaning is hidden or unfathomable." As Sanday and Headlam observe (Rom. xi. 25), with St. Paul it is a mystery revealed. Again, as to μέγα, the English versions—not only the incorrect AV., "this is a great mystery," but the grammatically correct RV., "this mystery is great"—convey the idea that what is said is, that the mysteriousness is great, or, that the mystery is in a high degree a mystery. This is not only inconsistent with the meaning of μυστήριον, assuming, as it does, that "hiddenness" is the whole of its meaning (for to speak of a thing as in a high degree a revealed secret would be unintelligible), but it assigns to μέγα a meaning which does not belong to it. In English we may speak of great facility, great folly, simplicity, (πολλὴ μωρία, εὐηθεία); great ignorance (πολλὴ ἄγνοια); great perplexity (πολλὴ ἀπορία): but μέγας is not so used, for it properly expresses magnitude, not intensity. These linguistic facts are sufficient to set aside a large number, perhaps the majority, of interpretations of the clause. The sense must be of this kind: "This doctrine of revelation is an important or profound one."

What, then, is the μυστήριον of which St. Paul thus speaks? Some suppose it to be this statement about marriage, which to the heathen would be new. But this requires us to take λέγω in the

sense "I interpret," or the like, which it does not admit. It is
better to understand it as referring to the comparison of marriage
with union of Christ with the Church. The latter clause, then,
expressly points out that the former does not refer to marriage in
itself, and λέγω has the same which it frequently has in St. Paul,
"I mean."

V. Soden takes τοῦτο to refer to what follows: "this secret, *i.e.*
that which I am about to say as the secret sense of this sentence, is
great, but I say it in reference to Christ and the Church," comparing
1 Cor. xv. 51, μυστήριον ὑμῖν λέγω. This would be very elliptical.

Hatch translates: "this symbol (*sc.* of the joining of husband
and wife into one flesh) is a great one. I interpret it as referring
to Christ and to the Church" (*Essays*, p. 61).

The rendering of the Vulgate is: "Sacramentum hoc magnum
est; ego autem dico in Christo et in ecclesia." There are several
other places in which μυστήριον is rendered "sacramentum," viz.
Eph. i. 9, iii. 3, 9; Col. i. 27; 1 Tim. iii. 16; Rev. i. 20.

It was, however, no doubt, the rendering in this passage which
led to marriage being entitled a sacrament. In an encyclical
of 1832 (quoted by Eadie) occurs the statement, "Marriage is,
according to St. Paul's expression, a great sacrament in Christ and
in the Church." But the greatest scholars of the Church of Rome
have rejected this view of the present passage. Cardinal Caietan
says: "Non habes ex hoc loco, prudens lector, a Paulo conjugium
esse sacramentum. Non enim dixit esse sacramentum, sed mysterium." And to the same effect Estius. Erasmus also says:
"Neque nego matrimonium esse sacramentum, sed ex hoc
loco doceri possit proprie dici sacramentum quemadmodum
baptismus dicitur, excuti volo." As to the question whether
marriage is properly to be reckoned a sacrament or not, this is
very much a matter of definition. If sacrament is defined as in
the Catechism of the Churches of England and Ireland and by
other Reformed Churches, it is not, for it was not instituted by
Christ. Even if we take Augustine's definition, "a visible sign of
an invisible grace," there would be a difficulty. But if every rite
or ceremony which either is, or includes in it, a sign of something
spiritual, is to be called a sacrament, then marriage is well entitled
to the name, especially in view of the apostle's exposition here.
But to draw any inference of this kind from the present passage is
doubly fallacious, for this is not the meaning of μυστήριον; and,
secondly, St. Paul expressly states that it is not to marriage that
he applies the term, but to his teaching about Christ and the
Church; or, according to the interpretation first mentioned, to the
meaning of the verse from Genesis.

33. πλὴν καὶ ὑμεῖς οἱ καθ' ἕνα ἕκαστος τὴν ἑαυτοῦ γυναῖκα οὕτως
ἀγαπάτω ὡς ἑαυτόν.

πλήν. "Howbeit—not to dwell on this matter of Christ and the Church, but to return to what I am treating of—."

καὶ ὑμεῖς, ye also, viz. after the pattern of Christ. AV. drops the καί, which is important. The precept is individualised by the ἕκαστος, so as to bring more home its force for each man. ὡς ἑαυτόν, as being himself, ver. 28.

ἡ δὲ γυνὴ, ἵνα φοβῆται τὸν ἄνδρα. ἡ γυνή is best taken as a nom. abs. and "the wife—let her see," etc. On φοβῆται, Oecum. rightly remarks: ὡς πρέπει γυναῖκα φοβεῖσθαι, μὴ δουλοπρεπῶς. "Nunquam enim erit voluntaria subjectio nisi praecedat reverentia," Calvin.

VI. 1-9. *Special injunctions to children and fathers, slaves and masters. Slaves are called on to regard their service as a service done to Christ; masters are reminded that they, too, are subject to the same Master, who has no respect of persons.*

1. τὰ τέκνα, ὑπακούετε τοῖς γονεῦσιν ὑμῶν ἐν Κυρίῳ. ἐν Κυρίῳ is omitted by B D* G, but added in ℵ A D^bc K L P, Vulg. Syr. etc. Origen expressly, who mentions the ambiguity of the construction, *i.e.* that it may be either τοῖς ἐν Κυρίῳ γονεῦσιν or ὑπακούετε ἐν Κ. If the words had been added from Col. iii. 20 they would probably have come after δίκαιον. Assuming that the words are genuine, as seems probable, the latter is the right construction. "In the Lord," not as defining the limits of the obedience, ἐν οἷς ἂν μὴ προσκρούσῃς (τῷ Κυρίῳ), Chrys., but rather showing the spirit in which the obedience is to be yielded. It is assumed that the parents exercise their authority as Christian parents should, and we cannot suppose that the apostle meant to suggest to the children the possibility of the contrary.

τοῦτο γάρ ἐστιν δίκαιον, *i.e.* καὶ φύσει δίκαιον καὶ ὑπὸ τοῦ νόμου προστάσσεται, Theoph. Compare Col. iii. 20. From the children being addressed as members of the Church, Hofmann infers that they must have been baptized, since without baptism no one could be a member of the Church (*Schriften*, ii. 2, p. 192). Meyer's reply, that the children of Christian parents were ἅγιοι by virtue of their fellowship with their parents (1 Cor. vii. 14), loses much of its point in the case of children who were past infancy when their parents became Christians. But no conclusion as to infant baptism can be deduced.

2. ἥτις ἐστὶν ἐντολὴ πρώτη ἐν ἐπαγγελίᾳ. ἥτις, "for such is," Alf. To translate "seeing it is" would be to throw the motive to obedience too much on the fact of the promise.

πρώτη ἐν ἐπ. has caused difficulty to expositors. The second commandment has something which resembles a promise attached. Origen, who mentions this difficulty, replies, first, that all the commandments of the Decalogue were πρῶται, being given first after the coming out of Egypt; or, if this be not admitted, that the promise in the second commandment was a general one, not specially attached to the observance of that precept. The latter reply has been adopted by most modern commentators. Others have supposed "first" to mean "first in the second table"; but the Jews assigned five commandments to each table, as we learn from Philo and Josephus. See also Lev. xix. 3 and Rom. xiii. 9. The position of the precept in the former passage and its omission in the latter agree with this arrangement. In either case this would be the only commandment with promise. Meyer and Ellicott suppose, therefore, that it is not the Decalogue alone that is referred to. Braune and Stier understand πρώτη as first in point of time, namely, the first which has to be learned. Compare Bengel (not adopting this view): "honor parentibus per obedientiam praesertim praestitus initio aetatis omnium praeceptorum obedientiam continet."

ἐν ἐπαγγελίᾳ. Ellicott, Meyer, and others take this to mean "in regard of, or, in point of, promise." "The first command we meet with which involves a promise" (Ell.). Meyer compares Diod. Sic. xiii. 37, ἐν δὲ εὐγενείᾳ καὶ πλούτῳ πρῶτος. But to make this parallel we should understand the words here: "foremost in promise," *i.e.* having the greatest promise attached, or, at least, "having the advantage in point of promise," which is not their interpretation. Chrysostom says: οὐ τῇ τάξει εἶπεν αὐτὴν πρώτην, ἀλλὰ τῇ ἐπαγγελίᾳ. But it is precisely τῇ τάξει that Ell. and Mey. make it first, only not of all the commandments. It is better, then, to take ἐν (with Alford) as = characterised by, accompanied with, so that we might translate "with a promise." But to what purpose is it to state that this is the first command in order accompanied with a promise, especially when it would be equally true, and much to the purpose, to say that it is the only command with a promise? On the whole, therefore, remembering that it is children who are addressed, the interpretation of Stier and Braune seems preferable. Westcott and Hort give a place in their margin to a different punctuation, viz. placing the comma after πρώτη, and connecting ἐπαγγελίᾳ with ἵνα.

3. ἵνα εὖ σοι γένηται, κ.τ.λ. The text in the Sept. proceeds: καὶ ἵνα μακροχρόνιος γένῃ ἐπὶ τῆς γῆς ἧς Κύριος ὁ Θεός σου δίδωσί σοι. The latter words are probably omitted purposely as unsuitable to those addressed. The future ἔσῃ is to be regarded as dependent on ἵνα,—a construction which is found elsewhere in St. Paul, as 1 Cor. ix. 18, ἵνα ἀδάπανον θήσω τὸ εὐαγγ.: Gal. ii. 4, ἵνα ἡμᾶς καταδουλώσουσιν. In Rev. xxii. 14 we have future and conjunctive, just as in classical writers future and conjunctive are used after ὅπως. It is possible that ἔσῃ is used here because there was no aor. conj. of the verb. In the passage referred to in Rev. the future is ἔσται.

4. καὶ οἱ πατέρες. καί marks that the obligation was not all on the side of the children. So καὶ οἱ Κύριοι, ver. 9. πατέρες, "patres potissimum alloquitur, nam hos facilius aufert iracundia," Bengel. μὴ παροργίζετε, Col. iii. 21, μὴ ἐρεθίζετε, "Do not irritate."

ἐν παιδείᾳ καὶ νουθεσίᾳ Κυρίου. παιδεία occurs only in one other place in St. Paul, viz. 2 Tim. iii. 16, πᾶσα γραφή ... ὠφέλιμος ... πρὸς παιδείαν τὴν ἐν δικαιοσύνῃ. The verb παιδεύω also, although used of chastening in 1 Cor. xi. 32; 2 Cor. vi. 9, is employed in a wider sense in 2 Tim. ii. 25; Tit. ii. 12. There is no sufficient reason, then, for supposing that the two substantives here are distinguished, as Grotius thinks: "παιδεία hic significare videtur institutionem per poenas: νουθεσία autem est ea institutio quae fit verbis," followed by Ellicott and Alford. Rather, παιδεία is, as in classical writers, the more general, νουθεσία more specific, of instruction and admonition. νουθεσία is a later form for νουθέτησις. Κυρίου is not "concerning the Lord," as Theodoret, etc.,—a meaning which the genitive after such a word as νουθ. can hardly have, but the subjective genitive; the Lord is regarded as the guiding principle of the education.

5. οἱ δοῦλοι, ὑπακούετε τοῖς κατὰ σάρκα κυρίοις. This is the order in ℵ A B P, etc. Rec. has τοῖς κυρίοις κατὰ σάρκα.

Bengel thinks that κ. σάρκα is added, because after the mention of the true κύριος it was not fitting to use κύριοι without qualification. In Col. iii. 22 a sentence intervenes, but still the reason holds good, for ὁ Κύριος was their κύριος also κατὰ πνεῦμα. δεσπότης is the word used for the master of slaves in the Pastorals and 1 Peter.

μετὰ φόβου καὶ τρόμου. These words are similarly associated in 1 Cor. ii. 3; 2 Cor. vii. 15; Phil. ii. 12, expressing only anxious solicitude about the performance of duty, so that there is no allusion to the hardness of the service. In Col. iii. 22 it is φοβούμενοι τὸν κύριον.

ἐν ἁπλότητι τῆς καρδίας. The word ἁπλότης is used several times by St. Paul (by him only in the N.T.), and always indicates singleness and honesty of purpose, sometimes showing itself in liberality. (See Fritzsche's note on Rom. xii. 8, vol. iii. p. 62.) Here the meaning is the obvious one, there was to be no double-heartedness in their obedience, no feeling of reluctance, but genuine heartiness and goodwill. ἔνι γὰρ καὶ μετὰ φόβου καὶ τρόμου δουλεύειν, ἀλλ᾽ οὐκ ἐξ εὐνοίας, ἀλλὰ κακούργως, Occum.

ὡς τῷ Χριστῷ, as ὡς τῷ Κυρίῳ, v. 22, "so that your service to your master is regarded as a service to Christ."

6. μὴ κατ᾽ ὀφθαλμοδουλίαν. "Not in the way of ὀφθ." The word is not found elsewhere except in Col. iii. 22, and may have been coined by St. Paul. The adjective ὀφθαλμόδουλος is found in the *Apost. Constit.*, but with reference to this passage (i. p. 299 A, ed. Cotel.). The meaning is obvious.

ὡς ἀνθρωπάρεσκοι. This word is not found in classical writers; it occurs in the Sept., Ps. lii. (liii.) 6; not as a rendering of our Hebrew text. It is also found in *Psalt. Sol.* iv. 8, 10. This is the opposite of ὡς τῷ Χριστῷ as well as of the following words.

ἀλλ' ὡς δοῦλοι Χριστοῦ ποιοῦντες τὸ θέλημα τοῦ Θεοῦ. τοῦ before Χριστοῦ rests on insufficient authority, D^r K L, etc., against א D* G L P, etc. Not subordinate to the following clause, as if it were "as servants who are doing," etc., for the words are clearly in contrast to the preceding, and ποιοῦντες τὸ θέλ. has much more force if taken as a separate character.

6, 7. ἐκ ψυχῆς μετ' εὐνοίας δουλεύοντες ὡς τῷ Κυρίῳ. ἐκ ψυχῆς may be connected either with what precedes or with what follows. The latter connexion (adopted by Syr. Chrys. Jerome, Lachm. Alf. WH.) seems preferable, for ποιοῦντες τὸ θέλημα τοῦ Θεοῦ does not require such a qualification, nor is there any tautology in taking ἐκ ψ. with the following, for these words express the source in the feeling of the servant towards his work; μετ' εὐνοίας his feeling towards his master (Harless). Compare Raphel's apt quotation from Xen.: οὐκοῦν εὔνοιαν πρῶτον, ἔφην ἐγώ, δεήσει αὐτὸν [τὸν ἐπίτροπον] ἔχειν σοι καὶ τοῖς σοῖς εἰ μέλλοι ἀρκέσειν ἀντὶ σοῦ παρών. (*Oecon.* xii. 5). Treg. puts a comma after εὐνοίας, WH. after δουλεύοντες.

ὡς before τῷ Κυρίῳ rests on preponderant evidence, א A B D* G P, Vulg. Syr. It is omitted by D^r K L. Internal evidence is in its favour, since δουλ. τῷ κ. would be tautologous with δοῦλοι Χριστοῦ.

8. εἰδότες ὅτι ἕκαστος ὃ ἂν ποιήσῃ ἀγαθόν, τοῦτο κομίσεται παρὰ Κυρίου.

> There is great uncertainty as to the reading.
> ὅτι ἕκαστος ὃ ἂν (or ἐὰν) ποιήσῃ, A D G P 17 37, Vulg. Arm.
> ὅτι ἕκαστος ἐάν τι, B, Petr. Alex.
> ὅτι ἐάν τι ἕκαστος, L* 46 115.
> ὃ ἐάν τι ἕκαστος ποιήσῃ, L** and most cursives. This is the Rec. Text.
> ὅτι (probably to be read ὃ τι) ἐὰν ποιήσῃ, א*, corrected by א^c by the insertion of ὃ before ἐάν.
> There are minor variations.
> The best supported reading is that first mentioned, which is adopted by Treg. and Tisch. 8; but Meyer and Ellicott think the Rec. better explains the others. WH. adopt the reading of B.
> In the reading of Rec. the relative is to be understood as separated from τι by tmesis. Cf. Plato, *Legg.* ix. 864 E, ἤν ἄν τινα καταβλάψῃ.
> κομίσεται, א A B D* G, is better attested than the Rec. κομιεῖται. τοῦ also of Rec. before Κυρίου is rejected on the authority of all the chief uncials.

κομίζεσθαι is to receive back, as, for example, a deposit, hence here it implies an adequate return. Compare 2 Cor. v. 10, ἵνα κομίσηται ἕκαστος τὰ διὰ τοῦ σώματος, and Col. iii. 25.

This lesson to slaves is equally a lesson for all kinds of service, as the following for all masters.

9. καὶ οἱ κύριοι. See on καί, ver. 4.

τὰ αὐτὰ ποιεῖτε. *I.e.* act in a similar manner, in the same spirit. De Wette refers it to ἀγαθόν. The Greek comm. pressed τὰ αὐτά as if it meant δουλεύετε αὐτοῖς.

ἀνιέντες τὴν ἀπειλήν. "Giving up your threatening." The article indicates the well known and familiar threatening, "quemadmodum vulgus dominorum solet," Erasmus.

εἰδότες, κ.τ.λ. Wetstein cites a remarkable parallel from Seneca, *Thyest.* 607, "Vos, quibus rector maris atque terrae Jus dedit magnum necis atque vitae, Ponite inflatos tumidosque vultus. Quicquid a vobis minor extimescit, Major hoc vobis dominus minatur! Omne sub regno graviore regnum est."

καὶ αὐτῶν καὶ ὑμῶν is supported by preponderant authority, ℵ* (ἑαυτῶν) A B D*, Vulg. Boh. Arm., Petr. Alex. etc. Dᶜ G have καὶ αὐτῶν ὑμῶν: K and most cursives, καὶ ὑμῶν αὐτῶν. Meyer thinks the mention of slaves (αὐτῶν) here appeared unsuitable, partly in itself and partly in comparison with Col. iv. 1. Whether this be a correct account of the causes of the variation, it cannot be doubted that the reading attested by the best MSS. here is the more forcible, expressing, not merely the fact that "ye also have a Master," but that both you and they are subjects of the same Master.

προσωποληψία, like **προσωπολημπτής,** and the verb **προσωπολημπτέω,** is found only in N.T. and ecclesiastical writers. The expression πρόσωπον λαμβάνειν has a different meaning in the N.T. from that which it had in the O.T. In the latter it only meant to show favour, in the former it is to show partiality, especially on account of external advantages.

10–12. *Exhortation to prepare for the spiritual combat by arming themselves with the panoply of God, remembering that they have to do with no mere mortal foes, but with spiritual powers.*

10. τοῦ λοιποῦ. So ℵ* A B 17.

τὸ λοιπόν. ℵᶜ D G K L P, Chrys. etc.

Meyer points out that B 17 have δυναμοῦσθε instead of ἐνδ., a variation which Meyer thinks may have arisen from a confusion of the N of λοιπόν with the N of ἐνδυν., thus pointing to the reading λοιπόν. Properly, τοῦ λοιποῦ means "henceforth, for the future," Gal. vi. 17, in which sense τὸ λοιπόν may also be used; but the latter alone is used in the sense "for the rest," Phil. iii. 1, iv. 8; 2 Thess. iii. 1. As the latter is the meaning here, we should expect τὸ λοιπόν.

ἀδελφοί μου is added in Rec. before ἐνδυν., with ℵᶜ K L P, most cursives, Syr. (both) Boh., but om. by ℵ* B D 17, Arm. Aeth. A G, Vulg. Theodoret have ἀδελφοί without μου. It has probably come in by assimilation to other passages in which τὸ λοιπόν occurs (see above). St. Paul does not address his readers thus in this Epistle.

ἐνδυναμοῦσθε. "Be strengthened." Cf. Rom. iv. 20. Not

middle but passive, as elsewhere in N.T. (Acts ix. 22; Rom. iv. 20; 2 Tim. ii. 1; Heb. xi. 34). The active occurs Phil. iv. 23; 1 Tim. i. 12; 2 Tim. iv. 17. The simple verb δυναμόω, which B 17 have here, is used in Col. i. 11, and according to א* A D* in Heb. xi. 34. ἐνδυναμοῦσθαι occurs once in the Sept. Ps. li. (lii.) 7 rather in a bad sense. There is no reason why a verb which occurs once in the Sept. and several times in the N.T. should be said to be "peculiar to the Alexandrian Greek."

καὶ ἐν τῷ κράτει τῆς ἰσχύος αὐτοῦ. Not a hendiadys. Compare i. 19.

11. ἐνδύσασθε τὴν πανοπλίαν τοῦ Θεοῦ. "Put on the panoply of God." πανοπλία occurs also in Luke xi. 22. The emphasis is clearly on παν. not on τοῦ Θεοῦ. Observe the repetition in ver. 13, "of God," *i.e.* provided by God, ἅπασιν διανέμει τὴν Βασιλικὴν πανrευχίαν, Theodoret. There is no contrast with other armour, nor is πανοπλία to be taken as merely = "armatura." The completeness of the armament is the point insisted on. St. Paul was, no doubt, thinking of the Roman soldiery, as his readers also would, although the Jewish armour was essentially the same. Polybius enumerates as belonging to the Roman πανοπλία, shield, sword, greaves, spear, breastplate, helmet. St. Paul omits the spears, and adds girdle and shoes, which, though not armour, were an essential part of the soldier's dress.

πρὸς τὸ δύνασθαι. "To the end that ye may be able." στῆναι πρός, "to hold your ground against," an expression suited to the military figure.

τὰς μεθοδείας. Cf. iv. 14. The plural expresses the concrete workings of the μεθοδεία. We can hardly press it as specially appropriate to the military metaphor and = "stratagems."

12. ὅτι οὐκ ἔστιν ἡμῖν ἡ πάλη πρὸς αἷμα καὶ σάρκα.

ἡμῖν, with א A Dᶜ K L P and most mss. and Vss.
ὑμῖν, B D* G, Goth. Aeth., adopted by Lach., and admitted to the margin by Treg. and WH. The second person would very readily occur to a scribe, the whole context being in the second person.

ἡ πάλη. "Our wrestling." The word is suitable to πρὸς αἷμα καὶ σ., but not to the struggle in which the πανοπλία is required. The word is indeed found in a more general sense (see Ellicott), but only in poetry, as "wrestling" also might be used in our own tongue. But as the word is here used to describe what the struggle is not, it is most natural to supply a more general word, such as ἡ μάχη or μαχετέον, in the following clause, according to an idiom frequent in Greek writers.

αἷμα καὶ σάρκα, in this order here only. Jerome understands this of our own passions; but that would be πρὸς τὴν σάρκα without αἷμα. Moreover, the contrast is clearly not between foes within and foes without, but between human and superhuman powers.

πρὸς τὰς ἀρχάς, πρὸς τὰς ἐξουσίας. See on i. 21.

πρὸς τοὺς κοσμοκράτορας. "World-rulers." The word κοσμοκράτωρ occurs in the *Orphica* (viii. 11, xi. 11), and is used by the Schol. on Aristoph. *Nub.* 397, Σεσάγχωσις ὁ βασιλεὺς τῶν Αἰγυπτίων κοσμοκράτωρ γεγονώς. It frequently occurs in Rabbinical writers (transliterated), sometimes of kings whose rule was world-wide, as "tres reges κοσμοκράτορες, dominatores ab extremitate mundi ad extremitatem ejus, Nebucadnesar, Evilmerodach, Belsazar" (*Shir Rab.* iii. 4, ap. Wetst.); also of the four kings whom Abraham pursued (Bereshith Rabba, fol. 57. 1). These are so called to add glory to Abraham's victory. Also the angel of death is so called, and by the Gnostics the Devil (Iren. i. 1). In the *Test. XII Patr.*, Test. Sol. the demons say: ἡμεῖς ἐσμεν τὰ λεγόμενα στοιχεῖα, οἱ κοσμοκράτορες τοῦ κόσμου τούτου. It appears, therefore, that it differs from "rulers" in implying that their rule extends over the κόσμος. Schoettgen supposes that St. Paul means the Rabbis and Doctors of the Jews, and he cites a passage from the Talmud where it is argued that the Rabbis are to be called kings; he also compares Acts iv. 26. But the context appears to be decisive against such a view. The contest is clearly a spiritual one. Compare the designation of Satan as ὁ Θεὸς τοῦ αἰῶνος τούτου, 2 Cor. iv. 4; ὁ ἄρχων τοῦ κόσμου τούτου, John xiv. 30.

τοῦ σκότους τούτου.

So, without τοῦ αἰῶνος, ℵ* A B D* G 17 67², Vulg. Boh. Syr-Pesh. and Harcl. (text), etc.

After σκότους, τοῦ αἰῶνος is added by ℵᶜᵃ Dᶜ K L P most mss. The words were not likely to be omitted because they seemed superfluous or difficult to explain; and an omission from homoeoteleuton is not to be supposed in the face of so many documents. They might, on the contrary, have been added as a gloss, the phrase σκότους τούτου being rare.

πρὸς τὰ πνευματικὰ τῆς πονηρίας. "Against the spirit forces of wickedness," which belong to or are characterised by πονηρία. RV. has "*hosts* of wickedness." So Alford, Ellicott, Meyer, comparing τὸ ἱππικόν, "the cavalry," Rev. ix. 16; τὸ πολιτικόν, Herod. vii. 103; τὰ λῃστρικά, Polyaen. v. 14. 141. But these are not really parallel; ἱππικόν, primarily meaning "appertaining to ἵπποι," hence "equestrian," was naturally used for brevity to designate the cavalry of an army, as πεζικά the infantry, just like our "horse and foot." Thus Polyb. xv. 3. 5, Ἀννίβας ἐλλείπων τοῖς ἱππικοῖς, "in the matter of cavalry"; *ib.* xviii. 5. 5, Αἰτωλοὶ . . . καθ᾽ ὅσον ἐν τοῖς πεζικοῖς ἐλλιπεῖς εἰσι . . . κατὰ τοσοῦτον τοῖς ἱππικοῖς διαφέρουσι πρὸς τὸ βέλτιον τῶν ἄλλων Ἑλλήνων: *ib.* iii. 114. 5, τὸ τῶν ἱππικῶν πλῆθος τὸ σύμπαν τοῖς Καρχηδονίοις εἰς μυρίους. . . . In Rev ix. 16 we have ὁ ἀριθμὸς τῶν στρατευμάτων τοῦ ἱππικοῦ. But πνευματικόν never had such a signification, nor would its etymology lead us to expect that it could be so used; for it does not mean what relates to πνεύματα, but to τὸ πνεῦμα. It would be almost as reasonable to conclude from the use of the English "horse" and "foot," that "spirit" could be used for a host of spirits, as to draw a like conclusion about πνευματικά from the use of ἱππικά, etc. Moreover, τὰ ἱππικά does not mean "hosts or armies" of horses or of horsemen; and, if we were to follow the analogy of its meaning, we should interpret τὰ πν. τῆς πον. as = the πνευματικόν constituent of πονηρία. τὰ λῃστρικά, too, does not mean "bands of robbers," but of "pirate ships," which are themselves called λῃστρικαί, Polyaenus, v. 14. 141; and τὸ πολιτικόν, in Herod. vii. 103, means that part of the population which consists of πολῖται. This word, like ἱππικόν, used in such a connexion as it has there, at once conveys this meaning. But to give πνευματικά here the meaning "spiritual armies, or hosts," is to depart wholly from the ordinary use of the word.

Giving up, therefore, this rendering as untenable, we may translate "the spiritual forces, or elements of wickedness."

ἐν τοῖς ἐπουρανίοις is connected by Chrysostom with ἡ πάλη ἐστίν. Thus: ἐν τοῖς ἐπ. ἡ μάχη κεῖται... ὡς ἂν εἰ ἔλεγεν, ἡ συνθήκη ἐν τίνι κεῖται: ἐν χρυσῷ, i.e. our contest is for the heavenly blessings, and so Theodoret, Oecum. al. But in the illustration cited it is the connexion with κεῖται that makes this sense possible; the idea is "rests in, or depends on," which does not suit ἡ πάλη ἐστίν.

The view generally adopted by modern expositors is that τὰ ἐπ. means the seat of the evil spirits or spiritual hosts referred to, corresponding to the τοῦ ἀέρος of ii. 2. As Alford expresses it, that habitation which in ii. 2, when speaking of mere matters of fact, was said to be in the ἀήρ, is, now that the difficulty and importance of the Christian conflict is being set forth, represented as ἐν τοῖς ἐπ.—over us and too strong for us without the panoply of God. He compares τὰ πετεινὰ τοῦ οὐρανοῦ, Matt. vi. 26. This comment seems to amount to this, that these spiritual hosts dwell in the air; but to impress us the more with the difficulty of the combat, the air is called "heaven." There is, however, no proof that τὰ ἐπουράνια meant the atmosphere, and this is not the meaning of the word elsewhere, e.g. i. 3, 20, ii. 6.

The view of Eadie, al., is that τὰ ἐπ. means the celestial spots occupied by the Church, and in them this combat is to be maintained, "These evil spirits have invaded the Church, are attempting to pollute, divide, and overthrow it." Barry, while adopting the former view of τὰ ἐπ., yet adds that the meaning points to the power of evil as directly spiritual, not acting through physical and human agency, but attacking the spirit in that higher aspect in which it contemplates heavenly things and ascends to the communion with God.

In the *Book of the Secrets of Enoch*, which is pre-Christian, and perhaps as early as B.C. 30, we have "a scheme of the seven heavens which, in some of its prominent features, agrees with that conceived by St. Paul. Paradise is situated in the third heaven as in 2 Cor. xii. 2, 3, whereas, according to later Judaism, it belonged to the fourth heaven. In the next place the presence of evil in some part of the heavens is recognised. Thus, in Eph. vi. 12, we meet with the peculiar statement, Against the spiritual hosts of wickedness in the heavens" (Morfill and Charles, p. xl). Charles points out other parallels between the Epistle and the *Book of the Secrets of Enoch*; *e.g.* Eph. iii. 10, iv. 10, 25 (pp. xxii, xli); and the possibility that the present passage has been influenced by these speculations must be admitted.

13–18. *Detailed description of the spiritual armour.*

13. ἐν τῇ ἡμέρᾳ τῇ πονηρᾷ. "The evil day," the day of the power of evil, when the conflict is most severe, "any day of which it may be said, 'this is your hour, and the power of darkness,'" Barry. Meyer understands it as referring to the great outbreak of Satanic power expected to occur before the second coming. ἅπαντα κατεργασάμενοι; Oecum. and Theoph. take this to mean "having overcome all," AV. marg.; but although the verb has this sense occasionally in classical writers, or rather "to despatch, to finish," "conficere," it never has it in St. Paul, who uses it twenty times. This would not be decisive if this meaning were more suitable here. But the conflict is perpetual in this world, it is ever being renewed. On the other hand, we cannot without tautology understand this clause as merely expressing preparation for the combat. κατεργάζεσθαι, too, means to accomplish a difficult work: "notat rem arduam," Fritzsche, and could hardly be used of mere arming for the fight. It appears, then, to mean having done all that duty requires, viz. from time to time. The Vulgate (not Jerome) has "omnibus perfecti," or, in some MSS., "in omnibus perfecti," following, as some think, the reading κατειργασμένοι. A has κατεργασμένοι, doubtless a mistake for κατεργασάμενοι, not meant for κατειργασμένοι. στῆναι, opposed to φεύγειν, "hold your ground."

14. στῆτε οὖν. This στῆτε cannot be taken in the same sense as the preceding, otherwise we should have the end there aimed at, here assumed as already attained when the arming begins.

In the following details of the figure, each part of the equipment has its appropriate interpretation, which, however, must not be pressed too minutely. In the case of the breastplate and the helmet, St. Paul follows Isa. lix. 17, ἐνεδύσατο δικαιοσύνην ὡς θώρακα, καὶ περιέθετο περικεφαλαιον σωτηρίου ἐπὶ τῆς κεφαλῆς, but the remainder of Isaiah's description was unsuitable, viz. καὶ περιεβάλετο ἱμάτιον ἐκδικήσεως καὶ τὸ περιβόλαιον ζήλου. The figure of Isaiah is more fully carried out in Wisd. v. 18, 20, λήψεται πανοπλίαν τὸν ζῆλον αὐτοῦ ... ἐνδύσεται θώρακα δικαιοσύνην, καὶ περιθήσεται κόρυθα κρίσιν ἀνυπόκριτον. λήψεται ἀσπίδα ἀκαταμάχητον ὁσιότητα, ὀξυνεῖ δὲ ἀπότομον ὀργὴν εἰς ῥομφαίαν. In Isa. xi. 5, δικαιοσύνη and ἀλήθεια are both girdles.

περιζωσάμενοι τὴν ὀσφὺν ὑμῶν ἐν ἀληθείᾳ. The aorists are properly used, since the arming was complete before the στῆτε. The present would mean that they were to be arming themselves when they took up their position, which would be rather a mark of unpreparedness. The girdle was a necessary part of the equipment of a soldier to make rapid movement possible; and, indeed, was commonly used to support the sword, though not in Homeric times. But there is no reference to that use here, the sword being not referred to until ver. 17. ἐν ἀληθείᾳ, ἐν, instrumental, "with"; "truth," not the objective truth of the gospel, which is the sword, ver. 17, but truth in its widest sense as an element of character. Compare ch. v. 9.

τὸν θώρακα τῆς δικαιοσύνης, genitive of apposition. δικ., as in ch. v. 9, Christian uprightness of character, which like a breast-plate defends the heart from the assaults of evil. Eadie (with Harless, *al.*) understands it of the righteousness of faith, *i.e.* Christ's justifying righteousness, remarking that the article has a special prominence. But the article is used in accordance with the ordinary rule, θώρακα having the article. The faith by which this justification is attained is mentioned in ver. 16. That no Christian possesses entire rectitude is not an objection, the breast-plate is not faultlessness, which would, in fact, be inconsistent with the figure, but the actual rightness of character wrought by Christ.

15. ὑποδησάμενοι τοὺς πόδας, no doubt referring to the "caligae" of the Roman soldier.

ἐν ἑτοιμασίᾳ. The more classical form is ἑτοιμότης, but Hippocr. has ἑτοιμασία. The word occurs in the Sept. in the sense of "preparedness" (Ps. ix. 41, x. 17), but more frequently as representing the Hebrew מָכוֹן, which they rendered according to their view of its etymology, not its meaning. It is quite erroneous to interpret it here by this use, or rather misuse, of it, as some expositors have done, taking it, for example, to mean "vel constantiam in tuenda religione Christi, vel religionem adeo ipsam certam illam quidem et fundamento cui insistere possis, similem," Koppe. This is also against the figure. Shoes are not the firm foundation on which one stands, but we may compare with them the readiness of mind with which one advances to the conflict, and which is wrought by the gospel τοῦ εὐαγ. It is not preparation to preach the gospel that is meant, for the apostle is addressing all Christians; and, moreover, this interpretation does not agree with the figure.

τῆς εἰρήνης, peace with God and amongst men, see ch. ii. 17; an oxymoron. ἂν τῷ διαβόλῳ πολεμῶμεν εἰρηνεύομεν πρὸς τὸν Θεόν, Chrys.

16. ἐν πᾶσιν. So ℵ B P 17, *al.*, Cat. text, Vulg. Boh. Syr-Harcl. Aeth.

ἐπὶ πᾶσιν, A D G K L most cursives, Syr-Pesh. Arm. etc.

<blockquote>There is a similar variety in Luke xvi. 26, where ℵ B L Boh. read ἐν, but A D X Δ *al.* ἐπί. This alone is sufficient to set aside Ellicott's suggestion that ἐν here was a correction for the ambiguous ἐπί. Meyer thinks it was substituted as the more common.</blockquote>

If ἐπί is read it is not to be rendered "above all," AV. Beza, nor "over all," but "in addition to all"; cf. Luke iii. 20, προσέθηκε καὶ τοῦτο ἐπὶ πᾶσι.

τὸν θυρεόν. θυρεός is used in Homer of a great stone placed against a door to keep it shut. In later writers, Plutarch, Polybius, etc., it means a large oblong shield, "scutum," according to Polyb. 4 ft. by 2½, differing from the ἀσπίς, which was small and round. But in Wisdom, quoted above, ὁσιότης is the ἀσπίς or "clypeus." St. Paul's purpose, however, is different, and he is describing a heavy armed warrior well furnished for defence.

τῆς πίστεως, genitive of apposition. Only where faith is weak does the enemy gain access. In 1 Thess. v. 8 faith and love are the breastplate.

ἐν ᾧ δυνήσεσθε. The future is properly used, not because the combat does not begin until the day of the great future conflict with evil, but because the whole duration of the fight is contemplated. At all times ye shall be able, etc.

τὰ βέλη τοῦ πονηροῦ τὰ πεπυρωμένα σβέσαι. The figure alludes to the darts or arrows tipped with tow dipped in pitch and set on fire, mentioned, for example, in Herod. viii. 52. Some of the older interpreters (Hammond, *al.*) understood the word to mean poisoned, the word "fiery" being used with reference to the sensation produced; but this is contrary to the grammatical meaning of the word. "Fiery darts" is a suitable figure for fierce temptations; beyond this there is no need to go.

σβέσαι is appropriate, since the shields alluded to were of wood covered with leather, in which when the arrow fixed itself the fire would go out. So Thucydides tells us of hides being used for this very purpose (ii. 75).

<blockquote>τά is omitted by B D* G, and bracketed by Treg. and WH.; omitted by Lachm. If omitted, the interpretation would be "fire tipped as they are." The authority for omission is small; but the insertion would be more easily accounted for than the accidental omission.</blockquote>

17. καὶ τὴν περικεφαλαίαν τοῦ σωτηρίου δέξασθε. This verse is separated from ver. 16 by a full stop in RV. as well as by Lachm. Tisch., not Treg. WH. But though the construction is changed, as in i. 22, this is only a result of the rapidity of thought for which a strict adherence to the participial construction might be a hindrance. The same vividness of conception leads the writer to put τὴν περικ. first.

Σωτήριον is not used elsewhere by St. Paul; here it is taken with the preceding word from the Sept. Theodoret understands it as masculine, referring to Christ; and so Bengel, "salutaris, *i.e.* Christi"; but this is refuted by the parallel, 1 Thess. v. 8, where the περικ. is the hope of salvation. Soden thinks that in that passage the apostle purposely corrects the σωτήριον of the Sept.

καὶ τὴν μάχαιραν τοῦ πνεύματος. This cannot well be a genitive of apposition, since the following clause explains the sword as ῥῆμα Θεοῦ. Olshausen, indeed, and Soden, take the relative ὅ as referring to πνεύματος. They understand the writer as speaking of the Holy Spirit in relation to man, as finding expression in the word of God. But there is no parallel for thus calling the Spirit ῥῆμα Θεοῦ. It is much more natural to interpret τοῦ πν. as "which is given by the Spirit"; nor is there any difficulty in taking this genitive differently from the others, since this alone is a genitive of a personal name. Chrysostom suggests the alternative: ἤτοι τὸ Πνεῦμά φησιν, ἤτοι ἐν τῇ πνευματικῇ μαχαίρᾳ (or ἤτοι τὸ χάρισμα τὸ πνευματικόν, διὰ γὰρ πνευματικῆς μαχαίρας, κ.τ.λ.).

ὅ ἐστιν ῥῆμα Θεοῦ. Compare Heb. iv. 12, ὁ λόγος τοῦ Θεοῦ ... τομώτερος ὑπὲρ πᾶσαν μάχαιραν δίστομον.

δέξασθε. "Accipite, oblatum a Domino," Bengel.

A Dᶜ K L, etc., read δέξασθαι, perhaps only by itacism. The verb is omitted by D* G, *al.*

18. διὰ πάσης προσευχῆς καὶ δεήσεως, κ.τ.λ. These words are best taken with the principal imperative στῆτε, not simply with the previous clause, for πάσης and ἐν παντὶ καιρῷ would not agree with the momentary act δέξασθε, which is itself subordinate to στῆτε. "With all prayer, *i.e.* prayer of every form."

προσευχή and δέησις differ in this respect, that the former is used only of prayer, whether supplication or not, to God, while δέησις means "request," and may be addressed to either God or man. Here, then, we may say that πρ. expresses that the prayer is addressed to God, and δ., that it involves a request. Compare Phil. iv. 6, ἐν παντὶ τῇ προσευχῇ καὶ τῇ δεήσει, and see on Lk. i. 13.

ἐν παντὶ καιρῷ corresponds with the ἀδιαλείπτως προσεύχεσθαι of 1 Thess. v. 17.

ἐν Πνεύματι. "In the Spirit" (cf. Jude 21) not = ἐκ ψυχῆς, for which interpretation St. Paul's usage supplies no justification, besides which it was not necessary to say that the prayer was to be from the heart. Chrysostom supposes ἐν πν. to be in contrast to βαττολογίαις, which is also open to the objection that he who has put on the specified armour must be assumed not to pray ἐν βαττολογίᾳ.

καὶ εἰς αὐτό. "Thereunto," *i.e.* to the προσευχόμενοι ἐν π. κ. ἐν πν.

Rec. has τοῦτο after αὐτό, with D^c J K, etc.; but αὐτό alone, ℵ A B (D* G, αὐτόν). The frequent occurrence of αὐτὸ τοῦτο in St. Paul accounts for the insertion.

ἀγρυπνοῦντες ἐν πάσῃ προσκαρτερήσει. Compare Col. iv. 2, τῇ προσευχῇ προσκαρτερεῖτε, γρηγοροῦντες ἐν αὐτῇ ἐν εὐχαριστίᾳ, "keeping watch," or "being watchful"; cf. Mark xiii. 33, ἀγρυπνεῖτε καὶ προσεύχεσθε: *ib.* 35, γρηγορεῖτε: Luke xxi. 36, ἀγρυπνεῖτε ἐν παντὶ καιρῷ δεόμενοι, κ.τ.λ.

Προσκαρτέρησις is not found elsewhere, but the verb προσκαρτερέω is frequent both in classical writers and N.T. always with the sense of continued waiting on, attention to, adherence, etc. Cf. Acts ii. 42, τῇ διδαχῇ: *ib.* 46, ἐν τῷ ἱερῷ: viii. 13, τῷ Φιλίππῳ: Mark iii. 9, ἵνα πλοιάριον προσκαρτερῇ αὐτῷ: Rom. xii. 12, προσευχῇ: *ib.* xiii. 6, εἰς αὐτὸ τοῦτο. It is clear, then, that Alford is not justified in rendering it "importunity" in order to avoid a hendiadys. Practically, there is a hendiadys.

περὶ πάντων τῶν ἁγίων, καὶ ὑπὲρ ἐμοῦ. καί, introducing a special case, see ch. v. 18. Harless and Eadie distinguish περί here from ὑπέρ, regarding the latter as more vague. "They could not know much about all saints, and they were to pray about them." Eadie admits, however, that such a distinction cannot be uniformly carried out. Meyer, to prove the prepositions synonymous, quotes Dem. *Phil.* ii. p. 74, μὴ περὶ τῶν δικαίων μηδ' ὑπὲρ τῶν ἔξω πραγμάτων εἶναι τὴν βουλήν, ἀλλ' ὑπὲρ τῶν ἐν τῇ χώρᾳ: but this passage rather indicates the contrary; "not about a question of justice, but in defence of." So also the similar one, οὐ περὶ δόξης οὐδ' ὑπὲρ μέρους χώρας πολεμοῦσι, *i.e.* "not about a matter of glory, but in defence of," etc. ὑπὲρ δόξης might have been used, but the idea would not be quite the same. Here, too, ὑπέρ expresses with more precision "on behalf of"; but the reason of the difference is probably not to be found in the difference between πάντων τῶν ἁγίων and ἐμοῦ, but in the fact that the special object of the latter prayer is stated: "and on behalf of me, that," etc. See Dale, Lect. xxiv. p. 437.

19, 20. *The apostle's request for their prayers for himself, that he may have freedom to proclaim the mystery of the gospel for which he is an ambassador.*

ἵνα μοι δοθῇ λόγος ἐν ἀνοίξει τοῦ στόματός μου. Λόγος, in the sense of utterance, as 2 Cor. xi. 2, ἰδιώτης τῷ λόγῳ. The words ἐν ἀνοίξει τοῦ στ. are by some connected with the following. Thus Grotius: "ut ab hac custodia militari liber per omnem urbem perferre possem sermonem," etc., but παρρησία never refers to external freedom, and its meaning here is further determined by παρρησιάσωμαι, ver. 20. To take παρρησίᾳ as merely epexegetical of ἀνοίξει τ. στ. would be very flat.

Taken with the preceding, the words may mean the opening of the mouth by God, as in Ps. li. 17. Or they may mean, "when I open my mouth." The latter is the interpretation adopted by Alford, Ellicott, Eadie, Meyer. But so understood, the words are superfluous, not to say trivial.

On the other hand, with the former interpretation they give a fulness of expression to the idea in δοθῇ λόγος, which is in harmony with the gravity of the thought; they complete from the subjective side what is expressed on the objective side in δοθῇ λόγος. This is the view of Harless, Olsh. Soden. The absence of the article is also in its favour. Compare Col. iv. 3, although there it is ἵνα ὁ Θεὸς ἀνοίξῃ ἡμῖν θύραν τοῦ λόγου. "Opening the mouth" is an expression used only where some grave utterance is in question.

ἐν παρρησίᾳ γνωρίσαι. "To make known with openness of speech"; cf. Phil. i. 20. The margin of RV. connects ἐν παρρησίᾳ with the preceding words, as the AV. had done. This involves a tautology with παρρησιάσωμαι.

δοθείη of Rec. rests on very slight evidence.

τὸ μυστήριον τοῦ εὐαγγ. See ch. i. 9.

20. ὑπὲρ οὗ πρεσβεύω ἐν ἁλύσει. οὗ refers to τὸ μυστ., for this is the object of γνωρίσαι, and γνωρίσαι is in substance connected with πρεσβεύω. Compare Col. iv. 3, λαλῆσαι τὸ μυστ. τοῦ Χριστοῦ δι' ὃ καὶ δέδεμαι. The simplest view is probably the best: "I am an ambassador in chains"; but Grotius understands the words to mean: "nunc quoque non desino legationem"; but this would require some emphasis on ἁλύσει, as, for example, καὶ ἐν ἁλ. πρεσβεύω: and there is no reference here, as in Phil. i. 12 ff., to the good effects of his imprisonment. The oxymoron is noted by Bengel and Wetstein: "alias legati, jure gentium sancti et inviolabiles, in vinculis haberi non poterant." So, indeed, Theoph., τοὺς πρέσβεις νόμος μηδὲν πάσχειν κακόν. ἐν ἁλύσει is in distinct opposition to ἐν παρρησίᾳ.

Paley and others have drawn attention to the use of ἅλυσις here as referring to the "custodia militaris" in which St. Paul was kept at Rome, Acts xxviii. 16, 20; cf. 2 Tim. i. 16. It is true the singular might possibly be used in a general sense, although the instances cited from Polyb. of εἰς τὴν ἅλυσιν ἐμπίπτειν (xxi. 3. 3, iv. 76. 5) are not parallel, since the article there is generic. Still it can hardly be denied that the term has a special suitability to the circumstances of this imprisonment, or rather custody. Of course, δεσμοί as the general term might also be used, and therefore the fact that it is used, Col. iv. 18, is no objection.

ἵνα ἐν αὐτῷ παρρησιάσωμαι. Co-ordinate with the preceding ἵνα. Soden, however, takes the clause as depending on the πρεσβεύω ἐν ἁλ., the meaning according to him being that St. Paul might have been set at liberty on condition that he did not preach the gospel, but remained in custody in hope that the result of the trial would be that he would be at liberty to preach. This, he adds, corresponds to ὡς δεῖ με λαλῆσαι, and escapes the tautology involved in the other interpretations.

21-24. *Personal commendation of Tychicus, who carries the letter, and final benediction.*

21. ἵνα δὲ εἰδῆτε καὶ ὑμεῖς. καί is probably simply "ye as well as others." Meyer and others suppose a reference to the Epistle to the Colossians, "ye as well as the Colossians"; cf. Col. iv. 7. But this seems forced, for this significance of καί could hardly occur to the readers. But it may mean, "although there are no personal relations between us." Alford understands: "as *I* have been going at length into the matters concerning *you*, so if *you also*, on your part, wish," etc.

τὰ κατ' ἐμέ = Col. iv. 7.

τί πράσσω, nearer definition of τὰ κατ' ἐμέ, "how I do," not "what I am doing," which they knew was the one thing that always engaged his thoughts.

Τύχικος ὁ ἀγαπητὸς ἀδελφὸς καὶ πιστὸς διάκονος. Tychicus is mentioned, Acts xx. 4, as accompanying St. Paul from Macedonia to Asia. His services as διάκονος are alluded to 2 Tim. iv. 12; Tit. iii. 12. It was only ἐν Κυρίῳ that he was Paul's διάκονος. In Col. iv. 7 σύνδουλος is added.

22. ὃν ἔπεμψα εἰς αὐτὸ τοῦτο (= Col. iv.), *i.e.* for the very purpose now to be mentioned: ἵνα γνῶτε τὰ περὶ ἡμῶν, κ.τ.λ. = Col. iv. 8 (where, however, there is a difference of reading).

23. Εἰρήνη τοῖς ἀδελφοῖς, κ.τ.λ. A truly apostolic benediction as to substance, but differing in form from St. Paul's final benedictions. First, it is in the third person, not the second, τοῖς ἀδελφοῖς instead of ὑμῖν, μετὰ πάντων τῶν ἀγ. instead of μεθ' ὑμῶν. The whole form, too, is markedly general. This agrees well with the view that the Epistle was addressed to a circle of Churches. Secondly, the benediction is in two parts, not, as elsewhere, one; and, thirdly, χάρις, which elsewhere comes first, here concludes, and εἰρήνη, elsewhere last, is here first. These points all speak for the genuineness of the Epistle, and against the hypothesis of imitation.

ἀγάπη μετὰ πίστεως. πίστις is presupposed, therefore it is not ἀγάπη καὶ π. Love is the characteristic of a true faith.

For ἀγάπη A has ἔλεος, suggested probably by recollection of 1 Tim. i. 1; 2 Tim. i. 1.

24. Ἡ χάρις μετὰ πάντων τῶν ἀγαπώντων τὸν Κύριον ἡμῶν Ἰησοῦν Χριστὸν ἐν ἀφθαρσίᾳ.

ἀφθαρσία elsewhere means the incorruptibility of future immortality; see, for example, Rom. ii. 7; 2 Tim. i. 10. The adjective ἄφθαρτος has a corresponding meaning. God is ἄφθαρτος, Rom. i. 23; 1 Tim. i. 17; the dead are raised ἄφθαρτοι, 1 Cor. xv. 52; the Christian's crown is ἄφθαρτος. So 1 Pet. iii. 4, the ornament of women is to be ἐν τῷ ἀφθάρτῳ τοῦ πραέος καὶ ἡσυχίου πνεύματος. The word, then, does not point merely to time but to character, and that suits very well here as an attribute of love. It is more than "sincerity" (ἀφθορία, Tit. ii. 7); it is "imperishableness, incorruptibility." It is a "spiritual, eternal love, and thus only is the word worthy to stand as the crown and climax of this glorious Epistle," Alford. Some connect the word with χάρις. Soden defends the connexion on the following grounds: first, that if connected with ἀγαπώντων, ἐν ἀφθ. must express a character of the ἀγάπη, in which case ἀγαπᾶν ἐν ἀφθ. would be an unsuitable form of expression for ἀγαπᾶν ἐν ἀγάπῃ ἀφθάρτῳ; and, secondly, that ἀφθαρσία almost always contains a point of contrast with the transitory nature which belongs to the creature in this world; it belongs to the sphere of heavenly existence, serving to designate eternal life as the highest blessing of salvation; and this is the gift of χάρις, which culminates in the bestowal of it. Bengel, who connects ἀφθ. with χάρις, remarks, however, well: "Congruit cum tota summa epistolae: et inde redundat etiam ἀφθαρσία in amorem fidelium erga Jesum Christum." The writer, in fact, returns to the fundamental thought of i. 3–14.

There is no analogy for the connexion with τὸν Κύριον ἡμῶν, adopted by some expositors.

Ἀμήν is added in א^c D K L P most mss., Amiat.** Syr. (both) Boh., not in א* A B G 17, Arm. Amiat.*

THE
EPISTLE TO THE COLOSSIANS.

ΠΡΟΣ ΚΟΛΟΣΣΑΕΙΣ.

The spelling of the name is uncertain. In the title the spelling Κολοσσαεις is given by ℵ B⁰ D G L 17 (Κολοσαεις), while A B* K P have Κολασσαεις, which ℵ also has twice at the top of the page, and so G once (once also Κολοσοαεις). In the subscription ℵ A B* C K 17 agree in Κολασσαεις, while B² D G L P have Κολοσσαεις.

In ver. 2 ℵ B D G L have Κολοσσαις, K P 17, *al.* Κολασσαις (A *non liquet*).
The versions also vary. Syr. (both) have *a*, with Boh., but Vulg. and Arm. *o*.

Coins give the spelling with *o*, and for the name of the people Κολοσηνων or Κολοσσηνων. But the form with *a* appears in Polyaenus and in some MSS. of Herodotus and Xenophon. The latter may have been a provincial pronunciation and spelling. WH. and Lightfoot adopt *a* in the title, *o* in ver. 2; Tregelles has *a* in both places, as well as in the subscription (which WH. omit). Tischendorf preserves the correct spelling with *o*, remarking, "videtur Κολασσαι scriptura sensim in usum abisse. At inde non sequitur iam Paulum ita scripsisse." As the heading did not proceed from the pen of St. Paul, this conclusion agrees practically with that of WH. and Lightfoot as to the spelling here.

I. 1. SALUTATION. Παῦλος ἀπόστολος, κ.τ.λ. See Eph. i. 1.

καὶ Τιμόθεος. Timothy's name is joined with that of Paul also in 2 Cor. Phil. 1 Thess. 2 Thess. Philemon. In Phil. and Philemon, however, the apostle proceeds in the singular, whereas here the plural is maintained throughout the thanksgiving.

ὁ ἀδελφός. This does not imply any official position (οὐκοῦν καὶ ἀπόστολος, Chrys.); it is the simplest title that could be employed to express Christian brotherhood. So it is used of Quartus, Rom. xvi. 23; of Sosthenes, 1 Cor. i. 1; and of Apollos, 1 Cor. xvi. 12; and of an unnamed brother, 2 Cor. viii. 18, xii. 18. Compare 2 Cor. ix. 3, 5.

2. τοῖς ἐν Κ. ἁγίοις καὶ πιστοῖς ἀδελφοῖς. ἁγίοις, as in all similar salutations, must be taken as a substantive. De Wette, however, and apparently Syr. and Vulg., connect it as an adjective with ἀδελφοῖς. πιστοῖς is more than "believing," which would add nothing to ἁγίοις and ἀδελφοῖς. It is "true, steadfast." Cf. Acts xvi. 15.

ἐν Χριστῷ. Closely connected with πιστοῖς ἀδ., but refers chiefly to πιστοῖς. Cf. πιστὸς διάκονος ἐν Κυρίῳ, Eph. vi. 21. Only in Christ were they "faithful brethren"; the article, therefore, is not required. ἐν Χρ. might, indeed, have been dispensed with; but it suits the formality of the introductory greeting.

After ἐν Χριστῷ, Ἰησοῦ is added in A D* G 17, Vulg. Boh., not in ℵ B D° K L P, Syr-Harcl. Arm. etc. (Syr-Pesh. has Ἰησοῦ before Χριστῷ).

It is remarkable that St. Paul's earlier Epistles are addressed τῇ ἐκκλησίᾳ, ταῖς ἐκκλησίαις; whereas here, as in Rom. and Eph., the address is to the saints and brethren. This can hardly be accidental. It certainly gives the address a more personal and less official aspect, and may have been adopted because the apostle had no personal relations with the heads of these Churches, to which he was personally unknown. It has been objected to this, that in iv. 16 the Church of the Laodiceans is mentioned; and, again, that the Epistle to the Philippians, to whom St. Paul was personally known, is similarly addressed. As to the former objection, it may be fairly replied that to speak of his Epistle being read in the Church is very different from addressing it to the Church; and as to the second, although the word ἐκκλησία is not used in the address to the Phil., we have what may be regarded as an equivalent, σὺν ἐπισκόποις καὶ διακόνοις. It is hardly satisfactory to say that the disuse of ἐκκλησία in the address is characteristic of the later Epistles; for, first, this is not an explanation; and, secondly, the word is used in Philemon, τῇ κατ' οἶκόν σου ἐκκλησίᾳ.

χάρις ὑμῖν καὶ εἰρήνη ἀπὸ Θεοῦ πατρὸς ἡμῶν = Eph. i. 2, where there follows καὶ Κυρίου Ἰησοῦ Χριστοῦ.

These words are added here also in ℵ A C G and most MSS. Boh. Arm., also P in a different order, Ἰησοῦ Χρ. τοῦ Κυρίου ἡμῶν. The words are absent from B D K L 17, al. Amiat. Fuld. Syr-Pesh. (text). Origen and Chrysostom both expressly attest the absence of the words. The latter, after quoting the preceding words, observes: τὸν υἱὸν ἐσίγησεν καὶ οὐ προσέθηκεν ὡς ἐν πάσαις ταῖς ἐπιστολαῖς· καὶ Κυρίου Ἰησοῦ Χριστοῦ. The addition has plainly come in by assimilation to Eph.

3–8. *Thanksgiving for their faith and love, passing on into the assurance that the gospel they were taught by Epaphras was the true universal gospel, which proved its genuineness by the fruit it produced, both among them and in all the world.*

3. εὐχαριστοῦμεν. In all St. Paul's Epistles to Churches, with the exception of that to the Galatians, the Salutation is followed by thanksgiving. In Eph. as in 2 Cor. this is in the form εὐλογητὸς ὁ

Θεός, elsewhere in some form of εὐχαριστῶ. On the verb, see Eph. i. 15.

τῷ Θεῷ πατρί. We have the same form of words in iii. 15; elsewhere, however, always ὁ Θεὸς καὶ πατήρ.

Here also καί is inserted by ℵ A C² Dᶜ K L P, and apparently all other mss. except those mentioned below; Vulg. Arm. Theodoret, al.
It is wanting in B C* D* G, Chrys. (D* G Chrys. have τῷ πατρί). Old Latin, Syr. (both) Boh. Eth.
Tisch. 8th ed. (in deference to ℵ), restores καί, which he had omitted in 7th ed. (WH. and RV. omit). Lachm. also omits, but reads τῷ with D* F G. Meyer thinks καί was omitted in a mechanical way after the preceding Θεοῦ πατρός.
It is observable that in iii. 17, ℵ A agree with B C in omitting καί, while D F G, with K L and nearly all others, as well as Syr-Pesh., insert it. The evidence for the omission there is decidedly preponderant. It is less so here, yet perhaps decisive enough when we consider how certainly the scribes would stumble at the unusual form. The reading τῷ πατρί appears to be another attempt to get rid of it. Compare i. 12 below, where ℵ 37, with other authorities, have Θεῷ before πατρί.

εὐχαριστοῦμεν ... πάντοτε περὶ ὑμῶν προσευχόμενοι. It is questioned whether πάντοτε is to be joined with εὐχαριστοῦμεν or with προσευχ. The latter connexion is adopted by the Greek commentators, also by Bengel, Olshausen, Alford, Ellicott, etc. But Eph. i. 16 is almost decisive for the other connexion, οὐ παύομαι εὐχαριστῶν ὑπὲρ ὑμῶν μνείαν ὑμῶν ποιούμενος ἐπὶ τῶν προσευχῶν μου. Compare 1 Cor. i. 4; 1 Thess. i. 2. προσευχ. is, in fact, a nearer definition of πάντοτε. "We give thanks on your account always in our prayers," or (as Meyer), "always when we pray for you." "Always praying for you" would require the addition of words specifying the object of the prayer.

The reading varies between περί and ὑπέρ. The latter is read by B D* G 17, al., but A C Dᶜ J K, with most mss., have περί. ὑπέρ would readily be introduced from ver. 9, where there is no variant.

4. ἀκούσαντες τὴν πίστιν ὑμῶν ἐν Χριστῷ Ἰησοῦ. Assigns the ground of his thanksgiving. He had heard from Epaphras, ver. 8. The addition of ἐν Χρ. Ἰησ. as a more precise definition of πίστις, which of itself expresses only a psychological conception, is quite natural here, where St. Paul is addressing for the first time those who were unknown to him. So in Eph. i. 15. In Rom. i. 8 the specification of πίστις had preceded vv. 2, 3. The article is unnecessary, as πίστις ἐν Χρ. is one notion. See Eph. l.c.

καὶ τὴν ἀγάπην ἣν ἔχετε εἰς πάντας τοὺς ἁγίους.

ἣν ἔχετε is read in ℵ A C D* G P 17 37 47, al. Old Latin, Vulg. Boh. Syr-Harcl. Arm. But Dᶜ K L and most mss Chrys. Theod. Syr-Pesh. have τὴν ἀγάπην τὴν εἰς, while B has τὴν ἀγάπην εἰς. The reading with ἣν ἔχετε might be a conformation to Philem. 5, while τὴν ἀγάπην τήν might be a conformation to Eph. i. 15.

5. διὰ τὴν ἐλπίδα. The Greek comm. and most moderns

connect this with the words immediately preceding, "the love which ye have to all the saints." ἀγαπᾶτέ, φησι, τοὺς ἁγίους οὐ διά τι ἀνθρώπινον ἀλλὰ διὰ τὸ ἐλπίζειν τὰ μέλλοντα ἀγαθά, Theoph. The reasons alleged are—(1) the remoteness of εὐχαριστοῦμεν; (2) the following clause, ἣν προηκούσατε, suggests that the words διὰ τὴν ἐλπίδα describe the motives of the Colossians for welldoing, rather than the reasons of the apostle for thanksgiving; (3) in other Epistles the ground of thanksgiving is the spiritual state of the persons addressed; (4) εὐχαριστεῖν is never used with διά in the N.T.; and (5) the connexion with εὐχ. would break up the triad of graces which St. Paul delights in associating together. (So Meyer, Soden, Alford, Ellicott, Lightfoot.) (1), (2), (5) are considered by Lightfoot decisive. Yet surely there is something strange in assigning the future hope as the motive of Christian love. As Eadie observes, if the apostle had said that they loved one another because of the common hope which they had in heaven, or that this prospect of a joint inheritance deepened their attachments, the meaning might have been easily apprehended; but why the hope in itself should be selected as the prop of such love, we know not. Of all the graces, love has the least of self in its nature. Such passages as 2 Cor. ix. 6, Gal. vi. 9 f. are not analogous; for what creates a difficulty is not the mention of expected reward as a motive for action, but as a motive for love. As ἐλπίς here is not the grace of hope, but the object (τὴν ἀποκειμένην), reason (5) loses its force; as ἐλπίς does not mean the same thing as in 1 Thess. i. 3, for example, it is quite natural that it should fall into a different connexion. Nor does there seem to be much weight in the second reason. The words ἣν προηκούσατε, κ.τ.λ., involve an appeal to the first teaching they had received, which was sound and full. This goes very well with εὐχαριστοῦμεν; but if the hope were described as the motive of their love, what appropriateness would there be in referring to their former instruction in it? As to (3) and (4), the clause ἀκούσαντες does imply that the ground of his thanksgiving was their faith and love; but it is consistent with this that what prompted him to feel thankful for these graces was the thought of the hope laid up for them, and hence with this connexion διά is not only admissible, but is alone suitable. The signification of εὐχαριστεῖν ὑπέρ (1 Cor. x. 30; Eph. v. 20) is not that required here. There is good reason, then, for Bengel's interpretation: "ex spe patet, quanta sit causa *gratias* agendi pro dono fidei et amoris." If ἣν ἔχετε be omitted the connexion with ἀγάπην is grammatically harsh.

Estius, De Wette, Olshausen, and others connect διὰ τὴν ἐλπ. with both πίστιν and ἀγάπην. This connexion is certainly awkward, and the sentiment not Pauline. Theodore Mops. connects the words with προσευχόμενοι.

ἐλπίς is clearly objective, as in Rom. viii. 24; Gal. v. 5.

τὴν ἀποκειμένην. The thought of the "hope," *i.e.* the blessing hoped for, being already prepared is not expressed in this form by St. Paul elsewhere, except perhaps 1 Tim. vi. 19, but is clearly put in 1 Pet. i. 4, κληρονομίαν ... τετηρημένην ἐν οὐρανοῖς. In substance it is involved in Phil. iii. 20, and, indeed, in Matt. vi. 20.

ἣν προηκούσατε. The προ- has reference, according to Meyer, to the future fulfilment. Bengel understands it simply as "antequam scriberem," but the context rather suggests that the reference is to their early teaching in contrast to the later errors. The apostle now is not teaching them anything new, but desires to confirm them in the true doctrine which they had already learned. Compare *vv.* 7, 23 and v. 6. Hence also the mention of the truth of the gospel in the following words:—

ἐν τῷ λόγῳ τῆς ἀληθείας τοῦ εὐαγγελίου. That εὐαγγελίου is the principal notion here is shown by the participle παρόντος, which agrees with it, and not with ἀληθείας. And this is confirmed by the connexion of ἐλπίς and εὐαγγέλιον in ver. 23. The genitive ἀληθείας then qualifies λόγος, and this compound notion is explained by εὐαγγ. ἡ ἀλ. τοῦ εὐαγγ., Gal. ii. 5, 14, is not exactly parallel, because there the formula has a direct polemical purpose. Here the point is that ὁ λόγος τοῦ εὐαγγ. is a λόγος τῆς ἀληθείας in opposition to those false teachers who would fain complete it by their παραδόσεις, ii. 8, which were κενὴ ἀπάτη.

6. τοῦ παρόντος εἰς ὑμᾶς. A quite classical use of παρεῖναι as implying "has come and remains." οὐ παρεγένετο καὶ ἀπέστη, ἀλλ' ἔμεινε καὶ ἔστιν ἐκεῖ, Chrys.; cf. Acts xii. 20. It needs, then, no further addition.

καθὼς καὶ ἐν παντὶ τῷ κόσμῳ ἐστὶν καρποφορούμενον. παντὶ τῷ κόσμῳ here is not an insignificant hyperbole, but intimates the catholicity of the true gospel in opposition to the merely local character of false gospels; compare ver. 23.

Tischendorf, ed. 8, places a comma after ἐστίν. This construction escapes the irregularity involved in the doubling back of the comparison by the second καθώς. The comparison then may be either as to the mere fact of the presence of the gospel, so that ἐστίν = "exists," or as to the contents of it, which agrees better with the designation of the gospel as λόγος τῆς ἀληθείας. The readers then are assured that the gospel which has come to and remains with them is the same as in the whole world; they need have no fear that it was imperfect; it is the false teachers that are not in agreement with the universal gospel. So Soden. But most comm. connect ἐστί with καρποφορούμενον καὶ αὐξ.

καί is prefixed to ἐστίν in D^bc G K L, etc. Old Lat. Vulg. Syr. (both) Chrys.

It is absent from ℵ A B C D* 17, *al.* Boh. Arm. Eth. The evidence against it, therefore, is quite decisive. It was doubtless added to simplify the construction, and is defended on the ground of this simplicity by Olshausen and Eadie. Ellicott, who had previously hesitated, thinking that it might have been omitted to modify the hyperbole, omitted the word in his 5th ed.

καρποφορούμενον. The middle voice is not elsewhere found; its force here is probably intensive, denoting the inherent energy, while the active (which is used below, ver. 10) would rather denote external diffusion (Lightfoot). Verbs like σιδηροφορεῖσθαι, τυμπανοφορεῖσθαι are not parallel, since in them φορεῖσθαι means "to wear."

Those comm. who connect ἐστίν with the participles explain this periphrastic present as expressing continuity of action, as in 2 Cor. ix. 12, οὐ μόνον ἐστὶν προσαναπληροῦσα, κ.τ.λ., and Phil. ii. 26, ἐπιποθῶν ἦν.

καὶ αὐξανόμενον rests on preponderant evidence, ℵ A B C D* G I, Vss. Rec. omits, with D^he K, etc.

αὐξανόμενον doubtless refers to the outward expansion, as καρποφ. to the personal, inner working. "The gospel is not like those plants which exhaust themselves in bearing fruit and wither away. The external growth keeps pace with the reproductive energy," Lightfoot. Observe the order; first the preservation of the gospel amongst those who received it, and after that its extension to new circles. Both are to the Colossians a proof of its truth and sufficiency.

καθὼς καὶ ἐν ὑμῖν, so that they did not come behind their brethren in this respect.

If we connect the participles with ἐστίν, the comparison is very curiously doubled back on itself. Moreover, as Olshausen observes (defending the addition of καί after κόσμῳ), the words καθὼς καὶ ἐν ὑμῖν do not fit the beginning of the proposition, καθὼς καὶ ἐν παντὶ τῷ κόσμῳ, since the Colossians are, of course, included with the rest in the whole world. Lightfoot explains the irregularity thus: "The clause reciprocating the comparison is an afterthought springing out of the apostle's anxiety not to withhold praise where praise can be given," and he compares 1 Thess. iv. 1 (not Rec.), παρακαλοῦμεν ἐν Κυρίῳ Ἰησοῦ ἵνα, καθὼς παρελάβετε παρ' ἡμῶν τὸ πῶς δεῖ ὑμᾶς περιπατεῖν καὶ ἀρέσκειν Θεῷ, καθὼς καὶ περιπατεῖτε, ἵνα περισσεύητε μᾶλλον. But that passage is not really parallel; for καθὼς καὶ περιπατεῖτε is entirely distinct from καθὼς παρελάβετε, and is a courteous admission that they were actually walking as they had been taught. Here there is nothing of the kind, and the difficulty (apart from that mentioned by Olshausen) is that we have the mere repetition, "in you as also in all the world, as also in you." The difficulty, of course, disappears in the

Rec. Text with the insertion of καί; or, since we are compelled to omit καί, with the adoption of the construction above referred to, as then the comparison in καθὼς καὶ ἐν ὑμῖν is with καρποφ. καὶ αὐξ.

ἀφ' ἧς ἡμέρας, κ.τ.λ. To be closely joined with καθὼς καὶ ἐν ὑμῖν; the fruitfulness and growth began at once, so that it was independent of these later παραδόσεις.

ἠκούσατε καὶ ἐπέγνωτε τὴν χάριν. There is no occasion to regard τὴν χάριν as the object of the latter verb only (as Meyer, Alford, Ellicott, Eadie understanding "it," i.e. the gospel, as the object of ἠκούσατε). χάρις was the content of the gospel message, which is called τὸ εὐαγγέλιον τῆς χάριτος τοῦ Θεοῦ (Acts xx. 24), and as such may be said to be heard. We can hardly, indeed, say, with Lightfoot, that St. Paul uses χάρις as a "synonyme for the gospel," of which use he gives as instances 2 Cor. vi. 1, viii. 9, γινώσκετε τὴν χάριν τοῦ Κυρίου ἡμῶν Ἰησοῦ Χριστοῦ, ὅτι δι' ὑμᾶς ἐπτώχευσε πλούσιος ὤν. Here the word suggests a contrast with the false gospel, which was one of δόγματα (ii. 14). Compare Gal. ii. 21, οὐκ ἀθετῶ τὴν χάριν τοῦ Θεοῦ.

ἐπέγνωτε implies not so much developed knowledge as active conscious recognition, or taking knowledge of; cf. Acts iii. 10, iv. 13, xxii. 24, 29, xxvii. 39, xxviii. 1; 1 Cor. xiv. 37; 2 Cor. i. 14 (ἐπέγνωτε ἡμᾶς ἀπὸ μέρους).

ἐν ἀληθείᾳ. Even although the gospel was itself λόγος τῆς ἀληθείας, there was the possibility that as known by them it was imperfect; hence this is added to guard them against the error of the false teachers, who insisted on supplementing it by their philosophy (ii. 8, 28).

7. καθὼς ἐμάθετε ἀπὸ Ἐπαφρᾶ. This gives them a further assurance as to the source of their Christianity; the apostle gives his seal to the teaching of Epaphras, which conveyed the full gospel of the grace of God, so that having received this in truth as they did, they had no need to listen to strange teachers.

Epaphras appears from iv. 12 to have been a Colossian; either a native, or now reckoned as an inhabitant of Colossae. From the present passage we gather that he was the founder of the Church there (compare the καθώς and ἀφ' ἧς ἡμέρας.) He was at this time a fellow-prisoner of St. Paul (Philemon 23): or perhaps συναιχμάλωτος there only means that he was so constantly with St. Paul as practically to share his captivity. As the name is a shortened form of Epaphroditus, it was natural to conjecture that the Epaphroditus of Phil. ii. 25 was the same person. But the names were common, occurring frequently in inscriptions; and as Epaphroditus appears to be in close connexion with the Philippians (whose ἀπόστολος he was), there is no sufficient ground for the identification.

τοῦ ἀγαπητοῦ συνδούλου ἡμῶν. So Tychicus (iv. 7) is called

σύνδουλος, the servitude being, of course, to Christ. This designation appears intended to command high respect for Epaphras, who is thus placed as near as possible to the apostle.

ὅς ἐστι πιστὸς ὑπὲρ ἡμῶν διάκονος τοῦ Χριστοῦ. See note on the reading. The reading ἡμῶν makes Epaphras a representative of St. Paul in preaching the gospel at Colossae; probably at the time when the apostle was dwelling for two years at Ephesus, at which time "all that dwelt in Asia heard the word of the Lord Jesus" (Acts xix. 10). This would explain the attitude of authority which St. Paul assumes in this Epistle towards a Church which he had not himself seen.

διάκονος has clearly its general meaning "minister," not the special sense "deacon," as the genitive τοῦ Χριστοῦ shows. This designation of him as πιστὸς ὑπὲρ ἡμῶν, κ.τ.λ., serves still further to confirm the confidence of the Colossians in their first teacher. If ὑμῶν is read, ὑπέρ ὑμῶν would mean "for your benefit," not "instead of you," for there is no personal reference here, as in Philemon 13, ἵνα ὑπὲρ σοῦ μοι διακονῇ. The genitive τοῦ Χριστοῦ is, indeed, decisive of this, for this implies that his ministry was one of spiritual benefit, which would not be suitable to a messenger from the Colossians to St. Paul.

There are two rather important varieties of reading in ver. 7. The Rec. Text has καί after καθώς on comparatively weak authority, viz. D^c 37 47 K L Syr-Harcl. Arm., against ℵ A B C D* G 17 P Vulg. Syr. Pesh. and other Vers. καί was doubtless added from assimilation to the two preceding καθὼς καί. καθὼς ἐμάθετε without καί can only mean that Epaphras was their first teacher.

The other important variation is between ὑπὲρ ἡμῶν and ὑπὲρ ὑμῶν, and with respect to this there is a remarkable conflict between MSS. and versions. ἡμῶν is read by ℵ* A B D* G.

Ambrosiaster (Comm. "qui eis ministravit gratiam Christi vice Apostoli"). ὑμῶν by ℵ^c C D^bc K L P and most MSS.

The versions, however, are nearly all on the side of ὑμῶν, Vulg. Syr. (both) Boh. Arm. Eth. Goth. Chrys. also interprets ὑμῶν. The other Greek comm. are silent as to the word in their comments, and the reading in their texts, which is ὑμῶν, may be due to editors. Of the old Latin, d (and e) with f have "vobis" (against the Greek D F), while g has "nobis" (agreeing with G).

Internal evidence favours ἡμῶν. First, "for your benefit" would hardly be expressed by ὑπὲρ ὑμῶν, but either by ὑμῶν, cf. διάκονον περιτομῆς, Rom. xv. 8, or ὑμῖν, as in 1 Pet. i. 12. The form of expression does not indicate that any emphasis on "for your benefit" is intended, as if the apostle meant to impress on the Col. that whatever Epaphras had done was for their good. Secondly, it is easy to understand how ὑμῶν might be substituted for ἡμῶν, partly on account of the recurrence of ὑπὲρ ὑμῶν in the neighbouring context (vv. 3, 9) and in connexion with this, from the significance of ἡμῶν not being understood. The two words being pronounced alike, these circumstances would naturally lead to ὑμῶν being written by mistake in the first instance, and the second to its preference when both readings were deliberately compared. On the other hand, Meyer thinks that ἡμῶν is due to the influence of the preceding ἡμῶν and the following ἡμῶν. Editors differ in their judgment;

Lachm. Treg. WH. Lightfoot, RV. Barry, Moule adopt ἡμῶν, ὑμῶν being given a place in the margin by WH. RV.

On the other hand, Tisch. Meyer, Ell. Eadie, Soden prefer ὑμῶν. Eadie in support of this points out that ἡμῶν would include Timothy. But there is no reason why Timothy should be so pointedly excluded, as would have been the case had ἐμοῦ been used, any more than with συνδούλου and δηλώσας.

8. ὁ καὶ δηλώσας ἡμῖν τὴν ὑμῶν ἀγάπην ἐν πνεύματι, viz. their love to St. Paul in particular. This appears clear from ἡμῖν τὴν ὑμῶν, as well as from the subsequent διὰ τοῦτο καὶ ἡμεῖς. The words may be regarded as a courteous justification of the didactic tone which the apostle adopts, and perhaps also as an indication that Epaphras had not made any complaint of the Colossians. Meyer (reading ὑμῶν) understands love to Epaphras; Ellicott, brotherly love.

ἐν πνεύματι expresses the ground of their love, which was not individual sympathy, personal acquaintance, or the like, but belonged to the sphere of the Holy Spirit's influence. It was οὐ σαρκική, ἀλλὰ πνευματική, Oecum. Compare ὅσοι οὐχ ἑωράκασι τὸ πρόσωπόν μου ἐν σαρκί (ii. 7).

9-12. *Prayer for their advancement in spiritual knowledge, not speculative, but practical.*

9. Διὰ τοῦτο. On account, namely, of all that has preceded from ver. 4; cf. 1 Thess. ii. 4. Chrys. strikingly observes: καθάπερ ἐν τοῖς ἀγῶσιν ἐκείνους μάλιστα διεγείρομεν τοὺς ἐγγὺς ὄντας τῆς νίκης· οὕτω δὴ καὶ ὁ Παῦλος τούτους μάλιστα παρακαλεῖ τοὺς τὸ πλέον κατωρθωκότας. Cf. Eph. i. 15. καὶ ἡμεῖς, "we also," by its position emphasises the transition from the conduct of the Colossians to its effect on the apostle and his friends.

ἀφ' ἧς ἡμέρας ἠκούσαμεν echoes the similar expression in ver. 6. So the apostle's prayer was, as it were, an echo of their faith. An encouragement to them to proceed as they had begun.

οὐ παυόμεθα προσευχόμενοι. Cf. Eph. i. 16. Called by Ellicott an "affectionate hyperbole"; yet it is hardly to be called a hyperbole, for it would at no moment be true to say that he had ceased to pray for them. It is not asserted that the expression of the prayer was uninterrupted. As they did not cease to grow and bear fruit, so he did not cease to pray. Cf. Acts v. 42, οὐκ ἐπαύοντο διδάσκοντες, κ.τ.λ., and *contra*, Acts xiii. 10, οὐ παύσῃ διαστρέφων, and 1 Sam. xii. 23. καὶ αἰτούμενοι, κ.τ.λ., adds the special request to the more general προσευχόμενοι. Compare Mk. xi. 24, ὅσα προσεύχεσθε καὶ αἰτεῖσθε.

ἵνα after words like θέλειν, αἰτεῖσθαι, signifies merely the purport of the wish or prayer; cf. Phil. i. 9, where τοῦτο as object of προσεύχομαι is explained by ἵνα πληρωθῆτε τὴν ἐπίγνωσιν. For the accusative, compare Phil. i. 11, πεπληρωμένοι καρπὸν δικαιοσύνης, "that ye may be perfected in," Oltramare. ἐπίγνωσιν, stronger than γνῶσις: see 1 Cor. xiii. 12. The difference, however, seems to be rather that the former word implies a more active exercise of a faculty, and hence lends itself better to the expression of practical knowledge. This distinction agrees well with Rom. i. 21, 28. Compare on the verb, ver. 6. Lightfoot remarks that ἐπίγνωσις is a favourite word in the later Epistles of St. Paul; but, in fact, although it occurs four times in this Epistle and twice in Eph., it is used only once in Phil. (i. 9), whereas it is thrice used in Rom. In the later Epistles, however, it is always used in reference to spiritual knowledge. See Trench, *Syn.* lxxv.

τοῦ θελήματος αὐτοῦ. The following context, *vv.* 10-12, shows that what is meant is the Divine will as to their conduct, as in iv. 12; 1 Thess. iv. 3, v. 18; Rom. xii. 2; not the χάρις mentioned as the object of their knowledge in ver. 6 (διὰ τοῦ υἱοῦ προσάγεσθαι ἡμᾶς αὐτῷ, οὐκέτι δι' ἀγγέλων, Chrys. etc.). The knowledge which is here meant is, in fact, the consequence of that which is there attributed to them. Knowing the χάρις, they should know also that what God required of them was nothing but conduct corresponding thereto. This in opposition to the false teachers and the doctrines of their φιλοσοφία.

ἐν πάσῃ σοφίᾳ καὶ συνέσει πνευματικῇ. "In all spiritual wisdom and understanding," ἐν introducing the manner in which the πληρωθῆναι is carried out, and πάσῃ and πνευματικῇ being taken with both substantives. To connect πν. with συνέσει alone would be to give the inappropriate meaning, "wisdom of all kinds and spiritual understanding."

On σοφία see Eph. i. 8, where the words are ἐν πάσῃ σοφίᾳ καὶ φρονήσει. These three, σοφία, φρόνησις, σύνεσις, are reckoned by Aristotle as the three intellectual ἀρεταί or excellences (*Eth. N.* i. 13), the first being the most general and thorough, embracing the knowledge of first principles as well as that of particulars; while he distinguishes φρόνησις as the practical knowledge of particulars from σύνεσις, which is critical; ἡ φρόνησις ἐπιτακτική ἐστιν . . . ἡ δὲ σύνεσις κριτική (*Eth. N.* vi. 7. 11). Demosth. (269. 24) defines σύνεσις, ᾗ τὰ καλὰ καὶ αἰσχρὰ διαγνώσκεται, which agrees with Aristotle's κριτική. It would appear, therefore, that σύνεσις was the faculty of deciding what was right or wrong in particular cases, while σοφία apprehended the general principles. But σύνεσις is used by St. Paul in a more general sense; see Eph. iii. 4; cf. Luke ii. 47. The two words frequently occur together in the O.T., *e.g.* Ex. xxxi. 3; Isa. xxix. 14; Eccles. xiv. 20; (1 Cor. i. 19 is a quotation), and the corresponding adjectives in Matt. xi. 25.

πνευματικῇ, given by the Spirit. Compare 1 Cor. xii. 8, ᾧ μὲν διὰ τοῦ πνεύματος δίδοται λόγος σοφίας.

The word is emphatic in this position, marking the contrast

with the false teaching, which had λόγον σοφίας, a pretence of wisdom (ii. 23) which really proceeded from ὁ νοῦς τῆς σαρκός (ii. 18). We have the apostle's σοφία σαρκική, 2 Cor. i. 12; ἀνθρωπίνη, 1 Cor. ii. 5, 13; τοῦ κόσμου τούτου, 1 Cor. ii. 6, etc.

10. περιπατῆσαι ὑμᾶς ἀξίως τοῦ Κυρίου. A similar expression occurs 1 Thess. ii. 12, ἀξίως τοῦ Θεοῦ: and Eph. iv. 1, τῆς κλήσεως, "in a manner worthy of," *i.e.* befitting your connexion with Him. The infinitive expresses the consequence (and proof) of πληρωθῆναι, ἀεὶ τῇ πίστει συζεύγνυσι τὴν πολιτείαν, Chrys.

If ὑμᾶς after περιπατῆσαι were genuine (Text. Rec.), the infinitive might conceivably be regarded as dependent on προσευχόμενοι; but it is certainly spurious, being omitted by ℵ* A B C D* G 17, *al.* Clem., Boh. It is added in ℵᶜ Dᶜ K L P, most mss. Chrys. Theodoret, Arm.

εἰς πᾶσαν ἀρεσκείαν. *I.e.* "so as to please God in every way." Compare 1 Thess. iv. 5, πῶς δεῖ ὑμᾶς περιπατεῖν καὶ ἀρέσκειν Θεῷ. In classical authors ἀρεσκεία has generally an unfavourable sense, "obsequiousness," and it is so defined both in *Eth. Eudem.* (τὸ λίαν πρὸς ἡδονήν, ii. 3) and by Theophrastus (*Char.* 5). Polybius uses it especially of trying to gain the favour of a sovereign. Similarly Philo, πάντα καὶ λέγειν καὶ πράττειν ἐσπούδαζεν εἰς ἀρεσκείαν τοῦ πατρὸς καὶ βασιλέως (i. p. 34), but he also uses it of pleasing God. The ἀνθρώποις ἀρέσκειν is disavowed by the apostle in Gal. i. 10; 1 Thess. ii. 4; compare ch. iii. 22. The verb is used, however, without any unfavourable connotation, in Rom. xv. 2 (τῷ πλησίον ἀρεσκέτω) and elsewhere.

ἐν παντὶ ἔργῳ ἀγαθῷ qualifies the following, as *ἐν πάσῃ δυνάμει* qualifies the following participle. Most commentators separate καρποφοροῦντες and αὐξανόμενοι; but then αὐξ. τῇ ἐπιγνώσει becomes tautologous with πληρωθῆτε τὴν ἐπίγνωσιν, ver. 9. Moreover, the combination καρποφορούμενον καὶ αὐξ. in ver. 6 seems to require that the two participles here also should be taken together. What is true of the gospel in the world and amongst the Colossians is also to hold good of those whose lives are inspired by its teaching. The participles refer to the logical subject of περιπατῆσαι, not to πληρωθῆτε (Beza, Bengel). Cf. Eph. iv. 2. **τῇ ἐπιγνώσει τοῦ Θεοῦ,** "by the knowledge of God," instrumental dative, a frequent use of the dative with αὔξαν. (So Alford, Eadie, Ellicott, Lightfoot, Soden, RV.mg.) The fruitfulness and growth are wrought through the ἐπίγνωσις τοῦ Θεοῦ, and this again results from the practice of his will, ver. 9.

Some commentators take the dative as one of reference, as in Rom. iv. 20 (?), "increasing in the knowledge of God" (Moule, RV. text), which, after πληρωθῆτε τὴν ἐπιγν., ver. 9, would be somewhat of a tautology.

τῇ ἐπιγνώσει is the reading of ℵ A B C D* G P 17, *al.* Amiat. Arm. *al.* ἐν is prefixed in ℵᶜ 47, and a few others, Chrys. Old Lat. and Vulg-Clem.

have "in scientia Dei," which is doubtful. Text. Rec. has εἰς τὴν ἐπίγνωσιν, with D^c K L most mss., Theodoret, Theoph. Oec. This appears to be an attempt to simplify the construction. Meyer, on the contrary, regards the dative as an explanation of the more difficult (?) εἰς τὴν ἐπ., which, he thinks, is also confirmed by the parallelism in structure of the other participial clauses, which conclude with a definition introduced by εἰς. He understands it as "in respect of," that is, always more fully attaining to a knowledge of God, εἰς indicating the final reference, or direction of the growth, comparing Eph. iv. 15 and 2 Pet. i. 8. As to the comparative difficulty of the readings, Alford's judgment, that the simple dative "is by far the most difficult of the three readings," is surely more correct than Meyer's. εἰς τὴν ἐπίγν. would, in fact, present no difficulty to the ordinary reader.

11. ἐν πάσῃ δυνάμει δυναμούμενοι. Theodoret takes this ἐν as instrumental, τῇ θείᾳ ῥοπῇ κρατυνόμενοι, and so Eadie, Ellicott, and Meyer. "Strengthened with all (every form of) strength," Ell. (a translation which is itself ambiguous).

It is simpler and more natural to understand ἐν π. δ. as "in (*i.e.* in the matter of) all strength" (Alford, Lightfoot). It thus corresponds with ἐν πάσῃ σοφίᾳ and ἐν παντὶ ἔργῳ, which are both subjective. δυναμούμενοι, present, "becoming strengthened." The simple verb is not used elsewhere by St. Paul, who, however, employs ἐνδυναμοῦσθαι several times. But δυναμοῦσθαι is in Heb. xi. 34, and B has it in Eph. vi. 10. It is frequently used by the Greek translators of the O.T., but is not a classical word. The connected virtues here, ὑπομονή and μακροθυμία, indicate that what is referred to in this clause is steadfastness under trial, as the former referred to active conduct.

κατὰ τὸ κράτος τῆς δόξης αὐτοῦ. "According to the might of His glory." Strength is supplied in a manner correspondent with the power which belongs to the glory of God, *i.e.* His majesty as manifested to men. Compare Eph. i. 19. The rendering of AV. (Beza, etc.), "His glorious power," is sufficiently refuted by αὐτοῦ. Thomas Aquinas understands by "His glory," "His Son Christ Jesus." But although the Son may be called ἀπαύγασμα τῆς δόξης αὐτοῦ, it would not be intelligible to use ἡ δόξα αὐτοῦ as a substitute for His name. Lightfoot remarks that κράτος in N.T. is "applied solely to God"; but see Heb. ii. 14, τὸν τὸ κράτος ἔχοντα τοῦ θανάτου, τοῦτ' ἔστι τὸν διάβολον.

εἰς πᾶσαν ὑπομονὴν καὶ μακροθυμίαν. "To all endurance and longsuffering." "Patience" is a very inadequate rendering of ὑπομονή, which includes perseverance or steadfast continuance in a course of action. Thus we have καρποφοροῦσιν ἐν ὑπομονῇ, Luke viii. 15; ὑπομονὴ ἔργου ἀγαθοῦ, Rom. ii. 7; δι' ὑπομονῆς τρέχωμεν, Heb. xii. 1. Even the ὑπομονή of Job, to which James refers, was by no means the uncomplaining endurance of suffering to which we give the name of "patience." Job was, in fact, the very reverse of "patient"; but he maintained his faith in God and his uprightness in spite of his sore trials. μακροθυμία comes much nearer to our notion of "patience" (cf. 1 Cor. xiii. 4); not so much, however, patience under suffering, but "the self-restraint which does not hastily retaliate a wrong." It is the opposite of ὀξυθυμία. Chrysostom distinguishes the two words thus: μακροθυμεῖ τις πρὸς ἐκείνους οὓς δυνατὸν καὶ ἀμύνασθαι· ὑπομένει δὲ οὓς οὐ δύναται ἀμύνασθαι; but this, though correct as to μακροθυμεῖ, is clearly inadequate for ὑπομένει.

11, 12. μετὰ χαρᾶς εὐχαριστοῦντες. μετὰ χαρᾶς is joined by many comm. to the preceding (Theodoret, Olsh. De W. Alf. Eadie, Lightfoot, RV.). In defence of this it is said that εὐχαριστεῖν of itself implies joyfulness, so that μετὰ χ. if attached to it would be flat and unmeaning; also that by joining the words with εὐχ. we lose the essential idea of joyful endurance. Lightfoot, quoting Jas. i. 2, 3, πᾶσαν χαρὰν ἡγήσασθε . . . ὅταν πειρασμοῖς περιπέσητε ποικίλοις, γινώσκοντες ὅτι τὸ δοκίμιον ὑμῶν τῆς πίστεως κατεργάζεται ὑπομονήν, remarks that this parallel points to the connexion with the preceding, and adds that the emphatic position of the words if connected with εὐχ. cannot be explained. It may be replied that εὐχαριστεῖν does not necessarily imply joy. See, for example, 1 Cor. xiv. 18, "I thank God, I speak with tongues more than you all," x. 30; Col. iii. 17. χαρᾶς is so far from being flat or unmeaning, that without it εὐχαριστοῦντες would be too weak. The idea of joyful endurance is not lost when the prayer passes from endurance to joyful thanksgiving; and the emphatic position of the words is sufficiently explained by the writer's desire to emphasise this characteristic of their thanksgiving with special reference to the trials implied in ὑπομονή and μακροθυμία. The words thus acquire greater significance than if they slipped in as it were after μακροθυμίαν. The connexion with εὐχαριστοῦντες is also favoured by the structure of the preceding clauses, each of which commences with a defining adjunct. This connexion is adopted by Chrys. Theoph. Oecum., also Ellicott, Meyer, Soden, Lachm. Tisch.

In any case εὐχ. is not to be connected with οὐ παυόμεθα, as Chrys. Theoph. al., which unnaturally separates this clause from the preceding, making them parenthetical. This interpretation was suggested by the reading ἡμᾶς: but even if that is correct, the transition from the second person to the first is quite in St. Paul's manner; cf. ii. 12, 13.

τῷ Πατρί. The designation of God thus absolutely as ὁ Πατήρ, when Christ has not been named immediately before (as in Rom. vi. 5; Eph. ii. 18; Acts i. 4, 7, ii. 33), is remarkable. But we have τοῦ Κυρίου in ver. 10, and, what is perhaps more to the point, τοῦ υἱοῦ τῆς ἀγάπης αὐτοῦ in ver. 13.

א 37 (G, Οεω τω πατρι), Vulg-Clem. Boh. al. prefix Θεῷ πατρί.

τῷ ἱκανώσαντι ὑμᾶς. "Who qualified you," or "made you competent," *i.e.* given you a title. The same verb occurs 2 Cor. iii. 6 (only). ὃς καὶ ἱκάνωσεν ἡμᾶς διακόνους καινῆς διαθήκης, "qualified us to be ministers," cf. *ib.* ver. 5. The adjective ἱκανός is of frequent occurrence in the N.T., always with the idea of reaching to a certain standard, "sufficient," and so when time or quantity is in question, "considerable." See Mark xv. 15; Luke xxii. 38, ἱκανόν ἐστι: Acts xxii. 6, φῶς ἱκανόν; 2 Cor. ii. 16, πρὸς ταῦτα τίς ἱκανός: 2 Tim. ii. 2, οἵτινες ἱκανοὶ ἔσονται καὶ ἑτέρους διδάξαι. It does not mean "dignus," "worthy," although with a negative that translation is not unsuitable in Matt. iii. 11, viii. 8. Here, then, ἱκάνωσεν is not "dignos fecit," Vulg., but "idoneos fecit."

> There is an important variety of reading. For ἱκανώσαντι (which is read by ℵ A C Dᵉ K L P most mss., Vulg. Boh. Syr. (both), Chrys. etc.) we have καλέσαντι in D* G 17 80, Goth. Arm. Eth., also Didymus (once), Ambrosiaster; while B has καλέσαντι καὶ ἱκανώσαντι, which is adopted by Lachm., but appears to be a combination of both readings. The confusion between ΤΩΙΚΑΝΩCANTI and ΤΩΙΚΑΛΕCANTI would be easy, and the latter word would naturally occur to a copyist.
> ὑμᾶς is the reading of ℵ B 4 23 80 115, Amiat. Syr-Pesh. marg. Eth. Didymus, Theoph. Ambrosiaster.
> ἡμᾶς, A C D G K L P most mss., Vulg-Clem. Fuld. Syr-Pesh. and Harcl. text, Chrys. Theodoret, etc.
> Internal evidence seems rather to favour ὑμᾶς. The natural tendency of scribes would be to generalise such a statement, and this would be assisted by ἡμᾶς which presently follows. On the other hand, it would be quite natural for St. Paul to enforce the exhortation involved in his prayer by such a personal application. In the next sentence, where he passes to a direct dogmatic statement, he naturally and of course uses ἡμᾶς. (Yet P, *al.* Amiat. Goth. have ὑμᾶς there also.) Compare Eph. iv. 32, v. 2. ὑμᾶς is adopted here by Tisch. WH. Soden, and is given a place in the margin by Tregelles, Lightfoot, RV.

εἰς τὴν μερίδα τοῦ κλήρου, "for, *i.e.* to obtain, the portion of the lot." Compare Ps. xv. 5, Κύριος μερὶς τῆς κληρονομίας μου. Κλῆρος (pp. "a lot") is not synonymous with κληρονομία, it does not designate the whole, but the allotted part; cf. Acts viii. 21, οὐκ ἔστι σοι μερὶς οὐδὲ κλῆρος: xxvi. 18, κλῆρον ἐν τοῖς ἡγιασμένοις. What is a μερίς in reference to the whole is a κλῆρος in reference to the possessor. The genitive, then, is one of apposition, "the portion which consists in the lot" (Lightfoot, Soden). It is, however, possible to understand it as partitive, "to have a share in the κλῆρος," and so most comm. Chrysostom observes: διὰ τί κλῆρον καλεῖ; δεικνὺς ὅτι οὐδεὶς ἀπὸ κατορθωμάτων οἰκείων βασιλείας τυγχάνει, referring to Luke xvii. 10. Compare also Luke xii. 32, εὐδόκησεν ὁ πατὴρ ὑμῶν δοῦναι ὑμῖν τὴν βασιλείαν.

ἐν τῷ φωτί. Chrys. Oec. Theoph. followed by Meyer, *al.*, connect with ἱκανώσαντι, "by the light," ἱκανοῦν ἐν τῷ φωτί being nothing else but καλεῖν εἰς τὸ φῶς (1 Pet. ii. 9) regarded in its moral efficacy, the result of which is that men are φῶς ἐν Κυρίῳ (Eph. v. 8). This light has power, it is the light of life (John

viii. 12); has its weapons (Rom. xiii. 12); produces fruit (Eph. v. 9), etc.; and without it men were incapable of partaking in the kingdom of Christ. But φῶς is not the means, but the result; and, moreover, the distance of ἐν τῷ φωτί from ἱκαν. forbids the connexion, for there is no such emphasis on the words as to account for their position. It is the deliverance that is the thought dwelt on, not the means. It is better to connect the word with τὴν μερίδα, κ.τ.λ. (Alf. Lightfoot), or, if with one of the three substantives, with κλήρου, which has a local sense (Ellicott, Soden). Thus ἐν τῷ φωτί = "in the kingdom of light." Compare 2 Cor. xi. 14; 1 Tim. vi. 16; 1 John i. 7; Rev. xxi. 24. κλῆρος ἐν τῷ φωτί, then, is equivalent to the ἐλπὶς ἀποκειμένη ἐν τοῖς οὐρανοῖς, φῶς being here chosen because the apostle had already in his thoughts the representation of the natural condition of men as σκότος. There is nothing, therefore, in the objection, that if this were the sense intended ἐν τοῖς οὐρανοῖς would have been used, or ἐν τῇ ζωῇ, or the like. Eadie's interpretation, "the inheritance which consists in light," is untenable, and is certainly not supported by his examples of κλῆρος ἐν from Acts viii. 21, xxvi. 18.

13 ff. *From the prayer for their increase in knowledge, St. Paul goes on to give them positive instruction which will be a safeguard against the false teaching which threatens them. They have already been translated from the kingdom of darkness to the kingdom of God's beloved Son, and it is in Him only that they have redemption.*

13. ὃς ἐρρύσατο (ἐρύσατο, B* G P Lightf.) ἡμᾶς ἐκ τῆς ἐξουσίας τοῦ σκότους. "Who rescued us from the power of darkness." ἐρρύσατο, δεικνὺς ὅτι ὡς αἰχμάλωτοι ἐταλαιπωρούμεθα. Theoph. ἐξουσία (from ἔξεστι), properly means "liberty of action," as in 1 Cor. ix. 5; hence in relation to others, "authority," generally "delegated authority" (but not always; see Jude 25). Lightfoot, following Wetstein, maintains that the word here means "arbitrary power, tyranny." But the instances he cites seem quite insufficient to support this. In Demosth., for example, *De Falsa Leg.* p. 428, τὴν ἄγαν ταύτην ἐξουσίαν, it is the word ἄγαν that introduces the idea of excess, just as we might speak of the "excessive exercise of authority." From the etymology of the word it is applicable, whether the ἐξεῖναι is assumed or rightfully derived. Whatever its use, however, in Plutarch or other writers, the usage of the N.T. gives no support to Lightfoot's view. It is a word of very frequent occurrence (being found nearly one hundred times), and always in the simple sense of "authority" (abstract or concrete). If the "idea of disorder is involved" in ἡ ἐξουσία τοῦ σκότους here and in Luke xxii. 53, it is suggested by σκότους, not by ἐξουσία. When Chrysostom, after explaining τῆς ἐξουσίας by τῆς τυραννίδος, adds: χαλεπὸν καὶ τὸ ἁπλῶς εἶναι ὑπὸ τῷ διαβόλῳ· τὸ δὲ καὶ μετ' ἐξουσίας, τοῦτο χαλεπώτερον, his meaning seems to be: "It is hard to be simply under the power of the devil; but that he should also have authority is still harder." This gives much more force to his words. That ἐξουσία is not opposed to βασιλεία, as an arbitrary tyranny to a well-ordered sovereignty, see Rev. xii. 10, ἡ βασιλεία τοῦ Θεοῦ ἡμῶν καὶ ἡ ἐξουσία τοῦ Χριστοῦ αὐτοῦ. The whole passage is strikingly parallel to Acts xxvi. 18, τοῦ ἐπιστρέψαι ἀπὸ σκότους εἰς φῶς καὶ τῆς ἐξουσίας τοῦ Σατανᾶ ἐπὶ τὸν Θεόν, τοῦ λαβεῖν αὐτοὺς ἄφεσιν ἁμαρτιῶν καὶ κλῆρον ἐν τοῖς ἡγιασμένοις. σκότος here is not to be regarded as personified, as if it were equivalent to "the devil" (Augustine); it is rather the characteristic and ruling principle of the region in which they dwelt before conversion to Christ.

καὶ μετέστησεν. The verb is appropriate, being that which is employed by classical writers to signify the removal of whole bodies of men. Yet it is doubtful whether such an idea is present here; cf. Plato, *Rep.* vii. p. 518 A, ἔκ τε φωτὸς εἰς σκότος μεθισταμένων καὶ ἐκ σκότους εἰς φῶς.

τοῦ υἱοῦ τῆς ἀγάπης αὐτοῦ. Not of angels, as the false teachers would have it. ὑπὸ τὸν κληρόνομον ἐσμέν, οὐχ ὑπὸ τοὺς οἰκέτας, Severianus.

τῆς ἀγάπης αὐτοῦ. Augustine understands this as a genitive "auctoris." "Caritas quippe Patris ... nihil est quam ejus ipsa natura atque substantia ... ac per hoc filius caritatis ejus nullus est alius quam qui de ejus substantia est genitus" (*De Trin.* xv. 19). He is followed by Olshausen and Lightfoot. But such a form of expression has no analogy in the N.T. Love is not the "substantia" or "natura" of God, but an essential attribute. An action might be ascribed to it, but not the generation of a person.

Theodore of Mopsuestia interpreted the expression in an opposite way: υἱὸν ἀγάπης αὐτὸν ἐκάλεσεν ὡς οὐ φύσει τοῦ Πατρὸς ὄντα υἱὸν ἀλλ' ἀγάπῃ τῆς υἱοθεσίας ἀξιωθέντα τούτων. But an explanation of the nature of the Sonship would be alien to the context. The simplest interpretation is, "the Son who is the object of His love." It corresponds exactly with Eph. i. 6, ἐν τῷ ἠγαπημένῳ ἐν ᾧ ἔχομεν, κ.τ.λ., only that it gives more prominence to the attribute. Love is not merely bestowed upon Him, but makes Him its own. υἱὸς ὀδύνης μου in Gen. xxxv. 18 (Meyer, Ellicott) is not parallel.

Lightfoot thinks this interpretation destroys the whole force of the expression; but it is not so. It is because Christ is the central object of God's love that those who have been translated into His kingdom are assured of the promised blessings thereof.

14. ἐν ᾧ ἔχομεν, κ.τ.λ. = Eph. i. 7.

The words διὰ τοῦ αἵματος αὐτοῦ of the Rec. Text are an interpolation from Eph. i. 7. They are found in many minuscules, and in Vulg-Clem.

Demid. Syr-Pesh. Arm., Theodoret, Oec.; but apparently not in any uncial nor in the other versions.

For ἔχομεν B, Boh. Arab. (Lips. Bedwell) read ἔσχομεν. In the parallel passage, Eph. i. 7, ℵ* D* (not the Latin d) Boh. Eth., Iren. (transl.) have ἔσχομεν. Lightfoot thinks that this reading in Eph. was a harmonistic change to conform to the text which these authorities or their predecessors found in Col., and judges that ἔσχομεν is possibly the correct reading here. WH. also give it a place in the margin. Yet it is hard to suppose that St. Paul wrote different tenses in the two places. Moreover, ἔσχομεν does not appear to be a suitable tense; if past time were to be expressed, we should expect ἐσχήκαμεν (cf. Rom. v. 2). Weiss rejects it.

τὴν ἄφεσιν τῶν ἁμαρτιῶν. This expression does not occur in the Epistles of St. Paul elsewhere, but twice in his speeches in Acts (xiii. 38, xxvi. 18). In Eph. i. 7 we have the equivalent, ἄφεσιν τῶν παραπτωμάτων; generally in the Epp. he prefers the more positive δικαιοσύνη. Lightfoot suggests that the studied precision in the definition of ἀπολύτρωσις points to some false conception of ἀπολ. put forward by the heretical teachers. Later Gnostics certainly did pervert the meaning of the term. Irenaeus relates of the Marcosians that they held εἶναι τελείαν ἀπολύτρωσιν αὐτὴν τὴν ἐπίγνωσιν τοῦ ἀρρήτου μεγέθους (i. 21. 4). Hippolytus says: λέγουσί τι φωνῇ ἀρρήτῳ ἐπιτιθέντες χεῖρα τῷ τὴν ἀπολύτρωσιν λαβόντι, κ.τ.λ. (*Haer.* vi. 41). In the baptismal formula of the Marcosians are the words: εἰς ἕνωσιν καὶ ἀπολύτρωσιν καὶ κοινωνίαν τῶν δυνάμεων (Iren. i. 21. 3), where the last words "surely mean communion with the (spiritual) powers." In an alternative formula, also given by Irenaeus, the words are εἰς λύτρωσιν ἀγγελικήν, which is explained by Clem. Alex. (*Exc. Theod.* p. 974) as ἦν καὶ ἄγγελοι ἔχουσιν. It is not likely that there was any historical connexion between these later Gnostics and the Colossian heretics; but, as Lightfoot observes, "the passages quoted will serve to show how a false idea of ἀπολύτρωσις would naturally be associated with an esoteric doctrine of angelic powers."

15–17. *The pre-eminence of Christ. In His essential nature He is above all created things, being the image of the invisible God; and more than that, all things have been created through Him and held together by Him.*

15. ὅς ἐστιν, κ.τ.λ. On this verse Lightfoot has a valuable excursus. The arrangement of the passage 15–20 is twofold. We have, first, the relation of Christ to God and the world, 15–17; and, secondly, His relation to the Church, 18 ff. This division is indicated in the construction of the passage by the repeated ὅτι ἐν αὐτῷ, 16, 19, introducing in each case the reason of the preceding statement. The relation to the Church begins with καὶ αὐτός, ver. 18.

Some commentators regard 15–17 as descriptive of the Word before the Incarnation, the Λόγος ἄσαρκος; and 18–20, of the Incarnate Word, Λόγος ἔνσαρκος. But this is inconsistent with ἔστιν, "is," which shows that St. Paul is speaking of Christ in His present glorified state. Compare 2 Cor. iv. 4, τὸν φωτισμὸν τοῦ εὐαγγελίου τῆς δόξης τοῦ Χριστοῦ, ὅς ἐστιν εἰκὼν τοῦ Θεοῦ. The exalted Christ is now and continues to be what He was in His own nature as the Word before He became incarnate, John xvii. 5.

εἰκών is primarily an image (so in Rev. often, comp. Matt. xxii. 20). It differs from ὁμοίωμα, which expresses mere resemblance, whereas εἰκών implies representation of an archetype. αὔτη γὰρ εἰκόνος φύσις μίμημα εἶναι τοῦ ἀρχετύπου (Greg. Naz. Orat. 30). It may be used, therefore, to express resemblance in some essential character. So in Heb. x. 1, εἰκών is contrasted with σκιά. Compare 1 Cor. xv. 49, τὴν εἰκόνα τοῦ χοϊκοῦ ... τὴν εἰκ. τοῦ ἐπουρανίου: Rom. viii. 29, συμμόρφους τῆς εἰκόνος τοῦ υἱοῦ αὐτοῦ, an idea expressed again 2 Cor. iii. 18, τὴν αὐτὴν εἰκόνα μεταμορφούμεθα: and Col. iii. 10, τὸν ἀνακαινούμενον κατ' εἰκόνα τοῦ κτίσαντος αὐτόν. An allusion to Gen. i. 26, 28. With the same allusion in 1 Cor. xi. 7 the apostle calls the man εἰκὼν καὶ δόξα Θεοῦ. This last passage, in particular, forbids our adopting the view of some commentators, that the expression denotes "the eternal Son's perfect equality with the Father in respect of His substance, nature, and eternity" (Ellicott, quoting Hil. De Syn. § 73: "perfectae aequalitatis significantiam habet similitudo."). As Lightfoot remarks: "The idea of perfection does not lie in the word itself, but must be sought from the context, e.g. πᾶν τὸ πλήρωμα, ver. 19."

The expression is frequently used by Philo in reference to the Logos, e.g. τὸν ἀόρατον καὶ νοητὸν θεῖον λόγον εἰκόνα λέγει Θεοῦ (De Mund. Op. 8, Opp. I. p. 6); λόγος δέ ἐστιν εἰκὼν Θεοῦ δι' οὗ σύμπας ὁ κόσμος ἐδημιουργεῖτο (De Monarch. ii. 5, II. p. 225); and notably De Somniis, I. p. 656, καθάπερ τὴν ἀνθήλιον αὐγὴν ὡς ἥλιον οἱ μὴ δυνάμενοι τὸν ἥλιον αὐτὸν ἰδεῖν ὁρῶσι ... οὕτως καὶ τὴν τοῦ Θεοῦ εἰκόνα, τὸν ἄγγελον αὐτοῦ λόγον, ὡς αὐτὸν κατανοοῦσι. Compare with this John xiv. 9, ὁ ἑωρακὼς ἐμὲ ἑώρακεν τὸν πατέρα.

Closely allied to εἰκών is χαρακτήρ, similarly applied to Christ in Heb. i, 3, ὧν ἀπαύγασμα τῆς δόξης καὶ χαρακτὴρ τῆς ὑποστάσεως αὐτοῦ.

τοῦ ἀοράτου. This word, which by its position also is emphatic, makes prominent the contrast with the εἰκών, the visibility of which is therefore implied. Compare Rom. i. 20, τὰ ἀόρατα αὐτοῦ ... τοῖς ποιήμασι νοούμενα καθορᾶται. Here Christ is the visible manifestation of the invisible. Chrysostom, indeed, and the Nicene and post-Nicene Fathers, argued that, as the archetype is invisible, so must the image be, ἡ τοῦ ἀοράτου εἰκὼν καὶ αὐτὴ ἀόρατος καὶ ὁμοίως ἀόρατος. But, as Lightfoot says, "the underlying idea of the εἰκών, and, indeed, of the λόγος generally, is the manifestation of the hidden." Compare John i. 18, Θεὸν οὐδεὶς ἑώρακε πώποτε· ὁ μονογενὴς υἱός (v.l. μονογενὴς Θεός), ὁ ὢν εἰς τὸν κόλπον τοῦ πατρός, ἐκεῖνος ἐξηγήσατο, and xiv. 9, quoted above.

πρωτότοκος πάσης κτίσεως. πρωτότοκος seems to have been a recognised title of the Messiah (see Heb. i. 6), perhaps derived from Ps. lxxxix. 28, ἐγὼ πρωτότοκον θήσομαι αὐτόν, which is interpreted of the Messiah by R. Nathan in Shemoth Rabba, 19, fol. 118. 4. Israel is called God's firstborn (Ex. iv. 22; Jer. xxxi. 9), and hence the term was readily transferred to the Messiah, as the ideal representative of the race.

The genitive here is not partitive, as the following context clearly shows, for ἐν αὐτῷ ἐκτίσθη τὰ πάντα. Setting this aside, commentators are not agreed as to the interpretation of πρωτότοκος. Eadie, Hofmann, *al.*, understand it of sovereignty. Alford and Lightfoot, while giving the first place to the idea of priority to all creation, admit sovereignty over all creation as part of the connotation. So Theodore of Mops., οὐκ ἐπὶ χρόνου λέγεται μόνον· ἀλλὰ γὰρ καὶ ἐπὶ προτιμήσεως (but he interprets κτίσεως of the new creation). In defence of this interpretation of the word Ps. lxxxviii. 28 is quoted, where after πρωτότοκον θήσομαι αὐτόν the explanation is added, ὑψηλὸν παρὰ τοῖς βασιλεῦσι τῆς γῆς: also what appears as a paraphrase of this, ἔθηκεν κληρόνομον πάντων, Heb. i. 2: also Ex. iv. 22; Rom. viii. 29, εἰς τὸ εἶναι αὐτὸν πρωτότοκον ἐν πολλοῖς ἀδελφοῖς. Job xviii. 13, "the firstborn of death," for "a fatal malady"; and Isa. xiv. 30, "the firstborn of the poor," for "the very poor," are also referred to. Lightfoot quotes R. Bechai, who calls God Himself the firstborn of the world, and he concludes that the words signify "He stands in the relation of πρ. to all creation," *i.e.* "He is the Firstborn, and as the Firstborn the absolute Heir and Sovereign Lord of all creation."

The passages cited do not justify this interpretation. In Ex. iv. 22 the word does not at all mean "sovereign," which would be quite out of place even apart from the prefixed "my," but "object of favour." In Ps. lxxxviii. 28, again, the added words, if taken as an explanation of πρωτ. simply, would go too far; but it is the πρωτότοκος of God, who is said to be "higher than the kings of the earth." θήσομαι αὐτὸν πρ. is, "I will put him in the position of a firstborn," and the following words are not an explanation of πρ., but state the result of God's regarding him as such. Compare the English phrase, "making one an eldest son by will." By no means would the words of the psalm justify such an expression as πρωτότοκος τῶν βασιλέων, unless it were intended to include the πρ. amongst the βασιλεῖς. As the context forbids our including the πρωτότοκος here amongst the κτίσις, the interpretation leaves the genitive inexplicable. It is called "the genitive of reference"; but this is too vague to explain anything, as will appear by substituting either κόσμου for κτίσεως, or μέγας for πρωτ. Thus πρωτότοκος τοῦ κόσμου for "sovereign in relation to the world," and μέγας πάσης κτίσεως are equally impossible. If by "genitive of reference" is meant "genitive of comparison," then we come back to the relation of priority in πρῶτος. In fact, the genitive after πρ. must be 1st, genitive of possession, as "my firstborn," 2nd, partitive, "firstborn" of the class, or 3rd, of comparison, as in John i. 15, πρῶτός μου ἦν. A moment's reflection will show that Isa. xiv. 30 is not parallel, for there "the firstborn of the poor" is included in the class. In Job xviii. 13 (which, moreover, is poetical) the genitive is possessive, "death's chief instrument." Rom. viii. 29, there is no genitive, but πρ. is included ἐν πολλοῖς ἀδελφοῖς.

Rabbi Bechai's designation of God as "firstborn of the world" is a fanciful interpretation of Ex. xiii. 2. R. Bechai probably meant by the expression "priority," not "supremacy." The firstborn were to be consecrated to God because He was the First of all. But it must be remembered that the Hebrew word is not etymologically parallel to πρωτότοκος.

Hence the only tenable interpretation of the words before us is "begotten before πᾶσα κτίσις," the genitive being like that in John i. 15, πρωτότοκον τοῦ Θεοῦ καὶ πρὸ πάντων τῶν κτισμάτων, Justin M. *Dial.* § 100. The only ideas involved are priority in time and distinction from the genus κτίσις. οὐχ ὡς ἀδελφὴν ἔχων τὴν κτίσιν, ἀλλ' ὡς πρὸ πάσης κτίσεως γεννηθείς, Theodoret; and so Chrysostom: οὐχὶ ἀξίας κ. τιμῆς ἀλλὰ χρόνου μόνον ἐστι σημαντικόν. Compare Rev. iii. 14, ἡ ἀρχὴ τῆς κτίσεως τοῦ Θεοῦ. πρωτόκτιστος or πρωτόπλαστος would have implied that Christ was created like πᾶσα κτίσις.

Isidore of Pelusium, in the interests of orthodoxy, assigns an active meaning to πρωτοτόκος (to be in that case thus accented), not, however, a meaning corresponding to the signification of πρωτοτόκος in classical writers, which is "primipara," and could yield no tolerable sense, but as "primus auctor." His words are: οὐ πρῶτον τῆς κτίσεως . . . ἀλλὰ πρῶτον αὐτὸν τετοκέναι τοῦτ' ἐστι πεποιηκέναι τὴν κτίσιν ἵνα ᾖ τρίτης συλλαβῆς ὀξυμένης, ὡς πρωτοκτίστος (*Ep.* iii. 31). Basil seems to adopt the same view, for, comparing ver. 19, he says: εἰ δὲ πρωτότοκος νεκρῶν εἴρηται, διὰ τὸ αἴτιος εἶναι τῆς ἐν νεκρῶν ἀναστάσεως, οὕτω καὶ πρωτότοκος κτίσεως, διὰ τὸ αἴτιος εἶναι τοῦ ἐξ οὐκ ὄντων εἰς τὸ εἶναι παραγαγεῖν τὴν κτίσιν (*Contra Eunom.* lib. iv. p. 292 D). (The true reading in ver. 19 is πρ. ἐκ τῶν νεκρῶν, but πρ. τῶν ν. is in Rev. i. 5.)

This interpretation is followed by Michaelis and some others. In addition, however, to the unsuitableness of τίκτειν in this connexion, πρῶτος is unsuitable, since there would be no possibility of a δευτεροτόκος.

πάσης κτίσεως. κτίσις in N.T. has three meanings: 1st, the act of creation (the primary meaning of κτίσις as of "creation"), Rom. i. 20, ἀπὸ κτίσεως κόσμου: 2nd, "creation" as the universe of created things, Rom. viii. 22, πᾶσα ἡ κτίσις συστενάζει: 3rd, "a creation," a single created thing, Rom. viii. 39, οὔτε τις κτίσις ἑτέρα. Here it may be questioned whether πάσης κτίσεως means "all creation" (RV. Alford, Lightfoot, *al.*) or "every creature" (AV. Meyer, Ellicott, *al.*). In favour of the latter rendering is the absence of the article, which we should expect after πᾶς in the former sense. It may be replied that κτίσις belongs to the class of nouns which from their meaning may sometimes dispense with the article, such as γῆ (Luke ii. 14; Heb. viii. 4), οὐρανός (Acts iii. 21, *al.*), κόσμος (Rom. v. 13, xi. 12, 15, *al.*). Yet it is very rarely, and only in particular combinations, that these words are without the article. As an instance of κτίσις = the aggregate of created things being without the article, is cited Mark xiii. 19, ἀπὸ ἀρχῆς κτίσεως, the parallel in Matt. xxiv. 21 having ἀπ' ἀρχῆς κόσμου. So also Matt. x. 6; 2 Pet. iii. 4.

But granting that κτίσις here = κόσμος (which might be questioned) the point to be noted is the anarthrous use, not of κτίσις, but of the compound term ἀρχὴ κτίσεως, like ἀρχὴ κόσμου; and this is precisely parallel to the similar use of καταβολὴ κόσμου, which we have several times with ἀπό and πρό, always without the article. So we have frequently ἀπ' ἀρχῆς, ἐν ἀρχῇ, ἐξ ἀρχῆς. Similarly, εἰς τέλος, ἕως τέλους, μέχρι τέλους. ἀπ' ἀρχῆς being regularly used without the article, it is in accordance with rule that in ἀπὸ ἀρχῆς κτίσεως the latter word should also be anarthrous. Moreover, even κόσμος and γῆ, which are cited as examples of words occasionally anarthrous, do not dispense with the article when πᾶς precedes, probably because of the possible ambiguity which would result. There appears, therefore, no sufficient justification for departing from the natural rendering, "every created thing." This furnishes an additional reason against the interpretation which would include the πρωτότοκος in πᾶσα κτίσις.

This exposition of the unique and supreme position of Christ is plainly directed against the errors of the false teachers, who denied this supremacy.

The history of the ancient interpretation of the expression πρωτότοκος τ. κτ., is interesting and instructive. The Fathers of the second and third centuries understand it correctly of the Eternal Word (Justin, Clem. Alex., Tert., Origen, etc.). But when the Arians made use of the expression to prove that the Son was a created being, many of the orthodox were led to adopt the view that the words relate to the Incarnate Christ, understanding, therefore, κτίσις and κτίζεσθαι of the new spiritual creation, the καινὴ κτίσις. (Athanasius, Greg. Nyss., Cyril, Theodore Mops.) As Lightfoot observes, this interpretation "shatters the context," for, as a logical consequence, we must understand ἐν αὐτῷ ἐκτίσθη τὰ πάντα ἐν τοῖς οὐρανοῖς καὶ ἐπὶ τῆς γῆς and ver. 17 of the work of the Incarnation; and to do this is "to strain language in a way which would reduce all theological exegesis to chaos." In addition to this, the interpretation disregards the history of the terms, and "takes no account of the cosmogony and angelology of the false teachers against which the apostle's exposition here is directed." Basil prefers the interpretation which refers the expression to the Eternal Word, and so Theodoret and Severianus, and the later Greek writers generally (Theoph. Oecumenius, etc.). Chrysostom's view is not clear.

16. ὅτι introduces the proof of the designation, πρωτότοκος πάσης κτ. It leaves, therefore, no doubt as to the meaning of that expression, and shows that the πρωτότοκος is not included in πᾶσα κτίσις, for τὰ πάντα is equivalent to πᾶσα κτίσις.

ἐν αὐτῷ is not simply = δι' αὐτοῦ, 1 Cor. viii. 6 (Chrys. etc.). The latter designates Christ as the mediate instrument, the former goes further, and seems to express that the conditioning cause of the act of creation resided in Him. The Eternal Word stood in the same relation to the created Universe as the Incarnate Christ to the Church. The latter relation is constantly expressed by ἐν, which is also used by classical writers to express that the cause of a relation exists in some person. Comp. ver. 17, ἐν αὐτῷ συνέστηκεν, and for the preposition, Acts xvii. 28, ἐν αὐτῷ ζῶμεν καὶ κινούμεθα καί ἐσμεν. The originating cause ἐξ οὗ τὰ πάντα is God the Father, Rom. xi. 36; 1 Cor. viii. 6.

The Schoolmen, following, indeed, Origen and Athanasius, interpreted the words of the *causa exemplaris*, viz. that the *idea omnium rerum* was in Christ. So that He was, as it were, the Archetypal Universe, the summary of finite being as it existed in the Eternal Mind. This view has been adopted by Neander, Schleiermacher, Olshausen, and others. Olshausen says: "The Son of God is the intelligible world, the κόσμος νοητός, that is, things in their Idea. In the creation they come forth from Him to an independent existence."

This would correspond to Philo's view of the Logos (which to him, however, was a philosophical abstraction), οὐδὲ ὁ ἐκ τῶν ἰδεῶν κόσμος ἄλλον ἂν ἔχοι τύπον ἢ τὸν θεῖον λόγον τὸν ταῦτα διακοσμήσαντα (*De Mundi Op.* iv. § 4, tom. i. p. 4), and again: ὅσα ἂν ἐνθυμήματα τέκῃ, ὥσπερ ἐν οἴκῳ τῷ λόγῳ διαθείς (*De Migr. Abr.* i. tom. i. p. 437). Lightfoot regards the apostle's teaching as "an enlargement of this conception, inasmuch as the Logos is no longer a philosophical abstraction, but a Divine Person," and he quotes, seemingly with assent, the words of Hippolytus: ἔχει ἐν ἑαυτῷ τὰς ἐν τῷ πατρὶ προεννοηθείσας ἰδέας ὅθεν κελεύοντος πατρὸς γίνεσθαι κόσμον τὸ κατὰ ἓν Λόγος ἀπετελεῖτο ἀρέσκων Θεῷ (*Haer.* x. 33).

But, however attractive this interpretation may be, it is inconsistent with ἐκτίσθη, which expresses the historical act of creation, not a preceding εἶναι ἐν αὐτῷ. Nor has it any support elsewhere in the N.T.

ἐκτίσθη, "were created." Schleiermacher (*Studien u. Kritiken*, 1832) alleges that the verb is never used in Hellenistic Greek of creation proper, and therefore understands it here of constitution and arrangement; and he interprets the statement as referring to the foundation of the Church. The word is often so used in classical writers. But in the N.T. κτίζω, κτίσις, κτίσμα are always used of original creation or production. See for the verb Mark xiii. 19; Rom. i. 25; 1 Cor. xi. 9; 1 Tim. iv. 3; Apoc. iv. 11, x. 6. Its use in Eph. ii. 10, 15, iv. 24 is not an exception, the καινὸς ἄνθρωπος being regarded as a new creation.

The tenses of ἐκτίσθη, ἔκτισται are to be noted; the former is suitable to the historical fact of creation, the latter to the permanent relations of the creation to the Creator; comp. συνέστηκεν, ver. 17.

τὰ πάντα, all things collectively, presently specified as to place and nature. ἐν τοῖς οὐρανοῖς καὶ ἐπὶ τῆς γῆς, an expression designating all created things, the heaven and earth themselves not excluded, as Wetstein would have it, who infers that not the physical creation is meant, but "habitatores ... qui reconciliantur." The compendious expression is adopted because the apostle has chiefly in view the heavenly beings; but τὰ πάντα shows that the statement is meant to be universal.

The τά of Text. Rec. before ἐν τοῖς οὐρ. is omitted by ℵ* B D* G P 17, al. d f g Vulg.
Inserted by ℵc A Dc K L and most mss.
τά before ἐπὶ τῆς γῆς is omitted by ℵ* B, d f g Vulg.
Inserted by ℵ* A C D G K L P.
It will be observed that the authority for omission is much greater in the first clause than in the second, although the one cannot be inserted or omitted without the other. It is possible, therefore, that τά was accidentally omitted in the first clause after πάντα, and then omitted from the second for the sake of uniformity. On the other hand, it may have been inserted in both places from the parallels in ver. 20 and in Eph. i. 10.

τὰ ὁρατὰ καὶ τὰ ἀόρατα, a Platonic division; θῶμεν οὖν, εἰ βούλει, ἔφη, δύο εἴδη τῶν ὄντων, τὸ μὲν ὁρατόν, τὸ δὲ ἀειδές. The latter term here refers to the spirit world, as the following context indicates. Chrys. Theoph. Lightfoot, etc., suppose human souls to be included, but it is more probable that man as a whole is included among the ὁρατά.

εἴτε θρόνοι, κ.τ.λ. In the parallel, Eph. i, 21, we have ὑπεράνω πάσης ἀρχῆς καὶ ἐξουσίας καὶ δυνάμεως καὶ κυριότητος. It will be noted that both the names and the order are different. Moreover, the addition in Eph., καὶ παντὸς ὀνόματος ὀνομαζομένου, shows that St. Paul is only adopting current terms, not communicating any incidental revelation about objective facts (see on Eph. i. 21). The gist of the passage is to make light of the speculations about the orders of angels, but to insist on the supremacy of Christ.

"His language here shows the same spirit of impatience with this elaborate angelology as in ii. 18," Lightfoot. It is said, indeed, that St. Paul "is glorifying the Son of God by a view of His relation to created being; and assuredly this would not be best done by alluding to phases of created being which might all the while be figments of the imagination" (Moule). But it is sufficient for the purpose that the existence of angelic beings in general should be a reality. If St. Paul accepts as true the fundamental assumption of the heretical angelology, it seems to follow that revelations about heavenly existences may be found elsewhere than in the Scriptures, for this system of the angelic hierarchy could not be derived either from the O.T. or from reason.

θρόνοι are not mentioned elsewhere in the N.T., but in *Test. XII. Patr.* (Levi 3) they are placed in the highest (seventh) heaven. Probably the name was meant as a designation of spirits who occupied thrones surrounding the throne of God. Comp. Rev. iv. 4. Clement of Alex. seems to regard them as so called because supporting or forming the throne of God (*Proph. Ecl.* 57), as the cherubim are represented in Ezek. ix. 3, x. 1, xi. 22; Ps. lxxx. 2, xcix. 1. For a summary of Jewish and Christian speculations as to the angelic hierarchy, Lightfoot's note may be consulted.

τὰ πάντα κ.τ.λ. This is properly separated from the foregoing by a colon after ἐξουσίαι. The sentence emphatically restates in a form applied to the present what had already been said of the relation of Christ to the creation. Thus what was described in 16 as a historical act by ἐκτίσθη, is here repeated, regarded as a completed and continuing fact; so ἐν αὐτῷ συνέστηκεν expresses what for the present existence of things is the logical consequence of their origin ἐν αὐτῷ; and, lastly, καὶ αὐτός ἐστιν πρὸ πάντων repeats πρωτότοκος πάσης κτίσεως. εἰς αὐτόν introduces a new idea.

εἰς αὐτόν. The conditions of existence of the created universe are so ordered that without Christ it cannot attain its perfection. This εἰς αὐτόν is nearly equivalent to δι' ὅν in Heb. ii. 10. He is Alpha and Omega, the ἀρχὴ καὶ τέλος (Apoc. xxii. 13). This εἰς αὐτὸν ἔκτισται is the antecedent condition of the subjection of all things to Christ, 1 Cor. xv. 24, 28. There is no inconsistency, then (as Holtzmann and others maintain), between this passage and 1 Cor. viii. 6 (where the subject of εἰς αὐτόν is not τὰ πάντα, but ἡμεῖς), or Rom. xi. 36, where it is said of God, ἐξ αὐτοῦ καὶ δι' αὐτοῦ καὶ εἰς αὐτὸν τὰ πάντα. Had ἐξ αὐτοῦ been used, there would have been an inconsistency; but as the passage stands, the subordination to the Father is fully indicated by the form of expression, δι' αὐτοῦ καὶ εἰς αὐτὸν ἔκτισται, implying that it was by the Father that He was appointed the τέλος. This double use of εἰς αὐτόν to express the immediate end and the final end, is parallel to the double use of δι' αὐτοῦ with reference to Christ in 1 Cor. viii. 6, and to God in Rom. xi. 36.

The thought in Eph. i. 10, ἀνακεφαλαιώσασθαι τὰ πάντα ἐν Χριστῷ, is very similar to the present; but, of course, we cannot quote Eph. in a question touching the genuineness of the present Epistle.

17. καὶ αὐτός ἐστιν πρὸ πάντων. αὐτός is emphatic, as always in the nom. "He himself," in contrast, namely, to the created things. πρὸ πάντων, like πρωτότοκος, is of priority in time not in rank (which would be ἐπὶ πάντων, ὑπὲρ πάντα, or the like). In Jas. v. 12; 1 Pet. iv. 8, πρὸ πάντων is adverbial, "above all," "especially," and if so taken here, we should render "He especially exists." The words repeat with emphasis the assertion of pre-existence. ἦν might have been used, but ἐστιν is more suitable to express immutability of existence. As we might say, "His existence is before all things"; compare John viii. 58, πρὶν Ἀβραὰμ γίνεσθαι, ἐγώ εἰμι. Lightfoot accentuates the verb αὐτὸς ἔστιν; but as the predicate is πρὸ πάντων, ἐστίν appears to be only the copula.

The Latin takes πάντων as masculine, "ante omnes," *i.e.* thronos, etc.; but the following τὰ πάντα is decisive against this.

συνέστηκε. "Consist," "maintain their coherence." "Corpus unum, integrum, perfectum, secum consentiens esse et permanere" (Reiske, *Index Demosth.*). ἐκ τοῦ Θεοῦ τὰ πάντα, καὶ διὰ Θεοῦ ἡμῖν συνέστηκεν (Aristot. *De Mundo*, vi. 471): ξυνεστάναι τῷ τοῦ οὐρανοῦ δημιουργῷ αὐτόν τε καὶ τὰ ἐν αὐτῷ (Plato, *Rep.* 530 A). Compare also Philo, ὁ ἔναιμος ὄγκος, ἐξ ἑαυτοῦ διαλυτὸς ὢν καὶ νεκρός, συνέστηκε καὶ ζωπυρεῖται προνοίᾳ Θεοῦ (*Quis Rer. Div. haeres.* p. 489). The Logos is called by Philo the δεσμός of the universe.

18–20. *Transition to Christ's relation to the Church.* ἀπὸ τῆς θεολογίας εἰς τὴν οἰκονομίαν, Theodoret. *Here also He is first, the firstborn from the dead, and the Head of the Church, all the fulness of God dwelling in Him. So that even the angelic powers are included in the work of reconciliation which has been wrought through Him.*

18. καὶ αὐτός, and He and none other, "ipse in quo omnia consistunt est caput."

ἡ κεφαλὴ τοῦ σώματος, τῆς ἐκκλησίας. τῆς ἐκκλησίας in apposition with σώματος; compare ver. 24, ὅ ἐστιν ἡ ἐκκλησία, and Eph. i. 23, τῇ ἐκκλ. ἥτις ἐστὶ τὸ σῶμα αὐτοῦ. σώματος is added in order to define more precisely the meaning of the figure, κεφαλὴ τῆς ἐκκλησίας. It shows that the writer is not using κεφαλή vaguely, but with the definite figure of the relation of head to body in his thoughts.

ὅς ἐστιν ἀρχή = "in that He is." In classical Greek γε would probably be added. ἀρχή has special but not exclusive reference to the following words, which express the aspect in which ἀρχή is here viewed. πρωτότοκος implies that other νεκροί follow; ἀρχή, that He it was who made possible that others should follow. He was the Principle and the first example, ἀρχή, φησίν, ἐστι τῆς ἀναστάσεως, πρὸ πάντων ἀναστάς, Theoph. Thus He was the ἀπαρχή, 1 Cor. xv. 20, 23; and the ἀρχηγὸς τῆς ζωῆς, Acts iii. 14. His resurrection is His title to the headship of the Church: cf. Rom. i. 4.

ἐκ τῶν νεκρῶν. Not "amongst," which would be πρ. τῶν νεκρ. as in Rev. i. 5, but "from among." That others were raised before Him is not regarded as an objection to this. Theophylact observes : εἰ γὰρ καὶ ἄλλοι πρὸ τούτου ἀνέστησαν, ἀλλὰ πάλιν ἀπέθανον· αὐτὸς δὲ τὴν τελείαν ἀνάστασιν ἀνέστη.

ἵνα γένηται. "That He may become," not "be," as Vulg. As ἐστί is used to express what He is, so γένηται of what as a consequence He is to become, viz. ἐν πᾶσιν, κ.τ.λ. "Himself in all things pre-eminent." πᾶσιν is not masculine, "inter omnes," as Beza and others take it, but neuter, as the following τὰ πάντα makes certain. πρωτεύειν does not occur elsewhere in the N.T., but is found in classical writers and in the Sept. Thus in a connexion similar to the present, Plutarch (*Mor.* p. 9), σπεύδοντες τοὺς παῖδας ἐν πᾶσι τάχιον πρωτεύειν. Demosthenes also has πρωτεύειν ἐν ἅπασι, but with ἅπασι, masc. (p. 1416). Chrysostom's explanation here is : πανταχοῦ πρῶτος· ἄνω πρῶτος, ἐν τῇ ἐκκλησίᾳ πρῶτος, ἐν τῇ ἀναστάσει πρῶτος. This πρωτεύειν is the final result of the state to which the πρωτότοκον εἶναι ἐκ τῶν νεκρῶν was the introduction, but is not involved in the word πρωτότοκος itself.

19. ὅτι. The correspondence with ὅτι in ver. 16, following ὅς ἐστιν of ver. 15, shows that this assigns a reason, not for ἵνα γένηται, but for ὅς ἐστιν, ver. 18. The indwelling of the Godhead explains the headship of the Church as well as that of the Universe.

εὐδόκησεν. The subject may be either ὁ Θεός or πᾶν τὸ πλήρωμα. The former view is adopted by most comm., including Meyer, Alford, Lightfoot, De Wette, Winer. In favour of it, the ellipsis of ὁ Θεός in Jas. i. 12, iv. 6, is quoted, and it is remarked that the omission here is the more easy, because "εὐδοκία, εὐδοκεῖν, etc. (like θέλημα), are used absolutely of God's good purpose, *e.g.* Luke ii. 14 ; Phil. ii. 13." But the verb εὐδοκεῖν is used by St. Paul even more frequently of men than of God (seven times to three). It cannot, therefore, be said that it was in any sense a technical term for the Divine counsel, so as to render the express mention of ὁ Θεός as the subject unnecessary ; nor is there any instance of its being used absolutely in this sense ; see 1 Cor. i. 21 ; Gal. i. 15, where ὁ Θεός is expressed with the verb. Indeed, except in Luke ii. 14, even the substantive εὐδοκία, when it refers to God, is always defined either by a genitive (Eph. i. 5, 9) or by ὁ Θεός being the subject of the sentence, as in Phil. ii. 13, where the article with an abstract noun after a preposition "necessarily brings in a reflexive sense,—to be referred to the subject of the sentence," Alford.

Here there is nothing in the context from which ὁ Θεός can be supplied, and clearness, especially in such an important passage, would require it to be expressed.

Further, although an example is cited from 2 Macc. xiv. 35 in which the subject of the infinitive after εὐδοκεῖν is different from the subject of the finite verb (σύ, Κύριε, εὐδόκησας ναὸν τῆς σῆς κατασκηνώσεως ἐν ἡμῖν γενέσθαι), yet in every instance in the N.T. (six) in which εὐδοκεῖν is followed by an infinitive, the subject of both is the same. The assumed change of subject to the two infinitives κατοικ. and ἀποκατ. is also harsh. Lastly, the words seem to be an echo of Ps. lxviii. 17, ὁ Θεὸς εὐδόκησε κατοικεῖν ἐν αὐτῷ, while in ii. 9 we have a close parallel in ὅτι ἐν αὐτῷ κατοικεῖ πᾶν τὸ πλήρωμα τῆς θεότητος.

For these reasons it seems best to take πᾶν τὸ πλ. as the subject. So Ewald, Ellicott, Scholefield, Soden, RV. marg.

A third interpretation, which has little to recommend it, is that of Tertullian (*adv. Marc.* v. 19), according to which the subject of εὐδόκησεν is ὁ Χριστός; and this is adopted by Conybeare and Hofmann. εἰς αὐτόν then would be "to Himself." But it was not to Christ but to the Father that all things were reconciled by Him; compare 2 Cor. v. 19. As Lightfoot observes, the interpretation "confuses the theology of the passage hopelessly."

Although the tense is the aorist, "hath been pleased to dwell" represents the sense better than "was pleased to dwell." For as the good pleasure must accompany the dwelling, instead of being a transient act, antecedent to it, the latter expression would be equivalent to "dwelt," and so would only refer to past time.

πᾶν τὸ πλήρωμα. If this is the subject of εὐδ. it, of course, means "all the fulness of the Godhead," τῆς θεότητος, as in ii. 9, "omnes divitiae divinae naturae" (Fritz.), πᾶν τὸ πλ. being personified. But even if ὁ Θεός is taken as the subject, it is most natural to interpret this expression by that in ii. 9, where κατοικεῖ is also used. It is, indeed, objected by Meyer and Eadie that the Divine essence dwelt in Christ "necessarily" ("nothwendig," Meyer) and "unchangeably" (Eadie), not by the Father's good pleasure and purpose. Hence they understand with Beza, "cumulatissima omnium divinarum rerum copia . . . ex qua in Christo tanquam inexhausto fonte, omnes gratiae in nos . . . deriventur." Alford, while adopting the interpretation, rightly sets aside the objection of Meyer and Eadie to the former view, saying that "all that is His own right is His Father's pleasure, and is ever referred to that pleasure by Himself."

Severianus and Theodoret interpret πλήρωμα of the Church, following Eph. i. 23. The latter says: πληρ. τὴν ἐκκλησίαν ἐν τῇ πρὸς Ἐφεσίους ἐκάλεσεν, ὡς τῶν θείων χαρισμάτων πεπληρωμένην. ταύτην ἔφη εὐδοκῆσαι τὸν Θεὸν ἐν τῷ Χριστῷ κατοικῆσαι, τουτέστιν αὐτῷ συνῆφθαι; and so many moderns. Similarly Schleiermacher, who, referring to πλήρωμα τῶν ἐθνῶν in Rom. xi. 12, 25, 26, explains the word here of the fulness of the Gentiles and the whole of Israel, whose indwelling in Christ is the permanent state which is necessarily preceded by the complete reconciliation of which the peacemaking was the condition. But there is nothing to support this either in the absolute use of πλ. or in the context here. It is clear that the κατοικῆσαι is stated as the antecedent, not the consequent of ἀποκατ., "haec inhabitatio est fundamentum reconciliationis," Bengel. Other interpretations may be found in De Wette and Meyer.

κατοικῆσαι implies permanent, or rather "settled" residence, not a mere παροικία. Cf. Gen. xxxvi. 44 (xxxvii. 1), κατῴκει δὲ Ἰακὼβ ἐν τῇ γῇ οὗ παρῴκησεν ὁ πατὴρ αὐτοῦ ἐν γῇ Χαναάν. That the word of itself does not always imply "permanent residence," see Acts vii. 4, κατῴκησεν ἐν Χαρράν· κἀκεῖθεν μετῴκισεν αὐτὸν εἰς τὴν γῆν ταύτην: see on Lk. xi. 26. The aorist seems to be usually employed in the sense, "take up one's abode in." Compare Matt. ii. 23, iv. 13; Acts vii. 2, 4; Eph. iii. 17. This, however, cannot be insisted on here, where the infinitive is dependent on an aorist.

It is probable, as Lightfoot remarks, that the false teachers maintained only a partial and transient connexion of the πλήρωμα with the Lord.

20. ἀποκαταλλάξαι. The ἀπο may be intensive, "prorsus reconciliare," or, as in ἀποκαθιστάναι, may mean "again" (so Alford, Ell., Lightfoot, Soden). "Conciliari extraneo possent, reconciliari vero non alii quam suo," Tertull. *adv. Marc.* v. 19. But καταλλάσσειν is the word always used by St. Paul in Rom. and Cor. of reconciliation to God; and of a wife to her husband, 1 Cor. vii. 11. See on Eph. ii. 16.

τὰ πάντα, defined as it is presently after by εἴτε τὰ ἐπὶ τῆς γῆς, κ.τ.λ., cannot be limited to the Church (as Beza), nor to men (especially the heathen, Olshausen), nor yet to intelligent beings generally. "How far this restoration of universal nature may be subjective, as involved in the changed perceptions of man thus brought into harmony with God, and how far it may have an objective and independent existence, it were vain to speculate," Lightfoot. Compare ἀποκαταστάσεως πάντων, Acts iii. 21; also Rom. viii. 21.

εἰς αὐτόν. If our interpretation of this were to be determined solely by considerations of language, we should have no hesitation in referring αὐτόν to the same antecedent as ἐν αὐτῷ, δι' αὐτοῦ, and αὐτοῦ after σταυροῦ, that is Christ, and that, whatever subject we adopt for εὐδόκησε, but especially if πᾶν τὸ πλ. is not taken as the subject. On this interpretation the ἀποκαταλλάξαι τὰ πάντα εἰς αὐτόν would refer back to τὰ πάντα εἰς αὐτὸν . . . ἔκτισται. If ἑαυτῷ was necessary in 2 Cor. v. 19, was it not more necessary here in order to avoid ambiguity?

It is, however, a serious objection to this view that we nowhere read of reconciliation to Christ, but only through Him to God.

This objection is, indeed, somewhat weakened by the consideration, first, that this is the only place in which the reconciliation of τὰ πάντα is mentioned. In 2 Cor. v. 19 the words which follow ἑαυτῷ, viz. μὴ λογιζόμενος αὐτοῖς τὰ παραπτώματα αὐτῶν, κ.τ.λ., show that κόσμος has not the wide significance of τὰ πάντα here. Secondly, that already in ver. 17 there is predicated of Christ what elsewhere is predicated of God, viz. δι' αὐτοῦ καὶ εἰς αὐτὸν τὰ πάντα (Rom. xi. 35). Thirdly, here only is εἰς used instead of the dative after (ἀπο) καταλλάσσειν. The difference is slight, and only in the point of view; but the change would be accounted for by the reference to ver. 17.

It deserves notice that some expositors who reject this view use language which at least approximates to the idea of reconciliation to Christ. Thus Alford, speaking of the "sinless creation," says it "is lifted into nearer participation and higher glorification of Him, and is thus *reconciled*, though not in the strictest yet in a very intelligible and allowable sense."

If πᾶν τὸ πλήρωμα is the subject, and αὐτόν be viewed as = τὸν Θεόν, this antecedent would be supplied from πᾶν τὸ πλ. in which, on this view, it is involved. On the other hand, if the subject of εὐδόκησε is ὁ Θεός understood, this, of course, is the antecedent. But the reference of αὐτόν (reflexive) to an unexpressed subject is harsh, notwithstanding Jas. i. 12.

εἰρηνοποιήσας belongs to the subject of the verb, the masc. being adopted κατὰ σύνεσιν, as in ii. 19. This was inevitable, since the personal character of ὁ εἰρηνοποιήσας could not be lost sight of.

As it is Christ who is specified in Eph. ii. 15 as ποιῶν εἰρήνην, Chrysostom, Theodoret, Oecum. and many moderns, although making ὁ Θεός the subject of εὐδόκησε, have so understood εἰρηνοποιήσας here "by the common participial anacoluthon"; but this is a very harsh separation of the participial clause from the finite verb, and introduces confusion amongst the pronouns.

δι' αὐτοῦ, repeated for the sake of emphasis, "by Him, I say." This repetition, especially in so pointed a connexion with τὰ ἐπὶ τῆς γῆς and τὰ ἐν τοῖς οὐρανοῖς, still further emphasises the fact that angelic mediators have no share in the work of reconciliation, nay, that these heavenly beings themselves are included amongst those to whom the benefit of Christ's work extends.

> The second δι' αὐτοῦ is read by ℵ A C D^bc K P and most mss., Syr. (both) Boh., Chrys. Theodoret. It is omitted by B D* G L, Old Lat. Vulg. Arm. Eth., Theophyl. Ambrosiaster, *al.* There would be a tendency to omit them as superfluous.

εἴτε τὰ ἐπὶ τῆς γῆς, εἴτε τὰ ἐν τοῖς οὐρανοῖς. There is much diversity of opinion as to the interpretation of this passage; "torquet interpretes," says Davenant, "et vicissim ab illis torquetur." First, are we to understand τὰ πάντα as limited to intelligent creatures, or as including also unreasoning and lifeless things? Alford, Meyer, and many others adopt the latter view, which, indeed, Alford says is "clearly" the apostle's meaning. Rom. viii. 19-22 is compared, where it is said that the κτίσις has been made subject to ματαιότης. But it is not easy to see how the reversal of this ματαιότης or the delivery from the δουλεία τῆς φθορᾶς can be called "reconciliation to God." Reconciliation implies enmity, and this cannot be predicated of unreasoning and lifeless things. The neuter τὰ πάντα does not bind us to this interpretation, it is simply the most concise and striking expression of universality. But, further, what is meant by the reconciliation of heavenly beings? Many commentators suppose the meaning to be that even good angels have need to be in some sense "reconciled." Calvin observes: "duabus de causis Angelos quoque oportuit cum Deo pacificari: nam quum creaturae sint, extra lapsus periculum non erant, nisi Christi gratia fuissent confirmati . . . Deinde in hac ipsa obedientia quam praestant Deo, non est tam exquisita perfectio ut Deo omni exparte et citra veniam satisfaciat. Atque huc procul dubio spectat sententia ista ex libro Job (iv. 18). 'In Angelis suis reperiet iniquitatem'; nam si de diabolo exponitur, quid magnum? pronuntiat autem illic Spiritus Summam puritatem sordere, si ad Dei iustitiam exigatur." Similarly De Wette, Bleek, Huther, Alford, Moule. The last named adopts Alford's statement: "No reconciliation must be thought of which shall resemble *ours* in its process, for Christ took not upon Him the seed of angels, nor paid any propitiatory penalty in the root of their nature. . . . But forasmuch as He is their Head as well as ours . . . it cannot be but that the great event in which He was glorified through suffering should also bring them nearer to God. . . . That such increase [of blessedness] might be described as a *reconciliation* is manifest: we know from Job xv. 15 that 'the heavens are not clean in His sight'; and *ib*. iv. 18, 'His angels He charged [charges] with folly.'" The general truth may be admitted without accepting Eliphaz the Temanite as a final authority. But imperfection is not enmity, and the difficulty is in the application of the term "reconciled" in the sense of "lifted into nearer participation and higher glorification" of God. Davenant, followed by Alexander, says that Christ has reconciled angels "analogically, by taking away from them the possibility of falling."

It is hardly necessary to dwell on the opinion of Origen, that the devil and his angels are referred to; or on that of Beza, van Til, *al.*, that τὰ ἐν τοῖς οὐρανοῖς are the souls of those who died in the Lord before the coming of Christ, and who are supposed to have been admitted into heaven by virtue of His work which was to come. Neither opinion has any support in Scripture. (Bengel notes that πάντα "continet etiam defunctos," but does not suppose them referred to as in heaven.)

A better view is that of Harless (adopted also by Reuss, Oltramare, *al.*), according to which the reconciliation proper applies only to τὰ ἐπὶ τῆς γῆς, but the apostle adds τὰ ἐν τοῖς οὐρ., "not as if there were in heaven any real need of redemption, nor as if heaven were only added as a rhetorical figure, but because the Lord and Creator of the whole body, whose members are heaven and earth, in restoring one member has restored the whole body; and herein consists the greatest significance of the reconciliation, that it is not only the restoration of the earthly life, but the restoration of the harmony of the universe" (Harless, *Eph.* p. 53).

Ritschl thinks that St. Paul refers to the angels concerned in the giving of the law, to whom he believes the apostle here and elsewhere attributes a certain lack of harmony with the Divine plan of redemption (*Jahrb. f. Deutsche Theol.* 1863, p. 522 f.). Compare ii. 15.

Meyer's solution is that the reference is to angels as a category, not as individuals. The original normal relation between God and these higher spirits no longer subsists so long as the hostile realm of demons still exists; whose power has indeed been broken by the death of the Lord, but which shall be fully destroyed at the Parousia.

Hammond argues at considerable length that "heaven and earth" was a Hebrew expression for "this lower earth." Chrysostom takes the accusatives to depend on εἰρηνοποίησας. This is clear from his question, τὰ δὲ ἐν τοῖς οὐρανοῖς πῶς εἰρηνοποίησε; His reply is that the angels had been made hostile to men, seeing their Lord insulted (or as Theodoret more generally says, on account of the wickedness of the many). God, then, not only made things on earth to be at peace, but brought man to the angels, him who was their enemy. This was profound peace. Why then, says the apostle, have ye confidence in the angels? So far are they from bringing you near, that had not God Himself reconciled you to them, ye would not have been at peace. So Augustine (*Enchir.* 62): "pacificantur coelestia cum terrestribus, et terrestria cum coelestibus." Erasmus adopts the same construction, amending the Latin version thus: "pacificatis et iis quae in terra sunt, et quae in coelis." Bengel's interpretation is similar, and he appears to adopt the same construction, for he compares Luke xix. 38, εἰρήνη ἐν οὐρανῷ: and comparing this again with Luke ii. 14, ἐπὶ γῆς εἰρήνη, he remarks that what those in heaven call peace on earth, those on earth call peace in heaven. This construction does not seem to be open to any grammatical objection. Only two instances of εἰρηνοποιεῖν are cited in the Lexicons, one from the Sept., Prov. x. 10, where it is intransitive; the other from Hermes, *ap. Stob. Ecl. Phys.* p. 984, where the middle is used transitively, τότε καὶ αὐτὴ τὸν ἴδιον δρόμον εἰρηνοποιεῖται. As to the form of the compound, Aristotle uses ὁδοποιεῖν with an accusative, *Rhet.* i. 1. 2, δῆλον ὅτι εἴη ἂν αὐτὰ καὶ ὁδοποιεῖν. So λογοποιεῖν takes an accus., *e.g.* συμφοράς, Lys. p. 165, 26; cf. Thuc. vi. 38, *al.* It is singular that this construction which yields an excellent sense has been entirely overlooked, and the interpretation of Chrys., etc., met with the objection that ἀποκαταλλάξαι . . . εἴτε τά . . . εἴτε τά cannot mean to reconcile these two with one another.

May it not be that the difficulty arises from attempting to turn what is practically a hypothetical statement into a categorical assertion? St. Paul has in his mind throughout this part of the Epistle the teaching of the false teachers at Colossae, who knew, forsooth, all about the celestial hierarchy, with its various orders, some of which were doubtless regarded as not entirely in harmony with the Divine will. The apostle no more adopts their view here than he adopts their hierarchical system. The point on which he insists is that all must be brought into harmony, and that this is effected through Christ.

Are we, however, justified in assuming that all τὰ ἐν τοῖς οὐρανοῖς (which is not necessarily equivalent to "in heaven") are holy angels, or were so conceived by St. Paul? If there are "other worlds than ours," would not their inhabitants be reckoned as ἐν τοῖς οὐρανοῖς?

21-23. *The Colossians are reminded that this reconciliation applies to them also, and that the object in view is that they may be blameless in the sight of God. But this depends on their holding fast by the truth which they have been taught.*

21. We must first note the difference of reading in the last word of the verse. ἀποκαταλλάγητε is read by B, 17 (ἀποκατηλλάκηται); ἀποκαταλλαγέντες, by D*G, the Latin d g m Goth., Iren. (transl.) *al.*; but all other authorities have ἀποκατήλλαξεν. Lachm., Meyer, Lightfoot, Weiss adopt ἀποκατηλλάγητε, which is given a place in the margin by Treg. WH. and Rev. It is argued that ἀποκαταλλαγέντες is an emendation, for grammatical reasons, of ἀποκατηλλάγητε (though a careless one, for it should be accus.). These two sets of authorities, then, may be taken together as attesting the passive. As between ἀποκατηλλάγητε and ἀποκατήλλαξεν, there is in favour of the former the consideration that, if the latter had been the original reading, the construction would be plain, and no reason would exist for altering it. Lightfoot regards this reading of B as perhaps the highest testimony of all to the great value of that MS.

With the reading ἀποκατήλλαξεν there is a slight anacoluthon, there being no direct protasis. Examples, however, are not infrequent of a clause with δέ following a participle which indirectly supplies the protasis. The anacoluthon might indeed be avoided by making ὑμᾶς depend on ἀποκαταλλάξαι; but this would be more awkward; and, besides, ver. 21 obviously begins a new paragraph, resuming the thought from which the apostle had digressed in 15.

With the reading ἀποκατηλλάγητε it is possible to regard the clause νυνὶ δέ—θανάτου as parenthetical. "And you who once were estranged (but now ye have been reconciled) to present you, I say," the second ὑμᾶς repeating the first; and so Lachmann, Lightfoot, Moule. But, considering the importance of the clause, it is perhaps better (with Meyer) to understand the construction as an anacoluthon, the apostle having begun the sentence with the active in his mind, and, in a manner not unusual with him, passing to a more independent form of statement. This, too, seems much more in St. Paul's manner than the parenthesis supposed by Lachmann.

καὶ ὑμᾶς, "and you also," ποτὲ ὄντας ἀπηλλοτριωμένους, "who were once in a state of estrangement." ὄντας expresses more forcibly the settledness of the alienation. For ἀπαλλοτριόω see on Eph. ii. 12. Here the remote object must be God, as of its opposite ἀποκαταλλάσσειν, and the word implies that they belonged to another (ἀλλότριος) (they were, in fact, subject to the ἐξουσία τοῦ σκότους), and that this was the consequence of movement away from Him (ἀπο-). Alford understands the verb here objectively, "banished"; but it seems more congruous to the whole context (ἀποκαταλ., ἐχθρούς) to understand it subjectively, "estranged (in mind)."

ἐχθροὺς τῇ διανοίᾳ. ἐχθρούς is taken passively by Meyer, "invisos Deo." But such a meaning is not justified either by the context here or by the use of the word elsewhere; cf. Rom. viii. 7, τὸ φρόνημα τῆς σαρκὸς ἔχθρα εἰς Θεόν. Even in Rom. v. 10, εἰ γὰρ ἐχθροὶ ὄντες κατηλλάγημεν τῷ Θεῷ, κ.τ.λ., it is best understood actively; there, as here, the sinner is spoken of as reconciled to God, not God to the sinner. Indeed, nowhere in the N.T. is the latter expression used. The fact that it occurs in Clement, in the *Const. Apost.*, and in the Apocrypha (Meyer), only makes its absence from the N.T. the more noticeable. As Lightfoot observes, "it is the mind of man, not the mind of God, which must undergo a change, that a reunion may be effected." It was not because God hated the world, but because He loved it, that He sent His Son. In Rom. xi. 28, where the Jews are said to be ἐχθροί in a passive sense, this is not absolute, but κατὰ τὸ εὐαγγέλιον, and they are at the same time ἀγαπητοί. Here, in particular, the active sense is required by the following τῇ διανοίᾳ, which Meyer indeed interprets as a "causal dative" (as if it were = διὰ τὴν διανοίαν). But in ἐχθρὸς τῇ διανοίᾳ the two notions must have the same subject (ὑμῶν not being added). Besides, if so intended, διανοίᾳ would surely be qualified by πονηρᾷ or the like. τῇ διανοίᾳ, then, is the dative of the part affected, as in ἐσκοτωμένοι τῇ διανοίᾳ, Eph. iv. 18; καθαροὶ τῇ καρδίᾳ, Matt. v. 8.

ἐν τοῖς ἔργοις τοῖς πονηροῖς, the practical sphere in which the preceding characteristics exhibited themselves. A striking contrast to the description of the Christian walk in ver. 10.

22. νυνὶ δέ, "now," *i.e.* in the present order of things, not "at the present moment." The aorist marks that the state of things

followed a given event. It is correctly rendered by the English perfect. So ver. 26; also Eph. ii. 13, iii. 5; Rom. v. 11, vii. 6, xi. 30, 31, xvi. 26; 2 Tim. i. 10; 1 Pet. i. 10, ii. 10, 25. We have the aorist similarly used in Plato, *Symp.* 193 A, πρὸ τοῦ, ὥσπερ λέγω, ἓν ἦμεν· νυνὶ δὲ διὰ τὴν ἀδικίαν διῳκίσθημεν ὑπὸ τοῦ Θεοῦ, and in Isaeus, *De Cleon. her.* 20, τότε μὲν . . . νυνὶ δὲ . . . ἐβουλήθη.

ἀποκατηλλάγητε or ἀποκατήλλαξεν. For reading and construction, see above.

ἐν τῷ σώματι τῆς σαρκὸς αὐτοῦ, ἐν pointing to the medium of the reconciliation. The addition of τῆς σαρκὸς αὐτοῦ, "consisting in His flesh," has been variously accounted for. Beza, Huther, Barry, *al.*, suppose the expression directed against Docetism; but there is no direct evidence of this form of error so early, nor does there appear to be any allusion to it in this Epistle. Others, as Bengel, Olshausen, Lightfoot, supposed the words added to distinguish between the physical and the spiritual σῶμα, *i.e.* the Church. But this would be irrelevant. Marcion, however, omitted τῆς σαρκός as inconsistent with his views, and explained ἐν τῷ σώματι of the Church. Tertullian, referring to this, says: "in eo corpore in quo mori potuit per carnem mortuus est, non per ecclesiam sed propter ecclesiam" (*Adv. Marc.* v. 19). The most probable explanation is that the words have reference to the opinion of the false teachers, that angels who were without a σῶμα τῆς σαρκός assisted in the work of reconciliation (so Alford, Ellicott, Meyer, Soden). διὰ τοῦ θανάτου expresses the manner in which the reconciliation was wrought.

After θανάτου, αὐτοῦ is added in ℵ A P *al.*, Boh. Arm. *al.*

παραστῆσαι ὑμᾶς. With the reading ἀποκατήλλαξεν this infinitive expresses the final purpose; comp. 2 Cor. xi. 2, ἡρμοσάμην ὑμᾶς ἑνὶ ἀνδρί, παρθένον ἁγνὴν παραστῆσαι τῷ Χριστῷ. Here, however, the verb has its judicial sense; comp. 2 Cor. iv. 14, ὁ ἐγείρας τὸν Κύριον Ἰησοῦν καὶ ἡμᾶς σὺν Ἰησοῦ ἐγερεῖ καὶ παραστήσει σὺν ὑμῖν. As this παραστῆσαι is thus included by God Himself in His work as the consequence of the reconciliation which He has accomplished, it follows that there is no room for anything to be contributed to this end by man himself.

With the reading ἀποκατηλλάγητε two constructions are possible. First, it may be taken as dependent on εὐδόκησεν, νυνὶ δέ—θανάτου being parenthetical (Lightfoot). This makes the sentence rather involved. Or, secondly, the subject of παραστῆσαι and that of ἀποκατ. may be the same, viz. ὑμεῖς, "ut sisteretis vos." Comp. Rom. vi. 13, παραστήσατε ἑαυτοὺς τῷ Θεῷ; 2 Tim. ii. 15, σπούδασον σεαυτὸν δόκιμον παραστῆσαι τῷ Θεῷ. There is here no emphasis on the reflexive sense (the words being nearly equivalent to "that ye may stand"), so that ἑαυτούς is not required.

Lightfoot regards παραστῆσαι here as sacrificial, paraphrasing thus: "He will present you a living sacrifice, an acceptable offering to Himself." But this is reading into the words something which is not suggested, nor even favoured, by the context. Though ἁγίους καὶ ἀμώμους may seem to be borrowed from the vocabulary of sacrifice, the combination does not carry any such connotation with it. Comp. Eph. i. 4 (ἐξελέξατο ἡμᾶς) εἶναι ἡμᾶς ἁγίους καὶ ἀμώμους κατενώπιον αὐτοῦ; *ib.* ver. 27 (in connexion with the same verb παραστῆναι, where the figure is that of a bride); Jude 24, στῆσαι κατενώπιον τῆς δόξης αὐτοῦ ἀμώμους. ἀνεγκλήτους, moreover, is not suitable to sacrifice. It is a judicial term, and thus determines the sense of the other two, παραστῆσαι being quite as much a judicial as a sacrificial word; cf. Acts xxiii. 33. May we not add that the thought expressed in Lightfoot's paraphrase has no parallel in the N.T.? For Rom. xii. 1 does not support the idea of God presenting believers to Himself as a sacrifice. Accordingly, this view is rejected by most commentators. The adjectives, then, are best understood of moral and spiritual character, the first expressing the positive aspect, the others the negative; and κατενώπιον αὐτοῦ being connected with the verb, which requires such an addition, not with the adjectives, nor with the last only.

23. εἴ γε, "assuming that." See Eph. iii. 2.

ἐπιμένετε, "ye abide, continue in," a figurative use of ἐπιμένειν, occurring several times in St. Paul (only), and always with the simple dative; cf. Rom. vi. 1, xi. 22, 23; 1 Tim. iv. 16. (In Acts xiii. 43 the genuine reading is προσμένειν.) The ἐπι- is not intensive, as if ἐπιμένειν were stronger than μένειν (cf. 2 Cor. ix. 9; 2 Tim. ii. 13; 1 Tim. ii. 15; Acts xviii. 20, ix. 43, xxviii. 12, 14). It adds the idea of locality.

τῇ πίστει, *i.e.* ὑμῶν, referring to i. 4.

τεθεμελιωμένοι καὶ ἑδραῖοι, the former word referring to the sure foundation (Eph. iii. 17), the latter to the firmness of the structure. ἑδραῖος occurs also in 1 Cor. vii. 37, ὃς δὲ ἕστηκεν ἐν τῇ καρδίᾳ αὐτοῦ ἑδραῖος, and in 1 Cor. xv. 58, ἑδραῖοι γίνεσθε, ἀμετακίνητοι.

μὴ μετακινούμενοι expresses the same idea on the negative side, but defined more precisely by the following words. It seems better taken as middle than passive, especially considering the present tense, "not constantly shifting." The use of μή implies that this clause is conditioned by the preceding (Winer, § 55. 1*a*).

ἀπὸ τῆς ἐλπίδος. As the three preceding expressions involve the same figure, Soden regards these words as connected (by zeugma) with the first two as well as with the third.

τοῦ εὐαγγελίου, subjective genitive, the hope that belongs to the gospel. Comp. ἡ ἐλπὶς τῆς κλήσεως, Eph. i. 18, iv. 4.

οὗ ἠκούσατε, κ.τ.λ. Three points to enforce the duty of not being moved, etc. They had heard this gospel; the same had been universally preached, and the apostle himself was a minister of it. πάλιν αὐτοὺς φέρει μάρτυρας, εἶτα τὴν οἰκουμένην ἅπασαν ... καὶ τοῦτο εἰς τὸ ἀξιόπιστον συντελεῖ. ... μέγα γὰρ αὐτοῦ ἦν τὸ ἀξίωμα λοιπὸν πανταχοῦ ᾀδομένου, καὶ τῆς οἰκουμένης ὄντος διδασκάλου, Chrys.

ἐν πάσῃ κτίσει, "in all creation," RV., or "among every creature," Coverdale, Lightfoot; cf. Mark xvi. 15 (where, however, κτίσις has the article), κηρύξατε τὸ εὐαγγέλιον πάσῃ τῇ κτίσει. In both places the thought is of proclamation and of reception by faith; and therefore we can hardly (with Lightfoot) bring in "all creation, animate and inanimate."

The expression κηρυχθέντος is probably not to be regarded as hyperbolical, but ideal, "it 'was' done when the Saviour ... bade it be done" (Moule).

After πάσῃ, τῇ is added in אᶜ Dᶜ K L P and most. It is absent from א* A B C D* G 17, etc.

οὗ ἐγενόμην ἐγὼ Παῦλος διάκονος. Returning to his introduction of himself in ver. 1, the apostle prepares to say some further words of introduction of himself and his calling, before entering on the main topic of the Epistle. It is not for the purpose of magnifying his office that he thus names himself, but to impress on his readers that the gospel which they had heard, and which was proclaimed in all the world, was the very gospel that he preached.

For διάκονος, א* P read κῆρυξ καὶ ἀπόστολος. A combines both readings.

24-29. *The apostle's own qualification as a minister of this gospel. To him has been given the privilege of knowing and proclaiming this mystery which was hidden from former ages, namely, that of Christ dwelling in them. It is his mission to make this known, and so to admonish and teach that he may present every man perfect. This he earnestly labours to do through the power of Christ.*

24. νῦν χαίρω. νῦν is not transitional ("quae cum ita sint," Lücke), which would require οὖν, or the like, but refers to present time. Now as a prisoner "with a chain upon my wrist" (Eadie). His active service as διάκονος is at present suspended, but the sufferings which it had brought upon him are a source of joy. Lightfoot understands it thus: "Now, when I contemplate the lavish wealth of God's mercy, now when I see all the glory of bearing a part in this magnificent work, my sorrow is turned into joy." But there is no indication of such a connexion of thought in the text.

ὅς is prefixed to νῦν in D* G, Vulg. *al.* (AV.). It is, doubtless, a repetition of the first syllable of διάκονος, assisted by the desire to supply a connecting link between the sentences. For examples of similar abruptness compare 2 Cor. vii. 9; 1 Tim. i. 12.

ἐν. Compare Phil. i. 18, ἐν τούτῳ χαίρω : Rom. v. 3, καυχώμεθα ἐν ταῖς θλίψεσιν.

After παθήμασιν, μου is added in Text. Rec. with א^c and many cursives, Syr-Pesh. Arm. Eth. al.

ὑπὲρ ὑμῶν, to be connected with παθήμασιν. His sufferings had been brought on him by his labours on behalf of the Gentiles, "propter vestrum gentium salutem," Estius, and so with a kindly personal reference he represents them as endured on behalf of the Colossians, who shared in the benefit of his ministry. The article is not required before ὑπὲρ ὑμῶν, τοῖς παθήμασιν being = οἷς πάσχω.

ἀνταναπληρῶ. This double compound is not found elsewhere in LXX or N.T. ἀναπληροῦν is found six times in N.T., twice in connexion with ὑστέρημα, 1 Cor. xvi. 17; Phil. ii. 30. προσαναπληροῦν also occurs twice with ὑστέρημα, but in a different sense, the former verb referring to a deficiency left by, the latter to one felt by, the persons mentioned. What modification is introduced in the meaning of ἀναπληροῦν by the addition of ἀντι- is disputed. ἀντι in composition with a verb does not imply "instead of another," as Photius here takes it (τουτέστιν, Ἀντὶ δεσπότου καὶ διδασκάλου ὁ δοῦλος ἐγώ, κ.τ.λ.), but "over against," which may be either in opposition, as ἀντιλέγω, ἀντίκειμαι, or in correspondence, in turn, as ἀντιμετρέω, ἀντικαλέω (Luke xiv. 12), ἀντιλαμβανόμαι, etc. Here the ἀντι- has been understood by some as referring to διακονία, the suffering now taking the place of the former active service, or as indicating that the apostle's afflictions were in response to what Christ had done for him. It is, perhaps, sufficient to say, with Wetstein, that it indicates the correspondence with the ὑστέρημα, "ἀντὶ ὑστερήματος succedit ἀναπλήρωμα." (So Meyer, Alford, Ellicott, Eadie, Soden.) Lightfoot objects that this practically deprives ἀντι of any meaning, for ἀναπληροῦν alone would denote as much. He adopts Winer's view, that ἀνταναπληροῦν is used of one who "*alterius ὑστέρημα de suo* explet," or, as Lightfoot puts it, "that the supply comes *from an opposite quarter* to the deficiency." Instances are cited in which this idea (or rather that of "a different quarter") is expressed in the context, for example, Dion Cass. xliv. 48, ἵν' ὅσον . . . ἐνέδει, τοῦτο ἐκ τῆς παρὰ τῶν ἄλλων συντελείας ἀνταναπληρωθῇ. The requirements of this passage seem to be fully met by the idea of correspondence, as will appear if we translate : "in order that . . . as much as was wanting . . . this might be correspondingly supplied." And in the two instances in which ἀναπληροῦν is used with ὑστέρημα, the supply is from a different quarter from the deficiency, so that there is no more reason for including this idea in ἀνταναπλ. than in ἀναπλ.

In Demosth. (*De Symm.* p. 182), τούτων τῶν συμμωριῶν ἑκάστην διελεῖν κελεύω πέντε μέρη κατὰ δώδεκα ἄνδρας, ἀνταναπληροῦντας πρὸς τὸν εὐπορώτατον ἀεὶ τοὺς ἀπορωτάτους, the idea is that the poorer members should balance the rich in each μέρος, so as to equalise the μέρη. It is this idea of balance that is expressed by the ἀντι-.

Similarly the substantive ἀνταναπλήρωσις in Diog. Laert. x. 48, καὶ γὰρ ῥεῦσις ἀπὸ τῆς τῶν σωμάτων ἐπιπολῆς συνεχὴς συμβαίνει, οὐκ ἐπίδηλος αἰσθήσει διὰ τὴν ἀνταναπλήρωσιν, *i.e.* on account of the counter-supply, *i.e.* the supply which "meets" the deficiency.

It is not, perhaps, an over-refinement to suggest that ἀνταναπληρῶ is more unassuming than ἀναπληρῶ, since part of the force of the word is thrown on the idea of correspondence.

τὰ ὑστερήματα. The plural is used because the afflictions are not regarded as a unity from which there is a definite shortcoming. Compare 1 Thess. iii. 10, τὰ ὑστερήματα τῆς πίστεως ὑμῶν, where the singular would suggest that their faith, as faith, was defective, while the plural suggests that there were points in which it needed to be made perfect.

τῶν θλίψεων τοῦ Χριστοῦ. By two classes of commentators these words are understood to mean the afflictions which Christ endured. First, many Roman Catholic expositors, including Caietan, Bellarmine, and more recently Bisping, find in the passage a support for the theory that the merits of the saints constitute a treasure of the Church from which indulgences may be granted. Estius, with his usual candour, while holding the doctrine to be Catholic and apostolic, yet judges that "ex hoc Ap. loco non videtur admodum solide statui posse. Non enim sermo iste, quo dicit Ap. se pati pro ecclesia, necessario sic accipiendus est, quod pro redimendis peccatorum poenis quas fideles debent, patiatur, quod forte nonnihil haberet arrogantiae; sed percommode sic accipitur, quomodo proxime dixerat 'gaudeo in passionibus meis pro vobis' ut nimirum utraque parte significet afflictiones et persecutiones pro salute fidelium ipsiusque ecclesiae promovendae toleratas." It has been more fully replied (*e.g.* by Lightfoot) that the sufferings of Christ may be regarded from two different points of view, either as *satisfactoriae* or *aedificatoriae*. In the former sense there can be no ὑστέρημα, Christ's sufferings and those of His servants are different in *kind*, and therefore incommensurable. But in this sense θλίψις would be an unsuitable word, and, in fact, it is never applied in any sense to Christ's sufferings. In the second point of view, however, that of ministerial utility, "it is a simple matter of fact that the afflictions of every saint and martyr do supplement the afflictions of Christ. The Church is built up by repeated acts of self-denial in successive individuals and successive generations" (Lightfoot).

It is no doubt true that these "continue the work which Christ began" (compare 2 Cor. i. 5; 1 Pet. iv. 13). But to say this is not to say that there was any "shortcoming" in the afflictions of Christ. His work, including His sufferings, was absolutely complete; and so far as others carry it on, their work is included in His (Phil. iv. 13). To say that He left something "behind" is to slur over the meaning of ὑστέρημα, which does not mean something left behind, but a want of sufficiency. Nowhere in the N.T. is anything of the kind suggested. And the Colossians were the last to whom St. Paul would use, without explanation, a phrase which would be so open to misconception, as tending to foster the delusion that either saints or angels could add anything to Christ's work. If affliction could do so, why not (it might be said) self-imposed suffering, asceticism, or gratuitous self-denial? Moreover, can it be supposed that St. Paul, who calls himself the least of saints, and not meet to be called an apostle, would express himself thus without some qualification? Lightfoot would mitigate the apparent arrogance by the remark that "the present tense, ἀνταναπληρῶ, denotes an inchoate, not a complete act." The term "inchoate" does not seem to be justified. The present, indeed, denotes an act continuing and therefore not finished, but not incomplete as far as the present moment is concerned. Compare the instances of ἀναπληρῶ itself: Matt. xiii. 14, ἀναπληροῦται αὐτοῖς ἡ προφητεία, κ.τ.λ.: 1 Cor. xiv. 16, ὁ ἀναπληρῶν τὸν τόπον τοῦ ἰδιώτου: 2 Cor. ix. 12, οὐ μόνον ἐστὶ προσαναπληροῦσα τὰ ὑστερήματα τῶν ἁγίων, ἀλλὰ καὶ περισσεύουσα, κ.τ.λ. Compare also the present of πληροῦν, Gal. v. 14; Eph. v. 18; Col. iv. 17.

A third view is adopted by Chrysostom, Theophylact, Augustine, and most expositors, ancient and modern. According to this, "the afflictions of Christ" are the sufferings of His Body, the Church, so called because "He really felt them." So Augustine on Ps. lxi. says of Christ, "qui passus est in capite nostro et patitur in membris suis, id est, nobis ipsis." And Leo, quoted by Böhmer (ap. Eadie), "passio Christi perducitur ad finem mundi," etc. This view is adopted amongst late commentators by Alford, Ellicott, De Wette, Olshausen. But the notion that Christ suffers affliction in His people is nowhere found in the N.T. Acts ix. 4, "Why persecutest thou Me?" is not an instance. There the persecution of His saints is represented as directed against Him, but He is not represented as suffering from it. The idea that the glorified Christ continues to suffer, and that " His tribulations will not be complete till the last pang shall have past" (Alf.) (an idea which, as Meyer observes, would seem to imply even the thought of Christ's dying in the martyrs), is inconsistent with the scriptural representations of His exalted state. It is true that He sympathises with the afflictions of His people; but sympathy is not affliction, nor can the fact of this sympathy justify the use of the term "afflictions of Christ," without explanation, to mean the afflictions of His Church. This would be particularly unsuitable in the present connexion, for it would make St. Paul say that he rejoiced in His sufferings because they went to increase the afflictions of Christ.

It remains that (with Meyer, Soden, *al.*) we take the expression to signify the apostle's own afflictions; and to this interpretation the readers are naturally led, first, by the word θλίψις, which is never used of Christ's sufferings, but often of the apostle's; and, secondly, by the defining words ἐν τῇ σαρκί μου, which are best connected with τῶν θλίψεων. For if the writer had intended them to be taken with the verb, he would doubtless have written ἀνταναπληρῶ ἐν τῇ σαρκί μου. It is said, indeed, that the words are placed here for the sake of the antithesis to τοῦ σώματος αὐτοῦ. But there would be no purpose served by emphasising this antithesis here, and to do so would only distract the attention of the reader.

Meyer, however, while adopting this view of θλ. τοῦ Χρ., connects ἐν τῇ σ. μου with the verb. On the other hand, Steiger, joining these words with θλ. τοῦ Χρ., connects both with the following: "the sufferings which Christ endures in my flesh for His body."

That St. Paul should call his own sufferings in the service of Christ the afflictions of Christ in his flesh, is quite in accordance with other expressions of his. For instance, in 2 Cor. i. 5 he speaks of the sufferings of Christ overflowing to him, περισσεύει τὰ παθήματα τοῦ Χριστοῦ εἰς ἡμᾶς. In Phil. iii. 10 he speaks of knowing κοινωνία τῶν παθημάτων αὐτοῦ συμμορφιζόμενος τῷ θανάτῳ αὐτοῦ. Again, 2 Cor. iv. 10, πάντοτε τὴν νέκρωσιν τοῦ Ἰησοῦ ἐν τῷ σώματι περιφέροντες.

The form of expression, then, need not cause any difficulty. The question what St. Paul means by calling his own troubles the afflictions of Christ in his flesh is a different one, and may be answered by saying that Christ's afflictions are regarded as the type of all those that are endured by His followers on behalf of the Church. So Theodoret: Χριστὸς τὸν ὑπὲρ τῆς ἐκκλησίας κατεδέξατο θάνατον . . . καὶ τὰ ἄλλα ὅσα ὑπέμεινε, καὶ ὁ θεῖος ἀπόστολος ὡσαύτως ὑπὲρ αὐτῆς ὑπέστη τὰ ποικίλα παθήματα. Compare Matt. xx. 23, τὸ μὲν ποτήριόν μου πίεσθε.

ὑπὲρ τοῦ σώματος αὐτοῦ. The use of this designation was probably suggested by the mention of σάρξ. ὑπέρ is clearly not "in the place of," but "on behalf of"; cf. ver. 7.

ὅ ἐστιν ἡ ἐκκλησία. The antithesis of σῶμα and σάρξ rendered necessary this explanation of the words σώματος αὐτοῦ. Besides, ἐκκλησία was required by the following ἐγενόμην διάκονος.

ὅ ἐστιν has not the same shade of meaning as ἥτις ἐστίν

(1 Tim. iii. 15, ἐν οἴκῳ Θεοῦ ... ἥτις ἐστὶν ἐκκλησία). The former is equivalent to *id est*; the latter to "and such is."

25. ἧς ἐγενόμην διάκονος resumes the οὗ ἐγεν. διάκ. of ver. 23, carrying out now the active side of the ministry, as ver. 24 the passive.

κατὰ τὴν οἰκονομίαν. "According to the stewardship in the house of God." On οἰκ. cf. Eph. i. 10. Here = the office or function of a steward, so that he is an οἰκονόμος Θεοῦ, cf. 1 Cor. ix. 17, οἰκονομίαν πεπίστευμαι, and Luke xvi. 2. So the apostles and other ministers of the Church are called οἰκονόμοι, 1 Cor. iv. 1, 7; Tit. i. 7; see also 1 Pet. iv. 10. The Church is οἶκος τοῦ Θεοῦ, 1 Tim. iii. 15. Chrysostom, *al.*, take οἰκ. in the sense "dispensation," which is inconsistent with τὴν δοθεῖσάν μοι.

εἰς ὑμᾶς, cf. ver. 24. Connected by Scholefield and Hofmann with the following πληρῶσαι. But compare Eph. iii. 2, τὴν οἰκονομίαν τῆς χάριτος τοῦ Θεοῦ τῆς δοθείσης μοι εἰς ὑμᾶς: and Rom. xv. 16, τὴν χάριν τὴν δοθεῖσάν μοι ὑπὸ τοῦ Θεοῦ εἰς τὸ εἶναί με λειτουργὸν Χριστοῦ εἰς τὰ ἔθνη.

πληρῶσαι, not infin. of design, but explanatory of οἰκ. τὴν δοθ. κ.τ.λ. The verb is found in a similar connexion Rom. xv. 19, ὥστε με ... μέχρι τοῦ Ἰλλυρικοῦ πεπληρωκέναι τὸ εὐαγγέλιον τοῦ Χριστοῦ. ὁ λόγος τοῦ Θεοῦ is frequently used by St. Paul for the gospel (1 Cor. xiv. 36; 2 Cor. ii. 17, iv. 2; 1 Thess. ii. 13; compare also Acts iv. 31, *al.*). The sense then is: "to carry out to the full the preaching of the gospel"; "ad summa perducere: Paulus ubique ad summa tendit," Bengel. There is doubtless a reference to St. Paul's special office as the apostle of the Gentiles, by virtue of which he gave full development to the "word of God." This is suggested by δοθεῖσάν μοι εἰς ὑμᾶς.

Beza takes the phrase to mean "to fulfil the promise of God" (cf. 2 Chron. xxxvi. 21), which does not suit the context. Fritzsche understands it as meaning "to complete the teaching begun by Epaphras." See on Lk. viii. 11.

26. τὸ μυστήριον. Lightfoot observes: "This is not the only term borrowed from the ancient mysteries, which St. Paul employs to describe the teaching of the gospel," and he mentions τέλειον, ver. 28; μεμύημαι, Phil. iv. 12; and (perhaps) σφραγίζεσθαι in Eph. i. 14. There is, he says, an intentional paradox in the employment of the image by St. Paul, since the Christian mysteries are not, like the heathen, confined to a narrow circle, but are freely communicated to all. But as μυστήριον in the singular is never used by Greek writers in connexion with the ancient mysteries, and on the other hand appears to have been an ordinary word for "secret" (see note on Eph. i. 9), there seems to be no ground for the assumption that the term is borrowed from the "mysteries." The plural is used thrice only by St. Paul, viz. 1 Cor. iv. 1,

xiii. 2, xiv. 2; but occurs in the Gospels, Matt. xiii. 11; Luke viii. 10. As to μέμνημαι, although the verb may have been originally borrowed from the mysteries, St. Paul found it already in use in the sense in which he employs it; cf. Alciphron, ii. 4, κυβερνᾶν μνηθήσομαι. For τέλειος, see on ver. 28.

τὸ ἀποκεκρυμμένον ... νῦν δὲ ἐφανερώθη. These are the two characteristics of a μυστήριον in the N.T. Compare Rom. xvi. 25, μυστηρίου χρόνοις αἰωνίοις σεσιγημένου, φανερωθέντος δὲ νῦν. πρὸ τῶν αἰώνων, used in 1 Cor. ii. 7 of God's purpose, could not properly have been said of its concealment. ἀπὸ τῶν αἰώνων, κ.τ.λ. ἀπό here is of time, being opposed to νῦν. So ἀπ' αἰῶνος, Acts iii. 21, xv. 18. An αἰών includes many γενεαί; compare Eph. iii. 21. The fact of the long concealment and recent disclosure of the mystery is not without point here; it explains the acceptance of the errors which the apostle is combating.

27. ἐφανερώθη. The anacoluthon gives more emphasis to the mention of the φανέρωσις; cf. ver. 22.

τοῖς ἁγίοις αὐτοῦ; *i.e.* Christians in general, not only the apostles and prophets of the N.T., as many both of the older and later commentators take it, in agreement with Eph. iii. 5. Cod. G even adds ἀποστόλοις (and F, of course, agrees).

οἷς, "quippe quibus." ἠθέλησεν ὁ Θεός. It was God's free choice, so that the γνωρίζειν was only to those to whom He chose to make it known.

τί τὸ πλοῦτος τῆς δόξης. Compare Rom. ix. 23, ἵνα γνωρίσῃ τὸν πλοῦτον τῆς δόξης αὐτοῦ: and Eph. i. 18, iii. 16. τί joined to a substantive of quantity signifies "how great." πλοῦτος (indifferently masculine and neuter in St. Paul) is a favourite term in these Epistles as applied to the dispensation of grace.

δόξα is not a mere attribute of πλοῦτος (Erasmus), nor μυστηρίον (Beza), but is the principal idea; it is of the δόξα τοῦ μυστηρίου that it is said that it has shown itself in rich measure. It is the glorious manifestation of God's dealings contained in this μυστήριον, "magniloquus est in extollenda evangelii dignitate," Calvin. σεμνῶς εἶπε καὶ ὄγκον ἐπέθηκεν ἀπὸ πολλῆς διαθέσεως, ἐπιτάσεις ζητῶν ἐπιτάσεων, Chrys. The latter, however, understands the words of the glorious results of the gospel amongst the heathen.

ἐν τοῖς ἔθνεσιν. It was amongst these especially that this πλοῦτος was displayed; φαίνεται ἐν ἑτέροις, πολλῷ δὲ πλέον ἐν τούτοις ἡ πολλὴ τοῦ μυστηρίου δόξα, Chrys. For the construction cf. Eph. i. 18.

ὅ ἐστιν Χριστὸς ἐν ὑμῖν. The antecedent may be either μυστήριον or πλοῦτος. The former (Vulg. Chrys.) is that generally favoured by expositors: "the mystery consists in this, that Christ is ἐν ὑμῖν"; and this seems on the whole the most natural.

Μυστήριον is the principal idea in the context (ver. 26, ii. 2), τὸ πλοῦτος τῆς δόξης being subsidiary to it. Again, the "mystery" is not something distinct from the riches of the glory of it; those to whom the former is revealed are made acquainted with the latter. This view also agrees with Eph. iii. 6, where the μυστήριον τοῦ Χριστοῦ is defined as εἶναι τὰ ἔθνη συγκληρονόμα, κ.τ.λ. The strongest objection to this view is that it seems to make ὅ ἐστιν, κ.τ.λ., a merely parenthetical definition, whereas it carries on the thread of the discourse. But this is more apparent than real; it is the thought of the μυστήριον that runs through the whole, and the clause is not parenthetical, but carries on the description of the μυστήριον begun in ver. 26, ἐν ὑμῖν. The parallelism with ἐν τοῖς ἔθνεσιν favours the interpretation "among you," rather than "in you."

ἡ ἐλπὶς τῆς δόξης. This δόξης is an echo of the former, but this does not require us to give both the same signification. Oltramare regards this, not as an apposition to ὁ Χρ., but as a second thought succeeding the former in a lively manner, and joining on to it, "It is Christ in the midst of you! the hope of glory!"

τί τὸ πλοῦτος is read by A B D^bc K L (τὸ πλοῦτος without τί, G), while ℵ C P have the masc. τίς ὁ πλ.

ὅ ἐστιν is read by A B G P 17 47 67², probably Lat. Vulg. (*quod est*); ὅς ἐστιν by ℵ C D K L and most, Chrys. Theodoret, *al.* With the latter reading, ὅς is attracted to the gender of Χριστός. But this interferes with the sense, for whether the antecedent be πλοῦτος or μυστήριον, it is not Χριστός that is predicated, but Χριστὸς ἐν ὑμῖν.

28. ὃν ἡμεῖς καταγγέλλομεν. "And Him we proclaim." Him, *i.e.* not Χριστόν only, but Χρ. ἐν ὑμῖν. ἡμεῖς, emphatic, in opposition to the heretical as well as to the Judaising teachers; "we," himself and Timothy in particular.

νουθετοῦντες . . . καὶ διδάσκοντες . . . "admonishing . . . and teaching." These, as Meyer observes, correspond to the μετανοεῖτε καὶ πιστεύετε of the gospel message. νουθεσία μὲν ἐπὶ τῆς πράξεως, διδασκαλία δὲ ἐπὶ δογμάτων.

πάντα ἄνθρωπον, thrice repeated, emphasises the universality of the gospel as taught by St. Paul (iii. 11), in opposition to the doctrine of an intellectual exclusiveness taught by the false teachers; probably also it points to the fact that each man individually was an object of the apostle's care, τί λέγεις; πάντα ἄνθρωπον; ναί, φησι, τοῦτο σπουδάζομεν, εἰ δὲ μὴ γένηται, οὐδὲν πρὸς ἡμᾶς, Theophylact.

ἐν πάσῃ σοφίᾳ, *i.e.* μετὰ πάσης σοφίας καὶ συνέσεως, Chrys. *al.*, expressing the manner of the teaching. The Latin Fathers understand the words as denoting the object of the teaching; so Moule: "in the whole field of that holy wisdom," etc. But in the N.T. the object of διδάσκειν is put in the accusative, not in the dative with ἐν.

There is no contradiction to 1 Cor. i. 17, ii. 1–16, for there is a Θεοῦ σοφία (1 Cor. ii. 7), a divine philosophy, the source of which is indicated in ch. ii. 3; cf. Eph. i. 8, τῆς χάριτος αὐτοῦ ἧς ἐπερίσσευσεν εἰς ἡμᾶς ἐν πάσῃ σοφίᾳ. Compare ver. 9 and iii. 16.

ἵνα παραστήσωμεν, as in ver. 22, refers to presentation before a tribunal, not as a sacrifice.

τέλειον. This is one of the words noted by Lightfoot as "probably borrowed from the ancient mysteries, where it seems to have been applied to the fully instructed, as opposed to the novices," and in 1 Cor. ii. 6, 7 he finds the same allusion. This technical sense of τέλειος as applied to persons does not seem sufficiently made out; in the passages cited by Lightfoot, with one exception, it is not to the persons, but to the mysteries, τελεταί, that the term is applied. The one exception is Plato, *Phaedr.* 249 C, τελέους ἀεὶ τελετὰς τελούμενος τέλεος ὄντως μόνος γίγνεται, which cannot be regarded as proving the usage. But even if this be granted, there seems no sufficient reason for introducing this sense here, where what is in question is not complete initiation, or knowledge, but maturity of faith and spiritual life. In this sense the word is used by St. Paul, Eph. iv. 13, μέχρι καταντήσωμεν εἰς ἄνδρα τέλειον: Phil. iii. 15, ὅσοι οὖν τέλειοι, τοῦτο φρονῶμεν: 1 Cor. xiv. 20, ταῖς φρεσὶ τέλειοι γίνεσθε. Compare Heb. v. 14; Matt. v. 48, xix. 21. And in the present Epistle, iv. 12, ἵνα σταθῆτε τέλειοι καὶ πεπληροφημένοι ἐν παντὶ θελήματι τοῦ Θεοῦ. Observe also here the defining addition τέλειον ἐν Χριστῷ. For the use of the term in early Christian writers to denote the baptized as opposed to the catechumens, see Lightfoot's note.

29. εἰς ὅ, viz. to present every man, etc.

καὶ κοπιῶ. I not only καταγγέλλω, κ.τ.λ., but carry this to the point of toiling. Hofmann understands it as meaning, "I become weary," comparing John iv. 6; Apoc. ii. 3, where, however, the verb is perfect. The sense, moreover, would be quite unsuitable here in connexion with the ἀγωνίζεσθαι in the power of Christ. The verb is frequently used by St. Paul of his toilsome labours in the Churches; *e.g.* 1 Cor. xv. 10; Gal. iv. 11; Phil. ii. 16; also of the labours of others; Rom. xvi. 12; 1 Cor. xvi. 16; 1 Thess. v. 12. But he also uses it of the labour of the hands; 1 Cor. iv. 12; Eph. iv. 28. The change to the singular has its ground in the personal experience described.

ἀγωνιζόμενος. Compare 1 Tim. iv. 10, εἰς τοῦτο κοπιῶμεν καὶ ἀγωνιζόμεθα. The reference here is to an inward ἀγών, as is shown by the following context; cf. iv. 12.

κατὰ τὴν ἐνέργειαν αὐτοῦ. Not by his own strength, but by that which Christ supplies. τὸν αὐτοῦ κόπον καὶ ἀγῶνα τῷ Χριστῷ ἀνατιθείς, Oecum. But Chrys. Theoph. understand the αὐτοῦ of God, against the immediate context. ἐνεργουμένην, middle, as always in St. Paul. Fritzsche on Rom. vii. 5 observes: "ἐνεργεῖν, *vim exercere* de *personis*, ἐνεργεῖσθαι *ex se* (aut suam) *vim exercere* de *rebus* collocavit, Gal. v. 6; Col. i. 29; 1 Thess. ii. 13; *al.* ut *h.l.* Passivo ... nunquam Paulus usus est."

ἐν δυνάμει, "in power"; cf. Rom. i. 8; 2 Thess. i. 11. Some understand this of the power of working miracles, which is quite inappropriate to the context, according to which the reference is to κοπιῶ ἀγωνιζόμενος.

II. 1-7. *The apostle's care and anxiety are not limited to those Churches which he had himself founded, or to which he had personally preached, but extended to those whom he had never seen. He is anxious that they should be confirmed in the faith and united in love, and, moreover, may learn to know the mystery, that is, the revealed will of God. It is no new doctrine they are to look for, but to seek to be established in the faith which they have already been taught, and to live in conformity thereto.*

1. Γάρ. "Striving, I say, for," etc. The general statement κοπιῶ ἀγωνιζόμενος is supported by this special instance of his anxiety for the Colossian Church; and thus although γάρ is not merely transitional, the transition to the personal application is naturally effected.

θέλω γὰρ ὑμᾶς εἰδέναι. So 1 Cor. xi. 3. More frequently οὐ θέλω ὑμᾶς ἀγνοεῖν. That either phrase does not necessarily commence a new section is clear from 1 Cor. xi. 3; Rom. xi. 25.

ἡλίκον, a classical word, not found in Sept. or Apocrypha, and in the N.T. only here and Jas. iii. 5.

ἀγῶνα ἔχω. As he was now a prisoner this ἀγών can only be an inward one. It is not to be limited to prayer (iv. 12), but includes anxiety, etc.

ὑπὲρ ὑμῶν. Here, as often, the reading varies between ὑπέρ and περί. The former is that of ℵ A B C D^b P; the latter of D*^c G K L.

καὶ τῶν ἐν Λαοδικίᾳ (*sic* ℵ A B* C D* G K L P).

The Laodiceans were probably exposed to the influence of the same heretical teaching as the Colossians. Hierapolis is probably alluded to in the words καὶ ὅσοι, κ.τ.λ., see iv. 13. καὶ τῶν ἐν Ἱεραπόλει is actually added in some mss. (10 31 73 118) and in Syr-Harcl.* It is clearly a gloss from iv. 13.

καὶ ὅσοι, κ.τ.λ. καί here introduces the general after the particular, as in Acts iv. 6 and often. It is only the context that decides whether this is the case or whether a new class is introduced. Here there would be no meaning in mentioning two particular Churches which had known him personally, and then in general all who had not known him. The inference is therefore certain that he had never visited Colossae, and this agrees with the incidental references in the Epistle as well as with the narrative in the Acts. See on αὐτῶν, ver. 2.

ἑώρακαν (Alexandrian) is better supported than the Attic ἑωράκασι. The spelling with ω is rather better supported here than that with ο.

ἐν σαρκί does not qualify the verb, as if "seeing in the flesh" were contrasted with "seeing in the spirit" (δείκνυσιν ἐνταῦθα ὅτι ἑώρων συνεχῶς ἐν πνεύματι, Chrys.), but goes with πρόσωπόν μου, giving vividness to the expression. Naturally it is implied that they had a knowledge of him, though not personal.

2. ἵνα παρακληθῶσιν αἱ καρδίαι αὐτῶν. "That their hearts may be strengthened." It can hardly be doubted that this is the meaning of παρακαλεῖν here, where there is no mention of, or allusion to, troubles or persecutions. The sense "comforted, consoled" is, indeed, defended by Meyer, Ellicott, Eadie, al. Ellicott observes: "surely those exposed to the sad trial of erroneous teachings need consolation"; but there is no trace of this view in the Epistle, nor would such consolation be the prime object of the apostle's prayer and anxiety. No; what made him anxious was the danger they were in of being carried away by this erroneous teaching. It was not consolation that was required, but confirmation in the right faith. For this sense of παρακαλεῖν cf. 1 Cor. xiv. 31 (RV. marg.).

αὐτῶν. We might have expected ὑμῶν, but αὐτῶν was suggested by the preceding ὅσοι. This is decisive as to the Colossians being included in the ὅσοι; for if excluded there, they are excluded here, and the writer returns to the Colossians in ver. 4 (ὑμᾶς) in a most illogical manner: "This I say about others who do not know me, in order that no man may deceive *you*."

συμβιβασθέντες. "United, knit together," the common meaning of the verb, and that which it has elsewhere in this Epistle (ver. 19) and in Eph. iv. 16, *q.v.* In the Sept. it always means to "instruct," cf. 1 Cor. ii. 16 (quotation) and Acts xix. 33. It is so rendered here by the Vulg. "instructi." The nominative agrees with the logical subject of the preceding.

It is read by ℵ A B C D* P *al.*, Vulg. Syr. (both). The genitive συμβιβ-ασθέντων is read in ℵᶜ Dᶜ K L and most mss., but is obviously a grammatical correction.

ἐν ἀγάπῃ. "In love," which is the "bond of perfection" (iii. 14). καὶ εἰς expresses the object of the συμβιβ.; connected by καί, because the verb contains the idea of motion.

πᾶν πλοῦτος τῆς πληροφορίας τῆς συνέσεως. "All riches of full assurance of the understanding." "Full assurance" seems the most suitable sense for πληροφορία, and it is also suitable in every other place in the N.T. where the word occurs (1 Thess. i. 5; Heb. vi. 11, x. 22). "Fulness" would also be suitable, except in 1 Thess. i. 5. The word does not occur in Sept. or Apocr., nor in classical authors. On σύνεσις cf. i. 9. It has an intransitive sense, and hence never takes a genitive of the object; here it appears to mean the faculty of judging. He desires their judgment to be exercised with full certainty. De Wette observes that πλοῦτος expresses a quantitative, πληροφορία a qualitative, characteristic.

εἰς ἐπίγνωσιν, κ.τ.λ., seems best taken as parallel to the preceding εἰς, so that it emphatically points out the special object on which the σύνεσις is to be exercised. Some, however, connect this with παρακληθῶσιν, on the ground that ἐπίγνωσις implies as an antecedent condition the συμβιβ. κ.τ.λ. For ἐπίγνωσις, "full knowledge," see Eph. i. 17.

τοῦ Θεοῦ Χριστοῦ. If this reading is adopted, there are three conceivable constructions: (a) Χριστοῦ in apposition to Θεοῦ, (b) Χριστοῦ dependent on Θεοῦ, (c) Χριστοῦ in apposition to μυστηρίου. The first (adopted by Hilary of Poitiers, also by Steiger and Bisping) is generally rejected, either on account of the context (Ell.) or because the phrase is destitute of Pauline analogy (Meyer, Moule, Lightfoot). But it appears to be inadmissible on other grounds. To point τοῦ Θεοῦ, Χριστοῦ, taking these in apposition and thus identifying ὁ Θεός and Χριστός, is obviously impossible, as it would mean, not that Θεός could be predicated of Χριστός, but that Χριστός could be predicated of ὁ Θεός, thus ignoring the distinction of Persons. On the other hand, if we point τοῦ Θεοῦ Χριστοῦ, and understand "the God Christ" (according to the rendering suggested, though not accepted, by Moule), the expression seems inconsistent with strict Monotheism. It defines Θεοῦ by the addition Χριστοῦ, and therefore suggests that other definitions are possible. ὁ Θεὸς πατήρ is not analogous, for two reasons; first, πατήρ only suggests υἱός, and, secondly, πατήρ expresses a relation proper to the Deity. Ellicott, who considers the construction not indefensible, takes it to mean "of God, even of Christ." This is rather to suppose μυστηρίου supplied before Χριστοῦ, which is certainly untenable. But this is clearly not what he means, and it suggests that he hesitated to accept either of the other renderings.

According to the third view, Χριστοῦ is in apposition to μυστηρίου, so that Christ personally is the mystery of God (Ellicott, Lightfoot, Moule, al.). If this is the apostle's meaning, he has expressed himself very obscurely. As μυστήριον is an abstract name, when it is explained as a person, we should expect ὅ ἐστιν as in i. 24, 27; 1 Cor. iii. 11. Lightfoot understands the "mystery" not as "Christ," but "Christ as containing in Himself all the treasures of wisdom," and in illustration of the form of the sentence compares Eph. iv. 15, εἰς αὐτόν... ὅς ἐστιν ἡ κεφαλή, Χριστός, ἐξ οὗ πᾶν τὸ σῶμα, κ.τ.λ. This passage, it is obvious, adds another example of the use of ὅς ἐστιν in such sentences, and it can hardly be said to furnish a parallel to Lightfoot's interpretation of ἐν ᾧ, for in Eph. iv. 15 a full stop might have been placed after Χριστός without impairing the figure. Moreover, the apostle has given a different definition of the μυστ. in i. 27 (to which he again alludes in iv. 3), and it is hard to suppose that he would give a different definition within a few lines, for different this certainly is. The second translation mentioned above, "the God of Christ," has its parallel in the phrase, ὁ Θεὸς καὶ πατὴρ Ἰησοῦ Χριστοῦ, and in Eph. i. 17, ὁ Θεὸς τοῦ Κυρίου ἡμῶν Ἰησοῦ Χριστοῦ. This construction is adopted by Meyer and v. Soden. The addition of Χριστοῦ is explained by the consideration that it is only through Christ that God's plan in this mystery is carried out; it is only because and in so far as God is the God of Christ that this μυστήριον could exist and be revealed. Meyer adds, "He that has recognised God as the God of Christ, to him is the Divine μυστήριον revealed." This, after all, is not quite satisfactory, and requires us to read into the text more than is expressed.

If the shorter reading τοῦ Θεοῦ (omitting Χριστοῦ) is adopted, the difficulty disappears; but the difficulty is not so obvious as to tempt the ordinary copyist to omit the word.

The different readings are as follow:—

(1) τοῦ Θεοῦ. Without any addition. D^b P 37 67** 71 80 116. Adopted by Griesbach, Tisch. 2, Olsh., De Wette, Alford.

(2) τοῦ Θεοῦ Χριστοῦ. B, Hilary of Poitiers (*De Trin.* ix. 62, "in agnitionem sacramenti dei Christi," adding, "Deus Christus sacramentum est"). Adopted by Lachmann, Tregelles, and Lightfoot without a comma after Θεοῦ; by Tisch. 8, RV. with a comma, also by Harless (*Eph.* p. 458), Ellicott, Meyer, and v. Soden.

(3) τοῦ Θεοῦ, ὅ ἐστιν Χριστός. D* "Dei quod est Christus," d e, Vigilius Thaps. So Augustine, *De Trin.* xiii. 24, "Dei quod est Christus Jesus."

(4) τοῦ Θεοῦ πατρός (add τοῦ, A C 4) Χριστοῦ, ℵ* A C 4, Vulg. in Codd. Amiat. Fuld. f. Boh. (add Ἰησοῦ, Lagarde).

(5) τοῦ Θεοῦ καὶ πατρὸς τοῦ Χριστοῦ, ℵ^c two of Scrivener's MSS. and a corrector in the Harclean Syriac.

(6) τοῦ Θεοῦ πατρὸς καὶ τοῦ Χριστοῦ, 47 73, Syr-Pesh. (ed. princeps and Schaaf).

(7) τοῦ Θεοῦ καὶ πατρὸς καὶ τοῦ Χριστοῦ (Rec. Text), D³ K L most cursives, Syr-Harcl. (text), Theodoret, etc.

Isolated readings are—

(8) τοῦ Θεοῦ καὶ Χριστοῦ, Cyril. *Thes.* p. 287.

(9) τοῦ Θεοῦ ἐν Χριστῷ, Clem. Alex. v. 10. 12, and with τοῦ before ἐν, 17. So Ambrosiaster, "Dei in Christo." τοῦ Χριστοῦ is given by Tisch. from his MS. of Euthalius, but with the remark, "sed non satis apparet."

As far as documentary evidence goes (4) seems the best attested, and is probably the source of (5) (6) (7). But it is most probably an attempt to remove the difficulty of the simpler reading (1) or (2). Of these (2) is preferred by the critics above named, as accounting for all the rest, (1) the witnesses for which are later, being supposed to have originated from an attempt to remove the difficulty of the former reading. Meyer thinks that the original reading must have involved some dogmatic difficulty, which (4) does not.

The short reading, τοῦ Θεοῦ (1), would account for the others, but the attestation of it is not sufficiently early. Wescott and Hort suspect some corruption.

3. ἐν ᾧ. The antecedent is probably μυστηρίου, not Χριστοῦ. What the apostle is dwelling on is the greatness of the "mystery" (i. 27), and the importance of the knowledge of it, in opposition to the supposed wisdom of the false teachers; hence the statement that "all the treasures," etc., are contained in it. This is confirmed by the use of ἀπόκρυφοι, which corresponds to μυστήριον. So Alford, Eadie, Meyer, Soden, De Wette, etc.; but Ellicott, Lightfoot, and many comm. refer the ᾧ to Christ. With this latter reference, the wisdom and knowledge are those possessed by Christ as a treasure which He communicates. With the reference to μυστ. the terms have an objective sense, these being characteristics of the Divine plan. These treasures St. Paul calls ἀπόκρυφοι, probably in allusion to the pretended hidden wisdom of the false teachers, which nevertheless was merely superficial and concerned external observances, whereas the true Christian wisdom was inward and profound. These treasures of wisdom are not "kept concealed," ἀποκεκρυμμένοι, they are "hidden, laid up," ἀπόκρυφοι; but capable of being discovered. For this reason, as well as on account of the position of the word, ἀπόκρυφοι is not to be construed with εἰσίν as the direct predicate,—a construction which would require it to come next to εἰσίν. Meyer and Alford take the word as attributive, "all the secret treasures." The absence of the article is against this, although not perhaps fatal; since, as Alford observes, οἱ ἀπόκρυφοι would imply that there were other treasures, only those that are secret being contained, etc. The position of the word, however, suggests that it is a secondary predicate (Ellicott, Lightfoot, v. Soden, *al.*), "all the treasures, etc., as hidden treasures," *i.e.* "hiddenly," ὥστε παρ' αὐτοῦ δεῖ πάντα αἰτεῖν. Chrys. "quo verbo innuitur quod pretiosum et magnificum est in Christo non prominere, aut protinus in oculos incurrere hominum carnalium, sed ita latere ut conspiciatur tantummodo ab illis quibus Deus oculos dedit aquilinos, id est, spirituales ad videndum," Davenant, quoted by Ellicott. The word occurs in connexion with θησαυροί in Isa. xlv. 3, δώσω σοι θησαυροὺς σκοτεινοὺς ἀποκρύφους: also 1 Macc. i. 23, ἔλαβε τοὺς θησαυροὺς τοὺς ἀποκρύφους. On the Gnostic use of the word to designate their esoteric writings, see Lightfoot's note.[1]

---

[1] Mr. Charles compares Book of Enoch, 46. 3, "the Son of Man who reveals all the treasures of that which is hidden."

The expression θησαυρὸς σοφίας is used by Plato, *Phileb.* 15 E, ὥς τινα σοφίας εἰρηκὼς θησαυρόν, and by Xen. *Mem.* iv. 2. 9, ἄγαμαί σου διότι οὐκ ἀργυρίου καὶ χρυσίου προείλου θησαυροὺς κεκτῆσθαι μᾶλλον ἢ σοφίας.

σοφίας καὶ γνώσεως. These terms occur together, Rom. xi. 33, and several times in Eccles. Sept. "While γνῶσις is simply *intuitive*, σοφία is *ratiocinative* also. While γνῶσις applies chiefly to the apprehension of truths, σοφία superadds the power of reasoning about them and tracing their relations," Lightfoot. Augustine's distinction is that σοφία is "intellectualis cognitio aeternarum rerum"; γνῶσις, "rationalis temporalium," so that the former pertains to contemplation, the latter to action (*De Trin.* xii. 20, 25). This, however, is quite opposed to usage. Aristotle, *Eth. Nic.* i. 1, opposed γνῶσις to πρᾶξις. And in 1 Cor. xiii. 2, St. Paul connects γνῶσις with the apprehension of eternal μυστήρια.

4. τοῦτο λέγω. In this expression τοῦτο often refers to what follows, but with ἵνα it refers to what precedes; cf. John v. 34. τοῦτο is not to be limited to ver. 3. Ver. 5 shows that 1–3 are included, if, indeed, the reference does not extend further back.

δέ is omitted in ℵ* Λ* (apparently) B, but added in ℵᶜ Aᶜᵒʳʳ· CDKLP, and apparently all other authorities. Weiss considers it certainly genuine.

ἵνα μηδείς. So ℵ* ABCD P *al.* ἵνα μή τις, ℵᶜ KL, most MSS.

παραλογίζηται. In N.T. only here and Jas. i. 22; frequent in Sept. and later Greek writers. It applies primarily to false reckoning, and thence to fallacious reasoning; hence, παραλογισμός, a fallacy or paralogism; cf. ἀπάτῃ τινὶ παραλογισάμενος ὑμᾶς, Aeschines, p. 16, 33.

ἐν πιθανολογίᾳ. "By persuasive speech," "a persuasive style," Moule. The word occurs in Plato, *Theaet.* p. 162 E (πιθανολογίᾳ τε καὶ εἰκόσι); the verb πιθανολογεῖν in Arist. *Eth. Nic.* i. 1; also Diog. Laert. x. 87, *al.* In classical writers the sense is only that of probable reasoning as opposed to demonstration; but see Demosth. 928, 14, λόγους θαυμασίως πιθανούς, and ἡ πιθανολογική = "the art of persuasion," Arrian, *Epict.* i. 8. 7.

Compare St. Paul, 1 Cor. ii. 4, οὐκ ἐν πειθοῖς σοφίας λόγοις, ἀλλ᾽ ἐν ἀποδείξει πνεύματος. πιθανολογία expresses the subjective means of persuasion, the personal influence; παραλογ. the objective, the appearance of logic.

5. εἰ γὰρ καί. The καί after εἰ does not belong to the whole clause introduced by εἰ, but emphasises the word immediately following; cf. 2 Cor. iv. 16, xi. 6.

τῇ σαρκὶ ἄπειμι. It has been inferred from this that St. Paul had been at Colossae; but with ut reason. The same expression, indeed, occurs 1 Cor. v. 3; but this proves nothing, γάρ.

ἀλλά introduces the apodosis, when it is contrasted with a hypothetical protasis; cf. Rom. vi. 5; 1 Cor. viii. 6; 2 Cor. v. 16, *al*. τῷ πνεύματι, "in spirit," not "by the spirit," as Ambrosiaster and Grotius, "Deus Paulo revelat quae Colossis fierent." The antithesis is the common one of body and spirit; cf. 1 Cor. v. 3, ἀπὼν τῷ σώματι, παρὼν δὲ τῷ πνεύματι.

σὺν ὑμῖν. Stronger than ἐν ὑμῖν, expressing union in a common interest.

χαίρων καὶ βλέπων. There is no need to suppose a logical transposition, or to separate the participles as if χαίρων meant "rejoicing at being with you in the spirit" (Meyer, Alford). The apostle's joy may have been due to many circumstances, and this joy led him to contemplate further their orderly array.

ὑμῶν τὴν τάξιν. The pronoun is placed emphatically first, not so much to accentuate this τάξις as an advantage which they possessed over others, as because the apostle's interest was in them personally and in the τάξις only as belonging to them.

τὴν τάξιν καὶ τὸ στερέωμα. Both terms are supposed by Hofmann, Lightfoot, Soden, *al*., to contain a military metaphor, perhaps suggested by St. Paul's enforced companionship with the praetorian guard, στερέωμα being rendered by Lightfoot "solid front, close phalanx"; by Soden, "bulwark," "Bollwerk." τάξις is frequently used of military array, *e.g.* Xen. *Anab*. i. 2. 18, ἰδοῦσα τὴν λαμπρότητα καὶ τὴν τάξιν τοῦ στρατεύματος ἐθαύμασεν: Plut. *Vit. Pyrrh*. 16, κατιδὼν τάξιν τε καὶ φυλακὰς καὶ κόσμον αὐτῶν καὶ τὸ σχῆμα τῆς στρατοπεδείας ἐθαύμασε. στερέωμα is found in the Sept. Ps. xviii. 2; Gen. i. 6, *al*. 1 Macc. ix. 14 is quoted in support of the military sense, εἶδεν ὁ Ἰούδας ὅτι Βακχίδης καὶ τὸ στερέωμα τῆς παρεμβολῆς ἐν τοῖς δεξίοις.

But neither word has this military sense of itself, but from the context, and here the context suggests nothing of the kind. τάξις is used equally of the organisation of a state or a household, *e.g.* Demosth. p. 200, 4, ταύτην τὴν τάξιν αἱρεῖσθαι τῆς πολιτείας. Compare also Plato, *Gorgias*, p. 504 A, τάξεως ... καὶ κόσμου τυχοῦσα οἰκία. St. Paul has it again, 1 Cor. xiv. 40, πάντα ... κατὰ τάξιν γινέσθω. Here the idea of a well-ordered state lies much nearer than that of an army. The apostle rejoices in the orderly arrangement of the Colossian Church. The opposite state would be ἀταξία, and of this he finds some instances in Thessalonica, where some walked ἀτάκτως, and he reminds them ὅτι οὐκ ἠτακτήσαμεν ἐν ὑμῖν (2 Thess. iii. 6, 8, 11).

With στερέωμα τῆς πίστεως compare Acts xvi. 5, ἐστερεοῦντο τῇ πίστει, and 1 Pet. v. 9, ᾧ ἀντίστητε στερεοὶ τῇ πίστει. It is most natural to take the word here as = the firm structure of your faith, *i.e.* the solidity of your faith. ὅτε πολλὰ συναγαγὼν συγκολλήσεις πυκνῶς καὶ ἀδιασπάστως, τότε στερέωμα γίνεται, Chrys.

We gather from this that the Church at Colossae was still substantially sound in the faith, and it is instructive to observe how here as in other Epistles St. Paul is careful to commend what he finds deserving of commendation.

It is worthy of notice that d e translate as if they read ὑστέρημα for στερέωμα "quod deest necessitatibus fidei vestrae." Augustine agrees, quoting, "id quod deest fidei vestrae" (*Ep.* 149, *Joh.* 98). So also Ambrosiaster.

6. ὡς οὖν παρελάβετε. "As, then, ye received, *i.e.* from your teachers" = καθὼς ἐμάθετε ἀπὸ Ἐπαφρᾶ, i. 7 ; καθὼς ἐδιδάχθητε, ver. 7. Compare 1 Thess. iv. 1, καθὼς παρελάβετε παρ' ἡμῶν τὸ πῶς δεῖ, κ.τ.λ.; 1 Cor. xv. 1, 2, xi. 23; Gal. i. 9, 12; Phil. iv. 9 (ἐμάθετε καὶ παρελάβετε).

Ellicott, however, and Moule understand it as meaning that they received "Christ *Himself*, the sum and substance of all teaching." The sense is good, but does not agree so well with the usage of παραλαμβάνειν or with the context, in which we have the contrast between true and false teaching in relation to the Christian walk (καθὼς ἐδιδάχθητε, κατὰ τὴν παράδοσιν τῶν ἀνθρ.).

τὸν Χριστὸν Ἰησοῦν τὸν Κύριον. As St. Paul does not use the phrase ὁ Χριστὸς Ἰησοῦς, this is naturally divided into τὸν Χριστόν and Ἰησοῦν τὸν Κύριον, so that τὸν Χρ. is the immediate object of παραλ. This is confirmed by the frequency of ὁ Χριστός in this Epistle, and by the designation of the object of the Christian preaching as ὁ Χριστός in Phil. i. 15, 17. Further, it will be observed that in what follows up to iii. 4 it is not the notion of Ἰησοῦς or of Κύριος that is prominent, but that of Χριστός. The Christ, rather than the gospel, is specified as the object of the instruction, because "the central point of the Colossian heresy was the subversion of the true idea of the Christ," Lightfoot. Ἰησοῦν τὸν Κύριον adds to the official designation the name of Him to whom it belongs, "even Jesus the Lord." Compare Eph. iv. 20, 21. The position of τὸν Κύριον after Ἰησοῦν (instead of the usual τὸν Κύριον Ἰησοῦν) points to the two elements of which the true doctrine of the Christ consists, viz. first, the recognition of the historical person, Jesus; and, secondly, the acceptance of Him as the Lord.

ἐν αὐτῷ περιπατεῖτε. This phrase does not occur elsewhere, but it corresponds to the idea of τὰς ὁδούς μου ἐν Χριστῷ, 1 Cor. iv. 17; ζῶντας ἐν Χριστῷ, Rom. vi. 11, etc.

7. ἐρριζωμένοι καὶ ἐποικοδομούμενοι. The propriety of the tenses is to be observed; the settled state, which is the antecedent condition of περιπατεῖν ἐν αὐτῷ, is expressed by the perfect; the continual development which is always advancing, by the present. The three figures are disparate, the apostle's thoughts being occupied with the lesson to be enforced, without regard to the consistency of his

metaphor; see Eph. iii. 18. Some commentators put a stop at περιπατεῖτε, connecting the participles with the following ver. 8 a construction which leaves ἐν αὐτῷ π. very isolated.

The ἐπι- in ἐποικοδ. probably does not convey "the accessory idea of the foundation," which would not agree well with ἐν; besides, it is clear from περιπατεῖτε and ἐρριζ. that the apostle has not before him the distinct figure of a building, but is using the word as St. Jude does, ver. 20, ἐποικοδομοῦντες ἑαυτοὺς τῇ ἁγιωτάτῃ ὑμῶν πίστει, in the derived ethical sense "being built up." Lightfoot remarks that in this Epistle and that to the Ephesians, Christ is represented rather as the binding element than as the foundation of the building; see Eph. ii. 20.

βεβαιούμενοι qualifies the idea of both the preceding participles. The present gives the idea "being more and more stablished."

τῇ πίστει is taken by Meyer and Lightfoot as an instrumental dative, "by your faith." "Faith," says the latter, "is, as it were, the cement of the building." But this is to press unduly the metaphor in ἐποικοδ., which, as we have seen, is not intended any more than the other two verbs to convey a definite picture. There is no question here of the instrument, and τῇ πίστει is better taken as a dative of reference, as in Jude 20. There πίστις was that which needed βεβαίωσις. καθὼς ἐδιδάχθητε, "even as ye were taught," *i.e.* so that ye continue firm and true to the lessons which ye were taught by Epaphras; cf. i. 7, not "taught to be established by or in your faith."

περισσεύοντες ἐν εὐχαριστίᾳ. "Abounding in thanksgiving." If ἐν αὐτῇ is read after περισσ., then ἐν εὐχ. is "with thanksgiving," although even with this reading some expositors interpret "in your faith abounding in thanksgiving."

<small>τῇ πίστει without ἐν, B D* 17 *al.*, Vulg., Ambrosiaster, Theoph. ἐν τῇ πίστει, ℵ D^c K L P, most mss., Chrys. *al.* ἐν πίστει, A C 67². ἐν would readily come in from the impression made by the repeated ἐν in the context.

ἐν αὐτῇ is added after περισσεύοντες in B D^c K L most mss., Syr-Pesh. Arm., Chrys. Also ℵ^c D* 1 d e f, Vulg. Syr. mg. have ἐν αὐτῷ. The words are absent from ℵ* A C 17 and some other mss., Amiat. Fuld. Eth. The words are omitted in the text of RV. but retained in the marginal reading. They may have been added originally from a recollection of iv. 2, where we have ἐν αὐτῇ ἐν εὐχαριστίᾳ. This is rather more probable than that they were omitted because περισσεύοντες was thought to be sufficiently defined by ἐν εὐχαριστίᾳ. So Weiss.</small>

8-15. *The apostle has reason to know (having, no doubt, been so informed by Epaphras) that there are amongst the Colossians teachers who are propagating mischievous heresies, dangerous to the faith, and inculcating precepts not consistent with their position as members of Christ's kingdom. These teachers make a professsion of philosophy, but it is a mere system of deceit and of human origin, and so far is it from being an advance on what they have been* taught that it really belongs to a more elementary stage of progress. Ye, he tells them, have been already made full in Christ, in whom dwells the whole fulness of the Godhead, and who is therefore far above all these angelic beings of whom they speak. Ye need no circumcision of the flesh, for ye have received in Christ the true circumcision of the spirit. By Him ye have been raised from death to life, and His work is complete; He has wholly done away with the bond that was against you.*

8. βλέπετε μή τις ὑμᾶς ἔσται. "Beware lest there be anyone," etc. For τις with the participle and article, cf. Gal. i. 7, εἰ μή τινές εἰσιν οἱ ταράσσοντες ὑμᾶς. As it gives prominence to the person and his action, it appears to point to some particular person whom the apostle has in view but does not wish to name. Compare Ignat. *Smyrn.* 5, ὅν τινες ἀγνοοῦντες ἀρνοῦνται ... τὰ δὲ ὀνόματα αὐτῶν ... οὐκ ἔδοξέ μοι ἐγγράψαι. The future indic. ἔσται indicates the reality of the danger, cf. Mark xiv. 2, μήποτε ἔσται θόρυβος, and Heb. iii. 12, βλέπετε μήποτε ἔσται ἔν τινι ὑμῶν, κ.τ.λ. ὑμᾶς before ἔσται is somewhat emphatic: "you who are such persons as I have thus commended."

This order, ὑμᾶς ἔσται, is that of B C K L P; but ℵ A D have ἔσται ὑμᾶς, which, as the more obvious order, was more likely to be written in error.

ὁ συλαγωγῶν. A later Greek word (not indeed found till after St. Paul) used by Aristaenetus (ii. 22) with οἶκον in the sense "plunder," in which sense it is understood here by Chrys. Theodoret, and some moderns. Theodoret supplies τὴν πίστιν, Theophyl. τὸν νοῦν. If this were the sense here, the object could hardly be omitted. But the proper meaning of the word seems to be "to carry off as spoil." So Heliodorus, *Aeth.* x. 35, ὁ τὴν ἐμὴν θυγατέρα συλαγωγήσας. And this meaning corresponds with that of the analogous compounds, δουλαγωγεῖν, σκευαγωγεῖν, λαφυραγωγεῖν. Von Soden remarks that it also corresponds better with the idea of a destroyed bond in ver. 14 to suggest that they might again be brought into bondage; cf. Gal. v. 1. The Vulgate "decipiat" is very inadequate.

διὰ τῆς φιλοσοφίας. A term not occurring elsewhere in the N.T., and no doubt adopted here because it was used by the false teachers themselves. The combination of it here with κενὴ ἀπάτη indicates that the sense is nearly "his philosophy, so called, which is a vain deceit." Compare ψευδώνυμος γνῶσις, 1 Tim. vi. 20. Chrysostom remarks: ἐπειδὴ δοκεῖ σεμνὸν εἶναι τὸ "τῆς φιλοσοφίας" προσέθηκε καὶ κενῆς ἀπάτης. That the word φιλοσοφία was in use in Jewish circles appears from Philo and Josephus. The former applies the word to the religion of the Jews and the law of Moses, perhaps for the purpose of giving dignity to them in the eyes of Gentile readers. He speaks of ἡ κατὰ Μωϋσῆν φιλοσοφία (*De Mut.*

Nom. 39), ἡ πάτριος φιλοσοφία (*Leg. ad Cai.* 23), ἡ Ἰουδαϊκὴ φιλοσοφία (*ib.* 33). Josephus calls the three Jewish sects τρεῖς φιλοσοφίαι (*Ant.* xviii. 1. 2). It is clear from the connexion with κενῆς ἀπάτης that St. Paul is not condemning philosophy in general, which, indeed, would be quite beside his purpose.

καὶ κενῆς ἀπάτης. The absence of the article shows that this is not a different thing from ἡ φιλοσοφία, but is a characteristic of it. ἀπάτη is opposed to λόγος τῆς ἀληθείας, i. 5, and to σοφία καὶ γνῶσις, ii. 3.

κατὰ τὴν παράδοσιν τῶν ἀνθρώπων. Probably to be connected with the immediately preceding words rather than with συλαγωγῶν. The teaching of the Colossian false teachers was essentially traditional and esoteric. The Essenes, their spiritual predecessors, as well as the Gnostics, subsequently claimed to possess such a source of knowledge. The oath taken by the full members of the former sect bound them not to communicate any of their doctrines to anyone otherwise than as he himself had received them, and, further, to guard carefully the books of their sect and the names of the angels (Josephus, *Bell. Jud.* ii. 8. 7; Lightfoot, pp. 89, 90). Compare the designation Kabbala, "tradition," applied by the Jews to their later mystic theology.

κατὰ τὰ στοιχεῖα τοῦ κόσμου. "According to the rudiments of the world" (?). This κατά with the following κατὰ Χριστόν may perhaps be best connected with συλαγωγῶν, as the ideas they introduce have a different logical relation to the main idea, and οὐ κατὰ Χριστόν is too brief to form the antithesis to the other two κατά clauses.

τὰ στοιχεῖα (= Gal. iv. 3) (originally = "letters of the alphabet") is generally understood by modern commentators as meaning "elementary teaching," "the A B C of religious instruction"; compare παιδαγωγός in Gal. Then τοῦ κόσμου would mean having reference to mundane, or material, not spiritual things (Alford, Lightfoot, *al.*). But De Wette takes κόσμος as = "humanity," as the subject of this instruction (John iii. 16; 2 Cor. v. 19). So Oltramare. Meyer, on the other hand, understands by it "the non-Christian world," "rudiments with which the world concerns itself" (= Bleek, Weiss, *al.*).

Neander judges that a comparison of all the Pauline passages and the Pauline association of ideas favour our understanding the phrase as denoting the earthly, elsewhere termed τὰ σαρκικά. Hence, ii. 20, στοιχεῖα τοῦ κόσμου and κόσμος may, he thinks, be considered as synonymous.

> An entirely different interpretation has been adopted by several recent commentators. According to this, τὰ στοιχεῖα τοῦ κόσμου are the personal elemental spirits. According to Jewish ideas, not only were the stars

conceived as animated by spiritual beings,[1] but all things had their special angels. In the Book of Enoch, 82. 10 ff., it is said with reference to the angels of the stars that they keep watch, that they may appear at their appointed times, in their proper orders, etc. There are, first, the four leaders who divide the seasons, then the twelve leaders of the orders (taxiarchs), who divide the months; and for the 360 days there are heads over thousands (chiliarchs), who divide the days. Anyone who is curious about the matter may learn the principal names in the book itself. In 18. 15 we read of stars which suffer punishment because they have transgressed the commandment of God as to their appearing. In the Book of Jubilees, cap. 2, amongst the creations of the first day are the Angels of the Presence, but also the angels of the winds, of clouds, of cold and heat, of hail, hoarfrost, thunder, etc. Perhaps Ps. civ. 4 may have some relation to this conception; certainly it seems to be illustrated by the Apocalypse, vii. 1, 2, xiv. 18, xvi. 5 (τοῦ ἀγγέλου τῶν ὑδάτων), xix. 17; and by the interpolation in John v. 4. It is obvious that the term properly used of the elements ruled by these spirits might readily be applied to the spirits themselves, especially as there was no other convenient term. It agrees with this that in Gal. iv. 1 ff. those who were δεδουλωμένοι ὑπὸ τὰ στοιχεῖα τοῦ κόσμου are compared to those who are under ἐπίτροποι καὶ οἰκονόμοι,—a comparison which suggests personality in the former. And again, ib. 8, 9, δουλεύειν τοῖς φύσει μὴ οὖσιν θεοῖς appears to be equivalent to δουλεύειν τοῖς στοιχείοις, κ.τ.λ.

In the present passage the observance of times and seasons, etc., is κατὰ τὰ στ. τ. κ., not κατὰ Χρ., a contrast which does not agree well with the conception of στ. as elements of instruction. This view of τὰ στοιχεῖα gives special pertinence to the proposition which follows, ὅτι ἐν αὐτῷ, κ.τ.λ., and ver. 10, ὅς ἐστιν ἡ κεφαλὴ πάσης ἀρχῆς καὶ ἐξουσίας. Ritschl defends this personal interpretation of στοιχεῖα at length (*Rechtfertigung u. Versöhnung*, 3rd ed. ii. p. 252), but needlessly limits the meaning to the angels of the lawgiving. Spitta adopts the more general reference (*Der Zweite Brief des Petrus u. der Brief des Judas*, 1885, 263 ff.). He quotes from the *Test. Levi*, c. 4, a passage which speaks of the burning up of τὰ ἀόρατα πνεύματα, just as 2 Pet. iii. 10 speaks of the burning up of στοιχεῖα. This view is unreservedly adopted by Kühl, the recent editor of the Epistles of Peter and Jude in Meyer's *Kommentar*, and by v. Soden in his comment on the present passage.[2]

9. ὅτι ἐν αὐτῷ κατοικεῖ πᾶν τὸ πλήρωμα. See i. 19; and on πλήρωμα, Lightfoot's dissertation, *Colossians*, p. 323 ff.

τῆς θεότητος, "of the Godhead," *i.e.* of the Divine nature. θεότης, the abstract of θεός, must not be confounded with θειότης, which is used with propriety in Rom. i. 20, and which means, not the essence, but the quality of divinity. θεότης is found in Lucian, *Icarom.* ix., τὸν μέν τινα πρῶτον Θεὸν ἐπεκάλουν, τοῖς δὲ τὰ δεύτερα καὶ τὰ τρίτα ἔνεμον τῆς θεότητος; and in Plutarch, *Mor.* p. 415 C, ἐκ δὲ δαιμόνων ὀλίγαι μὲν ἔτι χρόνῳ πολλῷ δι' ἀρετῆς καθαρθεῖσαι παντάπασι θεότητος μετέσχον. The δαίμονες were always θεῖοι, but a few became in course of time θεοί. The same author, *Mor.* p. 857 A, says, πᾶσιν Αἰγυπτίοις θειότητα πολλὴν καὶ δικαιοσύνην μαρτυρήσας,

---

[1] A notion which, it may be remembered, was shared by the great astronomer Kepler.

[2] In *Test. Solomonis* (Fabricius, *Cod. Pseudep. Vet. Test.* i. 1047) we read: ἡμεῖς ἐσμὲν τὰ λεγόμενα στοιχεῖα, οἱ κοσμοκράτορες τοῦ κόσμου τούτου, ἀπάτη, ἔρις, κλώθων, ζάλη, πλάνη, δύναμις, κ.τ.λ. This, however, is a very late document.

II. 10] THEIR COMPLETENESS IN CHRIST 249

i.e. a Divine faculty. The Versions generally, including the Vulgate, fail to mark the distinction, doubtless for want of a word to express θεότης. The word *deitas* was a later coinage (not quite according to Latin analogy). Trench quotes from Augustine, *De Civ. Dei*, vii. § 1, "Hanc divinitatem, vel, ut sic dixerim *deitatem*: nam et hoc verbo uti jam nostros non piget, ut de Graeco expressius transferant id quod illi θεότητα appellant."

σωματικῶς, "bodilywise, corporeally." Not ἀσωμάτως as in the λόγος before the Incarnation, but in His glorified body σῶμα τῆς δόξης αὐτοῦ, Phil. iii. 21. Chrysostom draws attention to the accuracy of the expression, μὴ νομίσῃς Θεὸν συγκεκλεῖσθαι, ὡς ἐν σώματι.

This interpretation, which is that adopted by most modern commentators, is the only one tenable, but many others have been suggested. Theophylact and Oecumenius took the word to mean "essentially," οὐσιωδῶς, *i.e.* not merely as an influence, as in the saints or as in the prophets. So Calvin, Beza, and, more recently, Olshausen and Usteri. But the word cannot have this meaning.

Augustine (*Epist.* 149) understands it to mean "really" not "typically," "vere non umbratice," not "umbratiliter," as in the temple made with hands; and so many moderns (including Bengel and Bleek), comparing ver. 17, where σῶμα is contrasted with σκιά. But there the idea is that of a body which cast a shadow, and the passage does not justify our rendering the adverb "really."

Others, again, understanding πλήρωμα of the Church, take σωματικῶς to mean, "so that the Church is related to Him as His body" (Baumgarten-Crusius, *al.*), thus making the body of Christ dwell in Christ, instead of Christ in the body.

10. καὶ ἐστὲ ἐν αὐτῷ πεπληρωμένοι. "And ye are in Him made full." Alford, Ellicott, and Lightfoot render, "ye are in Him, made full," regarding the clause as containing two predications. But the connexion seems to require the fact to be emphasised, that it is "in Him" that the πεπληρωμένον εἶναι rests; for on this depends the inference that nothing more is lacking in our relation to God. The πεπληρωμένοι obviously corresponds with the πλήρωμα. Christ is πεπληρωμένος: ye being in Him share in His πλήρωμα, and are therefore yourselves πεπληρωμένοι. Compare John i. 16, ἐκ τοῦ πληρώματος αὐτοῦ ἡμεῖς πάντες ἐλάβομεν : Eph. iii. 9, ἵνα πληρωθῆτε εἰς πᾶν τὸ πλήρωμα τοῦ Θεοῦ, also *ibid.* iv. 13 and i. 23.

ὅς ἐστιν. So ℵ A C K L P and nearly all mss. with the Latin e f g Vulg. and Chrys. Theodoret, *al.* But B D G 47* with d have ὅ ἐστιν, perhaps a correction made on the supposition that αὐτῷ referred to πλήρωμα, or by oversight c was lost before e c. Lachmann adopts it, placing καὶ to ἐν αὐτῷ in a parenthesis. The image, however, would be quite confused if the πλήρωμα were represented as the head; ἡ κεφαλή is always Christ. Besides, we should be obliged to refer ἐν ᾧ also to πλήρωμα, and this would not yield any tolerable sense. Ewald, adopting ὅ ἐστιν, takes it as = "scilicet," comparing i. 24, 27 and iii. 17; but this would require τῇ κεφαλῇ.

ἡ κεφαλὴ πάσης ἀρχῆς καὶ ἐξουσίας. He is the head of all those angelic powers to whose mediation the false teachers would teach you to seek. As they are subordinate to Christ, ye have nothing to expect from them which is not given you in full completeness in Christ.

11. ἐν ᾧ καὶ περιετμήθητε. "In whom also ye were (not 'are,' as A.V.) circumcised." "Ye have received the circumcision of the heart, by which ye have put off the whole body of the flesh, and therefore ye have no need of the symbolical circumcision of the flesh."

The aorists point to the time of their reception into the Christian Church by baptism.

περιτομῇ, "with a circumcision," not "the circumcision."

ἀχειροποιήτῳ, "not wrought by hands," not physical: cf. Mark xiv. 58; 2 Cor. v. 1; and Eph. ii. 11, where we have the other side of the contrast, οἱ λεγόμενοι ἀκροβυστία ὑπὸ τῆς λεγομένης περιτομὴ ἐν σαρκὶ χειροποιήτου. The idea of spiritual circumcision is frequent in the O.T.; see note on the passage in Eph. In St. Paul, compare Rom. ii. 28; Phil. iii. 3. At first sight it might appear from this clause that the Colossians had been tempted like the Galatians to submit to circumcision. But in that case we should find, as in the Epistle to the Galatians, some direct condemnation of the practice; whereas in 16-23 there is no reference to it. Possibly the allusion here is to some claim to superiority on the part of the false teachers.

ἐν τῇ ἀπεκδύσει. ἐν specifies that in which the περιτομή consisted. The substantive ἀπέκδυσις has not been found in any earlier writer (for the verb, see ver. 15). It expresses a complete putting off and laying aside, and was probably chosen with reference to the figure of circumcision. The connexion requires it to be understood passively, not "ye have put off," but "was put off from you."

τοῦ σώματος τῆς σαρκός, *i.e.* "the body which consists in the flesh," "the fleshly body," so that we are no more ἐν τῇ σαρκί (Rom. vii. 5, viii. 8, 9). The change is ideally represented as complete, which it is in principle.

Some expositors take σῶμα in the sense of "mass, totality" (Calvin, Grotius, *al.*); but this is against N.T. usage, and does not agree so well with the context, the images in which are connected with the body, "buried, raised." The expression σῶμα τῆς σαρκός, i. 22, has a different meaning.

<small>The Rec. Text after σώματος adds τῶν ἁμαρτιῶν, with ℵ^c D^{bc} K L and most mss., Syr., Chrys. etc.

The words are absent from ℵ* A B C D* G P some good cursives, Old Lat. Vulg. Boh. etc. They are clearly a gloss.</small>

ἐν τῇ περιτομῇ τοῦ Χριστοῦ. The simplest and most natural

interpretation is: "the circumcision which belongs to Christ, and is brought about by union with Him," in contrast to the circumcision of Moses and of the patriarchs. Thus it is nearly equivalent to "Christian circumcision," but expresses the idea that the source of this circumcision is in Christ.

Some commentators have taken Χριστοῦ as the genitive of the object, the thought being supposed to be that in the circumcision of Christ we are circumcised. So Schöttgen: "Circumcisio Christi qui se nostri causa sponte legi subjecit, tam efficax fuit in omnes homines, ut nulla amplius circumcisione carnis opus sit, praecipue quum in locum illius baptismus a Christo surrogatus sit." This is not only without support from Scripture analogy, but is foreign to the context, in which the circumcision spoken of is ἀχειροποίητος. The baptism mentioned in ver. 12, in which we are buried with Him, is our baptism. Soden also takes Χριστοῦ as an objective genitive, understanding, however, περιτομή in the sense of ἀπέκδυσις τοῦ σώματος τῆς σαρκός just specified, which echoes i. 22.

Chrysostom and Theophylact understand the genitive as subjective, ὁ Χριστὸς περιτέμνει ἐν τῷ βαπτίσματι ἀπεκδύων ἡμᾶς τοῦ παλαιοῦ βίου, Theoph. This does not harmonise with the following συνταφέντες αὐτῷ.

12. συνταφέντες αὐτῷ, κ.τ.λ. We have the same figure in Rom. vi. 3, 4, which may almost be regarded as a commentary on this passage. The figure was naturally suggested by the immersion in baptism, which St. Paul interprets as symbolical of burial, the emersion similarly symbolising the rising again to newness of life.

συνταφέντες is to be connected with περιετμήθητε, and specifies when and how this was brought about.

ἐν τῷ βαπτίσματι. So most authorities, ℵ* A C Dᵉ K L P, etc. But ℵᶜ B D* F G 47 67² 71 have βαπτισμῷ, which Lightfoot prefers on the ground that it is the less usual word in this sense. That it might be so used is shown by its occurrence in Josephus, *Ant.* xviii. 5. 2, of the baptism of John. But in two of the other three passages in which it occurs in the N.T., it means lustration or washing, *e.g.* of vessels: Mark vii. 4 (in Rec. also 8); Heb. ix. 10. The third passage, Heb. vi. 2, is doubtful. In the Latin version as well as in the Latin Fathers, "baptisma" and "baptismus" are used indifferently. St. Paul uses the substantive "baptism" in only two other places (Rom. vi. 4; Eph. iv. 5), and this is not sufficient to supply any basis for inference as to his usage. Etymologically βαπτισμός would signify rather the act of dipping, βάπτισμα the act as complete. Weiss thinks the former more suitable here.

ἐν ᾧ, viz. βαπτίσματι. This seems clearly required by the analogy between συνταφέντες ἐν and συνηγέρθητε. Chrysostom, however, and most comm. understand ἐν Χριστῷ. Meyer defends this on the ground, first, of the parallelism of ἐν ᾧ καί—ἐν ᾧ καί; secondly, because, if baptism were intended, ἐν would not be suitable to the rising again, and we should expect ἐξ, or at least the non-local διά; and, lastly, because as συνταφέντες is defined by ἐν τῷ βαπτ., so is συνηγέρθητε by διὰ τῆς πίστεως; and, therefore, the text suggests no reason for continuing to it the former definition also. To the second objection (adopted also by Eadie), it may be replied that βάπτισμα (βαπτισμός) includes the whole act. It is only when we take in the two things signified, the "death unto sin" and the "new birth unto righteousness," or the putting off of the old man and the putting on of the new, that βάπτισμα can be identified with περιτομὴ ἀχειροποίητος; for περιτομή also signified the entrance into a holy state as well as the separation from the state of nature. The first objection has really no weight, for it is much more natural to connect συνηγέρθητε with συνταφέντες than with περιετμήθητε; and this is strongly confirmed by the passage in Rom. just referred to: συνετάφημεν αὐτῷ διὰ τοῦ βαπτίσματος ... ἵνα ὥσπερ ἠγέρθη Χριστός ... οὕτως καὶ ἡμεῖς ἐν καινότητι ζωῆς περιπατήσωμεν, κ.τ.λ. Further, as Lightfoot observes, the idea of Χριστῷ must be reserved for συνηγέρθητε, where it is wanted: "ye were raised together with Him." (So Alford, Beza, De Wette, Ellicott, Lightfoot, Soden, al.)

συνηγέρθητε. Compare Gal. iii. 27, ὅσοι εἰς Χριστὸν ἐβαπτίσθητε Χριστὸν ἐνεδύσασθε. The Χριστὸν ἐνδύσασθαι presupposes the ἀπέκδυσις τοῦ σώματος τῆς σαρκός.

διὰ τῆς πίστεως τῆς ἐνεργείας τοῦ Θεοῦ. "Through your faith in the working of God." Bengel, De Wette, al., understand ἐνεργείας as a genitive of cause, "faith produced by the operation of God." But the genitive after πίστις, when not that of the person, is always that of the object. Cf. Mark xi. 22; Acts iii. 16; Rom. iii. 22; Gal. ii. 16, 20; Eph. iii. 12; Phil. i. 27, etc. Eph. i. 19 is cited in favour of this interpretation, but κατὰ τὴν ἐνεργείαν there is not to be joined to τοὺς πιστεύοντας; see note on the passage. The former interpretation is also more suitable to the context. The πίστις here is specified as faith in the resurrection, πιστεύοντες γὰρ τῇ τοῦ Θεοῦ δυνάμει προσμένομεν τὴν ἀνάστασιν, ἐνέχυρον ἔχοντες τοῦ δεσπότου Χριστοῦ τὴν ἀνάστασιν, Theodoret. πίστεως ὅλον ἐστίν· ἐπιστεύσατε ὅτι δύναται ὁ Θεὸς ἐγεῖραι, καὶ οὕτως ἠγέρθητε, Chrys. Faith is the subjective means by which the grace is received; only by a belief in the resurrection can the rising again with Christ be appropriated by the individual. By belief in the resurrection of Christ we believe in the power of God, of which it is an evidence; and this belief, again, is the means by which that power works in the life and produces an effect analogous to that resurrection. Compare Rom. iv. 24, vi. 8, x. 9.

B D G 17 and most mss. have τῶν before νεκρῶν; ℵ A C K L P and several cursives omit it. In most instances of this or similar phrases ἐκ νεκρῶν is used without τῶν, and with no variety in codd. (In Eph. i. 20 L and some twenty-five mss. prefix τῶν.) But in 1 Thess. i. 10 ℵ B D G L P and many mss., with Chrys. Theodoret, *al.*, have τῶν, A C K and many mss. omitting it. It seems, therefore, more probable that τῶν was omitted here in conformity with usage than that it was wrongly added. See on Lk. xx. 35.

13. καὶ ὑμᾶς, νεκροὺς ὄντας τοῖς παραπτώμασι ... ὑμῶν. See Eph. ii. 1.

καὶ τῇ ἀκροβυστίᾳ τῆς σαρκὸς ὑμῶν. Some commentators understand σαρκός as a genitive of apposition, or "epexegetical," "the uncircumcision which consisted in your carnal, sinful nature"; "*exquisita* appellatio peccati originalis," Bengel. But the apostle could hardly have said νεκροὺς τῇ σαρκὶ ὑμῶν without some further definition. If, indeed, he were addressing Jews, the expression in this sense would be intelligible, since it would be at once obvious that ἀκροβ. was figuratively used, and therefore σαρκός also. But though intelligible it would be very strange, as it would imply a hidden contrast between the literal and figurative meanings of σάρξ. As addressed to Gentiles, who had the literal ἀκροβυστία τῆς σαρκός, the words can hardly be understood otherwise than as referring to the external fact. But it is referred to only on account of its symbolical significance. Dead in your trespasses and your alienation from God, of which the uncircumcision of your flesh was a symbol. τῆς σαρκός appears to be added in contrast to the περιτομὴ ἀχειροποίητος, and at the same time to suggest the symbolical sense. Hence the apostle does not say ἡμῶν, although presently after he introduces the first person.

The Rec. Text has ἐν before τοῖς παραπτώμασιν, with ℵ*ᵃ* A C D F G K P and most mss. It is omitted by Tisch. Lightfoot, with ℵ* B L 17 and some other mss. Chrys. D* G and a few others, with the Latin d e g, prefix ἐν to τῇ ἀκροβυστίᾳ also.

συνεζωοποίησεν ὑμᾶς. ὑμᾶς is repeated for emphasis.

So ℵ* A C K L and about fifty cursives, Syr. Eth. etc. B 17 37 and more than twenty other cursives read ἡμᾶς, conforming to the following ἡμῖν. ℵᶜ D G P and many mss. Old Lat. Vulg. Boh., Chrys. etc. omit. The reasons for omission may have been the desire to simplify the grammar, and to avoid the proximity of ὑμᾶς and ἡμῖν.

As B reads ἡμᾶς here for ὑμᾶς, so ℵᶜ L P and many others, with Vulg. Eth., Theodoret, *al.*, have ὑμῖν for ἡμῖν.

On συνεζωοποίησε, see Eph. ii. 5. What is the subject? Ellicott, following Chrysostom, replies: Christ; partly on account, first, of "the logical difficulty of supplying a nom. from the subordinate gen. Θεοῦ"; secondly, of the prominence given to Christ throughout the preceding context, the acts described in the participles (ἐξαλ. κ.τ.λ., compared with Eph. ii. 15, and χαρισ. with Col. iii. 13); and, lastly, the difficulty of referring *vv*. 14 and 15 to God the Father. On the other hand, the reasons for adopting ὁ Θεός as the subject seem decisive. (1) There is really less logical difficulty in supplying ὁ Θεός from τοῦ Θεοῦ τοῦ ἐγείραντος than in supplying ὁ Χριστός from αὐτῷ or αὐτόν, where it is the object, or from τοῦ Χριστοῦ. (2) καὶ ὑμᾶς makes it almost necessary to understand the same subject to συνεζωοποίησε as to ἐγείραντος. (3) This is further confirmed by the συν in συνεζωοποίησεν, and by σὺν αὐτῷ. He that quickened you along with Him must surely be the same who is said to have raised Him. (4) In St. Paul it is always God, not Christ, who is the subject of ἐγείρει, συνεγείρει, ζωοποιεῖ, συνζωοποιεῖ. (5) Lastly, in Eph. ii. 4, which is so closely parallel, ὁ Θεός is the subject of συνεζωοποίησε. Hence we seem compelled to take ὁ Θεός here as the subject, whatever the difficulty of *vv.* 14, 15. And so Meyer, Alford, Lightfoot, v. Soden.

χαρισάμενος, "having forgiven." Moule prefers "forgiving," *i.e.* in the act of quickening. There is no grammatical objection to this; but logically, at least, the χαρίζεσθαι must precede the ζωοποιεῖν. The verb χαρίζεσθαι properly means "to grant as a favour" (see on Eph. iv. 32). Compare in the N.T. Luke vii. 21, ἐχαρίσατο βλέπειν: Acts iii. 14, φονέα χαρισθῆναι: xxv. 11, οὐδείς με δύναται αὐτοῖς χαρίσασθαι: *ib.* 16, xxvii. 24, κεχάρισταί σοι ὁ Θεὸς πάντας τοὺς πλέοντας μετὰ σοῦ. Phil. i. 29; Philem. 22.

It does not seem necessary to suppose that its use in the sense "forgive an offence" is derived from that of "forgiving a debt"; but even if so, there is no reason to think that it continued to suggest the latter idea. Here at all events, notwithstanding χειρόγραφον, it would appear not to have been so intended, else παραπτώματα would hardly be used, which would interfere with the figure. See on Lk. vii. 21, 42.

ἡμῖν is here the right reading, with ℵ* A B C D G K and most mss., d e g Goth. Syr. (both), Boh. Arm., Chrys. *al.*

ὑμῖν is read by ℵ^c L P and many mss. f, Vulg. Eth. The apostle at the earliest moment, as we may say, includes himself, claiming his share in the transgression and in the forgiveness. Such transition is frequent with him; cf. i. 10–13, iii. 3, 4; Eph. ii. 2, 3, 13, 14, iv. 31, 32, v. 2. For the converse transition see Gal. iii. 25, 26, iv. 5, 6. If χαρισάμενος were simultaneous with συνεζωοποίησεν, St. Paul must have used ὑμῖν here.

14. ἐξαλείψας, "blotting out" (because simultaneous with χαρισάμενος, and specifying the act by which the χαρ. was carried out). Strictly, it means "wiping out or away," "cera obducta delere." It is used of "sins," Acts iii. 19; of a "name," Rev. iii. 5; of "tears," Rev. vii. 17, xxi. 4. It is used also in classical writers of blotting out or wiping out a writing, *e.g.* Plato, *Rep.* p. 386 C, p. 501 B, and hence of abolishing a law, *Dem.* p. 468, 1, etc.

τὸ καθ' ἡμῶν χειρόγραφον. "The bond that was against us." χειρόγραφον, properly an autograph, was in later Greek a technical term for a written acknowledgment of debt, for which the older term was συγγραφή or γραμματεῖον. "Chirographum" became the usual Roman legal term; cf. Cic. *Fam.* vii. 18; Juvenal, *Sat.* xvi. 41.

Here the χειρόγραφον is the Mosaic Law, which being unfulfilled is analogous to an unpaid "note of hand." But the figure must not be pressed too far, for in this case the χειρόγραφον was not written by the debtor. Nor is it necessary to suppose that the apostle had in view the assent of the Jewish people; Deut. xxvii. 14–26; Ex. xxiv. 3 (Chrys. Oecum. Theoph. Lightfoot, etc.), or in the case of the Gentiles the assent of conscience to the moral law. The fact of obligation is sufficient to justify the use of the figure. Hence it is τὸ καθ' ἡμῶν χειρόγραφον, but not ἡμῶν χειρόγραφον. Although the Gentiles had not the written law, they had "the work of the law written in their hearts," and therefore come under the same obligation.

For a detailed account of other views of χειρόγραφον, see Eadie.

δόγμασιν, "consisting in δόγματα, *i.e.* ordinances," compare Eph. ii. 15, τὸν νόμον τῶν ἐντολῶν ἐν δόγμασι, where see note on the meaning of δόγμα, which in the N.T. is always "a decree."

The dative is best regarded as closely connected with χειρόγραφον only, being dependent on the idea of γεγραμμένον involved in the word. Compare Plato, *Ep.* vii. p. 243 A, ὃ δὴ πάσχει τὰ γεγραμμένα τύποις. So Meyer, Alford, Eadie, Lightfoot, Soden. The explanation is not without difficulty, as χειρογ. is a synthetic compound; and Lightfoot thinks it possible that ἐν may have dropped out after the similar termination -ον. If so, it must have been in the earliest ages that the error occurred, since no trace remains of the reading ἐν.

Two or three other explanations deserve notice; first, that of Winer, *al.*, followed by Ellicott, according to which δόγμασι is a nearer definition of the whole, τὸ καθ' ἡμῶν χειρόγραφον expressing at the same time what the χειρόγραφον was, and in what respect it was against us. For this we should expect τὸ τοῖς δόγμασιν καθ' ἡμῶν χ., or τὸ καθ' ἡμῶν χ. τῶν δογμάτων, or the like.

Erasmus, Olshausen, Conybeare, and others connect τοῖς δόγμασιν with the following clause: "the handwriting, which by its ordinances, was against us," a very unnatural construction, for which Acts i. 2 affords no parallel.

The Greek commentators (Chrysostom, Severianus, Theodore Mops., Theodoret, Oec., Theoph.) connect δόγμασιν with ἐξαλείψας, understanding the word to mean the doctrines or precepts of the gospel, as the instrument by which the blotting out was effected. Jerome adopts this view; and so, amongst moderns, Grotius, Estius, Bengel, Fritzsche.

But this is not only opposed to the use of δόγμα in the N.T., but, what is of more importance, it is inconsistent with fact.

For it is not by precepts or doctrines (ἡ εὐαγγελικὴ διδασκαλία, Theoph.), nor by faith (Theodoret), that the handwriting, *i.e.* the Mosaic Law, is abrogated. Moreover, the cognate verb δογματίζεσθε in ver. 20 has obvious reference to the δόγματα here, and it is implied that such δόγματα are obsolete. It is remarkable that the Greek commentators named above do not even allude to the correct interpretation, adopting without question that construction which was grammatically simplest. Irenaeus, however (quoted by Lightfoot), appears to have taken the more correct view.

The term δόγματα is used here instead of νόμος, doubtless in order to fix attention on the formal element, the plurality of precepts, an element which was common to it and the δογματίζειν of the false teachers. It thus prepares for the τί δογματίζεσθε of ver. 20. See on Lk. ii. 1.

ὃ ἦν ὑπεναντίον ἡμῖν. "Which was directly opposed to us." Here first the idea of the hostility of the χειρόγραφον is expressed, the καθ' ὑμῶν only asserting its validity with reference to us.

ὑπεναντίος occurs again Heb. x. 27. The ὑπό does not in this word imply either secrecy (Beza, *al.*) or mitigation, as = "subcontrarius," a signification which ὑπό in composition often has, but which does not belong to ὑπεναντίος either in the Sept. or in classical writers. For the Sept. cf. Gen. xxii. 27; Ex. xxiii. 27; and for classical usage, two passages cited by Lightfoot, viz. Arist. *De Gen. et Corr.* i. 7, ἐοίκασι οἱ τοῦτον τὸν τρόπον λέγοντες ὑπεναντία φαίνεσθαι λέγειν, where it means "self-contradictory," and [Plato] *Alcib. Sec.* 138 C, ΣΩ. Τὸ μαίνεσθαι ἄρα ὑπεναντίον σοι δοκεῖ τῷ φρονεῖν; ΑΛ. Πάνυ μὲν οὖν ... 139 B, ΣΩ. Καὶ μὴν δύο γε ὑπεναντία ἑνὶ πράγματι πῶς ἂν εἴη, where the argument turns on the sense of direct opposition involved in the word.

καὶ αὐτὸ ἦρκεν ἐκ τοῦ μέσου. "And it (emphatic) He hath taken out of the way." The χειρόγραφον, the writing on which had been blotted out, has now been itself removed out of the way. αἴρειν ἐκ τοῦ μέσου or ἐκ μέσου was a classical expression for removing out of the way, as, on the contrary, ἐν μέσῳ εἶναι meant "to be in the way." For the former, compare Dem. *De Corona*, p. 354, τὸ καταψεύδεσθαι καὶ δι' ἐχθράν τι λέγειν ἀνελόντας ἐκ μέσου; also Acts xvii. 33 and 2 Thess. ii. 7, μόνον ὁ κατέχων ἄρτι ἕως ἂν ἐκ μέσου γένηται. The idea "from between us and God" is not implied, but only that of an obstacle, as these and other passages show. The change of structure from the participles to the finite verb is to be noted, as well as the perfect ἦρκεν. The perfect fixes attention on the present state of freedom resulting from the action which was especially before the apostle's mind. "It is suggested," says Lightfoot, "by the feeling of relief and thanksgiving which rises up in the apostle's mind at this point." This is quite sufficient to account for the change of construction; but there was another and more imperative reason in the necessity for adding a further participial definition to the "taking away." It is clear that ἄρας... προσηλώσας would not have conveyed the same idea.

Lightfoot and others suppose a change of subject at ἦρκεν, viz. from ὁ Θεός to ὁ Χριστός. A new subject, it is thought, must be introduced somewhere, because "no grammatical meaning can be assigned to ἀπεκδυσάμενος by which it could be understood of God the Father," and the severance created here by the change of construction suggests this as the best point of transition, the alternative point being at ἀπεκδυσάμενος. Barry observes that such grammatical anomalies are not uncommon in St. Paul. But certainly this cannot be said of such a misleading confusion or hidden change of subject as this would be. Lightfoot compares the transition in i. 17–19. If the interpretation given in the note there is correct, there is no hidden transition, the subject of εὐδόκησεν being expressed. But even if ὁ Θεός is the subject of εὐδόκησεν in i. 19, there is no analogy. For the change of subject there is not concealed, and the only peculiarity is that ὁ Θεός is not expressed; and the very ground on which commentators defend this view of the construction is that the verb εὐδοκεῖν and the substantive εὐδοκία are so often used absolutely of God's good pleasure that the verb itself suggests "God" as its subject. Here, on the contrary, there is nothing in the words to indicate or suggest a new subject. On the contrary, ἦρκεν ἐκ τοῦ μέσου only expresses a different aspect of the same idea that is presented in ἐξαλείψας. No intelligible reason has been alleged why St. Paul should say, "God blotted out the handwriting, Christ removed it out of the way." Indeed, had this been stated with the subjects expressed, it would have created a difficulty.

Further, this view is open to the fatal objection, that it dissociates χαρισάμενος and ἐξαλείψας from the Cross. It inevitably suggests that the forgiveness and the blotting out of the χειρόγραφον ascribed to God are one thing, and the removal, etc., ascribed to Christ a distinct and subsequent work. V. Soden, indeed (who, however, does not suppose any change of subject), suggests such a distinction as possible. He remarks that in the figure itself αἴρειν προσηλώσαντα denotes a step beyond ἐξαλείφειν, so that we might regard the ἐξαλ. as accomplished in the sending of Christ, the αἴρειν ἐκ τοῦ μέσου in His death. He considers it more probable, however, that both expressions are figures for one and the same thing, the χαρίζεσθαι τὰ παραπτώματα, the former applying to it in its effect, the latter adding the means by which the effect is accomplished.

προσηλώσας αὐτὸ τῷ σταυρῷ. The aorist expresses the historical fact. The verb does not occur elsewhere in the N.T., but is found in classical writers, and with σταυρῷ in 3 Macc. iv. 9, and Joseph. *Bell. Jud.* ii. 14. 9. The thought expressed is similar to that in Gal. iii. 13. As Meyer observes, "since by the death of Christ on the Cross the law which condemned men lost its penal authority, inasmuch as Christ by His death endured for men the curse of the Law and became the end of the Law, hence in the fact that Christ as a ἱλαστήριον was nailed to the Cross, the Law itself was nailed thereon, whereby it ceased to be ἐν μέσῳ." The figure in προσηλώσας is suggested simply by the idea of the crucifixion; there is no reason to suppose, with Grotius, any allusion to a custom of driving a nail through obsolete laws or decrees, and so hanging them up in public, a custom which seems to be unproved.

15. ἀπεκδυσάμενος τὰς ἀρχὰς καὶ τὰς ἐξουσίας, ἐδειγμάτισεν,

κ.τ.λ. The verb ἀπεκδύεσθαι appears not to occur in any writer before St. Paul; its occurrence, therefore, here and in iii. 9, as well as that of ἀπέκδυσις in ver. 11, is remarkable. It is, no doubt, chosen in order to express more emphatically the completeness of the action. Both ἀποδύειν and ἐκδύειν occur in classical authors in the sense "strip," hence of enemies, "strip of arms, spoliare." For ἐκδύειν in the sense "strip," see Matt. xxvii. 28, 31; Mark xv. 20; Luke x. 30. The middle occurs 2 Cor. v. 4 of putting off the mortal body. In this Epistle, iii. 19, ἀπεκδυσάμενοι occurs again in the sense "strip off and put away," viz., τὸν παλαιὸν ἄνθρωπον. It is very difficult to decide in what sense the word is used here.

First, it has been taken absolutely, "having put off from himself his *body*, he made a show," etc., as RV. marg. This, which supposes ὁ Χριστός to be the subject, is the interpretation adopted by Hilary, Ambrose, Augustine, and some other Latins. Probably, however, they had before them a Latin counterpart of the reading found in G, viz. τὴν σάρκα καὶ τὰς ἐξουσίας. The Latin of G has the same. Thus Hilary has twice, "exutus carnem et potestates ostentui fecit" (773, 990); once, however, he has "spolians se carne et principatus et potestates ostentui fecit" (204).

Novat. also has "exutus carnem potestates dehonestavit" (*De Trin.* 16). It will be observed that these quotations, except the third from Hilary, agree with G in omitting τὰς ἀρχάς. This reading may have originated from the eye or ear error of a copyist, aided by the suggestion of ἀπεκδ.; but more probably was a gloss, which was supposed to be a correction, and so substituted for the correct text. There is a trace either of the reading or the interpretation in a Docetic work quoted by Hippolytus, *Haer.* viii. 10, p. 267, ψυχὴ ἐκείνη ἐν τῷ σώματι τραφεῖσα, ἀπεκδυσαμένη τὸ σῶμα καὶ προσηλώσασα πρὸς τὸ ξύλον καὶ θριαμβεύσασα δι' αὐτοῦ τὰς ἀρχάς, κ.τ.λ. The Syriac Peshitto has the same interpretation, "by the putting off of his body"; and so the Gothic also.

In support of this interpretation 2 Cor. v. 4 is referred to, where the cognate verb ἐκδύσασθαι is used absolutely of putting off the body. But there the metaphor is not abruptly introduced, the verb only carrying out the figure introduced with its explanation in *vv.* 2, 3. Here it would be quite isolated, being neither explained nor suggested by anything in the context, with which, indeed, the idea would have no apparent connexion. Some expositors, indeed, have found an allusion to the metaphorical use of ἀποδύεσθαι, "to prepare for a contest," as in Plut. *Mor.* 811 E, πρὸς πᾶσαν ἀποδυόμενοι τὴν πολιτικὴν πρᾶξιν. This explanation is very far-fetched, and entirely unsuitable.

2. Ellicott, Lightfoot, *al.*, adopt the interpretation of the Greek commentators, Chrysostom, Severianus, Theodore Mops., and

Theodoret, viz. taking τὰς ἀρχάς, κ.τ.λ., as governed by ἀπεκδ., the sense being, "having stripped off from himself the hostile powers of evil." "Our Lord by His death stripped away from Himself all the opposing Powers of Evil (observe the article) that sought in the nature which He had condescended to assume to win for themselves a victory," Ell. Similarly Lightfoot, "Christ took upon Himself our human nature with all its temptations (Heb. iv. 15). The powers of evil gathered about Him. Again and again they assailed Him; but each fresh assault ended in a new defeat." "The final act in the conflict began with the agony of Gethsemane; it ended with the Cross of Calvary. The victory was complete. The enemy of man was defeated. The powers of evil, which had clung like a Nessus robe about His humanity, were torn off and cast aside for ever. And the victory of mankind is involved in the victory of Christ. In His Cross we too are divested of the poisonous clinging garments of temptation and sin and death; τῷ ἀποθέσθαι τὴν θνητότητα, says Theodore, ἣν ὑπὲρ τῆς κοινῆς ἀφεῖλεν εὐεργεσίας, ἀπεδύσατο κἀκείνων (i.e. τῶν ἀντικειμένων δυνάμεων) τὴν αὐθεντείαν ᾗπερ ἐκέχρηντο καθ᾽ ἡμῶν."

But this interpretation is open to serious if not fatal objections. In the first place, as the verb means to divest of clothing, it requires us to regard these hostile powers in the light of a clothing of God or Christ, a "Nessus robe," as Lightfoot expresses it.

If the interpretation, "putting off the body," is to be rejected on the ground that the metaphor, though a natural one, is not suggested or explained by the context, the objection applies more strongly to the view in question, which supposes a metaphor by no means easy to understand and not elsewhere paralleled. The putting off the old man, ch. iii. 9, is not at all parallel. Lightfoot compares Philo, *Quod det. pot. ins.* 13 (i. p. 199), where the image in the context is that of a wrestling bout, ἐξαναστάντες δὲ καὶ διερεισάμενοι τὰς ἐντέχνους αὐτῶν περιπλοκὰς εὐμαρῶς ἐκδυσόμεθα; but there the figure is sufficiently explained by the context. Here (and this is the second objection) the figure would be irrelevant to the context. As Alford observes, "is it in any way relevant to the fact of the law being antiquated by God in the Great Sacrifice of the atonement, to say that He in that act (or, according to others, Christ in that act) spoiled and triumphed over the *infernal potentates*?" Lastly, there is another very strong objection. If it was only by putting off His human body on the Cross that He could put off from Himself the powers of evil that beset His humanity, this would not be victory, but retreat.

3. Alford observes, and apparently with justice, that the terms ἀρχαί and ἐξουσίαι are general; and a specific reference to "infernal powers" is not to be assumed unless it is determined by the context, as in Eph. vi. 12. "Now the words have occurred before

in this very passage, ver. 10, where Christ is exalted as κεφαλὴ πάσης ἀρχῆς καὶ ἐξουσίας, and it is hardly possible to avoid connecting our present expression with that, seeing that in τὰς ἀρχὰς καὶ τὰς ἐξουσίας the articles seem to contain a manifest reference to it." Taking the words, then, in a more general sense, he explains the whole by reference to passages in which the Law is said to have been administered by angels, Gal. iii. 19, διαταγεὶς δι' ἀγγέλων : Heb. ii. 2, ὁ δι' ἀγγέλων λαληθεὶς λόγος : Acts vii. 53, ἐλάβετε τὸν νόμον εἰς διαταγὰς ἀγγέλων. Compare Jos. *Ant.* xv. 5. 3, ἡμῶν τὰ κάλλιστα τῶν δογμάτων, καὶ τὰ ὁσιώτατα τῶν ἐν τοῖς νόμοις δι' ἀγγέλων παρὰ τοῦ Θεοῦ μαθόντων, "they were the promulgators of the χειρόγραφον τοῖς δόγμασιν." That writing was first wiped out, and then nailed to the Cross—abrogated and suspended there. "Thus God ἀπεξεδύσατο τὰς ἀρχὰς καὶ τὰς ἐξουσίας—divested Himself of, put off from Himself, that ἀγγέλων διαταγή, manifesting Himself henceforward without a veil in the exalted Person of Jesus." It is no objection to this "that thus more prominence would be given to angelic agency in the law than was really the fact; the answer is, that the prominence which is given is owing to the errors of the false teachers, who had evidently *associated the Jewish observances* in some way *with the worship of angels.*" With reference to this, the statement of Theodoret quoted below on ver. 18 is important, τοὺς ἀγγέλους σέβειν εἰσηγοῦντο, διὰ τούτων λέγοντες δεδόσθαι τὸν νόμον. "St. Paul's argument will go only to this,—that whatever part the angelic powers may have *had*, or be supposed to have had in the previous dispensation, all such interposition was now at an end, that dispensation itself being once for all antiquated and put away." Ritschl's view is similar. Ellicott's objection to this view is that it rests on the assumption that the verse refers to Θεός, not Χριστός. But, in fact, it only assumes that the contrary is not proved. The principal objection to taking ὁ Θεός as the subject throughout is the supposed difficulty or impossibility of interpreting ἀπεκδυσάμενος, κ.τ.λ., of God the Father. It is not logical to adopt this argument, and then to reject an interpretation which meets this difficulty on the ground that the subject must be ὁ Χριστός.

4. The foregoing interpretations assume that ἀπεκδυσάμενος, being in the middle voice, must mean "stripping from himself." But the middle often only expresses a personal interest, and the cognate verb ἀπεδυσάμεθα occurs in Plato, *Rep.* p. 612 A (quoted by Meyer), in the sense "nudavimus." Nor does the fact that in iii. 9 the same verb in the same voice means "strip from oneself," decide the question as to its meaning here. As Bp. Perowne observes (*apud* Moule), there are classical parallels to such a varying use of the middle in neighbouring contexts. See Soph. *Ajax*, 245, 647. It is allowable, therefore, to take the verb here in the sense

"spoil, disarm," the middle conveying the idea "sibi exspoliare." This sense, accordingly, is adopted by Bengel, De Wette, Meyer, Moule, Eadie, Soden. Most of these, however, understand as in (1) (2) by the ἀρχαὶ καὶ ἐξουσίαι the infernal powers. Some of the objections made to (2) apply to this view also. First, that if these were intended we should expect this to be specified; and, secondly, that it does not harmonise with the context. What had the disarming of the infernal powers to do with the abolition of the δόγματα? or what connexion had the assertion of it with the warning against the θρησκεία τῶν ἀγγέλων? Meyer's explanation is that it was in sin that these powers had their strength in their hostility to God, and "the power of sin was in the Law" (1 Cor. xv. 56); hence with the law "the infernal power stands and falls." Surely a faulty argument. The abolition of the law does not do away with sin. Moule, again, says, "He who is King of all orders of good angels is here presented as Conqueror of their evil counterpart." This supposes that τὰς ἀρχάς, κ.τ.λ., here are actually contrasted with πάσης ἀρχῆς, κ.τ.λ., in ver. 10, of which contrast there is no indication.

5. V. Soden adopts the translation "spoiled," *i.e.* "disarmed," but adopts a view of ἀρχαὶ καὶ ἐξουσίαι similar to that of Alford and Ritschl, viz. that they are the angelic powers in so far as they represent the Law, and thereby have power over men, and doubly over those who do not fulfil it, that is (since ideally the law was valid for all men), not Jews only, but Gentiles also (Gal. iv. 3, 9, iii. 19; 1 Cor. viii. 5 sqq.). The fact, which in ver. 14 was described on the side of men, is now carried out in its significance for the angelic powers who represented those δόγματα, having in view the fact that the δογματίζειν taught in Colossae, which the apostle is combating, was ultimately a θρησκεία τῶν ἀγγέλων (18, 23).

This view is equally tenable whether the subject is taken to be ὁ Θεός or ὁ Χριστός, and it seems less open to objection than the former. The remark quoted above from Alford as to the prominence given to angelic action is equally applicable to this interpretation.

ἐδειγμάτισεν. A rare word, which, perhaps, is also to be read in Matt. i. 19, μὴ θέλων αὐτὴν δειγματίσαι:[1] and Lightfoot also quotes a passage from *Acta Pauli et Petri*, in which it occurs, ἵνα μὴ μόνον ἀπὸ τῆς τοῦ Σίμωνος ἀπάτης φύγωσιν, ἀλλὰ καὶ δειγματίσουσιν αὐτόν, where it is explained in the context as "to proclaim." The substantive δειγματισμός occurs in the Rosetta inscription. The idea involved in δειγματίζειν is only that of public exhibition, not of shame (παραδειγματίζειν).

ἐν παρρησίᾳ. The rendering "openly," as in AV. and retained

---

[1] The Text. Rec. there has παραδειγματίσαι,—a word which frequently occurs in Polyb. etc.; also Num. xxv. 4; Isa. iv. 17; Jer. xiii. 22; Ez. xxviii. 17.

in RV., is approved by Bengel, De Wette, Olsh., Wordsworth, and Eadie. δημοσίᾳ, πάντων ὁρώντων, Theoph., Alford would preserve the idea of "openness of speech," "declaring and revealing by the Cross that there is none other but Christ the Head πάσης ἀρχῆς καὶ ἐξουσίας." "Openness of speech," however, seems unsuitable to the connexion. As to the sense "openly, publicly," it seems to be supported by John vii. 4, where ἐν παρρησίᾳ εἶναι is opposed to ἐν κρυπτῷ ποιεῖν, and xi. 54, Ἰησοῦς οὐκέτι παρρησίᾳ περιεπάτει ἐν τοῖς Ἰουδαίοις ἀλλὰ ἀπῆλθεν ἐκεῖθεν, κ.τ.λ. In St. Paul, however, it always means "with boldness, or confidence" (an idea which is also present in the places cited), and so it is understood here by Meyer, Ellicott, Lightfoot, Soden. Hofmann connects ἐν παρρησίᾳ in the sense "openly" with θριαμβεύσας, which, however, already contains that idea.

θριαμβεύσας αὐτούς. αὐτούς, masc. of the ἀρχαὶ καὶ ἐξ., because they are treated as personal existences, not with any reference to their possible designation as ἀγγέλους.

θριαμβεύσας, "triumphing over them," or, rather, "leading them in triumph," as in 2 Cor. ii. 14. This is the usual signification of the verb with accus. of person. *E.g.* Plut. *Thes. et Rom.* 4, βασιλεῖς ἐθριάμβευσε καὶ ἡγεμόνας. Wetstein, on Cor. *l.c.*, gives other examples.

ἐν αὐτῷ. Bengel, De Wette, *al.*, take this as = ἐν Χριστῷ. But Christ is not mentioned in ver. 14. Most commentators understand it as = ἐν σταυρῷ. To this Soden objects that σταυρός in ver. 14 is only a secondary idea; and he refers the pronoun to χειρόγραφον. In doing away with the χειρόγραφον God triumphed over those who administered it. (Meyer, ed. 4 (1874), does not mention this view, which is attributed to him by Ellicott (1857) and Eadie (1855).) The Vulgate has "in semetipso," and so RV. margin. G reads ἐν ἑαυτῷ.

The metaphor is a very bold one whether understood of God or of Christ. If αὐτῷ refers to σταυρῷ, the words would certainly be more suitable to Christ, and in that case the antithesis between θριάμβευσας and ἐν σταυρῷ would be extremely striking. "The violence of the metaphor," says Lightfoot, "is its justification. The paradox of the Crucifixion is thus placed in the strongest light—triumph in helplessness and glory in shame. The convict's gibbet is the victor's car." No doubt this way of putting the thought is very striking; but if this had been the meaning of the apostle, might we not expect that he would express it more distinctly, instead of almost hiding it, as we may say, in an unemphatic pronoun with an ambiguous preposition ἐν? We might have expected some such expression, for instance, as σταυρωθεὶς ἐθριάμβευσε. But, in fact, the contrast suggested would be quite irrelevant to the apostle's purpose, and the more striking it is the less likely is it that he would introduce it in this way as a side-thought, thus tending to draw the reader's attention from the argument.

For ἐν αὑτῷ Origen (in several places) reads ἐν τῷ ξύλῳ. So also his translator (*Int.* ii. 416), commenting on "in ligno crucis," says: "licet in aliis exemplaribus habeatur *triumphans in semetipso,* sed apud Graecos habetur *in ligno.*"

16–23. *Practical application of these principles to the ascetic precepts and the angel-worship of the false teachers. With their precepts about eating and drinking and observance of days, they would have you attach yourselves to the shadow, whereas you are in possession of the reality. The cult of angels is inculcated as a becoming exercise of humility; but this is a false humility, and is really the fruit of carnal pride, vaunting itself in the pretended knowledge of these angelic powers, and is derogatory to Christ the Head, on whom alone we depend for spiritual health and growth.*

16. Μὴ οὖν τις ὑμᾶς κρινέτω. "Therefore," seeing that the law of ordinances has been done away with, "let not any one," not μηδείς, but μή τις, as in ver. 8, pointing to some definite persons; κρινέτω, not "condemn," but "judge you, take you to task." Compare Rom. xiv. 3, 4; 1 Cor. x. 29.

ἐν βρώσει ἢ ἐν πόσει. "In eating or in drinking," *i.e.* in the matter of eating or drinking. Compare Rom. xiv. 17, οὐ γάρ ἐστιν ἡ βασιλεία τοῦ Θεοῦ βρῶσις καὶ πόσις. βρῶσις in St. Paul is always the action of eating (1 Cor. viii. 4; 2 Cor. ix. 10), not the thing eaten (βρῶμα, 1 Cor. vi. 13, viii. 8, x. 3, *al.*; Heb. ix. 10). In Homer, indeed, βρῶσις is used for "food" (*Il.* i. 210, *al.*); and so in St. John iv. 32; cf. 34, vi. 27, 55. There is a similar difference between πόσις and πόμα.

The Mosaic Law contained no prohibition respecting drinks except in special cases, namely, those of Nazirite vows and of priests ministering in the tabernacle (Num. vi. 3; Lev. x. 9). There was also a prohibition of drinking from vessels rendered unclean by the dead bodies of unclean animals (Lev. xi. 34). We know, however, that the Essenes, the prototypes of the Colossian false teachers, went far beyond the Mosaic code, abstaining wholly from wine and from animal food (see Lightfoot, p. 86).

Lightfoot reads καὶ ἐν πόσει, with B, Syr-Pesh. Boh., Tertull. Origen. Tertullian, however, reads *et* in all four places, therefore his evidence in this instance is valueless. The Syriac also has "and" in three of the four places, "or" only in the second; its evidence also, therefore, counts for nothing. The apostle might have written καί not ἤ, because βρῶσις and πόσις naturally belong together (but so, indeed, do the following three), and the occurrence of ἤ in the other three clauses would easily lead a copyist to substitute it here. But the authority for καί is too slight.

Compare 1 Cor. xi. 27, ἐσθίῃ τὸν ἄρτον ἢ πίνῃ τὸ ποτήριον, κ.τ.λ., where A, some cursives, Syr-Pesh. Boh. Eth., Origen, al. have καί.

ἢ ἐν μέρει, "in the matter of"; compare ἐν τούτῳ τῷ μέρει, 2 Cor. iii. 10, ix. 3; μέρος often denotes the class or category, especially with verbs like τιθέναι, as in Plato, *Rep.* i. 348 E, ἐν ἀρετῆς καὶ σοφίας τίθης μέρει τὴν ἀδικίαν. Chrys. and Theodoret take it here in the sense "part," οὐ γὰρ δὴ πάντα κατεῖχον τὰ πρότερα, Chrys.

ἑορτῆς ἢ νουμηνίας ἢ σαββάτων. The words specify the annual, monthly, and weekly celebrations; cf. Gal. iv. 10.

σάββατα, though plural, means "a Sabbath day," being, in fact, a Greek transliteration of the Aramaic, and from its form mistaken for a plural. Thus Josephus distinctly, *Ant.* iii. 10. 1, ἑβδόμην ἡμέραν ἥτις σάββατα καλεῖται; also *ib.* i. 1. 1. Compare Hor. *Sat.* i. 9. 69, "hodie tricesima Sabbata." See on Lk. iv. 31.

B G have the spelling νεομηνίας, and so the Vulg.

17. ἅ ἐστιν σκιὰ τῶν μελλόντων, τὸ δὲ σῶμα Χριστοῦ. σκιά does not mean an outline or sketch (as understood by Calvin and many others), which would be σκιαγραφία or σκιαγράφημα, and is excluded by the antithesis of σῶμα. A sketch would be contrasted with the complete picture. It is simply "shadow," having in itself no substance, but indicating the existence of a body which casts the shadow. σῶμα accordingly retains its proper signification "body," not "substance." Compare Philo, *De Conf. Ling.* p. 434, τὰ μὲν ῥητὰ τῶν χρησμῶν σκιάς τινας ὡσανεὶ σωμάτων εἶναι: opposed to τὰ ὑφεστῶτα ἀληθείᾳ πράγματα. Josephus, *Bell. Jud.* ii. 2. 5, σκιὰν αἰτησόμενος βασιλείας, ἧς ἥρπασεν ἑαυτῷ τὸ σῶμα. Compare also Heb. x. 1, σκιὰν ἔχων ὁ νόμος τῶν μελλόντων ἀγαθῶν, οὐκ αὐτὴν τὴν εἰκόνα τῶν πραγμάτων: *ib.* viii. 5, σκιᾷ λατρεύουσι τῶν ἐπουρανίων. The figure expresses both the unsubstantiality and the supersession of the Mosaic ritual. But the thought found in it by some Greek commentators, and adopted by Meyer and Lightfoot, that the shadow comes *before* the substance (ἡ σκιὰ προτρέχει τοῦ σώματος), is not contained in the text; for it is no part of the idea of a shadow that it goes before the body, or is seen before it. Theodoret presses the figure still further: προλαμβάνει ἡ σκιὰ τὸ σῶμα ἀνίσχοντος τοῦ φωτός· ὡς εἶναι σκιὰν μὲν τὸν νόμον σῶμα δὲ τὴν χάριν, φῶς δὲ τὸν δεσπότην Χριστόν.

Meyer again presses the tense of ἐστι so far as to infer that τὰ μέλλοντα are not the already then existing Christian relations, the καινὴ διαθήκη (rather τὰ τῆς καινῆς διαθήκης), but belong "wholly" to the αἰὼν μέλλων. The present, however, is sufficiently explained by the remark of Davenant (*apud* Ellicott), "loquitur de illis ut considerantur *in suâ naturâ*, abstractae a circumstantiis temporis." Yet it may be used in its temporal sense quite as well as the presents in Heb. x. 1. sqq. For the observance of these times and seasons had not ceased, although that of which they were the shadow had come. Meyer's interpretation would vitiate the apostle's reasoning, for if τὰ μέλλοντα were still wholly future, the σκιά would not be superseded, and the observances referred to would retain their importance.

V. Soden regards σῶμα as denoting τὰ μέλλοντα in their concrete organisation, *i.e.* the Church (cf. ver. 19).

τοῦ Χριστοῦ, *i.e.* belongs to Christ; the blessings typified by these observances are found in Him. The article is prefixed in ℵ* A C P 17 *al.*, Oec.; omitted in ℵᶜ D G K L most mss., Chrys. etc. Chrysostom mentions a strange punctuation: οἱ μὲν οὖν τοῦτο στίζουσι· τὸ δὲ σῶμα, Χριστοῦ, ἡ δὲ ἀλήθεια ἐπὶ Χριστοῦ γέγονεν· οἱ δέ, τὸ δὲ σῶμα Χριστοῦ μηδεὶς ὑμᾶς καταβραβευέτω, τουτέστιν, ἐπηρεαζέτω. So Augustine, *Ep.* 59, "Corpus autem Christi nemo vos convincat," confessing that he does not understand it. This connexion is also supported by A B P (apparently ℵ also) *al.*, Eth.

18. Μηδεὶς ὑμᾶς καταβραβευέτω. καταβραβεύειν is an extremely rare word. Jerome reckoned it as one of St. Paul's Cilicisms, but it has been found in two other places. First in Demosth. *Mid.* p. 544 (not as used by the orator, but in a statement of witnesses), διὰ ταύτην τὴν αἰτίαν ἐπιστάμεθα Στράτωνα ὑπὸ Μειδίου καταβραβευθέντα καὶ παρὰ πάντα τὰ δίκαια ἀτιμωθέντα. Strato had been arbitrator in a cause between Demosthenes and Meidias, and as the latter did not appear, gave judgment against him. On this account Meidias contrived to have Strato condemned to ἀτιμία. The other passage quoted in the Lexicons and commentators is in Eustathius on Hom. *Il.* Α. 402 sqq. Speaking of the assistance which Briareus, son of Poseidon, rendered to Zeus, when Poseidon, with two other deities, conspired against him, Eustathius observes that as amongst men sons often differ from their fathers, οὕτως οὐδὲ ὁ μυθικὸς Βριάρεως φίλα φρονεῖ τῷ πατρί, ἀλλὰ καταβραβεύει αὐτόν, ὥς φασιν οἱ παλαιοί, τοῦ φυσικοῦ θεσμοῦ προθέμενος τὸ δίκαιον. Here the word clearly means "decides, or takes part, against," and from the words ὥς φασιν οἱ παλαιοί, may be regarded as almost a definition of the word by a scholar to whom it was familiar. It will be observed that neither in this passage nor in the former is there any question of a prize.

This meaning of the verb is confirmed by its etymology. The simple verb βραβεύειν, which, of course, signifies primarily "to act as βραβεύς or umpire," awarding the prize, βραβεῖον (1 Cor. ix. 24 : Phil. iii. 14), seems, in all the examples that we have of its use, to have dropped all reference to a prize, and to mean only "to decide." For instance, Isocr. *Areop.* p. 144 B, ἐν τῇ κληρώσει τὴν τύχην βραβεύσειν. The same writer, *Phil.* c. 29, uses τὰ παρά (τινος) βραβευόμενα to express regulations made by a person. In

Demosthenes, again, *Ol.* p. 36, 7, τὰ τῶν ἄλλων δίκαια βραβεύειν is "to arbitrate or decide on the rights of others." So p. 1231, 11, of the unequal treatment of rich and poor, τοῦτον τὸν τρόπον ὑμῶν ταῦτα βραβευόντων. Josephus, *Ant.* ix. 1. 1, has: παρεκελεύσατο μηδενὸς οὕτως ὡς τοῦ δικαίου προνοουμένους κρίνειν τοῖς ὄχλοις ... βραβεύειν δὲ ἅπασι τὸ ἴσον; and *Ant.* xiv. 9. 5, ὡς εἰ καὶ πολέμου ῥοπὰς βραβεύει τὸ θεῖον. Compare also Col. iii. 15, ἡ εἰρήνη τοῦ Χριστοῦ βραβευέτω ἐν ταῖς καρδίαις ὑμῶν. In accordance with this meaning of βραβεύειν, καταβρ. would mean "to decide or give judgment against"; and it is so interpreted by Photius (*ap.* Oec.) and Hesychius, κατακρινέτω. So also the Syriac Versions.

This gives an excellent sense here, the phrase being stronger than the similar one in ver. 16, κρινέτω. It is adopted instead of κατακρινέτω, probably in order to suggest the idea of assumption of authority. This is the interpretation adopted by Reiche, Bleek, Field (*Otium Norvicense*), and many others. Bengel's interpretation is: "ne quis brabeutae potestatem usurpans, atque adeo abutens, vos currentes moderetur, perperamque praescribat quid sequi quid fugere debeatis praemium accepturi"; and similarly a-Lapide and Beza. This seems to put too much into the word.

The Greek commentators, who seem to have had no independent knowledge of the word, take it to be equivalent to παραβραβεύειν, which occurs in Polybius and Plutarch, and means to assign the prize unfairly. Zonaras (*ap.* Suicer) says: καταβραβεύειν ἐστὶ τὸ μὴ νικήσαντα ἀξιοῦν τοῦ βραβείον, ἀλλ' ἑτέρῳ διδόναι αὐτό. This implies that ὁ καταβραβεύων is the judge. Suidas' words are: τὸ ἄλλου ἀγωνιζομένου ἄλλον στεφανοῦσθαι λέγει ὁ ἀπόστολας καταβραβεύεσθαι. Meyer, adopting this view, supposes the apostle to mean "willing (θέλων) to bring it about that the prize may be withheld from you and given to him and his." As their obtaining the prize would not involve others losing it, this would imply folly as well as malice. The meaning assigned by recent commentators generally, viz. "rob or beguile you of your prize," *i.e.* "cause you to lose your reward by defeat," or the like, does not agree either with Suidas or Zonaras, and it increases the difficulty of θέλων. It results from the desire to retain a reference to a βραβεῖον, which, as we have seen, is not generally retained in the simple verb, nor, as far as we can judge, in the compound.

θέλων ἐν ταπεινοφροσύνῃ. These words are very difficult. Many commentators (including Augustine, Estius, Olshausen, Bleek, Lightfoot) explain them as a Hebraism in imitation of the Hebrew "ב חפץ, "taking delight in," or rather (since the Hebrew verb does not mean θέλειν, but εὐδοκεῖν), of the occasional Septuagint rendering of that expression (1 Sam. xviii. 22; 2 Sam. xv. 26; 1 Kings, x. 9; 2 Chron. ix. 8; Ps. cxi. 1, cxlvii. 10). In 1 Chron. xxviii. 4, the same words occur as a rendering

of "רצה ב. Lightfoot also quotes from the *Test. XII. Patr.* Asher
i., ἐὰν οὖν ἡ ψυχὴ θέλῃ ἐν καλῷ.

The main objection to this, and it is a fatal one, is that St. Paul does not use Hebraisms which so violate Greek grammar. The fact of such an expression occurring in the Sept., especially in Sam. Kings and Chron., is not a reason for attributing it to St. Paul. Indeed, except in Ps. cxlvii. 10, the object in the Sept. is always a person. In the Apocrypha, θέλειν ἐν is not found. The expression θελητὰς νόμου, 1 Macc. iv. 42, is not parallel. Nor is this interpretation relevant to the context, for it is not the pleasure which the false teacher takes in his humility, etc., that is in question.

Alford connects θέλων with the participle, translating "of purpose," and comparing 2 Pet. iii. 5, λανθάνει γὰρ αὐτοὺς τοῦτο θέλοντας. He also quotes Theophylact as apparently supporting this view, θέλουσιν ὑμᾶς καταβραβεύειν διὰ ταπεινοφρ. But both this comment and the passage in 2 Pet. are equally, if not more, applicable to the following interpretation.

Other expositors connect θέλων with the following words, supplying καταβραβεύειν. So Theodoret: τοῦτο τοίνυν συνεβούλευον ἐκεῖνοι γίνεσθαι, ταπεινοφροσύνῃ δῆθεν κεχρημένοι (compare Theoph. above); and so Photius, Buttmann, Eadie, Ellicott, and many others. Theodoret, indeed, presses θέλων too far; the purpose of the false teachers was not directly, but indirectly hostile to the Colossians.

RV. marg. has: "of his own mere will, by humility," etc. This agrees nearly with Beza: "hoc munus sibi a nullo tributum exercens," Reiche, Tittmann, *al.* It also corresponds well with ἐθελοθρησκεία below, and, on the whole, appears to deserve the preference. The construction (which is the same as Alford's) is simpler grammatically than that last mentioned, and the sense obtained is more satisfactory. Luther (followed by Ewald and Tyndale) gives a similar sense to θέλων, but connects it with ἐμβατεύων.

Lightfoot quotes two conjectural emendations, viz. θέλγων, suggested by Leclerc (*ad loc.*) and Bentley (*Crit. Sacr.* p. 59), and more plausibly ἐλθών, suggested by Toup (*Emend. in Suidam*, ii. p. 63). We can hardly suppose, however, that if ἐλθών had stood here originally it could be corrupted into θέλων. Hort conjectures ἐν ἐθελοταπεινοφροσύνῃ. The last word is actually employed by Basil, and compounds of ἐθελο- were used freely when St. Paul wrote. Compare Aug. *Ep.* 149, § 27: "Sic enim et vulgo dicitur qui divitem affectat *thelodives*, et qui sapientem *thelosapiens*, et cetera hujusmodi. Ergo et hic *thelohumilis*, quod plenius dicitur *thelon humilis*, id est *volens humilis*, quod intelligitur 'volens videri humilis,' 'affectans humilitatem.'"

ἐν ταπεινοφροσύνῃ καὶ θρησκείᾳ τῶν ἀγγέλων. ταπ. is elsewhere (except ver. 23) treated as a virtue, and so in this Ep. iii. 12. But there is false as well as true humility, and here it is defined by the following θρησκείᾳ τῶν ἀγγ., which again is illustrated by it. What is referred to, then, is the humility which finds expression in the worship of angels, and this worship again is that which is inspired by this false humility. Perhaps the false teachers made much of humility in inculcating this θρησκεία, chiefly from false notions as to the power of the angels; but partly, it may be, from an idea that God Himself was too high and unapproachable for men, who must therefore use the mediation of angels. This is the explanation given by Theodoret: λέγοντες ὡς ἀόρατος ὁ τῶν ὅλων Θεός, ἀνεφικτός τε καὶ ἀκατάληπτος, καὶ προσήκει διὰ τῶν ἀγγέλων τὴν θείαν εὐμένειαν πραγματεύεσθαι. Compare Augustine, *Conf.* x. 42, "Quem invenirem qui me reconciliaret tibi? Ambiendum mihi fuit ad angelos? Multi conantes ad te redire, neque per se ipsos valentes, sicut audio, tentaverunt haec, et inciderunt in desiderium curiosarum visionum, et digni habiti sunt illusionibus." Zonaras, again, in commenting on the 35th Canon of the Council of Laodicaea, says there was an ancient heresy of some who said that we should not call on Christ for help or access to God, but on the angels, ὡς τάχα τοῦ τὸν Χριστὸν ἐπικαλεῖσθαι πρὸς τὰ εἰρημένα μείζονος ὄντος τῆς ἡμετέρας ἀξίας (Suicer, i. p. 45). So also Chrysostom and Theophylact. This latter view, however, would place Christ high above the angels, and therefore cannot have been that of the Colossians, who required to be taught the superiority of Christ. Nor can Theodoret's explanation be adopted without hesitation, since there is nothing in the context about the mediation of angels or of Christ; nor does this view of ταπεινοφρ. agree with the following ἃ ἑώρακεν, κ.τ.λ. Theodoret, however, throws light on the passage when he states that οἱ τῷ νόμῳ συνηγοροῦντες καὶ τοὺς ἀγγέλους σέβειν αὐτοῖς εἰσηγοῦντο, διὰ τούτων λέγοντες δεδόσθαι τὸν νόμον, for which reason, he adds, the Council at Laodicaea forbade praying to angels: καὶ μέχρι δὲ τοῦ νῦν εὐκτήρια τοῦ ἁγίου Μιχαὴλ παρ' ἐκείνοις καὶ τοῖς ὁμόροις ἐστὶν ἰδεῖν.

ἃ ἑώρακεν ἐμβατεύειν or ἃ μὴ ἑώρακεν ἐμβατεύων. ἐμβατεύειν is properly to step or stand on (as an ἐμβάτης). So with gen. Soph. *Oed. Tyr.* 845, ἐμβατεύειν πατρίδος. Hence "to dwell in," Eurip. *Heracl.* 875, κλήρους δ' ἐμβατεύσεσθε χθονός: and similarly of a god, to "haunt" a place. Soph. *Oed. Col.* 671, ἵν' ὁ βακχειώτας ἀεὶ Διόνυσος ἐμβατεύει. It also means to "enter upon" a country, "to invade." Later, it is found in a figurative sense of "entering into" a subject of inquiry. So Philo, *De Plant. Noe.* ii. 19, "As some of those who open up wells often fail to find the sought-for water," οὕτως οἱ προσωτέρω χωροῦντες τῶν ἐπιστημῶν καὶ ἐπιπλέον ἐμβατεύοντες αὐταῖς, ἀδυνατοῦσι τοῦ τέλους ἐπιψαῦσαι: and so perhaps 2 Macc. ii. 30, τὸ μὲν ἐμβατεύειν καὶ περὶ πάντων ποιεῖσθαι λόγον . . . τῷ τῆς ἱστορίας ἀρχηγέτῃ καθήκει (but RV. "to occupy the ground"). Athanas. on Matt. xi. 27, τολμηρὸν ἐμβατεύειν τὴν ἀπερινόητον φύσιν. Nemes. *De Nat. Hom.* (p. 64, ed. Matth.), οὐρανὸν ἐμβατεύει τῇ θεωρίᾳ.

If we read ἑώρακεν the sense will be, "dwelling in," as RV. "taking his stand upon," as RV. marg. or "poring over, busying himself with," or with the idea of pride in his possession, "making parade with." "What he hath seen" is then to be understood ironically, his "visions."

Hilgenfeld (quoted by Meyer) understands the words to mean, without irony, "taking his stand on the ground of sense"; but against this is the perfect ἑώρακεν as well as the expressive ἐμβατεύων. Besides, the error in question was based on a supposed knowledge of angels.

The Rec. Text ἃ μὴ ἑώρακεν conveys the idea, "intruding into things which he hath not seen." At first sight this is easier. But, as Alford remarks, it "would be a strange and incongruous expression for one who was advocating a religion of *faith*—whose very charter is μακάριοι οἱ μὴ ἰδόντες καὶ πεπιστευκότες—to blame a man or a teacher for ἃ μὴ ἑώρακεν ἐμβατεύειν." We should rather expect it to be regarded as a fault in a teacher that he took his stand in the realm of sight.

If, however, the negative was written from the apostle's point of view, we should expect the objective οὐχ to be used; if, on the other hand, it is from the false teacher's point of view, "intruding" would not be a suitable translation, but "searching," or the like.

As to the reading, the evidence is as follows:—
Without the negative:
MSS.: ℵ* A B D* 17 28 67² codd. mentioned by Jerome (*Ep.* 121 *ad Alg.* i. p. 880); codd. mentioned by Augustine (*Ep.* 149, ii. p. 514).
Versions: Old Latin d e m Boh. Arab. (Leipz.) Eth.
Fathers, etc.: Tertullian (*cont. Marc.* v. 19, "ex visionibus angelicis," and apparently Marcion himself also); Origen once (in the Latin translation. *In Cant.* iii. p. 63, "in his quae videt"). Also, *cont. Cels.* i. p. 583 (Greek, the editions prior to De la Rue); Lucifer's *De non conv. c. haer.* p. 782, Migne; Ambrosiaster (explaining thus: "inflantur motum pervidentes stellarum, quas angelos vocat." In the citation of the text editions differ). Pseudo-Augustine, *Quaest. ex N.T.* ii. 62, iii. App. p. 156.
With the negative μή:
MSS.: C K L P and all cursives except those above mentioned.
Versions: Old Latin fg Vulg. Goth. Syr. (both) Arm.
Fathers, etc.: Origen once (in the Latin transl. *In Rom.* ix. § 42, iv. p. 665). Also, *cont. Celsum*, as above (Greek as edited by De la Rue, who, however, says nothing about MSS., but remarks: "at Gelenius legit." ἃ μὴ ἑώρακεν, Tisch.); Ambrose. *In Ps.* 118, *Exp.* 20 (i. p. 1222), Pelagius, Chrysostom, Theodore Mops., Theodoret, John Dam.
With οὐ, ℵᶜ C Dˡˣ G.

It will be observed that no MS. older than the ninth century reads μή, and with the exception of C none older than the seventh has a negative in either form. It is open to question whether οὐ, inserted by way of correction in ℵ and D, was derived from MS. authority or was merely a conjecture.

The "deliberate preference" of Jerome and Augustine cannot rightly be reckoned as "evidence" in favour of μή. The words of the former are: "Quae nec ipse vidit qui vos superare desiderat, sive vidit (utrumque enim habetur in Graeco)." The words of Augustine are: "Quae non vidit inculcares, vel sicut quidam codices habent, quae vidit inculcares." Their evidence amounts simply to this, that some of the MSS. they consulted or were acquainted with had the negative and some had not. As to their judgment, that is a different thing. Jerome's "utrumque habetur in Graeco" expresses none. Even Augustine's do not contain any direct or decided expression of preference, nor does he say anything as to the respective value of the MSS. which he quotes.

The reading which omits the negative is preferred by Tisch. Treg. WH. (see *post*), Alford, Meyer, Soden, Lightfoot (but see *post*). Burgon thinks the Rec. Text "cannot seriously be suspected of error" (*Revision Revised*, p. 356).

Lightfoot concludes from a review of the evidence that the negative is a later insertion; but as the combination "invading what he has seen" is so hard and incongruous as to be hardly possible, he suspects a corruption of the text prior to all existing authorities; and in this Hort and Taylor agree with him. He conjectures αἰώρᾳ (or ἐώρᾳ) κενεμβατεύων, "raised aloft, treading on empty air," the existing text, αεωρακενεμβατευων, being "explained partly by an attempt to correct the form ἑώρᾳ into αἰώρᾳ, or conversely, and partly by the perplexity of transcribers when confronted with such unusual words." κενεμβατεύειν does not itself occur, but κενεμβατεῖν is not infrequent. It is used by Plutarch, Basil, and others in a figurative sense, *e.g.* Basil, i. p. 135, τὸν νοῦν . . . μυρία πλανηθέντα καὶ πολλὰ κενεμβατήσαντα; i. p. 596, σοῦ δὲ μὴ κενεμβατείτω ὁ νοῦς. The other word, αἰώρα, which is used in a literal sense, either of the instrument for suspending or of the position of suspension, as the floating of a boat, the balancing on a rope, the poising of a bird, etc., is used figuratively by Philo, *De Somn.* ii. 6 (i. p. 665), ὑποτυφούμενος ὑπ' αἰώρας φρενῶν καὶ κενοῦ φυσήματος; *Quod Deus Immut.* § 36 (i. p. 298), ὥσπερ ἐπ' αἰώρας τινὸς ψευδοῦς καὶ ἀβεβαίου δόξης φορεῖσθαι κατὰ κενοῦ βαίνοντα.

Dr. C. Taylor (*Journal of Philology*, 1876, xiii. 130), followed by Westcott and Hort, prefers ἀέρα κενεμβατεύων. There is an earlier conjecture which involves even less change, or none, in the text, viz. ἃ ἑώρα (or ἃ ἑώρακεν) κενεμβατεύων. ἑώρακεν is better than ἑώρα, and the emendation only supposes the common error of omission of a repeated syllable. Ingenious, however, as these conjectures are, it does not seem necessary to depart from the text of the best MSS. (Blass thinks κενεμβατεύων fairly certain, *Gram.* p. 67.)

εἰκῆ φυσιούμενος. εἰκῆ is by some comm. connected with the preceding clause (De W., Conybeare, *al.*) in the sense "rashly, uselessly." But εἰκῆ in St. Paul precedes the words it qualifies (Rom. xiii. 4; 1 Cor. xv. 2; Gal. iv. 11), except Gal. iii. 4, where there is a special reason for placing it after ἐπάθετε. Its usual meaning in St. Paul is "to no purpose, fruitlessly"; and so it is understood here by v. Soden; but it equally admits the other sense, "without reason," which it has in Matt. v. 22, and this is more suitable to φυσιούμενος. The false teachers were without reason puffed up with the idea of their superior knowledge. There

II. 19]   FALSE HUMILITY OF ANGEL WORSHIP   271

is a sharp irony in the contrast between ταπεινοφροσύνη and φυσιούμενος. τὸ δέ γε φυσιούμενος τῇ ταπεινοφροσύνῃ ἐνάντιον οὐκ ἔστι· τὴν μὲν γὰρ ἐσκήπτοντο, τοῦ δὲ τύφου τὸ πάθος ἀκριβῶς περιέκειτο, Theodoret.

ὑπὸ τοῦ νοὸς τῆς σαρκὸς αὐτοῦ. "By the mind of his flesh." The νοῦς as a natural faculty is in itself indifferent, and may be under the influence either of σάρξ or πνεῦμα; cf. Rom. i. 28, xii. 2 ; 1 Tim. vi. 5; Tit. i. 15, and Rom. vii. 25; 1 Cor. xiv. 14, 15. The expression here used, "mind of, or belonging to, the flesh" (possessive genitive), seems to continue the irony. The false teachers claimed a higher intelligence, perhaps a deeper spiritual insight; whereas the apostle declares that it was carnal, not spiritual. Compare Rev. ii. 24, "which know not the deep things of Satan, as they say," where "as they say" refers to "deep things," which are then bitterly characterised as "of Satan."

19. καὶ οὐ κρατῶν. "And not holding fast." For this sense of κρατεῖν with accus., compare Mark vii. 3, 4, 8, κρ. τὴν παράδοσιν: Acts ii. 24, οὐκ ἦν δυνατὸν κρατεῖσθαι αὐτὸν ὑπ' αὐτοῦ: iii. 11, κρατοῦντος δὲ αὐτοῦ τὸν Πέτρον καὶ Ἰωάννην: 2 Thess. ii. 15 ; Rev. ii. 1, 13, 14, 15, 25, iii. 11, vii. 1. Frequently, however, it means "to seize"; but that sense is inapplicable here.

τὴν κεφαλήν, ἐξ οὗ. The relative is masculine, because it is a person that is referred to as the Head; not because Χριστοῦ is implied; cf. ver. 15. Meyer, however, followed by Eadie, regards οὗ as neuter, referring to the Head, not personally, but in an abstract sense "from which source." To understand it as referring to Christ, Eadie thinks, would destroy the harmony of the figure. The objection does not apply to the explanation just given. It is to be noted that D* Syr-Harcl. Arm. add Χριστόν.

ἐξ is causal, "from whom as the source," and the relative clause expresses the perverseness of the οὐ κρατῶν, κ.τ.λ., as much as to say "whereas from this," etc.

διὰ τῶν ἁφῶν καὶ συνδέσμων. For the meaning of these words see note on Eph. iv. 16. σύνδεσμος means in general any of the connecting bands in the body, whether ligaments proper, or tendons, or muscles; but in its special sense is limited to the "ligaments," as appears from a passage in Galen quoted by Lightfoot. But in a passage like the present this technical sense is not to be pressed; the purpose of the figure is to express the complete dependence of the Church as a whole, and of all its members as parts of an organised body, on Christ directly, angels not intervening.

ἐπιχορηγούμενον καὶ συμβιβαζόμενον. Compare Eph. iv. 16, συναρμολογούμενον καὶ συμβιβαζόμενον. There, the main purpose was to insist on the vital cohesion and union of the parts with each other; here, on dependence on the Head. Here as there the present participles are to be noted; the process is a continuing one. For ἐπιχορ. cf. 2 Cor. ix. 10; Gal. iii. 5; 2 Pet. i. 5, 11. ἐπί indicates rather direction than intensity. ἐπιχορ. seems to be the function of the ἀφαί, συμβιβ. of the σύνδεσμοι. For the passive of ἐπιχορ., compare Polyb. iv. 77. 2, πολλαῖς ἀφορμαῖς ἐκ φύσεως κεχορηγημένος. Arist. *Pol.* iv. 1, σῶμα κάλλιστα πεφυκὸς καὶ κεχορηγημένον.

αὔξει τὴν αὔξησιν, cognate accusative; not a periphrasis, nor added "to give force to the meaning of the verb," but because it was desired to define the nature of the αὔξησις as τοῦ Θεοῦ, a growth having its root in God, belonging to God; cf. 1 Cor. iii. 6, ὁ Θεὸς ηὔξανεν. In Eph. iv. 16 also "growth" is the result aimed at; but there, in accordance with the difference in the points of view just referred to, it is τὸ σῶμα itself which τὴν αὔξησιν τοῦ σώματος ποιεῖται εἰς οἰκοδομὴν ἑαυτοῦ ἐν ἀγάπῃ. Lightfoot remarks that the discoveries of modern physiology have invested the apostle's language with far greater distinctness and force than it can have worn to his own contemporaries. "The volition communicated from the brain to the limbs, the sensations of the extremities telegraphed back to the brain, the absolute mutual sympathy between the head and the members, the instantaneous paralysis ensuing on the interruption of continuity,—all these add to the completeness and life of the image." He quotes several very interesting passages from Hippocrates, Galen, and others as illustrating ancient speculation on the subject, and he reminds us that one of the apostle's most intimate companions at this time was "the beloved physician" (iv. 14). It may be remarked, however, that the apostle is speaking of supply and binding together rather than of volition and sensation (unless we adopt Meyer's view of ἀφαί (see on Eph.)). Theophylact also remarks: ἀπὸ τῆς κεφαλῆς πᾶσα αἴσθησις καὶ πᾶσα κίνησις.

20. εἰ ἀπεθάνετε σὺν Χριστῷ. "If ye died with Christ" (not "if ye be dead," as AV.). They had died with Christ in baptism, *vv*. 11, 12, and had risen again with Him. Comp. Jn. vi. 49, 58.

ἀπὸ τῶν στοιχείων τοῦ κόσμου. ἀποθνήσκειν ἀπό occurs here only in the N.T. The dative is used Rom. vi. 2; Gal. ii. 19. Here the preposition is more suitable, inasmuch as what is referred to is liberation from a dominating power.

τί ὡς ζῶντες ἐν κόσμῳ, not merely as being in the world, but living your life in the world. Their true "life was hid with Christ in God," iii. 3. To live in the world would be εἶναι ἐν τῇ σαρκί.

δογματίζεσθε. Probably best taken with RV. as middle. "Why do ye subject yourselves (or allow yourselves to be subjected) to ordinances?" The middle, indeed, implies some blame to the readers. But they were not compelled by force, so that even if the verb be understood as passive, it is implied that they submitted to the yoke.

The verb δογματίζειν occurs frequently in Sept. and Apocr., meaning "to issue a decree." Elsewhere it is used of the precepts of philosophers. In the active it takes the indirect object in the dative, 2 Macc. x. 8, which therefore may become the subject of the passive.

οὖν of the Rec. Text has little support, of uncials only ℵ* and ℵᶜ.
τῷ before Χριστῷ scarcely any.

21. "μὴ ἅψῃ μηδὲ γεύσῃ μηδὲ θίγῃς." Examples of the δόγματα, "Handle not, neither taste, nor touch." ἅπτεσθαι is stronger than θιγγάνειν, suggesting rather "taking hold of" than merely "touching." Thus Themist. *Paraphr. Arist.* 94, ἡ τῶν ζώων ἀφὴ κρίσις ἐστὶ καὶ ἀντίληψις τοῦ θιγγάνοντος. Compare Xen. *Cyrop.* i. 3. 5, ὅτι σε, φάναι, ὁρῶ, ὅταν μὲν τοῦ ἄρτου ἅψῃ, εἰς οὐδὲν τὴν χεῖρα ἀποψώμενον, ὅταν δὲ τούτων τινὸς θίγῃς εὐθὺς ἀποκαθαίρει τὴν χεῖρα εἰς τὰ χειρόμακτρα. In the N.T. comp. Matt. viii. 3, ἥψατο αὐτοῦ ὁ Ἰησοῦς: *ib.* 15, τῆς χειρὸς αὐτῆς: John xx. 17, μή μου ἅπτου (often in the Gospel): 1 Cor. vii. 1, γυναικὸς μὴ ἅπτεσθαι: 2 Cor. vi. 17, ἀκαθάρτου μὴ ἅπτεσθε. θιγγάνειν occurs in N.T. only here and Heb. xi. 28, xii. 20 (a quotation). Hence there is a climax of prohibitions, reversed in the AV., following perhaps (through Tyndale) the Latin, which has "tangere" for ἅπτεσθαι, and "contrectare" for θιγεῖν. Coverdale renders well (except as to the order), "as when they say, touch not this, taste not that, handle not that." There were such prohibitions in the Mosaic law, and these were, doubtless, not only re-enacted, but exaggerated by the Colossian false teachers, as they had been by the Jewish. The form of the Rabbinical precepts was just that here given. The Essenes also abstained from the use of wine, oil, and animal food, and would not touch food prepared by defiled hands.

Some commentators have suggested a special object for each of the three verbs; for example, for ἅψῃ (γυναικός), which others have supplied to θίγῃς. This form of asceticism, which also was practised by the Essenes, is referred to in 1 Tim. iv. 3, κωλυόντων γαμεῖν; but it is not suggested by anything in the present context, and would hardly be referred to so obscurely. Other suggestions have been offered which do not deserve mention, since it is clear that St. Paul is only citing typical forms of prohibition. For the same reason we must not suppose the prohibitions limited to food.

It is a singular illustration of the asceticism of a later date, that some Latin commentators (Ambrose, Hilary, Pelagius) regarded these prohibitions as the apostle's own. In the words of Augustine, who argues against this view: "tanquam praeceptum putatur apostoli, nescio quid tangere, gustare, attaminare, prohibentis" (*Epist.* cxix., ii. p. 412). Jerome gives the correct interpretation, which he illustrates from the Talmud, i. 84.

22. (ἅ ἐστι πάντα εἰς φθορὰν τῇ ἀποχρήσει.) The clause is parenthetical. "Which things (the objects which it is forbidden to touch) are all (destined) for corruption in their consumption." For εἶναι εἰς compare Acts viii. 20, εἴη εἰς ἀπώλειαν: 2 Pet. ii. 12, γεγεννημένα ... εἰς ἅλωσιν καὶ φθοράν. φθορά has its proper sense of decomposition, referring to the physical dissolution of such things in their natural use; ἀπόχρησις meaning "using up," "consumption." The thought is that these things which are merely material, as is shown by their dissolution in the ordinary course of nature, have in themselves no moral or spiritual effect. The argument is strikingly similar to that in Matt. xv. 17, εἰς ἀφεδρῶνα ἐκβάλλεται: so much so, indeed, that we might suppose that the apostle had this discourse in his mind. Compare also 1 Cor. vi. 12, where the same consideration is differently applied; and *ib*. viii. 8, where the principle is expressed, "Meat will not commend us to God; neither, if we eat not, are we the worse; nor if we eat, are we the better." This is the view taken by the Greek commentators as well as by most moderns. Theodoret says: οὐ σκοπεῖτε ὡς μόνιμον τούτων οὐδέν· εἰς κόπρον γὰρ ἅπαντα μεταβάλλεται: and Oecumenius: φθορᾷ γάρ, φησίν, ὑπόκειται ἐν τῷ ἀφεδρῶνι.

Other interpretations are as follow:—

First, the antecedent of ἅ is taken to be the precepts referred to: "which δόγματα all by their use tend to (everlasting) destruction." So Ambrose, Augustine, Corn. a Lapide, *al*. For this sense of φθορά, see Gal. vi. 8. But ἀπόχρησις never means simply "use," but "using up," "consumption"; nor, indeed, would the simple χρῆσις be suitable in the sense of "observance," τήρησις. Moreover, the addition τῇ ἀποχρήσει would, on this view, be quite superfluous.

Secondly, it is held by some that these words are those of the false teachers, repeated in irony by St. Paul: "omnia haec (vetita) usu suo perniciem afferunt." Or, again—

Thirdly, the words, similarly interpreted, are connected with the following: κατὰ τὰ ἐντάλματα, κ.τ.λ. "Which things tend to destruction"; "scil. si ex doctorum Judaicorum praeceptis et doctrinis hac de re judicium feratur." So Kypke, De Wette, and others.

Against both these interpretations the objection from the meaning of ἀπόχρησις holds good, for it was not the "using up" of these things, but their simple use, that these teachers condemned.

κατὰ τὰ ἐντάλματα καὶ διδασκαλίας τῶν ἀνθρώπων. To be connected with *vv*. 20, 21. The article covers both nouns, which belong to the same category, and is generic. These δόγματα were of human invention, not founded on the Divine commands and

II. 23] FALSE WISDOM OF THE ASCETIC PRECEPTS 275

teaching. διδασκαλίας is a term of wider application than ἐντάλματα, "precepts and in general teachings." The expression is taken from Isa. xxix. 13, μάτην δὲ σέβονταί με, διδάσκοντες ἐντάλματα ἀνθρώπων καὶ διδασκαλίας. Compare Matt. xv. 9; Mark vii. 7.

23. ἅτινά ἐστιν λόγον μὲν ἔχοντα σοφίας. ἅτινα = "which are such things as," or "which kind of things." The position of ἐστιν seems to forbid our separating it from ἔχοντα, as Lightfoot and others do, joining it with οὐκ ἐν τιμῇ. Bengel connects it with πρὸς πλησμονήν, κ.τ.λ.

ἐστιν ἔχοντα is not quite the same as ἔχει; the former marks that the character of the precepts is such that a λόγος σοφίας belongs to them. Dem. 31. 11, οὐδὲ λόγον τὸ πρᾶγμ᾽ ἔχον ἐστί.

λόγον σοφίας = "the repute of wisdom." For this sense of λόγον ἔχειν, compare Plato, *Epinomis*, p. 987 B, ὁ μὲν γὰρ ἑωσφόρος ἕσπερός τε ὢν αὐτὸς Ἀφροδίτης εἶναι σχεδὸν ἔχει λόγον: Herod. v. 66, Κλεισθένης . . . ὥσπερ δὴ λόγον ἔχει τὴν πυθίην ἀναπεῖσαι.

This repute is explained by the professed basing of these precepts on φιλοσοφία, ver. 8. The addition of μέν suggests at once that this repute was not well founded. The contrasted character which we expect to be introduced with δέ appears to be replaced by the negative characteristic οὐκ ἐν τιμῇ, κ.τ.λ. which, of course, implies the absence of true wisdom, but is not opposed to λόγον σοφίας, but to ἐν ἐθελοθρ. κ.τ.λ. This use of μέν without the δέ clause following is frequent. See Jelf, § 766; Winer, § 63. 2. e.

ἐν ἐθελοθρησκείᾳ. ἐν indicating on what this repute for wisdom rests. The substantive ἐθελοθρησκεία is not found elsewhere (except in eccles. writers), but the verb ἐθελοθρησκεῖν is explained by Suidas, ἰδίῳ θελήματι σέβειν τὸ δοκοῦν. Epiphanius explains the name of the Pharisees: διὰ τὸ ἀφωρισμένους εἶναι αὐτοὺς ἀπὸ τῶν ἄλλων διὰ τὴν ἐθελοπερισσοθρησκείαν παρ᾽ αὐτοῖς νενομισμένην (*Haer*. i. 16). Similar compounds, however, are frequent in Greek, as ἐθελοδουλεία (Plato *Conv.* 184 C; *Rep.* 562 D); ἐθελοπρόξενος, Thuc. iii. 70. 2, where the Schol. explains: ἀφ᾽ ἑαυτοῦ γειόμενος καὶ μὴ κελευσθείς, κ.τ.λ. The meaning of ἐθελοθρ. is therefore clear; it is "self-imposed worship."

καὶ ταπεινοφροσύνῃ, viz. what the false teachers called so; see ver. 18. Lightfoot supposes the force of ἐθελο. to be carried on; but this seems unnecessary.

καὶ ἀφειδίᾳ σώματος. "And unsparing treatment of the body." The substantive ἀφειδία occurs in the definition of ἐλευθερία in [Plato] *Def.* 412 D, ἀφειδία ἐν χρήσει καὶ ἐν κτήσει οὐσίας. The verb ἀφειδεῖν βίου occurs in Thuc. ii. 43; ἀφ. σωμάτων in Lys. *Or. Fun.* 25; cf. ἀφειδῶς ἐχρῶντο τοῖς ἰδίοις σώμασιν εἰς τὴν κοινὴν σωτηρίαν, Diod. Sic. xiii. 60. A frequent Latin rendering here was "vexatio," but Vulg. has "ad non parcendum." Augustine mentions both (*Ep.* 149).

After ταπεινοφροσύνῃ, τοῦ νοός is added in G d e f g Vulg. Syr-Harcl., Hil. al. καί before ἀφειδίᾳ is omitted by B m Origen (Latin transl. iv. 665), Hil. al. Lachmann and Lightfoot bracket it, the latter saying it should probably be omitted, ἀφειδίᾳ being then taken as an instrumental dative.

ἀφειδία is the spelling in אB*CDGL and most mss.

οὐκ ἐν τιμῇ τινὶ πρὸς πλησμονὴν σαρκός. These words are among the most difficult in the Epistle. The Greek commentators understand ἐν τιμῇ τινι of the honour to be paid to the body (suggested by the preceding ἀφειδίᾳ σώματος), and πλησμ. τῆς σ. of the satisfaction of bodily appetites.

This view has been adopted by many modern expositors, including Corn. a Lapide, Calvin, De Wette, and Scholefield. Estius expresses it thus: "Sentit apostolus sapientiam illam aut praecepta talia esse, per quae corpori debitus honor, pertinens ad expletionem, i. e. justam refectionem carnis, subtrahatur." It is a decisive objection to this interpretation that it assigns an impossible sense to πλησμονή, which is never used in the sense of moderate satisfaction, but always in that of "repletion" or "excessive indulgence." It is expressly so defined by Galen, *Op.* xv. p. 113 (quoted by Lightfoot), who says that not only physicians but the other Greeks apply the word μᾶλλόν πως . . . ταῖς ὑπερβολαῖς τῆς συμμέτρου ποσότητος. Here, where it would stand in contrast to the asceticism of the false teachers, it would be particularly inappropriate. Moreover, this view supposes σάρξ to be used in an indifferent sense as equivalent to σῶμα, and that in a context in which it has just occurred with an ethical meaning. The change from σώματος to σαρκός can be explained only by the latter having an ethical meaning here as in ver. 18.

Lightfoot (followed by RV. and Moule) adopts and ably defends the interpretation given by Conybeare (*Life and Epistles of St. Paul*), and before him by Sumner, viz. "yet not really of any value to remedy indulgence of the flesh," or more literally as RV. "*but are* not of any value against the indulgence of the flesh." St. Paul "allows that this πλησμονή is the great evil to be checked, . . . but he will not admit that the remedies prescribed have any substantial and lasting efficacy."

But this interpretation is open to serious objection from the linguistic point of view. First, as to the meaning assigned to πρός. It is, no doubt, often convenient to translate it "against"; but the idea of hostility or opposition is not in the preposition itself, which only means "with a view to," "looking to," etc., but in the words with which it is joined, as in Acts vi. 1, xxiv. 19; Eph. vi. 11.

Lightfoot shows also that it is frequently used by Aristotle, and especially by Galen, after words denoting utility, etc., to introduce the object, to check or prevent which the thing is to be employed. Thus Aristotle, *Hist. An.* iii. 21, συμφέρει πρὸς τὰς διαρροίας: *De*

Respir. 8, βοηθεῖ πρὸς ταύτην τὴν φθορμίν: Galen, *De Compos. Medic., Opp.* xii. p. 420, τοῦ δόντος αὐτὰ πρὸς ἀλωπεκίας φαλακρώσεις: p. 476, βραχυτάτην ἔχοντι δύναμιν ὡς πρὸς τὸ προκείμενον σύμπτωμα: and so very frequently. This use is very parallel (as Lightfoot indeed observes) to that of the English "for." Compare "good for a cold, for a hurt."

Here the sense of the preposition seems to be "with reference to," the object being a state or condition. On the other hand, if the object is a word signifying action or the production of an effect, "for" and πρός still signifying "with reference to" can only suggest "with a view to (producing)." For example, "good for cutting, good for the satisfaction of thirst."

Hence it seems to follow that unless πλησμονή be taken in the sense of "a state of repletion," which would be unsuitable, πρὸς πλησμονήν could only mean "so as to produce πλ."

Secondly, as to the sense of ἐν τιμῇ τινί, "of real value." Lightfoot, after Wetstein, quotes Lucian, *De Merc. Cond.* 17, τὰ καινὰ τῶν ὑποδημάτων ἐν τιμῇ τινί καὶ ἐπιμελείᾳ ἐστίν, and Hom. *Il.* ix. 319, ἐν δὲ ἰῇ τιμῇ, κ.τ.λ. But in these and similar passages τιμή means "estimation," not objectively "real value," and ἐν τιμῇ εἶναι is to be "in esteem," not to be "of value." Hence also the use of τιμή in the sense of "price." Sometimes the two ideas, "estimation" and "value," may approximate, as, indeed, our word "value" is sometimes incorrectly used as "valuation." But here the interpretation in question supposes τιμή to mean "real value," as opposed to mere "estimation." No instance has been produced which would justify such a supposition.

Thirdly, as to οὐ . . . τινί. This can hardly mean "not any" in the sense of "none," *i.e.* οὐδεμία. τις means "aliquis," not "ullus" (except in poetry). So here the Latin: "in honore aliquo."

The οὐκ contradicts the combination ἐν τιμῇ τινί, implying that on the other side this had been said or assumed. Thus the words would mean: "not for some (supposed) τιμή."

These last two objections are fatal to all interpretations which require οὐκ ἐν τιμῇ τινί to be understood as "not of any real value." Eadie regards λόγον to τινί as participial, and joins ἐστιν with πρὸς πλ., which is very harsh.

Alford connects πρὸς πλησμ. κ.τ.λ. with δογματίζεσθε, treating all between as parenthetical, and understanding οὐκ ἐν τιμῇ τινί as = "not in any real honour done to the body." "Why are ye suffering yourselves to be thus dogmatised, and all for the satisfaction of the flesh," for the following out of a διδασκαλία, the ground of which is in the φυσιοῦσθαι ὑπὸ τοῦ νοὸς τῆς σαρκός, ver. 18. Then follow most naturally the exhortations of the next chapter, *vv.* 2, 5. To the objection that the antithesis presented by οὐκ ἐν τιμῇ τινί is thus not to ἐθελοθρ. κ.τ.λ. but merely to ἀφειδίᾳ σώματος, he replies that "if the apostle wished to bring out a negative antithesis to these last words only, he could hardly do so without repeating the preposition, the sense of which is carried on to ἀφειδίᾳ." This interpretation yields a very appropriate sense, and gives τινί its proper sense. But it is difficult to admit so long a parenthesis separating the verb from its qualification. It is not analogous to other Pauline parentheses.

It remains that we take τιμή in the sense of "honour," and πρὸς πλ. τῆς σαρκός as = "for the full satisfaction of the flesh." The words suggest that the observation of such precepts was supposed to bring honour, and in contradicting this St. Paul with abrupt and sharp irony declares that the only honour would be such as satisfied the carnal nature, and that their boasted ἀφειδία σώματος was in very truth πλησμονὴ τῆς σαρκός: and this striking contrast explains the adoption of πλησμονή in this unusual sense.

This is the view adopted by Soden and (nearly) by Meyer. Ellicott and Barry take a similar view of the connexion, but understand τιμή as "value."

III. 1–4. *Ye must have a loftier aim ; ye have risen with Christ and your life is hid with Christ in God. Seek therefore those things that are above, where He is, seated at God's right hand.*

1. εἰ οὖν συνηγέρθητε τῷ Χριστῷ. Not "if ye be risen," AV., but "if ye were raised," viz. at the definite point of time when they became Christians, and were in baptism symbolically buried and raised again with Him, ch. ii. 12. The death as a death from τὰ στοιχεῖα τοῦ κόσμου is mentioned in ii. 20. εἰ does not express a doubt, but, as in ii. 20, the ground of an inference.

τὰ ἄνω ζητεῖτε, κ.τ.λ. There is no longer any direct reference to the precepts of the false teachers (as if τὰ ἐπὶ τῆς γῆς, ver. 2, were τὰ περὶ βρωμάτων καὶ ἡμερῶν, Theoph.). These have been cast aside as concerning only those living in the world, and the apostle rises into a higher region. Your thoughts should be on things above, on spiritual things, and the precepts you have to follow concern moral conduct. Compare "treasure in heaven," Matt. vi 20 ; τὸ βραβεῖον τῆς ἄνω κλήσεως, Phil. iii. 14.

οὗ ὁ Χριστός ἐστιν, κ.τ.λ. ἐστιν is not the copula: "where Christ is, seated," etc. "Par enim illuc tendere studia curasque membrorum, ubi jam versator caput," Erasm.

2. τὰ ἄνω φρονεῖτε. "Set your mind on the things above," RV., an advance on ζητεῖτε. In the AV. "set your affection," etc. The word "affection" was doubtless intended to bear the sense of "affectus," "tendency or bias of the mind." The bishops' Bible had "affections." The Vulgate has "sapite," "savour," as Wyclif renders. We have the opposite state of mind in Phil. iii. 19, οἱ τὰ ἐπίγεια φρονοῦντες. Compare Rom. viii. 5.

3. ἀπεθάνετε γάρ. Not "ye are dead," as AV., but "ye died." Conybeare, indeed, urges that the associated κέκρυπται shows that the aorist is here used for the perfect; but this is erroneous. The aorist expresses what occurred at a particular moment in the past, while the perfect κέκρυπται expresses the resulting and now existing state. Nor does the nature of the verb θνήσκω preclude a rigorous translation, as even Ellicott suggests. True, in ordinary narrative, ἀπέθανε, "died," implies, though it does not express, "is dead"; but not so when there is reference to a possible afterlife. Accordingly, Plato in the *Phaedo* never confounds θνήσκειν or ἀποθανεῖν with τεθνάναι. For example, p. 72 C, εἰ ἀποθνήσκοι μὲν πάντα, ὅσα τοῦ ζῆν μεταλάβοι, ἐπειδὴ δὲ ἀποθάνοι, μένοι ἐν τούτῳ τῷ σχήματι τὰ τεθνεῶτα καὶ μὴ πάλιν ἀναβιώσκοιτο ἆρ᾽ οὐ πολλὴ ἀνάγκη τελευτῶντα πάντα τεθνάναι καὶ μηδὲν ζῆν; τὸ τεθνάναι having been defined in 71 C as the opposite of τὸ ζῆν, while ἀποθνήσκειν was the opposite of ἀναβιώσκεσθαι, *ib.* E.

So Homer, *Il.* ψ. 365, uses τέθναθι with critical accuracy, not "die," but "lie dead."

Here "are dead" would contradict συνηγέρθητε. They died, indeed, but at the same time rose again, and that to a life spiritual and heavenly. They were, indeed, νεκροὶ τῇ ἁμαρτίᾳ, but ζῶντες τῷ Θεῷ, Rom. vi. 11.

ἡ ζωὴ ὑμῶν, your true life, not merely your resurrection life. They are seated ἐν τοῖς ἐπουρανίοις, Eph. ii. 4–6.

κέκρυπται. "Neque Christum neque Christianos novit mundus; ac ne Christiani quidem plane seipsos," Bengel. Compare Rom. ii. 29, ὁ ἐν τῷ κρυπτῷ Ἰουδαῖος.

4. ὅταν ὁ Χριστὸς φανερωθῇ, ἡ ζωὴ ἡμῶν. "When Christ shall be manifested, who is our life," not "shall be manifested in the character of our life," as Bengel and Eadie. Compare ὁ ἔχων τὸν υἱὸν ἔχει ζωήν, 1 John v. 12. He is Himself the essence of the life; cf. Gal. ii. 20; Phil. i. 21. The absence of δέ or καί makes the expression more striking and vivid. Bengel observes on this: "Sermo absolutus lectorem totum . . . repentina luce percellit." For the transition to the first person cf. ii. 13.

φανεροῦσθαι is used here with propriety instead of ἀποκαλύπτεσθαι, which does not so distinctly imply actual present existence.

τότε καὶ ὑμεῖς σὺν αὐτῷ φανερωθήσεσθε ἐν δόξῃ. Compare 1 John iii. 2, οἴδαμεν ὅτι ἐὰν φανερωθῇ ὅμοιοι αὐτῷ ἐσόμεθα, and Rom. viii. 19, τὴν ἀποκάλυψιν τῶν υἱῶν τοῦ Θεοῦ ἀπεκδέχεται: and on ἐν δόξῃ, Rom. viii. 17, ἵνα καὶ συνδοξασθῶμεν, and 18, τὴν μέλλουσαν δόξαν ἀποκαλυφθῆναι εἰς ἡμᾶς.

For the reading; ἡμῶν is read in B D^bc K L most mss., Syr. (both), Boh., Origen.

ὑμῶν in ℵ C D* G P 17 47, Vulg. Goth. Arm. Eth.

ὑμῶν was very likely to be substituted for ἡμῶν on account of the preceeding ὑμῶν and the following ὑμεῖς. Tischendorf and Tregelles prefer ὑμῶν; WH. and Lightfoot ἡμῶν; and so Weiss.

5–11. *Sins to be destroyed, as well the more subtle sins of temper as the grosser ones of appetite.*

5. Νεκρώσατε οὖν. "Make dead, therefore." As ye died, and your true life is hidden, carry out this death to the world, and kill whatever is carnal in you.

τὰ μέλη τὰ ἐπὶ τῆς γῆς. Meyer understands by μέλη the literal members, hand, foot, eye, etc. (Matt. v. 29), of course, taking the verb in an ethical sense. But this would be too strong a figure, and is not sufficiently supported by the passage in St. Matt., where the precept is not, as here, unqualified and absolute, and the verbs, moreover, are used in as literal a sense as the substantives. The whole precept there is symbolical, but the words have their natural sense. Besides, this interpretation of μέλη makes the connexion with the following more difficult. It is more natural to explain the word by the idea of the "old man," "In the σῶμα τῆς σαρκός." And this is suggested by the added qualification τὰ ἐπὶ τῆς γῆς. The members spoken of are those which belong to the body as the instrument of the carnal mind.

With the whole precept compare θανατοῦτε: Rom. viii. 13, εἰ δὲ πνεύματι τὰς πράξεις τοῦ σώματος θανατοῦτε ζήσετε: and Gal. v. 24, οἱ τοῦ Χριστοῦ τὴν σάρκα ἐσταύρωσαν σὺν τοῖς παθήμασι καὶ ταῖς ἐπιθυμίαις.

πορνείαν, κ.τ.λ. Usually taken in apposition with μέλη, either directly, as if πορνεία, etc., were themselves called μέλη, "membra quibus vetus homo, i. e. ratio ac voluntas hominis depravata perinde utitur ac corpus membris," Beza; "naturam nostram quasi massam ex diversis vitiis conflatam imaginatur," Calvin; or indirectly, *i.e.* "when I say νεκρώσατε τὰ μέλη, I mean νεκρώσατε πορνείαν, κ.τ.λ., of which τὰ μέλη are instruments." On either view the apposition of the instruments and the activities is extremely harsh. Severianus (followed by many moderns) regards sin as the body of which the special sins enumerated are the members: σῶμα καλεῖ τὴν ἁμαρτίαν, ἧς καὶ τὰ μέλη καταριθμεῖ; but this only evades the difficulty. Alford regards the construction as an instance of that form of the double accusative where the first denotes the whole, the second a part of it, as in ποῖόν σε ἔπος φύγεν ἕρκος ὀδόντων,—an explanation which does not touch the difficulty. Braune thinks the body in question is the body of the Church.

Lightfoot proposes to meet the difficulty by placing a colon after γῆς. Then πορνείαν, κ.τ.λ., will be viewed as prospective accusatives, which should be governed directly by some such word as ἀπόθεσθε: but several dependent clauses interpose, and the last of these suggests incidentally a contrast between the past and the present, the thought of which predominating in the apostle's mind leads to a recasting of the sentence, νυνὶ δὲ ἀπόθεσθε καὶ ὑμεῖς τὰ πάντα. Lightfoot illustrates this dislocation of the construction occasioned by the contrast of ποτέ and νῦν by reference to i. 22, νυνὶ δὲ ἀποκατηλλάγητε (or ἀποκατήλλαξεν): and 26, νῦν δὲ ἐφανερώθη: and to Eph. ii. 1–5, καὶ ὑμᾶς ... ἐν αἷς ποτέ ... ἐν οἷς καί ... ποτε ... ὁ δὲ Θεός ... καὶ ὄντας ἡμᾶς ... συνεζωοποίησεν. This construction has been characterised as "extremely difficult"; but the difficulty is only of the same kind as that in the passages cited.

After ὑμῶν the Rec. Text adds ὑμῶν, with ℵ* A C³ D G H K L P most mss., Vulg. Goth. other versions, Chrys. al.
It is omitted by ℵ B C* 17 67² 71, Clem. al.

πάθος is used by classical writers of any passive emotion. Thus, Aristotle distinguishes these three ἐν τῇ ψυχῇ γινόμενα: πάθη, ἕξεις, δυνάμεις. πάθη he defines as οἷς ἕπεται ἡδονὴ ἢ λύπη, including ἐπιθυμία, ὀργή, etc. But it is specially used of a violent emotion or "passion."

In the other two places in which the word occurs in St. Paul it is defined by a genitive (πάθη ἀτιμίας, Rom. i. 26; ἐν πάθει ἐπιθυμίας, 1 Thess. iv. 5). Here the enumeration appears to proceed from the more special to the more general, so that πάθος probably means not specially "lustfulness." Still less the πάθη ἀτιμίας of Rom. i. 26,—an interpretation which has no linguistic justification,—but generally "passion," as RV.

ἐπιθυμίαν κακήν. This includes all evil longings, and so is wider than πάθος. ἰδού, γενικῶς τὸ πᾶν εἶπε· πάντα γὰρ ἐπιθυμία κακή, βασκανία, ὀργή, λύπη, Chrys. ἐπιθυμία in the N.T. has a wide sense; cf. John viii. 44; hence the necessity for κακήν.

καὶ τὴν πλεονεξίαν, κ.τ.λ. See on Eph. iv. 19, v. 5.

ἥτις ἐστίν. "Seeing it is."

6. δι' ἅ. This is undoubtedly the correct reading, but a few authorities (C* D* G) read δι' ὅ.

ἔρχεται ἡ ὀργὴ τοῦ Θεοῦ. After Θεοῦ, Rec. adds: ἐπὶ τοὺς υἱοὺς τῆς ἀπειθείας, as in Eph. v. 6.

> The evidence for the addition is extremely strong, as they are contained in all manuscripts except B. In D, however, the words are written in a smaller character at the end of the line, an indication apparently that they were not present in its archetype. Of Versions the Sahidic omits them, and the Roman ed. of the Ethiopic. Clement 294 (mss.) and 531 quotes from νεκρώσατε to Θεοῦ: but it would be unsafe to infer that his copy did not contain the addition; he may well have stopped short of it as not necessary for his purpose.
> Ambrosiaster omits them in his text, but his comment appears to recognise them.
> With these exceptions the addition is supported by all MSS., Versions, and Fathers. Its genuineness would be certain were it not that the same words occur in the parallel passage Eph. v. 6. It is very credible that they were added from that place at a very early period. On the other hand, they

seem required to complete the sense; certainly without them the thought is not the same as in the parallel in Eph. In the one case the words are a general warning as to the consequence of these sins; in the other a lesson is drawn from the example of others. The καὶ ὑμεῖς, ver. 7, seems to assume a previous mention of the unbelieving Gentiles.

The evidence in favour of the omission being so slight, it may be considered equally probable that the omission was accidental. The words are omitted by Tischendorf, Tregelles, WH., Alford, Weiss, and bracketed by Lachm. They are retained by Ellicott, Meyer, RV. (om. marg.).

7. ἐν οἷς καὶ ὑμεῖς περιεπατήσατέ ποτε, ὅτε ἐζῆτε ἐν τούτοις. The reading τούτοις is certain, being that of ℵ A B C D* *al.* αὐτοῖς is read in D^c G K L, most mss., Chrys. Theodoret, *al.*

If the doubtful words in ver. 6 are omitted, οἷς and τούτοις are of necessity both neuter, and refer to the vices mentioned. If the words are retained, the pronouns may be both neuter, or the first masculine and the second neuter, or the first neuter, and the second masculine. To the last view, which is that of Huther and others, it may be objected, that ζῆν ἐν is never used in the N.T. of living amongst persons, while it is frequently used with things, ἐν ἁμαρτίᾳ, Rom. vi. 2; ἐν κόσμῳ, ii. 20; ἐν σαρκί, Phil. i. 22. So in classical writers, ἐν ἀρετῇ, ἐν φιλοσοφίᾳ, etc. Meyer, De Wette, Braune, and Ellicott take οἷς as masc., τούτοις neuter. In favour of this seems to be the partial parallel, Eph. ii. 2, 3, εἰ τοῖς υἱοῖς τῆς ἀπειθείας ἐν οἷς καὶ ἡμεῖς πάντες ἀνεστράφημέν ποτε, a parallel which Ellicott thinks leaves no room for doubt. Of course, περιπατεῖν ἐν would then be understood to denote not mere outward living amongst, but participation in a course of life. Alford and Lightfoot argue that, independently of the rejection of the doubtful words, it is better to take οἷς as neuter, since περιπατεῖν ἐν is most commonly used of things, not of persons, especially in this and the companion Epistle, iv. 5, Eph. ii. 2, 10, iv. 17, v. 2. In 2 Thess. iii. 11, indeed, we have τινας περιπατοῦντας ἐν ὑμῖν ἀτάκτως: but the addition of ἀτάκτως there makes the expression not quite parallel. So Eph. ii. 3 Lightfoot regards as not parallel on account of the addition ἐν ταῖς ἐπιθυμίαις τῆς σαρκὸς ἡμῶν. But this addition does not affect the connexion of ἐν οἷς ἀνεστρ. And Alford admits that, if the clause ἐπὶ τ. υἱ. τ. ἀπ. is retained, this parallel goes far to decide the matter.

ὅτε ἐζῆτε ἐν τούτοις, *i.e.* before ye died to the world; ἐζῆτε being in contrast with ἀπεθάνετε. The change of tense is to be observed, περιεπατήσατε, aorist, because denoting single acts, ἐζῆτε expressing the containing state. For the difference in sense, compare Gal. v. 25, εἰ ζῶμεν πνεύματι, πνεύματι καὶ στοιχῶμεν. "Vivere et ambulare inter se differunt, quemadmodum potentia et actus; vivere praecedit, ambulare sequitur," Calvin.

8. νυνὶ δέ, in contrast to the ποτε above. καὶ ὑμεῖς, "ye also," as well as other Christians. As in the former verse they were

compared with the heathen society from which they had separated, so here with the Christian society which they had joined. Holtzmann strangely supposes the καί to refer to the Christians addressed in Eph. ii. 22.

τὰ πάντα, "all of them," everything that belongs to the old man. The asyndeton is thus less harsh than if τὰ πάντα be understood to be only retrospective (as Meyer, *al.*).

ἀπόθεσθε, "put ye away."

ὀργήν, κ.τ.λ. See on Eph. iv. 31.

αἰσχρολογία occurs in the N.T. here only. The connexion here shows that it means "abusive" rather than "filthy" language. It denotes the form in which the injurious βλασφημία finds expression. Chrysostom takes it in the sense of "obscene talk" (which he calls ὄχημα πορνείας), and so many moderns; but the sins of uncleanness have been dealt within ver. 5, and the other substantives here regard want of charity. The word is used by Polybius, viii. 13. 8, in this sense of "abusive language," ἡ κατὰ τῶν φίλων αἰσχρολογία: cf. xxxi. 10. 4. The verb has a similar meaning in Plato, *Rep.* iii. p. 395 E, κακηγοροῦντάς τε καὶ κωμῳδοῦντας ἀλλήλους καὶ αἰσχρολογοῦντας. Compare αἰσχρὰ ἔπεα, Hom. *Il.* γ. 38.

ἐκ τοῦ στόματος ὑμῶν, not "proceeding from," but dependent on ἀπόθεσθε, and belonging to both βλασφ. and αἰσχρ.

9. μὴ ψεύδεσθε εἰς ἀλλήλους. "Do not lie towards one another." εἰς does not express hostility, but direction. In Hist. Sus. 55 we have ἐψεύσαι εἰς τὴν σεαυτοῦ ψυχήν: but this is clearly not parallel.

ἀπεκδυσάμενοι, κ.τ.λ. This may be understood either as "putting off," "exuentes," Vulg., so as to form part of the exhortation, or "seeing that ye have put off." The former view is adopted by Olshausen, De Wette, etc. Lightfoot also defends it, observing (1) that though both ideas are found in St. Paul, the imperative is the more usual; cf. Rom. xiii. 12; Eph. vi. 11, with ver. 14; 1 Thess. v. 8, νήφωμεν ἐνδυσάμενοι, κ.τ.λ.; (2) that in the parallel, Eph. iv. 24, the "putting on" is imperative; and (3) that the participles here are followed by an imperative, ver. 12. Grammatically, there is no difficulty in thus understanding the aorist participle as synchronous with the present imperative. The aorist would, in fact, express a thing done once for all, and would be better represented in Latin by an ablative absolute than by a present participle. Nevertheless, the other view (adopted by Theodoret, and amongst moderns by Meyer, Alford, Ellicott), according to which the participles contain the motive for the preceding exhortation (from ἀπόθεσθε), seems the more probable, first, because in what precedes there is nothing to correspond with ἐνδυσάμενοι, as the Christian graces are not referred to; secondly, because ver. 11 does not fit in so well with an exhortation as with an argument; and thirdly, because the imperative in ver. 12 is introduced by οὖν. On ἀπεκδυσάμενοι see ii. 11, 15.

τὸν παλαιὸν ἄνθρωπον. See Eph. iv. 22.

10. καὶ ἐνδυσάμενοι τὸν νέον. In the parallel, Eph. iv. 24, it is ἐνδύσασθαι τὸν καινὸν ἄνθρ. νέος, unlike καινός, only expresses newness in point of time, but the idea of καινότης is supplied by the participle.

As the result of ἐνδύσασθαι τὸν νέον ἄνθ. is that Christ is τὰ πάντα καὶ ἐν πᾶσιν, and as the apostle speaks elsewhere of Χριστὸν ἐνδύσασθαι, Gal. iii. 27, Rom. xiii. 14, some commentators infer that the νέος ἄνθρ. here is Christ; and hence, again, that ὁ παλαιὸς ἄνθρ. is Adam, whose image men bear, 1 Cor. xv. 49. Ignatius, *Eph.* 20, has the expression εἰς τὸν καινὸν ἄνθρωπον Ἰησοῦν Χριστόν. If this had been the thought in St. Paul's mind here, he would probably have expressed it more distinctly. It seems better, then, to rest satisfied with the interpretation of the "new man" as "the regenerate man formed after Christ." The ultimate meaning is the same.

ἀνακαινούμενον, present participle, because although "created" once for all (κτισθέντα, Eph. iv. 24), its growth and development are continually going on. Compare 2 Cor. iv. 16, ὁ ἔσω ἡμῶν [ἄνθρωπος] ἀνακαινοῦται ἡμέρᾳ καὶ ἡμέρᾳ, and the opposite, τὸν παλαιὸν ἄνθρ. τὸν φθειρόμενον, Eph. iv. 22. The ἀνα does not suggest the restoration of the original state, but the contrast to that which has lately existed.

ἀνακαινόω is not used by Greek authors, nor by the Sept., but ἀνακαινίζω. The substantive ἀνακαίνωσις (Rom. xii. 2; Tit. iii. 5) is also peculiar to the N.T.

εἰς ἐπίγνωσιν. "Unto thorough knowledge." Meyer connects this with the following words: "unto a knowledge which accords with the image of God," *i.e.* which is in accordance with the Divine knowledge. But the Divine knowledge would hardly be set forth in this general way as an ideal to be attained; we should expect some limitation to moral or spiritual knowledge. It is more natural to connect κατ' εἰκόνα with ἀνακαιν. and to supply the object of ἐπίγνωσις from the context, viz. the knowledge of God and the mystery of the gospel; cf. i. 9, ἵνα πληρωθῆτε τὴν ἐπίγνωσιν τοῦ θελήματος αὐτοῦ, and ii. 2, εἰς ἐπίγνωσιν τοῦ μυστηρίου, κ.τ.λ.

κατ' εἰκόνα, κ.τ.λ. To be connected with ἀνακαινούμενον as above. An allusion to Gen. i. 26, 28.

τοῦ κτίσαντος αὐτόν. ὁ κτίσας according to Chrysostom, *al.* is Christ; but ὁ κτίσας is always God, and so here especially, where the passage in Genesis is alluded to. αὐτόν is the new man, not τὸν ἄνθρωπον generally. Compare κτισθέντα in Eph. iv. 24, and καινὴ κτίσις, 2 Cor. v. 17. Soden, who interprets the "new man" of Christ, refers αὐτόν to τὸν ἀνακαινούμενον. As Christ is the εἰκών of God, 2 Cor. iv. 4, Col. i. 15, so Christians, when Christ is formed in them, become renewed after the image of God.

Olshausen presses the designation of Christ as the εἰκών of God, and accordingly interprets, "after the pattern of Him who is the Image of God." But this does not agree with the allusion to Genesis. It is true the Alexandrian school interpreted the expression in Genesis of the Logos, but only in a sense borrowed from the Platonic doctrine of ideas as τὸ ἀρχέτυπον παράδειγμα, ἰδέα τῶν ἰδεῶν ὁ Θεοῦ λόγος: and this conception is certainly not in the spirit of St. Paul. Besides, the absence of the definite article before εἰκόνα obliges us to take κατ' εἰκόνα in its natural sense as "after the likeness of." Those commentators who understand κατὰ Θεόν, Eph. iv. 24, as = "after the likeness of," of course understand the expression here as only a more precise definition.

11. ὅπου οὐκ ἔνι. Compare Gal. iii. 28. This ἔνι is not, as formerly used to be stated, a contraction of ἔνεστι, although it is often used in that sense; it is simply the longer form of the preposition ἐν, with ἐστι understood, as in πάρα, ἄνα. The fact that ἐν is used with it in 1 Cor. vi. 5 is not inconsistent with this, since the word came to be looked upon as equivalent to ἔνεστι. That passage, however, shows that we are not to press here the idea of "impossibility," οὐκ ἔνι ἐν ὑμῖν οὐδεὶς σοφός. The word here simply states the objective fact.

The distinctions enumerated as abolished are first those of birth, involving national privileges; secondly, of legal or ceremonial standing (which might be gained by adoption); thirdly, those of culture; and fourthly, of social caste.

Ἕλλην καὶ Ἰουδαῖος. In contrast with Ἰουδαῖος, Ἕλλην means simply "Gentile"; and, indeed, even to the present day the Jews sometimes speak of other nations as Greeks.

περιτομὴ καὶ ἀκροβυστία. Abstract for concrete. This clause and the former have special reference to the Judaising tendency of the heretical teachers.

βάρβαρος, properly one who did not speak Greek (probably with the idea of talking "gibberish." Strabo explains it as onomatopoetic.) Hence the Greeks applied the term to all other nations. Even the older Roman poets (as Plautus) used the term of themselves; but later writers excluded the Romans from the class "barbari," and even included them under the term Ἕλληνες (Dion. Hal. *Ant. Rom.* v. 8).

Lightfoot quotes a striking passage from Professor Max Müller: "Not till that word *barbarian* was struck out of the dictionary of mankind, and replaced by *brother*, not till the right of all nations of the world to be classed as members of one genus or kind was recognised, can we look even for the first beginnings of our science (of language). . . . This change was effected by Christianity"

(Lectures on the Science of Language, 1st Ser. p. 81. The whole passage is too long to cite).

Σκύθης. The natural antithesis to βάρβαρος would be Ἕλλην (cf. Rom. i. 14); but as that has already been used the apostle substitutes for an antithesis a climax, for the Scythians were regarded as "barbaris barbariores," Bengel. The earlier Greek writers, indeed, on the principle "omne ignotum pro magnifico," described them as εὔνομοι (Aesch. *Frag.* 189); but Josephus says they are βραχὺ τῶν θηρίων διαφέροντες (*contra Ap.* ii. 37). Cicero uses a climax similar to that before us, "quod nullus in barbaria, Quis hoc facit ulla in Scythia tyrannus?" (*In Pisonem*, viii.). The word Σκύθης was used of any rough person, like our "Goth." This clause has reference, perhaps, to the stress laid by the Gnostic teachers on their γνῶσις.

δοῦλος, ἐλεύθερος. There was a special reason for St. Paul's thoughts being directed to the relation of master and slave, in the incident of Onesimus' conversion and return to his master.

πάντα and τὰ πάντα are very frequently used by classical writers as predicates of persons. Wetstein on 1 Cor. xv. 28 quotes many examples. One or two may suffice here. Dem. *De Cor.* p. 240, πάντ' ἐκεῖνος ἦν αὐτοῖς : *cont. Ariston*, p. 660, πάντα ἦν Ἀλέξανδρος; Lucian, *De Morte Peregr.* 11, προφήτης καὶ ξυναγωγεύς, καὶ τὰ πάντα μόνος αὐτὸς ὤν.

12-17. *Virtues to be cultivated, kindness, love, forgiveness, in which God's forgiveness of us is to be the pattern; mutual teaching and admonition, and in everything thankfulness, everything being done in the name of Jesus Christ.*

12. ἐνδύσασθε οὖν, having put on the new man, put on also these virtues.

ὡς ἐκλεκτοὶ τοῦ Θεοῦ. Cf. Rom. viii. 33; Tit. i. 1. In St. Paul κλητοί and ἐκλεκτοί, κλῆσις and ἐκλογή (Rom. xi. 28, 29), are coextensive, as indeed they seem to be in other N.T. writers (cf. Rev. xvii. 14) except the Gospels, where κλητοί and ἐκλεκτοί are distinguished (Matt. xxiv. 22, 24, 31 *al.*). ὡς ἐκλεκτοί has a significant connexion with what precedes, since the ἐκλογή is presupposed in what is said in *vv.* 10, 11.

ἅγιοι καὶ ἠγαπημένοι are best taken as predicates of ἐκλέκτοι, which with and without τοῦ Θεοῦ is used in several places as a substantive.

<small>καί is om. by B 17 Sah., and Lightfoot brackets it, thinking that the sentence gains in force by the omission; cf. 1 Pet. ii. 6.</small>

σπλάγχνα οἰκτιρμοῦ. "A heart of compassion." σπλάγχνα, like "viscera," denoted especially the nobler inward parts, heart, liver, and lungs, and figuratively the seat of the emotion, as we use the word "heart."

The singular οἰκτιρμοῦ is supported by very preponderant authority.

χρηστότητα, cf. Eph. ii. 7.
ταπεινοφροσύνη. Eph. iv. 2, πραΰτητα μακροθυμίαν, *ibid*.
13. ἀνεχόμενοι ἀλλήλων, *ibid*.
καὶ χαριζόμενοι ἑαυτοῖς. For the variation from ἀλλήλων to ἑαυτοῖς, see Eph. iv. 32. The latter word marks more strikingly than ἀλλήλοις would the correspondence with ὁ κύριος ἐχαρίσατο ὑμῖν.

μομφή, not found elsewhere in the N.T. nor in Sept. or Apocr. In classical writers ἔχειν μομφήν is frequent. "Quarrel" of the AV. is an archaism.

καθὼς καὶ ὁ Κύριος ἐχαρίσατο ὑμῖν. To be connected with the following words, οὕτω καὶ ὑμεῖς (as RV.), supplying, therefore, not χαριζόμενοι, but χαρίζεσθε (ἑαυτοῖς). Assuming, as is probable, that ὁ Κύριος = ὁ Χριστός, this is the only place where Christ is directly said to forgive (see on ii. 13). In the parallel in Eph. iv. 32, the subject is ὁ Θεὸς ἐν Χριστῷ. Meyer remarks that the very frequent ἡ χάρις τοῦ κυρίου ἡμῶν corresponds with the present expression. It is perhaps pressing the technical sense of Κύριος too much to suppose, with Lightfoot, that it suggests the duty of fellow-servant to fellow-servant, recalling the lesson of the parable of the Unforgiving Servant, Matt. xviii. 27; compare below, iv. 1. It must be observed that the καθώς has reference only to the fact of forgiveness, not to the manner of its exhibition in the death of Christ (as Chrys. Theoph. *al*.).

The reading cannot be regarded as certain. For ὁ κύριος are A B D* G 213 d e f g Vulg. Pelag.
For ὁ Χριστός, אᵃᶜ C D^{bc} K L P almost all mss. Syr. (both), Sah. Boh. Eth. Arab. (Bedwell), Clem. Chrys. Euthal. (cod. Tisch.), Theodoret, *al*. א* has ὁ Θεός, while 17 Arm. have ὁ Θεὸς ἐν Χριστῷ. Augustine also has the latter reading in one place (*Ep*. 148), but in another ὁ Κύριος.
It is suggested, on the one hand, that Χριστός has been substituted (as in other places) as an interpretation of Κύριος, especially as it occurs in Eph. iv. 32 (but not in the same connexion); and, on the other side, it has been suggested that Κύριος originated in an attempt at conformation with the passage in Eph.
Lachmann, Treg. WH. Alford, Meyer, Lightfoot, RV. Weiss read Κύριος. Tisch. Ellicott read Χριστός, to which RV. and WH. give a place in the margin.

14. ἐπὶ πᾶσι δὲ τούτοις. "And over all these," the figure of clothing being retained, as the verb ἐνδύσασθε has still to be carried on.

ὅ ἐστιν. The pronoun is not without difficulty. The illustrations cited by Lightfoot from Ignatius are hardly parallel, *Rom*. 7, ἄρτον Θεοῦ θέλω, ὅ ἐστιν σὰρξ Χριστοῦ: *Magn*. 10, νέαν ζύμην ὅ ἐστιν Ἰησοῦς Χριστός. In these cases the words following ὅ ἐστιν are an explanation of the words preceding, and ὅ ἐστιν = "id est," or "by which is to be understood." So in Mark xii. 42, λεπτὰ δύο, ὅ ἐστι κοδράντης: xv. 42, παρασκευή, ὅ ἐστι προσάββατον. In none of these cases does ὅ ἐστιν, κ.τ.λ. predicate a property or character of the antecedent. In order that the present instance should be parallel, τ. ἀγάπην and σύνδ. τ. τελ. should change places. Eph. v. 5 is nearer, πλεονέκτης, ὅ ἐστιν εἰδωλολάτρης, and Ign. *Trall.* 7, ἀνακτήσασθε ἑαυτοὺς ἐν πίστει ὅ ἐστιν σὰρξ τοῦ Κυρίου: yet neither are these quite parallel. εἰδωλολάτρης is not, indeed, an explanation of the word πλεονέκτης, but it expresses his true character. Probably the form of expression is to be accounted for by the figure. σύνδεσμος, κ.τ.λ., explains the view taken of ἀγάπην when ἐπὶ πᾶσι τούτοις is applied to it. An alternative is to suppose the antecedent to be τὸ ἐνδύσασθαι τὴν ἀγάπην: and so Huther and Soden. But this certainly does not suit the sense so well.

σύνδεσμος τῆς τελειότητος. Love binds the virtues into a harmonious whole, not as if they could exist without it, for it might be called by a different figure—the root of all; but the figure of clothing here adopted required that its relation to the other virtues should be put in a different aspect. πάντα ἐκεῖνα, says Chrysostom, αὕτη συσφίγγει· ὅπερ ἂν εἴπῃς ἀγαθόν, ταύτης ἀπούσης οὐδέν ἐστιν, ἀλλὰ διαρρεῖ, to which Theoph. adds ὑπόκρισις ὄντα.

τῆς τελειότητος. As it is the σύνδεσμος here that makes all perfect, the genitive comes rather under the head of the possessive than of the objective. Lightfoot seems to take the latter view, explaining "the power which unites and holds together all those graces and virtues which together make up perfection." This not only involves a very questionable meaning of τελειότης, as if = τὰ τὴν τελειότητα ποιοῦντα, Chrys., but gives an inadequate representation of the function of ἀγάπη.

Wetstein quotes from Simplicius, in *Epict.* p. 208 A, a strikingly parallel expression of the Pythagoreans: καλῶς οἱ Πυθαγόρειοι περισσῶς τῶν ἄλλων ἀρετῶν τὴν φιλίαν ἐτίμων καὶ σύνδεσμον αὐτὴν πασῶν τῶν ἀρετῶν ἔλεγον.

Grotius, Erasmus, Estius and many others take the genitive to be one of quality, "the perfect bond," which is not only feeble, but leaves σύνδεσμος undefined. Bengel, De Wette, Olshausen, *al.* understand by σύνδεσμος the "totality," as in Herodian, iv. 12. 11, πάντα τὸν σ. τῶν ἐπιστολῶν, "the whole bundle o letters." But there is no instance of σύνδεσμος being used figuratively in this sense; nor does it agree with the context, in which ἀγάπη is represented as put on ἐπὶ πᾶσι, not to say that it would require the article. In Eph. iv. 3 the gen. after σύνδεσμος is one of apposition.

For τελειότητος D* G d e g and Ambrosiaster have ἑνότητος.

15. καὶ ἡ εἰρήνη τοῦ Χριστοῦ. The peace of Christ is the peace which He gives and has left to His Church, εἰρήνην τὴν ἐμὴν δίδωμι ὑμῖν, John xiv. 27. But it is Christ's peace in another sense, as the peace which belongs to His kingdom by virtue of His sovereignty; compare the expression, "the King's peace." The immediate reference here is not to the inward peace of the soul, but to peace one with another, as the context shows. But it cannot be limited to this, the moment the words are uttered or heard they suggest the other reference.

βραβευέτω, only here in N.T.; see on καταβραβευέτω, ii. 18. As there observed, βραβεύω had dropped, for the most part, the reference to a contest, and was used of deciding or governing in general. Josephus, *Ant.* iv. 3. 2, uses it as synonymous with διοικεῖν; Moses, in his prayer, says: πάντα σῇ προνοίᾳ διοικεῖται, καὶ μηδὲν αὐτομάτως, ἀλλὰ κατὰ βούλησιν βραβευόμενον τὴν σὴν εἰς τέλος ἔρχεται. Again, *ib.* βραβεύων ὁμονοίαν καὶ εἰρήνην. Philo, *Quis Rer. Div.* i. p. 494 A, οὐ θαυμαστὸν δὲ παρ' ἀληθείᾳ βραβευούσῃ.

The transition of meaning is exactly parallel to that of the Latin "arbitrium," which from meaning the sentence of an arbitrator comes to signify "will and pleasure." "Jovis nutu et arbitrio caelum terra mariaque reguntur," Cic. *pro Rosc. Amer.* c. 45. Obtinere arbitrium rei Romanae," Tac. *Ann.* vi. c. ult.

Hence there is no necessity to insist on the idea of a contest of opposing parties, and the attempt to introduce it by reference to a conflict of motives, etc., really forces on the text more than is suggested by it. Chrysostom carries this to an extreme, στάδιον ἔνδον ἐποίησεν ἐν τοῖς λογισμοῖς, καὶ ἀγῶνα καὶ ἄθλησιν καὶ βραβευτήν.

The sense then appears to be, "let the peace of Christ be the ruling principle in your hearts."

ἐν ταῖς καρδίαις ὑμῶν. In order that this principle may govern your actions and your words, it must first govern in your hearts.

Χριστοῦ is the reading of ℵ* A B C* D* G P 37 47, Vulg. Syr. (both), Boh. Sah. Arm. Eth.

Θεοῦ is in ℵc C² Dc K L 17, Goth. As ἡ εἰρήνη τοῦ Θεοῦ occurs in Phil. iv. 7, the substitution of Θεοῦ for Χριστοῦ is readily accounted for. The latter is clearly more suitable to the present context, since εἰρήνη τοῦ Θεοῦ could not well be understood of anything but our peace with God. In Phil. iv. 7, A has Χριστοῦ. Bengel and others who defend the reading Θεοῦ here, suppose Χριστοῦ to have come in from 13 or 16.

εἰς ἣν καὶ ἐκλήθητε. This is nearly equivalent to "for to that we were also called." Comp. 1 Cor. vii. 15, ἐν εἰρήνῃ κέκληκεν ἡμᾶς ὁ Θεός.

ἐν ἑνὶ σώματι. Not = εἰς ἓν σῶμα, but expressing the result of their calling; they are so called that they are in one body. It is on the fact that this is their present condition that the stress is placed. As there is one body, there should be one spirit; cf. Eph. iv. 3, 4, τηρεῖν τὴν ἑνότητα τοῦ πνεύματος ἐν τῷ συνδέσμῳ τῆς εἰρήνης, Ἓν σῶμα καὶ ἓν πνεῦμα, κ.τ.λ.

καὶ εὐχάριστοι γίνεσθε. "And become thankful." Thankfulness for this calling is the strongest motive for the preservation of the peace to which they were called. The mention of this leads on to what follows. γίνεσθε is used because the ideal is not yet reached. εὐχάριστος does not occur elsewhere in N.T. It is not uncommon in classical writers, both in the sense "thankful" and "pleasant" (so usually of things). It occurs once in Sept., and then in the latter sense, Prov. xi. 16, γυνὴ εὐχάριστος. Some commentators take it here in the latter sense (cf. Eph. iv. 32, χρηστοί). So Jerome, Beza, a Lapide, Olshausen, Reiche; "in mutuo vestro commercio *estote gratiosi, amabiles, comes* . . . qua virtute pax et concordia saepe servantur," Reiche. This sense is certainly not inappropriate; and in favour of it it may be observed that the duty of thankfulness is brought in as the final exhortation in ver. 17.

16. ὁ λόγος τοῦ Χριστοῦ. In 1 Thess. i. 8, iv. 15 St. Paul has ὁ λόγος τοῦ Κυρίου, but more usually ὁ λ. τοῦ Θεοῦ. The change here is probably owing to the apostle's purpose of exalting the position of Christ, which is characteristic of this Epistle. The gen. may be either objective, as in εὐαγγέλιον Χριστοῦ, or subjective (as most comm.), "the word delivered by Christ." It is generally understood as = the gospel, but Lightfoot interprets it as denoting "the presence of Christ in the heart as an inward monitor. Comp. 1 John ii. 14, ὁ λόγος τοῦ Θεοῦ ἐν ὑμῖν μένει, with *ib.* i. 10, ὁ λόγος αὐτοῦ οὐκ ἔστιν ἐν ὑμῖν: and so perhaps Acts xviii. 5, συνείχετο τῷ λόγῳ (the correct reading)." Probably the "teaching of Christ" generally is meant; and so apparently Chrysostom, τουτέστιν, ἡ διδασκαλία, τὰ δόγματα, ἡ παραίνεσις. See on Lk. viii. 11.

ἐν ὑμῖν. Not "among you," which would not agree with the idea of "indwelling." Yet it cannot well be understood of each individual, as if referring to the faith and knowledge of each. Since the context speaks of oral communication one with another, ἐν ὑμῖν then means, probably, "in you as a collective body." This is not the same as "among you."

πλουσίως. The fulness of this indwelling exhibits itself in the following words.

ἐν πάσῃ σοφίᾳ. Lightfoot joins these words with the foregoing, comparing for their position ch. i. 9 and Eph. i. 8, which, however, determine nothing. He thinks this connexion is favoured by the parallel in Eph. v. 18, 19; but this only decides that ψαλμοῖς, κ.τ.λ., are to be connected with the preceding words. On the other hand, it may be observed that ἐνοικείτω is already qualified by πλουσίως, which emphatically stands at the end. Ch. i. 28 is strongly in favour of the connexion with the following, νουθετοῦντες πάντα ἄνθρωπον καὶ διδάσκοντες πάντα ἄνθρωπον ἐν πάσῃ σοφίᾳ. Here the correspondence in meaning is surely of more weight than the position of the words, which precede in the one case as appropriately as they follow in the other.

On διδάσκοντες and νουθετοῦντες comp. i. 28; and on ψαλμοῖς, κ.τ.λ., Eph. v. 18. Here as there the reference does not appear to be exclusively or chiefly to public worship, for mutual instruction is what is prescribed.

καί both before and after ὕμνοις is omitted by ℵ A B C* D* F G, d e f g Vulg. (best mss.) Syr-Pesh. Goth. al.
It was much more likely to be added than omitted erroneously, and the omission is quite Pauline.

ἐν [τῇ] χάριτι.

τῇ is inserted in ℵᶜ B D G 67², Chrys. comm.
Omitted in ℵ A K L (to which we may perhaps add C, in which εν χαρι is written but expunged by dots above and below), Chrys. text.

The reading with the article is adopted by critical editors generally, but Reiche argues strongly in favour of the omission. If it is read there are two interpretations possible, for χάρις may mean either the Divine grace, or thanksgiving. The former meaning is adopted by Meyer, Alford, Ellicott, Lightfoot, etc. For ἡ χάρις = the grace of God, compare ch. iv. 18, ἡ χάρις μεθ' ὑμῶν: Acts xviii. 27, τοῖς πεπιστευκόσι διὰ τῆς χάριτος: 2 Cor. iv. 15; Gal. v. 4; Eph. iv. 7; Phil. i. 7, συγκοινωνούς μου τῆς χάριτος. It must, however, be admitted that none of these passages is parallel to the present. In all of them ἡ χάρις is spoken of as something conferred, and therefore can only be ἡ χ. τοῦ Θεοῦ. It is different here, where the readers are directed to do something ἐν τῇ χάριτι.

Hence the other interpretation, "with thankfulness," which is that of Anselm, De Wette, Bleek (omitting τῇ), Soden, seems preferable. For χάρις in this sense see 1 Cor. x. 30, εἰ δὲ ἐγὼ χάριτι μετέχω, where the apostle himself interprets χάριτι in the following clause: ὑπὲρ οὗ ἐγὼ εὐχαριστῶ. The article is sufficiently accounted for by the reference to the previous εὐχαριστοί. Meyer, on the supposition that χάρις is understood as "thanksgiving," would interpret the article as meaning "that which is due."

It is not a valid objection to this view of χάρις that the idea of thanksgiving is introduced in the next verse; on the contrary, the precept there is an extension of this one; what is here said of singing is there said of everything.

Theophylact's interpretation is different; he takes χάρις in the sense "venustas," "pleasingness," μετὰ χάριτος καὶ ἡδονῆς πνευματικῆς ὥσπερ γὰρ τὰ ἀνθρώπινα ᾄσματα χάριν ἔχειν δοκοῦσιν, εἰ μὴ πνευματικήν, οὕτω τὰ θεῖα, πνευματικήν; so also Bengel. Compare for this use of χάρις Ps. xlv. 3, ἐξεχύθη χάρις ἐν χείλεσί σου; Eccles. x. 12, λόγοι στόματος σοφοῦ χάρις; Luke iv. 22, ἐθαύμαζον ἐπὶ τοῖς λόγοις τῆς χάριτος; also ch. iv. 6, ὁ λόγος ὑμῶν πάντοτε ἐν χάριτι. Compare also Demosth. p. 51 (*Phil.* i. 38), ἡ τῶν λόγων χάρις, and so in classical writers frequently. Reiche, adopting this interpretation, remarks: "recte et perspicue ἐν χάριτι ᾄδοντες ii dicuntur, qui carmina sacra cantant et modulantur venuste, decore, suaviter, ita ut etiam cultioribus et pulchri sensu praeditis placeant." To the objection that the following words show that the apostle is speaking of silent singing in the heart, he replies by defending the reading ἐν τῇ καρδίᾳ and interpreting it as = "*ex animo, i.e.* non ore tantum sed etiam cum animi assensu," a questionable sense of ἐν τῇ καρδίᾳ ὑμῶν. See on Lk. iv. 22 and Rom. i. 5.

In conformity with the connexion assigned to ἐν πάσῃ σοφίᾳ, ἐν τῇ χάριτι is to be joined to what follows. Lightfoot naturally takes it with the preceding.

ᾄδοντες ἐν ταῖς καρδίαις ὑμῶν. These words may either specify another effect of the ἐνοικεῖν, κ.τ.λ. (Alford, *al.*), or they may denote the inward disposition which was to accompany the διδάσκοντες, κ.τ.λ. If τῇ χάριτι is understood as above, the latter view would be the more suitable (Soden). It is preferred apart from that by Lightfoot.

ἐν ταῖς καρδίαις is supported by preponderant authority, ℵ A B C D* G, d e f g Vulg. Goth. Syr. (both), Sah. Boh. Arm., Chrys.
ἐν τῇ καρδίᾳ is supported by D^c K L most mss., Eth., Clem. Ephr. Theodoret. Compare Eph. v. 19, where the singular appears to be the genuine reading. The singular here, as the plural there, is probably due to an attempt to harmonise Eph. and Col.
τῷ Θεῷ is the reading of ℵ A B C* D* G 17 47 67² *al.*, d f g Vulg. Sah. Syr. (both), Arm., Clem. *al.*
τῷ Κυρίῳ is that of C² D^c K L most mss., Goth. Boh., Ephr. Theodoret, *al.* (Chrys. varies). This, again, is harmonistic, the parallel in Eph. having τῷ Κυρίῳ without variation.

17. καὶ πᾶν ὅ τι ἐὰν ποιῆτε ἐν λόγῳ ἢ ἐν ἔργῳ. A nominative absolute. Comp. Matt. x. 32, πᾶς οὖν ὅστις ὁμολογήσει . . . ὁμολογήσω κἀγὼ ἐν αὐτῷ: Luke xii. 10. As πᾶν would become the object in the following clause, it is replaced by πάντα.

πάντα. We might supply to this ποιοῦντες, parallel to the other participles; but it is much better to supply ποιεῖτε, especially as εὐχαριστοῦντες is subordinate.

ἐν ὀνόματι Κυρίου Ἰησοῦ. Comp. Eph. v. 20. "In the name of" here means, not "calling on for aid," as Chrys. etc., nor "in honorem," as Jerome, but in the spirit which regards Christ as all and in all, the spirit which belongs to those who bear His name. "Ut perinde sit, ac si Christus faciat, ver. 11 [this is too strong] vel certe, ut Christo omnia pobetis. Qui potest dicere; *Hoc in tuo, Jesu Christe, nomine feci*, is certe actionem suam Christo probat," Bengel.

There is here another difference of reading.

Κυρίου Ἰησοῦ is the reading of B D⁰ K 17 37 most mss., f. Amiat. Tol. Goth. Syr-Pesh. Arm., Chrys.

Ἰησοῦ Χριστοῦ, A C D* G g.

Κυρίου Ἰησοῦ Χριτοῦ, ℵ, d e Vulg. (Clem.), Field, *al*. Syr. (Harcl.), Sah. Boh. Eth.

Before πατρί, καί is added in D G K L and nearly all mss., d e f g Vulg. Syr-Pesh. Arm., Chrys. (cf. Eph. v. 20). It is absent from ℵ A B C, Sah. Boh. Syr. (Harcl.), Eth. Goth.

18-IV. 1. *Special precepts for the several relations of life, the motive being in each, that what is done is done "in the Lord."*

18. αἱ γυναῖκες, κ.τ.λ. Comp. Eph. v. 22.

ἰδίοις, prefixed in Rec. Text to ἀνδράσιν, has but slight support, and has probably come from Eph. v. 22.

ὡς ἀνῆκεν, imperfect, as often in Greek writers with similar verbs. Comp. Eph. v. 4, ἃ οὐκ ἀνῆκεν: Acts xxii. 22, οὐ γὰρ καθῆκεν αὐτὸν ζῆν. It is not implied here that the duty has not hitherto been rightly performed, but only that the obligation existed previously.

The use of the past tense in the English "ought" is not quite parallel, since the present "owe" cannot be used in this sense.

ἐν Κυρίῳ is to be joined with ἀνῆκεν, not with ὑποτάσσεσθε: see ver. 20, εὐάρεστόν ἐστιν ἐν Κυρίῳ, "for those who are in the Lord."

19. οἱ ἄνδρες, κ.τ.λ. = Eph. v. 25.

μὴ πικραίνεσθε. "Become not embittered," or rather, as this would seem to imply a lasting temper, "show no bitterness." The word occurs frequently in classical writers. Plato has (*Legg.* 731 D), τὸν θυμὸν πραΰνειν κ. μὴ ἀκραχολοῦντα, γυναικείως πικραινόμενον, διατελεῖν: Pseudo-Dem. 1464, μηδενὶ μήτε πικραίνεσθαι μήτε μνησικακεῖν. The adjective πικρός is used by Euripides in a strikingly illustrative passage, *Helen.* 303, ὅταν πόσις πικρὸς ξυνῇ γυναικί ... θανεῖν κράτιστον. Plutarch observes that it shows weakness of mind when men πρὸς γύναια διαπικραίνονται. Philo uses πικραίνεσθαι of just anger. *De Vita Moysis*, ii. pp. 135, 20, and 132, 34. The word would seem, then, to correspond more nearly with the colloquial "cross" than with "bitter."

20. τὰ τέκνα, κ.τ.λ. See Eph. vi. 1. Disobedience to parents is mentioned as a vice of the heathen, Rom. i. 30, κατὰ πάντα. There would be no propriety in suggesting the possibility in a Christian family of a conflict between duty to parents and duty to God.

εὐάρεστον. There is no need to supply τῷ Θεῷ; the adjective is taken absolutely, like προσφιλῆ in Phil. iv. 8, and is sufficiently defined by ἐν Κυρίῳ. In Rom. xii. 2 εὐάρεστον seems also to be absolute, τὸ θέλημα τοῦ Θεοῦ τὸ ἀγαθὸν καὶ εὐάρ. καὶ τέλειον.

The Rec. Text has, instead of ἐν Κυρίῳ, τῷ Κυρίῳ, with many cursives, Boh. Eth., Clem. *al.*

ἐν Κυρίῳ is the reading of all the uncials, most cursives, and versions.

The Rec. arose from a desire to give a dative to εὐάρεστον.

21. μὴ ἐρεθίζετε. "Do not irritate." The verb means to "excite, provoke," not necessarily to anger, or in a bad sense; and in 2 Cor. ix. 2 it is used in a good sense.

There is another reading, παροργίζετε, very strongly supported, being read in ℵ A C D* G K L *al*. Euthal. (Tisch. cod.), Theodoret (cod.), Theoph.

ἐρεθίζετε is read in B D^le K, most mss., Syr. (both, but Harcl. marg. has the other reading), Clem. Chrys.

παροργίζετε occurs in the parallel Eph. vi. 4 (with no variety), and to this is obviously due its introduction here.

ἵνα μὴ ἀθυμῶσιν. "That they may not lose heart." "Fractus animus pestis juventutis," Bengel. A child frequently irritated by over-severity or injustice, to which, nevertheless, it must submit, acquires a spirit of sullen resignation, leading to despair.

22. οἱ δοῦλοι, κ.τ.λ. Comp. Eph. vi. 5 ff. Here it is observable that the duties of masters and slaves occupy nearly twice as much space as those of husbands and wives, parents and children, together. The circumstance is perhaps explained by the incident of Onesimus, a Colossian, who was now returning to his master, Philemon, in company with the bearer of the Epistle.

φοβούμενοι τὸν Κύριον, *i.e.* the one Lord and Master, contrasted with τοῖς κατὰ σάρκα Κυρίοις. Observe that these words are not preceded by ὡς, whereas ἀνθρωπάρεσκοι is. It is taken for granted that they fear the Lord.

ἐν ὀφθαλμοδουλείαις, the plural is read with ℵ C K L most mss., Clem. Theodoret, Oecum., Syr-Harcl.

A B D G, *al.*, Boh. have the singular. Chrysostom varies.

Κύριον is the reading of ℵ* A B C D* G L *al*., fg Amiat. Fuld. Syr. (both), Arm., Clem. Chrys. *al.*

Θεόν is read in ℵ^c D^c K most mss., d Goth. Boh., Theodoret. This reading spoils the contrast.

23. ὃ ἐὰν ποιῆτε. This is the correct reading, with ℵ* A B C (D* G) 17 *al.*, Old Lat. Vul. Goth. Boh. Arm. etc. (D* G have ἄν for ἐάν).

The Rec. Text has καὶ πᾶν ὅ τι ἐάν, with D^b K L most mss., Syr. (both), Theodoret, Chrys. (without καί). This reading obviously comes from ver. 17.

ἐκ ψυχῆς. Eph. vi. 6. μετὰ εὐνοίας. Μὴ μετὰ δουλικῆς ἀνάγκης, ἀλλὰ μετὰ ἐλευθερίας καὶ προαιρέσεως, Chrys.

ἐργάζεσθε. "Do the work." Not used as particularly appropriate to slaves, but because the things done are ἔργα.

ὡς τῷ Κυρίῳ, κ.τ.λ. Eph. vi. 7, 24, ἀπὸ Κυρίου. Lightfoot notes the absence of the article here, while it is studiously inserted in the context, *vv.* 22-24. In the parallel in Eph. the preposition is παρά. Some commentators and grammarians distinguish the two prepositions as expressing respectively the immediate (παρά) and

III. 24, 25] SPECIAL PRECEPTS 295

the ultimate source; but this distinction is untenable. See Lightfoot on Gal. i. 12.

24. τὴν ἀνταπόδοσιν. "The full recompense." The word is frequently used both in the Sept. and in classical writers, but not elsewhere in N.T.

τῆς κληρονομίας. Genitive of apposition, the reward which consists in the inheritance. There is a special point in the word, inasmuch as slaves could not be inheritors of an earthly possession. Comp. Rom. viii. 15–17; Gal. iv. 1–7.

τῷ Κυρίῳ Χριστῷ δουλεύετε. γάρ, which in the Rec. Text is inserted after τῷ, must be rejected.

<blockquote>
In favour of the insertion are D^{bc} K L most mss., Syr. (both), Arm. Goth. For the omission, ℵ A B C D* 17 al., Vulg. Copt. Euthal. (Tisch. cod.). It was clearly added to make the connexion easy. G d and Ambrosiaster have τοῦ κυρίου (ἡμῶν Ἰησοῦ) Χριστοῦ ᾧ δουλεύετε, but d and Ambr. omit the words in brackets.
</blockquote>

γάρ being omitted, the verb is best taken as imperative, "To the Master Christ do service." The combination Κύριος Χριστός is not to be taken in the technical sense as = the Lord Jesus Christ, a use to which there is no parallel. In Rom. xvi. 18, where we have τῷ Κυρίῳ ἡμῶν Χριστῷ, some MSS. omit ἡμῶν: but its genuineness is beyond question. In 1 Pet. iii. 15 Κύριον is predicate of τὸν Χριστόν. This suggests that we should take Κυρίῳ here as relative to δουλεύετε. The sentence is not so much a summary of what precedes as an introduction to the fresh point added in ver. 25; Lightfoot.

Lightfoot takes δουλεύετε as indicative, on the grounds, first, that the indicative is wanted to explain the previous ἀπὸ Κυρίου (but is it?); and, secondly, that the imperative would seem to require ὡς τῷ Κυρίῳ, as in Eph. vi. 7. On the other hand, however, he adds, see Rom. xii. 11, τῷ Κυρίῳ δουλεύοντες. If the interpretation above given is correct, ὡς is rightly absent, and in any case the indicative would be very abrupt and unconnected. Moreover, with this view the connexion of ver. 25 (γάρ) would be hardly intelligible. Lightfoot passes it over in silence.

25. ὁ γὰρ ἀδικῶν κομιεῖται ὃ ἠδίκησεν, καὶ οὐκ ἔστι προσωποληψία. The first clause is, of course, a general maxim, but the application here chiefly intended appears from the words οὐκ ἔστι προσωποληψία, which presuppose that the person punished is one higher in position. ὁ ἀδικῶν, also, is much more suitable to the master than the slave; and this view is further confirmed by the mention of τὸ δίκαιον in iv. 1. Hence ὁ ἀδικῶν in the present case is the master, and the words are designed to encourage the slave to regard himself as the servant of Christ, and as such not to be disheartened by unjust treatment, knowing that before the final tribunal there will be no respect of persons. So Theodoret, κἂν μὴ τύχητε ἀγαθῶν ἀνταποδόσεων παρὰ τοῦ δεσπότου, ἐστὶ δικαιοκριτής· ὃς οὐκ οἶδε δούλου καὶ δεσπότου διαφοράν, ἀλλὰ δικαίαν εἰσφέρει τὴν ψῆφον. But Chrys. Bengel, and others suppose the ἀδικῶν to be the slave. "Tenues saepe putant, sibi propter tenuitatem ipsorum esse parcendum. Id negatur," Bengel; cf. Lev. xix. 15. It must be observed, however, that some of those who adopt this view have had before them the reading ὁ δὲ ἀδικῶν (so Chrys.).

Erasmus, Lightfoot, and many others (following Jerome) suppose both masters and slaves to be referred to, as in Eph. vi. 8. On the other hand, ib. ver. 9, προσωποληψία οὐκ ἔστι παρ' αὐτῷ, is said with respect to the masters only.

κομιεῖται. "Shall be requited for"; cf. Eph. vi. 8, and for προσωποληψία, ib. 9.

ἠδίκησεν. The tense is past, from the point of view of the time referred to in κομιεῖται.

For the reading the authorities are:
For γάρ, ℵ A B C D* G 17 al., Old Lat. Vulg. Goth. Boh., Clem. al.
For δέ, D^c K L, most mss., Syr. (both), Chrys. Theodoret, al.

IV. 1. τὸ δίκαιον καὶ τὴν ἰσότητα. "Justice and fairness." ἰσότης differs from τὸ δίκαιον nearly as our "fair" from "just," denoting what cannot be brought under positive rules, but is in accordance with the judgment of a fair mind. Compare Philo, *De Creat. Princ.* ii. p. 401, ἰσότης μὲν οὖν τὴν ἐκ τῶν ὑπηκόων εὔνοιαν καὶ ἀσφαλείαν ἀμοιβὰς δικαίας ἀντεκτινόντων ἀπεργάσεται. Meyer and others suppose the meaning to be that slaves are to be treated as equals, not as regards the outward relation, but as regards the Christian brotherhood (see Philem. 16). It would be a very obscure way of expressing this thought to say τὸ δίκ. καὶ τὴν ἰσότητα παρέχεσθε: nor does it agree well with the following clause, καὶ ὑμεῖς ἔχετε Κύριον, not as in Eph., αὐτῶν καὶ ὑμῶν. Perhaps, indeed, we may regard τὰ αὐτά in Eph. (οἱ κύριοι, τὰ αὐτὰ ποιεῖτε πρὸς αὐτούς) as illustrating ἰσότης here. The same moral principles were to govern both. ἰσότητα οὐ τὴν ἰσοτιμίαν ἐκάλεσεν, ἀλλὰ τὴν προσήκουσαν ἐπιμέλειαν, ἧς παρὰ τῶν δεσποτῶν ἀπολαύειν χρὴ τοὺς οἰκετάς, Theodoret. Erasmus, Corn. a Lapide understand the word of impartiality, not treating one slave differently from others; but this would be consistent with harsh treatment of all.

παρέχεσθε. "Supply on your side."

2–6. *Exhortation to constant prayer and thanksgiving, to which is added the apostle's request that they would pray for himself in his work. Practical advice as to wisdom in action and speech.*

2. τῇ προσευχῇ προσκαρτερεῖτε = Rom. xii. 12; cf. 1 Thess. v. 17. We have the same verb similarly used in Acts i. 14, ii. 46, vi. 4.

γρηγοροῦντες ἐν αὐτῇ. "Being watchful in it," *i.e.* not careless in the act. ἐπειδὴ γὰρ τὸ καρτερεῖν ἐν ταῖς εὐχαῖς ῥᾳθυμεῖν πολλάκις ποιεῖ, διὰ τοῦτό φησι γρηγοροῦντες τούτεστι νήφοντες, μὴ ῥεμβόμενοι (wandering), Chrys.

ἐν εὐχαριστίᾳ. With thanksgiving (as an accompaniment; cf. ii. 7). αὕτη γὰρ ἡ ἀληθινὴ εὐχὴ ἡ εὐχαριστίαν ἔχουσα ὑπὲρ πάντων ὧν ἴσμεν καὶ ὧν οὐκ ἴσμεν, ὧν εὖ ἐπάθομεν ἢ ἐθλίβομεν, ὑπὲρ τῶν κοινῶν εὐεργεσιῶν, Theophylact.

3. προσευχόμενοι ἅμα καὶ περὶ ἡμῶν. "Praying at the same time also for us," including, namely, Timothy, named with St. Paul as sending the Epistle, but also, no doubt, including all who helped him in his work (vv. 10–14).

ἵνα. The prayer is not for the personal benefit of the apostle and his companions, but for the promotion of their work.

θύραν τοῦ λόγου. A door of admission for the word of the gospel, *i.e.* the removal of any hindrance which might be in the way. The same figure is employed 1 Cor. xvi. 9; 2 Cor. ii. 12.

Corn. a Lapide, Beza, Bengel, and others interpret θύραν τοῦ λόγου as "the door of our speech," *i.e.* our mouth,—an interpretation suggested by Eph. vi. 19, ἵνα μοι δοθῇ λόγος ἐν ἀνοίξει τοῦ στόματός μου, but certainly not consistent with τοῦ λόγου, which must mean "the word."

λαλῆσαι, infinitive of the end or object, "so as to speak" τὸ μυστήριον, κ.τ.λ., i. 26, ii. 2; see Eph. i. 9.

δι' ὃ καὶ δέδεμαι. For it was his preaching the free admission of the Gentiles that led to his imprisonment.

This is the only place in which St. Paul uses δέειν in the literal sense; but he uses δεσμοί, Phil. i. 7, 13, and elsewhere, as well as δέσμιος. The transition to the singular was inevitable when he passed from what was common to himself with others to what was peculiar to himself.

4. ἵνα φανερώσω, κ.τ.λ. Generally taken as dependent on the previous clause, "that God may open a door ... in order that," etc. Beza, De Wette, *al.*, however, make it dependent on προσευχόμενοι, which, on account of the change from plural to singular, is improbable. Bengel joins it with δέδεμαι, "vinctus sum ut patefaciam; paradoxon." In this he follows Chrysostom, τὰ δεσμὰ φανεροῖ αὐτόν, οὐ συσκιάζει: but this is quite untenable. V. Soden, who also makes the clause dependent on δέδεμαι, proposes a different interpretation. He observes that φανεροῦν is never used of St. Paul's preaching, nor does the notion of μυστήριον account for its use here. It must therefore have a special significance, and this is to be found in its immediate reference to δέδεμαι. St. Paul, as a prisoner awaiting trial, had to explain what his preaching was. How this turned out, he relates in Phil. i. 12 ff. The sense then, according to v. Soden, is: "in order that I may make it manifest, how I am bound to speak," the emphasis being on δεῖ, not ὡς. He desires to make clear to his judges, not only what he preaches, but that he cannot do otherwise; compare 1 Cor. ix. 16; Acts iv. 20.

δι' ὅ is the reading of ℵ A C D K L nearly all MSS., d e f Vulg. Goth., Clem. Chrys. etc. But B G, g have δι' ὅν, apparently a correction to suit Χριστοῦ, but destroying the point of the sentence.

5. ἐν σοφίᾳ = practical Christian wisdom; cf. Matt. x. 16.

πρός. "With respect to," or "in relation to," *i.e.* your behaviour towards them.

τοὺς ἔξω. Those outside the Church; compare 1 Cor. v. 12, 13; 1 Thess. iv. 12. The expression is borrowed from the Jews, who so designated the heathen. On the precept Chrys. says, πρὸς τὰ μέλη τὰ οἰκεῖα οὐ τοσαύτης ἡμῖν δεῖ ἀσφαλείας, ὅσης πρὸς τοὺς ἔξω· ἔνθα γὰρ ἀδελφοί, εἰσὶ καὶ συγγνῶμαι πολλαὶ καὶ ἀγαθαί.

τὸν καιρὸν ἐξαγοραζόμενοι. See Eph. v. 16, where is added a reason for the injunction, viz. ὅτι αἱ ἡμέραι πονηραί εἰσιν.

6. ὁ λόγος ὑμῶν πάντοτε ἐν χάριτι. Still referring to behaviour, πρὸς τοὺς ἔξω. On χάρις = pleasingness, see above, iii. 16. χάρις λόγων is frequent in classical writers.

ἅλατι ἠρτυμένος. "Seasoned with salt"; cf. Mark ix. 49, 50; pleasant but not insipid, nor yet coarse. Compare Plut. *Mor.* p. 514 F, χάριν τινὰ παρασκευάζοντες ἀλλήλοις, ὥσπερ ἁλσὶ τοῖς λόγοις ἐφηδύνουσι τὴν διατριβήν: and again, p. 669 A, ἡ δὲ τῶν ἁλῶν δύναμις ... χάριν αὐτῷ καὶ ἡδονὴν προστίθησι. ἅλας is a later form.

εἰδέναι, infinitive of object, as in ver. 3, πῶς δεῖ ἑνὶ ἑκάστῳ ἀποκρίνεσθαι, "to each one," according, namely, to the character, purpose, spirit, etc., of the inquirer. Compare the apostle's description of his own behaviour, 1 Cor. ix. 22, τοῖς πᾶσι γέγονα πάντα ἵνα πάντως τινὰς σώσω. His discourses and answers at Athens, and before Felix, Festus, and the Jews at Rome, supply the best illustrations.

7-18. *Personal commendations and salutations.*

7. τὰ κατ' ἐμέ = Phil. i. 12, "my matters"; cf. Acts xxv. 14. Not a noun absolute, but the object of γνωρίσει.

On Tychicus, see Eph. vi. 21, and compare Lightfoot's very full note here.

ὁ ἀγαπητὸς ἀδελφός = Eph. *l.c.*

καὶ πιστὸς διάκονος καὶ σύνδουλος ἐν Κυρίῳ. ἐν Κυρίῳ is probably to be taken with both substantives, as both require some specifically Christian definition, which ἀδελφός does not; and, moreover, in Eph. *l.c.* we have πιστὸς διάκονος ἐν Κυρίῳ. σύνδουλος is perhaps added in order to place Tychicus on a level with Epaphras, who is so designated i. 7, and who was in high repute at Colossae. πιστός probably covers both substantives.

8. ὃν ἔπεμψα, κ.τ.λ. = Eph. vi. 22

As to the reading, the Rec. Text has ἵνα γνῷ τὰ περὶ ὑμῶν, with אᶜ C Dᵇᶜ K L and most MSS., f Vulg. Goth. Syr. (both), Boh., Chrys. (expressly), Jerome (on Philemon), Ambrosiaster, al.

ἵνα γνῶτε τὰ περὶ ἡμῶν, A B D* G P a few cursives, d e g Arm. Eth., Theodore Mops. Theodoret, Jerome (on Eph. vi. 21), Euthalius (cod. Tisch.).

א* has γνῶτε with ὑμῶν. אᶜ at first corrected ὑμῶν to ἡμῶν to suit γνῶτε, but afterwards deleted this correction and substituted γνῷ for γνῶτε. The context, with the emphatic εἰς αὐτὸ τοῦτο, so obviously requires γνῶτε . . . ἡμῶν, that, considering the weight of authority, we cannot regard this as an alteration made in conformity with Eph. vi. 22. Besides, it is very unlikely that the writer himself should, to the Ephesians, say, εἰς αὐτὸ τοῦτο ἵνα γνῶτε, κ.τ.λ., and to the Colossians of the same messenger, εἰς αὐτὸ τοῦτο ἵνα γνῷ, κ.τ.λ. On the hypothesis that Eph. is not by the author of Col., it is equally improbable that the former should be written instead of the latter. The error may have arisen from τε accidentally dropping out before τα, or, as Lightfoot suggests, when ὑμῶν had once been written in error for ἡμῶν (as in א*), γνῶτε would be read γνῷ τε, as in 1 11 and John Dam. Op. ii. p. 214, and then the superfluous τε would be dropped. These authorities, however, seem too late to be used to explain so early a corruption.

Alford defends the Rec. Text, in which he is followed by Klöpper; but most critics and commentators adopt the other reading.

9. σὺν Ὀνησίμῳ τῷ πιστῷ καὶ ἀγαπητῷ ἀδελφῷ. Observe the delicacy with which Onesimus is given, as far as possible, the same predicates as Tychicus and Epaphras, he and Tychicus being, moreover, associated as subject of γνωριοῦσιν. He was not διάκονος or σύνδουλος, but as a faithful and beloved brother he is not placed below them. Compare Rom. xvi. 6, 12.

ὅς ἐστιν ἐξ ὑμῶν, who is of you, *i.e.* belongs to Colossae; hitherto, indeed, only a slave, but now a brother beloved, Philem. 16. It deserves notice how St. Paul assumes that Onesimus will be welcomed as such by his former master and by the Church. Calvin's very natural remark, "Vix est credibile hunc esse servum illum Philemonis, quia furis et fugitivi nomen dedecori subjectum fuisset," serves to put in strong relief this confidence of the apostle in the Colossians.

πάντα ὑμῖν γνωριοῦσιν τὰ ὧδε. This is not a formal restatement of τὰ κατ' ἐμέ, but includes more than that phrase, and τά περὶ ἡμῶν, namely, all that concerned the Church at Rome. This would naturally include an account of the conversion of Onesimus, who would be to them a living illustration of the success of St. Paul's preaching in Rome. Note the change from γνωρίσει to γνωριοῦσιν, in order more expressly to commend Onesimus to their confidence.

G d e f g Vulg. Jerome, Ambrosiaster add after ὧδε, πραττόμενα, a gloss which looks as if it originated in the Latin, which could not literally render τὰ ὧδε.

10. Ἀσπάζεται ὑμᾶς Ἀρίσταρχος. Of Aristarchus we know that he was a Macedonian of Thessalonica, Acts xix. 20, xx. 4; a member of the deputation to Jerusalem (*ib.*), and a companion of St. Paul in the first part, at least, of his journey to Rome, Acts xxvii. 2. Lightfoot (*Philippians*, p. 35) thought it probable that he parted from St. Paul at Myra, having accompanied him at first only because he was on his way home to Macedonia. If the centurion in whose charge St. Paul was had not accidentally fallen in at Myra with a ship sailing to Italy, their route would have taken them through Philippi. If this view is correct, Aristarchus must have rejoined St. Paul at Rome at a later date. In any case, the notices in Acts show that he would be well known in proconsular Asia.

ὁ συναιχμάλωτός μου. αἰχμάλωτος properly means a captive taken in war, and hence it has been supposed that it may here have reference to spiritual captivity; cf. Rom. vii. 23; 2 Cor. x. 5; Eph. iv. 8. But none of these passages justify such an interpretation. In Rom. the verb is used of captivity to sin; in Eph. it is in a quotation from a Psalm; while in Cor. it is the thoughts that are brought into captivity so as to be obedient to Christ. There is no analogy to support the supposed use of αἰχμάλωτος absolutely in the sense supposed. It would be particularly unlikely to be so used in a letter actually written from prison.

On the other hand, St. Paul speaks of the service of Christ in terms of military service; cf. 2 Tim. ii. 3, and συστρατιώτης, Phil. ii. 25; Philemon 2. It is in accordance with this that he should use the term συναιχμάλωτος here (and of Epaphras in Philem. 23). It has been conjectured that St. Paul's helpers may have voluntarily shared his imprisonment in turn; for Epaphras, who is here a συνεργός, is in Philemon a συναιχμ., and Aristarchus here συναιχμ. is there a συνεργός.

Μάρκος ὁ ἀνεψιὸς Βαρνάβα, "cousin," so defined by Pollux, iii. 28, ἀδελφῶν παῖδες ἀνεψιοί, εἴτε ἐκ πατραδέλφων εἰσί, εἴτε ἐκ μητραδέλφων εἴτε ἐξ ἀδελφοῦ καὶ ἀδελφῆς, εἴτ' ἐκ δυοῖν ἀρρένων ἀδελφῶν εἴτ' ἐκ δυοῖν θηλειῶν. The use of it for "nephew" is very late.

The relationship explains why Barnabas was more ready than Paul to condone Mark's defection, Acts xv. 37–39. At the same time, the passage throws light in turn on the rather remarkable form of commendation here, "if he comes unto you, receive him." The Pauline Churches, which were aware of the estrangement, might not be very ready to give a very hearty welcome to Mark. Comp. 2 Tim. iv. 11. δέχεσθαι is a regular term for hospitable reception. See, for example, Matt. x. 14; John iv. 45; often also in classical writers.

περὶ οὗ, κ.τ.λ. These injunctions probably had reference to the friendly reception of Mark, so that their purport is repeated in the following words.

11. Ἰησοῦς ὁ λεγόμενος Ἰοῦστος. Not mentioned elsewhere. The surname Justus is applied to two other persons in the

N.T., namely, Joseph Barsabbas, Acts i. 23, and a proselyte at Corinth, Acts xviii. 7. It was a frequent surname amongst the Jews.

οἱ ὄντες ἐκ περιτομῆς. These words are best connected with the following, οὗτοι μόνοι, κ.τ.λ. The sense then is, "of those of the circumcision, these alone are," etc. Otherwise, οὗτοι μόνοι would not be true (see *vv.* 12–14), and οἱ ὄντες ἐκ π. would have no significance. This construction, in which the more general notion stands first as in a nominative absolute, and the particular notion follows with the verb, is used by classical writers.

On this οὗτοι μόνοι comp. Phil. ii. 20, οὐδένα ἔχω ἰσόψυχον.

συνεργοί is the predicate, so that the apostle does not apply the term to the opponents.

οἵτινες as usual specifies, not the individuals, but the character, "men that proved." See on Lk. ii. 4. The aorist ἐγενήθησαν seems to refer to some definite recent occasion.

παρηγορία, "comfort," only here in N.T., frequent in Plutarch. There is no ground for Bengel's distinction, that παραμυθία refers to domestic, and παρηγορία to forensic trouble. So far as the latter word has a technical sense, it is medical (cf. "paregoric"); but it is commonly used of consolation in general.

12. Ἐπαφρᾶς, see i. 7.

ὁ ἐξ ὑμῶν. "Who is one of you."

δοῦλος Χριστοῦ Ἰησοῦ. A title frequently used by St. Paul of himself, once of Timothy in conjunction with himself, Phil. i. 1, but not elsewhere of any other.

πάντοτε ἀγωνιζόμενος, κ.τ.λ. Compare i. 29.

ἵνα στῆτε τέλειοι καὶ πεπληροφορημένοι. "That ye may stand fast, perfect and fully assured." στῆναι, as in Eph. vi. 11, 13, *al.*, conveys the idea of standing firm; hence τέλειοι καὶ πεπλ. are secondary predicates, the first expressing the objective moment, the second the subjective; they were not only to be τέλειοι ἐν Χριστῷ, i. 28, but to have full assurance; cf. ii. 2. πληροφορεῖν in N.T. means either "to fulfil," as in 2 Tim. iv. 5, 17, or, "to persuade fully," as in Rom. iv. 21, πληροφορηθεὶς ὅτι . . . δυνατός ἐστιν; xiv. 5, ἐν τῷ ἰδίῳ νοῒ πληροφορείτω. It is read in Rom. xv. 13, in B F G, where the sense is "fill"; but the better attested reading is πληρῶσαι. The Rec. Text here has πεπληρωμένοι. See on Lk. i. 1.

ἐν παντὶ θελήματι τοῦ Θεοῦ. "In all the will of God" is not quite correct, yet we cannot say "every will of God." Lightfoot renders "in everything willed by God." The words are best connected with τελ. καὶ πεπλ., not with στῆτε, as the order of the words shows. παντί probably has reference to the variety of circumstances in which the Christian may find himself, with perhaps a hint at the contrast with the definite external precepts of the false teachers.

στῆτε is the reading of ℵ^c A C D G K L P and most mss., Chrys. Theodoret. σταθῆτε, ℵ* B 23 71 *al.*, Euthal. (cod. Tisch.). Comp. Matt. ii. 9, xxvii. 11, in both which passages B C 1 33 have ἐστάθη for the Rec. ἔστη. The passive is adopted by the critical editors in all three places.

πεπληροφορημένοι, ℵ A B C D* G *al.*, Syr-Harcl. marg., Euthal. (cod. Tisch.).

πεπληρωμένοι, D^c K L P most mss., Syr-Harcl. text. and Pesh. Arm., Chrys. Theodoret. As, however, πληροφορεῖν is sometimes used with the meaning "fill," the versions cannot be quoted with certainty for the latter reading, which probably slipped in as the more familiar and simpler word.

13. μαρτυρῶ γὰρ αὐτῷ. The apostle confirms by his testimony what he has just said of Epaphras.

ὅτι ἔχει πολὺν πόνον. "That he has much labour." πόνος is not found elsewhere in N.T. except in the Apocalypse. It is, however, a common word for struggle in battle, and hence corresponds with the ἀγών of the apostle himself, ii. 1, and with the ἀγωνιζόμενος of ver. 12. The two words occur in juxtaposition in Plato, *Phaedr.* 247 B, ἔνθα δὴ πόνος τε καὶ ἀγὼν ἔσχατος ψυχῇ πρόκειται.

πολὺν πόνον, ℵ A B C P 80, Euthal. (cod. Tisch.), Old Lat. Vulg. Goth. Boh. Arm.

ζῆλον πολύν, Rec., with K L most mss., Syr. (both), Chrys. Theodoret. D^{bc} *al.* have πολὺν ζῆλον ; D* G, πολὺν κόπον.

Five cursives have πόθον, and two (6 67²) ἀγῶνα.

No doubt the rarity of πόνος in the N.T. is responsible for the variety of reading. It is found in the Apocalypse only.

ὑπὲρ ὑμῶν καὶ τῶν ἐν Λαοδικείᾳ καὶ τῶν ἐν Ἱεραπόλει. Laodicea and Hierapolis stood on opposite sides of the valley at a distance of about six miles from one another, and twice as far from Colossae. From the conjunction of the three names here it appears probable that Epaphras stood in the same relation, as evangelist, to the three, and also that they were threatened by the same dangers; as, indeed, their near neighbourhood and consequent frequent intercourse would suggest. Compare ii. 2.

14. ἀσπάζεται ὑμᾶς Λουκᾶς ὁ ἰατρὸς ὁ ἀγαπητός. "Luke the physician, the beloved." Beyond question the evangelist, named also 2 Tim. iv. 11 as well as Philem. 24. It is interesting to find two of the evangelists in St. Paul's company here. The reason of his calling being specified may be that he was attending on St. Paul in his professional capacity. It has been observed that his first appearance in company with St. Paul, Acts xvi. 10, "nearly synchronises with an attack of the apostle's constitutional malady (Gal. iv. 13, 14), so that he may have joined him partly in a professional capacity" (Lightfoot). From the manner in which he is separated from the group in ver. 10 it is clear that he was a Gentile. This is fatal, not only to the tradition that he was one of the Seventy (which, indeed, is hardly consistent with the preface to his Gospel), but also to the conjecture that he was the author of the Epistle to the Hebrews. See on Lk. i. 2, x. 1–16, xxiv. 13–32.

καὶ Δημᾶς. Probably a contraction for Demetrius. It is remarkable that he is named without any epithet of commendation, which is the more striking as coming after ὁ ἀγαπητός. In Philem. 24 he is named with Mark, Aristarchus, and Luke as a συνεργός of St. Paul. But in 2 Tim. iv. 10 he is mentioned as having deserted St. Paul, ἀγαπήσας τὸν νῦν αἰῶνα. Perhaps the curt mention here foreshadows that desertion.

15. ἀσπάσασθε τοὺς ἐν Λαοδικείᾳ ἀδελφούς, καὶ Νυμφᾶν, καὶ τὴν κατ' οἶκον αὐτῶν (or αὐτοῦ) ἐκκλησίαν. Nymphas (if this reading is correct) is probably a short form of Nymphodorus; cf. Artemas for Artemidorus, Zenas for Zenodorus (Tit. iii. 12, 13), Olympas for Olympiodorus (Rom. xvi. 15), and perhaps Lucas for Lucanus.

τὴν κατ' οἶκον, κ.τ.λ., *i.e.* the Church that assembled in their house. The same expression occurs, Rom. xvi. 5 and 1 Cor. xvi. 19, of the house of Prisca and Aquila at Rome and at Ephesus respectively; also Philem. 2. Compare Acts xii. 12. Separate buildings for the purpose of Christian worship seem not to be traced earlier than the third century. Bingham, *Antiq.* viii. 1. 13, shows that special rooms were so set apart, but gives no instances of separate buildings. Probst (*Kirchliche Disciplin*, p. 181 f.) is referred to by Lightfoot as affording similar negative evidence. It is curious that Chrysostom understands the expression to refer only to the household of Nymphas. ὅρα γοῦν πῶς δείκνυσι μέγαν τὸν ἄνδρα, εἴ γε ἡ οἰκία αὐτοῦ ἐκκλησία.

αὐτῶν is difficult. Alford, Lightfoot, *al.*, understand it as referring to οἱ περὶ Νυμφᾶν. Alford compares Xen. *Mem.* i. 2. 62, ἐάν τις φανερὸς γένηται κλέπτων ... τούτοις θάνατός ἐστιν ἡ ζημία, which is clearly not parallel, for τις is one of a class, and τούτοις all those belonging to that class. Lightfoot compares Xen. *Anab.* iii. 3. 7, προσῄει (Μιθριδάτης) πρὸς τοὺς Ἕλληνας· ἐπεὶ δ' ἐγγὺς ἐγένοντο, κ.τ.λ., and iv. 5. 33, ἐπεὶ δ' ἦλθον πρὸς Χειρίσοφον, κατελάμβανον καὶ ἐκείνους σκηνοῦντας. These also are not parallel, since here, as in other languages, the force is called by the name of its commander. Hence Meyer says that the plural cannot without violence be referred to anything but "the brethren in Laodicea and Nymphas." He thinks, then, that by these brethren is meant a Church distinct from that of Laodicea, but in filial relation to it, and meeting in the same house. Lightfoot also suggests (as an alternative to his first-mentioned view) that the "brethren in Laodicea" may refer to a family of Colossians settled in Laodicea.

<small>The reading varies between αὐτῶν, αὐτοῦ, and αὐτῆς.

For the plural, ℵ A C P 5 9 17 23 34 39 47 73, Boh. (wrongly quoted by Tisch. *al.* for αὐτοῦ, see Lightfoot), Arab. (Leipz.), Euthalius (cod. Tisch.).

For αὐτοῦ are D G K L. 37 (cod. Leic.) nearly all cursives, Goth., Chrys. Theodoret (expressly), Ambrosiaster.

For αὐτῆς, B 67².

The Latin versions have the singular "ejus," and so both Syriac. In the</small>

latter the gender would be indicated only by a point. The Pesh. is pointed inconsistently, making Nympha feminine (Nŭmphē) and the suffix (corresponding to αὐτοῦ or αὐτῆς) masculine. The Harclean, again, has the suffix feminine in the text, masculine in the margin. How the translator intended the proper name to be taken is uncertain; it may be either masc. or fem. Lightfoot thinks probably the latter. The Greek name is accented as feminine (Νύμφαν) in B° and Euthalius (cod. Tisch.).

Νύμφαν as a feminine name would be Doric, and the occurrence of such a form here is highly improbable. αὐτῆς, then, is probably a correction suggested by this misunderstanding of Νύμφαν. But it seems more probable that the scribe who made the correction had αὐτοῦ before him than αὐτῶν. αὐτῶν, again, might readily have been suggested to the mind of a copyist by his recollection of Rom. xvi. 5 and 1 Cor. xvi. 19 assisted by the occurrence of ἀδελφούς just before.

αὐτῆς is adopted by Lachmann, Tregelles (margin), WH., v. Soden, Weiss. Νύμφαν being accentuated accordingly.
αὐτῶν, by Tischendorf, Alford, Meyer, Tregelles (text).
αὐτοῦ, by De Wette (who designates αὐτῶν "false and unmeaning"), Ellicott.

16. καὶ ὅταν ἀναγνωσθῇ παρ' ὑμῖν ἡ ἐπιστολή. Obviously the present Epistle, as Rom. xvi. 22, Τέρτιος ὁ γράψας τὴν ἐπιστολήν: 1 Thess. v. 27, ἀναγνωσθῆναι τὴν ἐπιστολήν: 2 Thess. iii. 14, διὰ τῆς ἐπιστολῆς, these latter verses being of the nature of a postscript.

ποιήσατε ἵνα. Cf. John xi. 37. ποιεῖν, in the sense "take care," is sometimes followed by ὅπως, as in Herod. i. 8, ποίεε ὅκως ἐκείνην θεήσεαι γυμνήν: ib. 209, ποίεε ὅκως ἐπεάν . . . ὥς μοι καταστήσῃς τὸν παῖδα. So with ὡς, Xen. *Cyrop*. vi. 3. 18.

ἵνα καὶ ἐν τῇ Λαοδικέων ἐκκλησίᾳ ἀναγνωσθῇ. See the similar direction 1 Thess. v. 27, ἀναγνωσθῆναι τὴν ἐπ. πᾶσι τοῖς ἀδελφοῖς. The present Ep. was to be read in the assembly of the Church, and a copy sent to Laodicea and similarly read there. Compare the address 2 Cor. i. 1, which implies the sending of copies to neighbouring Churches.

καὶ τὴν ἐκ Λαοδικείας. Chrysostom says that some understood this of a letter written from Laodicea to St. Paul. The Syriac-Pesh. also renders "written from L."; and so Theodore Mops., Theodoret, and many others, including Beza, a Lapide, Estius, and some recent commentators. But why should St. Paul direct the Colossians to get from Laodicea the letter written to him, of which he could not assume even that the Laodiceans had retained a copy? and how would the letter of the Laodiceans edify the Colossians? Moreover, καὶ ὑμεῖς obviously implies that the Laodiceans were the receivers of the letter. Theophylact supposes the first Epistle to Timothy to be meant, which, according to the subscription, was written from Laodicea. This subscription, indeed, probably owes its origin to the theory, which was earlier than Theophylact, and appears in the margin of the Philoxenian Syriac. Other Epistles of St. Paul have been similarly said in some of the Versions to be "written from Laodicea" (see Lightfoot). It is fatal to all such hypotheses that St. Paul had not been at Laodicea before this time (ii. 1), and, even had he been there, had now been some time in prison, and therefore could not have written any letter recently from Laodicea.

These hypotheses are obviously founded on the error that ἡ ἐκ Λ. must mean "the letter written from 'L.'" But this is not so. When the article with a preposition expresses a substantival notion, it is often proleptic, a construction which is called the attraction of prepositions (Jelf, § 647), Thucyd. ii. 34, θάπτουσι τοὺς ἐκ τῶν πολέμων: iii. 22, ᾔσθοντο οἱ ἐκ τῶν πύργων φύλακες: vi. 32, ξυνεπεύχοντο δὲ καὶ ὁ ἄλλος ὅμιλος ὁ ἐκ τῆς γῆς. Most of the instances, indeed, cited by Jelf, *l.c.*, and others are with verbs implying motion, as in Luke xi. 13, xvi. 26.

Assuming, then, as certain that the Epistle was one written by St. Paul to Laodicea, we have three alternatives to choose from. First, there is extant an Epistle actually bearing the title "To the Laodiceans." It is extant only in Latin, but must have been originally written in Greek. Of it Jerome says (*Vir. Ill.* 5): "legunt quidam et ad Laodicenses, sed ab omnibus exploditur." It is, indeed, abundantly condemned by internal evidence. It is a mere cento of Pauline phrases put together with no definite connexion or purpose, and absolutely destitute of any local allusion, except in the last line, which is obviously borrowed from the verse before us, viz.: "et facite legi Colosensibus et Colosensium vobis." As Erasmus truly and strikingly expresses it: "nihil habet Pauli praeter voculas aliquot ex caeteris ejus epistolis mendicatas. . . . Non est cujusvis hominis Paulinum pectus effingere. Tonat, fulgurat, meras flammas loquitur Paulus. At haec, praeterquam quod brevissima est (about as long as this ch. iv.), quam friget, quam jacet! . . . Nullum argumentum efficacius persuaserit eam non esse Pauli quam ipsa epistola." It is found, however, in many copies of the Latin Bible from the sixth to the fifteenth century, and, as Lightfoot observes, for more than nine centuries it "hovered about the doors of the sacred canon, without either finding admission or being peremptorily excluded," until at the revival of learning it was finally condemned on all sides. The Latin text of the Epistle will be found on p. 308. A full account of its history with a collation of the principal MSS., also a translation into Greek, will be found in Lightfoot.

Secondly, it may be a lost Epistle. We have no reason to question the possibility of St. Paul having written letters which have not come down to us (compare, perhaps, 1 Cor. v. 9); but in the present case we may observe, first, that the Epistle referred to was one to which some importance was attached by St. Paul himself, so that he himself directs that it be read publicly in two distinct Churches (for the passage justifies us in assuming that it was publicly read in Laodicea as well as Colossae); and, secondly, that in consequence of this direction not only must it have been copied, but great publicity was, in fact, assured to it. The Epistle to Philemon, which was in itself unimportant, and private, was not allowed by the Colossians to be lost, how much less an important public letter? Again, we know of three Epistles sent at this time to Asia Minor, namely, those to the Ephesians, to the Colossians, and to Philemon. It is best not to assume a fourth unless we are compelled to do so, which it will be seen we are not. In any case it could hardly have been an Epistle addressed to the Laodiceans, since if it had been we should not have salutations to the Laodiceans in this Epistle, not to say that it would be called τὴν πρὸς Λαοδικέας rather than τὴν ἐκ Λ.

The third alternative is that the Epistle is one of those that we possess under another title. As early as the fourth century the claim was put forward on the part of the Epistle to the Hebrews by Philastrius, apparently from conjecture only, and one or two modern writers have adopted the same hypothesis. But in spite of some partial coincidences, it is really impossible to suppose these two Epistles to have been written at the same time by the same author to the same neighbourhood.

The Epistle to Philemon has also been suggested, and Wieseler (*Chronol. des Apost. Zeitalter*, p. 450 ff.) speaks of this identification as scarcely open to doubt; but that Epistle is entirely private, and the delicacy of its appeal would be destroyed if St. Paul directed it to be read in public.

There remains the Epistle to the Ephesians, which we know to have been written about the same time as the Epistle to the Colossians, and conveyed by the same messenger, and which, on quite distinct grounds, is, with high probability, regarded as a circular letter (see Introduction).

ἵνα καὶ ὑμεῖς ἀναγνῶτε. "See that ye also read." It would be rather awkward to make this ἵνα depend directly on ποιήσατε. It may be taken independently, as in Gal. ii. 10, μόνον τῶν πτωχῶν ἵνα μνημονεύωμεν: 2 Cor. viii. 7, ἵνα καὶ ἐν ταύτῃ τῇ χάριτι περισσεύητε (John ix. 3; 2 Thess. iii. 9; 1 John ii. 19 are not quite parallel).

ὅπως is frequently used by classical writers in a similar manner. Here, however, as ποιήσατε has just preceded followed by ἵνα, it is perhaps more natural to understand before this ἵνα, "see that," taken out of ποιήσατε by a sort of zeugma.

17. καὶ εἴπατε Ἀρχίππῳ. Archippus, called by St. Paul his συστρατιώτης (Philem. 2), was probably a son of Philemon, and a leading presbyter at Colossae (to suppose him to be a regular bishop would be an anachronism), or perhaps an "evangelist" (Eph. iv. 11). Lightfoot thinks it more probable that he resided at Laodicea (of which place the *Apostolic Constitutions* make him bishop), and accounts thus for St. Paul not addressing him directly. Contrast the direct address, Phil. iv. 3. But there the request addressed to the "true yokefellow" is a special one; here it is general, and the form adopted gives it an official character which is natural and suitable; in fact, a direct address would have the appearance of harshness and discourtesy to the Colossians, and this the more the greater the authority he possessed. Would not this be the impression inevitably produced, if after animadverting on the heretical teaching in Colossae, the apostle had added, "and thou, see that thou fulfil thy office"?

βλέπε, "look to"; compare 1 Cor. i. 26, βλέπετε τὴν κλῆσιν ὑμῶν: x. 18, βλέπετε τὸν Ἰσραὴλ κατὰ σάρκα. In Phil. iii. 2, βλέπετε τοὺς κύνας, κ.τ.λ., the idea is of being on one's watch (against).

τὴν διακονίαν. Clearly some office more important than the diaconate, properly so called, is intended here. So 2 Tim. iv. 5, τὴν διακονίαν σου πληροφόρησον: compare Acts xii. 25, πληρώσαντες τὴν διακονίαν (of a special mission to Jerusalem).

ἣν παρέλαβες ἐν Κυρίῳ. The qualification ἐν Κυρίῳ probably belongs both to the person and to the reception of the office; as living in the Lord, he received it, and he received it as committed to him in the service of the Lord.

ἵνα αὐτὴν πληροῖς. For the construction, compare 2 John 8; and for the sense, 2 Tim. iv. 5 quoted above.

The admonition reminds us, indeed, of the admonitions to Timothy and Titus. If Archippus was a young man, and recently appointed to his office, it would be a natural reminder of its greatness and its difficulty; and there is no need to suppose that a covert censure on his previous laxity is implied.

18. ὁ ἀσπασμὸς τῇ ἐμῇ χειρὶ Παύλου = 1 Cor. xvi. 21; 2 Thess. iii. 17. In the latter passage St. Paul states that this was his usual custom.

μνημονεύετέ μου τῶν δεσμῶν. An appeal, touching in its brevity, and one which could not proceed from an imitator. He does not ask specially for their prayers, their sympathy, that they should spare him further anxiety, or the like; but all these are included in the request that they "were ever to keep before them the fact that one who so deeply cared for them, and loved them, and to whom their perils of false doctrine occasioned such anxiety, was a prisoner in chains," Alford; who adds, "when we read of 'his chains' we should not forget that they moved over the paper as he wrote. His hand was chained to the soldier that kept him." This circumstance perhaps explains the singular abruptness of the request.

ἡ χάρις μεθ' ὑμῶν. This short form of benediction is used also in 1 Tim. vi. 21 and 2 Tim. iv. 22. ἡ χάρις used thus absolutely occurs only in the later Epistles. In the earlier it is defined by the addition of τοῦ Κυρίου [ἡμῶν] Ἰησοῦ [Χριστοῦ].

'Ἀμήν is added in ℵ^c D K L P and most mss., d e f Vulg. Goth. Syr. (both), Boh. etc.
Omitted in ℵ* A B C F G 17 67², g al.
For the subscription, ℵ A B C D G L P al. have πρὸς Κολασσαεις (or Κολοσσαεις, B^{cor} D F G L P, etc.), to which A B° add ἀπὸ ῥωμης (ῥωμη A), and so Syr. (both); but Boh. has "scripta Athenis."
Some later authorities, K L and many cursives, add διὰ Τυχικοῦ καὶ Ὀνησίμου. For other varieties and additions, see Tischendorf.

Here follows the text of the spurious Epistle from a MS. in the Library of Trinity College, Dublin.

AD LAODICENSES.

Paulus Apostolus non ab hominibus neque per hominem; sed per Jhesum Christum fratribus qui sunt Laodicie. Gratia vobis et pax a Deo patre nostro et Domino Jhesu Christo.
Gratias ago Deo meo per omnem orationem meam quod permanentes estis in eo et perseverantes in operibus eius, promissum expectantes in die iudicii. Neque destituant vos quorundam vaniloquia insinuantium, ut vos avertant a veritate evangelii quod a me praedicatur etsi faciet Deus ut qui sunt ex me ad perfectum veritatis evangelii et servientes et facientes benignitatem operum salutis vite eterne. Et nunc palam sunt vobis vincla mea quae patior in Christo quibus laetor et gaudeo et hoc mihi est ad salutem perpetuam quod ipsum factum orationibus vestris et administrante Spiritu Sancto, sive per vitam sive per mortem, est enim michi vivere vita in Christo et mori gaudium et in id ipsum vobis faciet misericordiam suam ut eandem dilectionem habeatis et sitis unanimes. Ergo dilectissimi ut audistis praesentia mei, ita retinete et facite in timore Dei et erit vobis vita eterna, est enim Deus qui operatur in vobis et facite sine retractu quecumque facitis et quod est [reliquum] dilectissimi gaudete in Christo et praecavete sordidos in lucro. Omnes sint petitiones vestre palam apud Deum et estote firmi in sensu Christi et quae integra sunt et vera et pudica et iusta et amabilia facite, et quae audistis et accepistis in corde retinete et erat [sic] vobis pax. Salutant vos sancti. Gratia Domini nostri Jhesu cum spiritu vestro. Et facite legi epistolam colosencium vobis.

INDEX TO THE NOTES.

I. Subjects and Names.

Aboth, 42.
Abstract for concrete collective, 41.
    plural, 32.
Acta Pauli et Petri, 261.
    Thomae, 165.
Aelian, 20, 25.
Aeons, lvi.
Aeschines, 34, 89, 151, 242.
Aeschylus, 69, 89, 101, 128, 136, 286.
"Affections," 278.
"Afflictions of Christ," 230.
Alexander, Abp., 222.
Alford on character of Ep. to Eph.,
    xi; Comm. *passim*.
Analogy, 172.
Angelology, 33, 215.
Angels of the law, 260.
Anger whether always unlawful, 140.
Antoninus, 40, 45, 160.
Apocalypse, relation to Eph., xxviii.
    to Col., lix.
Aorist, 48, 49, 215, 225, 279, 282, 283.
    infinitive, 136 *n*.
    participle, 257.
Apocrypha, 16, 57, 136, 144, 145, 184,
    219, 243, 249, 267, 268, 283, xxii.
Apollonius, 153.
Apostles, 72, 117.
Apostolic Constitutions, 307.
Archippus, 306.
Arians, 213.
Aristaenetus, 246.
Aristarchus, 147, 299.
Aristophanes, 44, 155.
Aristotle, 14, 18, 29, 36, 44, 96, 149, 161,
    203, 217, 224, 242, 256, 272, 276.
Arrian, 64, 143.
Artemidorus, 154.

Article, 51, 213, 291, ix, x.
    absence of, 58, 135.
    generic, 274.
Asceticism of a later age, 273.
Athanasius, 27, 94, 213, 268, 269.
Athenaeus, 57, 59, 89.
Atonement, the, 146.
Augustine, St., 39, 162, 208, 223,
    230, 242, 244, 265, 267, 268, 273.
Ausonius, 16.

Baptism, infant, 176.
Barnabas, Ep., 11, 26, 300, l.
Basil, St., 93, 162, 212, 270, i.
Baur, 40, 82, xiv, liv sqq.
"Being in," 128.
Bengel's maxim, Proclive scriptioni
    praestat ardua, xlv.
    remark, saepe vis modi, etc., 140.
Bentley, 267.
Bernhardy, 64, 89.
Bingham, 303.
Bishops' Bible, 138.
Bisping, 230.
Blaikie, 164.
Bloomfield, 164.
"Body" not = "totality," 250.
Bugenhagen, 167.
Building, the, 73.
Bullinger, 152.
Butler, Bp., 95, 140, 153.

Caesarea, whether Eph. written from,
    xxx.
"Captivity is captive led," 113.
Cerinthus, xlix, liv.
Chains, St. Paul's, 189, 307.
Charles, Mr., 241.

"Children of wrath," 44.
Christ as sacrifice, 147.
    whether afflicted in His people, 231.
    whether the mystery of God, 239.
Christology of Ep. to Eph., xxii.
Chrysostom on character of Ep. to Eph., xiii ; Comm. *passim.*
Cicero, 14, 16, 44, 64, 98, 131, 132, 255, 286, 289.
Cilicism, supposed, 265.
Circumcision, spiritual, 57, 251.
Clemens Alex., 10, 21, 39, 161, 209, xii, l.
Clemens Rom., viii.
Cockerell, xlix.
Coleridge on Eph., xiv.
Colossae, xlvii.
Colossian heresy, xlviii.
Colossians had not heard St. Paul, 238.
Colossians, relation of Ep. to Eph., xxiii.
Conybeare, 255, 260.
Coverdale, 273.
Covetousness, 133.
Creature, reconciliation of, 222.

Davenant, 221, 241, 264.
Delitzsch, 139.
Demas, 303.
Demiurge, liv.
Demosthenes, 12, 34, 53, 89, 128, 145, 187, 202, 207, 218, 229, 243, 258, 265, 266, 286, 292, 293.
Descent into hell, 115.
De Wette on language of Eph., xv.
Didaché, viii.
Dio Cassius, 229.
Diodorus, 12, 177, 275.
Diogenes Laertius, 42, 144, 230, xlix.
Dionysius Halic., 285.
Dionysius (pseudo), 33.
Dispensation of the grace of God, 79.
Dissen, 149.
Dobree, 101.

Earthquakes in Lycus Valley, xxxi.
"Element" or "sphere," 108, 122, 128.
Enoch, Book of, 17, 241, 248.
Epaphras, 199, 298, 300, 302, xlviii.
Ephesians, to whom written, i, 25, 78.
    external evidence of genuineness, ix.
    objections from language, xiv.
        from line of thought, xix.

Ephesians, relation to Col., xxiii ; to I Pet., xxiv ; to Heb., xxvi ; to Apocalypse, xxviii.
Ephrem Syrus, 33.
Epictetus, 48, 136.
Epiphanius, 275, xiii, liv.
Erasmus, xlix.
Eratosthenes, 265.
Essenes, 247, 273.
Estius, iv ; Comm. *passim.*
Eubulus, 89.
Eucharist, 172.
Euripides, 35, 69, 89, 144, 268, 293.
Eusebius, 93, xxxi, xlvii.
Eustathius, 265.
Euthymius, 102.
Evangelists, 118.
Ewald, 11, 111, 250, viii, xiii.
Excitement, spiritual, 162.

"Father of," 27.
Field, Dr., 143, 266.
Findlay, 164.
Firstborn of all creation, 211.
    History of the interpretation, 213.
Forgiveness in Christ, 146.
Foundation of apostles and prophets, 271.
Fritzsche, 9, 34, 35, 48, 54, 71, 104, 106, 152, 159, 161, 178, 237.
Future with "see lest," 246.

Galen, 126, 271, 276.
"Genitive of reference," 211.
Gnostics, 13, 40, 182, 209, 241, 247, xlix ; on Gnostic conceptions in Col., lv sq.
"Going off at a word," 62, xxii.
Grace, 10.
Greek, modern, 26, 50.
Gregory Naz., 144.
Gregory Nyss., 89.
Grimm, 20.
Grotius on Ep. to Eph., xiv.

Hammond, 133, 223.
Hausrath, xxiv.
Heavens, 116.
    things in, 222.
Heavenly powers, 32.
Hebrews, Ep. to, xxvi.
Hebraism supposed, 40, 42, 117, 150, 223, 266.
Heliodorus, 246.
Hermann, 48, 141, iv.
Hermas, xii.
Hermes, 224.

I. SUBJECTS AND NAMES 311

Herodian, 288.
Herodotus, 94, 129, 148, 183, 186, 275, xlvii.
Hesychius, 61, 98, 131, 266.
Hierapolis, 237, 302, xlix
Hierarchy, celestial, 33.
Hilary, 258.
Hilgenfeld, 269, xiv.
Hippocrates, 20, 144, 185, 272.
Hippolytus, 214, 258, xii.
Hitzig, 139.
Hofmann, 176, 233.
Holtzmann, 40, 216, xiii, xiv xxiii, li, *al.*
"Holy Apostles," 82.
Homer, 11, 41, 53, 74, 118, 147, 186, 277, 279.
Hope and love, 196.
Hort, 80, 136, iv, xx, xxii, xxxi.
Humility, 105.

Ignatius, 246, 284, 287, viii xi.
"Imitators of God," 146.
"Incidental revelation," 33.
"In the Lord," 103.
Infinitive of end, 317.
    of object, 297, 298
Irenaeus, 13.
Isaeus, 226.
Isidore of Pelusium, 212.
Isocrates, 170, 265.
"It saith," 111, 156.

Jelf, 48, 305.
Jeremiah, vi, 10, 57.
Jewish notions, 116, 142, 247, 298.
Jerome, xxxi; Comm. *passim.*
John St., Gospel of; its relation to Eph., xxviii.
"Joint," ambiguity of, 125.
Josephus, 12, 45, 121, 247, 257, 260, 264, 266, 286, 289, xlviii.
Judaic element in Colossian Church, xlviii.
Jülicher, xiv, xvi, lii.
Justin, 93, 212.
Juvenal, 255.

Kepler, 248.
Kiene, x.
Kneeling in prayer, 93.
Kühl, 248.

Labour, Christian, object of, 142.
Laodicea, Council of, 268.
    Epistle from, 237, 302, 304, iii, v, vii, xii, *al.*

Le Clerc, 267.
Life of God, 130.
Lightfoot, "Biblical Essays," v, xiii.
Liturgy, whether quoted, 158.
Liturgies, 164.
Locke, 19, 88.
"Lower parts of the earth," 115.
Lucian, 12, 36, 98, 248, 277, 286.
Luke, 302.
Lycus Valley, natural phenomena, xlix.
    Churches of, xlviii.
Lysias, 224, 275.

Mahaffy, Dr., lii, liii.
Maialas, 85.
Mangold, xiii, xxx.
Marcion, 227, ii, xiii, li.
Marcosians, 13, 209.
Mark, 300.
Marriage; why called a "Sacrament," 175.
Mayerhoff, li.
Metaphors, mixture of, 97, 119, 245.
Middle voice, 18, 38, 156, 272.
Middleton, 153.
Milligan, Dr., vii.
Milton, 33.
Monro, *Homeric Gram.*, 78.
Müller, Max, 285.
Muratorian Canon, v, li.
"Mystery," 15.
Mystery of God, 239.
Mysteries, words supposed to be borrowed from, 236.

Name, "in the name of," 163.
Neander, 247.
Nemesius, 269.
Nominative, irregular, 96.
Nympha or Nymphas, 303.

Onesimus, 299.
Onthovius, 103.
Original sin, 45.
Origen on the address of Ep. to Eph., ii.
    on redemption, 13.
    on angels, 33.
    a peculiar reading of his, 263.

Paley, 189, xx.
Pandects, 68.
"Paradox of the Crucifixion," 262.
Participle, paraphrases with, 275.
Paul, St., his style, a singularity of, xxi.
Pearson, Bp., 109, x.
Perfect tense, 26.

312 INDEX TO THE NOTES

Perowne, Bp., 260.
Persians, 148.
Philemon, Ep. to, lvii, lviii.
Philippians, Ep. to, lvii, lviii.
Philo, 12, 14, 35, 36, 44, 45, 76, 96, 203, 210, 214, 217, 246, 259, 264, 268, 289, 293, 296.
Philostratus, 120.
Photius, 129, 229, 266.
Phrynichus, 69, 73, 84.
Pindar, 31, 149.
Plato, 12, 14, 16, 26, 29, 53, 58, 59, 64, 83, 90, 95, 124, 149, 151, 179, 215, 217, 226, 236, 242, 243, 256, 260, 264, 275, 279, 283.
Plautus, 149, 285.
Pliny, xlvii.
Plutarch, 11, 12, 14, 38, 41, 107, 141, 143, 149, 161, 170, 218, 243, 248, 258, 262, 293, 298.
Platonic doctrine of Ideas, 285.
Polyaenus, 183.
Polybius, 12, 39, 120, 122, 128, 131, 136, 155, 160, 181, 182, 272, 283.
Polycarp, 133, 139, xi.
    Martyrdom of, 160.
Present tense, 73.
Principalities, 88, 259.
Probst, 303.
"Proclivi scriptioni," etc., xlv.
"Prophesy," 10, 117.
Pythagoreans, 42, 141, 288.

Quintilian, 18.
Quotations from O.T., 110, 157.

Rabbinic views, 42, 60, 142, 151, 182, 210.
Ramsay, Prof., 159, xlviii.
Rashi, 113.
Reading, the more difficult, xlv.
Reconciliation of things in heaven, 222.
Reiche, 114, 172, 290, 292, viii.
Reiske, 217.
Renan, xvi.
Reuss, li, lviii.
"Right hand of God," 32.
Ritschl, 12, 223, 248, 260.
Robertson (Arch.), xv, xvi.
Rosetta Stone, 261.
"Rudiments of the world," 247.

Sacrificial words, 227.
Salmon, Dr., xxvi, xxvii, lii, lviii.
Sanday and Headlam, 78, 174.
Scaliger, 9.

Schleiermacher, 214, 219, xiii.
Scholefield, 233.
Schöttgen, 147, 151, 182, 251.
Schott, xxvii.
Schwegler, xiv.
Scythians, 286.
Self-love, 171.
Seneca, 178.
Seufert, xxvi.
Seventy (LXX), the fallacious mode of reference to, 14.
Seventy, the, termed apostles, 117.
Shadow of things to come, 264.
Shakespeare, 11, 15.
Simplicius, 288.
Sophocles, 58, 59, 84, 97, 170, 260, 268.
Spitta, 248.
Stobaeus, 165.
Stoics, 144.
Strabo, xlvii.
Suidas, 36.
Subject, change of, 257.
Sumner, 276.
Svoboda, xlix.

Tacitus, 40, 289, xxxi.
Targum, 112.
Taylor, Dr. C., 270.
Tenses, 73, 136, 144, 244, 279, 284.
Tertullian, 117, 219, 220, 226, ii, l.
Testaments of the XII. Patriarchs, 33, 42, 145, 182, 216, 267.
Testamentum Salomonis, 148.
Themistius, 273.
Theophrastus, 203.
Thrones, etc., 216.
Thucydides, 128, 186, 224, 275, 305.
Toup, 267.
Trench, 104, 106, 133, 161, 249.
Trophimus, 61.
"Truth as it is in Jesus," 135.
Tychicus, 190, 298.

Ussher, vi.
Usteri, xiii.

Vail of the Court of Gentiles, 61.
Valentinians, xii, lvi.
Virtue, threefold division, 153.
Vitringa, 32.

Weiss on "in Christ," 5.
Westcott on Heb. cited, 12.
    on St. John cited, 13.
Wetstein, 215, 262, 277, 286, 288, *al.*

Wieseler, 306.
Winer, 26, 100, 103, 228, 229, 255.

Xenophon, 35, 36, 45, 61, 83, 84,

129, 134, 145, 150, 179, 242, 243, 273, 303, xlvii, lii.

Zonaras, 266, 268.

II. GREEK WORDS.

E. stands for Ephesians, C. for Colossians.

ἀγαθωσύνη, E. v. 9.
ἅγιοι, E. i. 2, ii. 19.
ἄθεος, E. ii. 12.
ἀθυμεῖν, C. iii. 21.
αἰσχρολογία, C. iii. 8.
αἰών, E. ii. 2.
ἅλας, C. iv. 6.
ἀληθεύειν, E. iv. 15.
ἀλλά, E. v. 24; C. ii. 5.
ἅλυσις, E. vi. 20.
ἄμωμος, E. i. 4, v. 27; C. i. 22.
ἀνα-, in compos., E. i. 10, iv. 23.
ἀνακαινοῦν, C. iii. 10.
ἀνακεφαλαιοῦσθαι, E. i. 10.
ἀναστροφή, E. iv. 22.
ἀνῆκεν, E. v. 4; C. iii. 18.
ἀνταναπληροῦν, C. i. 24.
ἀνταπόδοσις, C. iii. 24.
ἀντι-, in compos., C. i. 24.
ἀντὶ τούτου, E. v. 31.
ἀπεκδύεσθαι, C. ii. 15, iii. 9.
ἀπέκδυσις, C. ii. 11.
ἀπηλλοτριωμένοι, E. ii. 12, iv. 18; C. i. 21.
ἁπλότης, E. vi. 5; C. iii. 22.
ἀποθνήσκειν ἀπό, C. ii. 20.
ἀποκαταλλάσσειν, E. ii. 16; C. i. 20, 22.
ἀπόκρυφος, C. ii. 3.
ἀπολύτρωσις, E. i. 7, 14, iv. 30; C. i. 14.
ἀπόχρησις, C. ii. 22.
ἀρραβών, E. i. 14.
ἀρχή, E. i. 21; C. i. 18, ii. 10.
ἀρχαί, E. iii. 10, vi. 12; C. i. 16, ii. 15.
ἀσέλγεια, E. iv. 19.
ἀσωτία, E. v. 18.
ἀφειδία, C. ii. 23.
ἄφεσις, E. i. 7.
ἁφή, E. iv. 16; C. ii. 19.
ἀφθαρσία, E. vi. 24.

βάπτισμα, βαπτισμός,, C. ii. 12.

βάρβαρος, C. iii. 11.
βλέπειν, C. iv. 17.
βούλομαι, E. i. 11.
βραβεύειν, C. iii. 5; and see on ii. 18.
βρῶσις, C. ii. 15.

γενηθῆναι, E. iii. 7.
γινώσκειν, pregnant, E. iii. 19.
γνῶσις, C. ii. 3.

δέειν, C. iv. 3.
δειγματίζειν, C. ii. 15.
δέχεσθαι, C. iv. 11.
διάβολος, E. iv. 27.
διακονία, C. iv. 17.
διάνοια, E. ii. 3.
διδασκαλία, C. ii. 22.
δίκαιος, C. iv. 1.
δόγμα, E. ii. 15; C. ii. 14.
δογματίζειν, C. ii. 20.
δόξα, E. i. 17.

ἔγειρε, E. v. 14.
ἐθελοθρησκεία, C. ii. 23.
εἴγε, Introd. iv; E. iii. 2, iv. 21.
εἰκῆ, C. iii. 18.
εἰκών, C. i. 15.
εἶναι εἰς, C. ii. 22.
εἰρηνοποιεῖν, E. i. 20.
ἐκλέγεσθαι, E. i. 4.
ἐλαχιστότερος, E. iii. 8.
ἐλέγχειν, E. v. 11, 13.
ἐμβατεύειν, C. ii. 18.
ἐν with dative, whether of the "element, or sphere," E. iv. 4, 14, 17.
ἐνέργεια, E. i. 19.
ἔνι, C. iii. 11.
ἐξουσία, E. i. 21; τοῦ ἀέρος, ii. 2; τοῦ σκότους, C. i. 13.
ἐξουσίαι, E. iii. 10, vi. 12; C. i. 16, ii. 15.
ἔξω, οἱ ἔξω, C. iv. 5.
ἐπί, with dative, E. ii. 10.
ἐπιγινώσκειν, C. i. 6.

INDEX TO THE NOTES

ἐπίγνωσις, C. i. 9.
ἐπιχορηγεῖν, C. ii. 19.
ἐπιχορηγία, E. iv. 16.
ἐποικοδομεῖν, E. ii. 20.
ἐπουράνιος, E. i. 3, 20, ii. 6, iii. 10, vi. 12.
ἐργάζεσθαι, C. iii. 23.
ἐργασία, E. iv. 19.
ἐρεθίζειν, C. iii. 21.
ἑτοιμασία, E. vi. 15.
εὐάρεστος, E. v. 10.
εὐδοκεῖν, C. i. 19.
εὐδοκία, E. i. 5, 9.
εὐλογητός, E. i. 3.
εὐτραπελία, E. v. 4.
εὐχαριστεῖν, E. i. 16.
εὐχαριστία, E. v. 4; C. ii. 7, iv. 2.
εὐχάριστος, C. iii. 15.
ἐχθρός, C. i. 21.

ζωή, E. iv. 18.

ἡλικία, E. iv. 13.

θέλειν, E. i. 11.
θέλων ἐν, C. ii. 18.
θεότης, C. ii. 9.
θιγγάνειν, C. ii. 21.
θριαμβεύειν, C. ii. 15.
θυσία, E. v. 2.

ἵνα, E. ii. 9; C. i. 19; position, E. iii. 18.
ἰσότης, C. iv. 1.
ἰσχύς, E. i. 19.

καθ᾽ ὑμᾶς, E. i. 15.
καί, special use of, E. i. 21, v. 18; C. ii. 1, 5.
καιρός, E. i. 10.
κατά, E. iv. 24.
καταβραβεύειν, C. ii. 18.
καταρτισμός, E. iv. 12.
κατοικεῖν, E. iii. 17; C. i. 19.
κενεμβατεύειν, ? C. ii. 18.
κληρονομία, C. ii. 24.
κλῆρος, C. i. 2.
κληροῦν, E. i. 11.
κομίζεσθαι, E. vi. 8.
κοσμοκράτωρ, E. vi. 12.
κρατεῖν, C. ii. 19.
κράτος, E. i. 19.
κρίνειν, C. ii. 16.
κτίζειν, E. ii. 10; C. i. 16.
κτίσις, C. i. 15.

λέγει, E. iv. 8, v. 14.

λόγον ἔχειν, C. ii. 23.
λυτροῦν, see on E. i. 6.

μακροθυμία, E. iv. 2; C. i. 11, iii. 12.
μαρτύρομαι, with infin., E. iv. 17.
ματαιότης, E. iv. 17.
μέγας, not = English "great," E. v. 32.
μέν, absent, E. v. 8.
μέρος, ἐν μέρει, C. ii. 16.
μέσος, ἐν μέσου, C. ii. 14.
μεσότοιχον, E. ii. 14.
μηδέ, μήτε, E. iv. 27.
μομφή, C. iii. 13.
μυστήριον, E. i. 9, iii. 3, 4, 9, v. 32, vi. 19; C. i. 26, 27, ii. 2.

νεκρός, E. ii. 1.

ξένος, with gen., E. ii. 12.

οἰκεῖος, E. ii. 19.
οἰκοδομή, E. ii. 21.
οἰκονομία, E. i. 10; Introd. xvii.
ὄνομα, E. i. 21.
ὀνομάζειν, E. i. 21, iii. 15.
ὁσιότης, E. v. 24.
ὅστις, E. iii. 13, iv. 19, vi. 1; C. iv. 11.
οὕτως, E. v. 28.
ὀφθαλμοδουλεία, E. vi. 6; C. iii. 22.

πάθος, C. iii. 5.
πανουργία, E. iv. 14.
παρακαλεῖν, E. iv. 1, vi. 22.
παραλογίζεσθαι, C. ii. 4.
παράπτωμα, E. i. 7, ii. 1; C. ii. 13.
παραστῆσαι, E. v. 27; C. i. 22.
παρηγορία, C. iv. 11.
πάροικος, E. ii. 19.
παροργισμός, E. vi. 4.
παρρησία, E. iii. 12, vi. 19; C. ii. 15.
παρρησιάζεσθαι, E. vi. 20.
πᾶς, without article, E. ii. 21, iii. 15.
πατήρ, E. iv. 17.
πατριά, E. iii. 15.
περί and ὑπέρ, E. vi. 18.
πεπληροφορημένοι, C. iv. 12.
περιπατεῖν ἐν, E. ii. 2; C. iii. 7.
περιποίησις, E. i. 14.
πιθανολογία, C. ii. 4.
πικραίνεσθαι, C. iii. 19.
πιστός ἐν, E. i. 1.
πλεονεξία, E. iv. 19, v. 3; C. iii. 5.
πληρούμενος, E. i. 13.
πληροῦν τὸν λόγον, C. i. 25.

πληροῦσθαι ἐν, E. v. 18; C. ii. 10.
πληροφορεῖν, C. iv. 12.
πληροφορία, C. ii. 2.
πλήρωμα, E. i. 10, 23, iii. 19, iv. 13; C. i. 19, ii. 9.
πλησμονή, C. ii. 23.
πλούσιος, C. iii. 16.
πλοῦτος, E. i. 7; C. i. 27; Introd. xxi.
πνευματικός, E. i. 3, vi. 12.
ποιεῖν, E. iii. 11.
ποιεῖν πρόθεσιν, E. iii. 12.
ποίημα, E. ii. 10.
ποιμήν, E. iv. 11.
πολιτεία, E. ii. 12.
πολυποίκιλος, E. iii. 10.
πρεσβεύω ἐν ἁλύσει, E. vi. 20; Introd. xxii.
προετοιμάζειν, E. ii. 10.
πρός, C. ii. 23.
πρὸς ὅ, E. iii. 4.
προσαγωγή, E. ii. 18, iii. 12.
προσευχή and δέησις, E. vi. 18.
προσφορά, E. v. 2.
προσωποληψία, E. vi. 9; C. iii. 25.
πρωτεύειν, C. i. 18.
πρῶτος, E. vi. 2.
πρωτότοκος, C. i. 15, 18.
πώρωσις, E. iv. 18.

ῥῆμα, E. v. 26.
ῥιζοῦν, E. iii. 18.

σαπρός, E. iv. 29.
σοφία, E. i. 8, 17; C. i. 9, ii. 3.
σπλάγχνα, C. iii. 12.
σπουδάζειν, E. iv. 3.
στερέωμα, C. ii. 5.
στῆναι, E. vi. 11, 13; C. iv. 12.
στοιχεῖα, C. ii. 8.
συλαγωγεῖν, C. ii. 8.
συμβιβάζειν, E. iv. 16.

συμμυστής, Introd. xi.
συναιχμάλωτος, C. iv. 10.
συναρμολογεῖν, E. iv. 16.
σύνδεσμός, E. iv. 16; C. ii. 19.
συνεργός, C. iv. 11.
σύνεσις, C. i. 9.
σῶμα, C. i. 22, ii. 11, 17.
σωματικῶς, C. ii. 9.

τάξις, C. ii. 5.
ταπεινοφροσύνη, E. iv. 2.
τέ, E. iii. 18.
τέλειος, C. i. 28, iv. 12.
τιμή, C. ii. 23.
τις, with particip. and article, C. ii. 8.

ὕμνος, E. v. 19; C. iii. 16.
ὑπεναντίος, C. ii. 14.
ὑπέρ and περί, E. vi. 18.
ὑπερ-, compounds with, E. iii. 20.
ὑπομονή, C. i. 11.

φανεροῦν, C. iv. 4.
φανεροῦσθαι, E. v. 13; C. i. 26, iii. 4.
φιλοσοφία, C. ii. 8.
φραγμός, E. ii. 14.
φρόνησις, E. i. 8.
φύσει, E. ii. 3.

χάρις, E. i. 6; C. iii. 16, iv. 6, *al.*
χαριτοῦν, E. i. 6.
χειρόγραφον, C. ii. 14.
χρεία, E. iv. 29.
χωρίς, E. ii. 12.

ψαλμός, E. v. 19; C. iii. 16.
ψεύδεσθαι, C. iii. 9.
ψεῦδος, E. iv. 25.
ψυχή, ἐκ ψυχῆς, E. vi. 6; C. iii. 23.

ᾠδή, E. v. 19; C. iii. 16.

III. LATIN WORDS.

aedificatoriae, 230.
arbitrium, 289.
causa exemplaris, 214.
chirographum, 251.
fumus, 147.

interpolare, ii.
luxuria, 161.
morologus, 149.
satisfactoriae, 230.
urbanitas, 149.

The International Critical Commentary.

"*A decided advance on all other commentaries.*" — THE OUTLOOK.

DEUTERONOMY.

By the Rev. S. R. DRIVER, D.D.,
Regius Professor of History, and Canon of Christ Church, Oxford.

Crown 8vo. Net, $3.00.

"No one could be better qualified than Professor Driver to write a critical and exegetical commentary on Deuteronomy. His previous works are authorities in all the departments involved; the grammar and lexicon of the Hebrew language, the lower and higher criticism, as well as exegesis and Biblical theology; . . . the interpretation in this commentary is careful and sober in the main. A wealth of historical, geographical, and philological information illustrates and elucidates both the narrative and the discourses. Valuable, though concise, excursuses are often given." — *The Congregationalist.*

"It is a pleasure to see at last a really critical Old Testament commentary in English upon a portion of the Pentateuch, and especially one of such merit. This I find superior to any other Commentary in any language upon Deuteronomy." — Professor E. L. CURTIS, of Yale University.

"This volume of Professor Driver's is marked by his well-known care and accuracy, and it will be a great boon to every one who wishes to acquire a thorough knowledge, either of the Hebrew language, or of the contents of the Book of Deuteronomy, and their significance for the development of Old Testament thought. The author finds scope for displaying his well-known wide and accurate knowledge, and delicate appreciation of the genius of the Hebrew language, and his readers are supplied with many carefully constructed lists of words and expressions. He is at his best in the detailed examination of the text." — *London Athenæum.*

"It must be said that this work is bound to take rank among the best commentaries in any language on the important book with which it deals. On every page there is abundant evidence of a scholarly knowledge of the literature, and of the most painstaking care to make the book useful to thorough students." — *The Lutheran Churchman.*

"The deep and difficult questions raised by Deuteronomy are, in every instance, considered with care, insight, and critical acumen. The student who wishes for solid information, or a knowledge of method and temper of the new criticism, will find advantage in consulting the pages of Dr. Driver." — *Zion's Herald.*

The International Critical Commentary.

"We believe this series to be of epoch-making importance."
— The N. Y. EVANGELIST.

JUDGES.

By Dr. GEORGE FOOT MOORE,
Professor of Hebrew in Andover Theological Seminary.

Crown 8vo.   Net, $3.00.

"The typographical execution of this handsome volume is worthy of the scholarly character of the contents, and higher praise could not be given it." — Professor C. H. TOY, *of Harvard University.*

"This work represents the latest results of 'Scientific Biblical Scholarship,' and as such has the greatest value for the purely critical student, especially on the side of textual and literary criticism." — *The Church Standard.*

"Professor Moore has more than sustained his scholarly reputation in this work, which gives us for the first time in English a commentary on Judges not excelled, if indeed equalled, in any language of the world." — Professor L. W. BATTEN, *of P. E. Divinity School, Philadelphia.*

"Although a critical commentary, this work has its practical uses, and by its divisions, headlines, etc., it is admirably adapted to the wants of all thoughtful students of the Scriptures. Indeed, with the other books of the series, it is sure to find its way into the hands of pastors and scholarly laymen." — *Portland Zion's Herald.*

"Like its predecessors, this volume will be warmly welcomed — whilst to those whose means of securing up-to-date information on the subject of which it treats are limited, it is simply invaluable." — *Edinburgh Scotsman.*

"The work is done in an atmosphere of scholarly interest and indifference to dogmatism and controversy, which is at least refreshing. . . . It is a noble introduction to the moral forces, ideas, and influences that controlled the period of the Judges, and a model of what a historical commentary, with a practical end in view should be." — *The Independent.*

"The work is marked by a clear and forcible style, by scholarly research, by critical acumen, by extensive reading, and by evident familiarity with the Hebrew. Many of the comments and suggestions are valuable, while the index at the close is serviceable and satisfactory." — *Philadelphia Presbyterian.*

"This volume sustains the reputation of the series for accurate and wide scholarship given in clear and strong English, . . . the scholarly reader will find delight in the perusal of this admirable commentary." — *Zion's Herald.*

The International Critical Commentary.

"We deem it as needful for the studious pastor to possess himself of these volumes as to obtain the best dictionary and encyclopedia."
— THE CONGREGATIONALIST.

ST. MARK.

By the Rev. E. P. GOULD, D.D.,
Professor of New Testament Exegesis, P. E. Divinity School, Philadelphia.

Crown 8vo. Net, $2.50.

"In point of scholarship, of accuracy, of originality, this last addition to the series is worthy of its predecessors, while for terseness and keenness of exegesis, we should put it first of them all." — *The Congregationalist.*

"The whole make-up is that of a thoroughly helpful, instructive critical study of the Word, surpassing anything of the kind ever attempted in the English language, and to students and clergymen knowing the proper use of a commentary it will prove an invaluable aid." — *The Lutheran Quarterly.*

"Professor Gould has done his work well and thoroughly. . . . The commentary is an admirable example of the critical method at its best. . . . The Word study . . . shows not only familiarity with all the literature of the subject, but patient, faithful, and independent investigation. . . . It will rank among the best, as it is the latest commentary on this basal Gospel." — *The Christian Intelligencer.*

"It will give the student the vigorously expressed thought of a very thoughtful scholar." — *The Church Standard.*

"Dr. Gould's commentary on Mark is a large success, . . . and a credit to American scholarship. . . . He has undoubtedly given us a commentary on Mark which surpasses all others, a thing we have reason to expect will be true in the case of every volume of the series to which it belongs." — *The Biblical World.*

"The volume is characterized by extensive learning, patient attention to details and a fair degree of caution." — *Bibliotheca Sacra.*

"The exegetical portion of the book is simple in arrangement, admirable in form and condensed in statement. . . . Dr. Gould does not slavishly follow any authority, but expresses his own opinions in language both concise and clear." — *The Chicago Standard.*

"In clear, forcible and elegant language the author furnishes the results of the best investigations on the second Gospel, both early and late. He treats these various subjects with the hand of a master." — *Boston Zion's Herald.*

"The author gives abundant evidence of thorough acquaintance with the facts and history in the case. . . . His treatment of them is always fresh and scholarly, and oftentimes helpful." — *The New York Observer.*

The International Critical Commentary

"It is hardly necessary to say that this series will stand first among all English serial commentaries on the Bible."
— The Biblical World.

ST. LUKE.

By the Rev. ALFRED PLUMMER, D.D.,

Master of University College, Durham. Formerly Fellow and Senior Tutor of Trinity College, Oxford.

Crown 8vo. Net, $3.00.

In the author's Critical Introduction to the Commentary is contained a full treatment of a large number of important topics connected with the study of the Gospel, among which are the following: The Author of the Book — The Sources of the Gospel — Object and Plan of the Gospel — Characteristics, Style and Language — The Integrity of the Gospel — The Text — Literary History.

FROM THE AUTHOR'S PREFACE.

If this Commentary has any special features, they will perhaps be found in the illustrations from Jewish writings, in the abundance of references to the Septuagint, and to the Acts and other books of the New Testament, in the frequent quotations of renderings in the Latin versions, and in the attention which has been paid, both in the Introduction and throughout the Notes, to the marks of St. Luke's style.

"It is distinguished throughout by learning, sobriety of judgment, and sound exegesis. It is a weighty contribution to the interpretation of the Third Gospel, and will take an honorable place in the series of which it forms a part." — Prof. D. D. SALMOND, in the *Critical Review*.

"We are pleased with the thoroughness and scientific accuracy of the interpretations. . . . It seems to us that the prevailing characteristic of the book is common sense, fortified by learning and piety." — *The Herald and Presbyter*.

"An important work, which no student of the Word of God can safely neglect." — *The Church Standard*.

"The author has both the scholar's knowledge and the scholar's spirit necessary for the preparation of such a commentary. . . . We know of nothing on the Third Gospel which more thoroughly meets the wants of the Biblical scholar." — *The Outlook*.

"The author is not only a profound scholar, but a chastened and reverent Christian, who undertakes to interpret a Gospel of Christ, so as to show Christ in his grandeur and loveliness of character." — *The Southern Churchman*.

"It is a valuable and welcome addition to our somewhat scanty stock of first-class commentaries on the Third Gospel. By its scholarly thoroughness it well sustains the reputation which the INTERNATIONAL SERIES has already won." — Prof. J. H. THAYER, of Harvard University.

This volume having been so recently published, further notices are not yet available.

The International Critical Commentary.

"For the student this new commentary promises to be indispensable." — The METHODIST RECORDER.

ROMANS.

By the Rev. WILLIAM SANDAY, D.D.,
Lady Margaret Professor of Divinity, and Canon of Christ Church, Oxford,

AND THE

Rev. A. C. HEADLAM, M.A.,
Fellow of All Souls' College, Oxford.

Crown 8vo. Net, $3.00.

"From my knowledge of Dr. Sanday, and from a brief examination of the book, I am led to believe that it is our best critical handbook to the Epistle. It combines great learning with practical and suggestive interpretation." — Professor GEORGE B. STEVENS, *of Yale University.*

"Professor Sanday is excellent in scholarship, and of unsurpassed candor. The introduction and detached notes are highly interesting and instructive. This commentary cannot fail to render the most valuable assistance to all earnest students. The volume augurs well for the series of which it is a member." — Professor GEORGE P. FISHER, *of Yale University.*

"The scholarship and spirit of Dr. Sanday give assurance of an interpretation of the Epistle to the Romans which will be both scholarly and spiritual." — Dr. LYMAN ABBOTT.

"The work of the authors has been carefully done, and will prove an acceptable addition to the literature of the great Epistle. The exegesis is acute and learned . . . The authors show much familiarity with the work of their predecessors, and write with calmness and lucidity." — *New York Observer.*

"We are confident that this commentary will find a place in every thoughtful minister's library. One may not be able to agree with the authors at some points, — and this is true of all commentaries, — but they have given us a work which cannot but prove valuable to the critical study of Paul's masterly epistle." — *Zion's Advocate.*

"We do not hesitate to commend this as the best commentary on Romans yet written in English. It will do much to popularize this admirable and much needed series, by showing that it is possible to be critical and scholarly and at the same time devout and spiritual, and intelligible to plain Bible readers." — *The Church Standard.*

"A commentary with a very distinct character and purpose of its own, which brings to students and ministers an aid which they cannot obtain elsewhere. . . . There is probably no other commentary in which criticism has been employed so successfully and impartially to bring out the author's thought." — *N. Y. Independent.*

"We have nothing but heartiest praise for the weightier matters of the commentary. It is not only critical, but exegetical, expository, doctrinal, practical, and eminently spiritual. The positive conclusions of the books are very numerous and are stoutly, gloriously evangelical. . . . The commentary does not fail to speak with the utmost reverence of the whole word of God." — *The Congregationalist.*

The International Critical Commentary.

"I have already expressed my conviction that the International Critical Commentary is the best critical commentary, on the whole Bible, in existence."—DR. LYMAN ABBOTT.

Philippians and Philemon

BY

REV. MARVIN R. VINCENT, D.D.

Professor of Biblical Literature in Union Theological Seminary, New York.

Crown, 8vo, Net $2.00.

"It is, in short, in every way worthy of the series."—*The Scotsman.*

"Professor Vincent's Commentary on Philippians and Philemon appears to me not less admirable for its literary merit than for its scholarship and its clear and discriminating discussions of the contents of these Epistles."—DR. GEORGE P. FISHER.

"The book contains many examples of independent and judicial weighing of evidence. We have been delighted with the portion devoted to Philemon. Unlike most commentaries, this may wisely be read as a whole."—*The Congregationalist.*

"Of the merits of the work it is enough to say that it is worthy of its place in the noble undertaking to which it belongs. It is full of just such information as the Bible student, lay or clerical, needs; and while giving an abundance of the truths of erudition to aid the critical student of the text, it abounds also in that more popular information which enables the attentive reader almost to put himself in St. Paul's place, to see with the eyes and feel with the heart of the Apostle to the Gentiles."—*Boston Advertiser.*

"If it is possible in these days to produce a commentary which will be free from polemical and ecclesiastial bias, the feat will be accomplished in the International Critical Commentary. . . . It is evident that the writer has given an immense amount of scholarly research and original thought to the subject. . . . . The author's introduction to the Epistle to Philemon is an admirable piece of literature, calculated to arouse in the student's mind an intense interest in the circumstances which produced this short letter from the inspired Apostle."—*Commercial Advertiser.*

The International Theological Library.

EDITORS' PREFACE.

THEOLOGY has made great and rapid advances in recent years. New lines of investigation have been opened up, fresh light has been cast upon many subjects of the deepest interest, and the historical method has been applied with important results. This has prepared the way for a Library of Theological Science, and has created the demand for it. It has also made it at once opportune and practicable now to secure the services of specialists in the different departments of Theology, and to associate them in an enterprise which will furnish a record of Theological inquiry up to date.

This Library is designed to cover the whole field of Christian Theology. Each volume is to be complete in itself, while, at the same time, it will form part of a carefully planned whole. One of the Editors is to prepare a volume of Theological Encyclopædia which will give the history and literature of each department, as well as of Theology as a whole.

The Library is intended to form a series of Text-Books for Students of Theology.

The Authors, therefore, aim at conciseness and compactness of statement. At the same time, they have in view that large and increasing class of students, in other departments of inquiry, who desire to have a systematic and thorough exposition of Theological Science. Technical matters will therefore be thrown into the form of notes, and the text will be made as readable and attractive as possible.

The Library is international and interconfessional. It will be conducted in a catholic spirit, and in the interests of Theology as a science.

Its aim will be to give full and impartial statements both of the results of Theological Science and of the questions which are still at issue in the different departments.

The Authors will be scholars of recognized reputation in the several branches of study assigned to them. They will be associated with each other and with the Editors in the effort to provide a series of volumes which may adequately represent the present condition of investigation, and indicate the way for further progress.

CHARLES A. BRIGGS.
STEWART D. F. SALMOND.

VOLUMES ALREADY PUBLISHED.

An Introduction to the Literature of the Old Testament.	By S. R. Driver, D.D., Regius Professor of Hebrew, and Canon of Christ Church, Oxford.
Christian Ethics.	By Newman Smyth, D.D., Pastor of the First Congregational Church, New Haven, Conn.
Apologetics.	By A. B. Bruce, D.D., Professor of New Testament Exegesis, Free Church College, Glasgow.
History of Christian Doctrine.	By G. P. Fisher, D.D., LL.D., Professor of Ecclesiastical History, Yale College, New Haven, Conn.
A History of Christianity in the Apostolic Age.	By Arthur C. McGiffert, D.D., Professor of Church History, Union Theological Seminary, New York.

The International Theological Library.

VOLUMES IN PREPARATION.

Christian Institutions.	By A. V. G. ALLEN, D.D., Professor of Ecclesiastical History, P. E. Divinity School, Cambridge, Mass. (*Now Ready.*)
The Study of the Old Testament.	By HERBERT EDWARD RYLE, B.D., President of Queen's College, Cambridge, England.
Old Testament History.	By HENRY PRESERVED SMITH, D.D., late Professor of Hebrew, Lane Theological Seminary, Cincinnati, Ohio.
Contemporary History of the Old Testament.	By FRANCIS BROWN, D.D., Professor of Hebrew, Union Theological Seminary, New York.
Theology of the Old Testament.	By A. B. DAVIDSON, D.D., LL.D., Professor of Hebrew, New College, Edinburgh.
An Introduction to the Literature of the New Testament.	By S. D. F. Salmond, D.D., Professor of Systematic Theology and New Testament Exegesis, Free Church College, Aberdeen.
Canon and Text of the New Testament.	By CASPAR RENÉ GREGORY, D.D., Professor of New Testament Exegesis in the University of Leipzig.
Contemporary History of the New Testament.	By Frank C. PORTER, PH.D., Professor of Biblical Theology, Yale University, New Haven, Conn.
Theology of the New Testament.	By GEORGE B. STEVENS, D.D., Professor of Systematic Theology, Yale University, New Haven, Conn.
The Ancient Catholic Church.	By ROBERT RAINY, D.D., LL.D., Principal of the New College, Edinburgh.
The Latin Church.	By ARCHIBALD ROBERTSON, D.D. Principal of King's College.
Philosophy of Religion.	By ROBERT FLINT, D.D., LL.D., Professor of Divinity in the University of Edinburgh.
Comparative Religion.	By A. M. FAIRBAIRN, D.D., Principal of Mansfield College, Oxford.
The Christian Pastor.	By WASHINGTON GLADDEN, D.D., Pastor of Congregational Church, Columbus, Ohio. (*In Press.*)
Rabbinical Literature.	By S. SCHECHTER, M.A., Christ's College, Cambridge, England.
Theological Encyclopædia.	By Charles A. BRIGGS, D.D., Professor of Biblical Theology, Union Theological Seminary, New York.
Life of Christ.	By WILLIAM SANDAY, D.D., Lady Margaret Professor of Divinity and Canon of Christ Church Oxford.

The International Theological Library.

History of Christian Doctrine.

BY

GEORGE P. FISHER, D.D.,

Titus Street Professor of Ecclesiastical History in Yale University.

Crown 8vo, 583 pages, $2.50 net.

"He gives ample proof of rare scholarship. Many of the old doctrines are restated with a freshness, lucidity and elegance of style which make it a very readable book."—*The New York Observer.*

"Intrinsically this volume is worthy of a foremost place in our modern literature . . . We have no work on the subject in English equal to it, for variety and range, clearness of statement, judicious guidance, and catholicity of tone."—*London Nonconformist and Independent.*

"It is only just to say that Dr. Fisher has produced the best History of Doctrine that we have in English."—*The New York Evangelist.*

"It is to me quite a marvel how a book of this kind (Fisher's 'History of Christian Doctrine') can be written so accurately to scale. It could only be done by one who had a very complete command of all the periods."—PROF. WILLIAM SANDAY, *Oxford.*

"It presents so many new and fresh points and is so thoroughly treated, and brings into view contemporaneous thought, especially the American, that it is a pleasure to read it, and will be an equal pleasure to go back to it again and again."—BISHOP JOHN F. HURST.

"Throughout there is manifest wide reading, careful preparation, spirit and good judgment."—*Philadelphia Presbyterian.*

"The language and style are alike delightfully fresh and easy . . . A book which will be found both stimulating and instructive to the student of theology."—*The Churchman.*

"Professor Fisher has trained the public to expect the excellencies of scholarship, candor, judicial equipoise and admirable lucidity and elegance of style in whatever comes from his pen. But in the present work he has surpassed himself."—PROF. J. H. THAYER, *of Harvard Divinity School.*

"It meets the severest standard; there is fullness of knowledge, thorough research, keenly analytic thought, and rarest enrichment for a positive, profound and learned critic. There is interpretative and revealing sympathy. It is of the class of works that mark epochs in their several departments."—*The Outlook.*

"As a first study of the History of Doctrine, Professor Fisher's volume has the merit of being full, accurate and interesting."
—Prof. MARCUS DODS.

". . . He gathers up, reorganizes and presents the results of investigation in a style rarely full of literary charm."
—*The Interior.*

The International Theological Library.

Apologetics;

Or, Christianity Defensively Stated.

By ALEXANDER BALMAIN BRUCE, D.D.,

Professor of Apologetics and New Testament Exegesis, Free Church College, Glasgow; Author of "The Training of the Twelve," "The Humiliation of Christ," "The Kingdom of God," etc.

Crown 8vo, 528 pages, $2.50 net.

Professor Bruce's work is not an abstract treatise on apologetics, but an apologetic presentation of the Christian faith, with reference to whatever in our intellectual environment makes faith difficult at the present time.

It addresses itself to men whose sympathies are with Christianity, and discusses the topics of pressing concern—the burning questions of the hour. It is offered as an aid to faith rather than a buttress of received belief and an armory of weapons for the orthodox believer.

"The book throughout exhibits the methods and the results of conscientious, independent, expert and devout Biblical scholarship, and it is of permanent value."—*The Congregationalist.*

"The practical value of this book entitles it to a place in the first rank."—*The Independent.*

"A patient and scholarly presentation of Christianity under aspects best fitted to commend it to 'ingenuous and truth-loving minds.'"—*The Nation.*

"The book is well-nigh indispensable to those who propose to keep abreast of the times."—*Western Christian Advocate.*

"Professor Bruce does not consciously evade any difficulty, and he constantly aims to be completely fair-minded. For this reason he wins from the start the strong confidence of the reader."—*Advance.*

"Its admirable spirit, no less than the strength of its arguments, will go far to remove many of the prejudices or doubts of those who are outside of Christianity, but who are, nevertheless, not infidels."—*New York Tribune.*

"In a word, he tells precisely what all intelligent persons wish to know, and tells it in a clear, fresh and convincing manner. Scarcely anyone has so successfully rendered the service of showing what the result of the higher criticism is for the proper understanding of the history and religion of Israel."—*Andover Review.*

"We have not for a long time taken a book in hand that is more stimulating to faith. . . . Without commenting further, we repeat that this volume is the ablest, most scholarly, most advanced, and sharpest defence of Christianity that has ever been written. No theological library should be without it."—*Zion's Herald.*

The International Theological Library.

AN INTRODUCTION TO
The Literature of the Old Testament

By Prof. S. R. DRIVER, D. D.
Canon of Christ Church, Oxford.

New Edition from New Plates.

Crown 8vo, 558 Pages, $2.50 net.

Canon Driver's work, first published in 1891, at once took its place as a standard, and the necessity for several editions soon showed that it satisfied a wide-spread need. In the present edition, the new matter was found to have outgrown the limits of an appendix, so the volume has been entirely reset. The text has been carefully revised, the bibliography has been brought up to date, and an account of the principal critical views on the Old Testament promulgated since 1891 has been inserted. The volume has been already translated into German, and in its new form it cannot fail to still further increase its sphere of influence.

"It is the most scholarly and critical work in the English language on the literature of the Old Testament, and fully up to the present state of research in Germany."—Prof. PHILIP SCHAFF, D.D.

"His judgment is singularly fair, calm, unbiassed, and independent. It is also thoroughly reverential. . . . . The service which his book will render in the present confusion of mind on this great subject can scarcely be overestimated."—*The London Times.*

"As a whole, there is probably no book in the English language equal to this 'Introduction to the Literature of the Old Testament,' for the student who desires to understand what the modern criticism *thinks* about the Bible."—Dr. LYMAN ABBOTT, in *The Outlook.*

"It contains just that presentation of the results of Old Testament criticism for which English readers in this department have been waiting. . . . . The whole book is excellent; it will be found helpful, characterized as it is all through by that scholarly poise of mind which, when it does not know, is not ashamed to present degrees of probability."—*New World.*

". . . Canon Driver's book is characterized throughout by thorough Christian scholarship, faithful research, caution in the expression of mere opinions, candor in the statement of facts and of the necessary inferences from them, and the devout recognition of the divine inworking in the religious life of the Hebrews, and of the tokens of divine inspiration in the literature which records and embodies it."—Dr. A. P. PEABODY, in *The Cambridge Tribune.*

The International Theological Library.

Christian Ethics,

By NEWMAN SMYTH, D.D., New Haven.

Crown 8vo, 508 pages, $2.50 net.

"As this book is the latest, so it is the fullest and most attractive treatment of the subject that we are familiar with. Patient and exhaustive in its method of inquiry, and stimulating and suggestive in the topic it handles, we are confident that it will be a help to the task of the moral understanding and interpretation of human life."
— *The Living Church.*

"This book of Dr. Newman Smyth is of extraordinary interest and value. It is an honor to American scholarship and American Christian thinking. It is a work which has been wrought out with remarkable grasp of conception, and power of just analysis, fullness of information, richness of thought, and affluence of apt and luminous illustration. Its style is singularly clear, simple, facile, and strong. Too much gratification can hardly be expressed at the way the author lifts the whole subject of ethics up out of the slough of mere naturalism into its own place, where it is seen to be illumined by the Christian revelation and vision." — *The Advance.*

"Far from narrowing the subject by the apparent limitation of the title, *Christian* Ethics, Dr. Smyth has broadened it as one broadens his landscape by ascending to the highest possible point of view. The subjects treated cover the whole field of moral and spiritual relations, theoretical and practical, natural and revealed, individual and social, civil and ecclesiastical. To enthrone the personal Christ as the true content of the ethical ideal, to show how this ideal is realized in Christian consciousness and how applied in the varied departments of practical life—these are the main objects of the book and no objects could be loftier." — *The Congregationalist.*

"It is a noble book. So far as I know Ethics have hitherto been treated exclusively from a philosophical point of view, as though there were no prophet of the Moral Law whose interpretation of it we accept as final and authoritative. In treating Ethics from the Christian point of view Professor Smyth has made a notable contribution both philosophically and practically. His well-balanced statement of the Christian sociological principles, his moderate and well-balanced statement of the relations of the Church to sociological evolution, and his exposition of the duties of an agnostic toward the God who is unknown to him, and yet whose existence is not denied, strike me as among the most admirable features of a book admirable throughout, which I hope may find its way into our Christian schools and seminaries as a text-book."
—*Extract from a letter of Dr. Lyman Abbott.*

The International Theological Library

A HISTORY OF
CHRISTIANITY IN THE APOSTOLIC AGE

BY

ARTHUR CUSHMAN McGIFFERT, Ph.D., D.D.

Washburn Professor of Church History in the Union Theological Seminary, New York.

Crown 8vo, 681 Pages, $2.50 Net.

"The author's work is ably done. . . . . This volume is worthy of its place in the series."—*The Congregationalist.*

"Invaluable as a resumé of the latest critical work upon the great formative period of the Christian Church."—*The Christian World.* (LONDON.)

"There can be no doubt that this a remarkable work, both on account of the thoroughness of its criticism and the boldness of its views."—*The Scotsman.*

"The ability and learning of Prof. McGiffert's work on the Apostolic Age, and, whatever dissent there may be from its critical opinion, its manifest sincerity, candid scholars will not fail to appreciate."—DR. GEORGE P. FISHER, of Yale University.

"Pre-eminently a clergyman's book; but there are many reasons why it should be in the library of every thoughtful Christian person. The style is vivid and at times picturesque. The results rather than the processes of learning are exhibited. It is full of local color, of striking narrative, and of keen, often brilliant, character analysis. It is an admirable book for the Sunday-school teacher. It deserves attentive study as an aid to any one who wishes fairly to understand the greatest epoch in human history."—*Boston Advertiser.*

"It is in his interpretation of the teachings of Paul, or, as he felicitously terms it, "the Christianity of Paul," that Dr. McGiffert has rendered his greatest service to the church of our time, and it is a very great one. Paul has been overlaid with layer on layer of the scholasticism of the Middle Ages. These layers Dr. McGiffert simply sweeps away, and brings out the great Apostle to the Gentiles as he was in his own personality and his original power. We can compare Dr. McGiffert's work to nothing so apt as the work of a restorer, who discovers an ancient and noble work of art buried beneath successive layers of plaster in some old cathedral, and removes the plaster and brings back the ancient and forgotten picture to the light; or that of a scholar, who finds, in a palimpsest manuscript, a document of the second century, and by his skill removes the monkish writing which obscures the original, and restores that original and deciphers it. It might almost be said that Dr. McGiffert has rediscovered Paul. . . . . In promoting the better understanding of this Gospel, as understood by Paul, and in bringing about that revival of true religion for which we look with hope, to follow the bold and consistent preaching of the Gospel. Dr. McGiffert's volume is, we trust, destined to play a large part."—DR. LYMAN ABBOTT, in *The Outlook.*

www.ingramcontent.com/pod-product-compliance
Lightning Source LLC
Chambersburg PA
CBHW020100020526
44112CB00032B/649